MOTIF-INDEX
OF
FOLK-LITERATURE

A Classification of Narrative Elements in
Folktales, Ballads, Myths, Fables, Mediaeval Romances,
Exempla, Fabliaux, Jest-Books, and
Local Legends

REVISED AND ENLARGED EDITION BY

STITH THOMPSON
Indiana University

VOLUME TWO
D-E

INDIANA UNIVERSITY PRESS
BLOOMINGTON & INDIANAPOLIS

Indiana University Press gratefully acknowledges
the support of the L.J. and Mary C. Skaggs Foundation
in the republication of the six volumes of the
Motif-Index of Folk-Literature.

Manufactured in the United States of America

ISBN 0-253-33882-4
7 8 9 99 98 97

complete set ISBN 0-253-33887-5

D. MAGIC

DETAILED SYNOPSIS

D0—D699 TRANSFORMATION

D10 —D99. Transformation of man to different man
- D10. Transformation to person of different sex
- D20. Transformation to person of different social class
- D30. Transformation to person of different race
- D40. Transformation to likeness of another person
- D50. Magic changes in man himself
- D90. Transformation: man to different man — miscellaneous

D100—D199. Transformation: man to animal
- D110—D149. Transformation: man to mammal
  - D110. Transformation: man to wild beast (mammal)
  - D130. Transformation: man to domestic beast (mammal)
  - D150. Transformation: man to bird
  - D170. Transformation: man to fish
  - D180. Transformation: man to insect
  - D190. Transformation: man to reptiles and miscellaneous animals

D200—D299. Transformation: man to object
- D210. Transformation: man to vegetable form
- D230. Transformation: man to mineral form
- D250. Transformation: man to manufactured object
- D270. Transformation: man to object — miscellaneous

D300—D399. Transformation: animal to person
- D310—D349. Transformation: mammal to person
  - D310. Transformation: wild beast (mammal) to person
  - D330. Transformation: domestic beast (mammal) to person
  - D350. Transformation: bird to person
  - D370. Transformation: fish to man
  - D380. Transformation: insect to person
  - D390. Transformation: reptiles and miscellaneous animals to persons.

D400—D499. Other forms of transformation
- D410. Transformation: one animal to another
- D420. Transformation: animal to object
- D430. Transformation: object to person
- D440. Transformation: object to animal
- D450—D499. Transformation: object to object
  - D450. Transformation: object to another object
  - D470. Transformation: material of object changed
  - D480. Size of object transformed

D500—D599. Means of transformation
- D510. Transformation by breaking tabu
- D520. Transformation through power of the word
- D530. Transformation by putting on skin, clothing, etc.
- D550. Transformation by eating or drinking
- D560. Transformation by various means

D600—D699. Miscellaneous transformation incidents
- D610. Repeated transformation

D620. Periodic transformation
D630. Transformation and disenchantment at will
D640. Reasons for voluntary transformation
D660. Motive for transformation of others
D670. Magic flight.
D680. Miscellaneous circumstances of transformation

D700—D799. Disenchantment
D710. Disenchantment by rough treatment
D720. Disenchantment by removing (destroying) covering of enchanted person
D730. Disenchantment by submission
D750. Disenchantment by faithfulness of others
D760. Disenchantment by miscellaneous means
D790. Attendant circumstances of disenchantment

D800—D1699. MAGIC OBJECTS

D800—D899. Ownership of magic objects
D800. Magic object
D810—D859. Acquisition of magic object
D810. Magic object a gift
D830. Magic object acquired by trickery
D840. Magic object found
D850. Magic object otherwise obtained
D860. Loss of magic object
D880. Recovery of magic object

D900—D1299. Kinds of magic objects
D900. Magic weather phenomena
D910. Magic body of water
D930. Magic land features
D940. Magic forests
D950. Magic tree
D960. Magic gardens and plants
D980. Magic fruits and vegetables
D990—D1029. Magic bodily members
D990. Magic bodily members — human
D1010. Magic bodily members — animal
D1030. Magic food
D1040. Magic drink
D1050. Magic clothes
D1070. Magic ornaments
D1080. Magic weapons
D1110. Magic conveyances
D1130. Magic buildings and parts
D1150. Magic furniture
D1170. Magic utensils and implements
D1210. Magic musical instruments
D1240. Magic waters and medicines
D1250. Miscellaneous magic objects

D1300—D1599. Function of magic objects
D1300—D1379. Magic objects effect changes in persons
D1300. Magic object gives supernatural wisdom
D1310. Magic object gives supernatural information
D1330. Magic objects works physical change
D1350. Magic object changes person's disposition
D1360. Magic object effects temporary change in person
D1380. Magic object protects
D1390. Magic object rescues person

D1400—D1439. Magic object gives power over other persons
D1400. Magic object overcomes person
D1410. Magic object renders person helpless
D1420. Magic object draws person (thing) to it
D1430. Magic object pursues or captures
D1440. Magic object gives power over animals
D1450. Magic object furnishes treasure
D1470. Magic object as provider
D1500. Magic object controls disease
D1520. Magic object affords miraculous transportation
D1540. Magic object controls the elements
D1550. Magic object miraculously opens and closes
D1560. Magic object performs other services for owner

D1600—D1699. Characteristics of magic objects
D1600—D1649. Automatic magic objects
D1600. Automatic object
D1610. Magic speaking objects
D1620. Magic automata
D1640. Other automatic objects
D1650. Other characteristics of magic objects

D1700—D2199. MAGIC POWERS AND MANIFESTATIONS

D1710—D1799. Possession and means of employment of magic powers
D1710. Possession of magic powers
D1720. Acquisition of magic powers
D1740. Loss of magic powers
D1750. Other characteristics of magic power
D1760. Means of producing magic power

D1800—D2199. Manifestations of magic power
D1800—D1949. Lasting magic qualities
D1810. Magic knowledge
D1820. Magic sight and hearing
D1830. Magic strength
D1840. Magic invulnerability
D1850. Immortality
D1860. Magic beautification
D1870. Magic hideousness
D1880. Magic rejuvenation
D1890. Magic aging
D1900. Love induced by magic
D1910. Magic memory
D1920. Other permanent magic characteristics
D1950—D2049. Temporary magic characteristics
D1960. Magic sleep
D1980. Magic invisibility
D2000. Magic forgetfulness
D2020. Magic dumbness
D2030. Other temporary magic characteristics
D2050—D2099. Destructive magic powers
D2060. Death or bodily injury by magic
D2070. Bewitching
D2080. Magic used against property
D2090. Other destructive magic powers
D2100—D2149. Other manifestations of magic power
D2100. Magic wealth
D2120. Magic transportation
D2140. Magic control of the elements
D2150—D2199. Miscellaneous magical manifestations

D. MAGIC

D0—D699. TRANSFORMATION

D0. Transformation (general). *MacCulloch Childhood 149ff.; *Wimberley 275ff.; Sébillot Incidents s.v. "métamorphose"; Burton Arabian Nights VIII 270, S IV 329. — *Tibbals "Elements of Magic in the Romance of William of Palerne" MPh I (1903) 355ff.; *Easter: a Study of Magic Elements in the Romans d'Aventure (Dissertation, Baltimore 1906); *Hegar Hessische Blätter f. Vksk. XXVIII 110ff. — Greek: Frazer Apollodorus I 251 n. 4 (Neleus); Irish myth: *Cross; Jewish: *Neuman; Icelandic: *Boberg.

D5. *Enchanted person.* See also the entire section on transformation. No real difference seems to exist between transformation and enchantment. A bewitched or enchanted person may, however, retain his original physical form, but may be affected mentally or morally. — *Type 400; Gr. Nos. 93, 163; BP II 335ff. — Greek: Frazer Apollodorus II 105 n. 1 (Minos); India: Thompson-Balys; Missouri French: Carrière.

B187.7. Magic bitches (in human form). D2070. Bewitching. F165.6.1. Otherworld (fairyland) as place of sorrowful captivity. F300. Marriage or liason with fairy. F375. Mortals as captives in fairyland. F768.2. City of enchanted people. Apparently dead. G241.2.2. Person enchanted by witch's salve so as to be ridden by witch. G263. Witch injures, enchants, or transforms. T154. Cruel stepmother enchants stepdaughter on eve of wedding.

D5.1. *Enchanted person cannot move.* Swiss: Jegerlehner Oberwallis 294 No. 8.

D2072. Magic paralysis.

D5.1.1. *Stepson cursed to stick in grave mound till pretty girl wants to substitute for him.* Icelandic: *Boberg.

D1792. Magic results from curse. T164. Cruel stepmother enchants stepdaughter.

D5.2. *Enchanted person on bier.* Italian: Basile Pentamerone, Introduction.

D6. *Enchanted castle (building).* Irish myth: *Cross; Missouri French: Carrière.

D1131. Magic castle. F163.1. Castle in other world. F222. Fairy castle. F725.3.2. Castle under lake. F766. Deserted city. F771. Extraordinary castle.

D7. *Enchanted valley.* Irish myth: Cross.

F151.1.1. Perilous valley. F756. Extraordinary valleys and plains.

D10—D99. Transformation: man to different man.

D10. Transformation to person of different sex. *H. Gaidoz "Du changement de sexe dans les contes celtiques" Revue de l'histoire des religions LVII 317ff.; *Chauvin VIII 43 No. 11; *Penzer VII 42ff., 223ff.; *Fb "menneske" II 577b, "kvinde" II 339b; *Brown JAOS XLVII 3;

*Hdwb. d. Abergl. III 752; Irish myth: *Cross; India: *Thompson-Balys.

D624.3. Yearly transformation to person of different sex. D658.3. Transformation of sex to seduce. E605.1. Reincarnation with change of sex. Q551.3.6.1. Punishment: man reborn as girl. T. Sex.

D10.1. *Ogre has unique powers of exchange of sex with human being.* India: Thompson-Balys.

G630. Characteristics of ogres.

D10.2. *Change of sex after crossing water.* McKay Beal III 139.

D11. *Transformation woman to man.* *Types 406, 514; BP II 79ff., 87, III 84; Gr. Nos 71, 134; *Loomis White Magic 80; Irish myth: *Cross; Chinese: Eberhard FFC CXX 165, No. 108; Eskimo (Cumberland Sound): Boas BAM XV 248, (Cape York) Rasmussen III 152; (Koryak) Jochelson JE VI 195, 323; Africa (Dahomé): Einstein 28.

K1322. Girl masked as man wins princess's love. K1837. Disguise of woman in man's clothes.

D11.1. *Transformation: ogress to man.* India: Thompson-Balys.

D11.2. *Woman transforms herself into a bird and lends her female organ to a boy.* He fails to return it and she becomes a man when she resumes human form. India: Thompson-Balys.

D12. *Transformation: man to woman.* Irish myth: *Cross; Spanish Exempla: Keller; Greek: Frazer Apollodorus I 364 n. 1 (Tiresias); French Canadian: Sister Marie Ursule; Jewish: Neuman; Hindu: Keith 147, 151. — Eskimo (Cumberland Sound): Boas BAM XV 249, (West Hudson Bay) Boas BAM XV 325; Africa (Ekoi): Talbot 247, (Dahomé) Einstein 27.

A1275.3. Of ten original men one magically changes sex. D513.1. Man looks at copulating snakes: transformed to woman. D658.3. Transformation to female to seduce. D695. Man transformed to woman has children. K1321. Seduction by man disguising as woman. T2. The relative pleasures of love. T332. Man tempted by fiend in woman's shape. T578. Pregnant man.

D12.1. *Transformation: god to giantess.* MacCulloch Eddic 131 (Loki to Thökk).

D20. Transformation to person of different social class. Irish myth: *Cross.

D22. *Transformation: common man to exalted personage.*

D22.1. *Transformation: common man to grand officer.* French Canadian: Barbeau JAFL XXIX 17.

D22.2. *Transformation: man of low caste takes on prince's appearance, and transforms prince to take on his.* India: Thompson-Balys.

K1931. Impostors abandon (or kill) their companion and usurp his place.

D23. *Transformation to artisan.*

D23.1. *Transformation into a boatman.* Breton: Sébillot Incidents s.v. "batelier".

D24. *Transformation to humble person.*

D24.1. *Transformation: king to menial.* Icelandic: Boberg.

D24.2. *Transformation: king and queen to peasant and wife.* Icelandic: Boberg.

P411. Peasant.

D24.3. *Transformation into a swineherd.* Irish myth: Cross (D23).

K1816.6. Disguise as herdsman. P412.2. Swineherd.

D24.4. *Transformation: rich man to tramp.* Smears hands and face. French Canadian: Sister Marie Ursule.

D25. *Transformation layman to professional man.*

D25.1. *Transformation to doctor.* French Canadian: Sister Marie Ursule.

D25.2. *Transformation into a cleric (monk).* Irish myth: Cross.

K1826.1. Disguise as monk.

D27. *Transformation into leper.* Irish myth: Cross.

K778.2. Amazonian woman disguised as leper seduces and binds enemies one by one. K1818.1. Disguise as leper. K2357.11. Disguise as leper to enter enemies' camp. P162. Leper.

D28. *Transformation into giant.* Irish myth: Cross (D29.1.)

F531. Giant. F531.6.1.2. Giant is transformed man.

D29. *Transformation to a person of different social class—miscellaneous.* Irish myth: Cross.

D29.1. *Transformation into a churl (bachlach).* Irish myth: *Cross.

K1816. Disguise as menial. K2357.14. Disguise as churl.

D29.2. *Transformation into juggler.* Irish myth: Cross (D26).

K2357.13. Disguise as juggler to enter enemy's camp.

D30. Transformation to person of different race.

F1082. Person changes color.

D31. *Transformation: white person to negro.* (Cf. D57) — Chauvin II 183 No. 23; *Fb "jomfru", "hvid" I 700b, "sort" III 467b, "pige" II 816b. — Spanish Boggs FFC XC 57 No. 425; Jewish: *Neuman.

D40. Transformation to likeness of another person. *Type 363; BP III 534 n. 1. — Wells 30 (Uther Pendragon); Icelandic: Boberg; Irish myth: *Cross; Italian Novella: Rotunda; India: Thompson-Balys; Jewish: Neuman; Greek: Grote I 80; Eskimo (Greenland) Rasmussen II 211, (Cape York) Rasmussen III 54; Africa (Fang): Tessman 141f.

D658.2. Transformation to husband's (lover's) form to seduce woman. F234.2. Fairy in form of person. K1952.0.1. Brahman takes shape of a prince.

D40.1. *Transformation to likeness of person whose shield one carries* (Cf. D1101.1). Norse: FSS 37, 38.

D1101.1. Magic shield. F824.2. Extraordinarily painted shield

D40.2. *Transformation to likeness of another woman.* India: Thompson-Balys.

D40.2.1. *Transformation to resemble man's mistress so as to be able to kill him.* India: Thompson-Balys.

K1321.3.1. Man disguised as woman beguiles hostile chief.

D41. *Humble man in guise of exalted.*

D1810. Magic knowledge.

D41.1. *Transformation to likeness of ruler.* Man so uses the last of three wishes granted to him. Italian Novella: Rotunda.

J2075.2. Two transferred wishes used unwisely: redeemed by wise use of third.

D42. *God in guise of mortal.* Irish: MacCulloch Celtic 56, *Cross; Greek: Iliad and Odyssey passim; Jewish: Neuman; India: Thompson-Balys; Marquesas: Handy 109.

A120.0.1. God as shape-shifter. A125. God in human form. K1811. Gods (saints) in disguise visit mortals.

D42.1. *God transformed to giant with three heads and six arms.* Chinese: Werner 236.

D42.2. *Spirit takes shape of man.* India: *Thompson-Balys; Chinese: Eberhard FFC CXX 167, 169.

D43. *Transformation: mortal to guise of deity.* Greek myth: Grote I 117; Chinese: Eberhard FFC CXX 166f; India: Thompson-Balys.

D43.1. *Animal transformed to a god.*

D43.1.1. *Dog turned into a god.* India: Thompson-Balys.

D44. *Mortal in guise of spirit.* Africa (Upoto): Einstein 142, (Buin) Wheeler 51. See also D47.

D44.1. *Transformation: man to angel.* Jewish: Neuman.

V230. Angels.

D45. *Persons exchange forms.* Icelandic: Boberg.

D45.1. *Kings exchange forms and kingdoms for a year.* Welsh: MacCulloch Celtic 93; Irish myth: Cross.

L411. Proud king displaced by angel. (Angel in form of the king.)

D45.2. *Gods exchange forms.* Irish: MacCulloch Celtic 56, Cross.

A120.0.1. God as shape-shifter. A160. Mutual relations of the gods.

D45.3. *Two friends exchange forms.* Italian Novella: Rotunda.

H111. Identification by garment. T351. Sword of chastity.

D45.4. *Girl exchanges form with sorceress in order to visit her brother and get a son by him.* Icelandic: Völsunga saga ch. 7.

D47. *Transformation to likeness of monster.* Irish myth: Cross (D94, D95); Icelandic: Boberg; Jewish: Neuman; India: Thompson-Balys.

D47.1. *Mortal temporarily takes shape of demon.* India: Thompson-Balys.

D630. Transformation and disenchantment at will.

D47.2. *Transformation: normal men to ogres.* Become ravenous. India: Thompson-Balys.

G0. Ogres.

D47.3. *Transformation: princess to ogress.* Icelandic: *Boberg.

D49. *Transformation to likeness of another person — miscellaneous.*

D49.1. *Dwarf assumes human form.* German: Grimm No. 64.

D49.2. *Spirit takes any form.* India: Thompson-Balys.

D49.3. *Fairy transforms herself into a monstrous being with head of an ape, thin legs, sharp claws, fish scales and bristles.* India: Thompson-Balys.

D50. Magic changes in man himself. Irish: Plummer clxxxiv (changes in form, complexion, height, and age).

D732. Loathly lady. D733. Loathly bridegroom. D1330. Magic object works physical change. D1891. Transformation to old man to escape recognition.

D52. *Magic change to different appearance.* Irish myth: *Cross; Jewish: Neuman.

D631.1.1. Person changes appearance at will. D1860. Magic beautification. D1870. Magic hideousness.

D52.1. *Transformation: man becomes hideous.* Africa (Upoto): Einstein 130.

D52.2. *Ugly man becomes handsome.* Samoa: Beckwith Myth 473.

D53. *Transformation in health.*

D53.1. *Transformation to sick man.* Icelandic: Sturlaugs saga 642; Africa (Boloki): Weeks Congo 200ff.

D2064. Magic sickness.

D55. *Magic change of person's size.* Irish myth: *Cross; Eskimo (West Hudson Bay): *Boas BAM XV 361 (No. 34); Africa (Togo): Einstein 8.

D480. Size of object transformed. D631.1. Person changes size at will.

D55.1. *Person becomes magically larger.* Tobler 90. — Irish myth: *Cross; Jewish: Neuman; Latin: Virgil Aeneid VI line 50; Africa (Fang) Trilles 184.

A526.6. Culture hero, when angry, subject to contortions (riastartha). F531.6.1.2. Giant is transformed man.

D55.1.1. *Man magically stretches self to overcome cliff.* Hawaii: Dixon 91; Melanesia: ibid. 91 n. 104; Micronesia: ibid. 91 n. 105.

D482. Transformation: stretching tree.

D55.1.1.1. *Man magically stretches self to overcome opponent in battle.* Irish myth: *Cross

A526.6. Culture hero, when angry, subject to contortions (riastartha).

D55.1.1.2. *Man magically stretches self to sink tent pole.* Irish myth: Cross.

D55.1.2. *Transformation: person to giant.* Hawaii: Beckwith Myth 539; Eskimo: Boas BAM XV 314; Africa (Fang): Einstein 61.

F531.6.1.2. Giant is transformed man.

D55.1.3. *Pygmy turns into a giant.* Finnish: Kalevala rune 2.

F531. Giant. F535. Pygmy.

D55.2. *Person becomes magically smaller.* Irish myth: Cross; Japanese: Ikeda.

D185.1. Transformation: woman (fairy) to fly. D491. Compressible object.

D55.2.1. *Dwarf contracts self to enter nostrils of cannibals.* Africa (Zulu): Callaway 154.

F451. Dwarf as underground spirit.

D55.2.2. *Devil (troll) makes self small.* *Fb "lille" II 428.

D55.2.3. *Giant changes to normal size.* Micmac: Michelson JAFL XXXVIII 39.

D55.2.4. *Ten serving-women carried in bottle.* They change size at will. Köhler-Bolte II 471ff.

D2177.1. Demon enclosed in bottle. D2185. Magician carries woman in glass coffin. She comes out at will. F401.3.4. Spirit as fly going into bottle. F1034.1. Husband concealed in wife's ear. F1034.2. Magician carries mistress with him in his body. She in turn has paramour in hers.

D55.2.5. *Transformation: adult to child.* Jewish: Neuman; India: *Thompson-Balys; Eskimo (Greenland): Rasmussen I 103, (Mackenzie Area) Jenness 40; Africa (Togo): Einstein 8, (Boloki) Weeks Congo 200ff.

D55.2.6. *Hero reduces in size small enough to get into mango seed.* India: Thompson-Balys.

D56. *Magic change in person's age.* India: Thompson-Balys.

D56.1. *Transformation to older person.* Jewish: Neuman; India: *Thompson-Balys.

D630. Transformation and disenchantment at will. D1881. Magic self-rejuvenation.

D57. *Change in person's color.* (Cf. D31.) — Jewish: Neuman.

F1082. Person changes color.

D57.1. *Man transformed to green knight.* *Kittredge Gawain.

D57.2. *Black man's color altered to white.* *Loomis White Magic 81.

D57.3. *Hair and skin turn to color of gold.* India: Thompson-Balys.

D57.4. *Transformation to black man.* German: Grimm No. 121, 137; Jewish: Neuman.

D57.5. *Transformation to person of rusty color.* German: Grimm No. 136.

D61. *Magic appearance of human limbs.* A boy has no hands and legs; his abandoned sister successfully commands them to appear or disappear. Kaffir: Theal 74.

A526.6. Demigod, when angry, subject to contortions. A526.8. Culture hero can turn feet and knees backward. D1375. Magic object causes (or removes) temporary growths.

D90. Transformation: man to different man — miscellaneous.

D91. *Transformation: normal man to cannibal.* Fb "blod" IV 48a.

D92. *Transformation: wild man to normal.* Italian Novella: Rotunda.

F567. Wild men.

D93. *Transformation: prince to old man.* Type 431.

P30. Princes.

D94. *Transformation: man to ogre.* Irish myth: Cross. Icelandic: *Boberg.

D96. *Transformation: normal man to ascetic.* India: Thompson-Balys.

D97. *Transformation: man to witch.* (Cf. G200) India: Thompson-Balys.

D98. *Transformation: children into horsemen.* India: Thompson-Balys.

D100—D199. Transformation: man to animal.

D100. Transformation: man to animal. *BP II 60, III 8f.; *Dh III 284ff., 429ff., 446ff., 464ff.; Cosquin Contes indiens 58ff.; *Goerke Ueber Tierverwandlungen in französischer Dichtung und Sage (Dissertation, Königsberg 1904); Type 325; *Chauvin VI 199 No. 371. — Irish myth: *Cross; MacCulloch Celtic 168; Slavic (general): Machal 229; French Canadian: Barbeau JAFL XXIX 13, 17; Missouri French: Carrière; Hindu: Penzer VI 5 n. 1, 40 n. 1, 56 n. 1, 2, VII 42 n. 1, 44 n. 1, IX 45; India: Thompson-Balys; Arabian: Burton Nights I 28, 35, 97, 126, 173, VII 83, 290, 296, 301, IX 310, S IV 329, 336. — Chinese: Frémine La Tradition Sept.-Oct. 1890; Indonesian: DeVries' list Nos. 152, 153;

Hawaii: Beckwith Myth 141; American Indian (Passamaquoddy): Prince PAES X 43 No. 9; (Amazon) Alexander Lat. Am. 301; Jamaica: Beckwith MAFLS XVII 271 No. 84.

A522. Culture hero in animal form. A1710. Creation of animals through transformation. B200. Animals with human traits. B313. Helpful animal an enchanted person. B640. Marriage to person in beast form. F234.1. Fairy in form of an animal. F401.3. Spirit in animal form. Q55. Reward for sparing life when in animal form. Q551.3.2. Punishment: transformation into animal.

D101. *Transformation: god to animal.* *Krappe Études 53ff. — Greek: *Frazer Apollodorus I 49 n. 2; Fox 178 (Apollo); Irish myth: *Cross, MacCulloch Celtic 56; Persian: Carnoy 269; Norse: De la Saussaye 261; India: *Thompson-Balys; Penzer VII 175 n. 1.

A113. Totemistic gods. A132. God in animal form. D142.2. God assumes form of a cat. D154.1.0.1. Transformation: god to dove. D658.1. Transformation to animal to seduce woman. D796. Divine beings assume their own shape in sleep. E611.2.1. Divinity reincarnated as bull. F234.1. Fairy in form of animal. Q554.6. Cheaters visited by god in animal form.

D102. *Transformation: devil to animal.* *Kittredge Witchcraft 175 nn. 12—21, 29, 30; Missouri French: Carrière.

D1421. Devil as cat. G211. Witch in animal form. G303.3.3. The devil in animal form.

D102.1. *Transformation: demon to animal.* India: *Thompson-Balys.

K1810. Deception by disguise. N773. Adventure from following animal to cave.

D103. *Assembly or group transformed to animals.* N. A. Indian (California): Gayton and Newman 98.

D110—D149. TRANSFORMATION: MAN TO MAMMAL

D110. Transformation: man to wild beast (mammal). *Dh III 446ff.; Greek: Fox 16, Frazer Apollodorus II 67 n. 6; Breton: Sébillot Incidents s.v. "bête"; Jewish: Neuman; Eskimo (Mackenzie Area): Jenness 85.

D112. *Transformation: man to feline animal (wild).*

D112.1. *Transformation: man to lion.* Irish myth: Cross; Icelandic: Bósa saga 91; Spanish: *Boggs FFC XC 62 No. 451; Missouri French: Carrière; Jewish: Neuman. — Africa (Hottentot): Bleek 57 No. 25, (Angola): Chatelain 245 No. 47.

E612.1. Reincarnation as lion.

D112.1.1. *Village of lion-men.* India: Thompson-Balys, Penzer I 67f.

D112.2. *Transformation: man to tiger.* Greek: Frazer Apollodorus II 67 n. 6; Chinese: Werner 266, 270; India: *Thompson-Balys.

D112.2.1. *Wer-tiger.* Like werwolf. (Cf. D113.1.) — India: *Thompson-Balys; Chinese: Graham; Korea: Zong in-Sob 58, 71, 74, 79, 85, 89, 91.

N399.7. Man discovers he is married to wer-tiger.

D112.2.1.1. *When a wer-tiger is injured, similar marks appear on the human body of man who has possessed it.* India: Thompson-Balys.

D112.2.1.2. *Village of tiger-men.* (Cf. B221.6.1.) — India: Thompson-Balys.

D112.3. *Transformation: man to lynx.* Africa (Bushman): Bleek and Lloyd 97.

D112.4. *Transformation: man to leopard.* India: Thompson-Balys; Africa (Mpongwe): Nassau 71 No. 15, (Angola): Chatelain 167 No. 15, (Wakweli): Bender 52.

D112.5. *Transformation: man to buffalo.* Africa (Weute): Sieber 220ff.

D112.6. *Transformation: man to jaguar.* S. A. Indian (Toba): Métraux MAFLS XL 61, (Eastern Brazil): Lowie I 397.

D113. *Transformation: man to canine animal (wild).*

D113.1. *Transformation: man to wolf.* *Type 428; Dh III, Fb "blod" IV 48; Child V 497 s.v. "stepmother". — Irish myth: *Cross; Eng., U.S.: *Baughman; Icelandic: Corpus poeticum Boreale I 136, 140, *Boberg; Italian Novella: Rotunda; Greek myth: Grote I 160; Finnish: Aarne FFC VIII 14 No. 75, XXXIII 53 No. 75; Estonian: Aarne FFC XXV 130 No. 73, 145 No. 38; Lappish: Qvigstad FFC LX 48 No. 75; India: Thompson-Balys.

Q551.3.1. Punishment: Loki's son transformed into wolf which tears to pieces. S73.1. Fratricide. T155. Old beggar transforms wedding party into wolves. T611.10.1. Girl suckled by wolf has nail "like a wolf's nail." E612.2. Reincarnation as wolf. G211.5. Witch in form of wolf.

D113.1.1. *Werwolf.* A man changes periodically into the form of a wolf. He is usually malevolent when in wolf form. **R. Andree Globus XXVII (1875); *C. T. Stewart Zs. f. Vksk. XIX 30ff.; Kristensen Danske Sagn II (1893) 227ff.; (1928) 148ff.; Lid Saga och Sed 1937, 3ff.; Odstedt Varulven i svensk folktradition (Uppsala 1944); **K. E. Smith An Historical Study of the Werwolf in Literature (PMLA IX, 1894); **E. O'Donnell Werewolves (Boston 1914); Summers The Werwolf (London, 1933); *O. Clemen Zs. f. Vksk. XXX—XXXII 141; *Kittredge Witchcraft 175 nn. 5—7; ibid. Arthur 169 n. 1; **Baring-Gould The Book of Werewolves (London, 1865); *v. Sydow Feilberg Festskrift 594ff.; **Jijena Sanchez; *Lévy-Bruhl La mentalité primitive 279ff.; *Frazer Ovid II 318ff.; *Fb "varulv". — Irish myth: *Cross; Norse: MacCulloch Eddic 291; Icelandic: *Boberg, Hrolfs saga Kraka 50, Volsungasaga 15, Sveinnson FFC LXXXIII p. liv; Norwegian: Solheïm Register 16; Finnish: Aarne FFC XXXIII 46; German: Wuttke Volksaberglaube 277; Dutch: Schrijnen Volkskunde I 97; English: Philippson Germanisches Heidentum bei den Angelsachsen 53, Child III 498a s.v. "werewolves", Wells 19 (William of Palerne); Swiss: Jegerlehner Oberwallis 323 No. 109, 325, No. 9; Breton: Sébillot Incidents s.v. "loupgarou"; Gascon: Bladé Contes pop. de Gascogne II 360 No. 4; Estonian: Aarne FFC XXV 131f. Nos. 74—77, Eisen Esthnische Mythologie 31ff, Loorits Grundzüge I 311—320; Livonian: Loorits FFC LXVI 63 Nos. 160—178; Lithuanian: Balys Index No. 3671; Slavic: Machal 228f.; Jewish: Neuman; India: Thompson-Balys; N. A. Indian (Okanagon): Gould MAFLS XI 98 No. 2; S. A. Indian (Amazon): Alexander Lat. Am. 301. — Africa: Frobenius Atlantis V 153, 165, VII 31ff, 56, XI 263, *Werner African 344; (Basuto) Jacottet 238 No. 35.

A737.1. Eclipse caused by werewolf devouring sun or moon. C311.1.4. Tabu: looking at werewolf. D620. Periodic transformation. D791.1.1. Disenchantment at end of seven years. E721.5.1. Wandering soul assumes shape of wolf. H64.1. Recognition of disenchanted person by thread in his teeth. As werewolf he has torn woman's apron and caught thread in teeth. H132. Recognition by knife. Man who is werewolf recognized by knife which was carried away by the wolf. R169.3. Boy saved by werewolf. V49.1. Werwolves hold mass.

D113.1.2. *God (goddess) assumes form of a wolf.* Irish myth: Cross; Greek myth: *Grote I 43.

A132.8. Dog (wolf)-god. F234.1.13. Fairy in form of wolf.

D113.2. *Transformation: man to bear.* *Dh II 99; Hdwb. d. Abergl. I 886 s.v. "Bär"; *Fb "bjørn" IV 43a, "hvidbjørn" I 701a; Lappish: Qvigstad FFC LX 48 No. 75a; Icelandic: *Boberg; Greek myth: Grote I 162; Hindu: Penzer VII 42 n. 1; India: Thompson-Balys; Chinese: Eberhard FFC CXX 217 No. 167; N. A. Indian (Joshua): Farrand-Frachtenberg JAFL XXVIII 241 No. 20; Eskimo (Cumberland Sound): Boas BAM XV 251f., (West Hudson Bay) Boas BAM XV 326, (Kodiak) Golder JAFL XX 297, XXII 10, (Cape York) Rasmussen III 124, 297, 211, (Greenland) Rink 193, (Bering Strait) Nelson RBAE XVIII 493, (West Greenland) Rasmussen II 96, 184, (East Greenland) Rasmussen I 184; Africa (Ba Ronga): Einstein 249.

G211.2.1. Witch in form of bear.

D113.2.1. *Wer-bear.* A bear-man like the werwolf. *Fb "bjørn" IV 43a; Fox: Jones PAES I 157.

D113.3. *Transformation man to fox.* *Fb "ræv" III 113a; *Hdwb. d. Abergl. III 179. — Irish myth: Cross; Swiss: Jegerlehner Oberwallis 337 s.v. "Hexe", *302 No. 15, 307 No. 27, 32; Icelandic: Þorsteins saga Vik. 417; Missouri French: Carrière; Chinese: Krappe CFQ III (1944) 137; Korean: Zong in-Sob 19, 56; N. A. Indian: *Thompson Tales 342 n. 233 (cf. B651.1); Eskimo (Mackenzie Area): Jenness 52, 56.

E612.4. Reincarnation as fox. G211.2.3. Witch in form of fox. G304.1.1.1. Troll as fox. K1823. Man disguises as animal. K2357. Disguise to enter enemy's camp (castle).

D113.4. *Transformation: man to jackal.* India: Thompson-Balys.

D113.4.1. *Transformation: deity to jackal.* India: Thompson-Balys.

D101. Transformation: god to animal.

D113.5. *Transformation: man to hyena.* Africa (Ba Ronga): Einstein 266.

D114. *Transformation: man to ungulate (wild).*

D114.1. *Transformation: man to bovine animal (wild).*

D114.1.1. *Transformation: man to deer.* (Cf. B641.2.) — *Type 450; *Fb "hjort" I 625, "hind" I 612, "blod" IV 48a; Irish myth: Cross; *Loomis White Magic 80; Icelandic: *Boberg; India: *Thompson-Balys; Chinese and Persian: Coyajee JPASB XXIV 182ff., Eskimo (Cape York): Rasmussen III 191; N. A. Indian (White Mountain Apache): Goddard PaAM XXIV 128; S. A. Indian (Tembe): Métraux RMLP XXXIII 140.

A511.10.1. Culture hero son of deer mother. B611.5. Deer paramour. E612.5. Reincarnation as deer.

D114.1.1.1. *Transformation: girl to deer (fawn) (by druid).* Irish myth: *Cross.

D114.1.1.2. *Transformation: woman to doe.* India: Thompson-Balys.

D114.1.2. *Transformation: man to eland.* Africa (Kaffir): Theal 87.

D114.1.3. *Transformation: man to hartebeest.* Africa (Bushman): Bleek and Lloyd 3.

D114.1.4. *Transformation: man to buffalo.* India: Thompson-Balys; N. A. Indian (Cheyenne): Campbell JAFL XXIX 407 No. 1; Africa (Weute): Sieber 229.

D114.1.5. *Transformation: man to musk ox.* Eskimo (Mackenzie Area): Jenness 82.

D114.1.6. *Transformation: man to carabou.* Eskimo (Mackenzie Area): Jenness 56.

D114.1.7. *Transformation: man to moose.* Eskimo (Mackenzie Area): Jenness 40.

D114.2. *Transformation: man to elephant.* Hindu: Penzer VI 162; Buddhist myth: Malalasekera II 40; Africa (Ekoi): Talbot 247, (Benga) Nassau 184 No. 24, (Basuto) Jacottet 90 No. 14, (Fang) Tessman 118.

D114.3. *Transformation: man to swine (wild).*

D114.3.1. *Transformation: man to peccary.* S. A. Indian (Cariri): Lowie BBAE CXLIII (1) 559.

D114.3.2. *Transformation: man to boar.* Loomis White Magic 80; Irish myth: Cross; Welsh: MacCulloch Celtic 187; Icelandic: *Boberg.

D136. Transformation: man to swine. E611.3.1. Man reincarnated as wild boar.

D114.3.2.1. *Transformation: god to boar.* (Cf. D101.) India: Thompson-Balys.

D114.4. *Transformation: man to wild goat.* Africa: Milligan 141.

D115. *Transformation: man to equine animal (wild).*

D115.1. *Transformation: man to zebra.* Africa (Ba Ronga): Einstein 262.

D117. *Transformation: man to rodent.* S. Am. Indian (Toba): Métraux MAFLS XL 120.

D117.1. *Transformation: man to mouse.* *Fb "mus" II 631b; Dh I 258ff. (cf. C12.5.1); Type 545 A, B (BP I 325, III 487). — Irish myth: Cross; Welsh: MacCulloch Celtic 102; Spanish Exempla: Keller; India: *Thompson-Balys, Panchatantra III 13 (tr. Ryder) 353; Africa (Ba Ronga): Einstein 249.

G211.2.5. Witch in form of mouse.

D117.2. *Transformation: man to hare (rabbit).* *Fb "hare" I 556, "blod" IV 48a; Irish myth: *Cross (D123).

D655.2. Witch transforms self to hare so as to suck cows. E612.3 Reincarnation as hare. F234.1.12. Fairy in form of hare. G211.2.7. Witch in form of hare. G304.1.1.2. Troll as hare.

D117.3. *Transformation: man to rat.* Hawaii: Beckwith Myth 17, 425f.

D117.3.1. *Transformation: man to bandicoot.* India: Thompson-Balys.

D117.4. *Transformation: man to marmot.* India: Thompson-Balys.

D118. *Transformation: man to simian.*

D118.1. *Transformation: man to ape.* *Dh II 100. — Greek: Frazer Apollodorus I 241 n. 3; Jewish: Neuman; Hindu: Penzer I 28, III 191, VI 59, VII 44 n. 1; India: *Thompson-Balys; Chinese: Eberhard FFC CXX 177 No. 119; S. A. Indian (Quiché): Alexander Lat. Am. 172, Chile: Pino Saavedra 402ff.

D118.2. *Transformation: man (woman) to monkey.* India: Thompson-Balys; Chinese: Graham.

T68.5. Girl marries hunter when he promises to return to monkey brothers their human form.

D124. *Transformation: man to wild animal — mustelidae.*

D124.1. *Transformation: man to weasel.* Fb "lækat" II 495a.

D124.2. *Transformation: man to ermine.* Eskimo (Mackenzie Area): Jenness 36a.

D124.3. *Transformation: man to marten.* Tobler 51.

D124.4. *Transformation: man to badger.* Irish myth: *Cross (D117.2).

K2023. Badgers treacherously slain in violation of pledge given by prince.

D127. *Transformation: man to sea mammal.*

D127.1. *Transformation: man to seal.* *Fb "sælhund"; Icelandic: *Boberg; Irish myth: *Cross; Eskimo (Greenland): Rink 222, 224, 450, 469, Boas RBAE V 621, (Mackenzie Area) Jenness 84, (Cape York) Rasmussen III 100.

B80.1. Seal-man. E612.6. Reincarnation as seal.

D127.2. *Transformation: man to otter.* Irish myth: Cross; Icelandic: Völsunga Saga ch. 14; Eskimo (Aleut): Golder JAFL XVIII 221, (Kodiak): Golder JAFL XX 139.

D127.3. *Transformation: man to whale.* (See references at D178.) Icelandic: *Boberg; German: Grimm No. 197. — Eskimo (Greenland): Holm 31, (Smith Sound): Kroeber JAFL XII 170, (Labrador): Hawks GSCan XIV 157, (Central Eskimo): Boas RBAE VI 625; Tuamotu: Stimson MS (P—G 13/10).

D127.4. *Transformation: man to walrus.* Eskimo (Greenland): Rasmussen I 184, II 96.

D127.5. *Transformation: man to dolphin.* Icelandic: Boberg; Greek: Grote I 32, 45, 70x, 178 (Apollo), Frazer Apollodorus I 333 n. 1.

D127.6. *Transformation: man to porpoise.* Marquesas: Handy 92; Tonga: Gifford 77.

D130. Transformation: man to domestic beast (mammal).

D131. *Transformation: man to horse:* *Types 314, 502, 531, 726*; BP III 18ff, 94ff.; *Fb "hest" I 598; "æble" III 1136a, "blod" IV 48a; Tobler 44, 50, 80; *Malone PMLA XLIII 441 n. 25; Kittredge Arthur 170 n. 3; Cosquin Études 512ff. — Irish myth: *Cross; Icelandic: *Boberg; Swiss: Jegerlehner Oberwallis 329 No. 52; Finnish: Aarne FFC XXXIII 40 No. 33, 45 No. 71; Estonian: Aarne FFC XXV 118, 120, 130 Nos. 25, 33, 72; Persian: Carnoy 269; Hindu: Penzer VI 5, 8; India: *Thompson-Balys; Buddhist myth: Malalasekera II 1205; Japanese: Ikeda. — Africa (Mpongwe): Nassau 68 No. 15.

D535. Transformation to horse by putting on bridle. E611.1. Reincarnation as horse. G211.1. Witch in form of horse. G241.2.1. Witch transforms man to horse and rides him.

D131.1. *Transformation: merman to horse.* (Cf. B82.) Fb "hest" I 599a.

D132. *Transformation: man to ass (mule, jennet, etc.).*

D132.1. *Transformation: man to ass.* (Cf. B641.4.) — *Types 430, 567; *Chauvin II 183 No. 23; *K. Weinhold Über das Märchen vom Eselmenschen (Sitzungsb. d. K. Pr. Akad. Berlin [1893] 475—488); Cosquin Études 512ff.; Wesselski Theorie 22. — Breton: *Sébillot Incidents s.v. "âne"; India: *Thompson-Balys; Japanese: Ikeda.

D693. Man transformed to ass plays the lyre.

D132.2. *Transformation: man to mule.* Spanish: *Boggs FFC XC 86 No. 754 C*.

D133. *Transformation to cow (bull, calf, etc.).* India: Thompson-Balys.

D133.1. *Transformation to cow.* *Type 473; *Fb "ko" II 240b. — Icelandic: Boberg; Greek: Grote I 80; India: *Thompson-Balys; Chinese: Eberhard FFC CXX 43, 52.

E611.2. Reincarnation as cow. Q501.6. Punishment of Io. Transformed to cow with gadfly ceaselessly pursuing.

D133.1.1. *Nisser in form of cows.* Fb "ko" II 240b; Kristensen Danske Sagn II (1893) 83ff., (1928) 63ff.

D133.2. *Transformation: man to bull.* (Cf. B641.3.) — Irish myth: *Cross; Icelandic: *Boberg; Greek: Frazer Apollodorus I 299 n. 2 (Europa), I 256 n. 3 (Achelous); Persian: Carnoy 269; Hindu: *Penzer VI 5 n. 1; Chinese: Werner 359.

E611.2.1. Divinity reincarnated as bull.

D133.3. *Transformation: man to ox.* Cosquin Études 512ff.; Norse: FSS 118f, MacCulloch Eddic 181; Spanish: *Boggs FFC XC 48, 63 Nos. 327D*, 453.

D133.4. *Transformation: man to calf.* Fb "kalv" II 79; Irish myth: Cross.

D133.4.1. *God assumes form of calf.* Irish myth: Cross; Jewish: Neuman; Chinese: Eberhard FFC CXX 136.

A132.9. Bull-god.

D133.5. *Transformation: man to steer* (bullock). German: Grimm No. 82a, 163.

D134. *Transformation: man to goat* (he-goat, she-goat, kid etc.) Irish myth: *Cross; Icelandic: Boberg; Greek: Grote I 238; Lappish: Qvigstad FFC LX 48 No. 75C; German: Grimm No. 163; Hindu: Penzer VI 56 nn. 1, 2; India: *Thompson-Balys.

A1614.1.2. Origin of "goat-heads" from curse of Ham. B24. Satyr. E611.4. Man reincarnated as goat.

D134.1. *Transformation: man to he-goat.*

D134.2. *Transformation: man to she-goat.* Hartland Science 247; Loomis White Magic 80. — Breton: Sébillot Incidents s.v. "chèvre"; India: Thompson-Balys.

D134.3. *Transformation: man to kid.* Greek: Frazer Apollodorus I 320 n. 4 (Dionysus); India: Thompson-Balys.

D134.4. *Transformations supernatural being into a goat.* Irish myth: Cross.

D135. *Transformation: man to sheep.* Breton: Sébillot Incidents s.v. "mouton"; India: Thompson-Balys.

D135.1. *Transformation: man to lamb.* German: Grimm No. 141; India: Thompson-Balys.

D136. *Transformation: man to swine.* Fb "svin" III 676a; *Dh II 102. — Icelandic: *Boberg; Irish: *Hartland Science 198, *Cross; Italian Novella: Rotunda; Missouri French: Carrière; Greek: Fox 137, Frazer Apollodorus II 287 n. 2 (Odysseus and Circe); Hindu: Keith 218; Chinese: Eberhard FFC CXX 217 No. 167; Tahiti: Beckwith Myth 37.

D122. Transformation: man to boar. E611.3. Man reincarnated as swine. F460.1.1.1. Mountain-man in shape of hog. F480.1. House-spirit in form of a sow. Q226.2. Mutinous clerics expelled in shapes of swine.

D141. *Transformation: man to dog.* (Cf. B641.1.) — *Type 652; BP II 121 (Grimm Nos. 76, 30a); Types 449*, 726*; *Fb "hund" I 676b, "blod"

IV 48a, "lys" II 483b; *Dh II 101; **Jijena Sanchez; *Kittredge Arthur 170 n. 3; Chauvin V 3 No. 2, *5 No. 443 — Icelandic: *Boberg; Irish: *Cross; Lithuanian: Balys Index No. 3655; Jewish: Neuman; India: Thompson-Balys, Penzer VIII 141; Buddhist myth: Malalasekera II 1205; Korea: Zong in-Sob 64 No. 35; Hawaii: Beckwith Myth 349; Tuamotu: Stimson MS (z-G. 13/52); Maori: Clark 50; Surinam: Alexander Lat. Am 274; N. A. Indian: *Thompson Tales 347 n. 247, 248, (Canadian Dakota): Wallis JAFL XXXVI 90 No. 22; Eskimo (Labrador): Hawkes GSCan XIV 152, (Cumberland Sound): Boas BAM XV 156.

B17.1.2.3. Transformed man as hostile dog. B182.1.0.2. Magic dog transformed person. E611.6. Man reincarnated as dog. G211.1.8 Witch in form of dog.

D141.0.1. *Kynanthropy.* Irish myth: Cross.

D113.1.1. Werwolf.

D141.0.2. *Men and women transformed to dogs by druidic spell.* Irish myth: *Cross.

D141.1. *Transformation: woman to bitch.* Irish myth: *Cross; Greek: Frazer Apollodorus II 241 n. 4 (Hecuba).

F302.5.2. Fairy mistress transforms man's human wife. K1351. The weeping bitch. T257.2.3. Jealous wife (mistress) transforms rival to hound.

D141.1.1. *Transformation: girl to puppy.* India: Thompson-Balys.

D142. *Transformation: man to cat.* Types 402, 566; Fb "blod" IV 48a, "kat" II 108a; Taylor MPh XVII (1919) 59 n. 8. — Breton: Sébillot Incidents s.v. "chat"; French: Cosquin No. 11; German: Grimm No. 130a; India: Thompson-Balys; Tonga: Gifford 20; N. A. Indian: Thompson CColl II 400 ff.

D825.1. Magic object received from cat-woman (i. e. woman transformed intermittently to cat). E611.5. Man reincarnated as cat. G211.1.7. Witch in form of cat.

D142.0.1. *Transformation: woman to cat.* Irish myth: *Cross.

D142.1. *Devil as cat.* *Kittredge Witchcraft 178 nn. 37—44 passim.

D102. Transformation: devil to animal. G303.3.3.3. Devil in form of a cat.

D142.2. *God assumes form of a cat.* Hindu: Penzer II 46, 197 n. 2; Tonga: Gifford 20.

D101. Transformation: god to animal.

D150. Transformation: man to bird. (Cf. B644.) — *Types 405, 432, 665; BP II 26ff., 69; Dh II 250 ff., III 406, 429ff.; Hartland Science 247; Chauvin V 87 No. 27; Cosquin Ėtudes 516ff., 526ff.; Irish: *Cross, MacCulloch Celtic 75, 79; Icelandic: De la Saussaye 261; Greek: Fox 15, 16 (Ceyx and Alcyone), 70 (Procne and Philomela), Frazer Apollodorus I 70 n. 1, II 67 n. 6 (Thetis); Jewish: Neuman; Finnish: Aarne FFC XXXIII 46 No. 77**; India: *Thompson-Balys; Chinese: Graham, Eberhard FFC CXX 48, 123ff., 125; Japanese: Ikeda; Korean: Zong in-Sob 64 No. 35; Maori: Dixon 79; Philippine (Tinguian): Cole 139, 151; Marquesas: Handy 55, 108; Hawaii: Beckwith Myth 115; Tuamotu: Stimson MS (T-G 3/619); Eskimo (Greenland): Rink 148, 287, 327, Rasmussen II 14; N. A. Indian (Thompson River): Alexander N. Am. 137; S. A. Indian (Kiangon): Métraux BBAE CXLIII (1) 47, (Toba): Métraux: MAFLS XL 24, 26; Africa (Fang): Trilles Proverbes 202, Einstein 52, 55f.

E613. Reincarnation as bird. E732. Soul in form of bird. F234.1.15. Fairy in form of bird. H78.2. Identification by feather taken from hero when he was transformed to bird.

D151. *Transformation: man to bird — passeriform.*

D151.1. *Transformation: man to swallow.* *Dh III 414ff.; Icelandic: Boberg; Korean: Zong in-Sob 65 No. 35.

E613.4. Reincarnation as swallow.

D151.2. *Transformation: man to finch.* Africa (Zulu): Callaway 119.

D151.2.1. *Transformation into snowbunting.* Eskimo (Cumberland Sound): Boas BAM XV 220.

D151.3. *Transformation: man to nightingale.* *Fb "blod" IV 48a. — Greek: Frazer Apollodorus II 98 n. 2, Pausanias V 226.

D151.4. *Transformation: man to crow.* Fb "krage" II 285b. — Irish myth: *Cross; Icelandic: *Boberg; Spanish: Boggs FFC XC 63 No. 453; India: *Thompson-Balys.

F531.1.8.4. Giantess in crow's shape. G211.4.1. Witch in form of crow. G304.1.1.4. Troll as crow.

D151.5. *Transformation: man to raven.* *Type 451; Fb "ravn" III 22b, 23a; Krappe Speculum XX (1945) 405—414; German: Grimm No. 93; Irish myth: *Cross; Koryak: Jochelson JE VI 14; Eskimo (Cumberland Sound): Boas BAM XV 177, 227, 229, 303.

A13.1. Raven as creator. A522.6. Raven as culture hero.

D151.6. *Transformation: man to titmouse.* Livonian: Loorits FFC LXVI 90 No. 80.

D151.7. *Transformation: man to blackbird.* Irish myth: Cross.

D151.8. *Transformation: man to sparrow.* German: Grimm No. 68.

D151.9. *Transformation: man to magpie.* Icelandic: Boberg.

D152. *Transformation: man to bird — falconiform.*

D152.1. *Transformation: man to hawk.* Irish myth: *Cross; Icelandic: *Boberg; India: *Thompson-Balys, Penzer I 84. — Eskimo (Ungava): Turner RBAE XI 263; S. A. Indian (Yuracare): Métraux BBAE CXLIII (3) 504, (Mundurucú): Horton ibid. 294; Africa (Gold Coast): Barker and Sinclair 128 No. 22.

B120.0.1. The oldest animals. E613.3. Reincarnation as hawk.

D152.1.1. *Transformation: god to hawk.* India: Thompson-Balys.

D101. Transformation: god to animal.

D152.2. *Transformation: man to eagle.* Irish myth: *Cross; Welsh: Mac Culloch Celtic 97; Icelandic: Boberg; Finnish: Kalevala rune 43; Italian novella: Rotunda; Missouri French: Carrière; India: Thompson-Balys; Eskimo (Kodiak): Golder JAFL XVI 94 No. 8.

B120.0.1. The oldest animals.

D152.3. *Transformation: man to vulture.* Icelandic: Boberg; India: Thompson-Balys, Penzer VIII 142; Africa (Fang): Trilles 167.

D152.4. *Transformation: girl to falcon.* Italian Novella: Rotunda.

D152.4.1. *Odin as falcon.* Icelandic: Hervarar saga 82, 140, *Boberg.

D152.5. *Transformation: man to osprey.* Irish myth: Cross.

D152.6. *Transformation: man to kite.* India: *Thompson-Balys.

D153. *Transformation: man to bird — coraciiform.*

A1952. Creation of hoopoe. Transformed person.

D153.1. *Transformation: man to woodpecker.* *Type 751A; Dh II 125. — Lappish: Qvigstad FFC LX 38 No. 50; Livonian: Loorits FFC LXVI 90 No. 80.

A1957.1. Woodpecker from devil's shepherd transformed.

D153.2. *Transformation: man to owl.* (Cf. A1710, A1958). — Dh II 123; *Fb "ugle" III 964b. — Irish myth: *Cross; Welsh: MacCulloch Celtic 97; India: Thompson-Balys; S. A. Indian (Chibcha): Kroeber BBAE CXLIII (2) 908.

E613.2. Reincarnation as owl.

D153.3. *Transformation: man to hornbill.* India: Thompson-Balys.

D154. *Transformation: man to bird — charadriiform.*

D154.1. *Transformation: man to dove.* German: Grimm No. 130A; Spanish: Boggs FFC XC 56 No. 408A*; Greek: Frazer Apollodorus II 180 n. 1; India: *Thompson-Balys; S. A. Indian (Chiriguano): Métraux RMLP XXXIII 178.

D154.1.0.1. *Transformation: god to dove.* India: Thompson-Balys.

D101. Transformation: god to animal.

D154.2. *Transformation: man to pigeon.* French Canadian: Sister Marie Ursule; India: *Thompson-Balys; Maori: Clark 36; Tuamotu: Stimson MS (z-G 13/52).

D154.3. *Transformation: man to snipe.* Tuamotu: Stimson MS (P-G 13/10).

D154.4. *Transformation: man to gull.* Eskimo (Ungava): Turner RBAE XI 262, (West Hudson Bay): Boas BAM XV 327.

D155. *Transformation: man to bird — ciconiiform.*

A1965.1. Bittern from Pilate transformed. A1965.2. Bittern from transformed shepherd.

D155.1. *Transformation: man to stork.* *Dh II 102; Wesselski Bebel II 49 No. 117. — Lithuanian: Balys Index Nos. 3131f., Legends Nos. 232, 234, 237, 239—242, 246f.

D624.1. Storks become men in Egypt in winter.

D156. *Transformation: man to cuckoo.* *Dh II 99, 101, 127, III 426ff.; Japanese: Ikeda.

D157. *Transformation: man to parrot.* *Bolte Reise der Söhne Giaffers 209; *Penzer V 27ff., VI 60; India: *Thompson-Balys.

D161. *Transformation: man to bird of anatidae group (duck).*

D161.1. *Transformation: man to swan.* *Type 451; **O. Rank Die Lohengrinsage (1911) 65f.; *Wehrhan Die Sage 50; *Wesselski Märchen 255 No. 64; *Chauvin VIII 206 No. 248; *G. Huet Romania XXXIV (1905) 206ff.; *Fb "svane" III 664ab; H. A. Todd A propos of La Naissance du chevalier au cygne (MLN VI 2); Krappe Apollon Kyknos (Classical Philology XXXVII 353—370); *BP I 427ff.; Hibbard 248, *251. — English Romance: Wells 97 (Chevalere Assigne); Irish: *Cross; Icelandic: Hrómundar saga Gr. 373—75 (Kára), Boberg; Greek: *Frazer Pausanias II 395.

C841.5. Tabu: killing a swan. D361.1. Swan Maiden. D536.1. Transformation to swans by taking chains off neck. V331.9. Swans (transformed children) do not suffer in harsh weather after conversion to Christianity.

D161.2. *Transformation: man to goose.* *Types 403, 450; *Fb "gås"; Hdwb. d. Abergl. VII 1279f.

G304.1.1.3. Troll as goose. K1911.2.1. True bride transformed by false.

D161.2.1. *Transformation: man to gander.* India: Thompson-Balys.

D161.3. *Transformation: man to duck.* Types 403, 434*; Fb "and" IV 12b, "fjer" I 301, "blod" IV 48a; Missouri French: Carrière; Eskimo (Mackenzie Area): Jenness 32a.

G211.3.2. Witch in form of duck. K1911.2.1. True bride transformed by false.

D162. *Transformation: man to crane.* Fb "trane"; Irish myth: *Cross; Icelandic: Boberg; India: Thompson-Balys; Maori: Dixon 79.

D166. *Transformation: man to gallinaceous bird.*

D166.1. *Transformation: man to chicken (cock, hen).*

G211.3.1. Witch in form of hen.

D166.1.1. *Transformation: man to cock.* Fb "kok" II 248b. — Breton: Sébillot Incidents s.v. "coq", Missouri French: Carrière; India: Thompson-Balys.

D166.2. *Transformation: man to peacock.* Hindu: Penzer VIII 142; India: Thompson-Balys.

D166.3. *Transformation: man to turkey.* Papua: Ker 107.

D166.4. *Transformation: person to ptarmigan.* Eskimo (Cumberland Sound): Boas BAM XV 220, 302.

D169. *Transformation: man to bird — miscellaneous.*

D169.1. *Transformation: woman to waterfowl.* India: Thompson-Balys.

D169.2. *Transformation: magician to paddy-bird.* India: Thompson-Balys.

D169.3. *Transformation: man to toucan.* S. A. Indian (Chiriguano): Métraux RMLP XXXIII 178.

D169.4. *Transformation: man to cassowary.* Papua: Ker 90.

D170. Transformation: man to fish. *Types 555, 665; BP I 139; *Fb "fisk"; Chauvin 57 No. 222 n. 3; *Loorits Pharaos Heer in der Volksüberlieferung (Tartu, 1935); Cosquin Études 516ff. — English: Child V 497 s.v. "stepmother"; Irish myth: Cross; Norse: De la Saussaye 261; Lappish: Qvigstad FFC LX 48 No. 75 D; Chinese: Eberhard FFC CXX 122, Graham; India: *Thompson-Balys; Tahitian: Dixon 65; Hawaii: Beckwith Myth XXIII 204, 525; Tuamotu: Stimson MS (z-G 3/1100); Marquesas: Handy 135; Easter Island: Métraux Ethnology 372; Tonga: Gifford 84; Eskimo (Kodiak): Golder JAFL XX 139; N. A. Indian (Seneca): Curtin-Hewitt RBAE XXXII 170 No. 32; S. A. Indian (Cashinawa): Métraux BBAE CXLIII (3) 684, (Toba): Métraux MAFLS XL 52, 150; Africa (Madagascar): Renel I 94ff.

D1281. Magic dead fish.

D171. *Transformation: man to carp.* India: Thompson-Balys; Chinese: Werner 339.

D173. *Transformation: man to eel.* Irish myth: Cross; Polynesian, Melanesian, Indonesian: Dixon 55, 56 nn. 75, 76; Hawaii: Beckwith Myth 21; Samoa: Clark 70.

D173.1. *God assumes form of an eel.* Irish myth: Cross.
A132. God in animal form

D174. *Transformation: man to cuttlefish.* Greek: Frazer Apollodorus II 67 n. 6 (Thetis).

D175. *Transformation: man to crab.* New Guinea: Dixon 138 (woman); Papua: Ker 21, 86.

D175.1. *Transformation: god to crab.* India: Thompson-Balys.

D176. *Transformation: man to salmon.* Irish myth: *Cross; Norse: MacCulloch Eddic 146.
E617.1. Reincarnation as salmon.

D177. *Transformation: man (woman) to catfish.* India: Thompson-Balys.
A2127. Origin of catfish.

D178. *Transformation: man to shark.* Hawaii: Beckwith Myth 140; Fiji: ibid. 131; Tonga: ibid. 130, Gifford 76, 184; Solomon Islands: Beckwith Myth 131.

D179. *Transformation: man to fish — miscellaneous.*

D179.1. *Transformation: man to trout.* Irish myth: Cross.

D179.2. *Transformation: man to pike.* Icelandic: Völsunga saga ch. 14.

D179.3. *Transformation: man to sardine.* India: Thompson-Balys.

D179.4. *Transformation: man to shrimp.* India: Thompson-Balys.

D179.5. *Transformation: man to sword-fish.* Mangaia (Cook Island): Clark 140.

D180. Transformation: man to insect. Cosquin Études 527ff.; Irish: *MacCulloch Celtic 79ff.; Chinese: Werner 363, Eberhard FFC CXX 127; Eskimo (Aleut): Golder JAFL XVIII 220; Africa (Wachaga): Gutman 34.
A2011.2. Creation of ant: avaricious man transformed. E616. Reincarnation as insect.

D181. *Transformation: man to spider.* Tobler 80; Chinese: Werner 364; Africa (Gold Coast): Barker and Sinclair 72 No. 10.
A2091. Origin of spider. A2091.1. Arachne transformed to spider.

D182. *Transformation: man to hymoptera.*

D182.1. *Transformation: man to bee.* Chinese: Werner 363; Indonesian: Dixon 219f.; Africa (Basuto): Jacottet 220 No. 32.
E616.1. Reincarnation as bee.

D182.1.1. *Transformation: man to bumblebee.* India: Thompson-Balys.

D182.2. *Transformation: man to ant.* French Canadian: Sister Marie Ursule; Italian Novella: Rotunda; German: Grimm No. 29; Philippine (Tinguian): Cole 104.

D183. *Transformation: man to orthoptera.*

D183.1. *Transformation: man to cicada.* Greek: Fox 246 (Tithonus).

D183.2. *Transformation: man to cricket.* Chinese: Eberhard FFC CXX 127; Africa (Fjort): Dennett 52 No. 8 (girl).

D184. *Transformation: man to coleoptera.*

D184.1. *Transformation: man to beetle.*

D184.2. *Transformation: man to firefly.* Philippine (Tinguian): Cole 57, 85, 92.

D185. *Transformation: man to diptera.*

D185.1. *Transformation: man to fly.* *Fb "flue" I 315. — Icelandic: De la Saussaye 261f., *Boberg; India: Thompson-Balys; Chinese: Werner 363; Gold Coast: Barker and Sinclair 42 No. 4.

F401.3.4. Spirit as fly going into bottle. F392. Fairy transforms self to fly, allows herself to be swallowed by woman and reborn as fairy. G211.12. Witch in form of fly. K952.2. Man transforms self to gadfly to enter giant's stomach and kill him. K952.2. Animal (monster) killed from within.

D185.1.1. *Transformation: woman (fairy) to fly.* Irish myth: *Cross.

D185.2. *Transformation: man to flea.* Norse: Flateyjarbók I 276; India: Thompson-Balys.

G211.5. Witch in form of insect.

D185.3. *Transformation: man to gnat.* Irish myth: Cross (D187).

D186. *Transformation: man to lepidoptera.*

D186.1. *Transformation: man to butterfly.* Chinese: Eberhard FFC CXX 172, No. 113.

D190. Transformation: man to reptiles and miscellaneous animals.

D191. *Transformation: man to serpent (snake).* (Cf. B642.1.) — *Type 433; *BP III 89 n. 2; *E Hoffmann-Krayer Zs. f. Vksk. XXV 120 n. 1; R. M. Meyer Zs. f. Vksk. XXI 4; Köhler-Bolte II 435ff.; *Krappe Études 53ff.; Hartland Science 244—7; *Fb "orm" II 759b. — Icelandic: MacCulloch Eddic 54 (Bolverk), Boberg; Greek: Frazer Apollodorus II 67 n. 6; Jewish: Neuman; India: *Thompson-Balys, Penzer IX 45. — English: *Child V 497 s.v. "stepmother"; Breton: Sébillot Incidents s.v. "serpent"; Swiss: Jegerlehner Oberwallis 296 No. 21; New Britain: Dixon 117; Philippine (Tinguian): Cole 135; Eskimo (Greenland): Thalbitzer Phonetic Study of Eskimo Language (København, 1904) 5; American Indian (Seneca): Curtin-Hewitt RBAE XXXII 112 No. 14; (Plains Ojibwa): Skinner JAFL XXXII 303 No. 7, (Ladino): Conzemius BBAE CVI 130f.

D449.9. Pieces cut of sorcerer turn into serpents. E614.1. Reincarnation as snake.

D191.1. *Lucifer as serpent.* Irish myth: *Cross.

A671.2.1. Serpents in hell. G303.3.3.6.1. The devil in form of snake.

D192. *Transformation: man to worm (often=snake).* Irish myth: *Cross; English: Child I 315f.; India: *Thompson-Balys.

D192.0.1. *Transformation: demon (in human form) to worm.* Irish myth: Cross.

H47. Demon recognized by corpse it occupies turning to worm when stake is driven through it.

D192.1. *Transformation: man to caterpillar.* India: *Thompson-Balys.

D192.2. *Transformation: man to centipede.* Korean: Zong in-Sob 99 No. 54; Philippine (Tinguian): Cole 99.

D193. *Transformation: man to tortoise (turtle).* *Dh II 128. — Breton: Sébillot Incidents s.v. "tortue". — India: *Thompson-Balys; Chinese: Werner 324; Hawaii: Beckwith Myth 137.

D194. *Transformation: man to crocodile.* (Cf. B642.2.) — India: *Thompson-Balys; Africa (Ekoi): Talbot 181, 401, (Kaffir): Theal 38, (Luba): DeClerq Zs. f. Kolonialsprachen IV 204.

D194.0.1. *Wer-crocodile.* Africa (Ekoi): Talbot 401.

D194.1. *Transformation: man to alligator.* India: Thompson-Balys.

D195. *Transformation: man to frog.* (Cf. B643). — *Type 440; *BP I 1ff.; *Fb "frø" I 378, "blod" IV 48 a; Tobler 80. — Lithuanian: Balys Index No. 3188, Legends No. 202; Spanish: Boggs FFC XC 97 No. 836A; Jewish: Neuman; Buddhist myth: Malalasekera I 289, II 390; Korean: Zong in-Sob V No. 2; Chile: Pino Saavedra 405; Africa (Bushman): Bleek and Lloyd 199, (Zulu): Callaway 211.

E615.1. Reincarnation as frog.

D196. *Transformation: man to toad.* Fb "tudse" III 889a; Hartland Science 51ff.; Tobler 26. — English: Lang Eng. Fairy Tales 190; Breton: Sébillot Incidents s.v. "crapaud"; Chinese: Graham; S. A. Indian (Guaporé Rivér): Lévi-Strauss BBAE CXLIII (3) 379.

G211.6.1. Witch in form of toad.

D197. *Transformation: man to lizard.* S. A. Indian (Warrau): Métraux RMLP XXXIII 146.

D197.1. *Transformation: man to iguana.* S. A. Indian (Toba): Métraux MAFLS XL 66.

D198. *Transformation: man to snail.* India: Thompson-Balys; Korean: Zong in-Sob 30 No. 13; Africa: Milligan 95.

D199. *Transformation: man to other animals than those already treated.*

D199.1. *Transformation: man to centaur.* (Cf. B21.) — Pauli (ed. Bolte) No. 413.

D199.2. *Transformation: man to dragon.* (Cf. B11.) — English: Wells 103 (Alliterative Alexander Fragment A); Irish myth: *Cross.

G211.9.1. Witch in form of dragon.

D199.2.1. *Magician fights as dragon.* Icelandic: *Boberg.

G211.9.1. Witch in form of dragon.

D199.3. *Transformation: woman to siren.* Jewish: Neuman.

D200—D299. Transformation: man to object.

D200. **Transformation: man to object.** Burton Nights I 69, 163, IX 318, S V 247f.; Tawney I 232, II 363; India: Thompson-Balys.

D210. **Transformation: man to vegetable form.**

A2610. Creation of plants by transformation.

D210.1. *Plants as transformed bodies of gods.* Hawaii: Beckwith Myth 93.

D211. *Transformation: man to fruit.* *Type 652; BP II 121ff., *125; Penzer VII 130f., 161.

D431.4. Transformation: fruit to person. D721.5. Disenchantment from fruit (flower) by opening it.

D211.1. *Transformation: man (woman) to orange.* *Type 408; India: Thompson-Balys.

D981.3. Magic orange.

D211.2. *Transformation: man (woman) to pomegranate.* *Type 408; India: *Thompson-Balys.

D211.3. *Transformation: woman (man) to belfruit.* India: Thompson-Balys.

D211.4. *Transformation: man (woman) to mango.* India: Thompson-Balys.

D211.5. *Transformation: man to apple.* Cheremis: Sebeok-Nyerges.

D211.6. *Transformation: man to peach.* Chinese: Graham.

D212. *Transformation: man (woman) to flower.* *Type 652; *BP II 125; *Type 407; BP I 501, III 259; Tobler 69. — India: *Thompson-Balys; Hawaii: Beckwith Myth 93.

D975. Magic flower. E631.1. Flower from grave.

D212.1. *Transformation: man (woman) to carnation.* *Type 652.

D212.2. *Transformation: man (woman) to rose.* *Fb "rose" III 80a; India: Thompson-Balys.

D212.3. *Transformation: woman to lotus.* India: *Thompson-Balys.

D213. *Transformation: man to plant.*

D213.1. *Transformation: man to cockscomb plant.* India: Thompson-Balys.

D213.2. *Transformation: man to rosebush.* German: Grimm Nos. 51, 113.

D213.3. *Transformation: man to turmeric plant.* Easter Island: Métraux Ethnology 365.

D213.4. *Transformation: man to vine.* Hawaii: Beckwith Myth 93, 99.

D213.5. *Transformation: man to thorns.* Chinese: Eberhard FFC CXX 23.

D213.6. *Transformation: man to plantain stalk.* Africa (Bulu): Krug 121f.

D214. *Transformation to grain.*

D214.1. *Transformation: man to rice-grain.* India: Thompson-Balys.

D214.2. *Transformation: man to maize.* Africa (Luba): DeClerq Zs. f. Kolonialsprachen IV 207.

D215. *Transformation: man to tree.* *Type 442; *Fb "træ" III 867b. — Greek: Fox 16; Hindu: Penzer VI 25 n. 1; India: *Thompson-Balys; English: Child V 497 s.v. "stepmother"; Chinese: Eberhard FFC CXX 48; Hawaii: Beckwith Myth XII 101, 254, 478, 495, 532; Philippine (Tinguian): Cole 193; Eskimo (Greenland): Holm 13; N. A. Indian (Seneca): Curtin-Hewitt RBAE XXXII 489 No. 106, (Crow): Lowie PaAM XXV 45; Africa (Fjort): Dennett 42 No. 6, (Basuto): Jacottet 68 No. 10, (Fang): Tessman 112.

D950. Magic tree. E631. Reincarnation in plant (tree) growing from grave.

D215.1. *Transformation: man (woman) to laurel.* Greek: Fox 181 (Daphne).

D215.2. *Transformation: man to pear tree.* Breton: Sébillot Incidents s.v. "poirier".

D215.3. *Transformation: man (woman) to ash tree.* Fb "rön" III 125a.

D215.4. *Transformation: man (woman) to linden tree.* Fb "lind" II 432b.

D215.5. *Transformation: man to apple tree.* Hdwb. d. Märchens s.v. "Apfel" n. 27.

D215.6. *Transformation: man (woman) to mulberry tree.* Hindu: Penzer VI 26 n. 3; Chinese: Eberhard FFC CXX 84.

D215.7. *Transformation: man (woman) to almond tree.* Greek: Frazer Apollodorus II 262 n. 2.

D215.8. *Transformation: man (woman) to mango tree.* India: Thompson-Balys.

D216. *Transformation: man to log.* Hawaii: Beckwith Myth 100; Menomini: Skinner and Satterlee PaAM XIII 317; Philippine (Tinguian): Cole 60; Missouri French: Carrière.

D217. *Transformation: man to stick.* Africa (Hausa): Equilbecq II 171ff.

D218. *Transformation: man to sheaf of grain.*

D218.1. *Transformation: man (woman) to paddy-sheaf.* India: Thompson-Balys.

D221. *Transformation: man to gourd (calabash).* India: Thompson-Balys; Indonesian: DeVries' list No. 155; Cook Islands: Beckwith Myth 268, 450f.; Africa (Basuto): Jacottet 262 No. 39.

D222. *Transformation: man to nut.* Icelandic: Boberg.

D222.1. *Transformation: man to peanut.* Africa: Weeks Jungle 462.

D223. *Transformation: man to grass.* Jewish: Neuman.

D224. *Transformation: man to reed.* Greek myth: Syrinx.

D225. *Transformation: man to seaweed.* Eskimo (Greenland): Holm 13.

D230. Transformation: man to a mineral form.

D231. *Transformation: man to stone.* *Types 303, 471, 516; *Fb "sten" III 553b; Köhler-Bolte I 572f.; *Chauvin VI No. 273, *58 No. 222, VII 83 No. 373bis n. 1, 98 No. 375; *Loomis White Magic 80. — Irish myth: *Cross; Icelandic: *Boberg; Lithuanian: Balys Legends Nos. 503f.; England: *Baughman; Italian novella: Rotunda; Greek: Frazer Apollodorus I 153 n. 3, 343 (Niobe); India: *Thompson-Balys, Tawney I 123; Chinese: Eberhard FFC CXX 94, 119, 209; Japanese: Ikeda; Philippine (Tinguian): Cole 61; Tuamotu: Stimson MS (T-G 3/6); Marquesas: Handy 106; Hawaii: Beckwith Myth 65, 191, 342, 422; Tonga: Gifford 183, Mono Alu: Wheeler 25, 66; New Hebrides: Codrington 367; — Eskimo (Greenland): Rink 219, 464, Rasmussen III 152, 194, (Smith Sound): Kroeber JAFL XII 172, (Mackenzie Area): Jenness 84, (Labrador): Hawkes GSCan XIV 159, (Bering Strait): Nelson RBAE XVIII 505, (Cumberland Sound): Boas BAM XV 172. — American Indian (Central Brazil): Ehrenreich Int. Cong. Americanists XIV 662, (Snuqualmi and Snohomish): Haeberlin JAFL XXXVII 378. — Africa (Basuto): Jacottet 260 No. 38, (Kaffir): Theal 101.

A974.1. Certain stones are druids transformed by power of saint. C331. Tabu: looking back. C452. Tabu: boasting of children. C961.2. Transformation to stone for breaking tabu. D471. Transformation: object to stone. D529.1. Petrification when woman's voice is heard. D581. Petrification by glance. F451.3.2. Dwarfs turn to stone at sunrise. F768.2. City of petrified people. Q551.3.4. Transformation to stone as punishment. Q551.5. Scoffers turned to stone by saint.

D231.1. *Transformation: man to millstone.* Africa (Zulu): Callaway 27.

D231.2. *Transformation: man to marble column.* *Type 707; India: *Thompson-Balys.

D231.2.1. *Mass transformation of wedding party to marble statues, etc.* India: Thompson-Balys.

D233. *Transformation: man to shell.* India: Thompson-Balys; Eskimo (Greenland): Rasmussen I 114; Africa (Zulu): Callaway 27, (Congo): Weeks 200 No. 1.

D235. *Transformation: man (woman) to golden object.*

D235.1. *Transformation: man (god) to shower of gold.* Greek: Fox 33 (Zeus).

C961.1. Transformation to pillar of salt for breaking tabu.

D235.2. *Transformation: woman to golden stool.* India: Thompson-Balys.

D237. *Transformation: man to coral.* India: Thompson-Balys; Tonga: Gifford 94, 100; Marquesas: Handy 106.

D241. *Transformation: man to salt.* Jewish: Neuman.

C961.1. Transformation to pillar of salt for breaking tabu.

D242. *Transformation: man to oil.* Philippine (Tinguian): Cole 61.

D244. *Transformation: man to pumice.* Hawaii: Beckwith Myth 215.

D250. Transformation: man to manufactured object.

D251. *Transformation: man to dish.* N. A. Indian: *Thompson Tales 300 n. 100.

E633. Reincarnation as dish. Bones made into dish.

D251.1. *Transformation: man to saucepan.* Africa (Congo): Weeks 200 No. 1.

D252. *Transformation: man to pot.* Africa (Basuto): Jacottet 240 No. 35.

D253. *Transformation: man to needle.* Africa (Gold Coast): Barker and Sinclair 127 No. 22.

D254. *Transformation: man to musical instrument.*

D254.1. *Transformation: man to fiddle.* India: Thompson-Balys.

D255. *Transformation: man to boat.* Breton: Sébillot Incidents s.v. "bateau".

D255.1. *Transformation: man to canoe.* Hawaii: Beckwith Myth 231, 478.

D256. *Transformation: man to wheel.* *Fb "hjul".

D257. *Transformation: man to hatchel.* Fb "hegle".

D258. *Transformation: man to fishhook.* Easter Island: Métraux Ethnology 364.

D261. *Transformation: man to altar.* Breton: Sébillot Incidents s. v. "autel".

D263. *Transformation: man to ornament.*

D263.1. *Transformation: man to ring.* *Fb "guldring" I 514b; Missouri French: Carrière; N. A. Indian: *Thompson Tales 341 n. 228a; Africa (Luba): DeClerq Zs. f. Kolonialsprachen IV 205.

D263.2. *Transformation: man to necklace.* India: Thompson-Balys.

D263.3. *Transformation: man (girl) to comb.* Hindu: Penzer VII 239.

D263.4. *Transformation: man to beads.* Philippine (Tinguian): Cole 60.

D263.5. *Transformation: man to crown.* German: Grimm No. 51.

D264. *Transformation: man (woman) to skein of silk.* Fb "silke" III 204a.

H1381.3.4. Quest for princess transformed into skein of silk.

D265. *Transformation: man to mat.* Africa (Gold Coast): Barker and Sinclair 127 No. 22.

D266. *Transformation: man to pick-handle.* Africa (Basuto): Jacottet 262 No. 39, (Congo): Weeks 200 No. 1.

D268. *Transformation: man to building.*

D268.0.1. *Transformation: man to church.* German: Grimm No. 51, 113.

D671. Transformation flight.

D268.1. *Transformation: man to housepost.* Tuamotu: Stimson MS (z-G. 13/276).

D268.2. *Transformation: man to figure on ridgepole of house.* Maori: Clark 110.

D270. Transformation: man to object — miscellaneous.

D271. *Transformation: man to meat..*

D271.1. *Transformation: man to lard.* Africa (Basuto): Jacottet 262 No. 39.

D275. *Transformation: man to feather.* Tahiti: Beckwith Myth 37; N. A. Indian: *Thompson Tales 310 n. 117a.

D276. *Transformation: man to egg.* Faroe islands: MacCulloch Eddic 151.

D281. *Transformation: man to storm.* Hottentot: Bleek 65 No. 28.

D905. Magic storm. G304.1.2.1. Troll in form of cloud.

D281.1. *Transformation: man to wind.* Hottentot: Bleek 65 No. 28; India: Thompson-Balys.

D281.1.1. *Transformation: man to whirlwind.* Africa (Basuto): Jacottet 140 No. 20.

E641. Reincarnation as whirlwind.

D281.2. *Transformation: man to lightning.* India: Thompson-Balys.

D281.3. *Transformation: man to thunder.* Madagascar: Renel Contes de Madagascar I 94ff. No. 14.

D283. *Transformation: man to water.*

D421.2.2. Transformation: doe to bubble of water.

D283.1. *Transformation: man (woman) to pool of water.* Irish myth: *Cross, MacCulloch Celtic 60; India: Thompson-Balys; Hawaii: Beckwith Myth 532.

A920.1.11. Woman transformed to pool of water.

D283.2. *Transformation to spring of water.* Hawaii: Beckwith Myth 17; Philippine (Tinguian): Cole 60.

E635. Reincarnation as fountain.

D283.3. *Transformation: watersprite to flood.* German: Grimm No. 181.

D283.4. *Transformation: person to seafoam.* Tuamotu: Stimson MS (z-D. 13/203).

D283.5. *Transformation: man to ocean wave.* Tuamotu: Stimson MS (z-G 13/249); Maori: Beckwith Myth 318.

D284. *Transformation: man (woman) to island.* Greek: Pauly-Wissowa: s.v. "Delos".

D285. *Transformation: man to fire.* India: Thompson-Balys, Penzer VIII 219; Hottentot: Bleek 65 No. 28.

D285.0.1. *Transformation: god to fire.* India: Thompson-Balys.

A170. Deeds of the gods.

D285.1. *Transformation: man to smoke.* German: Grimm No. 163; Chinese: Werner 196.

D286. *Transformation: man to ashes.* Hindu: Keith 115.

D287. *Transformation: man to mound.* Africa (Bondei): Woodward FL XXXVI 367ff. No. 12.

D287.1. *Transformation: man to ant-hill.* India: Thompson-Balys.

D287.2. *Transformation: man to pillar of earth.* Africa (Loango): Pechuël-Loesche 110.

D291. *Transformation: man to mountain.* Africa (Bakuba): Einstein 160.

D292. *Transformation: man to hair.* *Charpentier 35 nn. 1, 2.

D293. *Transformation: man to star.* Jewish: Neuman; Tuamotu: Stimson MS (T-G 3/1005).

A761. Ascent to stars.

D294. *Transformation into puff of dust.* Tuamotu: Stimson MS (z-G. 13/203).

D295. *Transformation: man to spittle.* Jewish: Neuman.

D300—D399. Transformation: animal to person.

D300. Transformation: animal to person. *Goerke Ueber Tierverwandlungen in französischer Dichtung und Sage (Königsberg, 1904); Tawney II 138; India: Thompson-Balys; N. A. Indian (Plains Cree): Skinner JAFL XXIX 345 No. 1 (1); Eskimo (Greenland): Rasmussen III 205, Rink 450.

B650. Marriage to animal in human form.

D310—D349. TRANSFORMATION: MAMMAL TO PERSON

D310. Transformation: wild beast (mammal) to person. Irish myth: *Cross.

D312. *Transformation: feline animal to person.*

D312.1. *Transformation: lion to person.* Hindu: Penzer II 147; Africa (Angola): Chatelain 145, 147 No. 15.

D312.2. *Transformation: tiger to person.* India: *Thompson-Balys; Chinese: Eberhard FFC CXX 62f.

D312.3. *Transformation: leopard to person.* Africa (Mpongwe): Nassau 68 No. 15.

D313. *Transformation: canine animal to person.* Chinese: Krappe CFQ III (1944) 26ff., 136f.

D313.1. *Transformation: fox to person.* Chinese: Werner 370—379, Ferguson 157; Japanese: Ikeda, Anesaki 327; Korean: Zong in-Sob 128; Eskimo (Greenland): Rasmussen II 11.

D313.2. *Transformation: wolf to man.* Irish myth: Cross; Eskimo (Mackenzie Area): Jenness 76.

D113.1.1. Werwolf.

D313.3. *Transformation: bear to person.* Korean: Zong in-Sob 3 No. 1; Eskimo (Greenland): Rasmussen I 134, II 11, III 52, 86, Rink 196, (Mackenzie Area): Jenness 54.

D313.4. *Transformation: hyena to man.* Jewish: Neuman.

D314. *Transformation: ungulate animal (wild) to person.*

D314.1. *Transformation: bovine animal (wild) to person.* Africa (Cameroon): Mansfield 235.

D314.1.1. *Transformation: antelope to person.* Africa (Fjort): Dennett 71 No. 15.

D314.1.2. *Transformation: caribou to person.* Eskimo (Mackenzie Area): Jenness 58, (Ungava): Turner RBAE XI 328f.

D314.1.3. *Transformation: deer to woman.* S. A. Indian (Maroja): Métraux BBAE CXLIII (3) 448.

D314.1.4. *Transformation: gazelle to person.* Africa: Weeks Jungle 450.

D314.3. *Transformation: elephant to person.* Africa (Gold Coast): Barker and Sinclair 126 No. 22.

D315. *Transformation: rodent to man.*

D315.1. *Transformation: rat to person.* Saintyves Perrault 151ff. (to coachman); Type 510. — Missouri French: Carrière; India: Thompson-Balys; Africa (Duala): Lederbogen Africa V140.

D411.6.1. Transformation mouse to horse. D452.1. Transformation pumpkin to carriage. D1111.1. Carriage produced by magic.

D315.2. *Transformation: mouse to person.* India: Thompson-Balys, Penzer V 109 n. 2, Panchatantra III 13 (tr. Ryder) 353; Spanish Exempla: Keller; Eskimo (Mackenzie Area): Jenness 58.

D315.3. *Transformation: badger to person.* Japanese: Anesaki 327.

D315.4. *Transformation: squirrel to person.* India: Thompson-Balys; Eskimo (Mackenzie Area): Jenness 74.

D315.5. *Transformation: hare (rabbit) to person.* Spanish: Boggs FFC XC 60 No. 438; Eskimo (Greenland): Rink 307; Africa (Ila, Rhodesia): Smith and Dale II 395 No. 28.

D318. *Transformation: simian to person.*

D318.1. *Transformation: monkey to person.* Spanish: Boggs FFC XC 72 No. 557; Chinese: Werner 327.

D327. *Transformation: sea-mammal to person.*

D327.1. *Transformation: otter to person.* Chinese: Eberhard FFC CXX 168.

D327.2. *Transformation: seal to person.* Eskimo (Greenland): Rink 456.

D330. Transformation: domestic beast (mammal) to person.

D332. *Transformation: equine animal (domestic) to person.*

D332.1. *Transformation: ass (donkey) to person.* German: Grimm No. 144.

D333. *Transformation: bovine animal to person.* (Cf. D658.4.)

D333.1. *Transformation: bull to man.* Am. Negro (Georgia): Harris Friends 81 No. 11.

D333.2. *Transformation: calf to person.* Chinese: Eberhard FFC CXX 33 No. 55.

D334. *Transformation: goat to person.* India: Thompson-Balys.

D336. *Transformation: swine to person.* *Dh II 191f. — Breton: Sébillot Incidents s.v. "cochon"; Missouri French: Carrière; Italian Novella: Rotunda.

A1371.3. Bad women from transformed hog and goose.

D336.1. *Transformation: pig to person.* Philippine (Tinguian): Cole 116.

D341. *Transformation: dog to person.* Irish myth: Cross (D343.1).

D341.1. *Transformation: bitches to women.* Irish myth: *Cross (D343).

B187.7. Magic bitches (in human form) enchanted by fairy music.

D342. *Transformation: cat to person.* Fb "kat" II 108a. — Italian Novella: Rotunda; India: *Thompson-Balys.

J1908.2. Cat transformed to maiden runs after mouse.

D350. Transformation: bird to person. Tobler 79. — Irish myth: *Cross; Chinese: Eberhard FFC CXX 49f.; Easter Island: Métraux Ethnology 373.

A1271.2. Sun and moon beget stones and birds: these transformed to first parents. B775. Stork is man while hibernating in Egypt. D624.2. Fairies become birds every other year. D1193.1. Magic bag made from skin of crane (transformed woman). F234.1.15. Fairy in form of bird.

D352. *Transformation: falconiform to person.*

D352.1. *Transformation: hawk to person.* Eskimo (Cumberland Sound): Boas BAM XV 210.

D352.2. *Transformation: eagle to person.* Africa: Milligan Jungle 100.

D352.3. *Transformation: falcon to person.* Italian Novella: Rotunda.

D353. *Transformation: coraciiform to person.*

D353.1. *Transformation: woodpecker to person.* Africa (Shangani): Bourhill and Drake 43ff. No. 5.

D354. *Transformation: charidiiform to person.*

D354.1. *Transformation: dove to person.* Dickson 52.

D354.2. *Transformation: gull to person.* Eskimo (Cumberland Sound): Boas BAM XV 216, 302, (Greenland): Rasmussen 219, Rink 451.

D357. *Transformation: parrot to person.* S. A. Indian (Carajá): Lowie BBAE CXLIII (1) 516.

D361. *Transformation: swan to person.* Irish myth: Cross.

D361.1. *Swan Maiden.* A swan transforms herself at will into a maiden. She resumes her swan form by putting on her swan coat. (It is difficult to tell in most Swan Maiden tales whether the primary form is swan or maiden: the incident may belong at D161.) — *Type 313, 400, 465A; *BP III 406; **H. Holmström Studier över svanjungfrumotivet i Volundarkvida och annorstädes (Malmö 1919); Cosquin Indiens 348, 387, 391ff.; *Köhler-Bolte I 444; G. de Raille RTP IV 312; *Penzer VIII 213; Fb "jomfru" II 43, "svane" III 664a. — Irish myth: Cross; Spanish: *Boggs FFC XC No. 400A; Germanic: Grimm Deutsche Mythologie I 354, Krappe Mod. Lang. Review .XXI 66, MacCulloch Eddic 258ff.; Boberg; French: Sébillot France II 198, III 207; U.S.: *Baughman. — Arabian: Burton Nights V 345ff., VIII 31 n.; Persian: Bricteaux Contes Persans 97; India: *Thompson-Balys; Chinese: Graham; Japanese: Anesaki 258. — Indonesian: *DeVries's list Nos. 151—153, Dixon 64, 138 nn. 13—18, 207ff.; Polynesian, Melanesian: ibid. 64, 138 nn. 13—18; Australian: ibid. 294f. — N. A. Indian: *Thompson Tales 356 n. 284; *Hatt Asiatic Influences 94ff.; Eskimo (Greenland): Rasmussen I 364, II 12, III 74, 199, (Central Eskimo): Boas RBAE VI 615, (Smith Sound): Kroeber JAFL XII 170, (Cumberland Sound): Boas BAM XV 179, (Kodiak): Golder JAFL XVI 95.

A132.6.2. Goddess in form of bird. B81. Mermaid. B602. Marriage to bird. B653.1. Marriage to swan maiden. D161. Transformation: person to swan. F234.1.15.1. Fairy as swan. F302.6.1. Celtic fairy mistress dominant F302.4.2. Fairy comes into man's power when he steals her wings. She leaves when she finds them. F387. Fairy captured. K1335. Seduction (or wooing) by stealing clothes of bathing girl. N572.2. Swan maidens as guardians of treasure. T16. Man falls in love with woman he sees bathing. T111. Marriage of mortal and supernatural being.

D361.1.1. *Swan Maiden finds her hidden wings and resumes her form.* Types 400, 465A.— U. S.: *Baughman; India: Thompson-Balys; Korean: Zong in-Sob 22ff. No. 11.

D364. *Transformation: goose to person.* *Dh II 191f; *Fb "gås" I 528b.

A1371.3. Bad women from transformed hog and goose.

D365. *Transformation: duck to person.* (Cf. D361.1.) India: Thompson-Balys.

D370. **Transformation: fish to man.** India: Thompson-Balys; Chinese: Graham, Eberhard FFC CXX 142 No. 96; Tuamotu: Stimson MS (z-G. 13/194); S. A. Indian (Brazil): Oberg 108; Africa (Ila, Rhodesia): Smith and Dale II 403.

D370.1. *Fish cleaned by girl becomes man.* Irish myth: Cross.

D373. *Transformation: eel to person.* Fb "ål" III 1190a. — Tonga: Gifford 182; New Hebrides: Codrington 375; Tuamotu: Stimson MS (z-G. 3/1295).

D375. *Transformation: crab to man.* India: Thompson-Balys.

D376. *Transformation: salmon to person.* Irish myth: Cross (D374).

D380. **Transformation: insect to person.**

D381. *Transformation: spider to man.* Chinese: Eberhard FFC CXX 168.

D382. *Transformation: hymenoptera to person.*

D382.1. *Transformation: bee to person.* Eskimo (Greenland): Thalbitzer Phonetic Study of Eskimo Language (København, 1904) 2.

D382.2. *Transformation: ant to person.* Italian Novella: Rotunda; Greek: Frazer Apollodorus II 53 n. 5; Fox 121.

D390. Transformation: reptiles and miscellaneous animals to persons.

D391. *Transformation: serpent (snake) to person.* Dickson 55 n. 71. — Italian Novella: Rotunda; India: *Thompson-Balys; Buddhist myth: Malalasekera II 389, 423; Chinese: Eberhard FFC CXX 169, 185; Africa (Kaffir): Theal 52, (Zulu): Callaway 321, (Basuto): Jacottet 134 No. 19, 146 No. 20.

D392. *Transformation: worm to person.* Tonga: Gifford 25.

D395. *Transformation: frog to person.* Tobler 77ff; Type 440. — Hindu: Keith 147; India: *Thompson-Balys; Chinese: Eberhard FFC CXX 76, 78.

D396. *Transformation: toad to man.* Chinese: Graham.

D397. *Transformation: lizard to person.* India: Thompson-Balys.

D398. *Transformation: snail to person.* Chinese: Eberhard FFC CXX 59f.

D399. *Transformation: other animals than those already treated to person.*

D399.1. *Transformation: water-dragon to person.* (Cf. B12.) — Chinese: Werner 233.

D400—D499. Other forms of transformation.

D400. Other forms of transformation.

D410. Transformation: one animal to another. India: Thompson-Balys; Jewish: Neuman.

B11.1.2. Dragon from transformed horse. White horse plunges into water and is changed into a dragon. B318. Helpful animals transformed from other animals.

D411. *Transformation: mammal (wild) to another animal.*

D411.1. *Transformation: squirrel to another animal.*

D411.1.1. *Transformation: squirrel to horse.* Breton: Sébillot Incidents s.v. "écureuil".

D411.2. *Transformation: rat to another animal.*

D411.2.1. *Transformation: white rat to white-winged elephant.* Chinese: Werner 121.

B45. Air-going elephant.

D411.3. *Transformation: hare (rabbit) to another animal.*

D411.3.1. *Transformation: hare to leopard.* Ila (Rhodesia): Smith and Dale II 359 No. 12.

D411.4. *Transformation: antelope to another animal.*

D411.4.1. *Transformation: antelope to dog.* Africa (Fjort): Dennett 71 No. 15.

D411.4.2. *Transformation: antelope to goat.* India: Thompson-Balys.

D411.5. *Transformation: monkey to other animal.* Chinese: Werner 331.

3*

D411.5.1. *Transformation: monkey to eagle.* Chinese: Werner 363.

D411.5.2. *Transformation: monkey to candle-moth.* Chinese: Werner 365.

D411.5.3. *Transformation: monkey to ant.* Chinese: Werner 366.

D411.5.4. *Transformation: monkey to ox.* Chinese: Werner 351, 360.

D411.6. *Transformation: mouse to another animal.*

D411.6.1. *Transformation: mouse to horse.* Saintyves Perrault 151ff.; Type 510.

D315.1. Transformation: rat to person. D452.1. Transformation: pumpkin to carriage. D1111.1. Carriage produced by magic.

D411.6.2. *Transformation: mouse to cat.* India: Thompson-Balys.

D411.7. *Transformation: seal to another animal.* Irish myth: Cross.

D411.7.1. *Transformation: seal to horse.* Irish myth: Cross.

D411.8. *Transformation: fox to snake.* Chinese: Eberhard FFC CXX 228.

D411.9. *Transformation: gorilla to eagle.* Africa: Milligan Jungle 100.

D411.10. *Transformation: bear to goose.*

D411.10.1. *Parts of bears fall off and become geese.* Eskimo (Cumberland Sound): Boas BAM XV 256f.

D412. *Transformation: mammal (domestic) to another animal.*

D412.0.1. *Transformation: domestic to wild animal.* India: Thompson-Balys.

D412.1. *Transformation: cat to another animal.*

D412.1.1. *Transformation: cat to horse.* Breton: Sébillot Incidents s.v. "chat".

D412.1.2. *Transformation: cat to toad.* *Kittredge Witchcraft 178 n. 36.

D412.1.3. *Transformation: cat to dog.* India: Thompson-Balys.

D412.2. *Transformation: cow (ox) to another animal.*

D412.2.1. *Transformation: herd of cattle to wolves.* Finnish: Kalevala rune 33.

D412.2.2. *Transformation: ox-demon to pig.* Chinese: Werner 361.

D412.2.3. *Transformation: ox-demon to tiger.* Chinese: Werner.

D412.2.4. *Transformation: ox-demon to leopard.* Chinese: Werner 361.

D412.2.5. *Transformation: ox-demon to bear.* Chinese: Werner 361.

D412.2.6. *Transformation: ox-demon to elephant.* Chinese: Werner 361.

D412.3. *Transformation: swine becomes another animal.*

D412.3.1. *Transformation: pig-fairy to fish.* Chinese: Werner 363.

D412.3.2. *Transformation: pig to fish.* Irish myth: Cross.

D412.3.3. *Transformation: boar-pigs into he-goats.* *Loomis White Magic 80.

D412.3.4. *Transformation: sows into she-goats.* *Loomis White Magic 80.

D412.3.5. *Transformation: pig to dragon.* Chinese: Eberhard FFC CXX 162.

D412.4. *Transformation: horse to another animal.* Irish myth: Cross.

D412.4.1. *Transformation: packhorse to palfrey.* Irish myth: Cross.
D1860. Magic beautification.

D412.5. *Transformation: dog to another animal.* Irish myth: Cross.

D412.5.1. *Transformation: dog to dove (transformed man).* Irish myth: Cross.

D412.5.2. *Transformation: hound to lap-dog.* Irish myth: Cross.

D412.5.3. *Transformation: dog to otter.* Irish myth: Cross.

D412.5.4. *Animal that is hound by day, sheep by night.* Irish myth: Cross.
D621. Daily transformation.

D412.5.5. *Transformation: dog to leopard.* India: Thompson-Balys.

D412.5.6. *Transformation: dog to spider.* Eskimo (Cumberland Sound): Boas BAM XV 226.

D412.5.7. *Transformation: dog to snake.* Eskimo (Greenland): Rasmussen III 75.

D412.6. *Transformation: ass to horse.* *Loomis White Magic 80; S. A. Indian (Toba): Métraux MAFLS XL 89.

D412.7. *Transformation: sheep to grasshoppers.* Mexico: Mendoza Santa Barbara; India: Thompson-Balys.

D413. *Transformation: bird to another animal.* Irish myth: Cross.

D413.1. *Transformation: hawk to salmon (transformed man).* Irish myth: Cross.

D413.2. *Transformation: raven to water bird.* Eskimo (Greenland): Rasmussen III 73.

D415. *Transformation: insect to another animal.*

D415.1. *Transformation: mantis to another animal.*

D415.1.1. *Transformation: mantis to hartebeest.* Africa (Bushman): Bleek and Lloyd 3.

D418. *Transformation: reptile to other animal.*

D418.1. *Transformation: serpent (snake) to other animal.*

D418.1.1. *Transformation: python to gorilla.* Africa: Milligan Jungle 100.

D418.1.2. *Transformation: snake to dragon.* Chinese: Eberhard FFC CXX 31.

D418.1.3. *Transformation: serpent to mosquito.* India: Thompson-Balys.

D418.2. *Transformation: worm to other animal.*

D418.2.1. *Transformation: worm to serpent.* Jewish: Neuman.

D418.2.2. *Transformation: worm to dog.* Chinese: Eberhard FFC CXX 72.

D419. *Transformation: miscellaneous animals to other animals.*
D491.1. Compressible magic animals.

D419.1. *Transformation: dragon to other animal.* (Cf. B11.)

D419.1.1. *Transformation: sea dragon to serpent.* Chinese: Werner 311.
D659.4.2. Sea dragon in serpent form to accompany hero.

D419.1.2. *Transformation: dragon to horse.* Korean: Zong in-Sob 64 No. 35.

D420. Transformation: animal to object. India: Thompson-Balys; Koryak: Jochelson JE VI 194, 196, 323; Eskimo (Greenland): Rasmussen I 185, (Central Eskimo): Boas RBAE VI 639.

D421. *Transformation: mammal (wild) to object.*

D421.1. *Transformation: wolf to object.*

D421.1.1. *Transformation: wolf to tree.* Swiss: Jegerlehner Oberwallis 323. No. 108.

D421.2. *Transformation: antelope to object.*

D421.2.1. *Transformation: antelope to nut.* Africa (Fjort): Dennett 71 No. 15.

D421.2.2. *Transformation: doe to bubble of water (enchanted woman).* Irish myth: Cross.

D421.3. *Transformation: elephant to object.* India: Thompson-Balys.

D421.3.1. *Transformation: elephant to lotus.* India: Thompson-Balys.

D421.3.2. *Transformation: elephant to stone.* India: Thompson-Balys.

D421.4. *Transformation: tiger to object.*

D421.4.1. *Transformation: tigress to mortar.* India: Thompson-Balys.

D421.5. *Transformation: deer to object.*

D421.5.1. *Transformation: stag to wind.* Chinese and Persian: Coyajee JPASB XXIV 182f.

D421.6. *Transformation: bear to object.*

D421.6.1. *Transformation: bear to bow.* N. A. Indian (Klikitat): Jacobs U. Wash. II 31.

D421.7. *Transformation: whale to object.*

D421.7.1. *Transformation: whale to skull.* Eskimo (Labrador): Hawkes GSCan XIV 155, (Greenland): Rink 128, Holm 44, Rasmussen II 18, III 84.

D422. *Transformation: mammal (domestic) to object.*

D422.1. *Transformation: horse to object.*

D422.1.1. *Transformation: horse to river.* Breton: Sébillot Incidents s.v. "rivière".

D422.1.2. *Transformation: horse to stone.* Irish myth: Cross; India: Thompson-Balys.

D422.2. *Transformation: dog to object.*

D422.2.1. *Transformation: dead dog to money.* Fb "hund" I 676a; Lithuanian: Balys Index No. 3629; Chinese: Eberhard FFC CXX 229f. No. 176, FFC CXXVIII 201f. No. 113.

D422.2.2. *Transformation: dog to pumpkin.* India: Thompson-Balys.

D422.2.3. *Transformation: dog to statue.* India: Thompson-Balys.

D422.3. *Transformation: pig to object.* Irish myth: Cross.

D422.3.1. *Transformation: pig to bread.* Irish myth: Cross.

D423. *Transformation: bird (fowl) to object.*

D423.1. *Transformation: goose to object.*

D423.1.1. *Transformation: flock of geese to stone.* Fb "gås" I 528b.

D423.2. *Transformation: quails to sticks and pebbles.* India: Thompson-Balys.

D423.3. *Transformation: duck to precious stone.* Chinese: Eberhard FFC CXX 196.

D423.4. *Transformation: buzzard to door flap.* Klikitat: Jacobs U. Wash. II 31.

D424. *Transformation: insect to object.*

D424.1. *Transformation: butterfly to bamboo.* Chinese: Eberhard FFC CXX 266.

D425. *Transformation: reptile to object.*

D425.1. *Transformation: snake to object.*
A182. Snake turns to gold in answer to dream.

D425.1.1. *Transformation: snake to stone.* India: *Thompson-Balys.

D425.1.2. *Transformation: snake to jewel.* India: Thompson-Balys.

D425.1.2.1. *Transformation: snake to gold.* Chinese: Eberhard FFC CXX 184.

D425.1.3. *Transformation: snake to garland.* India: Thompson-Balys.

D425.1.4. *Transformation: snake to ship.* Buddhist myth: Malalasekera II 1160.

D426. *Transformation: fish to object.*

D426.1. *Transformation: eel to object.*

D426.1.1. *Transformation: eel to stone.* Hawaii: Beckwith Myth 21.

D426.1.2. *Transformation: eel to dry land.* Tuamotu: Stimson MS (z-G 13/221).

D426.2. *Transformation: octopus to stone.* Hawaii: Beckwith Myth 22.

D428. *Transformation: amphibian to object.*

D428.1. *Transformation: frog to object.*

D428.1.1. *Transformation: frog to tree.* Chinese: Graham.

D429. *Transformation: animal to object — miscellaneous.*

D429.1. *Transformation: water monster to Milky Way.* Raratonga: Beckwith Myth 439.

A778. Origin of Milky Way.

D429.2. *Transformation: dragon to object.* (Cf. B11.)

D429.2.1. *Transformation: dragon-king to gust of wind.* Chinese: Werner 311.

D429.2.2. *Transformation: dragon to stone.* Irish myth: Cross.

B11. Dragon.

D429.2.2.1. *Transformation: man-eating giantess to stone.* India: Thompson-Balys.

B11. Dragon. F531. Giant. G100. Giant ogre.

D430. Transformation: object to person.

A1271.2. Sun and moon beget stones and birds: these transformed to first parents.

D431. *Transformation: vegetable form to person.*

A2611. Plants from body of slain person or animal.

D431.1. *Transformation: flower to person.* *BP II 126f.; India: *Thompson-Balys; Chinese: Graham.

E251.2.2. Prince plucks from grave of vampire a flower which later becomes a girl.

D431.1.1. *Transformation: rose to person.* Spanish: *Boggs FFC XC 82 No. 708a; India: Thompson-Balys.

D431.1.2. *Transformation: carnation to person.* Spanish: Boggs FFC XC 59 No. 425D.

D431.2. *Transformation: tree to person.* Irish myth: Cross; Jamaica: *Beckwith MAFLS XVII 263 No. 67; Chinese: Eberhard FFC CXX 168.

T543.1. Bird from a tree.

D431.3. *Transformation: leaf (of tree) to person.* Africa (Yoruba): Ellis 257 No. 4, (Fjort): Dennett 43 No. 6, (Upoto): Einstein 141.

D431.4. *Transformation: fruit to person.* India: *Thompson-Balys.

D211. Transformation: man to fruit. F562.4. Girl lives in fruit and comes out only to be bathed by her 20 sisters.

D431.5. *Transformation: grass to person.*

D431.5.1. *Transformation: grass to soldiers.* Chinese: Graham.

D431.6. *Transformation: plant to person.* Hawaii: Beckwith Myth 515; Papua: Ker 131.

D431.6.1. *Woman emerges from plant.* India: *Thompson-Balys.

D431.7. *Transformation: reed to person.* Africa (Ba Ronga): Einstein 259.

D431.8. *Transformation: corn to person.* Jewish: Neuman.

D431.9. *Transformation: root (bulb) of plant to person.* Chinese: Eberhard FFC CXX 168.

D431.10. *Transformation: sections of bamboo to persons.* Papua: Ker 138.

D431.11. *Transformation: nut to person.* Papua: Ker 86; Philippine (Tinguian): Cole 121.

D432. *Transformation: mineral form to person.* Irish myth: Cross.

D432.1. *Transformation: stone to person.* Irish myth: Cross; India: Thompson-Balys; Chinese: Eberhard FFC CXX 69; Philippine (Tinguian): Cole 179.

D931. Magic rock (stone). F585.2. Magic phantom army. Created out of puffballs and leaves.

D432.2. *Transformation: shell to person.*

D432.2.1. *Every piece of shattered cowrie-shell turns into an armed man.* India: Thompson-Balys.

F585.2. Magic phantom army.

D432.3. *Transformation: jewel to person.*

D432.3.1. *Transformation: ruby to person.* India: Thompson-Balys.

D434. *Transformation: manufactured object to person.*

D434.1. *Transformation: utensil to person.* Chinese: Eberhard FFC CXX 169.

D434.2. *Transformation: rope to person.* Hawaii: Beckwith Myth 465.

D434.3. *Transformation: canoe-bailer to person.* Hawaii: Beckwith Myth 233.

D434.4. *Transformation: coffin cover to person.* Chinese: Eberhard FFC CXX 168.

D435. *Transformation: image to person.* (Cf. D445.) Korean: Zong in-Sob 213; Eskimo (Bering Strait): Nelson RBAE XVIII 517.

J2186. Trickster's false creations fail him.

D435.1. *Transformation: statue to person.*

D435.1.1. *Transformation: statue comes to life.* *Type 945, cf. Type 165*; *BP III 53 n. 2; D. E. MacKay The Double Invitation in the Legend of Don Juan (1943); *Loomis White Magic 81; Hdwb. d. Märchens s.v. "Baum"; Köhler-Bolte I 531. — Greek: Fox 200 (Galateia); Finnish: cf. Kalevala rune 37; Germanic: MacCulloch Eddic 188; Breton: Sébillot Incidents s.v. "statue"; Lithuanian: Balys Index No. *701; Hindu: Benfey Panchatantra I 490; India: Thompson-Balys; Babylonian: Meissner Babylonien und Assyrien II 96; Semitic: bin Gorion Born Judas V 180ff.; Jewish: Neuman; Indonesian: DeVries's list No. 184, Dixon 200, *201 n. 38; Torres Straits: Dixon 142 n. 25; German New Guinea: ibid. 141; Australian: ibid. 274; Eskimo (Bering Strait): Nelson RBAE XVIII 479, 485, 497, (Central Eskimo): Boas RBAE VI 619, (Koryak): Jochelson JE VI 22, 286, 370; N. A. Indian: Thompson Tales 357 n. 287i, Hatt Asiatic Influences 97.

A1241.3. Man made from clay image and vivified. A1245.2. Mankind from vivified stone image. A1252.1. Mankind from vivified wooden image. F1023. Creation of a person by cooperation of skillful men. T376. Young man betrothed to statue.

D435.1.2. *Transformation: dolls change to fairies when flute is played.* India: Thompson-Balys.

D523. Transformation through song. D786. Disenchantment by music. E55. Resuscitation by music.

D435.1.3. *Image of boy made of flowers comes to life.* India: Thompson-Balys.

K1924. Barren wife makes child by magic and claims it as her own.

D435.1.4. *Wax prince animated by serpent becomes human being.* India: Thompson-Balys.

D435.1.5. *Transformation: stone lion to man.* Chinese: Eberhard FFC CXX 169.

D435.2. *Transformation: picture to person.*

D435.2.1. *Picture comes to life.* Chauvin VII 101 No. 376. — India: Thompson-Balys; Chinese: Eberhard FFC CXX 61f.; N. A. Indian: Thompson Tales 357 n. 287i, Hatt Asiatic Influences 100.

D1266.2. Magic picture.

D436. *Transformation: manufactured object to person.*

D436.1. *Transformation: utensil to person.* Chinese: Eberhard FFC CXX 169.

D436.2. *Transformation: rope to person.* Hawaii: Beckwith Myth 465.

D436.3. *Transformation: canoe-bailer to person.* Hawaii: Beckwith Myth 233.

D436.4. *Transformation: coffin cover to person.* Chinese: Eberhard FFC CXX 168.

D437. *Transformation: part of animal or person to person.*

D437.1. *Human bone transforms self to person.* Africa (Pahouine): Largeau 198.

D437.2. *Animal bone transforms self to person.* Papua: Ker 13.

D437.3. *Transformation: feather to person.* Africa (Shangani): Bourhill and Drake 43ff. No. 5.

D437.4. *Transformation: excrements to person.* Eskimo (Greenland): Rasmussen III 85.

D437.5. *Transformation: spittle to person.* India: Thompson-Balys.

D439. *Transformation: miscellaneous objects to persons.*

C963.2. Person returns to original egg form when tabu is broken.

D439.1. *Transformation: tow to person.* Breton: Sébillot Incidents s.v. "filasse".

D439.2. *Transformation: coal to person.* Africa (Kaffir): Theal 87.

D439.3. *Transformation: water bubble to person.* Jewish: Neuman.

D439.4. *Transformation: egg to person.* India: Thompson-Balys; Africa (Duala): Lederbogen Märchen 384.

D439.4.1. *Woman emerges from egg.* India: Thompson-Balys.

D721.5. Disenchantment from fruit (flower) by opening it. T542. Birth of human being from an egg.

D439.5. *Transformation: heavenly body to person.*

D439.5.1. *Transformation: moon to person.* Samoa: Clark 118; S. A. Indian (Amuesha): Métraux RMLP XXXIII 150.

D439.5.2. *Transformation: star to person.* Philippine (Tinguian): Cole 15 n. 2, 109.

D439.6. *Fire takes the form of a woman and runs away.* India: Thompson-Balys.

D440. **Transformation: object to animal.** India: Thompson-Balys.

D441. *Transformation: vegetable form to animal.* Irish myth: Cross.

D441.1. *Transformation: tree to animal.* Hdwb. d. Märchens s.v. "Baum"; BP I 146f.

D441.2. *Transformation: fruit to animal.*

D441.2.1. *Transformation: fruit to birds.* Trees grow fruits. Those which fall on ground ripen and are normal; those that fall into water become birds and fly away. — *Pauli (ed. Bolte) II 445 No. 879.

D981. Magic fruit.

D441.3. *Transformation: branch of tree to animal.* S. A. Indian (Ceuici): Alexander Lat. Am. 304.

D954. Magic bough.

D441.3.1. *Transformation: faggots to chargers.* India: Thompson-Balys.

D441.3.2. *Transformation: log to bear.* India: Thompson-Balys.

D441.4. *Transformation: plant to animal.* Jewish: Neuman.

D441.4.1. *Transformation: fern to animal.* Irish myth: Cross.

D441.5. *Transformation: leaves to animal.*

D441.5.1. *Transformation: leaves to eels.* New Hebrides: Codrington 396.

D441.5.2. *Transformation: banana leaf to fish.* Africa (Duala): Lederbogen JAS IV 71.

D441.6. *Transformation: embers into animal.* (Cf. D562.2) — India: Thompson-Balys.

D441.6.1. *Transformation: ashes into animals.*

K2351.2.2. Ashes transferred into bees, wasps, scorpions and snakes drive invading army away from hero.

D441.7. *Transformation: sticks of wood to animal.* Jewish: Neuman; Philippine (Tinguian): Cole 17, 33, 52, 58; S. A. Indian (Apapocuvú-Guarani): Métraux RMLP XXXIII 138.

D441.7.1. *Transformation: rod to serpent.* Hebrew: Exodus 7:10.

D441.8. *Transformation: piece of cotton to snake.* India: Thompson-Balys.

D441.9. *Transformation: straw to snake.* India: Thompson-Balys.

D441.9.1. *Transformation: wisp of hay to horse.* (Cf. D451.5.7.) — Gering Islendzk Æfentyri II 167; Grimm Irische Elfenmärchen No. 11. — Malay: Hambruch Malaiische Märchen 215.

D441.10. *Transformation: chips of wood to animal.* Eskimo (Labrador): Hawkes GSCan XIV 152.

D442. *Transformation: mineral form to animal.*

D442.1. *Transformation: stone to animal.* Irish myth: Cross (D449.6); Hawaii: Beckwith Myth 22; Eskimo (Cumberland Sound): Boas BAM XV 163, 228.

D442.2. *Transformation: earth (dirt) to animal.* India: Thompson-Balys (D446.1.)

D442.2.1. *Transformation: earth to lice.* Jewish: Neuman.

D442.2.2. *Transformation: grave to animal.* Eskimo (Kodiak): Golder JAFL XVI 21.

D442.3. *Transformation: gold to animal.* Chinese: Eberhard FFC CXX 229f.

D444. *Transformation: manufactured object to animal.*

D444.1. *Transformation: money of the hard-hearted to scorpions.* (Cf. D444.2, D444.4, D469.11, D471.1). — Bolte Zs. f. Vksk. XXIX 69; cf. BP III 168, 462.

D661. Transformation as punishment. Q286. Uncharitableness punished.

D444.2. *Transformation: meat to toad.* Punishment for ungrateful son. Dh IV 262; Japanese: Ikeda.

D1032. Magic meat.

D444.3. *Transformation: pill to white rabbit.* Chinese: Werner 185.

D444.4. *Transformation: bread to serpents.* (Cf. D444.1, D444.2, D469.11, D471.1.) — BP III 462.

D444.5. *Transformation: book-satchel to bird.* Irish myth: Cross.

D444.6. *Transformation: drinking horn to dragon.* Norse: Herrmann Saxo Gr. II 596.

D444.7. *Transformation: armring to serpent.* Norse: Herrmann Saxo Gr. II 596.

D444.8. *Transformation: mortar to tigress.* India: Thompson-Balys.

D444.9. *Transformation: pouch to parts of body of ptarmigan.* Eskimo (Cumberland Sound): Boas BAM XV 320.

D444.10. *Transformation: dress to animal.*

D444.10.1. *Transformation: dress to butterfly.* Chinese: Eberhard FFC CXX 264.

D444.10.2. *Transformation: mitten to dog.* Eskimo (Bering Strait): Nelson RBAE XVIII 510.

D444.10.3. *Duck's sandals transformed to part of his feet.* S. A. Indian (Chiriguano): Métraux RMLP XXXIII 178.

D444.11. *Transformation: oars and masts to serpents.* Greek: Frazer Apollodorus I 333 n. 1.

D445. *Transformation: image of animal vivified.* (Cf. D435) — Dh. II 72ff. — India: Thompson-Balys; Chinese: Eberhard FFC CXX 234; N. A. Indian: Thompson Tales 357 n. 287i.

D445.1. *Image of horse vivified.* Chinese: Eberhard FFC CXX 231f.

D445.1.1. *Image of horse will be vivified only for one person.* India: Thompson-Balys.

D1651. Magic object obeys master alone. H31. Recognition by unique ability.

D445.2. *Images of parrots vivified.* India: Thompson-Balys.

D445.3. *Image of golden calf vivified.* Jewish: Neuman.

D447. *Transformation: parts of animal or human body to animal.*

D447.1. *Transformation: hair to animal.*
D991. Magic hair.

D447.1.1. *Transformation: hair to monkey.* Chinese: Werner 366.

D447.1.2. *Transformation: hair to insect.* Chinese: Werner 364.

D447.1.3. *Transformation: hair to serpent.* Sébillot France III 257; Eitrem Opferritus und Voropfer der Griechen und Römer 359. — England, U.S.: Baughman.

D447.2. *Transformation: skull to water-monster.* Africa (Angola): Chatelain 115 No. 9.

D447.3. *Transformation: blood to animal.*
D454. Transformation: blood to another object.

D447.3.1. *Transformation: blood drops to toads.* India: Thompson-Balys.

D447.3.1.1. *Transformation: blood drops to serpents.* Greek: Fox 34.
D1016. Magic blood of animal.

D447.3.2. *Transformation: blood of gorgon to flying horse.* Greek: Grote I 7.

D447.4. *Transformation: fishtail to shark.* Hawaii: Beckwith Myth 134.

D447.5. *Transformation: toes of sorceress to dogs.* Eskimo (Cumberland Sound): Boas BAM XV 248.

D447.6. *Transformation: tooth to fox.* Eskimo (Greenland): Rasmussen I 185.

D447.7. *Transformation: pig's bones to pig.* Papua: Ker 13.

D447.8. *Transformation: bone to dog.* Eskimo (Greenland) Rasmussen III 119.

D447.9. *Parts of sorcerer's body turn into serpents.* Icelandic: Boberg.
D191. Transformation: man to serpent.

D447.10. *Transformation: brain to giant serpent.* Irish myth: Cross (D449.7).

D449. *Transformation: miscellaneous objects to animals.*

D449.1. *Magic charm turns sweets into bugs.* (Cf. D522). India: Thompson-Balys.

D449.2. *Transformation: corpse to serpent.* Jewish: Neuman.

D449.3. *Transformation: treasure to ducks.* Chinese: Eberhard FFC CXX 196.

D449.4. *Transformation: snow to dogs.* Eskimo (Cumberland Sound): Boas BAM XV 324.

D450—D499. TRANSFORMATION: OBJECT TO OBJECT

D450. Transformation: object to another object. India: Thompson-Balys; Icelandic: Boberg.

D451. *Transformation of vegetable form.*

D451.1. *Transformation: tree to other object.* *Loomis White Magic 95; Africa (Loango): Pechuël-Loesche 109.

D451.1.0.1. *Transformation: branch of tree to palace.* India: Thompson-Balys.

D451.1.1. *Transformation: ash to hazel.* Irish myth: Cross (D469.17).

D451.2. *Transformation: plant to other object.* Irish myth: Cross (D452).

D451.2.1. *Transformation: rush to leek.* Irish myth: Cross (D462.1).

D451.2.1.1. *Transformation: rushes to grain.* Irish myth: Cross (D462.1.1).

D451.2.2. *Transformation: wheat to barley.* Irish myth: Cross (D462.2).

D451.2.3. *Transformation: oats to wheat.* Irish myth: Cross (D462.3).

D451.2.4. *Transformation: cotton to leaves.* India: Thompson-Balys.

D451.3. *Transformation: fruit to other object.* Irish myth: Cross (D463).

D451.3.1. *Transformation: apples to grain.* Irish myth: Cross (D463.1).

D451.3.2. *Transformation: cocoanut to philosopher's stone.* India: Thompson-Balys.

D451.3.3. *Transformation: pumpkin to carriage.* Type 410. — Breton: Sébillot Incidents s.v. "carosse"; Missouri French: Carrière.

D451.3.4. *Transformation: apples to pig bristles (frog legs).* German: Grimm No. 165.

D451.4. *Transformation: flowers to other object.*

D451.4.0.1. *Transformation: flowers to gold beads.* India: Thompson-Balys.

D451.4.1. *Transformation: lotus to human hand.* Penzer VIII 54.

D451.4.2. *Hibiscus blossom transformed to canoe.* Hawaii: Beckwith Myth 405.

D451.5. *Transformation: grass to other object.*

D451.5.1. *Transformation: blade of grass to horse.* Africa (Fjort): Dennett 63 No. 12.

D451.5.2. *Transformation: blade of grass to knife.* Africa (Fjort): Dennett 63 No. 12.

D451.5.3. *Transformation: blade of grass to gun.* Africa (Fjort): Dennett 63 No. 12.

D451.5.4. *Transformation: grass to beard.* Irish myth: Cross (D457.4).
K1821.4. Youths wear false beards (of grass, wool).

D451.5.5. *Transformation: pieces of grass turned into stone steps.* Chinese: Graham.

D451.5.6. *Transformation: roll of grass into gold.* Buddhist myth: Malalasekera II 210.

D451.5.7. *Transformation: wisp of hay to bridge.* — Maliseet: Mechling JAFL XXVI 251.

D451.6. *Transformation: stick (log) to other object.*

D451.6.1. *Transformation: wand to other object.*

D451.6.1.1. *Transformation: wand to bridge.* Breton: Sébillot Incidents s.v. "pont". — Cherokee: Mooney RBAE XIX 319 No. 67.

D451.6.2. *Stick thrust in ground changes into spirit hut.* Philippine (Tinguian): Cole 62.

D451.6.3. *Transformation: stick to weapon.* Africa (Loango): Pechuël-Loesche 109.

D451.7. *Transformation: nut to another object.*

D451.7.1. *Transformation: nut to palace.* Spanish: Boggs FFC XC 54 No. 400B.

D451.8. *Transformation: leaf to another object.* Buddhist myth: Malalasekera I 109; Hawaii: Beckwith Myth 478.

D451.8.1. *Transformation: leaves to cotton.* India: Thompson-Balys.

D451.8.2. *Transformation: leaf to knife.* Africa (Loango): Pechuël-Loesche 109.

D451.9. *Transformation: vegetable to other object.*

D451.9.1. *Transformation: peas to stones.* (Cf. D444.4, D471.1.) — BP III 462.

D452. *Transformation of mineral form.*

D452.1. *Transformation: rock (stone) to other object.*

D452.1.1. *Transformation: rock to hut.* Africa (Kaffir): Theal 83.

D452.1.2. *Transformation: stone to mountain.* Regular in D672, where references are given.

D452.1.3. *Transformation: stone to salt.* *Loomis White Magic 81; Irish myth: *Cross (D456.3); Jewish: Neuman.

D452.1.4. *Transformation: stone into jewel.* Lithuanian: Balys Index No. *1670.

D452.1.5. *Transformation: rock to glass.* *Loomis White Magic 81.

D452.1.6. *Transformation: stones to peas.*

D452.1.6.1. *Christ asks woman what she is cooking; she replies that she is boiling stones to make her children think they are peas and that they will have food. Christ changes the stones to peas.* England: Baughman.

D452.1.7. *Transformation: stone to firebrand.* Africa (Duala): Lederbogen JAS IV 71.

D452.1.8. *Transformation: stone to island.* Tonga: Gifford 191.

D452.1.9. *Transformation: stone to pillow.* Jewish: Neuman.

D452.1.10. *Transformation: rock to water.* Jewish: Neuman.

D452.1.11. *Transformation: stones to weapons.* Jewish: Neuman.

D452.1.12. *Transformation: stones to dust.* Jewish: Neuman.

D452.2. *Transformation: shell to another object.*

D452.2.1. *Transformation: shell to boat.* Breton: Sébillot Incidents s.v. "bateau".

D452.3. *Transformation: sand to another object.*

D452.3.1. *Transformation: sand to rice.* India: Thompson-Balys; Africa (Duala): Lederbogen Märchen 82.

D452.4. *Transformation: earth (dirt) to another object.*

D452.4.1. *Transformation: dirt to pepper.* Africa (Duala): Lederbogen JAS IV 71.

D454. *Transformation of manufactured object.*

D454.1. *Transformation: box to another object.*

D454.1.1. *Transformation: box to carriage.* Spanish: Boggs FFC XC 72 No. 557.

D454.1.2. *Transformation: box to ship.* Breton: Sébillot Incidents s.v. "boîte".

D454.2. *Transformation: bread to another object.* (Cf. D471).

D454.2.1. *Transformation: bread to flower.* Breton: Sébillot Incidents s.v. "fleur".

D454.2.2. *Bread tree springs from crumb of bread.* India: Thompson-Balys.

D1782. Sympathetic magic. Magic results obtained by imitating desired action.

D454.3. *Transformation: clothing to other object.*

D454.3.1. *Transformation: one article of clothing to another.* Irish myth: Cross (D469.16).

D454.3.1.1. *White chasuble suddenly turned into red.* *Loomis White Magic 81.

D454.3.2. *Transformation: handkerchief to other object.*

D454.3.2.1. *Transformation: handkerchief with three knots to clod, potsherd, and charcoal.* India: Thompson-Balys.

D1282.1. Magic knot.

D454.3.2.2. *Transformation: handkerchief with three knots to golden leopard, golden snake, and golden monkey.* India: Thompson-Balys.

B100. Treasure animals.

D454.3.3. *Transformation: belt to bridge* N. A. Indian (Quinault): Farrand JE II 115.

D1057. Magic belt. D1258. Magic bridge.

D454.3.4. *Transformation: cloak to other object.*

D454.3.4.1. *Transformation: cloak to mountain.* Tuamotu: Stimson MS (z-G. 13/420).

D454.3.4.2. *Transformation: cloak to vessel.* Saintyves Saints Successeurs 254f.

D454.4. *Transformation: needle to other object.* India: Thompson-Balys.

D454.4.1. *Transformation: thread to other object.* Africa (Vai): Ellis 191 No. 8.

D454.5. *Transformation: milk sack to other object.*

D454.5.1. *Transformation: milk sack to sheet of water.* Africa (Kaffir): Theal 87.

D454.6. *Transformation: pot to other object.* Africa (Kaffir): Theal 88.

D454.6.1. *Transformation: bowl to other object.* India: Thompson-Balys.

D454.7. *Transformation: brush to mountain.* German: Grimm No. 79.

D454.7.1. *Transformation: comb to mountain.* German: Grimm No. 79.

D454.8. *Transformation: ornament to other object.*

D454.8.1. *Transformation: necklace to other object.* India: Thompson-Balys.

D454.8.2. *Transformation: ring to other object.*

D454.8.2.1. *Transformation: ring to saber.* Breton: Sébillot Incidents s.v. "bague".

D454.9. *Transformation: weapon to other object.*

D454.9.1. *Transformation: spear to other object.*

D454.9.1.1. *Transformation: spear becomes mighty tree when driven into ground.* India: Thompson-Balys.

D454.9.2. *Transformation: sling-stick to boat.* Irish myth: Cross (D469.18).

D454.10. *Transformation: ship to other object.*

D454.10.1. *Transformation: ship to mountains.* Maori: Beckwith Myth 467.

D454.10.2. *Transformation: canoe into rock.* Tonga: Gifford 76.

D454.11. *Transformation: writing tablets to bundle.* Irish myth: Cross (D469.15).

D454.12. *Transformation: mirror to glass mountain.* German: Grimm No. 79

D454.13. *Transformation: pieces of chalk into tins of oil.* India: Thompson-Balys.

D454.14. *Transformation: ink to beams of light.* Jewish: Neuman.

D454.15. *Transformation: statue to drinking vessels.* Jewish: Neuman.

D454.16. *Transformation: instruments of torture to lotus flowers.* Chinese: Werner 268.

D457. *Transformed parts of person or animal to object.*

D457.1. *Transformation: blood to another object.*

D457.1.1. *Transformation: blood to rubies.* Turns to rubies as it drops. *Cosquin RTP XXVIII 194, *Contes indiens 18ff.; India: Thompson-Balys.

D475. Transformation: objects to treasure.

D457.1.2. *Transformation: blood to milk.* Bird caught and told to make milk bleeds and blood turns to milk. Africa (Kaffir): Theal 34 No. 1.

D457.1.3. *Transformation: drops of blood to flowers.* India: Thompson-Balys.

D457.2. *Transformation: milk to blood.* Irish myth: *Cross (D454.2.1).

D474.5. Transformation: butter (milk) to blood.

D457.3. *Transformation: calf's head to death's head.* *BP I 276 n. 2, II 535; Sébillot Incidents s.v. "tête".

D457.4. *Transformation: hair to other object.* Jewish: Neuman.

D457.4.1. *Transformation: hair to stream.* *Fb "hår" I 771b.

D457.4.2. *Transformation: hair to forest.* *Fb "hår" I 771b; Jewish: Neuman.

D457.4.3. *Transformation: hair to bridge.* Köhler-Bolte I 195.

D457.5. *Transformation: meat to other object.*

D457.5.1. *Transformation: stolen meat to roses.* Italian Novella: Rotunda.

V410. Charity rewarded.

D457.5.2. *Meat received from spirits transformed to banana leaves.* Africa (Wachaga): Gutman 105.

D457.6. *Transformation: scurf from body to palm tree.* India: Thompson-Balys.

D457.7. *Transformation: feather to tree.* Africa (Shangani): Bourhill and Drake 43ff. No. 5.

D457.8. *Transformation: tooth to ax head.* Cheremis: Sebeok-Nyerges; Norse: Herrmann Saxo II 596.

D457.9. *Transformation: finger to ax handle.* Cheremis: Sebeok-Nyerges; Chinese: Eberhard FFC CXX 131 No. 89.

D457.9.1. *Transformation: cut-off hand to plant.* Chinese: Eberhard FFC CXX 130 No. 85.

D457.10. *Transformation: moustache into grass.* (Cf. D562.2.) India: Thompson-Balys.

D457.11. *Transformation: eye to another object.*

D457.11.1. *Transformation: bull's eye to hornets.* India: Thompson-Balys.

B524.2.1. Enemies driven away by helpful hornets, bees, etc.

D457.11.2. *Transformation: eyeballs to torches.* Jewish: Neuman.

D457.12. *Transformation: bone to other object.*

D457.12.1. *Transformation: bone-dust becomes blazing fire.* India: Thompson-Balys.

D457.12.2. *Transformation: bone to skeleton.* Eskimo (Greenland): Holm 26.

D457.13. *Transformation: animal dung to other object.* Africa (Duala): Lederbogen Märchen 82.

D457.14. *Transformation: tongue to other object.*

D457.14.1. *Transformation: ogress's tongue to surfboard.* Hawaii: Beckwith Myth 194.

D457.14.2. *Transformation: tongue to flame.* Jewish: Neuman.

D457.15. *Transformation: animal heart to other object.*

D457.15.1. *Transformation: fox's heart to rattle.* S. A. Indian (Toba): Métraux MAFLS XL 138.

D457.16. *Transformation: saint's relics to other object.*

D457.16.1. *Saint's relics assume form of Buddha.* Buddhist myth: Malalasekera II 500f.

D457.17. *Transformation: flesh to other object.*

D457.17.1. *Transformation: flesh to fire.* Jewish: Neuman.

D457.18. *Transformation: tears to other object.*

D457.18.1. *Transformation: tears to fountain.* Jewish: Neuman.

D457.18.2. *Transformation: tears to river.* Jewish: Neuman.

D457.19. *Transformation: ear tips (animal) into pelts.* Eskimo (Bering Strait): Nelson RBAE XVIII 471, 541.

D469. *Transformation: miscellaneous object to other objects.*

D469.1. *Transformation: egg to mist.* Africa (Kaffir): Theal 87.

D469.1.1. *Transformation: egg to house.* Africa (Duala): Lederbogen Märchen 83.

D469.2. *Transformation: smoke to bridge.* Africa (Vai): Ellis 191 No. 8.

D469.3. *Transformation: chain of arrows to bridge.* Africa (Vai): Ellis 191 No.8.

D469.4. *Transformation: sea-scum to ice.* Eskimo (Greenland) Rasmussen III 260.

D469.5. *Transformation: furnace of fire to garden.* Jewish: Neuman.

D470. **Transformation: material of object changed.** India: Thompson-Balys.

D471. *Transformation: object to stone.*

D231. Transformation: man to stone. F934.3. Lake petrifies wood.

D471.1. *Transformation: bread to stone.* As punishment. (Cf. D441.1, D444.2, D444.4, D476.) — Type 368*; *BP III 168, 462; Fb "sten" III 553b, 554a; Hdwb. d. Abergl. I 1599; Icelandic: *Boberg.

D471.2. *Transformation: house to stone.* N. A. Indian (Seneca): Curtin-Hewitt RBAE XXXII 212 No. 41, 398 No. 70, 409 No. 73.

D471.2.1. *Transformation: house-door to stone.* N. A. Indian (Shasta): Farrand-Frachtenberg JAFL XXVIII 216 No. 6.

D471.3. *Transformation: ship to stone.* Greek: Fox 211.
V421. Shipman refuses alms: ship turned to stone.

D471.4. *Transformation: cheese to stone.* *Loomis White Magic 79; Irish myth: *Cross.

D471.4.1. *Transformation: milk to stone.* *Loomis White Magic 79.
D746.2.3.2. Milk transformed into lye.

D471.5. *Transformation: salt to stone.* Irish myth: Cross.
D1039.2. Magic salt. Q591.2. Punishment: man says salt he carries is stones; immediately becomes so.

D471.6. *Transformation: tree to stone.* Irish myth: Cross.

D471.7. *Transformation: poison to stone.* Irish myth: Cross.

D471.8. *Animals turned into stones.* *Loomis White Magic 80f.

D471.8.1. *Stolen chickens turned to stones in cooking.* *Loomis White Magic 79.
Q212.6. Stolen animal's meat impossible to cook.

D471.9. *A candle becomes stone.* *Loomis White Magic 81.

D471.10. *Water becomes rocks.* (Cf. D478). Jewish: Neuman.

D472. *Transformation: object to muck.*

D472.1. *Transformation: food to muck.* As punishment. Fb "mog" II 603; India: Thompson-Balys.
G265.8.1.1. Witch bewitches food in house.

D473. *Transformation: object to wood.*

D473.1. *Transformation: sword to wood.* Chauvin V 173 No. 96 n. 1.
H215. Magic manifestation at execution proves innocence.

D474. *Transformation: object becomes bloody.* Irish myth: *Cross.
D1003. Magic blood — human. D1016. Magic blood — animal. D1317. Magic object warns of danger. D1500.1.9. Magic healing blood. E761.1.1. Life token: water turns to blood. F961.1.8. Sun appears color of blood. F961.3.1. Moon turns to blood. F991. Object bleeds.

D474.1. *Tranformation: key becomes bloody.* *Type 311, 312; BP I 404ff.
C913. Bloody key as sign of disobedience.

D474.2. *Transformation: water becomes bloody.* Loomis White Magic 78; Irish myth: *Cross; Spanish Exempla: Keller; Jewish: Neuman; Buddhist myth: Malalasekera I 358.
F930. Extraordinary occurrences concerning seas or waters.

D474.3. *Transformation: cake becomes bloody.* Irish myth: *Cross.
F991.3. Bleeding cake. Bleeds when cut.

D474.4. *Egg becomes bloody.* German: Grimm No. 46.

D474.5. *Transformation: butter (milk) to blood.* Irish myth: *Cross.

D474.6. *Tears change to blood.* Jewish: Neuman.

D474.7. *Spittle changes to blood.* Jewish: Neuman.

D474.8. *Fruit juice turns to blood.* Jewish: Neuman.

D474.9. *Eyes of stone lion become bloody.* Chinese: Eberhard FFC CXX 83.

D475. *Transformation: object to treasure (or vice versa).*

B100. Treasure animals. D457.1.1. Transformation: blood to rubies. D1450. Magic objects furnish treasure. D2100. Magic wealth. F340. Gifts from fairies. K236.3. Tribute paid in enchanted snow: after payment snow takes proper form.

D475.1. *Transformation: objects to gold.* Encyc. Religion and Ethics s.v. "Alchemy"; *Loomis White Magic 79, 81. — Irish: Cross, Plummer xliv, clxxxv; German: Hartland Science 49; India: *Thompson-Balys; Chinese: Werner 383.

C911. Golden finger as sign of opening forbidden chamber. C912. Hair turns to gold as punishment in forbidden chamber. D565.1. Midas's golden touch. Everything touched turns to gold. D1450. Magic objects furnish treasure. D1466.1. Magic stone turns everything to gold. D2102. Gold magically produced. E501.15.4. Wild huntsman repays with leaves (shavings) that turn to gold. F342.1. Fairy gold. F348.0.1. Fairy gift disappears or is turned to something worthless when tabu is broken. F451.5.1.4. Dwarf's gold. Seemingly worthless gift given by dwarfs turns to gold. V411.4. Stones turn to gold for charitable money-lender.

D475.1.1. *Transformation: coals to gold.* Fb. "kul", "guld". — Swiss: Jegerlehner Oberwallis 322 No. 80.

F342.1. Fairy gold. Fairies give coals (wood, earth) that turns to gold.

D475.1.1.1. *Transformation: ashes to gold.* India: Thompson-Balys.

D475.1.2. *Transformation: shavings to gold.* Fb "høvlspån".

D475.1.3. *Transformation: dead leaves to gold.* Grimm Deutsche Mythologie 2, 246, 452.

D475.1.3.1. *Banyan leaves turn to gold.* Buddhist myth: Malalasekera II 1262.

D475.1.4. *Transformation: spittle to gold.* Hindu: Williams 11.

D1001. Magic spittle. D1454.3. Treasure from spittle.

D475.1.5. *Transformation: fire to gold.* Fb "ild" II 11b.

D475.1.6. *Transformation: rice to gold.* India: Thompson-Balys; Japanese: Mitford 180ff.

D475.1.6.1. *Transformation: grain to gold.* *Loomis White Magic 79; Irish myth: **Cross.

D475.1.7. *Transformation: brick (tile) to gold.* India: *Thompson-Balys; Chinese: Werner 382.

D475.1.8. *Transformation: earth to gold.* Fb "jord" II 45b.; India: Thompson-Balys.

D475.1.9. *Transformation: copper to gold.* India: Penzer III 162 n.

D475.1.10. *Transformation: hair to gold.* India: *Thompson-Balys.

C912. Hair turns to gold as punishment in forbidden chamber.

D475.1.11. *Paste (smeared on princess's body) turns to gold.* India: Thompson-Balys.

D475.1.12. *Transformation: putrescence to gold.* Irish myth: *Cross.

D475.1.13. *Mucus turns to gold to reward piety.* Irish myth: Cross.

D475.1.14. *Transformation: bottle to gold.* French Canadian: Sister Marie Ursule.

D475.1.15. *Transformation: palace to gold.* Buddhist myth: Malalasekera II 210.

D475.1.16. *Transformation: food to gold.* India: Thompson-Balys.

D475.1.17. *Transformation: axe becomes golden.* India: Thompson-Balys.

D475.1.18. *Transformation: flowers to gold and silver.* India: Thompson-Balys.

D475.1.19. *Transformation: leaves on which meal is served turn to gold plates.* India: Thompson-Balys.

D475.1.20. *Transformation: straw to gold.* German: Grimm No. 55.

D475.1.21. *Transformation: fingernails to gold.* Chinese: Eberhard FFC CXX 165 No. 108.

D475.2. *Transformation: object to money (or vice versa).*

D475.2.1. *Transformation: stones to gold coins.* Tobler 71.

D475.2.2. *Transformation: water to money.* Africa (Kpelle): Westermann Zs. f. afrikan., ozean., u. ostasiat. Spr. VI 161 No. 29a.

D475.2.3. *Transformation: money to ashes (leaves).* Fb "penge"; India: Thompson-Balys.

A1715. Animals from men transformed for discourtesy to God (Jesus). Q221.1. Discourtesy to God punished.

D475.2.4. *Transformation: money to pewter.* Chinese: Werner 373.

D475.3. *Transformation: objects to silver.*

D475.3.1. *Transformation: earth to silver.* Africa (Mossi): Frobenius Atlantis VIII 274ff. No. 20.

D475.3.2. *Tin changed into silver.* *Loomis White Magic 81.

D475.3.3. *Transformation: stone to silver.* India: Thompson-Balys; Chinese: Graham.

D475.3.4. *Transformation: iron in axe to silver.* German: Grimm No. 99.

D475.3.5. *Transformation: silver dish becomes wooden.* Irish myth: Cross (D479.16).

D475.4. *Transformation: object to jewels (or vice versa).* *Loomis White Magic 81.

D475.4.1. *Transformation: stones into jewels.* *Loomis White Magic 81; India: Thompson-Balys.

D475.4.2. *Transformation: lice into gems.* *Loomis White Magic 81.

D475.4.3. *Transformation: dishes to jewels.* India: Thompson-Balys.

D475.4.4. *Transformation: peas to pearls.* India: Thompson-Balys.

D475.4.5. *Tears become jewels.* German: Grimm No. 179; Greek: Grote 134; Jewish: Neuman; India: Thompson-Balys.

D475.4.6. *Transformation: fingernails into jewels.* India: Thompson-Balys.

D475.4.7. *Transformation: hairs to jewels.* India: Thompson-Balys.

D475.4.8. *Water dripping off person becomes agates.* Philippine (Tinguian): Cole 43, 55.

D475.4.9. *Oil changed to jewels.* Jewish: Neuman.

D475.5. *A cup of marble changed into one of crystal.* *Loomis White Magic 81.

D476. *Food transformed.*

D476.1. *Inedible substance transformed into edible.*

D476.1.1. *Bread made from mud.* *Loomis White Magic 81.

D476.1.2. *Loaf of bread made from the leaf of a tree.* *Loomis White Magic 81.

D476.1.3. *Wood turned into grain.* *Loomis White Magic 81.

D476.1.4. *Lard made from tree bark.* *Loomis White Magic 81.

D476.1.5. *Butter made from nettles.* *Loomis White Magic 81.

D476.1.6. *Pancakes made of snow.* *Loomis White Magic 78.

D476.1.7. *Rock changed into milk.* *Loomis White Magic 81.

D476.1.8. *Stream changed to egg.* Jewish: Neuman.

D476.1.9. *Transformation: ice becomes grease.* N. A. Indian (Menomini): Skinner and Satterlee PaAM XIII 270, (Crow): Lowie PaAM XXV 23ff., (Southern Ute): Lowie JAFL XXXVII 11 No. 5.

D476.1.10. *Bone-powder changed into cheese.* *Loomis White Magic 81.

D476.1.11. *Transformation: sand to rice.* India: Thompson-Balys.

D476.2. *Edible substance changed to inedible.*

D476.2.1. *Transformation: food to dust.* Jewish: Neuman.

D476.2.2. *Cooked meat changed to raw.* (Cf. D476.4.) — Jewish: Neuman.

D476.2.3. *Milk transformed into other substance.* *Loomis White Magic 79.

D476.2.3.1. *Milk transformed into blood.* *Loomis White Magic 79.

D476.2.3.2. *Milk transformed into lye.* *Loomis White Magic 79.

D476.2.4. *Transformation: sugar to ashes.* India: Thompson-Balys.

D476.3. *Meat transformed.*

D476.3.1. *Meat takes on taste of any dainty desired.* Jewish: Neuman.

D476.3.2. *Bacon changed to iron.* Irish myth: Cross (D479.5).

D476.3.2.1. *Bacon changed to different foods.* Loomis White Magic 79; Irish myth: *Cross (D479.5.1).

D476.3.3. *Transformation: horse meat to mutton.* Irish myth: Cross (D479.6).

D476.3.4. *Meat miraculously turned into fish on a feast day, and vice versa.* *Loomis White Magic 79.

D476.4. *Bread becomes cake.* German: Grimm No. 64.

D477. *Transformation: object becomes wine (or vice versa).* Irish myth: *Cross.

D477.0.1. *Wine miraculously changed into other object.* *Loomis White Magic 78.

D477.0.1.1. *Wine becomes blood* (Cf. D471.4.1). — *Loomis White Magic 78.

D477.0.1.2. *Wine becomes honey.* *Loomis White Magic 78.

D477.0.1.3. *Spiced wine becomes bitter.* Jewish: Neuman.

D477.1. *Transformation: water becomes wine.* Fb "vand" III 1000a.; St. John 2:9; Grimm Deutsche Mythologie I 486; Hartland Science 69; Farnell Cults of the Greek States V 156; Wuttke Volksaberglaube (Berlin 1900) 66ff.; *Toldo VI 310ff.; *Saintyves Essais 206ff.; Günter 246 s.v. "Wein"; *Loomis White Magic 78; Irish myth: *Cross; Icelandic: Boberg; Spanish Exempla: Keller.

B119.1. Dog turns water to wine. B183.8. Magic pig turns water to wine. E761.1.1. Life token: water turns to blood. E761.6.5. Life token: wine turns to vinegar.

D477.1.1. *Devil takes man waiting for water to turn to wine at midnight on Old Christmas Eve.* U. S.: Baughman.

D477.1.2. *Woman loses eye when she goes to well at midnight on Old Christmas Eve when the water turns to wine.* England: Baughman.

D477.2. *Transformation: brine becomes wine.* Irish myth: Cross.

D477.3. *Beer becomes wine.* German: Grimm No. 64.

D478. *Water changed to other substance (or vice versa).*

D478.1. *Transformation: water to milk.* Irish myth: *Cross (D479.4); Sébillot France II 213.

D478.2. *Transformation: water to ale.* Irish myth: *Cross (D479.4.1).

D478.3. *Transformation: water to fire.* Irish myth: *Cross (D479.4.2); Jewish: Neuman.

D478.4. *Transformation: water to marvelous drink.* Irish myth: *Cross (D479.4.3).

D478.5. *Transformation: water to honey.* *Loomis White Magic 78; Irish myth: *Cross (D479.4.4).

D478.6. *Transformation: water to mead.* Irish myth: *Cross (D479.4.5).

D109.1.2. Dog (whose skin) turns water to wine (mead).

D478.7. *Transformation: water changed into oil.* *Loomis White Magic 78.

D478.8. *Water changed into balsam.* *Loomis White Magic 78.

D478.9. *Water in river transformed to copper by magician.* Spanish Exempla: Keller.

D478.10. *Salty water turned into fresh liquid.* *Loomis White Magic 78; Jewish: Neuman.

D478.11. *Transformation: water to butter and cream.* Buddhist myth: Malalasekera II 460.

D478.12. *Transformation: water to rocks.* Jewish: Neuman.

D478.13. *Transformation: water to brimstone.* Jewish: Neuman.

D478.14. *Boiling pitch reduced to cold water.* *Loomis White Magic 81.

D479. *Transformation: miscellaneous objects change material.*

D479.1. *Transformation: bog to flowery mead (through power of saint).* Irish myth: Cross (D479.6).

D937. Magic plain.

D479.2. *Transformation: iron tools to earth.* India: Thompson-Balys.

D479.3. *Transformation: magic charm makes root bitter.* India: Thompson-Balys.

D479.4. *Transformation: goose egg becomes hen's egg.* Irish myth: Cross (D479.17).

D479.5. *Transformation: basket of things to iron.* India: Thompson-Balys.

D479.6. *Wax turned into earth.* *Loomis White Magic 81.

D479.7. *Evil smells transformed into sweet fragrances, and vice versa.* *Loomis White Magic 81.

D479.8. *Hut transformed into golden palace.* India: Thompson-Balys.

D480. Size of object transformed. Irish myth: Cross.

D55. Magic change of person's size. D631.1. Size changed at will.

D480.0.1. *Things miraculously stretched or shortened if needed by a saint.* *Loomis White Magic 89.

D482. *Stretching objects.*

D482.1. *Transformation: stretching tree. A tree magically shoots upward.* — India: Thompson-Balys; Batak: Warneck Religion der Batak 50; Melanesian: Codrington 165. — N. A. Indian: Thompson Tales 332 n. 199; S. A. Indian (Mataco): Métraux MAFLS XL 35; Africa (Ekoi): Talbot 188, 306.

D950. Magic tree. D1520.1.1. Transportation by stretching and swaying tree. D1576.1. Magic song causes tree to rise to sky. F54.1. Tree stretches to sky. F811. Extraordinary tree. K1113. Abandonment on stretching tree. A man is induced to get into a tree which magically shoots upward. R251. Flight on tree which ogre tries to cut down. S11.2. Jealous father sends son to upper world on stretching tree.

D482.2. *Stretching lily plant. Miraculously quick growing.* India: Thompson-Balys.

D965. Magic stick of wood.

D482.3. *Magic stretching lance* (Cf. D1086). Jewish: Neuman.

D482.4. *Transformation: stretching cliff. A cliff magically shoots up into the air.* Breton: Sébillot Incidents s.v. "precipice". — Hawaii: Dixon 90; Calif. Indian: Gayton and Newman 76.

D482.5. *Stretching sepulchre. Magically becomes longer.* Irish myth: Cross (D484).

D1299.2. Magic sepulchre (grave).

D482.5.1. *Grave equals five times length of any person's foot.* Irish myth: Cross (D484.1).

D482.5.2. *Tomb gate magically enlarged.* Jewish: Neuman.

D483. *Sea formed from giant's spittle.* (Cf. D1001.) — Indonesian: DeVries Volksverhalen II 285.

D483.1. *River expands and becomes sea.* S. A. Indian (Apapocuvú-Guaraní): Métraux RMLP XXXIII 138.

D485. *Transformation: stretching fingers to make ladder.* French Canadian: Sister Marie Ursule.

D486. *Person becomes larger.*

D486.1. *Demon becomes larger.* Tuamotu: Stimson MS (z—G. 13/420).

D487. *Animal becomes larger.*

D487.1. *Snake grows to 300 leagues length.* Buddhist myth: Malalasekera II 859.

D487.2. *Monkey becomes 100,000 feet high.* Chinese: Werner 361.

D487.3. *Ox-demon becomes 10,000 feet long.* Chinese: Werner 361.

D488. *Houses magically made larger.* Eskimo (Greenland): Rink 219.

D489. *Objects made larger — miscellaneous.*

D489.1. *Small leaves become larger.* Buddhist myth: Malalasekera II 1205.

D489.2. *Amulet enlarged to become cloak.* Jewish: Neuman.

D490. Miscellaneous forms of transformation.

D491. *Compressible objects.* N. A. Indian: Thompson Tales 336 n. 210a.

D55.2. Person becomes magically smaller. D55.2.4. Ten serving women carried in bottle. They change size at will. D631. Size changed at will. D631.3. Size of object changed at will. D631.3.1.1. Compressible ship. D2185. Magician carries woman in glass coffin. She comes out at his will.

D491.1. *Compressible magic animals.*

D491.1.1. *Herd of cattle put into magic cup.* (Cf. B182.) — Greek: Fox 86.

D491.1.2. *Magic folding mule.* Folds up like a sheet of paper. (Cf. B184.1.) — Chinese: Werner 294.

D491.1.3. *Magic dog shrinks in size.* Irish myth: Cross.

D491.2. *Compressible magic objects.*

D491.2.1. *Compressible magic box.*

D491.2.1.1. *Compressible magic box containing many people and objects.* East Africa: Frobenius Atlantis IV 134ff. No. 13.

D1476.1. Magic calabash furnishes slaves. D1477.1. Magic calabash furnishes livestock.

D491.2.2. *Compressible table.* Irish myth: *Cross.

D491.3. *Saint confined a large quantity of water in a small ditch.* *Loomis White Magic 41.

D491.4. *Iceflake made small by magic.* Eskimo (Greenland): Rasmussen III 270.

D491.5. *Castle magically made smaller.* German: Grimm No. 163.

D491.6. *Twelve stones unite to make one.* Jewish: Neuman.

D491.7. *Ship becomes small boat.* Tuamotu: Stimson MS (T—G 3/900).

D492. *Color of object changed.*

D492.1. *Cock's comb becomes white.* Jewish: Neuman.

D492.2. *Blood turns black.* Jewish: Neuman.

D492.3. *Color of hair suddenly changed.* Jewish: Neuman.

D493. *Spirit changes to animal.* Tuamotu: Stimson MS (T—G 3/1001, z-G. 3/1353).

D494. *Transformation: person to monster.* Eskimo (Greenland): Rasmussen III 154.

D500—D599. Means of transformation.

D500. Means of transformation — general.

D502. *Inability to transform self in presence of others.* Chinese: Graham.

D510. Transformation by breaking tabu. Tahiti: Beckwith Myth 468; Eskimo (Mackenzie Area): Jenness 154.

C960. Transformation for breaking tabu. D565.1. Transformation by sexual intercourse.

D511. *Transformation by breaking name tabu.* (Cf. C430.)

D511.1. *Man calls wife "my swallow"; she becomes swallow.* (Cf. A1917.) — Dh III 414.

C32. Tabu: offending supernatural husband. C435. Tabu: uttering spouse's name.

D512. *Transformation by expressing astonishment at marvel.* India: Thompson-Balys.

C32.1. Tabu: looking at supernatural husband.

D512.1. *Transformation when one expresses astonishment at smith drawing water in an egg-shell.* (Cf. C491.) — *Köhler-Bolte I 220.

D513. *Transformation by violation of looking tabu.* (Cf. C300.)

D513.1. *Man looks at copulating snakes: transformed to woman.* (Cf. D12.) — Greek: Frazer Apollodorus I 364 n. 1.

C300. Looking tabu.

D515. *Transformation by plucking flowers in enchanted garden.* Type 451.

C515. Tabu: plucking flowers. D961. Magic garden.

D516. *Transformation through excessive grief.* Greek: Roscher s.v. "Itys"; Japanese: Ikeda; N. A. Indian (Thompson): Alexander N. Am. 137.

C762.2. Tabu: too much weeping for dead. E361. Return from the dead to stop weeping.

D517. *Transformation because of disobedience.* India: Thompson-Balys.

D518. *Woman transformed for nourishing an animal.* Eskimo (Smith Sound): Kroeber JAFL XII 176, (Greenland): Rink 413, Rasmussen III 81, (West Hudson Bay): Boas BAM XV 638.

D520. Transformation through power of the word.

D521. *Transformation through wish.* Type 451; Irish myth: Cross; Jewish: Neuman; N. A. Indian (Seneca): Curtin-Hewitt RBAE XXXII 398 No. 70, 409 No. 73, (Shasta): Farrand-Frachtenberg JAFL XXVIII 216 No. 6; Eskimo (Cumberland Sound): Boas BAM XV 172.

D1761. Magic results produced by wishing.

D521.1. *Transformation through thoughtless wish of parent.* BP I 430 (Grimm Nos. 9, 27, 49).

S11. Cruel father.

D522. *Transformation through magic word (charm).* (Cf. D1273.) — Irish myth: Cross; India: *Thompson-Balys, Penzer I 136, II 20, VI 8, 59. — Tuamotu: Stimson MS (z-G. 13/203); Jamaica: *Beckwith MAFLS XVII 271 No. 84.

D1273. Magic formula (charm).

D523. *Transformation through song.* (Cf. D1275.) — Jamaica: Beckwith MAFLS XVII 273 No. 87.

D523.1. *Transformation by playing musical instrument.*

D523.1.1. *Transformation by playing flute.* Chinese: Graham.

E55.2. Resuscitation by playing flute.

D525. *Transformation through curse.* Irish myth: Cross; India: Thompson-Balys, Penzer VI 16, VIII 140ff.; Icelandic: *Boberg.

D1711.4. Druid as magician. D1713. Magic power of hermit (saint). D1792. Magic results from curse. D2062.2.2. Person suffers from "crookedness in his eyes" as result of curse. D2175. Cursing by magic. M400. Curses. M400.1. Satire. M430. Curses on person.

D525.1. *Despondent mother curses herself and children into trees.* Lithuanian: Balys Index No. *425D.

D526. *Transformation through greeting: first creature to be greeted will be transformed.* (Cf. A1371.3.) — *Dh II 191ff.

N125.2. Districts named from first person met in each. S241.1. Unwitting bargain with devil evaded by driving dog over bridge first. The child has been unwittingly promised (the first thing that goes over the bridge).

D527. *Transformation by scolding.* Eskimo (Greenland): Rink 468.

D529. *Transformation through power of the word — miscellaneous.*

D529.1. *Petrification when woman's voice is heard.* India: Thompson-Balys.

D321. Transformation: man to stone.

D530. Transformation by putting on skin, clothing, etc.

D113.1.1. Werwolf. D1025. Magic skin of animal. G270. Witch overcome or escaped.

D531. *Transformation by putting on skin.* By putting on the skin, feathers, etc. of an animal, a person is transformed to that animal. — Fb "and"; Icel.: Völsunga saga ch. 8; Irish myth: *Cross; English: Child II 494, III 518, IV 495a, V495 s.v. "seals"; India: *Thompson-Balys; Chinese: Graham; Japanese: Ikeda; N. A. Indian: *Thompson Tales 313 n. 132; Eskimo (Greenland): Rasmussen I 364, II 13, III 75, 143, 262, Rink 146, (Cumberland Sound): Boas BAM XV 181, (Central Eskimo): Boas RBAE VI 617, (Bering Strait): Nelson RBAE XVIII 468, (Kodiak): Golder JAFL XVI 95; Jamaica: Beckwith MAFLS XVII 271 No. 84; North Carolina Negro: Parsons JAFL XXX

187; Surinam: Alexander Lat. Am. 274. — See also all references under D361.1 (Swan Maiden).

D361.1. Swan Maiden. D721. Disenchantment by removing skin (covering).

D532. *Transformation by putting on claw, feather, etc. of helpful animal.* Types 552A, 553; *BP III 434; Eskimo (Kodiak): Golder JAFL XXII 13.

B501. Animal gives part of body as talisman for summoning its aid. B505. Magic object received from animal. D684. Transformation by helpful animal. D1021. Magic feather. D1023. Magic hair of animal.

D533. *Transformation to fish by catching in fish-trap.* India: Thompson-Balys.

D535. *Transformation to horse (ass. etc.) by putting on bridle (halter).* *Fb "hest" I 598b, "grime" I 484, "bidsel" IV 37b; Köhler-Bolte I 220, 586. — Estonian: Aarne FFC XXV 130 No. 71; Finnish: Aarne FFC XXXIII 45 No. 71; Lithuanian: Balys Index No. 3656; India: Thompson-Balys, Penzer VI 56 n. 2, *59.

C837. Tabu: loosing bridle in selling man transformed to horse. D131. Transformation: man to horse. D132. Transformation man to ass. D722. Disenchantment by taking off bridle. D1209.1. Magic bridle. G211.1.2. Witch as horse shod with horseshoes.

D535.1. *Transformation to horse by being horse-shod.* Köhler-Bolte I 220, 586.

G221.1.2. Witch as horse shod with horseshoes.

D536. *Transformation by removing chains from neck.*

D536.1. *Transformation to swans by taking chains off neck.* (Cf. D161.) — **O. Rank Die Lohengrinsage (1911) 65f.; *Wehrhan 50; *Wesselski Märchen 255 No. 64; *Chauvin VIII 206 No. 248; *G. Huet Romania XXXIV (1905) 206ff.; H. A. Todd MLN VI 2. — Norse: MacCulloch Eddic 263; English Romance: Wells 97 (Chevalere Assigne).

D723.1. Disenchantment by putting chain around neck. D1078. Magic chain.

D537. *Transformation by changing clothes.* Icelandic: Árnason (Powell and Magnusson tr.) II 246, Boberg. — N. A. Indian (Micmac): Rand Nos. 5, 16, 17. (Caughnawaga): Harrington JAFL XIX 127f., cf. (Yana): Curtin Creation Myths of Primitive America (Boston 1898) 312ff. — Cf. Fb. "klæder" II 200a.

D537.1. *Transformation by donning hood.* (Cf. D1067.3.) Irish myth: *Cross.

D537.2. *Transformation by donning cloak.* Irish myth: Cross.

D1053. Magic mantle (cloak).

D537.2.1. *Giantess's cloak makes man grow.* Eskimo (Greenland): Rink 430.

D537.3. *Transformation by putting on moustache.* French Canadian: Sister Marie Ursule.

D537.4. *Transformation by donning wig.* French Canadian: Sister Marie Ursule.

D550. Transformation by eating or drinking. *MacCulloch Childhood 158. — Japanese: Ikeda; N. A. Indian: *Thompson Tales 313 n. 132a.

C200. Tabu: eating. C250. Tabu: drinking. D764. Disenchantment by eating or drinking.

D551. *Transformation by eating.* *MacCulloch Childhood 158; *Penzer VI 56.

D551.1. *Transformation by eating fruit.* (Cf. D981.) Cf. Type 566. India: Thompson-Balys.

D1375.1.1. Magic fruit causes horns to grow on person.

D551.1.1. *Transformation by eating apple.* *Fb "æble" III 1136a; Hdwb. d. Märchens s.v. "Apfel" n. 11. — Icelandic: Boberg; Breton: Sébillot Incidents s.v. "pomme"; Spanish: Boggs FFC XC 62 No. 449. Cf. Type 566.

D981.1. Magic apple.

D551.1.2. *Transformation by eating apricot.* Chinese: Werner 203.

D551.1.3. *Transformation by eating pear.* Hdwb. d. Märchens s.v. "Birnbaum".

D551.2. *Transformation by eating vegetable.* (Cf. D983.) — Type 567; *BP III 6; *Aarne MSFO XXV 143ff. (Cf. D132.1.)

D551.2.1. *Transformation by eating cabbage.* Spanish: Boggs FFC XC 48 No. 327*D.

D551.2.2. *Transformation by eating cicuta.* Spanish: Boggs FFC XC 63 No. 453.

D551.2.3. *Transformation through eating magic seeds.* (Cf. D971). — Hindu: Penzer VI 56 n. 1, 62f.

D551.2.4. *Transformation by eating flower.* India: Thompson-Balys.

D551.2.5. *Transformation by eating onions.* Korean: Zong in-Sob 21.

D551.2.6. *Transformation by eating garlic.* Korean: Zong in-Sob 3.

D551.2.7. *Transformation by eating manioc.* Africa (Dahomé): Einstein 27.

D551.3. *Transformation by eating flesh.* Icelandic: Boberg. — Chinese: Eberhard FFC CXX 162; Japanese: Ikeda; American Indian (Creek): Swanton BBAE LXXXVII 32f., (Ladino): Conzemius BBAE CVI 130f.; Argentina: Jijena Sanchez 23.

D551.4. *Transformation by eating bread.* India: Thompson-Balys.

D551.5. *Transformation by eating leaf from a tree. Falcon is returned to form of girl.* Italian Novella: Rotunda.

D551.6. *Transformation by eating — miscellaneous.*

D551.6.1. *Transformation by placing pill in mouth.* (Cf. D1243.) — Hindu: Penzer VII 42 n. 1, 222; India: Thompson-Balys.

D765.1.1. Disenchantment by removal of enchanting pill from mouth.

D551.6.2. *Transformation by eating rice mixed with perspiration.* Africa (Bushman): Bleek and Lloyd 85.

D551.6.2.1. *Transformation by eating sticky rice.* Chinese: Eberhard FFC CXX 60.

D551.6.3. *Transformation by eating snake eggs.* India: Thompson-Balys.

A2145: Creation of snake (serpent).

D555. *Transformation by drinking.* *Type 450; BP I 86ff.; MacCulloch Childhood 159. See also references to D550. — Italian Novella: Rotunda; Greek: Frazer Apollodorus II 287 n. 2; India: Thompson-Balys.

D1040. Magic drink.

D555.1. *Transformation by drinking from animal's track.* (Cf. D578.) — *Type 450; *Sartori Zs. f. Vksk. IV 41ff.

D555.2. *Transformation by drinking wine.* Korean: Zong in-Sob 27.

D560. Transformation by various means.

D561. *Transformation by jumping over. The person, animal, or object jumped over is transformed.* American Indian (Zuñi): Parsons JAFL XXXI 243 No. 16, (Canadian Dakota): Wallis JAFL XXXVI 97 No. 26, (Cheyenne): Campbell JAFL XXIX 407 No. 1.

E13. Resuscitation by jumping (stepping) over.

D561.1. *Transformation by rolling.* N. A. Indian (California): Gayton and Newman 81.

D561.2. *Transformation by somersault.* Chinese: Graham; Argentina: Jijena Sanchez 31, 38, 59.

D561.3. *Transformation by jumping three times.* Korean: Zong in-Sob 58.

D562. *Transformation by bathing.* *Chauvin V 4 No. 2, VIII 43f. No. 11; English: Child V 499 s.v. "transformations"; Irish myth: *Cross. — Indonesian: Dixon 216; India: *Thompson-Balys; Africa (Kaffir): Theal 87.

D1788. Magic results from bathing. D1866. Beautification by bathing. D1887. Rejuvenation by bathing. D1895. Magic aging by bathing.

D562.1. *Transformation by application of water.* India: *Thompson-Balys.

D562.2. *Transformation by urine.* (Cf. D441.5, D441.6, D564.4, D1006.) — India: Thompson-Balys.

D562.2.1. *God's urine makes chilly fiery.* India: Thompson-Balys.

D562.2.2. *Human urine softens rock.* India: Thompson-Balys.

D563. *Transformation by encircling object thrice.* Fb "rundt" III 96a. — N. A. Indian (Zuñi): Parsons JAFL XXXI 243 No. 16 (four times).

D1791. Magic power by circumambulation.

D564. *Transformation by smelling.* India: Thompson-Balys.

D132. Transformation: man to ass (mule, jennet, etc.).

D564.1. *Self-transformation by smelling stick.* India: Thompson-Balys.

D564.2. *Transformation by smelling flower.* India: Thompson-Balys.

D564.3. *Transformation by smelling powders.* India: Thompson-Balys.

D564.4. *Transformation by smelling wine.* (Cf. D562.2.) — Korean: Zong in-Sob 56.

D565. *Transformation by touching.* India: Thompson-Balys.

C500. Tabu: Touching.

D565.0.1. *Transformation by touching ground on return from fairyland.* Irish myth: Cross.

F378.1. Tabu: touching ground on return from fairyland.

D565.1. *Midas' golden touch.* Everything touched turns to gold. Greek: Roscher s.v. "Midas"; India: Thompson-Balys.

D1076. Magic ring. D1466. Magic stone furnishes wealth. D1466.1. Magic stone turns everything to gold. D1761. Magic results produced by wishing, J2072.1. Short-sighted wish: Midas' touch. M430. Curses on persons.

D565.2. *Transformation by touching with rod.* Irish myth: *Cross; Greek: *Frazer Apollodorus I 70 n. 1, II 287 n. 2; Jewish: Neuman.

D475.1. Transformation: object to gold. D1355.16. Magic rod produces love. D1254.1. Magic wand. D1664.26. Silver rods cause magic sleep. D2100. Magic wealth. P427.10.6. Poet's rod (flesc filed).

D565.3. *Transformation by licking.* Irish myth: *Cross.

A511.10.1. Culture hero soon of deer mother. B635.3.1. Culture hero licked by deer mother. D1775. Magic results from licking.

D565.4. *Transformation by seizing ears.* Spanish: Boggs FFC XC 86 No. 754C*.

D565.4.1. *Transformation by twisting one's own ear.* India: Thompson-Balys.

D565.5. *Transformation by kiss.* Spanish: Boggs FFC XC 56 No. 408A*; Irish myth: Cross; English: Child V 499 s.v. "transformations."

D735. Disenchantment by kiss. D1794. Magic results from kissing.

D565.5.1. *Transformation by sexual intercourse.* Irish myth: *Cross.

D732. Loathly lady. D735. Disenchantment by kiss.

D565.6. *Transformation by touching water.* Irish myth: Cross.

D1788.1. Magic results from contact with water.

D565.7. *Transformation at touch of magic dogskin.* Irish myth: Cross.

D1025.6. Magic dogskin.

D565.8. *Transformation by touching with flower.* India: Thompson-Balys.

D565.8.1. *Transformation by pinching flower (life token).* German: Grimm No. 9.

D565.9. *Bag of stones becomes auks on touching ground.* Eskimo (Smith Sound): Kroeber JAFL XII 172.

D565.10. *Transformation by scratching.* Brazil: Jijena Sanchez 37.

D566. *Transformation by striking.* Livonian: Loorits FFC LXVI 90 No. 80.

D712.3. Disenchantment by striking. E11. Resuscitation by beating.

D566.1. *Transformation by striking wolf-skin glove.* Icelandic: Hrólfs saga Kraka 50.

D566.2. *Transformation by striking with stone.* Irish myth: Cross.

D566.3. *Transformation of horse by spurring.* India: Thompson-Balys.

D566.4. *Transformation by decapitation.* India: Thompson-Balys.

D567. *Transformation by sunlight.* *BP III 89 n. 2.

T521. Conception from sunlight.

D568. *Transformation by turning magic hood.* Irish: MacCulloch Celtic 175, *Cross.

D571. *Transformation by throwing object or person.*

D571.1. *Transformation by throwing rice on person.* India: Thompson-Balys.

D572. *Transformation by magic object.* Irish myth: Cross.

D572.1. *Transformation by magic stick.* Hawaii: Beckwith Myth 276, 280.

D572.2. *Transformation by ring.* Icelandic: Boberg.

D572.3. *Transformation by cloth.* German: Grimm No. 99.

D572.4. *Transformation by wand.* German: Grimm No. 56, 60.

D572.5. *Transformation by means of magic stone.* Icelandic: *Boberg; Africa (Fang): Einstein 53.

D572.6. *Transformation by magic powder.* Korean: Zong in-Sob 230 No. 99.

D572.7. *Transformation by celestial dew.* Jewish: Neuman.

D573. *Transformation by spell (charm).*

D1273. Magic formula (charm).

D573.1. *Transformation by written spell.* Korean: Zong in-Sob 85.

D573.2. *Petrification by magic written formula.* India: Thompson-Balys.

D574. *Transformation by crossing water.* Scotch: McKay Beal III 139.

D575. *Transformation by fumigations. Burning of magic perfume transforms.* (Cf. D1245.) — Chauvin V 87 No. 27.

D575.1. *Transformation by throwing ashes.* Africa: Milligan 141.

D576. *Transformation by being burned.* (Cf. D1787.) — N. A. Indian: *Thompson Tales 349 n. 256, also most of references in n. 259. — Indonesian: DeVries list 239, DeVries Volksverhalen Iï 356 No. 100; Africa (Kaffir): Theal 87.

D577. *Transformation by braiding hair.* Africa (Ila, Rhodesia): Smith and Dale II 395 No. 18.

D578. *Transformation by stepping in footprint.* (Cf. D555.1.) — Africa (Kaffir): Theal 87.

D579. *Transformation by looking in a mirror.* Icelandic: *Boberg.

D1163. Magic mirror.

D581. *Petrification by glance.* Fb "öje" III 1167b. — Greek: Frazer Apollodorus I 152 n. 3 (Gorgon).

A974.1. Certain stones are druids transformed by power of saint. D231. Transformation: man to stone. D2061.2.1. Death-giving glance. D2071. Evil Eye. F526.3. Gorgon. Heads turned about, scales of dragon, tusks of swine, brazen hands, golden wings. G263.2.1. Witch transforms to stone.

D581.1. *Damsel whose voice turns her suitors to stone.* India: Thompson-Balys.

D231. Transformation: man to stone.

D582. *Transformation by sticking magic pin into head.* (Cf. D765.1.2., D1182.) — Fb "knappenål" II 211b; *Cosquin Indiens 58ff.; Penzer VI 61.

D582.1. *Transformation by sticking nails into feet.* India: Thompson-Balys.

D765.1.2. Disenchantment by removal of enchanting pin (thorn).

D582.2. *Transformation by magic needle.* India: Thompson-Balys.

D583. *Transformation by lousing.* Maori: Dixon 55.

D1962.2. Magic sleep by lousing. Q41.2. Reward for cleansing loathsome person.

D584. *Transformation by contemplation.* Penzer VI 20f.

D585. *Transformation by binding with string around neck.* India: *Thompson-Balys, Penzer VI 39f., 56ff., VII 44 n. 1.

D621.1. Animal by day, man by night.

D585.1. *Transformation by tying charm around person's neck.* India: Thompson-Balys.

D586. *Transformation to fish by throwing into sea.* N. A. Indian (California): Gayton and Newman 100; Madagascar (Antankarana): Renel I 94ff. No. 14.

D170. Transformation: man to fish.

D587. *Transformation by baptism.* Irish myth: Cross.

V81. Baptism.

D588. *Transformation by blowing.* Irish myth: Cross.

D1005. Magic breath.

D591. *Transformation by immersing in magic well.* Irish myth: Cross.

D926. Magic well.

D592. *Transformation to likeness of another by sleeping with arms about him under the same mantle.* Irish myth: Cross.

D52. Magic changes to different appearance.

D593. *Change of sex by exchange with a yaksa (ogre).* (Cf. D10.) India: Thompson-Balys.

D594. *Transformation by rubbing with ointment.* India: Thompson-Balys.

D595. *Transformation by application of blood.* India: Thompson-Balys.

D596. *Transformation by placing something on head.* India: Thompson-Balys.

D596.1. *Transformation by placing bewitched flower on head.* India: Thompson-Balys.

D599. *Transformation by various means — miscellaneous.*

D600—D699. Miscellaneous transformation incidents.

D600. Miscellaneous transformation incidents.

G263. Witch enchants or transforms.

D601. *Offer to make pups born of woman in shape of hound human.* Irish myth: Cross.

T554.1. Woman transformed to animal bears animal.

D610. Repeated transformation. Transformation into one form after another. — Köhler-Bolte I 265; *Type 325; *Norlind 73ff.; *Scott Thumb 124ff.; Cosquin Études 516ff; Chauvin II 183, V 199. — Irish myth: *Cross; Icelandic: *Boberg; English: Child I 337, *V 499 s.v. "transformations, successive"; French Canadian: Barbeau JAFL XXIX

16f.; Missouri French: Carrière; Greek: Fox 87 (Nereus), 92 (Periklymenos), 122 (Thetis), Frazer Apollodorus II 67 n. 6, Roscher s. v. "Acheloos"; Persian: Carnoy 270, 272; Turkish: Radloff IV 81ff.; India: Keith 152, Tawney II 168, 510ff., *Thompson-Balys. — Chinese: Werner 361, Eberhard FFC CXX 48; Japanese: Ikeda; Indonesian: DeVries Volksverhalen Nos 63, 69, 132. — Cape Verde Islands: Parsons MAFLS XV (1) 213 No. 73; Central Caroline Islands: Dixon 258; American Indian (Aztec): Alexander Lat. Am. 83. — Africa (Angola): Chatelain 72 No. 3, (Bushman): Bleek and Lloyd 3, (general): Frobenius Atlantis II 38ff, III 116ff., Meinhof African. Märchen No. 35.

D735.2. Three redeeming kisses. D757. Disenchantment by holding enchanted person during successive transformations. E151. Repeated resuscitation. A person dies and is resuscitated repeatedly. E607.2. Person transforms self, is swallowed and reborn in new form. E670. Repeated reincarnation. F420.4.1.1. Protean transformation of waterspirit. S401. Unsuccessful attempts to kill person in successive reincarnations (transformations).

D610.1. *Goddess repeatedly transforms herself.* India: Thompson-Balys.

D611. *Protean beggar: Person assumes successive forms in order to beg.* — N. A. Indian: *Thompson Tales 310 n. 117d.

K1834. Multiple disguise. K1982. Ubiquitous beggar. In disguise obtains alms three times from same person.

D612. *Protean sale: man sells youth in successive transformations.* — *Type 325; *BP II 60ff.; *Cosquin Études 567ff.; India: *Thompson-Balys; *Kittredge Witchcraft 184 n. 98 -- Missouri French: Carrière.

C837. Tabu: loosing bridle in selling man transformed to horse. K1834. Multiple disguise.

D612.1. *Illusory transformation of animals in order to sell and cheat.* (Cf. D2031, K1870.) — Kittredge Witchcraft 184 n. 100.

D615. *Transformation combat.* Fight between contestants who strive to outdo each other in successive transformations. — *Penzer III 195 n. 1, 203ff., VIII 80 n. 1; Mitra *The Magical Conflict in Santali, Ao Naga Folklore (Man in India IX 173—80); Chauvin V 2 No. 2, 5 No. 443, 199 No. 116, VI 86 No. 252, 110 No. 274; Cosquin Études folkloriques 570ff.; Köhler-Bolte I 138, 588. — Egypt: Müller 126 (Horus and Seth); Greek: Frazer Apollodorus I 256 n. 3 (Hercules and Achelous); Irish myth: *Cross; Welsh: MacCulloch Celtic 110; Finnish: Kalevala rune 28; Buddhist myth: Malalasekera I 289; India: *Thompson-Balys; Chinese: Werner 361; Hawaii: Dixon 90f; Tuamotu: Stimson MS (T-G. 3/1001); N. A. Indian: *Thompson Tales 311 n. 117e; Eskimo (Cumberland Sound): Boas BAM XV 220, (West Hudson Bay): Boas BAM XV 319, (Mackenzie Area): Jenness 85, (Greenland): Rasmussen II 96; S. A. Indian (Eastern Brazil): Lowie BBAE CXLIII 1 434.

D642.2. Transformation to escape death. D651. Transformation to defeat enemies. D659.2. Transformation to animals to fight. D785. Disenchantment by magic contest. D928.1. Serpent transforms self to staff, is picked up and bites enemy. D1719.1. Contest in magic. R251. Flight on a tree which ogre tries to cut down.

D615.1. *Transformation contest between magicians.* Finnish: Kalevala rune 27; Lappish: Qvigstad FFC LX 50 No. 89; Jewish: Neuman; India: Thompson-Balys; Chinese: Eberhard FFC CXX 169, 242; Africa: Milligan Jungle 100.

D615.2. *Transformation contest between master and pupil.* *Type 325; *BP II 68; *Köhler-Bolte I 138, 556; English: Child V 499 s.v. "transformation"; India: *Thompson-Balys; Missouri-French: Carrière.

D150. Transformation: man to bird.

D615.3. *Transformation combat between lover and maid.* BP II 68; Child V 499 s.v. "transformations".

D642.3. Transformation to escape lover. K1310. Seduction by disguise or substitution.

D615.4. *Men transformed to animals fight.* BP III 261 (Grimm No. 163).

D615.4.1. *Fairies (gods?) transformed to animals fight.* Irish myth: Cross.

D615.5. *Transformation combat between saints.* Irish myth: Cross.

V220. Saints.

D616. *Repeated transformations to deceive wives.* A husband thus makes each of his many wives believe that he is always with her. Hindu: Keith 166.

D620. **Periodic transformation.** A person or thing is transformed at definite intervals. *Types 432, 652; *BP II 125; R. M. Meyer Zs. f. Vksk. XXI 4. — Irish myth: *Cross; Icelandic: Völsunga saga ch. 8—9, Boberg; India: Thompson-Balys; Indonesian: Dixon 219f.; N. A. Indian (Menomini): Skinner and Satterlee PaAM XIII 317; S. A. Indian (Surinam): Alexander Lat. Am. 274, (Guaporé): Lévi-Strauss BBAE CXLIII (3) 379. — Africa (Angola): Chatelain 145 No. 15, (Mpongwe): Nassau 68 No. 15.

D113.1.1. Werwolf. E155. Periodic resuscitation.

D621. *Daily transformation.* German: Grimm No. 49, 123; India: Thompson-Balys; S. A. Indian (Argentina): Jijena Sanchez 55, 59.

D412.5.4. Animal that is hound by night, sheep by day. F811.12. Trees grow and "ungrow" each day. T113.1. Sorceress marries a man every morning and transforms him to some kind of animal in the evening.

D621.0.1. *One shape by day; another by night.* Child V 490 s.v. "one".

D621.1. *Animal by day; man by night.* *Types 425, 552A; *Köhler-Bolte I 315ff.; *Fb "hund" I 678a, "bjørn" IV 43a. — Irish myth: Cross; Icelandic: Hrólfs saga Kraka 50; Spanish: *Boggs FFC XC 62 No. 451; Bohemian: Hartland Science 246. — India: *Thompson-Balys; Hawaii: Beckwith Myth 135; Mangaia (Polynesia), Samoa, Union Group, Tahiti: Dixon 55f.; Melanesian, Indonesian: ibid. 56 nn. 75, 76; N. A. Indian: Thompson Tales 347 nn. 247, 248; S. A. Indian (Arawak): Jijena Sanchez 23.

D640.1. Marriage to beast by day and man by night. D658. Transformation to seduce woman.

D621.1.1. *Man by day; animal by night.* *Taylor MPh XVII 59 n. 8. — Icelandic: Boberg; Finnish: Aarne FFC XXXIII 45 No. 71; Estonian: Aarne FFC XXV 130 No. 71; Hawaii: Beckwith Myth 135; Eskimo (Mackenzie Area): Jenness 52.

D659.1. Transformation to snakes at night in order to sleep.

D621.2. *Tree by day; man by night.* Fb "træ" III 867b; India: Thompson-Balys.

F252.3.1. Soldiers of fairy king are trees by day and men by night. T117.5.1. Marriage to tree by day, man by night.

D621.2.1. *Bush by day; woman by night.* Italian: Basile I No. 2.

D621.2.2. *Flower by day; girl by night.* India: *Thompson-Balys.

D431.1. Transformation: flower to person.

D621.3. *Ugly by day; fair by night.* *Köhler-Bolte II 435ff.; Irish myth: Cross.

D1860. Magic beautification. D1870. Magic hideousness.

D621.4. *Size of object transformed at night.*

D621.4.1. *Magic dog shrinks at night.* Irish myth: Cross.

D491. Compressible objects.

D621.5. *Sheep by day; dog by night.* Irish myth: *Cross.

B187.5. Dog that is hound by day and flame of fire by night.

D621.6. *Young man issues from conch-shell every evening.* India: Thompson-Balys.

D622. *Weekly transformation.* See all references to C31.1.2 (Melusine). — Jijena Sanchez 42.

C31.1.2. Tabu: looking at supernatural wife on certain occasion (Melusine). The husband must not see the wife when she is transformed.

D622.1. *Transformation to werwolf every Friday night.* S. A. Indian (Brazil): Jijena Sanchez 42.

D623. *Transformation every ten days.* Icelandic: Volsungasaga 15.

D624. *Yearly transformation:* Irish myth: *Cross.

D624.1. *Storks become men in Egypt in the winter* (Cf. D155.1.) — Wesselski Bebel II 138 No. 117.

D624.2. *Fairies become birds every other year.* Irish myth: *Cross.

F234.1.15. Fairy in form of bird. F241.7. Fairy birds.

D624.3. *Yearly transformation to person of different sex.* Irish myth: Cross.

D10. Transformation to person of different sex.

D630. Transformation and disenchantment at will. See, in general, references throughout D610—D629, D640—D659, D670—D699, nearly all of which motifs involve the idea of voluntary transformation. — *Types 652, 665; Hdwb. d. Märchens s.v. "Baum"; *Bolte Reise der Söhne Giaffers 215; *Chauvin VII 83 No. 373bis n. 1. — German: Grimm Nos. 51, 56, 68, 181; Irish myth: *Cross; Greek: Frazer Apollodorus I 84 n. 2, Grote I 105; Icelandic: De la Saussaye 298f., MacCulloch Eddic 46ff. (Odin), *Boberg; Jewish: Neuman; India: *Thompson-Balys, Keith 156, 218; Arabian: Burton Nights I 134ff., 220f., III 126f., 236, VII 76, 300, IX 331, X 30, S II 86, 105, S V 88, S VII 239; Buddhist myth: Malalasekera I 420, II 676; Chinese: Werner 327, Coyajee JPASB XXIV 182, Jameson The Chinese Art of Shifting Shape (JAFL LXIV 275—80), Graham; Korean: Zong in-Sob 85; Indonesian: De Vries's list No. 152, 153; New Guinea: Dixon 138; Hawaii: Beckwith Myth 401ff. note; New Hebrides: Beckwith 131; Easter Island: Métraux Ethnology 363. — S. A. Indian (Argentina): Jijena Sanchez 53; Jamaica: Beckwith MAFLS XVII 271 No. 84. — Africa (Cold Coast): Barker and Sinclair 42 No. 4, (Ekoi): Talbot 247.

A165.2.0.1. Deity's messenger can assume any size he wishes. A527.3.1. Culture hero can transform self. D46.1. Mortal temporarily takes shape of demon. D659.2. Transformation to animals to fight. D1700. Acquisition of magic power. F234.0.1. Fairy transforms self. F531.1.8. Giant in animal form. F531.6.5. Giants as magicians. G210. Form of witch. G303.3.3. The devil in animal form. T555.1. Woman gives birth to a fruit. Can transform itself to girl.

D630.1. *Power of self-transformation received from wood spirit.* *Type 667.

B11.5.1. Dragon's power of self-transformation.

D630.1.1. *Power of self-transformation received from demon.* Jewish: Neuman.

D630.2. *Power of self-transformation received from a god.* Greek: *Frazer Apollodorus I 84 n. 2; India: Thompson-Balys.

D630.2.1. *Power of self-transformation received from an angel.* Jewish: Neuman.

D630.3. *Power of self-transformation received from fairy parent.* Irish myth: Cross.

F305. Offspring of fairy and mortal.

D630.4. *Deity has power of self-transformation.* Hawaii: Beckwith Myth 93, 117ff, 172ff., 186, 276—83, 512.

A527.3.1. Culture hero can transform self.

D631. *Size changed at will.* India: Thompson-Balys.

B91.5.1. Sea-serpent dilates and contracts. B750. Fanciful traits of animals. D55. Magic change of person's size. D480. Size of object transformed.

D631.1. *Person changes size at will.* Irish myth: Cross; Marquesas: Handy 106; Eskimo (Greenland): Rasmussen III 77, 241, Rink 402, (Mackenzie Area): Jenness 84; Africa (Zulu): Callaway 154 (see D55.2.1.).

A526.6. Culture hero, when angry, subject to contortions. D55. Magic change of person's size. D1377. Magic object changes person's size.

D631.1.1. *Person changes appearance at will.* Irish myth: Cross.

A120.0.1. God as shape-shifter. D52. Magic changes to different appearance. F234.0.2. Fairy as shape-shifter.

D631.2. *Animal's size changed at will.* Eskimo (Bering Strait): Nelson RBAE XVIII 516.

B91.5.1. Sea-serpent dilates and contracts.

D631.2.1. *Dogs large or small at will.* N. A. Indian (Micmac): Michelson JAFL XXXVIII 52.

D631.3. *Size of object changed at will.* Eskimo (Greenland): Rasmussen 235, III 173.

D491. Compressible objects.

D631.3.1. *Compressible canoe.* Can be made pocket size. N. A. Indian: *Thompson Tales 275 n. 14c.

D631.3.1.1. *Compressible ship.* Can be put into vest pocket. (Cf. D1123.) — Fb "skib" III 243a. — Icelandic: MacCulloch Eddic 109, Boberg.

D631.3.2. *Compressible tent.* Large or small at will. Chauvin VI 135 No. 286 n. 1.

D1138. Magic tent. F923. Tent-house folded and swallowed as means of carrying it.

D631.3.3. *Sword large or small at will.* (Cf. D1081.) Fb "sværd" III 690b; Irish myth: Cross.

D1081. Magic sword.

D631.3.4. *Compressible load.* India: Thompson-Balys.

D631.3.5. *Compressible hammer.* (Cf. D1209.4.) — Norse: MacCulloch Eddic 79, Boberg.

D631.3.6. *Cloth large or small at will.* Indonesian: DeVries Volksverhalen II 103.

D631.3.7. *Bed large or small at will.* Irish myth: Cross (D631.6); India: Thompson-Balys.

D1154.1. Magic bed.

D631.3.8. *Spear large or small at will.* Icelandic: Sturlaugs saga st. 625—26, Boberg.

D631.4. *Supernatural creatures change size at will.*

D631.4.1. *Dwarfs change size at will.* Eskimo (Greenland): Rasmussen III 248.

D631.4.2. *Angels change size at will.* Jewish: Neuman.

D631.4.3. *Demons change size at will.* Jewish: Neuman.

D631.4.4. *Creature born from egg changes size at will.* Marquesas: Handy 124.

D632. *Boat transforms self at will of master.* Breton: Sébillot Incidents s.v. "bateau".

D632.1. *Island canoe.* An island that becomes a canoe at will. N. A. Indian: *Thompson Tales 275 n. 14.

D640. Reasons for voluntary transformation.

D1891. Transformation to old man to escape recognition. F601.6. Extraordinary companions are transformed animals. T235. Husband transforms himself to test his wife's faithfulness.

D641. *Transformation to reach difficult place.* *Types 329, 665, 434. — Irish myth: *Cross; Icelandic: De la Saussaye 261; Finnish: Kalevala rune 43; Greek: Fox 178; India: *Thompson-Balys; Chinese: Werner 270, 273, 365, Ferguson 159; Maori: Dixon 79; N. A. Indian: *Thompson Tales 310 n. 117; S. A. Indian (Toba): Métraux MAFLS XL 26.

R115. King transformed to parrot frees captured parrots. R152.7. Transformed wife takes husband out of captivity.

D641.1. *Lover as bird visits mistress.* *Type 432; Child V 39ff. — Irish myth: *Cross; Greek: Grote I 86; India: Thompson-Balys.

B614. Bird paramour. B620. Animal suitor. T33. Man transformed to animal kept as pet by heroine.

D641.1.1. *Girl as bird visits lover.* Irish myth: *Cross.

F234.1.15. Fairy in form of bird.

D641.1.2. *Transformation to be able to woo maiden.* Greek: Grote I 139; India: Thompson-Balys.

D658.1. Transformation to animal to seduce woman. K1346. Hero flies to maiden's room.

D641.2. *Transformation to gain access to enemy's camp (fortress).* Irish myth: *Cross.

K1800. Deception by disguise or illusion. K1930. Treacherous impostors. K2350. Military strategy.

D641.2.1. *Transformation to spy out enemy's camp.* Korean: Zong in-Sob 64.

D641.3. *Transformation in order to enter rival's stomach.* (Cf. D651.2.) Tonga: Gifford 76.

K952.2. Man transforms self to gadfly to enter giant's stomach.

D641.4. *Transformation to travel to otherworld.* S. A. Indian (Toba): Métraux MAFLS XL 24.

F0. Journey to otherworld.

D642. *Transformation to escape difficult situation.* Type 461; Irish myth: *Cross; Icelandic: *Boberg; India: *Thompson-Balys; Jamaica:

Beckwith MAFLS XVII 258 No. 40; Africa (Basuto): Jacottet 238 No. 35.

D671. Transformation flight. K520. Death escaped through disguise, shamming or substitution. R210. Escapes. S365. Maltreated children transformed.

D642.1. *Transformation to escape from captivity.* Finnish: Kalevala rune 16; Italian Novella: Rotunda; Chinese: Werner 366.

D642.2. *Transformation to escape death.* *Type 316. — Greek: *Frazer Apollodorus I 49 n. 2, 251 n. 4; Icelandic: MacCulloch Eddic 146, *Boberg; Jewish: Neuman; India: Thompson-Balys; Chinese: Werner 324. — N. A. Indian: *Thompson Tales 310 nn. 117a, 117b.; S. A. Indian (Toba): Métraux MAFLS XL 120; Aztec: Alexander Lat. Am. 83; Eskimo (Greenland) Rasmussen II 211; Africa (Ekoi): Talbot 247.

D642.3. *Transformation to escape lover.* Greek: Frazer Apollodorus I 22 (Mitis), II 54 n. 1 (Psamathe), 67 n. 6 (Thetis); Chinese: Graham.

D615. Transformation combat. D664. Transformation of woman by goddess to preserve chastity. R210. Escapes. T320. Escape from undesired lover.

D642.3.1. *Pursued sweetheart becomes tree.* (Cf. D215.) — Greek: Fox 181 (Daphne); India: Thompson-Balys; N. A. Indian (Crow): Lowie PaAM XXV 45.

D615.3. Transformation combat between lover and maid.

D642.4. *Transformation to escape ambush.* Irish myth: *Cross.

D642.5. *Transformation to escape notice.* Greek: Grote I 43; India: *Thompson-Balys.

D642.5.1. *Transformation to hide from ogress.* India: Thompson-Balys.

D642.6. *Transformation to escape ogress.* India: Thompson-Balys.

D642.7. *Transformation to elude pursuers.* (Cf. D671, D672.) Jewish: Neuman.

D643. *Transformation so as to rescue.*

D643.1. *Transformation to falcon in order to rescue condemned man at the gallows.* India: Thompson-Balys.

D643.2. *Man transformed to deer decoy for people at execution of saint's friend.* India: Thompson-Balys.

D644. *Transformation to travel fast.* Icelandic: Boberg; N. A. Indian (Seneca): Curtin-Hewitt RBAE XXXII 317, 323, 331; Eskimo (Bering Strait): Nelson RBAE XVIII 516.

D645. *Transformation to test heroes.* Irish myth: Cross.

H1550. Tests of character.

D646. *Transformation to be picked up (caught).* Africa (Basuto): Jacottet 262 No. 39.

D646.1. *Transformation to fish to be caught.* Chinese: Werner 273, 363.

D646.2. *Transformation to child or pet to be adopted.* N. A. Indian: Thompson Tales 281 n. 42 (many of the references).

D647. *Transformation to seek lost (or unknown) person.* India: Thompson-Balys.

H1230. Accomplishment of quests. H1231. Large boot-supply for journey.

D647.1. *Faithful brother transforms self to deer to seek sister.* India: Thompson-Balys.

H1385.6. Quest for lost sister.

D647.2. *Transformation to eagle so as to scour country for lovely woman as bride for king.* India: Thompson-Balys.

H1381.3.1. Quest for bride for king.

D651. *Transformation to defeat enemies.* (Cf. D615.) Irish myth: Cross; Welsh: MacCulloch Celtic 189; Middle English Romance: Wells 103 (Alliterative Alexander Fragment A); Icelandic: *Boberg; Greek: Fox 219 (Dionysus); India: *Thompson-Balys.

D651.1. *Transformation to kill enemy.* India: *Thompson-Balys; Eskimo (Aleut): Golder JAFL XVIII 220; S. A. Indian (Yuricare): Métraux BBAE CXLIII (3) 504, (Mundurucú): Horton ibid. (3) 294, (Apapocuva-Guaraní): Métraux RMLP XXXIII 238; N. A. Indian: *Thompson Tales 278 n. 26, (Plains Ojibwa): Skinner JAFL XXXII 303 No. 7.

D651.1.1. *Transformation of magic object to animal which kills enemy.* Irish myth: Cross.

D651.1.2. *Demons assume human form to revenge brother's death.* India: Thompson-Balys.

D651.1.3. *Queen transforms herself to defeat god of death.* India: Thompson-Balys.

A487. God of death.

D651.2. *Transformation to frighten enemy.* (Cf. D641.3.) Icelandic: Egils saga einhenda XII 9—10; India: Thompson-Balys; Ila (Rhodesia): Smith and Dale II 359 No. 12.

K952.2. Man transforms self to gadfly to enter giant's stomach and kill him. K1700. Deception through bluffing.

D651.3. *Transformation to destroy enemy's property.* Africa (Angola): Chatelain 245 No. 47.

D651.4. *Transformation to ant in order to gnaw bow-strings of enemy.* *Charpentier Kleine Beiträge 35 n. 3.

D651.5. *Transformation to spy enemy's camp.* Icelandic: *Boberg; Korean Zong in-Sob.

D651.6. *Transformation so as to protect hero from enemy.* India: Thompson-Balys.

D655. *Transformation to receive food.* N. A. Indian: *Thompson Tales 300 n. 100, 310 n. 117c.; S. A. Indian (Toba): Métraux MAFLS XL 124f; Africa (Hottentot): Bleek 57 No. 25, (Angola): Chatelain 145 No. 15.

K300. Thefts and cheats.

D655.1. *Transformation to buffalo so as to eat grass.* Cheyenne: Campbell JAFL XXIX 407 No. 1.

D655.2. *Witch transforms self to animal (hare, pig) so as to suck cows.* Kittredge Witchcraft 166, 484 nn. 21, 22; England, Ireland, U.S.: *Baughman.

G211.2.7. Witch in form of hare.

D657. *Transformation to steal.* (Cf. K300.) — Icelandic MacCulloch Eddic 54; Chinese: Werner 360f.; N. A. Indian: *Thompson Tales 306 n. 109x, (Calif.): Gayton and Newman 63; Africa (Basuto): Jacottet 220 No. 32.

D657.1. *Transformation to be put in food-bag.* Cape Verde Islands: *Parsons MAFLS XV (1) 323.

D657.2. *Transformation to flying horse so as to abduct king.* India: Thompson-Balys.

D657.3. *Transformation in order to steal fire.* S. A. Indian (Toba): Métraux MAFLS XL 7, (Choco): ibid. 112.

A1415. Theft of fire.

D658. *Transformation to seduce.* Greek: Frazer Apollodorus I 319 n. 2. 395; India: Thompson-Balys. — N. A. Indian: *Thompson Tales 305 n. 109v.

D615.3. Transformation combat between lover and maid. D621.1. Animal by day; man by night. K1300. Seduction. K1301. Mortal woman seduced by a god. K1326. Attempted seduction by transformation. K1915. The false bridegroom. R16.1. Maiden abducted by transformed hero. R16.3. Maiden abducted by (transformed) fairy. T0. Love.

D658.1. *Transformation to animal to seduce woman.* *Krappe Études 53ff. — Irish myth: *Cross; Greek: Frazer Apollodorus I 209 n. 2 (Europa), Fox 24, 33, 60, 166, 223; Hindu: Keith 76 (Prajapati); N. A. Indian (Iroquois): Alexander N. Am. 26; Am. Negro (Georgia): Harris Friends 81 No. 11, 91 No. 12; Africa (Zulu): Callaway 211, (Congo): Weeks 219 No. 14, (Fjort): Dennett 71 No. 15. Cf. Chinese: Werner 363.

A188.1. Philandering god. B611.4. Bull paramour. B641.3. Marriage to god in bull form. D101. Transformation: god to animal. D641.1. Lover as bird visits mistress. K1310. Seduction by disguise or substitution. T33. Man transformed to animal kept as pet by heroine.

D658.2. *Transformation to husband's (lover's) form to seduce woman.* *Penzer III 126f.; *Toldo Zs. f. Vksk. XV 367; *Frazer Apollodorus I 174 n. 1; *Hdwb. d. Märchens s.v. "Betrüger überführt"; Roscher Lexikon s.v. "Alkmene"; Euphorion I 589f.; Zachariae Zs. f. Vksk. XVI 138ff.; Wells 30 (Geoffrey of Monmouth), 32 (Layamon's Brut), 43 (Arthour and Merlin), 103 (Alliterative Alexander, Fragment A). — Irish myth: *Cross, MacCulloch Celtic 52, 56, 63, 75; Welsh: ibid. 185; German: Boberg; Indonesian: DeVries's list No. 150.

A180. Gods in relation to mortals. D40. Transformation to likeness of another person. D41. God in guise of mortal. K1311. Seduction by masking as woman's husband. K1915.2. Through power of saint, man is caused to assume lover's form and sleep with princess, etc.

D658.3. *Transformation of sex to seduce.* Irish myth: *Cross; Danish: Boberg; Eskimo (Greenland): Rasmussen III 49.

A1275.3. Of ten original men one magically changes sex. D10. Transformation to person of different sex.

D658.3.1. *Transformation to seduce man.* Irish myth: Cross; Icelandic: *Boberg; Hindu: Keith 151.

K1321. Seduction by man disguising as woman.

D658.3.2. *Transformation of animal to woman to seduce man.* India: *Thompson-Balys.

D658.3.2.1. *God as mare seduces stallion.* Icelandic: De la Saussaye 261 (Loki); India: Thompson-Balys.

D658.3.3. *Seven girls in guise of seven parrots come to boy who has spurned them.* India: Thompson-Balys.

D659. *Miscellaneous reasons for voluntary transformation.*

D1891. Transformation to old man to escape recognition.

D659.1. *Transformation to snakes at night in order to sleep.* (Cf. D621.1.1.) Done by otherworld people. — New Britain: Dixon 117.

F170. Otherworld — miscellaneous motifs.

D659.2. *Transformation to animals to fight.* (Cf. D615) — Icelandic: Boberg; Irish myth: *Cross; Persian: Carnoy 269; Eskimo (Mackenzie Area): Jenness 38.

D630. Transformation and disenchantment at will. F531.1.8. Giant in animal form. F531.6.5. Giants as magicians. G210. Form of witch.

D659.3. *Transformation to show displeasure.* India: Thompson-Balys; Africa (Basuto): Jacottet 94 No. 14.

D659.4. *Transformation to act as helpful animal.*

B11. Dragon D611. Protean beggar. D612. Protean sale. Man sells youth in successive transformations.

D659.4.1. *Transformation to lion in order to guard palace.* (Cf. D112.1, D621.1.) — Spanish: Boggs FFC XC 62 No. 451.

D659.4.2. *Sea dragon in serpent's form to accompany hero.* (Cf. D419.1.1, B11.) — Chinese: Werner 311.

D659.4.3. *Transformation to eagle to carry hero to safety.* Africa (Hausa): Equilbecq II 171ff.

B313. Helpful animal an enchanted person. B542.1.1. Eagle carries man to safety.

D659.4.4. *Transformation to eagle in order to guard princess.* Icelandic: Boberg.

D659.5. *Transformation to obtain blessing.* Irish myth: *Cross.

K1810. Deception by disguise.

D659.6. *Transformation to friar to instruct mankind.* Italian Novella: Rotunda.

Z110. Abstractions personified.

D659.7. *Transformation: wife to mistress.* Transformed wife substitutes for husband's mistress. — Italian Novella: Rotunda.

K1840. Deception by substitution.

D659.8. *Transformation to test fidelity.* Irish myth: Cross.

H1556. Tests of fidelity.

D659.9. *Transformation to another form to persuade man to go to battle.* Irish myth: Cross.

D659.10. *Transformation to lure hunters to certain place.* Usually fairyland. Irish myth: *Cross; India: *Thompson-Balys.

B172.6. Magic birds lure hunters to certain place. F159.1. Otherworld reached by hunting animal. F241.0.1. Fairy animal hunted. F320. Fairies carry people away to fairyland. F370. Visit to fairyland. K700. Capture by deception. N771. King (prince) lost on hunt has adventures.

D659.11. *Transformation to recover stolen goods.* French Canadian: Sister Marie Ursule.

D659.12. *Transformation to tramp to escape recognition.* French Canadian: Sister Marie Ursule. (Cf. D23.1.)

D659.13. *Transformation in order to drive buffaloes to milking.* India: Thompson-Balys.

D659.14. *Transformation: woman to fly so as to help hero pick out weapons from among many.* India: Thompson-Balys.

D185. Transformation: man to fly. H161. Recognition of transformed persons among identical companions. Prearranged signal. H324. Suitor test: choosing princess from others identically clad.

D660. Motive for transformation of others.

K1911.2.1. True bride transformed by false. K2213.6. Faithless wife transforms husband.

D661. *Transformation as punishment.* *Dh II 99ff., 123ff., III 284ff., 404ff., 426ff., IV 262; *Type 751A, 368*, 402*; *Fb "fisk" I 296b, "sten" III 553b, 554a; *BP III 168, 462; Köhler-Bolte I 154; Bolte Zs. f. Vksk. XXIX 69; Pauli (ed. Bolte) No. 413. — Icelandic: *Boberg; Finnish: Kalevala rune 33; Spanish: Boggs FFC XC 97 No. 836A*; Breton: Sébillot Incidents s.v. "amoureux"; Swiss: Jegerlehner Oberwallis 313 No. 82; Greek: Frazer Apollodorus I 343 (Niobe), Fox 29 (Io); Jewish: Neuman; Tahiti: Dixon 65; Africa (Fjort): Dennett 89 No. 22, 105 No. 29.

A974.1. Certain stones are druids transformed by power of saint. A1965.1. Bittern from Pilate transformed. C961.1. Transformation to pillar of salt for breaking tabu. D444.1. Transformation: money of the hard-hearted to scorpions. D444.2. Transformation: meat to toad. Punishment for ungrateful son. D471.1. Transformation: bread to stone. As punishment. Q226.2. Mutinous clerics expelled in shape of swine. Q. Rewards and punishments. Q415.1.1. Punishment: transformation to deer which is eaten by dogs. Q501.6. Punishment of Io. Transformed to cow with gadfly ceaselessly pursuing. Q551.3. Punishment: transformation of lovers into lion and lioness for desecrating temple. Q551.4. Punishment: calf's head in murderer's hand turns to corpse's head. Q551.5. Scoffers turned to stone by saint. Q551.13. Transformation of a man to animal as punishment. Q584. Transformation as fitting punishment.

D661.1. *Transformation as revenge for repulsing amorous advances.* Irish myth: Cross.

F302.3.3. Fairy avenges herself on man who scorns her love.

D661.2. *Transformation as punishment for denouncing saint.* Der Heiligen Leben und Leiden 100ff. (Santa Barbara).

Q227. Punishment for opposition to holy person.

D661.3. *Transformation for violation of vow.* Greek: Grote I 162.

M100. Vows and oaths.

D662. *Transformation to cure inconstant husband.* He falls in love with another woman: his wife changes him to negro. He then falls in love with negress: wife changes him to ass. He then falls in love with she-ass. Finally restored to his original form. — *Chauvin II 183 No. 23.

K1535. Adulteress transforms her husband into an animal to get rid of him. T230. Faithlessness in marriage.

D663. *Transformation as reward.* Italian Novella: Rotunda.

D664. *Transformation of woman by goddess to preserve chastity.* India: Thompson-Balys.

D642.3. Transformation to escape lover.

D665. *Transformation of enemy to be rid of him.* Irish myth: *Cross.

D665.1. *Transformation of rival in love (marriage) to be rid of him.* Irish myth: *Cross.

F302.5.2. Fairy mistress transforms man's human wife. T92. Rivals in love. T257.2. Jealousy of rival wives.

D665.2. *Transformation of stepchild to be rid of him.* Irish myth: Cross.

D665.3. *Jealous co-wife transforms the other.* India: Thompson-Balys.

K2222. Treacherous co-wife (concubine).

D666. *Transformation to save a person.* Icelandic: Hjálmtèrs saga ok Ölvers 472, Boberg; Jewish: Neuman.

D666.1. *King of birds transforms his quails into sticks and pebbles so king and his hunters and hawks cannot kill them.* India: Thompson-Balys.

D423.2. Transformation: quails to sticks and pebbles.

670D. Magic flight. Irish myth: Cross; *Krappe The Legend of Walther and Hildegund (Journal of English and Germanic Philology XXII [1923] 75—88).

D1611. Magic object answers for fugitives. R220. Flights.

D671. *Transformation flight.* Fugitives transforms themselves in order to escape detection by the pursuer. — *Types 313, 325, 327; **Aarne Die magische Flucht (FFC XCII); *Fb "and" IV 12b, "rose" III 80a. — Irish myth: *Cross; English: Child V 499 s.v. "transformations"; Greek: Grote I 182; Jewish: Neuman; Arabian: Burton Nights V 353; India: *Thompson-Balys; Japanese: Ikeda; Philippine (Tinguian): Cole 75, 17 n. 1; Eskimo (Greenland): Rasmussen I 327, 367, III 124, Rink 195, (Cumberland Sound): Boas BAM XV 182; N. A. Indian: *Thompson Tales 334 n. 205b; S. A. Indian (Sharanti, Comacan, Mashacalí): Horton BBAE CXLIII 3 294, (Mundurucu): Horton ibid. 3 281; Jamaica: Beckwith MAFLS XVII 274 No. 86. — Africa (Kaffir): Theal 98, (Zulu): Callaway 21, (Basuto): Jacottet 206 No. 30, Casalis Les Bassoutos (Paris 1859) 349.

D642. Transformation to escape difficult situation. K521.1. Escape by dressing in animal (bird) skin. R210. Escapes.

D671.0.1. *Fugitive transforms self to stone.* Thrown to safety by pursuer. Africa (Zulu): Held 144ff., (Bechuana): Brown, J. T. Among the Bantu Nomads (London, 1926) 181ff., (Northern Rhodesia): Worthington The Little Wise One (London, 1930) 135ff. No. 19, (Gan): Westermann Die Sprache der Guang (Berlin, 1922) 86f.

D671.0.2. *Fugitive transformed by helper to escape detection.* Irish myth: Cross; Greek: Grote I 238.

N800. Helpers.

D671.1. *Reversed transformation flight.* Transformed pursuer. Koryak: Jochelson JE VI 363.

D672. *Obstacle flight.* Fugitives throw objects behind them which magically become obstacles in pursuer's path. — *Types 313, 314, 325, 327, 502; **Aarne Die Magische Flucht (FFC XCII); **BP II 140; Fb "hår" I 771b, "flaske" I 309a, "hvidtorn" I 703a; *Wesselski Theorie 31; *Hdwb. d. Märch. I 151a; *Hdwb. d. Abergl. II 1655; Cosquin Etudes 166, 193ff. — England, Scotland, U.S.: *Baughman; Irish myth: Cross; Breton: Sébillot Incidents s.v. "objets"; Swiss: Jegerlehner Oberwallis 304 No. 30; Icelandic: Boberg; Hungarian: Solymossy Hongaarsche Sagen (Zutphen, 1929) 403; French Canadian: Barbeau JAFL XXIX 11; Jewish: Neuman; India: *Thompson-Balys, Penzer II 21, III 227 n. 1, 236ff., IX 151; Chinese: Eberhard FFC CXX 234f.; Korean: Zong in-Sob 173f.; Japanese: Ikeda; Indonesian: Dixon 236 nn. 48, 49, DeVries Volksverhalen Nos. 16, 17, 63, 116; Philippine (Tinguian): *Cole 75, 17 n. 1; Marquesas: Handy 117; N. A. Indian: *Thompson Tales 333 n. 205, (Yuchi): Speck UPa I 141 n. 5, Hatt Asiatic Influences 92ff.; S. A. Indian (Mundurucú, Carajá): Lowie BBAE CXLIII (3) 55, (Amuesha): Métraux RMLP XXXIII 149; Eskimo (Mackenzie Area): Jenness 79, (Greenland): Rasmussen I 106; Jamaica: Beckwith MAFLS XVII 274 No. 86; Africa (Duala): Lederbogen Märchen 145, (Basuto): Jacottet 4 No. 1, 220 No. 32, (Mpongwe): Nassau 74 No. 15, (Kaffir): Theal 87; Frobenius Atlantis IV 220, V 308. Cf. Ceiuci: Alexander Lat. Am. 304.

D1175.1. Magic tinder. D1175.2. Magic fire-steel (flint, strike-a-light). D1390. Magic object rescues. D1593.1. Magic flower thrown down creates mountains. F636.1. Remarkable thrower of iron: makes field full of scissors. F636.2. Remarkable thrower of chips: makes forest. F636.3. Remarkable pourer of water: makes a river. H331.5.1.1. Apple thrown in race with bride. Distracts girl's attention, and as she stops to pick it up, suitor passes her (Atalanta). R231. Obstacle flight — Atalanta type. Objects are thrown back which the pursuer stops to pick up while the fugitive escapes.

D672.1. *Magic objects as decoy for pursuer.* Date palms are dropped which are transformed into animals which the pursuer stops to pick up. S. A. Indian (Ceiuci): Alexander Lat. Am. 304.

J351.1. Beaver sacrifices scrotum to save life. Cuts it off and leaves it for pursuers.

D673. *Reversed obstacle flight.* Magic obstacles raised in front of fugitive. — Type 450; BP III 205. — Arabic: A. Jahn Die Mehri-Sprache in Südarabien (Wien, 1902) 124 No. 28, D. H. Müller Mehri und Hadrami-Texte (Wien, 1909) 99 No. 39, ibid. Mehri und Soquotri Sprache (Wien, 1905) II 99 No. 20.

D674. *Magic flight with the help of a he-goat.* Speaking he-goat saves the girl promised to the devil. Lithuanian: Balys Index No. *314B.

B211.2. Speaking goat. B413. Helpful goat.

D675. *Sea turns to ice to permit flight.* Eskimo (Greenland): Rasmussen I 328, 367, III 124, 260, Rink 195, (Cumberland Sound): Boas BAM XV 182.

D680. Miscellaneous circumstances of transformation.

A1710. Creation of animals through transformation. A2260. Animal characteristics from transformation. B11.5.1. Dragon's power of self-transformation. G241.2.1. Witch transforms man to horse and rides him. H61. Recognition by ornaments under skin. H62. Recognition of person transformed to animal. H64. Recognition of disenchanted person by physical attributes.

D681. *Gradual transformation.* (Cf. D701.) — Köhler-Bolte I 573. — Greek: Hahn Gr. and alb. Märchen No. 29; Russian: v. Löwis of Menar Russische Märchen No. 29: Norwegian: Aasen Norske Minnestykke No. 62; India: Thompson-Balys; N. A. Indian (Seneca): Curtin-Hewitt RBAE XXXII 170 No. 32, (White Mountain Apache): Goddard PaAM XXIV 128, (Joshua): Farrand-Frachtenberg JAFL XXVIII 241 No. 20; — Eskimo (Mackenzie Area): Jenness 85.

D682. *Partial transformation.* Tobler 54, 59ff., 80; Jewish: Neuman.

J1908.2. Cat transformed to maiden runs after mouse.

D682.1. *Partial transformation: person with animal head.* Hartland Science 198; India: Thompson-Balys; Eskimo (Greenland): Rasmussen I 150, (Central Eskimo): Boas BAM XV 182, 253, (Mackenzie Area): Jenness 49.

D682.2. *Partial transformation: person with animal hair.* Irish: MacCulloch Celtic 168.

A511.10.1.1. Culture hero with deer's hair on temple. B635.3. Child of mortal and deer; he has deer's hair on temple.

D682.3. *Partial transformation: animal with human mind.* Irish myth: *Cross; Penzer VI 5 n. 1.

B212. Animal understands human speech. B773. Animals with human emotions.

D682.3.1. *Animals in human form retain animal food and habits.* Eskimo (Greenland): Rink 456, Rasmussen III 73, (Smith Sound): Kroeber JAFL XII 173, (Central Eskimo): Boas BAM XV 217.

D682.3.2. *Animal with human eyes.* Icelandic: *Boberg.

D682.4. *Partial transformation — color changed.* Irish myth: Cross.

D57. Change in person's color. F985 Animals change color. F1082. Person changes color.

D682.4.1. *Magic mantle changes color hourly.* Irish myth: Cross.

D1053. Magic mantle (cloak).

D682.4.2. *"Spirit of poetry" as hideous youth becomes beautiful.* Irish myth: *Cross.

D1860. Magic beautification. Z117. Poetry personified.

D683. *Transformation by magician.* Kittredge Witchcraft 184 n. 97; Irish myth: *Cross; See also all notes to D615.1.

D1711. Magician. S31.2. Children enchanted by stepmother.

D683.1. *Transformers.* Demigods who transform things at will so that they assume present form. See all references for motifs A900—A999 for work of transformers. (Cf. D272.) — Marshall Islands: Davenport JAFL LXVI 222.

D683.2. *Transformation by witch (sorceress).* *Types 403, 405, 410, 450, 451; *Kittredge Witchcraft 183f. nn. 91—96; *Fb "grime" I 484. — Irish myth: *Cross; Italian Novella: Rotunda; Greek: Fox 137 (Circe); Spanish: *Boggs FFC XC No. 449; India: Thompson-Balys.

G200. Witch. G210. Form of witch. S31.2. Children enchanted by stepmother.

D683.3. *Transformation by troll.* Fb "trold" III 852b.

G304. Troll.

D683.4. *Transformation by saint.* *Toldo Studien zur vgl. Littgsch. V 343; Irish myth: *Cross; Jewish: Neuman.

D1713. Magic power of hermit (saint). H1573.3.3. Transformation by saint as proof of power of Christianity before druid. Q551.5. Scoffers turned to stone by saint. V220. Saints. V223.1. Saint changes maggots in the sores of a nun into precious stones.

D683.5. *Transformation by god (goddess).* Italian Novella: Rotunda.

D683.6. *Transformation by evil spirits.* Irish myth: Cross.

D683.7. *Transformation by fairy.* Irish myth: *Cross.

D1719.5. Magic power of fairy. F343.11. Fairy offers man change of form and feature for aid in battle.

D683.7.1. *Transformation by offspring of fairy and mortal.* Irish myth: Cross.

F305. Offspring of fairy and mortal.

D683.8. *Transformation by angel (God).* Irish myth: *Cross; Jewish: Neuman.

V230. Angels.

D683.9. *Transformation by druid.* Irish myth: Cross.

D141.0.2. Men and women transformed to dogs by druidic spell. D1711.4. Druid as magician.

D684. *Transformation by helpful animals.* *Type 329.

B191. Animal as magician. B500. Magic power from animal. B505. Magic object received from animal. D532. Transformation by putting on claw, feather, etc. of helpful animal.

D684.0.1. *Transformation by magic animal.* Irish myth: Cross.

B119.1. Dog (whose skin) turns water to wine (mead).

D686. *Transformed animal refuses to touch meat of that animal.* Jamaica: Beckwith MAFLS XVII 102 No. 84.

C221.2. Tabu: eating totem animal.

D686.1. *Person transformed to animal refuses human food.* Will eat only food suitable for his enchanted form. Scottish: Campbell-McKay No. 1 and note.

D688. *Transformed mother suckles child.* *Types 403, 450; BP I 79ff., 99ff. — India: Thompson-Balys; Jewish: Neuman; Japanese: Ikeda. — Africa (Bushman): Bleek and Lloyd 87, (Kaffir): Theal 61.

E323.1.1. Dead mother returns to suckle child. F322.3. Stolen mother returns from fairy land each Sunday to minister to her children. S410. Persecuted wife.

D688.1. *Transformed cow advises daughter.* Chinese: Graham.

D691. *Daily beating of men transformed to dogs.* Necessary unless hero himself is to be transformed. — Chauvin V 3 No. 2, *5 No. 443.

D712.5. Disenchantment by beating.

D692. *City's inhabitants transformed to fish.* Different classes to different colored fish. — Chauvin VI 57 No. 222 n. 3.

D693. *Man transformed to ass plays the lyre.* *Type 430; *BP III 166.

D132.1. Transformation: man to ass. J512.4. Ass tries in vain to play lyre. J2413.1. Ass tries to caress his master like the dog. He is driven off.

D694. *Food left for transformed person.* India: Thompson-Balys.

D695. *Man transformed to woman has children.* Irish myth: Cross.

D12. Transformation: man to woman. T578. Pregnant man.

D696. *Transformation during sleep.* Irish myth: Cross.

D697. *Magic object can transform self.*

D697.1. *Magic loin cloth can transform itself into anything.* India: Thompson-Balys.

D698. *Gods have power to transform themselves.* Greek myth: passim; Hawaii: Beckwith Myth 2, and chapt. 1 passim.

D699. *Additional transformation motifs.*

D699.1. *Eyes of hero's buffalo friend turn into two powerful dogs that protect his wife.* India: Thompson-Balys.

B520. Animals save person's life.

D700—D799. Disenchantment.

D700. **Person disenchanted.** Types 314, 402, 434*, 442, 502; *Hdwb. d. Abergl. II 925 s.v. "Erlösung". — Irish myth: Cross; Breton: Sébillot Incidents s.v. "métamorphose"; India: *Thompson-Balys; Chinese: Werner 285, 356, 364.

F302.3.2.2. Fairy offers to disenchant mortal wife if man will marry her. F383.5. Transformed soldiers of fairy army disenchanted when overcome. H61.2. Recognition of disenchanted person by ornaments under his skin. H64. Recognition of disenchanted person by physical attributes. H1199.5. Task: disenchantment.

D701. *Gradual disenchantment.* (Cf. D617.) — *Type 307; Wimberly 381; Moe Samlede Skrifter I 52; German: Grimm Nos. 108, 121, 137; India: Thompson-Balys.

D702. *Partial disenchantment.*

D702.1. *Disenchantment with missing member.* While in transformation a person loses a bodily member. When disenchanted, he still lacks the member. — Many of the references to E33 may refer to this motif.

E33. Resuscitation with missing member. G252. Witch in form of cat has hand cut off.

D702.1.1. *Cat's paw cut off: woman's hand missing.* A man spends a night in a haunted mill, where he cuts off a cat's paw. In the morning the miller's wife has lost her hand. (Cf. D142, D621.1.1.) — *Taylor MPh XVII 59 n. 8; Tobler 43; Eng., Ire., U.S.: *Baughman; India: Thompson-Balys; Japanese: Ikeda.

G252. Witch in form of cat has hand cut off. Recognized next morning by missing hand. H57. Recognition by missing member.

D702.1.2. *Hog's forefoot cut off: woman's hand missing.* Scotland, U.S.: *Baughman.

D702.2. *Person restored to human form retains certain animal features.* German: Grimm No. 49.

D705. *Place disenchanted.*

D705.1. *Castle disenchanted.* India: Thompson-Balys.

D6. Enchanted castle.

D710. Disenchantment by rough treatment. Types 507A, 507C; India: Thompson-Balys; Irish myth: Cross.

E10. Resuscitation by rough treatment.

D711. *Disenchantment by decapitation.* *Types 314, 402, 425, 440, 441, 471, 506, 507, 531, 545A, 545B, 550, 708; *Fb "hoved" I 655a, "løse" II 517a; **Kittredge JAFL XVIII 1; BP I 9, III 60; Hartland Science 241. — Irish myth: *Cross; French Canadian: Barbeau JAFL XXIX 17; French: Sébillot France III 52, 140; India: Thompson-Balys; Africa (Fjort): Dennett 39 No. 5.

D566.3. Transformation by decapitation. D1865.1. Beautification by decapitation and replacement of head. E12. Resuscitation by decapitation. E446.3. Ghost laid by decapitating body. M221. Beheading bargain. S110. Murders.

D711.1. *Disenchantment by decapitation and replacement of head.* Type 531; Fb "hund" I 678a.

D711.1.1. *Head transferred from one man to another; second man's head in first man's hand.* Irish myth: Cross.

E783.1. Head cut off and successfully replaced. F511.0.6. Beheaded man's head replaced crooked.

D711.2. *Disenchantment by cutting person in two.* Type 506, 507, BP III 537; India: Thompson-Balys.

D711.3. *Disenchantment from bird by cutting off bill.* Fb "næb".

D711.4. *Disenchantment from flower by breaking stalk.* Type 407. — Lithuanian: Balys Index Nos. *368, 407; India: Thompson-Balys.

D431.1. Transformation: flower to person.

D711.4.1. *Disenchantment from flower by plucking it.* India: *Thompson-Balys.

D711.5. *Disenchantment from leaf by breaking it from tree.* Africa (Fjort): Dennett 42 No. 6.

D711.6. *Disenchantment from fruit by plucking it from tree.* India: Thompson-Balys.

D712. *Disenchantment by violence.*

D712.1. *Disenchantment by cutting off and reversing bodily members.* (Cf. D711.1.) — Kittredge JAFL XVIII 13; Fb "flå"; Irish myth: Cross.

D712.1.1. *Disenchantment by cutting off animal's limb.* German: Grimm No. 57.

D712.1.2. *Disenchantment by cutting in two.* India: Thompson-Balys.

D712.2. *Disenchantment by slinging against something.* Type 440; Hartland Science 242. — Eskimo (Bering Strait): Nelson RBAE XVIII 510; Chile: Pino Saavedra 402.

D712.2.1. *Disenchantment by throwing into fire.* (Cf. E15.) India: Thompson-Balys.

D712.3. *Disenchantment by striking.* Wimberly 343. — Spanish: Boggs FFC XC 57 No. 412; Missouri-French: Carrière; Chinese: Werner 309; India: Thompson-Balys.

D566. Transformation by striking. N592. Treasure from striking animal (or person) and disenchanting him.

D712.3.1. *Disenchantment by striking with a missile.* Irish myth: *Cross.

D566.2. Transformation by striking with a stone.

D712.3.2. *Disenchantment by throwing a stone.* India: Thompson-Balys.

D712.3.3. *Disenchantment by throwing a flower.* India: Thompson-Balys.

D712.4. *Disenchantment by drawing blood.* *Fb "blod" IV 48a; Child I 178, 337 n.; Wimberly 342; *Jijena Sanchez 19f., 36.

D712.4.1. *Disenchantment by drinking blood.* Child I 178, 337 n.; Wimberly 341.

D766.2. Disenchantment by application of blood.

D712.5. *Disenchantment by beating.* N. A. Indian: *Thompson Tales 348 n. 249a; Eskimo (Cumberland Sound): Boas BAM XV 187, (Ungava): Turner RBAE XI 265, (Central Eskimo): Boas RBAE VI 630, (Labrador): Hawkes GSCan XIV 158, (Greenland): Rink 93, Rasmussen II 38, III 104.

D691. Daily beating of transformed dogs. Necessary unless hero is to be transformed. E11. Resuscitation by beating.

D712.6. *Disenchantment by wounding.* Kittredge JAFL XVIII 11; *Jijena Sanchez 35, 49; Chinese: Graham.

D712.7. *Disenchantment by shooting.* Kittredge JAFL XVIII 11; Fb "and" IV 12b. — Africa (Mpongwe): Nassau 76 No. 15.

D712.8. *Disenchantment by ripping armor.* Penzer Sigfrid 113.

D712.9. *Disenchantment by killing.* Eskimo (Greenland): Rasmussen III 252.

D712.9.1. *Lizard in human form killed; corpse is lizard.* India: Thompson-Balys.

D712.10. *Disenchantment by driving stake through body.* Irish myth: Cross.

D712.11. *Disenchantment by throwing objects at transformed person.* India: Thompson-Balys.

D714. *Disenchantment by rubbing.* French Canadian: Barbeau JAFL XXIX 17.

D716. *Disenchantment by overcoming enchanted person in fight (contest).* Type 406*; Hartland Science 243.

G33.1. Cannibal disenchanted by overcoming it. Becomes maiden.

D717. *Disenchantment by assembling bones.*

E30. Resuscitation by arrangement of members. E607.1. Bones of dead collected and burned.

D717.1. *Disenchantment by laying collected bones in a seven-fold cloth and spreading another above it.* India: Thompson-Balys.

D718. *Disenchantment by shaving.* Fb "løse" II 517a.

D719. *Disenchantment by rough treatment — miscellaneous.*

D719.1. *Disenchantment by burying victim and sowing grain over him.* Fb "levende" II 404ab.

D719.1.1. *Disenchantment through burial and revival.* Chinese: Graham.

D719.2. *Girl destroys crab shape of husband and disenchants him permanently.* India: Thompson-Balys.

D720. Disenchantment by removing (destroying) covering of enchanted person.

D721. *Disenchantment by removing skin (or covering).* See all references to D361.1, Swan Maiden. — Irish myth: *Cross: India: *Thompson-Balys; Chinese: Graham; Eskimo (Kodiak): Golder JAFL XX 299, (Mackenzie Area): Jenness 51; Koryak: Jochelson JE VI 131, 156, 335; Africa (Pangwe): Tessman 368f.

E221. Dead spouse's malevolent return.

D721.1. *Disenchantment by flaying.* Fb "flå"; Kittredge JAFL XVIII 12.

D721.2. *Disenchantment by hiding skin (covering).* When the enchanted person has temporarily removed the covering, it is stolen and the victim remains disenchanted until it is found. *Type 400; *Fb "sælhund". — Scandinavian: Krappe Scandinavian Studies XVIII (1944) 156—162; Slavic: Machal 258; India: Thompson-Balys; Chinese: Graham; Surinam: Alexander Lat. Am. 274; Indonesian: DeVries's list No. 151; Africa (Basuto): Jacottet 146 No. 30, (Kaffir): Theal 38.

F302.4.2. Fairy comes into man's power when he steals her wings. She leaves when she finds them.

D721.3. *Disenchantment by destroying skin (covering).* *Type 425, 430, 440, 441; Köhler-Bolte I *319, 511; *Chauvin VII 37 No. 212B. — Icelandic: *Boberg; Turkish: Giese Türkische Märchen (Jena 1925) 120; India: *Thompson-Balys; Chinese: Graham; Korean: Zong in-Sob 177. — Eskimo (Kodiak): Golder JAFL XVI 89, (Mackenzie Area): Jenness 55, (Cumberland Sound): Boas BAM XV 224; N. A. Indian: *Thompson Tales 347 n. 249; S. A. Indian: Jijena Sanchez 23; Africa: Frobenius Atlantis IV 69, 287.

C757.1. Tabu: destroying animal skin of enchanted person too soon. D531. Transformation by putting on skin.

D721.4. *Disenchantment by holding temporarily disenchanted person.* India: *Thompson-Balys.

D757. Disenchantment by holding enchanted person during successive transformations.

D721.5. *Disenchantment from fruit (flower) by opening it.* Type 408; India: *Thompson-Balys.

D431.1.1. Woman emerges from flower. D431.6.1. Woman emerges from plant. D439.4.1. Woman emerges from egg. D981.3. Magic orange. F562.4. Girl lives in fruit and comes out only to be bathed by her twenty sisters.

D722. *Disenchantment by taking off bridle.* Man transformed to horse (ass) thus released. — See references in D535. — *Type 325; *BP

II 67; Chauvin V 150 No. 73. — French Canadian: Barbeau JAFL XXIX 17; Missouri French: Carrière; India: Thompson-Balys.

C837. Tabu: loosing bridle in selling man transformed to horse. D535. Transformation to horse (ass, etc.) by putting on bridle. D1209.1. Magic bridle.

D723. *Disenchantment by putting on (removing) chain from neck.*

D723.1. *Disenchantment by putting chain around neck.* See all references to D536.1.

D536.1. Transformation to swans by taking chains off neck. D1078. Magic chain.

D723.2. *Disenchantment by removing chain from neck.* French Canadian: Barbeau JAFL XXIX 17; India: *Thompson-Balys.

D723.2.1. *Disenchantment by removing string from neck.* India: Thompson-Balys.

D730. Disenchantment by submission. The helper must submit to the will of the enchanted person. Icelandic: Hjalmþers saga ok Ölvis 510, 515; French Canadian: Barbeau JAFL XXIX 17.

D731. *Disenchantment by obedience and kindness.* *Type 431.

D732. *Loathly Lady.* Man disenchants loathsome woman by embracing her. — Maynadier The Wife of Bath's Tale; Taylor Washington Univ. Studies IV (2) (1917) 177 n. 9; Vogt MLN XXXVII 339; Coomaraswamy On the Loathly Bride (Speculum 1945, 391ff.); Krappe Philological Quarterly XXVI 352ff. — Irish myth: *Cross; Icelandic: *Boberg. — Ila (Rhodesia): Smith and Dale II 404 No. 1; India: Thompson-Balys.

D1860. Magic beautification. D1870. Magic hideousness. F302. Fairy mistress. K1815. Humble disguise. Usually in rough clothing. T110. Unusual marriage. Z116. Sovereignty of Ireland personified.

D732.1. *Disenchantment of girl by carrying her on back.* Hartland Science 237, 243.

D733. *Loathly bridegroom.* Woman disenchants loathsome man by embracing him. — India: *Thompson-Balys; Eskimo (Kodiak): Golder JAFL XVI 16; N. A. Indian: *Thompson Tales 329 n. 188; S. A. Indian (Toba): Métraux MAFLS XL 44, 87.

D1860. Magic beautification. D1870. Magic hideousness. F301. Fairy lover. F471.2. Incubus. K1815. Humble disguise. Usually in rough clothing. L112.4. Dirty boy as hero. Q41.2. Reward for cleansing loathsome person. Cleansing eyelids, bathing, lousing, etc. T110. Unusual marriage. T216. Loathly bridegroom carried on back in basket by wife.

D733.1. *Hairy anchorite.* Beast-like man seduced by beautiful woman becomes human and handsome. — *C. A. Williams Oriental Affinities of the Legend of the Hairy Anchorite (U. of Illinois, 1925) 15; Gaster Oldest Stories 43.

F526.4. Beast-like anchorite. Walks on all fours; covered with hair like beast; has horns like beast. T330. Anchorites under temptation. T338. Virtuous man seduced by woman.

D733.2. *Swine bridegroom.* Bride disenchants him by her love. He returns to original form. Italian Novella: Rotunda.

B601.8. Marriage to swine.

D733.3. *Loathly husband a god in disguise.* Buddhist myth: Malalasekera I 648.

D734. *Disenchantment of animal by admission to woman's bed.* *BP I 9; Type 440; Fb "løse" II 517a. — English: Child I 298, II 502b, IV

454a, V 213a, 215b; Indonesian: Dixon 210; Africa (Zulu): Callaway 63, 321, 327.

B640. Marriage to person in animal form. K1361.1. Transformed person sleeps before girl's door, at foot of bed, in the bed. Is disenchanted upon admission to the bed.

D735. *Disenchantment by kiss.* *Type 410; BP I 9, II 236 n., 271, 561; Wimberly 335ff.; Hartland Science 238 f., 241; Taylor Washington Univ. Studies IV (2) (1917) 177 n. 9; Klapper 112. — Irish myth: *Cross; English: Child I 306ff., Icelandic: Sveinsson FFC LXXXIII xxxv, *Boberg; France: Sébillot France I 244, III 291; India: *Thompson-Balys; Philippine: Fansler MAFLS XII 247 No. 29; Africa: Frobenius Atlantis I 108.

C120. Tabu: kissing. D565.5. Transformation by kiss. D1794. Magic results from kissing. D1978.5. Waking from magic sleep by kiss.

D735.1. *Beauty and the beast.* Disenchantment of animal by being kissed by woman (man). — *Type 402, 425, 433A, 440; Fb "kys"; Dickson 55 nn. 70, 72; Tobler 53; Zs. f. Vksk. XIV 245; Studien zur vgl. Littgsch. II 360, 472 n. 4. — English: Child V 486 s.v. "kiss";Chile: Pino Saavedra 404f.; India: Cowell Jātaka V 141; Philippine: Fansler MAFLS XII 303; Africa (Kaffir): Theal 38.

D735.2. *Three redeeming kisses.* (Die weisse Frau.) A woman can be disenchanted from animal form if man will kiss her three times, each time when she is in the form of a different terrifying animal. — Tobler 69; **M. Waehler Die weisse Frau (Erfurt 1931); *Hdwb. d. Abergl. II 928. — Swiss: Jegerlehner Oberwallis 298 No. 3, 307 No. 24, 314 No. 103, 322 No. 93, 325 No. 3, 329 No. 32; Lithuanian: Balys Index No. 3592.

D610. Repeated transformation. D759.9.1. Girl disenchants animal husband by enduring his embraces without fear. E425.1. Revenant as lady in white.

D735.3. *Disenchantment from tree form by embrace of lover.* Greek: Frazer Apollodorus II 262 n. 2 (Demophon and Phyllis).

D735.4. *Disenchantment by enduring animal's embrace.*

D735.4.1. *Girl disenchants animal husband by enduring his embraces without fear.* Africa (Bantu): Theal Zambesi 279ff.

D735.2. Three redeeming kisses. H360. Bride test. H1400. Fear test.

D735.4.2. *Son disenchants animal father by enduring his caresses without fear.* Africa (Suto): Hoffman Zs. f. Eingeborenen-Spr. XXII 172 No. 11.

D741. *Disenchantment of monster when prince promises to marry the monster's mother.* The prince imagines falsely that the mother is also a monster. — Type 708.

D741.1. *Disenchantment of monster when his mother acknowledges him as son.* Type 708. Cf. Hupa: Goddard UCal I 147.

D741.2. *Disenchantment of monster child when baptized.* *Hibbard 45ff. (King of Tars).

V81. Baptism.

D742. *Disenchantment by promise to marry.* Lithuanian: Balys Historical.

D743. *Disenchantment by sexual intercourse.* Man disenchants woman in form of a bear. Cheremis: Sebeok-Nyerges.

D745. *Disenchantment by feeding enchanted animals.* Fb "løse" II 517a.

D750. Disenchantment by faithfulness of others. Irish myth: Cross.

E62. Resuscitation by vigil at tomb.

D753. *Disenchantment by accomplishment of tasks.* Type 518; Irish myth: Cross; Lithuanian: Balys Index No. *422; Prussian: Plenzat 21; Rumanian: Schullerus FFC LXXVIII No. 308*; Hungarian: Honti FFC LXXXI No. 4011.

H900. Tasks imposed.

D753.1. *Disenchantment by sewing shirts for enchanted brothers.* *Type 451; Fb "skjorte" III 268b.

D753.2. *Disenchantment of another by weeping jug of tears.* Italian: Basile introduction.

E58. Resuscitation by weeping (tears).

D753.3. *Disenchantment by obeying directions received in a dream.* Lithuanian: Balys Historical.

D753.4. *Disenchantment by climbing glass mountain.* German: Grimm No. 93.

F751. Glass mountain.

D754. *Disenchantment by serving transformed person.* German: Grimm No. 106.

D755. *Disenchantment of long absent spouse by faithfulness of partner.* India: Thompson-Balys.

D757. *Disenchantment by holding enchanted person during successive transformations.* *Types 403, 450; *MacCulloch Childhood 45; Hartland Science 242. — Greek: Fox 122 (Thetis); English: Child V 499 s.v. "transformation, successive"; Eskimo (Greenland): Rink 326. — See also, in general, references to D610.

D610. Repeated transformation. D721.4. Disenchantment by holding temporarily disenchanted person.

D758. *Disenchantment by maintaining silence.* *Type 451; Hartland Science 242.

C401. Tabu: speaking during certain time. D1741.3. Silence under punishment breaks power of enchantment. D2020. Magic dumbness. Q451.3. Loss of speech as punisnment.

D758.1. *Disenchantment by three nights' silence under punishment.* *Type 400; cf. Type 307; *BP II 330; *Fb "tie" III 792a; Hartland Science 246.

D758.2. *Disenchantment by maintaining silence for a year or more.* German: Grimm Nos. 9, 49, 137.

D759. *Disenchantment by faithfulness of others — miscellaneous.*

D759.1. *Disenchantment by taking key from serpent's mouth at midnight.* The disenchanter is to take the key (three keys) from the mouth of the woman in serpent form with his own mouth. — Hartland Science 240; Tobler Epiphanie der Seele 74.

D759.2. *Disenchantment from bird when queen milks own milk into bird's beak.* (Cf. D764.1.) — Fb "trane".

D759.3. *Disenchantment by naked virgin undergoing frightful journey at midnight.* She must come naked and alone on St. John's night between twelve and one, climb the castle walls, and enter the treasure chamber. — Hartland Science 236.

D1796. Magic from maiden walking naked in public.

D759.4. *Disenchantment if twelve men will not leave castle for a year.* Hartland Science 246.

D759.5. *Disenchantment by following enchanted woman through lake to underwater castle.* Hartland Science 241.

D759.6. *Disenchantment by maidens walking with lighted candles in procession.* Spanish: Boggs FFC XC 59 No. 425*D.

D759.7. *Disenchantment by maiden sitting at head of enchanted king's bed on morning of St. John's day.* — Spanish: Boggs FFC XC No. 445B.

D759.8. *Snake disenchanted by being allowed to wrap itself three times around person's neck.* Tobler 21.

D759.9. *Failure to disenchant by not watching sleeping princess long enough.* Lithuanian: Balys Index No. *422B.

D759.10. *Three soldiers in the enchanted manor.* Curiosity overcoming them they forfeit the power of disenchanting the princesses. Seven seven-year-old boys break the spell and save the princess. Lithuanian: Balys Index No. *422B.

D760. Disenchantment by miscellaneous means.

D762. *Disenchantment by proper person waking from magic sleep.* The enchanted person appears three times and if the sleeper does not wake by the third time the enchantment must last. — *Type 403, 450; Cosquin 166f., 170. — Spanish: Boggs FFC XC 61 No. 445A; Lithuanian: Balys Index No. *422A; Russian: Andrejev No. *400B.

D1971. Three-fold magic sleep. Husband (lover) put to sleep by false bride. Only on the third night (the last chance) he wakes. D1978.4 Hero wakened from magic sleep by wife who has purchased place in his bed from false bride. H1481. Thumb cut and salt put on it in order to remain awake.

D762.1. *Disenchantment by causing enchanted person to speak.* Lithuanian: Balys Historical.

D762.2. *Disenchantment by being wakened from magic sleep by proper agent.* German: Grimm Nos. 50, 163.

D763. *Disenchantment by destroying enchanter.* Chauvin VI 88 No. 252. — Irish myth: Cross; Eskimo (Kodiak): Golder JAFL XVI 28, (Cumberland Sound): Boas BAM XV 325.

D763.1. *Disenchantment by eating enchanter's heart.* Fb "løse" II 517a. — Penobscot (European borrowing): Speck JAFL XXVIII 58 No. 4; India: Thompson-Balys.

D763.2. *Disenchantment by defeating enchanter in single combat.* Irish myth: Cross.

D764. *Disenchantment by eating or drinking.* Irish myth: Cross.

D550. Transformation by eating or drinking. D1793. Magic results from eating or drinking.

D764.1. *Disenchantment by drinking milk of queen who has borne two boys.* (Cf. D759.2.) — *Fb "lose" II 517a.

D764.2. *Disenchantment by biting certain twig.* *Hdwb. d. Märchens sv. "Baum".

D764.3. *Disenchantment by eating certain salmon.* Irish myth: Cross.

D764.4. *Disenchantment by eating apple.* Cheremis: Sebeok-Nyerges.

D764.5. *Disenchantment by eating whale meat.* Eskimo (Cumberland Sound): Boas BAM XV 327.

D764.6. *Disenchantment by eating certain plant.* German: Grimm No. 122; Apulejus Golden Ass.

D764.7. *Disenchantment by refusing to eat for three days.* German: Grimm No. 93.

D764.8. *Disenchantment by eating head of serpent.* Jewish: Neuman.

D765. *Disenchantment by reversing (undoing) enchantment.*

D2071.1.5. Countermagic against evil eye: returning glance of evil eye blights the original glance.

D765.1. *Disenchantment by removing cause of enchantment.*

D765.1.1. *Disenchantment by removal of enchanting pill from mouth.* (Cf. D551.4.1.) — Penzer VII 42 n. 1, 222.

D765.1.1.1. *Disenchantment by removing ring from under dead girl's tongue.* Lover is thus freed from loving her. Italian Novella: Rotunda.

D765.1.2. *Disenchantment by removal of enchanting pin (thorn).* (Cf. D582.) — Fb "løse" II 517a. — Spanish: Boggs FFC XC 59, 62 Nos. 435, 449; Missouri-French: Carrière; India: *Thompson-Balys.

D582.1. Transformation by sticking nails in feet. D1978.3. Waking from magic sleep by removal of enchanting instrument. E21. Resuscitation by withdrawal of wounding instrument.

D765.2. *Disenchantment by untying enchanting knot.* Fb "knude" II 228.

D766. *Disenchantment by liquid.*

D766.1. *Disenchantment by bathing (immersing) in water.* Type 433B; Taylor Washington Univ. Studies IV (2) (1917) 176 n. 8; Wimberly 388; Child I 308, 338 n., II 505, III 505, V 39f. — India: *Thompson-Balys.

F717.2. Poison pool.

D766.1.1. *Disenchantment by water and command.* India: *Thompson-Balys.

D1765. Magic results produced by command.

D766.1.2. *Disenchantment by touching water.* India: Thompson-Balys.

D766.1.3. *Disenchantment by pouring water into ear.* Eskimo (Mackenzie Area): Jenness 40.

D766.2. *Disenchantment by application of blood.* (Cf. D712.4, D712.4.1). — *Type 516; *Rösch FFC LXXVII 138; *Fb "blod" IV 46b, 47a; Child I 337 n.; Penzer I 97; Wesselski Mönchslatein 148 No. 119. — Irish myth: *Cross; Spanish: Boggs FFC XC 53 No. 400A*; India: *Thompson-Balys.

D1003. Magic blood — human. E113. Resuscitation by blood.

D766.2.1. *Disenchantment by rubbing with pig's blood.* Irish myth: Cross.

D766.3. *Disenchantment by tears.* *Type 425. — Africa (Angola): Chatelain 35 No. 1.

D766.4. *Disenchantment by bathing in milk.* Wimberly 372; Type 433B and 507 (Danish forms); India: Thompson-Balys.

E80.1.1. Resuscitation by bathing in milk.

D771. *Disenchantment by use of magic object.*
D1442. Magic object tames or restrains animal.

D771.1. *Disenchantment by burning magic hair.* Köhler-Bolte I 573.
D991. Magic hair. D1787. Magic results from burning.

D771.2. *Disenchantment by rubbing with magic grease.* Cape Verde Islands: Parsons MAFLS XV (1) 219 No. 73; Greek Odyssey 10 line 394.
D1244. Magic salve.

D771.3. *Disenchantment by using powder.* Chauvin VI 8 No. 273.
D1246. Magic powder.

D771.4. *Disenchantment by using wand.* MacCulloch Childhood 205; India: *Thompson-Balys.
D1254.1. Magic wand.

D771.5. *Disenchantment by drinking from golden vessel.* Irish myth: Cross.
D1171. Magic vessel.

D771.6. *Disenchantment by medicine.* India: Thompson-Balys.
D1242. Magic fluid.

D771.7. *Disenchantment by rosary or scapular.* Lithuanian: Balys Historical.

D771.8. *Disenchantment and transformation by means of a magic sword.* India: Thompson-Balys.

D771.9. *Disenchantment by sprinkling consecrated rice.* India: Thompson-Balys.

D771.10. *Disenchantment by ring.* German: Grimm No. 123.

D771.11. *Disenchantment by flower.* German: Grimm No. 69.

D771.12. *Disenchantment by use of crystal ball.* German: Grimm No. 196.

D772. *Disenchantment by naming.* Wimberly 345; *Fb "varulv" III 1015a.
C430. Name tabu.

D772.1. *Disenchantment by recognition.* German: Grimm Nos. 62, 160.

D775. *Disenchantment by feeding transformed creature.* This is done contrary to commands. — Estonian: Aarne FFC XXV 130 No. 72.

D777. *Disenchantment by placing handkerchief between horns.* Breton: Sébillot Incidents s.v. "mouchoir".

D777.1. *Disenchantment by covering with cloth.* German: Grimm No. 76; India: *Thompson-Balys.

D778. *Disenchantment by blowing on victim.* Chauvin V 236 No. 134; Eskimo (Greenland): Rasmussen III 105.

D778.1. *Disenchantment from berry by blowing on it.* Lithuanian: Balys Index No. *702.

D778.2. *Disenchantment by blowing medicine on victim.* Cheremis: Sebeok-Nyerges.

D781. *Disenchantment by prayer (mass) of Pope.* Meyer Zs. f. Vksk. XXI 4.
V50. Prayer.

D781.1. *Disenchantment by blessing.* German: Grimm No. 141.

D782. *Disenchantment by physical contact.* Kittredge Gawain 205f., 216f. — Spanish: Boggs FFC XC 70 No. 535; Irish myth: Cross; German: Grimm No. 49, 56, 60, 76, 96.

D782.1. *Disenchantment by touch of holy man.* India: Thompson-Balys.

D782.2. *Disenchantment by touching earth.* India: Thompson-Balys.

D783. *Disenchantment by being found when lost.* Type 451.

D784. *Disenchantment by lighting fire.* Type 727*.

D785. *Disenchantment by magic contest.* Cape Verde Islands: Parsons MAFLS XV (1) 330.

D615. Transformation combat. Fight between contestants who strive to outdo each other in successive transformations.

D785.1. *Disenchantment produced by hero winning series of contests with seven demons.* India: Thompson-Balys.

D786. *Disenchantment by music.* Wimberly 332.

D1275.1. Magic music.

D786.1. *Disenchantment by song.* Eskimo (Greenland): Holm 63; Africa (Swazi): Bourhill and Drake 212ff. No. 18.

D1275. Magic song.

D787. *Disenchantment by encircling.* Wimberly 363.

D1272. Magic circle. D1791. Magic power by circumambulation.

D788. *Disenchantment by sign of cross.* (Cf. D1766.6.) Wimberly 367.

D789. *Other means of disenchantment.*

D789.1. *Disenchantment by covering with deliverer's clothing.* Wimberly 390.

D789.2. *Disenchantment by breaking lamp.* Spanish: Boggs FFC XC 54 No. 400B*.

D789.3. *Disenchantment by sight of old home.*

D789.3.1. *Frog-woman disenchanted by sight of water.* Hindu: Keith 147.

C300. Looking tabu.

D789.4. *Disenchantment by breaking tabu.* (Cf. C.) — Hindu: Keith 147.

C968. Disenchantment for breaking tabu.

D789.5. *Disenchantment by throwing golden objects into water.* German: Grimm No. 181.

D789.6. *Disenchantment by repeating magic formula.* South Africa: Bourhill and Drake 237ff. No. 20.

D1273. Magic formula (charm).

D789.6.1. *Disenchantment by speaking proper words.* Lithuanian: Balys Historical.

D789.7. *Disenchantment by shaking certain tree.* Irish myth: Cross.

D789.8. *Disenchantment of enchanted (sunken) castle (town, inhabitants) by digging it out.* Lithuanian: Balys Historical.

D789.9. *Girl disenchants her tiger-husband by putting a garland around his neck, sprinkling sand and water over him.* India: Thompson-Balys.

D789.10. *Disenchantment by ringing bell.* Korean: Zong in-Sob 97.

D790. Attendant circumstances of disenchantment.

D791. *Disenchantment possible under unique conditions.* Only one combination of time place and person will serve. — For many of these combinations see Hartland Science 240, 244, 248. — Lithuanian: Balys Index No. 3593.

M313. Man transformed into swine will regain human form after third marriage.

D791.1. *Disenchantment at end of specified time.* Irish myth: *Cross; *Jijena Sanchez 35, 36, 68, 70.

A570. Culture hero still lives. D1960.2.1. King asleep in mountain will awake when his horse's shoes are worn down.

D791.1.1. *Disenchantment at end of seven years.* Spanish: Boggs FFC XC No. 453.

D791.1.2. *Disenchantment when superhuman task is finished. Enchanted person appears every seven years in human form and puts one stitch in a smock.* When it is finished, she will be delivered. Hartland Science 240.

H1110. Tedious tasks.

D791.1.3. *The deliverer in the cradle.* Enchanted person can be delivered by child rocked in a cradle made from an oak sapling after it has grown great. **Ranke Der Erlöser in der Wiege; Hartland Science 244f; *Pauli (ed. Bolte) No. 80.

D791.1.4. *Disenchantment at end of two hundred years.* Irish myth: Cross.

D791.1.5. *Disenchantment at end of nine hundred years.* Irish myth: Cross.

D791.1.6. *Disenchantment possible at the end of seven hundred years.* Lithuanian: Balys Historical.

D791.1.7. *Disenchantment at cock crow.* Jijena Sanchez 38, 55.

D791.1.8. *Disenchantment at midnight after owl hoots three times.* German: Grimm No. 179.

D791.2. *Disenchantment by only one person.*

D732. Loathly lady. D2161.4.10.2. Wound healed only by person who gave it. H1313. Quest for person who can withdraw sword. Z300. Unique exceptions.

D791.2.1. *Disenchantment of girl only by lover.* BP II 125.

D791.2.2. *Disenchantment can be done by wife.* India: Thompson-Balys.

D791.2.2.1. *Disenchantment promised if girl may marry transformed man.* India: Thompson-Balys.

D791.3. *Disenchantment fails because conditions are not fulfilled.* Lithuanian: Balys Historical.

D791.4. *Disenchantment by finding key to enchanted castle.* Lithuanian: Balys Historical.

D1176. Magic key.

D792. *Transformed mother called by her child.* Comes and is rescued. — Africa (Ekoi): Talbot 333.

D793. *Disenchantment made permanent.*

D793.1. *Disenchantment made permanent by holding to a hair.* Italian: Basile I No. 2.

D793.2. *Disenchantment made permanent by burning cast-off skin.* Cf. D721.3.

D794. *Enchanted person attracts attention of rescuer.*

D794.1. *Enchanted person attracts attention by dancing.* South Africa: Bourhill and Drake 237ff. No. 20.

D2006.1. Forgotten fiancée reawakens husband's memory.

D795. *Maiden disenchanted, deserted, and refound.* *BP II 325.

D796. *Divine beings assume their own shape in sleep.* Penzer III 92 n. 2, VIII 25 n. 2.

D101. Transformation: god to animal.

D797. *Disenchantment as proof of truth.* The prodigy convinces judge that witness is speaking truth. India: Thompson-Balys.

H210. Test of guilt or innocence.

D798. *Disenchantment by passing between human being's legs.* Argentina, Paraguay: Jijena Sanchez 45.

D799. *Disenchantment by other means.* Irish myth: Cross.

D799.1. *Children disenchanted after long period are aged.* Irish myth: Cross.

D799.2. *Valley disenchanted rises to level of surroundings.* Irish myth: Cross.

D799.3. *Attendants of disenchanted person automatically disenchanted.* German: Grimm Nos. 50, 106, 127, 169, 179.

D800—D1699. MAGIC OBJECTS

D800—D899. Ownership of magic objects.

D800. **Magic object.** *Toldo Studien zur vgl. Littgsch. VIII 60ff.; *Siuts 89ff.; *Penzer I 25ff., V 3 n 1, IX 142; *Tibbals "Elements of Magic in the Romance of William of Palerne" MPh I (1903) 355 ff.; *Easter A Study of Magic Elements in the Romans d'Aventure (Dissertation, Baltimore 1906).

F166.4. Magic objects in other world.

D801. *Ownership of magic object.* Irish myth: Cross.

D1710. Possession of magic powers.

D801.1. *Magic objects possessed by witch, sorcerer or evil dwarf.* (Cf. F451.7, G234, D1711.) German: Grimm Nos. 53, 56, 60, 191.

D803. *Magic objects created by deity.*

D803.1. *Magic objects created by God on sixth day.* (Cf. A0). Jewish: Neuman.

D804. *Ineffable name written on object renders it magic.* (Cf. C431.) Jewish: Neuman.

D805. *Magic object to be used only in extreme need.* Italian: Basile introduction.

D806. *Magic object effective only when exact instructions for its use are followed.*

D806.1. *Magic object effective when struck on ground once only.* Second blow renders useless. Africa (Bulu): Krug JAFL XXV 113 No. 9.

C757. Tabu: doing things too soon. D1470.1.37. Magic wishing ivory tusk. When struck on ground (only once) provides treasure.

D806.2. *Magic charm (formula) used injudiciously brings death to owner's wife, children, himself.* India: Thompson-Balys.

D810—D859. ACQUISITION OF MAGIC OBJECT

D810. Magic object a gift. *BP I 361; *Aarne JSFO XXVII 1—96. — Irish myth: Cross; Icelandic: *Boberg; India: *Thompson-Balys.

B310. Acquisition of helpful animal. B505. Magic object received from animal. D1720. Acquisition of magic powers. Q140. Miraculous or magic rewards.

D811. *Magic object received from God (a god).* *Toldo IX 451ff. — Irish myth: *Cross; Icelandic: Örvar-Odds saga 138—41, Boberg; Finnish: Kalevala rune 36; Breton: Sébillot Incidents s.v. "baguette"; Greek: Fox 40, *Grote I 88.

V227.1. God gives staff of Christ to saint.

D811.1. *Magic object received from goddess.* Hartland Perseus III 109; India: *Thompson-Balys.

D811.2. *Magic object falls down from the heaven.* India: Thompson-Balys.

F1037. Footstool thrown from heaven.

D811.2.1. *Magic needle and thread fall from heaven as result of prayer.* (Cf. D1766.1.) India: Thompson-Balys.

D812. *Magic object received from supernatural being.* Japanese: Ikeda.

D812.1. *Magic object received from saint.* BP I 361. — Irish myth: *Cross; Icelandic: *Boberg; French Canadian: Barbeau JAFL XXIX 15f.; India: *Thompson-Balys; Chinese: Eberhard FFC CXX 25, 50.

V220. Saints.

D812.2. *Magic object received from demigod.* Africa (Ekoi): Talbot 18.

D812.3. *Magic object received from devil.* *Aarne MSFO XXV 39. — Irish myth: Cross; Breton: Sébillot Incidents s.v. "baguette"; Hindu: Penzer IX 45 n. 1.

G303. Devil.

D812.4. *Magic object received from ghost.* *Aarne MSFO XXV 39; *Chauvin V 78 No. 22 n. 1. — Icelandic: *Boberg; Chinese: Eberhard FFC CXX 25; Africa (Ekoi): Talbot 47, 211.

E373. Ghosts bestow gifts on living.

D812.4.1. *Magic object received from the dead in lower world.* Africa (Cameroons): Mansfeld 229f. No. 16, (Ekoi): Talbot 46.

E341. The grateful dead.

D812.4.2. *Magic object acquired as reward for burial of the dead.* French Canadian: Sister Marie Ursule.

E341.1. Dead grateful for having corpse ransomed.

D812.5. *Magic object received from genie.* *Type 561; *BP II 547. — India: *Thompson-Balys; Chinese: Eberhard FFC CXX 109.

N813. Helpful genie.

D812.5.1. *Magic object received from temple demons.* Chinese: Graham.

D812.6. *Magic object received from witch or wizard.* Type 576*****, 576***.

G284. Witch as helper.

D812.7. *Magic object received from dragon king.* Japanese: Anesaki 315.

B11. Dragon.

D812.8. *Magic object received from lady in dream.* (Cf. D825.) — Hdwb. d. Märchens s.v. "Baum"; BP II 544. — Irish myth: Cross; Greek: Fox 40; India: Thompson-Balys.

D825. Magic object received from maiden.

D812.8.1. *Magic object received from giantess in dream.* Norse: *Boberg.

D812.8.2. *Magic object received from man in dream.* India: *Thompson-Balys.

D812.9. *Magic object received from wild man.* Italian: Basile I No. 1.

F567. Wild man.

D812.10. *Magic object received from angel.* Irish myth: Cross; Jewish: Neuman; India: Thompson-Balys.

V232. Angel as helper.

D812.10.0.1. *Angel reveals location of magic object.* Irish myth: Cross.

D1810.5. Magic knowledge from angel. D1816. Magic discovery of desired place.

D812.11. *Magic object received from giant.* Icelandic: *Boberg; Irish myth: *Cross.

D838.6. Magic object stolen from giant. D845.2. Magic object found in giant's cave. F531.5.1. Giant friendly to man. G610. Theft from ogre. N511.3.1. Treasure from defeated giant. N812. Giant or ogre as helper.

D812.12. *Magic object received from dwarf.* Icelandic: *Boberg; German: Grimm Nos. 28, 64, 91, 97, 165.

D817.1.1. Magic object received from dwarf in return for rescue of child or kindness to child. F451.5.1.6. Other gifts from dwarfs. F451.7. Possessions of dwarfs.

D812.12.1. *Magic sword received from dwarf in dream.* Icelandic: *Boberg.

D812.8. Magic object received from lady in dream. F1068.2. Objects received in dream.

D812.13. *Magic objects gifts of magician.* India: Thompson-Balys.

D812.14. *Magic object received from ascetic.* India: Thompson-Balys; Buddhist myth: Malalasekera I 849, II 210, 656.

D812.15. *Magic object received from maiden-spirit.* India: *Thompson-Balys.

D813. *Magic object received from fairy.* *Type 510. — Irish myth: *Cross; Icelandic: Boberg; Breton: Sébillot Incidents s.v. "baguette"; Missouri French: Carrière.

F340. Gifts from fairies.

D813.1. *Magic object received from river-nymph.* Hartland Perseus III 109.

F424. River-spirit.

D813.1.1. *Magic sword received from Lady of Lake.* (Cf. D878.1.) — Irish myth: *Cross; English: Wells 50 (Le Morte Arthur); Indo-Chinese: Scott Indo-Chinese 303.

D878.1. Magic sword returned to lake whence it was received. D1081. Magic sword. F343.3. Fairy smith gives knight magic sword.

D813.1.2. *Magic cauldron received from lake spirit.* (Cf. D1171.2.) — Welsh: MacCulloch Celtic 100.

D813.2. *Magic object received from grateful fairy.* Hero has cured sick fairy by making her laugh. English: Baughman; Italian Novella: Rotunda.

D1723. Magic power from fairies. F330. Grateful fairies. F340.Gifts from fairies.

D813.3. *Magic object received from maiden in otherworld island.* Irish myth: Cross.

D814. *Magic objects received from sun, moon, and stars, etc.* Köhler-Bolte I 188.

D814.1. *Magic object received from wind.* German: Grimm No. 88.

D815. *Magic object received from relative.*

D815.1. *Magic object received from mother.* (Cf. D842.) — *Type 510; Icelandic: MacCulloch Eddic 301, Boberg; Africa (Kaffir): Theal 145.

B313.1. Helpful animal reincarnation of parent. Dead mother appears to heroine in form of animal. E323. Dead mother's friendly return.

D815.2. *Magic object received from father.* Hartland Perseus III 199. — Irish myth: Cross; Icelandic: MacCulloch Eddic 308 (Tyrfing), *Boberg.

D815.3. *Magic object received from godmother.* Breton: Sébillot Incidents s.v. "baguette"; Missouri French: Carrière.

D815.4. *Magic object received from sister.* Hartland Perseus III 199; Icelandic: Boberg.

D815.5. *Magic object received from father-in-law.* Hartland Perseus III 199.

D815.6. *Magic object received from daughter.* Icelandic: Boberg.

D815.7. *Magic object received from foster-parents.* Icelandic: Boberg.

P271. Foster-father. P272. Foster-mother.

D815.7.1. *Magic object received from girl's foster-mother.* Icelandic: *Boberg.

P272. Foster-mother.

D815.8. *Magic object received from wife.* German: Grimm No. 92.

D816. *Magic object inherited.* MacCulloch Childhood 376; Icelandic: *Boberg.

P230. Parents and children.

D817. *Magic object received from grateful person.* *Type 560; *Aarne MSFO XXV 40; BP II 39. — Icelandic: *Boberg; Missouri French:

Carrière; N. A. Indian (Malecite, Penobscot): Thompson CColl II 411ff. (European borrowings).

D855. Magic object acquired as reward. Q140. Miraculous or magic rewards. W27. Gratitude.

D817.1. *Magic object received from man in return for rescue of child.* *Types 560, 611; Aarne MSFO XXV 38—56 passim; India: *Thompson-Balys.

D817.1.1. *Magic object received from dwarf in return for rescue of child or kindness to child.* Icelandic: *Boberg.

D812.12. Magic object received from dwarf. F337.1. Fairy grateful to mortal for saving children's life. F451.5.1.6. Other gifts from dwarfs.

D817.1.2. *Magic object received from grateful father of redeemed snake.* India: Thompson-Balys.

D817.2. *Magic object received in return for being shaved.* India: Thompson-Balys.

D818. *Magic object received from astrologer.* Irish myth: Cross.

D818.1. *Magic object received from magician.* India: Thompson-Balys.

D821. *Magic object received from old woman.* Hartland Perseus III 199. — Italian Novella: Rotunda; Missouri French: Carrière; Cape Verde Islands: Parsons MAFLS XV (1) 123.

N825.3. Old woman helper.

D822. *Magic object received from old man.* Hartland Perseus III 199. — Icelandic: *Boberg; U.S.: Baughman.

N825.2. Old man helper.

D823. *Magic object received from huntsman.*

D823.1. *Magic object received from green-clad huntsman.* Type 304.

D825. *Magic object received from maiden.* Hartland Perseus III 199. — Icelandic: *Boberg; Irish myth: Cross.

D812.8. Magic object received from lady in dream. N831. Girl as helper.

D825.1. *Magic object received from cat-woman; i.e. woman transformed intermittently to cat.* — French: Cosquin No. 11; N. A. Indian: Thompson CColl II 400f.

D142. Transformation: man to cat. F771.4.2. Cat castle. Castle occupied by cats (enchanted women.)

D826. *Magic object received from monster.*

D826.1. *Magic object vomited by conquered monster.* India: Thompson-Balys.

D827. *Magic object received through particular intermediaries.* Only one person can help secure it. — *Chauvin V 59 No. 19 n. 1.

B501. Animal gives part of body as talisman for summoning its aid. B505. Magic object received from animal. B505.1. Magic object received from animal brother-in-law. D2161.4.10.2. Wound healed only by person who gave it.

D828. *Magic object received from child.* Type 425.

D829. *Acquisition of magic object — miscellaneous.*

D829.1. *Magic object received by apprentice from master.* German: Grimm Nos 36, 111, 129.

D830. Magic object acquired by trickery. *Chauvin VII 38 No. 212B; Icelandic: MacCulloch Eddic 268; Buddhist myth: Malalasekera I 289.

D830.1. *Attempt to learn about magic object by spying.* Chinese: Graham.

D831. *Magic object acquired by trick exchange.* By means of second magic object hero recovers first. (Often mixed with D832). — *Types 302, 400, 507, 569; BP I 464; Penzer I 25ff. — India: *Thompson-Balys; Indonesian: DeVries Volksverhalen Nos. 3, 104.

A1415.3. Theft of fire — trick exchange. D851. Magic object acquired by exchange (no trick).

D832. *Magic objects acquired by acting as umpire for fighting heirs.* When hero gets hold of objects he refuses to return it. — *Types 400, 518; *BP II 331ff.; Cosquin Indiens 371ff.; Saintyves Perrault 287ff.; Hdwb. d. Märchens I 97. — Icelandic: Boberg; India: *Thompson-Balys; Indonesian: DeVries Volksverhalen No. 104; Chinese: Chavannes 500 Contes III 259 No. 470; Africa: Frobenius Atlantis II 113, 175, III 336, IV 110.

A183. Mortal as umpire of quarrel between gods. F451.5.23. Dwarfs seek human help in their fights and troubles. K342. Thief as umpire in contest. K452. Unjust umpire misappropriates disputed goods. K671. Captive throws his hat to lions who fight over it while he escapes. K2127.1. Desiring woman they quarrel over, man accuses group of men of having abducted his wife.

D833. *Magic object acquired by tricking giant.* Giant is persuaded to give the objects to the hero. (Cf. D831, where the person tricked is often a giant.) — Type 328.

D834. *Magic object acquired by tricking devil.* Man gets shelter in storm; devil gets wet. Devil gives man magic object in return for information as to how he kept dry. — Köhler-Bolte I 416.

D851. Magic object acquired by exchange (no trick).

D835. *Magic object acquired through trickery: child forced to cry till object is given.* Icelandic: Egils saga ok Asm., ch. XIV 10, Boberg.

D836. *Magic object acquired by exchanging letters.* (Cf. K511). India: Thompson-Balys.

D837. *Magic object acquired through foolish bargain.* Type 590. — N. A. Indian (Micmac) (European borrowing): Thompson CColl II 412.

J2080 Foolish bargains. K232.2.1. Fairy (god?) loses stronghold by consenting to lend it for "a day and a night." M200. Bargains and promises. N421. Lucky bargain.

D838. *Magic object acquired by stealing.* Types 576******, 581*; Irish myth: *Cross; Icelandic: *Boberg; Missouri French: Carrière; India: Thompson-Balys.

D861. Magic object stolen. D1651.11. Only master able to bend bow. K300. Thefts and cheats. K331.5. Trickster steals magic doll while owner is asleep.

D838.1. *Stolen objects powerful in magic.* *Fb "stjæle" III 576a, "tigge" III 793b.; India: Thompson-Balys.

D838.2. *Magic object taken from ogre's house.* Hartland Perseus III 201; Icelandic: *Boberg; Japanese: Ikeda; India: *Thompson-Balys.

D838.3. *Magic object stolen in Thor's temple.* Icelandic: Sturlaugs saga 617—31, Boberg.

D838.4. *Magic object taken in the serpents' country.* Icelandic: FSS 69—79, Boberg.

D838.5. *Magic object taken from barrow.* (Cf. E461.1, F352.) — Icelandic: *Boberg.

F352. Theft of cup (drinking horn) from fairies.

D838.6. *Magic object stolen from giant.* (Cf. F531.6.7.3.) — Icelandic: *Boberg.

D812.11. Magic object received from giant. D845.2. Magic object found in giant's cave. F531.6.7. Giant's treasure. G610. Theft from ogre. N511.3.1. Treasure from defeated giant.

D838.7. *Magic armor stolen from dwarf by giant.* Icelandic: Boberg.

D838.8. *Magic helmet taken directly from bystander.* Icelandic: Boberg.

D838.9. *Boy overhears witches' conversation about magic objects, which he gets possession of.* Lithuanian: Balys Index No. *613A.

N440. Valuable secrets learned.

D838.10. *Prince procures magic object from bathing fairy when he steals her clothes.* India: Thompson-Balys.

K1335. Seduction by stealing clothes of bathing girl.

D838.11. *Man poisons couple, owners of magic gong, and gains possession of it.* India: Thompson-Balys.

D838.12. *Magic object taken from dead enemy.* German: Grimm No. 166.

D838.13. *Magic object stolen at night.* Korean: Zong in-Sob 28 No. 12.

D839. *Magic object acquired by trickery — miscellaneous.*

D839.1. *Magic root acquired by tricking mother bird into searching for it in order to disentangle her young.* India: Thompson-Balys.

D839.2. *Fairy dun acquired by tricking owner.* Irish myth: Cross.

D840. Magic object found. Types 561, 590; Hartland Perseus III 201; India: Thompson-Balys.

N200. The good gifts of fortune.

D841. *Magic object accidentally found.* German: Grimm No. 122; Chinese-Persian: *Coyajee JPASB XXIV 197.

D842. *Magic object found on grave.*

D842.1. *Magic object found on mother's grave.* (Cf. D815.1.) — Type 510; Saintyves Perrault 41; Cox 477.

E323. Dead mother's friendly return. N810. Supernatural helpers.

D842.2. *Magic object found on father's grave.* Type 314.

D842.3. *Magic object found on grave of slain helpful animal.* Cox 477; Saintyves Perrault 37; Hdwb. d. Märchens s.v. "Baum". — Japanese: Ikeda.

B313.1. Helpful animal reincarnation of parent. Dead mother appears to heroine in form of animal. B330. Death of helpful animal. E610. Reincarnation as animal.

D845. *Magic object found in underground room.* Type 562. — India: Thompson-Balys.

D845.1. *Magic object found in giant's cave.* Icelandic: Boberg.

D812.11. Magic object received from giant. D838.6. Magic object stolen from giant. F531.5.1. Giant friendly to man. F531.6.7. Giant's treasure. G610. Theft from ogre. N511.3.1. Treasure from defeated giant. N812. Giant or ogre as helper.

D846. *Magic object found in magic castle.* *BP III 113 n. 4.

D846.1. *Golden cot found in magic castle.* India: Thompson-Balys.

D847. *Magic object found in chimney.* Breton: Sébillot Incidents s.v. "cheminée".

D848. *Magic object dug from ground.* Hartland Perseus III 201f. — Korean: Zong in-Sob 43.

D849. *Magic object found — miscellaneous.*

D849.1. *Magic object found in fort.* Chinese: Werner 312.

D849.2. *Magic object pointed out by bird.* *Norlind: Skattsägner 19ff., 29ff.

D849.3. *Magic object found on an island.* Aarne MSFO XXV 120; Icelandic: *Boberg.

D849.4. *Magic object found in a wood.* *Aarne MSFO XXV 120.

D849.4.1. *Magic object found in garden.* German: Grimm No. 121.

D849.5. *Magic object found in fish.* Italian Novella: Rotunda.

D849.5.1. *Magic object found in heart of whale.* Irish myth: Cross.

D849.6. *Magic object found under dead girl's tongue.* Italian Novella: Rotunda.

D849.7. *Magic object pointed out by divine voice.* Italian Novella: Rotunda.

D849.8. *Magic object found on ground.* French Canadian: Sister Marie Ursule.

D850. Magic object otherwise obtained.

D851. *Magic object acquired by exchange.* (No trick). — Hartland Perseus III 200; Irish myth: Cross; N. A. Indian (Ponca, Ojibwa, European borrowings): Thompson CColl II 329f.

B312.2. Helpful animals obtained by exchange. D831. Magic object acquired by trick exchange. D837. Magic object acquired through foolish bargain. K100. Deceptive bargain. M200. Bargains and promises.

D851.1. *Magic object purchased.* India: Thompson-Balys.

D852. *Magic object acquired by wishing.* *Type 675.

D1131.1. Castle produced by magic. D1720.1. Man given power of wishing. D1761. Magic results produced by wishing. D2100. Magic wealth.

D853. *Magic object forged by smith to order.* *Hartland Perseus III 200. — Icelandic: MacCulloch Eddic 268.

D853.1. *Magic horse (wooden) made by carpenter.* India: Thompson-Balys.

D855. *Magic object acquired as reward.* Icelandic: Boberg.

D817. Magic object received from grateful person. Q10. Deeds rewarded.

D855.1. *Magic object acquired as reward for vigil.* *BP III 111. — Chinese: Graham.

D855.2. *Magic object acquired as reward for religious austerities.* Chinese: Werner 277.

D1735.1. Magic power by fasting. P623. Fasting as a means of distraint. V462. Asceticism.

D855.3. *Magic object acquired as reward for quest into grave.* Icelandic: Boberg.

D855.4. *Magic object as reward for faith.* Jewish: Neuman.

D855.5. *Magic object as reward for good deeds.* Chinese: Eberhard FFC CXX 107 No. 62.

D856. *Magic object acquired by gaining love of owner.* Type 580.

T0. Love.

D857. *Magic object born with hero.* *Hartland Perseus III 198. — Africa (Fjort): Dennett 60 No. 12.

B311. Congenital helpful animal. Born at same time as hero and (usually) by same magic means. T589.3. Birth trees. Spring forth as hero is born, act as life tokens, etc. E761. Life-token. E765.2. Life bound up with that of animal. T589.7.1. Simultaneous birth of (domestic) animal and child.

D858. *Magic object acquired by singing.* Type 650***.

D859. *Magic object obtained — miscellaneous means.*

D859.1. *Magic object acquired by rapping on tree.* Fb "lind" II 432a.

D859.2. *Quest to hell for magic object.* Aarne FFC XXIII 130, JSFO XXVII 48. — Icelandic: Boberg.

H1270. Quest to lower world. V520. Salvation.

D859.2.1. *Magic object received from other world.* Jewish: Neuman.

D859.3. *Magic object obtained by reaching in certain cardinal direction.* N. A. Indian: *Kroeber JAFL XXI 224, (California): Gayton and Newman 75.

D2178. Objects produced by magic.

D859.4. *Magic object eaten unwittingly.*

D859.4.1. *Magic bird-heart eaten unwittingly.* Scottish: Campbell-McKay No. 15; Icelandic: Herrmann Saxo II 33.

D859.4.2. *Magic bird-liver eaten unwittingly.* Scottish: Campbell-McKay No. 15.

D859.5. *Magic object to be chosen from among identical worthless objects.* Insect helps in choice. East Africa: Torrend Zs. f. afrikan. u. ozean. Spr. I 247ff.

D1658.3.2. Grateful objects help in choice of caskets. H511.1. Three caskets. L211. Modest choice: three caskets type.

D859.6. *Magic object obtained as compensation for loss of entire herd* — the spirit of the herd resides in the last goat's tail, which old woman keeps. India: Thompson-Balys.

D859.7. *Magic object left by frightened demons.* Korean: Zong in-Sob 144.

D859.8. *Magic object as ransom of captive.* Greek: Grote I 139; Icelandic: Boberg.

D860. Loss of magic object. *Aarne MSFO XXV I — 200 passim; Bolte Zs. f. Vksk. XVIII 452 n. 3. — Chinese: Werner 348, Graham.

F948.3. Magic object sinks into earth.

D860.0.1. *Death to follow loss of magic object.* Irish myth: Cross.

D860.0.2. *Loss of magic object causes madness.* India: Thompson-Balys.

D861. *Magic object stolen.* Fansler MAFLS XII 17; Italian Novella: Rotunda; Jewish: Neuman; India: *Thompson-Balys; Georgia Negro: Harris Nights 30; S. A. Indian (Toba): Métraux MAFLS XL 130.

D838. Magic object acquired by stealing. D1651. Magic object obeys master alone. F451.5.2.2.1. Dwarfs steal magic objects. K300. Thefts and cheats. K331.5. Trickster steals magic doll while owner is asleep. K1935. Impostors steal rescued princess.

D861.0.1. *Magic object stolen from local deity.* Chinese: Graham.

D861.1. *Magic object stolen by host (at inn.)* *Type 563; *BP I 349ff.; **Aarne JSFO XXVII 1—96. — Breton: Sébillot Incidents s.v. "aubergiste"; French Canadian: Barbeau JAFL XXIX 24; Missouri French: Carrière; India: Thompson-Balys; Seneca: Curtin-Hewitt RBAE XXXII 264 No. 50 (not at inn).

K1837.9. Wife disguises as a man and outwits landlord of inn when he tries same trick he has played on her husband to get all of his goods, etc. K2241. Treacherous inn-keeper.

D861.2. *Magic object stolen by neighbor.* **Aarne JSFO XXVII 1—96, especially 48; *BP I 349ff.; Type 564. — India: Thompson-Balys.

D861.3. *Magic object stolen by brothers.* Type 563; BP I 349ff.

K2211. Treacherous brother. Usually elder brother. L10. Victorious youngest child.

D861.4. *Magic object stolen by rival for wife.* *Type 560, 561; *Aarne MSFO XXV 3—83; India: Thompson-Balys.

K2221. Treacherous rival lover. Wife's paramour or rival in love.

D861.4.1. *Magic object stolen by rival's emissary.* India: Thompson-Balys.

D861.5. *Magic object stolen by hero's wife.* *Type 560; **Aarne MSFO XXV 3—83.

K2213. Treacherous wife.

D861.5.1. *Magic object stolen by owner's fiancée.* German: Grimm No. 122.

D861.6. *Magic object stolen in card game.* *Type 566; BP I 470ff.; Aarne MSFO XXV 85—97.

K330. Means of hoodwinking the guardian or owner.

D861.7. *Magic object carried off by bird.* (Cf. D865.)

D861.7.1. *Magic horn carried off by bird.* India: Thompson-Balys.

D861.8. *Magic object stolen by relatives.* Madagascar: Renel I 209ff. No. 40.

D861.8.1. *Magic objects stolen from owner by his daughter, with whom he spends the night.* India: Thompson-Balys.

D861.9. *Magic object stolen by giants.* French Canadian: Sister Marie Ursule.

D861.10. *Magic object carried away; child allowed to play with it.* India: Thompson-Balys.

A1411.2. Theft of light by being swallowed and reborn. D883. Magic (marvelous object) given back to placate crying child. K331.5. Trickster steals magic doll while owner is asleep.

D862. *Magic object taken away by force.* India: Thompson-Balys.

D863. *Magic object mysteriously disappears.* Korean: Zong in-Sob 44.

D865. *Magic jewel carried off by bird.* This happens when the jewel is examined by daylight. (Cf. D861.7.) — *Chauvin V 211 No. 120; *Gerould PMLA XIX 392ff.; Krappe Neophilologus XIV 90; Italian Novella: Rotunda.

N352.2. Jewel (garment) carried off by bird from bather.

D865.1. *Magic ring carried off by bird.* Irish myth: Cross; India: Thompson-Balys.

D866. *Magic object destroyed.* Japanese: Ikeda.

D866.1. *Woman cooks the magic fruits.* (Cf. D981.) — Indonesia: DeVries's list No. 195.

D866.2. *Magic object destroyed because of feigned sickness.* India: Thompson-Balys.

B335.2. Life of helpful animal demanded as cure for feigned sickness. H1212. Quest assigned because of feigned illness. S268.1. Sacrifice of child demanded as cure for feigned sickness.

D867. *Magic object mysteriously disappears.* Korean: Zong in-Sob 44.

D867.1. *Magic object disappears at owner's death.* Irish myth: Cross (D857).

D868. *Magic object returns to original place.*

D868.1. *Magic mango returns to tree for broken tabu.* India: Thompson-Balys.

C900. Punishment for breaking tabu. D1602. Self-returning magic object.

D871. *Magic object traded away.*

J2080. Foolish bargains. M200. Bargains and promises.

D871.1. *Magic object exchanged for worthless.* Foolish brother (wife) exchanges old object for new. *Type 561; *BP II 205. — Breton: Sébillot Incidents s.v. "bague"; India: Thompson-Balys.

K266. New bags for old! Recovery of the old bag (containing money or having magic power) which the stupid wife has given away. The husband exchanges a new bag for it.

D871.1.1. *Exchange of common cow for gold-dropping cow made by daughter when her father stops at her home for the night.* India: Thompson-Balys.

D876. *Magic treasure animal killed.* (Goose that laid the golden egg). Greek fable: Wienert FFC LVI 64 (ET 283), 106 (ST 182); Babrius 123; Halm Aesop No. 343. — India: Keith 145 (gold-producing boy), Thompson-Balys; Panchatantra III 6 (tr. Ryder) 331; Cowell Jātaka I 292 No. 136; Japanese: Ikeda; Indonesian: Dixon 238 n. 51; N. A. Indian: *Thompson-Tales 306 n. 109z.

B100. Treasure animal. B103.2.1. Treasure-laying bird. B192. Magic animal killed. B330. Death of helpful animal. D1019. Magic egg. D1901.1. The overfed hen. A woman wants her hen to lay many eggs. Overfeeds her and she stops laying altogether. J700. Forethought in provision for life (general). J2129.3. Getting all the eggs at once. A peasant kills his hen so that he can immediately get all the eggs she will lay during the next year. N515. Treasure found in goose's stomach. Q272. Avarice punished.

D877. *Magic object loses power by overuse.* *Chauvin V 11 No. 7; India: Thompson-Balys; Chinese: Eberhard FFC CXX 106, 109. — Jamaica: Beckwith MAFLS XVII 248 No. 24.

C762.1. Tabu: using magic power too often. C762.4. Tabu: taking more than one fruit from a certain tree. D1651. Magic object obeys master alone.

D877.1. *Magic wishing-ring loses power by touching water.* Irish myth: Cross.

C532. Tabu: touching water. D1470.1.15. Magic wishing-ring. D1788.1. Magic results from contact with water.

D877.2. *Extraordinary flower preserves its freshness so long as it remains unperceived by anyone other than owner.* India: Thompson-Balys.

D878. *Magic object voluntarily restored to giver.* Irish myth: Cross.

D878.1. *Magic sword returned to lake whence it was received.* Taken back by lake spirit. (Excalibur). (Cf. D813.1.1.) — English: Wells 50 (Le Morte Arthur); Indo-Chinese: Scott 303.

D813.1.1. Magic sword received from Lady of the Lake. D1081. Magic sword.

D878.2. *Magic sword thrown into lake by dying hero.* Irish myth: Cross.

D880. Recovery of magic object. *Bolte Zs. f. Vksk. XVIII 452 n. 3; *Aarne MSFO XXV 3ff. — Chinese: Werner 348; India: Thompson-Balys.

D1601.10.1. Self-cooking pot.

D880.0.1. *Recovery of magic object cures madness.* India: Thompson-Balys.

D2161. Magic healing power. K420. Thief loses his goods or is detected.

D881. *Magic object recovered by using second magic object.* *Type 561; *Aarne MSFO XXV 3—83; *BP II 547ff. — Jewish: Neuman; India: Thompson-Balys; French Canadian: Barbeau JAFL XXIX 24.

D1375.1. Magic object causes horns to grow on person.

D881.1. *Recovery of magic object by use of magic apples.* These apples cause horns to grow. (Cf. D895.) *Type 566; BP I 470ff; Aarne MSFO XXV 85—97.

Q212. Theft punished. Q400. Kinds of punishment — general.

D881.2. *Recovery of magic object by use of magic cudgel.* (Cf. D1094.) — *Types 563, 564; BP I 349ff.; *Aarne JSFO XXVII 1—96. — India: *Thompson-Balys; Jamaica: Beckwith MAFLS XVII 248 No. 25.

D882. *Magic object stolen back.*

D882.1. *Stolen magic object stolen back by helpful animals.* Korean: Zong in-Sob 28.

D882.1.1. *Stolen magic object stolen back by helpful cat and dog.* They steal the ring from the thief's mouth. — *Type 560; **Aarne MSFO XXV 3—82; BP II 455. — India: Thompson-Balys; Indonesian: DeVries Volksverhalen Nos. 67, 170 notes.

B548. Animal retrieves lost object. B548.1. Animals recover lost wishing ring. B548.2. Fish brings lost object from bottom of sea. B548.2.1. Fish recovers ring from sea. K431. Mouse's tail in mouth of sleeping thief causes him to cough up swallowed magic ring.

D882.1.2. *Magic object recovered with lioness's help.* French Canadian: Sister Marie Ursule (D887).

D882.2. *Recovered magic articles dropped by rescuing animals into the sea.* Köhler-Bolte I 437; India: Thompson-Balys.

D882.3. *Magic object stolen back by servant.* Cheremis: Sebeok-Nyerges.

D882.4. *Stolen magic object stolen back by man in disguise.* India: Thompson-Balys.

K331.8. Theft by disguise as son of owner.

D883. *Magic (marvelous object) given back to placate crying child.* India: Thompson-Balys.

D861.10. Magic object carried away; child allowed to play with it.

D884. *Thief forced to vomit up stolen magic object.* India: Thompson-Balys.

D885. *Magic object recovered with devil's help.* Types 360, 361, 475; BP II 423.

D885.1. *Magic object recovered with witch's help.* Georgia Negro: Harris Nights 30.

D886. *Magic object recovered through recitation of magic formula.* Chinese: Werner 358.

D1273. Magic formula.

D895. *Magic object returned in payment for removal of magic horns.* (Cf. D881.1). — *Type 566.

D1375.1. Magic object causes horns to grow on person.

D900—D1299. Kinds of magic objects.

D900. Magic weather phenomena.

A280 Weather-God. A1130. Establishment of present order: weather phenomena. D1540. Magic object controls elements. D2140. Magic control of the elements. F790. Extraordinary sky and weather phenomena. F960. Extraordinary nature phenomena.

D900.0.1. *Prognostications from weather phenomena.* Irish myth: *Cross.

D1812.5.0.15.1. Prognostications for year from winds blowing on January 1.

D901. *Magic cloud.* *Chauvin V 230; Fb "sky"; Jewish: *Neuman.

D1311.6.2. Magic cloud answers questions. D1380.25. Magic cloud protects. D1445.6.1. Magic clouds burn animals. D1469.16. Clouds fetch precious stones. D1520.2. Magic transportation by cloud. Q552.15. Punishment: cloud cuts off view of man promised all he can see for expelling saint. Z156. Cloud (mist) as symbol of misfortune.

D902. *Magic rain.* (Cf. D910.) *Basset RTP XXXIII 167f. — Irish: Cross, Plummer clxxx; Chinese: Werner 205.

A1131. Origin of rain. D1242.1. Magic water. D1353.1. Magic rain makes people foolish. D1391.1. Miraculous rain extinguishes. D1541.4. Magic fountain causes rain. D1542. Magic object controls rain. D2143.1.1. Rain produced by pouring water.

D902.1. *Magic mist.* *Fb "tåge" III 945a; *Cox Cinderella 477; Irish: *Cross; Icelandic: *Boberg; English: Wimberly 321; Breton: Sébillot Incidents s.v. "brume"; N. A. Indian: *Thompson Tales 339 n. 221b.

D1361.1. Magic mist of invisibility. D1381.22 Magic mist protects against attack. D1418.1. Magic mist causes person to become lost. D2163.4. Magic mist as defense in battle. F61.3. Transportation from heaven in mist. K532.1. Escape in mist of invisibility. R236. Fugitive aided by magic mist.

D902.1.1. *Druidic mist.* Irish myth: *Cross.

P427. Druid (magus).

D902.2. *Magic dew.* *Fb "Sankt Hansdag" III 161a.

D1500.1.18.1. Dew from saint's grave as cure. D1505.5.2. Dew falling on St. John's Night restores sight. D1599.6. Magic dew destroys enemy's books.

D902.3. *Magic hail.* Irish myth: Cross.

A938. Twelve chief rivers of Ireland left by hail-storm. D1469.4. Magic hail on lake causes treasure to spring from it. F962.5. Storm of gigantic hailstones.

D903. *Magic snow.* Koryak: Jochelson JE VI 170.

D904. *Magic ice.* Eskimo (Bering Strait): Nelson RBAE XVIII 516.

D905. *Magic storm.* *Fb "storm" III 595b, 596a, "skål" III 352b, "vand" III 1001b; *Penzer IV 213; Morgan MPh. VI 331; Nitze MPh. VII 145. — Babylonian: Spence 77; Irish myth: *Cross, MacCulloch Celtic 44; Welsh: ibid. 191; Icelandic: *Boberg; Middle English: Wells 65 (Ywain and Gawain); Jewish: *Neuman; India: Thompson-Balys; Buddhist myth: Malalasekera II 1269; Korean: Zong in-Sob 170f.

D281. Transformation: man to storm. D1331.2.8. Magic storm blinds enemy troops. D1400.1.23. Magic storm conquers enemies. D1541. Magic object controls storms. D1541.4. Magic fountain causes storm. D2141.1. Storm produced by magic. F141.2.1. Storm as barrier to otherworld. F962.12. Electric storm breaks island into three parts. F1041.20. Man dies when he learns storm is magic. Q222.1. Magic storm conceived as punishment for desecrating temple. Q552.14. Fortress built on Sunday destroyed by tempest.

D906. *Magic wind.* *Fb "wind", "vindknude"; Frazer Golden Bough I 119ff.; Icelandic: *Boberg; Lappish: Holmberg Lappalaisten uskonto 75; Estonian: Eisen Estnische Mythologie 100; Spanish Exempla: Keller; Jewish: Neuman; Chinese: Graham; Africa (Ekoi): Talbot 344.

C984. Great wind because of broken tabu. D282. Transformation: man to wind. D429.1.1. Transformation: dragon-king to gust of wind. D1311. Divination from sound of wind. D1331.2.9. Magic wind blinds. D1402.26. Magic wind kills. D1408.2. Magic red wind devastates country. D1400.1.23.1. Magic wind sinks five pursuing demons in sea. D1414.3. Magic wind causes arms to fall from warriors' hands. D1520.28. Magic transportation in whirlwind. D1524.9. Magic wind catches hero up and transports him across immense sea. Q551.11. Drowning caused by magic wind as punishment for threatful braggart.

D908. *Magic darkness.* *Fb "tåge" III 945a; Irish myth: *Cross; Icelandic: *Boberg; Greek: Homer Iliad III 382, V 23, Odyssey XXIII 372; Jewish: *Neuman; Japanese: Ikeda.

F965. Premature darkness.

D910. Magic body of water. *A. Hertel Verzauberte Oertlichkeiten (Hannover 1908). — Irish myth: *Cross; Jewish: Neuman.

A910. Origin of water features. D1242.1. Magic water. D1432. Waters magically pursue man. D1551. Waters magically divide and close. D1614.4. Singing water. D1618.1. Magic weeping waters.

D911. *Magic sea.* Irish myth: *Cross; Breton: Sébillot Incidents s.v. "tonneau"; Jewish: Neuman; Africa (Zulu): Callaway 82.

D2151.1. Magic control of seas. D2151.3.1. Magic tidal wave. F711. Extraordinary sea. F931. Extraordinary occurrence connected with sea.

D911.1. *Magic wave.* Irish myth: Cross.

D1310.7. Singing of wave gives supernatural information. F931.4. Extraordinary behavior of waves.

D911.1.1. *Magic virtue of nine waves.* Irish myth: *Cross.

Z71.6. Formulistic number: nine.

D915. *Magic river.* Irish myth: Cross; Breton: Sébillot Incidents s.v. "rivière"; Jewish: *Neuman; Ila (Rhodesia): Smith and Dale II 416; Hottentot: Bleek 75 No. 36; Zulu: Callaway 90.

D1300.3.1. Streams of wisdom flow from magic well. D1311.11. Oracular river. D1318.17. River rises to drown liars. D1389.2.2. Thieves cannot cross a river because the water suddenly becomes too hot for them

D1500.1.18.6. Magic healing river. D1551.0.1. Water becomes shallow so man is able to cross river. D1610.35. Speaking river. D1658.1.1. River grateful for being praised even when ugly. D1658.1.6. River grateful for being given color. D2151.2. Magic control of rivers. E434.3. Ghosts cannot cross rapid stream. F715. Extraordinary river. F932. Extraordinary occurrences connected with rivers.

D915.1. *River produced by magic.* Irish myth: *Cross; Breton: Sébillot Incidents s.v. "rivière".

F636.3. Remarkable pourer of water. Makes a river.

D915.2. *River contained under cock's wings.* *Type 715.

B171. Demi-coq. A cock is cut in two and made magic. Carries robbers, foxes, and stream of water under wings. D1382.8. Magic stream quenches fire.

D915.2.1. *River contained in bird's ears.* India: Thompson-Balys.

D915.3. *River contained in box.* Breton: Sébillot Incidents s.v. "rivière".

D915.4. *Intermittent river.* River flows at stated intervals. *Chauvin VII 44 No. 153.

D915.4.1. *Sabbatical river.* Dry on Sabbath. *Chauvin VII 44 No. 153; Gaster Exempla 188 No. 15; India: Thompson-Balys.

D1676. Mill refuses to work on Sunday. F716.1. Fountain gives water on Wednesdays and Fridays. F932.6. River ceases to flow.

D915.5. *River issuing from cave controlled by race of Amazons.* Hartland Science 202.

F112. Journey to land of women. Island of women, land of maidens, country of the Amazons, etc.

D915.6. *Magic flood.* India: Thompson-Balys.

D921. *Magic lake (pond).* *Krappe Bulletin Hispanique XXXV (1933) 107ff.; Icelandic: *Boberg; Jewish: Neuman; Chinese: Werner 137 (lake of gems).

D1338.1.1.1. Magic lake rejuvenates. D1470.1.45. Magic lake: whoever dies in it will have his desires fulfilled in future birth. D1500.1.18.4. Magic healing lake. D1500.4.3. Magic pond causes disease. D1641.12. Lake removes itself. F713. Extraordinary pond (lake). K1072. Fairy induces hero to dive into lake which makes person old.

D921.1. *Lake (pond) produced by magic.* Breton: Sébillot Incidents s.v. "étang"; Irish myth: *Cross.

D921.2. *Lake produced by belches after magic draught.* Irish myth: Cross.

A920.1.5.1. Lakes originate from belches.

D921.3. *Lake under which supernatural smith lives.* Irish myth: *Cross.

F212. Fairyland under water. F271.3. Fairies skillful as smiths. F531.6.2.2.2. Giants live under lake. F725.5. People live under sea.

D921.3.1. *Lake of milk created through merit of saint.* Irish myth: Cross.

A920.1.13. Lake of milk formed through virtue of saint.

D921.4. *Magic tank.* India: Thompson-Balys.

D1500.4.3.1. Magic tank causes disease. D1549.9.1. Not a drop of water will remain in tank no matter how hard laborers work.

D925. *Magic fountain.* (Cf. D926, D927.) *Dh II 154; *Wünsche Die Sagen vom Lebensbaum und Lebenswasser (Leipzig, 1905); *Hopkins JAOS XXVI 1—67, 411—413; *Fb "ungdom" III 979b; Penzer IV 145; *Patch PMLA XXXIII 670 n. 67. — Irish myth: *Cross, Plummer cl—clii, clxxii; Breton: Sébillot Incidents s.v. "fontaine"; French Canadian: Barbeau JAFL XXIX 10—12; Tirol: Zingerle 588; Jewish: Neuman;

N. A. Indian: *Thompson Tales 284 n. 50a.; Lat. American: Alexander Lat. Am. 20 n. 6, 349.

D1311.3. Oracular fountain. D1313.11. Magic fountain indicates road for saint by removing itself. D1338.1.1. Fountain of youth. D1341.1. Magic fountain makes person old. D1346.2. Fountain of immortality. D1364.1. Fountain causes magic sleep. D1402.24. Water from magic fountain kills. D1467.1. Magic fountain produces gold. D1472.1.1. Fountain miraculously supports life. D1500.1.1. Magic healing fountain. D1505.5.3. Magic fountain restores sight. D1541.1.3. Magic fountain causes storm (rain). D1543.1. Fountain insures favorable wind when drained . D1641.1. Fountain removes itself. D1647. Fountain magically dries up. D1663.4. Fountains poison and cure. One with bronze vessel, tastes sweet and poisons; other, with iron vessel, tastes bitter and cures. D1812.2.3. Power of prophecy from accidental drinking of water from magic fountain. E80.1. Resuscitation by bathing. F716. Extraordinary fountain.

D925.0.1. *Magic oil-spouting fountain.* Italian: Basile introduction.

D925.0.2. *Miraculous well yielding milk, beer or wine.* *Loomis White Magic 38.

D925.1. *Fountain magically made.* Irish: Plummer cl, Cross; French Canadian: Barbeau JAFL XXIX 12; Jewish: *Neuman, Gaster Exempla 225 No. 206.

A941.5. Spring breaks forth through power of saint. D1549.5. Magic staff draws water from stone. D1567. Magic object produces fountain. D1567.6. Stroke of staff brings water from rock. D1766.1.1. Magic fountain produced by prayer. D1766.6.1. Fountain produced from sign of the cross. D1816.1. Location of fountain revealed in dream.

D925.1.0.1. *Fountain bursts forth where water is not available for baptismal ceremonies of future saint.* *Loomis White Magic 23.

D925.1.1. *Saint produces fountain by means of his tears.* *Loomis White Magic 37.

D925.1.2. *Fountain gushes up at place where saint's head was cut off.* *Loomis White Magic 37.

D925.1.3. *Samson makes sweet water flow from jawbone.* *Loomis White Magic 37.

D925.2. *Fountain is inhabited by sacred oracular fish.* *Loomis White Magic 38.

B150. Oracular animal.

D926. *Magic well.* (Cf. D925, D927.) Pauli (ed. Bolte) No. 54. — Irish myth: *Cross; Jewish: Neuman; Chinese: Eberhard FFC CXX 106f.; Eskimo (Greenland): Rink 189.

D591. Transformation by immersing in magic well. D1341.0.1. Magic well makes person's hair grey. D1380.15. Magic well protects. D1402.0.2.1. Magic well causes person to be drowned. D1403.2. Magic well maims. D1420.2. Person follows magic receding well. D1472.1.27. Magic well supplies grain. D1500.1.1.1. Magic healing well dug by saint. D1503.7. Magic well heals wounds. D1563.2.2.1. Well (river) polluted by blood shed in battle. D1645.9. Well shines at night. D1652.15. Inexhaustible well. D1663.3. Well of life and death. D1663.5. Well rises or sinks to indicate long or short life. E80.1. Resuscitation by bathing. F718. Extraordinary well. V232.3.1. Angel shows saint where to dig for water.

D926.1. *Well produced by magic.* Jewish: Neuman.

D926.1.1. *Well produced by saint invoking heaven.* *Loomis White Magic 37.

D927. *Magic spring.* (Cf. D925, D926.) *Fb "blind" IV 45b; *Herbert III 238; *Oesterley No 253; Child I 192. — Irish myth: Cross; Jewish: *Neuman.

D1300.3.1. Streams of wisdom flow from magic well. D1311.3.1. Spring gives omens. D1323.12. Clairvoyant spring. D1500.1.1.2. The water of spring which saint caused to flow has curative powers. D1505.5.4. Holy spring restores sight. D1563.0.1. Magic springs fertilize or sterilize earth. E761.7.2. Life token: spring goes dry. F933. Extraordinary occurrences connected with spring. H411.11. Magic spring as chastity test.

D927.1. *Spring made by magic.* P. Saintyves Le Miracle de l'apparition des eaux (Revue de l'Université de Bruxelles 1912, 265—94). — Germanic: De la Saussaye 254 (Balder); French Canadian: Barbeau JAFL XXIX 12; Jewish *Neuman.

A941. Origin of springs. A941.3.1. Spring breaks forth where magic spear strikes ground. A941.5. Spring breaks forth through power of saint. D1567.6. Stroke of staff brings water from rock. F933.1. Miraculous spring bursts forth for holy person.

D927.1.1. *Saint causes water to issue from cut in a tree.* *Loomis White Magic 37.

D927.2. *Magic spring guarded by demons (monsters).* Irish myth: Cross.

A1111. Impounded water. Water is kept by a monster so that mankind cannot use it. B11.7.1. Dragon controls water-supply. B11.7.2. Dragon guards lake. G302. Demons. G308.4. Lake made dangerous by haunting serpent.

D927.2.1. *Magic spring guarded by druids.* Irish myth: Cross.

P427. Druid (magus).

D927.3. *Spring augments milk of nursing mothers who drink its water.* *Loomis White Magic 38.

D927.4. *Spring follows saint to his country.* *Loomis White Magic 38.

D927.5. *Spring runs dry (as result of fratricide).* Irish myth: *Cross.

D1647. Fountain magically dries up. H251.3.9.1. Magic spring detects parricide and idolatry. Q211.9. Fratricide punished.

D928. *Magic water-hole.*

D928.1. *Water-hole made by magic.* Eskimo (Greenland): Rasmussen I 180; Southern Paiute (Maopa): Lowie JAFL XXXVII 168 No. 5a.

D930. Magic land features. *Hertel Verzauberte Oertlichkeiten (Hannover, 1908).

A950. Origin of the land.

D931. *Magic rock (stone).* *Type 593, 870A; Köhler-Bolte I 114, 572; *Fb "sten" III 553a, 554a, "ønske" III 1178b; Hartland Science 242; *Penzer III 161 n. 1, 162 n., V 177; Reinhart PMLA XXXVIII 458 n. 108. — Greek: Fox 111, 137, (modern): Hahn No. 34; German: Grimm No. 163; Irish: Plummer clv—clvii, *Cross; Swiss: Jegerlehner 309 No. 9; Icelandic: Boberg; Jewish: *Neuman; Chinese: Graham, Werner 383. — Aztec: Alexander Lat. Am. 118; N. A. Indian: *Thompson Tales 275 n. 15; Southern Paiute: Lowie JAFL XXXVII 143f. No. 15. Africa (Ekoi): Talbot 366, (Kaffir): Theal 36, 161, (Angola): Chatelain 47 (version B), (Zulu): Callaway 143, (Fang): Trilles Légendes 140, Einstein 99.

B722. Magic stone in animal's head. B785. Animals know about or have magic stone. C91.1. Tabu: stealing garment from rock. Rock pursues. D449.6. Transformation: magic stone to eel. D1262. Magic grinding-stone. D1300.4. Stone gives magic wisdom. D1311.16. Oracular stone. D1316.1. Stone reveals truth. D1317.12. Magic stone gives warning. D1318.1.1. Stone bursts as sign of unjust judgment. D1332.1.1. Magic stone causes deafness. D1331.1.4. Stone gives magic sight. D1331.2.4. Magic stone causes blindness. D1356.3. Magic stone represses lust. D1361.2. Magic stone gives invisibility. D1381.25.1. Dextrosum circuit (around sacred stone) insures victory. D1382.1. Magic pebble prevents burning. D1382.1.0.1. Magic stones from holy well protect against loss by fire or water. D1382.12. Magic blue stone protects against frost. D1385.21. Magic stone makes demons despair. D1388.2. Magic stone keeps flood from overflowing earth. D1389.1. Magic stone protects church from oppression. D1400.1.14. Magic stone (jewel) gives victory. D1401.5. Magic stone hits everything and returns by itself. D1402.21. Magic stone kills person whom it strikes. D1413.17. Magic adhesive stone. D1429.1. Magic stone turned thrice compels person to return to it. D1431.1. Rock (stone) pursues person. D1466. Magic stone furnishes wealth. D1466.1. Magic stone turns everything to gold. D1470.1.1. Magic wishing stone. D1472.1.2.1. Stone provides food. D1472.1.2.2. Rock produces wine. Herder sees resemblance of stone to wine cask. He strikes it and wine flows. D1472.1.2.3. Magic pebble provides food. D1472.1.2.4. Magic rock supplies water. D1482.1. Oil comes out of sacred white stone. D1486.1. Magic stone makes rivers and lakes. D1500.1.2. Sacred healing stone. D1500.1.18.5. Water from bullaun (hollowed out stone) as remedy. D1505.17. Magic stone restores sight. D1515.4.2. Snake stone applied to snake bite absorbs poison. D1515.5.1. Stone as antidote for mad dog bite. D1520.36. Transportation by magic stone. D1524.3. Magic stone serves as boat. D1524.6. River crossed by means of magic stone. D1531.4. Magic stone under tongue gives power of flying. D1539.1. Magic elevator. Stone on which one steps carries one underground. D1540.2. Magic white, red and yellow stone causes hail, sunshine, or fire, according to which side it is scratched on. D1540.3. Magic stone controls water. D1542.1.1. Magic stone produces rain. D1543.2. Magic stone causes favorable wind. D1549.5.1. Rock beaten by sword provides water. D1552. Mountains or rocks open and close. D1552.11. Magic stone opens treasure mountain. D1553. Symplegades. Rocks that clash together at intervals. D1561.1.6. Food left on magic stone brings good luck thereafter. D1561.1.7. Magic stone brings good luck. D1564.1. Magic pebble splits wood. D1602.1. Stones, being removed, return to their places. D1610.18. Speaking rock. D1617.1. Magic laughing stone. D1618.2. Magic weeping stone. D1641.1. Stones remove themselves. D1641.2.4. Stone moves at midnight. D1643.2. Rock travels. D1646.4. Dancing stones. D1648.1.4. Stones prostrate themselves before certain persons. D1649.3. Stones for heating water heated automatically in other world. D1654.0.2. Magic stone, hitting object, renders it immovable. D1654.1. Stone refuses to be moved. D1654.1.1. Immovable stone moved by saint. D1654.1.1.1. Stone rolls off well-top after saint has prayed. E64.17. Resuscitation by magic stone. E761.5.5. Life token: stone breaks. F235.4.3. Fairies made visible through use of magic stone on eyes. F800. Extraordinary rocks and stones. H171.5. Stone of Destiny. H251.2. Stone of truth. H411.1. Magic stone as chastity test. H1572.1. Stone under fertile woman issues milk; under barren woman, issues blood.

D931.0.1. *Stone produced by magic.* Irish myth: Cross.

V111.2. Stones for building church (chapel) miraculously supplied.

D931.0.2. *Stones fixed in the earth have certain magic powers.* *Fb II 47 s.v. "jordfast (sten)"; Örvar-Odds saga 136.

D931.0.2.1. *Location of magic stone determines race of king of country.* Irish myth: Cross.

F244.1. The Four Jewels of the Tuatha Dé Danann. H171.5. Stone of Destiny.

D931.0.3. *Stone on which saint is baptized (is born) has magic powers.* Irish myth: *Cross.

D1713. Magic power of hermit (saint).

D931.0.4. *Magic stone as amulet.* (Cf. D1274.1.) Eskimo (Greenland): Rink 148, Rasmussen II 233.

D931.1. *Magic coal.* Irish: O'Suilleabhain 69, Beal XXI 326.

D1380.6. Magic coal protects. D1500.1.2.1. Magic healing coal. D1552.10. Magic soot causes mountain to open.

D931.1.1. *Magic soot.* Africa (Washaga): Gutman 137.

D1380.7. Magic soot protects. D1500.1.2.3. Magic healing soot.

D931.1.2. *Magic ashes.* Jewish: Neuman; India: Thompson-Balys; Japanese: Mitford 180ff.

D1361.44. Magic ashes render invisible. D1380.8. Magic ashes protect. D1421.0.2. Magic ashes summon helper. D1469.10. Magic ashes produce jewelry. D1470.2.8. Supplies from magic ashes. D1472.1.30. Magic ashes produce food. D1500.1.2.2. Magic healing ashes. D1500.4.6. Ashes cause leprosy.

D931.1.3. *Magic lampblack.* India: Thompson-Balys.

D1361.42. Magic lampblack renders invisible.

D931.1.4. *Magic lime.*

D1500.1.2.4. Magic healing lime. D1500.1.10.6. Lime used in building church as cure.

D931.2. *Magic pebble.* Jewish: Neuman.

D932. *Magic mountain.* *Type 676; Fb "rundt".

A960. Creation of mountains. D1552. Mountains or rocks open and close. D1552.0.1. Door opens in mountain. D1641.2.2. Mountain moved by prayer so as to make room for church. D2136.1.0.1. Mountains or hills magically transported. D2152. Magic control of mountains. F750. Extraordinary mountains and other land features.

D932.0.1. *Mountain created by magic.* India: Thompson-Balys.

D932.1. *Magic cliff.*

D1610.33. Speaking cliffs.

D932.2. *Magic hill.*

D933. *Magic sink-hole.* Fb "grøft".

D1610.1. Speaking sink-hole.

D934. *Magic turf.* *Fb "græstørv".

D1323.7. Turf from church roof gives clairvoyance.

D934.1. *Magic sod.* Irish myth: Cross.

D1316.7. Magic sod indicates falsehood by turning grassy surface downward, truth by turning it upward. D1524.7. Magic sod serves as boat.

D935. *Magic earth (soil).* *Fb "muld" II 619. — Irish: Plummer clxxx, *Cross, O'Suilleabhain 92, Beal XXI 329; Jewish: *Neuman; Hindu: Penzer III 227f.; Chinese: Eberhard FFC CXX 161f.

D1278.1. Magic churchyard mould. D1318.6. Speaking earth reveals murder. D1385.1. Earth from Saints's grave expels demons. D1413.20. Magic earth-mould holds person fast. D1500.1.28. Earth as remedy. D1500.1.28.2. Consecrated clay as remedy. D1503.12. Magic earth heals wounds. D1610.19. Earth speaks.

D935.0.1. *Magic earth from crossroads.* (Cf. D1786.) Seligmann 151.

D935.1. *Magic sand.*

D1449.5. Magic sand causes crocodile to go ashore. D1524.1.4. Sand permits man to walk on water.

D935.2. *Magic clay.* India: Thompson-Balys.

D935.3. *Magic dust.* India: Thompson-Balys.

D1402.27. Magic dust kills. D1594.1. Magic dust vitalizes seeds and they become insects.

D935.4. *Magic brick.* India: Thompson-Balys.

D1532.13. Magic brick bears person to moon. D1551.8. Magic brick causes waters to divide.

D936. *Magic island.* Irish myth: Cross.

A955.2. Island created by shooting arrow. D1524.4. Island canoe. Magic island acts as canoe or boat. D1610.19.1. Speaking island. D1643.3. Magic island moves about as owner wishes. F730. Extraordinary islands.

D936.1. *Island made by magic.* Greek: Pauly-Wissowa s.v. "Anaphe".

D481. Transformation: stretching cliff.

D937. *Magic plain.* Irish myth: Cross.

D479.7. Transformation: bag to flowery mead. D1413.19. Magic plain to which one sticks. D1562.5. Hero crosses impassable plain in path of magic object. F756.2. Plain that is earthly paradise.

D940. Magic forests.

D941. *Magic forest.* Saintyves Perrault 65; Wimberly 124. — Irish myth: Cross; Icelandic: Boberg; Jewish: Neuman; Hindu: Penzer VIII 222 n. 2.

C51.2.2. Tabu: cutting sacred trees or forests. D1368.2. Magic forest seems to stretch farther as mortals travel within. D1554. Magic forest opens and closes for hero to pass. F151.1.3. Perilous forest on way to otherworld. F636.2. Remarkable thrower of chips. Makes forest. F812. Extraordinary forest. V1.1. Worship of trees. V114. Sacred groves (forests.)

D941.1. *Forest produced by magic.* Saintyves Perrault 92. — Irish myth: *Cross; Breton: Sébillot Incidents s.v. "forêt"; India: Thompson-Balys.

F979.8. Forest springs up from twig (twigs).

D945. *Magic hedge.* *Type 410; BP I 440. — Irish: Plummer clxi, *Cross.

D902.1. Magic mist. D1381.1. Druid's hedge prevents attack.

D950. Magic tree. *Types 330, 510, 511; BP II 188 n. 1; Dh II 10, 30ff.; A. F. Schmidt Hultræer i Danmark (Danske Studier 1932 33ff.); Köhler Aufsätze 19ff.; *Fb "træ" III 866a, 867a; Chauvin VII 95 No. 375; Penzer I 144, *VIII 69 n. 1. — Irish: Plummer cliii, *Cross; German: Grimm No. 123; Persian: Carnoy 281, Coyajee JPASB XXIV 185f., 194; Chinese: Ferguson 104, Eberhard FFC CXX 46. — Indonesian: Dixon 238 n. 51; Quiché: Alexander Lat. Am. 172; N. A. Indian: *Thompson Tales 297 n. 86a, (Seneca): Curtin-Hewitt RBAE XXXII 391 No. 70; Africa (Zulu): Callaway 146, 218, (Upoto): Einstein 123.

A652. World tree. A878. Earth tree. C510. Tabu: touching tree. C621.1. Tree of knowledge forbidden. D215. Transformation: person to tree. D482. Transformation: stretching tree. A tree magically shoots upward. D940. Magic forests and trees. D971. Magic seed. D1311.4. Oracular tree. D1313.4. Blinded trickster directed by trees. D1316.5. Magic speaking reed (tree) betrays secret. D1316.5.1. Voice comes forth from tree, revealing truth. D1317.20. Tree warns of danger. D1338.3.3. Rejuvenation by fruit of magic tree. D1338.3.3.1. Year added to life by eating fruit of magic tree. D1346.4. Tree of immortality. D1359.3.3. Fruit of magic tree exhilarating. D1368.4. Tree of delusion. D1380.2. Tree (plant) protects. D1381.28. Magic tree protects from attack. D1393.1. Tree opens and conceals fugitive. D1393.4. Tree points way to fugitive but misdirects enemy. D1413.1. Tree from which one cannot descend. D1461. Magic tree furnishes treasure. D1461.0.2. Tree with silver branches. D1470.1.2. Magic wishing-tree. D1470.1.3. Magic wishing-laurel. D1470.2.1. Provisions received from magic tree. D1472.1.28. Magic stump supplies drink. D1500.1.3. Magic tree heals. D1500.2.7. Magic tree bears prophylactic fruit. D1503.11. Wounds healed by eating fruit of magic tree. D1505.18. Tree restores sight. D1520.1.2. Transportation by hollow tree. D1532.7. Magic tree bears person through air. D1556. Self-opening tree trunk. D1602.2. Felled tree raises itself again. D1602.2.2. Chips from tree return to their places as cut. D1610.2. Speaking tree. D1612.1.2. Banana tree tells who cut its branches. D1612.6.1. Singing tree when touched wakes master. D1615.1. Singing tree. D1641.4. Forest cleared by magic. D1648. Tree bends to certain person. D1658.1.5. Apple-tree grateful for being shaken. D1658.1.5.2. Tree grateful for having milk poured on roots. D1663.6. Magic tree gives money to good — poisonous animals to bad brothers. D1667.1. Magic tree shoots forth leaf, flower and fruit at once. D1668. Magic tree continually in fruit. E761.3. Life token: tree (flower) fades. F162.3. Tree in otherworld F811. Extraordinary tree. H411.2. Magic tree as chastity test. T532.2. Conception from embracing magic tree.

D950.0.1. *Magic tree guarded by serpent (dragon) coiled around its roots.* Irish myth: *Cross; Greek: Fox 87f. (Apples of Hesperides).

B11.6.2. Dragon guards treasure. B11.7.2. Dragon guards lake. F152.0.1. Bridge to otherworld guarded by animals. F323. Fairy women take body of dead hero to fairyland. H1333.6. Quest for branches of tree guarded by dragon.

D950.0.1.1. *Magic tree guarded by giant ogre.* Irish myth: *Cross.

G100. Giant ogre.

D950.0.2. *Magic tree at bottom of lake.* Irish myth: Cross.

F725. Submarine world.

D950.1. *Magic hazel tree.* *BP III 477. Irish: Plummer cliii, *Cross.

A2711.4.1. Hazel gives Virgin Mary shelter: blessed. D985.3. Magic hazel nut. D1311.4.1.2. Hazel used by druids for divination. D1402.1. Rod from magic hazel tree kills snake immediately. D1500.1.3.1. Magic healing hazel tree. F811.4.2. Tree under sea. J165. Tree of knowledge.

D950.2. *Magic oak tree.* Type 577. — Irish myth: *Cross; Greek: Fox 109.

D1610.2.1. Speaking oak.

D950.3. *Magic peach tree.* Chinese: Werner 173.

D950.4. *Magic cherry tree.* Breton: Sébillot Incidents s.v. "cerisier".

D1413.1.1. Cherry tree from which one cannot descend.

D950.5. *Magic pear tree.* Fb "pæretræ"; cf. Type 1423; *Hdwb. d. Märchens s.v. "Birne".

D1413.1.2. Pear tree from which one cannot descend.

D950.6. *Magic ash tree (quicken, rowan).* *Fb "usynlig"; Irish myth: *Cross.

D950.0.1. Magic tree guarded by serpent (dragon). D1311.4.1.1. Ash (quicken, rowan) used by druids for divination. D1361.3. Magic ash-tree renders invisible. D1385.2.2. Ash (quicken, rowan) proof against spells and enchantments. F971.4.1. Ash tree bears apples. P427.6.1. Druids "went on their hurdles of rowan" in order to reach decision. S139.2.2.10. Ash stakes thrust through bodies of slain warriors. V11.1.2. Ash as sacred tree.

D950.7. *Magic lime tree.* Irish: Plummer cliii, *Cross.

D1472.1.3. Magic lime tree distills sustenance for saint.

D950.8. *Magic fig tree.* Italian Novella: Rotunda.

D1413.1.3. Fig tree from which one cannot descend.

D950.9. *Magic olive tree.* Jewish: *Neuman.

D950.10. *Magic apple tree.* Irish myth: *Cross; French Canadian: Sister Marie Ursule.

F162.3.4. Magic apple tree in otherworld. F813.1. Extraordinary apple. F971.4.1. Ash (alder, willow, etc.) tree bears apples ("fair fruit").

D950.11. *Magic alder tree.* Irish myth: *Cross.

F971.4.1. Ash (alder, willow etc.) tree bears apples ("fair fruit").

D950.12. *Magic birch tree.* Irish myth: Cross.

D953.2. Magic birch twig.

D950.13. *Magic hawthorn.* Irish myth: *Cross.

D1385.2.3. Hawthorn protects traveler.

D950.14. *Magic yew tree.* Irish myth: *Cross.

D1311.15.1. Magic yew rod used by druid to discover whereabouts of woman carried off by fairies to underground retreat. D1816.5.1. Druid by magic discovers whereabouts of abducted wife. F262.3.1.2. Fairy harper in yew tree. F811.2.1. (Three) marvelous trees of extraordinary age. V1.1.1.3. Yew as sacred tree.

D950.14.1. *Magic yew tree created by fairies.* Irish myth: Cross.

D950.15. *Magic bamboo tree.* India: Thompson-Balys; Chinese: Eberhard FFC CXX 80.

D1380.2.2. Tree as guardian of girl.

D950.16. *Magic nut tree.* Jewish: Neuman.

D950.17. *Magic laurel tree.* Jewish: Neuman.

D950.18. *Magic cedar tree.* Jewish: Neuman.

D950.19. *Magic palm tree.* Jewish: Neuman.

D951. *Tree produced by magic.* Irish myth: Cross.

D951.1. *Magic tree springs from fairyland berry.* Irish myth: Cross.

D952. *Magic tree-bark.*

D1408.1.1. Magic bark sets a creek on fire and burns it up.

D953. *Magic twig.* Irish myth: *Cross; India: Thompson-Balys.

D1311.4.0.1. Oracular twig. D1311.4.0.1.1. Sight of magic twigs gives foreknowledge of day's events. D1313.5.2. Reed as direction-finder. D1648.1.2.2. Twig of a tree bows down and releases a bag with relics when the man makes a promise. F979.8. Forest springs up from twig (twigs).

D953.1. *Origin of magic twig.* Irish myth: Cross.

D953.1.1. *Magic twigs grow from buried magic vessel.* Irish myth: Cross.

D1171. Magic vessel.

D953.2. *Magic birch twig.* (Cf. D950.12.) Irish myth: Cross.

D954. *Magic bough.* *Chauvin V 229 No. 130; Fb "finkelrut". — Irish: MacCulloch Celtic 114f.; *Cross; Spanish: Boggs FFC XC 51 No. 340; India: Thompson-Balys.

D441.3. Transformation: branch of tree to animal. D1314.2. Magic wand (twig) locates hidden treasure. D1351.2. Magic branch of peace. Warfare ceases when it is shaken. D1355.8. Olive branch insures fidelity of husband. D1359.1.1. Magic olive branch makes woman master in household. D1359.3.1.2. Magic musical branch soothes listeners. D1364.25.0.1. Musical branch causes sleep. D1444.1.3. Magic branch catches fish. D1520.1. Magic transportation by bough. D1542.3.3. Branch which dries up water in great river so person can cross it. D1563.1.6. Magic branch when used as a threshing pole produces marvelous harvest of rice. D1615.2. Magic musical branch. D1641.6. Branch leaps from hand to hand. D1658.1.5.1. Tree grateful for having boughs trimmed.

D955. *Magic leaf.* Type 612; *BP I 128; *Fb "blad" IV 44a. — Irish myth: Cross; Icelandic: Völsunga saga ch. 8, Boberg; Jewish: Neuman; India: Thompson-Balys; Africa (Ibo, Nigeria): Basden 280, (Ekoi): Talbot 115, 188, (Zulu): Callaway 191.

B512. Medicine shown by animal. C511. Tabu: touching leaves. D1337.6. Magic leaves turn white bird black. D1470.2.1.1. Leaves turn into fish to feed family. D1472.1.3.2. Food-providing leaf. D1500.1.4.2. Magic healing leaves. D1501.7. Leaves assist in childbearing. D1524.8.1. Leaf serves as boat for saint. D1531.10. Palmetto leaves give power of flying. D1532.9. Magic leaf bears person aloft. E105. Resuscitation by herbs (leaves). E761.7.3. Life token: leaves fall from tree. G242.3. Witch flies through air on leaf. T532.3. Impregnation by leaf of lettuce.

D956. *Magic stick of wood.* BP II 527; Jewish: *Neuman.

D1342.3. Magic wood gives health. D1393.1.1. Woman charms stick of wood so she can hide inside it. D1401.8. Log of wood animated by spirit of malignant holy man strikes left and right to kill offending villagers. D1402.10.2. Rod from magic hazel-tree kills snake immediately. D1469.8. Treasure from magic stick. D1483.3. Magic stick: when planted in ground, palace rises. D1531.6. Witch flies with aid of magic stick. D1551.6. Magic stick causes waters to divide. D1610.30. Speaking timber. D1649.4. Dung and wood burst into flames of their own accord. D1649.7. Magic wood stick makes noise at night. D1673.1. Tree grows from stick saint has used and thrown aside. D1688. Marvelous post wears down at top instead of rotting from bottom.

D957. *Magic faggot.* Irish myth: Cross.

D1324.2. Magic faggot drips at ebb tide.

D958. *Magic thorn.* *Köhler-Bolte I 261. — Icelandic: *Boberg; English: Child V 496 s.v. "sleep"; Hindu: Penzer III 227f.; India: Thompson-Balys.

D1313.14. Magic thornbush points out road. D1364.2. Sleep thorn.

D960. Magic gardens and plants.

D961. *Magic garden.* *Type 550; BP II 232. — Irish myth: *Cross; India: Thompson-Balys, Penzer I 66f.; N. Am. Indian (Tsimshian): Boas RBAE XXXI 182; Africa (Benga): Nassau 208 No. 33.

D515. Transformation by plucking flowers in enchanted garden. D1664. Summer and winter garden. D1667. Magic garden grows at once. E481.4.1. Avalon. F130. Location of otherworld. F162.1. Garden in otherworld. F971.5. Flowers bloom in winter.

D961.1. *Garden produced by magic.* (Cf. D2178.) Irish myth: Cross; Italian Novella: Rotunda; Penzer VIII 92.

H352. Suitor test: to make garden bloom in winter. H1023.16. Task: making garden bloom in winter.

D962. *Magic vineyard.* Jewish: Neuman.

D964. *Magic bush.* (Cf. D960, D965.) Basile Pentamerone IV 6; Irish: O'Suilleabhain 74, Beal XXI 326; Jewish: *Neuman.

D1610.2.2. Speaking bush. D1672.2. Self-burning bush. V222.2. Brake in which saint loses tooth bursts into flames.

D965. *Magic plant.* *BP I 128; Fb "blad" IV 44a, "vild" III 1052b; *Chauvin II 193 No. 12, V 14 No. 9; VI 73f. No. 239. — Breton: Sébillot Incidents s.v. "herbe"; Greek: Frazer Apollodorus I 312 n. 2, Fox 263; Jewish: Neuman; Babylonian: Spence 158, 160, 178; India: Thompson-Balys, Penzer; Chinese: Werner 299.

B217.2. Animal languages learned from eating plant. B512. Medicine shown by animal. D482.1. Stretching lily plant. D1310.4.2. Magic plant bears fruit to indicate that heroine is ready to marry. D1311.13. Plant used for divination. D1314.1. Magic plant shows location of treasure. D1337.2.2. Magic herbs render hideous. D1338.2. Rejuvenation by plant. D1346.5. Plant of immortality. D1355.17. Herb bath produces love. D1355.22. Love-producing magic plant. D1364.31. Plant produces sleep. D1365.1. Plant causes forgetfulness. D1367.1. Magic plant causes insanity. D1385.2.1. Herbs worn in ears keep off power of evil spirits. D1386.2. Magic herb keeps off demon lover. D1388.1.2. Magic herb protects from storms at sea. D1389.13. Magic plant banishes fear. D1402.1. Magic plant kills. D1447.3. Plant protects against snakes. D1469.1. Magic flower pot bears plants with gold letters on leaves. D1500.1.4. Magic healing plant. D1501.3. Magic plant makes childbirth easy. D1503.10. Magic plant heals wounds. D1505.1. Herbs restore sight. D1557.2. Magic herb causes door to open. D1585.2. Magic plant saves cut-off limbs from corruption. D1610.3. Speaking plant. E105. Resuscitation by herbs (leaves). E501.17.5.7. Wild hunt avoided by holding certain plant. E631. Reincarnation in plant (tree) growing from grave. F815. Extraordinary plants. G272.2. Magic herb protects from witch. H411.3. Magic plant as chastity test. T543. Birth from plant.

D965.0.1. *Honeysuckle "king of trees."* Irish myth: Cross.

D965.1. *Magic mandrake.* **Starck Der Alraun; *Taylor JAFL XXXI 561f.; Penzer III 153f.; F. Ohrt Dragedukker i Danmark (Danske Studier 1930 63ff., 186); *Fb "alrunerot" IV 10a; *Frazer Old Testament II 372ff.; Hdwb. d. Abergl. I 311 s.v. "Alraun". — Irish myth: Cross; Jewish: *Neuman.

A2611.5. Mandrake from blood of person hanged on gallows. D1311.13.1. Mandrake as magic forecaster. D1314.7.1. Mandrake shows location of treasure. D1344.10. Magic mandrake gives invulnerability. D1385.2.6. Mandrake protects from evil spirits. D1463.1. Magic mandrake furnishes treasure. F992.1. Mandrake shrieks when uprooted. T511.2.1. Conception from eating mandrake.

D965.2. *Magic calabash (gourd).* Chinese: Werner 347; Korean: Zong in-

Sob 288; Africa (Ekoi): Talbot 27, 34, (Yoruba): Ellis 246, (Benga): Nassau 208 No. 33.

D1361.4. Magic calabash renders invisible. D1380.2.1. Calabash as guardian of girl. D1431.5. Pursuit by magic calabash. D1463.2. Magic calabash furnishes treasure. D1470.1.4. Magic wishing-calabash. D1472.2.7. Magic calabash causes food to be furnished. D1475.6. Magic soldier-producing calabash. D1476.1. Magic calabash furnishes slaves. D1477.1. Magic calabash furnishes livestock. D1541.1.7. Magic calabash holding bones raises storm. D1543.7. Magic calabash (gourd) controls winds. D1601.1. Magic calabash cooks and cares for child. D1610.3. Speaking gourd. H335.2. Suitor task: cutting open magic gourd.

D965.3. *Magic rosebush.* BP II 527.

D1611.1. Magic rosebush answers for fugitive.

D965.4. *Magic mistletoe.* *K. v. Tubeuf Monographie der Mistel (München, 1923); *Frazer Golden Bough XII 373 s.v. "mistletoe", XI 78ff. — Irish myth: *Cross.

Z312. Unique deadly weapon. Only one thing will kill a certain man.

D965.4.1. *Mistletoe used by druids.* Irish myth: Cross.

D1501.1.1. Mistletoe used by druids to prevent barrenness.

D965.5. *Moly: magic plant.* *Taylor JAFL XXXI 561. — Greek: Frazer Apollodorus II 288 n. 1.

D1385.2. Moly as antidote to spells and enchantments.

D965.6. *Magic lotus plant.* (Cf. D975.1.) Greek: Frazer Apollodorus II 280 n. 2; Japanese: Ikeda.

D1365.1.1. Lotus causes forgetfulness.

D965.7. *Magic four-leaf clover.* *BP III 201; Fb "firkløver".

D1323.14. Four-leaf clover gives clairvoyance. D1561.1. Four-leaf clover brings good luck. G254. Witch known by inability to rise from chair with four-leaf clover under it.

D965.8. *Magic corn.* (Cf. D973.) Irish myth: *Cross; Jewish: *Neuman.

D973. Magic grains. D1652.1.3.2. Inexhaustible corn. F1099.4. Corn takes root in man's hair. H1022.6.1. Task: making ale derived from a single grain of corn.

D965.8.1. *Magic rice (plant.)*

D1667.3. Million-fold rice which ripens in one night.

D965.9. *Magic laurel (plant).* Hartland Science 204.

D1365.1.3. Laurel causes forgetfulness.

D965.10. *Magic myrtle.* Hartland Science 204.

D1365.1.2. Myrtle causes forgetfulness.

D965.11. *Magic plantain.* Ibo (Nigeria): Thomas 126.

D1375.4.1.1. Magic plantain causes four tails to grow.

D965.12. *Magic grass.* Irish myth: Cross; Jewish: Neuman; Chinese: Graham.

D1312.3. Speaking grass gives advice. D1355.21. Magic grass produces love when girl sleeps on it. D1413.21. Magic grass holds person fast. D1463.6. Magic grass furnishes treasure. D1500.1.4.1. Magic healing grass.

D965.13. *Magic flax.* Lithuanian: Balys Legends Nos. 673ff., Index No. 3697.

D965.14. *Magic fern blossom.* May be obtained on St. John's eve. Lithuanian: Balys Index 3644.

D965.15. *Magic barley plant.* (Cf. D973.2.) India: Thompson-Balys.

D1310.4.3. Barley plant droops if prince is in trouble.

D965.16. *Magic rue.*

D1385.2.2. Rue when burned keeps evil spirits at a distance.

D965.17. *Magic tobacco plant.*

D1463.4. Magic tobacco plant hides treasure.

D965.18. *Magic weeds.*

D1311.13.2. Weeds used for divination.

D965.19. *Magic myrtle.* Jewish: Neuman.

D967. *Magic roots.* Jewish: Neuman; India: Thompson-Balys; Africa (Baholoholo): Einstein 233.

D1314.15. Druid root sprouts when planted to indicate spot where holy man should set up his abode. D1316.12. Magic root reveals truth when water is poured over it. D1338.2.2. Root of eternal youth. D1355.21.1. Love charm from tuber. D1385.2.5. Roots protect from evil spirits. D1518.2. Root restores amputated hands and feet. D1547.1. Magic root floats against the current. D1551.3. Magic root causes waters to divide and close. E104.1. Resuscitation by magic root.

D971. *Magic seed.* Danish: Fb "frø" I 378b; Jewish: Neuman; Hindu: Penzer VI 62ff; Chinese: Eberhard FFC CXX 36f.; Africa (Ekoi): Talbot 178.

D1355.3.1. Seed mixed with blood as love charm. D1410.1. Seed cast on lions and tigers render them helpless. D551.2.3. Transformation through eating magic seeds. D1318.4. Magic seed indicates guilt. D1463.3. Magic seed produces golden gourd seed.

D971.1. *Magic mustard-seed.* Penzer VI 5, 29, 109, 123f.

D1402.16. Magic mustard-seed cause man to turn to ashes. D1531.1. Mustard seeds give power of flying.

D971.2. *Magic hemp-seed.* Breton: Sébillot Incidents s.v. "chenevis"; English: Child V 59, 286a.

D1331.1.1. Hempseed sown to acquire magic sight.

D971.3. *Magic fern-seed.* *Cox Cinderella 517.

D1361.5.1. Magic fern-seed renders invisible.

D971.4. *Magic black cummin.* India: Thompson-Balys.

D973. *Magic grains.* Irish myth: *Cross; Jewish: Neuman; India: Thompson-Balys.

D965.8. Magic corn. D1033.2. Magic wheat. D1500.1.10.4. Consecrated grain as remedy.

D973.1. *Magic rice-grains.* Tawney II 453; India: Thompson-Balys; Chinese: Graham.

D1335.1.1. Magic strength-giving rice-grains. D1338.13. Rejuvenation by magic rice.

D973.1.1. *Rice-grains magically produced by gourd.* India: Thompson-Balys.

D973.2. *Magic barley.* (Cf. D965.15.) Jewish: Neuman; Hindu: Penzer VI 55 n. 2.

D974. *Magic plant-sap.* Dh II 154.

D1338.2.1. Rejuvenation by juice of plant.

D975. *Magic flower.* *Basset 1001 Contes I 143; Irish myth: *Cross; Jewish: *Neuman; Chinese: Eberhard FFC CXX 108; Japanese: Ikeda.

D212. Transformation: man (woman) to flower. D1314.7. Magic flower shows location of treasure. D1361.6. Magic flower renders invisible.

D1364.3. Flowers cause magic sleep. D1375.1.4. Blossoms cause horns to grow on person. D1375.2.5. Blossoms remove horns from person. D1463.5. Treasure-giving magic flower (gold and silver). D1503.10.1. Grass and flowers which grew upon a saint's grave are good for cures. D1505.9. Magic flower restores sight. D1547.2. Magic flower thrown into lake causes waters to follow in the footsteps of the one who throws it in. D1593.1. Magic flower thrown down creates mountains. D1610.4. Speaking flower. D1645.11. Extraordinary flower; rays of golden light fall from it. D1648.1.3. Flower bends only to certain person. D1652.7. Unfading garlands. F814. Extraordinary flower. F979.10. Flower from otherworld. H432. Flower as chastity index. T532.1. Conception from plucking flower.

D975.1. *Magic lotus-flower.* (Cf. D965.6, D1641.15.) India: Thompson-Balys; Chinese: Werner 322.

D1610.4.1. Speaking lotus flower. D1641.15. Lotus disappears whenever anyone tries to pluck it. H432.3. Lotus flowers as chastity index.

D975.2. *Magic rose.* Köhler-Bolte II 447.

D1619.4. Laughing roses. H432.1. Rose as chastity index.

D976. *Magic thorn.*

D1601.27. Magic thorns make road through marsh.

D977. *Magic stalk.*

D1648.1.1. Magic stalk assures good weather.

D978. *Magic herbs.* (Cf. D965.) India: Thompson-Balys; Irish myth: Cross.

D980. Magic fruits and vegetables.

F810. Extraordinary trees, plants, fruits, etc. H1333.2.2. Quest for magic tobacco.

D981. *Magic fruit.* *Type 566; *Aarne MSFO XXV 122; Fb "næse" II 716b; *Penzer VI 216; *Basset 1001 Contes I 143; *Chauvin VI 74 No. 239. — Irish myth: *Cross; Jewish: *Neuman; Hindu: Tawney I 259f., 310n., 382, II 142n., 198n., 596n.; Chinese: Eberhard FFC CXX 105; Japanese: Ikeda; Indonesian: DeVries's list No. 195.

D441.2.1. Transformation: fruit to birds. D551.1. Transformation by eating fruit. D886.1. Woman cooks the magic fruits. D1310.10. Magic fruit gives supernatural knowledge. D1335.14. Eaten fruit causes sexual desire. D1338.3. Rejuvenation by fruit. D1338.3.3. Rejuvenation by fruit of magic tree. D1346.6. Fruit of immortality. D1346.9. Magic fruit gives immortality. D1355.3.3. Fruit pierced with pins as love charm. D1359.3.3. Fruit of magic tree exhilarating. D1364.4. Fruit causes magic sleep. D1375.1.1. Magic fruit causes horns to grow on person. D1375.4.2. Magic fruit causes tail to grow. D1376.1.1. Magic fruit makes nose long (restores it). D1461.1. Magic fruit furnishes treasure. D1500.1.5. Magic healing fruit. D1501.4. Magic fruit from Yggdrasil placed in fire makes childbirth easy. D1610.10. Speaking fruit. D1619.3. Fruits that laugh or cry. D1665.3. Fruit has any taste desired. F813. Extraordinary fruits.

D981.0.1. *Magic fruit juice.*

D1531.7. Witch flies with aid of magic juice.

D981.1. *Magic apple.* *Types 400, 500, 590, 708, 709; *Aarne MSFO XXV 121; *BP I 463, 482, III 97; *Köhler-Bolte I 118, 143; *Fb "guldæble" I 516a, "æble" III 1135f, "ønske" III 1178b; *Chauvin VI 74 No. 239, 133 No. 286. — Irish myth: *Cross; Icelandic: De la Saussaye 280, *Boberg; Breton: Sébillot Incidents s.v. "cornes", "pomme"; English: Child I 364; Jewish: Neuman; Arabian: Burton Nights S IV 434ff.

D551.1.1. Transformation by eating apple. D1310.10.1. Magic apple gives supernatural knowledge. D1313.6. Magic apple indicates road. D1318.18. Apples which grow from tree under which murder was done have red centers. D1335.15. Magic strength-giving apple. D1336.2.1. Magic apple gives weakness. D1337.1.10. Magic apple makes beautiful. D1338.3.1. Rejuvenation by apple. D1342.2. Magic apple gives health. D1346.6.2. Apple of immortality. D1347.1. Magic apple produces fecundity. D1349.2.3.

Magic apple produces immunity from old age. D1355.7. Apple produces love. D1364.4.1. Apple causes magic sleep. D1367.4. Magic apple causes insanity. D1375.1.1.1. Magic apples cause horns to grow on person. D1375.2.1.1. Magic apples remove horns from person. D1376.1.1.1. Magic apple makes nose long (restores it). D1470.1.5. Magic wishing apple. D1472.1.26. Magic apple satisfies hunger. D1500.1.5.1. Magic healing apple. D1520.4. Magic transportation by golden apple. D1602.14. Self-returning magic apple. D1611.14. Magic apple answers for fugitive. D1615.3. Singing apple. D1646.1. Dancing apple. D1651.10. Apple (or ball) containing man's soul can be split only by man's own sword. D1652.1.7. Inexhaustible apple. D1654.2. Immovable apple. D1889.4. Rejuvenation by smelling apple. E106. Resuscitation by magic apple. F402.5. Demon formed from charmed apples. F813.1. Extraordinary apple. H434.1. Apple as chastity index. H1323.1. Quest for magic apple. T511.1.1. Conception from eating apple.

D981.1.1. *Magic apple from Garden of the Hesperides.* Irish myth: *Cross.

A692. Islands of the blest. F111. Journey to earthly paradise. F134. Otherworld on island. F162.1. Garden in otherworld. F213. Fairyland on island. F343.15. Magic apple as fairy gift. H1151.1. Task: stealing golden apples. H1323. Quest for marvelous apple.

D981.2. *Magic peach.* Chinese: Werner 270, Eberhard FFC CXX 210.

D1338.3.2. Magic peach gives immunity from age. D1346.9.1. Magic peach gives immortality. D1349.1.1. Magic peach produces immunity from hunger and thirst. D1349.2.1. Magic peach produces immunity from old age. D1375.1.1.2. Magic peaches cause horns to grow on person.

D981.3. *Magic orange.* *Type 408. — Breton: Sébillot Incidents s.v. "orange".

D211.1. Transformation: person to orange. D1375.1.1.3. Magic orange causes horns to grow on person. D1375.2.1.2. Magic orange removes horns from person.

D981.4. *Magic cherry.* Aarne MSFO XXV 121; Fb "kirsebær"; Penzer I 27.

D1375.1.1.4. Magic cherry causes horns to grow on person. D1376.1.1.2. Magic cherry makes nose long (restores it).

D981.5. *Magic fig.* (Cf. D1375.1.1.5.) Aarne MSFO XXV 121. — Spanish: Boggs FFC XC 56, 116 Nos. 408*A, 970; Jewish: *Neuman; Hindu: Penzer I 27.

D1310.10.2. Magic fig gives supernatural knowledge. D1364.4.2. Figs cause magic sleep. D1502.8.3. Magic figs cure boils. D1610.10.3. Speaking fig. D1658.1.2. Figs grateful for being praised even when ill-tasting.

D981.6. *Magic pear.* (Cf. D1375.1.1.6, D1375.2.1.3.) Aarne MSFO XXV 121; Hdwb. d. Märchens s.v. "Birne".

D981.7. *Magic plum.* (Cf. D1375.1.1.7.) Aarne MSFO XXV 121.

D981.8. *Magic grape.* (Cf. D1375.1.1.8.) Aarne MSFO XXV 121; Jewish: *Neuman.

D1310.10.3. Magic grape gives supernatural knowledge. D1610.10.1. Speaking grapes. F813.2.1. Clusters of diamond and emerald grapes. F813.2.2. Gigantic grapes.

D981.9. *Magic date (fruit).* (Cf. D1375.1.1.9.) Aarne MSFO XXV 121.

D981.10. *Magic berry.* (Cf. D1375.1.1.10.) Aarne MSFO XXV 122; Irish myth: *Cross.

H1333.3. Quest for berries from tree guarded by giant (monster).

D981.10.1. *Magic cranberry.* Eskimo (Kodiak): Golder JAFL XVI 91.

D1564.5. Magic cranberry opens wedge and frees hero.

D981.11. *Magic pumpkin.* India: Thompson-Balys; Chinese: Eberhard FFC CXX 58, 67, 221.

D1463.2.1. Magic pumpkin furnishes treasure. D1472.2.6. Magic pumpkin yields year's supply of rice. D1482.2. Magic pumpkin holds streams of oil.

D981.12. *Magic pomegranate.* Jewish: Neuman; India: Thompson-Balys.

D981.13. *Magic bananas.*

D1610.10.2. Speaking bananas. D1641.16. Bananas run and hide when stone thrown at them.

D983. *Magic vegetable.* *Aarne MSFO XXV 143n., *BP III 6; Type 567.

D551.2. Transformation by eating vegetable. D960. Magic gardens and plants. D1034. Magic vegetable (as food). D1375.1.2. Magic vegetable causes horns to grow on person.

D983.1. *Magic bean.* *BP II 527. — Spanish: Boggs FFC XC 124 No. 1374A; Breton: Sébillot Incidents s.v. "fève".

D1610.4. Speaking bean. D1611.4. Magic beans answer for fugitive. D1619.1. Speaking beans rebuke wife for misdeed.

D983.2. *Magic yam.* Africa (Gold Coast): Barker and Sinclair 90 No. 16.

D983.3. *Magic leek.* Icelandic: *Boberg.

D1383.5. Leek in beer protects against poison. D1389.12. Leek put under the tongue of supposed dead person prevents him from harm by the burial.

D983.4. *Magic garlic.* Jewish: Neuman.

D1385.2.7. Garlic protects from evil spirits.

D983.5. *Magic egg-plant.*

D1610.3.4. Speaking egg-plant.

D985. *Magic nut.* Cox Cinderella Nos. 6, 72, 76, 88 and passim; Fb "nød" II 719a. — Irish myth: *Cross; Breton: Sébillot Incidents s.v. "noix"; French Canadian: Barbeau JAFL XXIX 10; Spanish: Boggs FFC XC 53 No. 400 B*; Italian: Basile introduction; Jewish: Neuman.

D1035. Magic nuts (as food). D1355.12. Magic nuts (eaten) produce love. D1375.2.2. Magic nut removes horns from person. D1470.1.6. Magic wishing-nut. D1524.11. Magic betelnut comes to one over water. D1610.22. Speaking nut. F715.1.1. River issues from magic nut. F813.3. Extraordinary nut.

D985.1. *Magic coconut-shell.* Sulka of New Britain: Dixon 132 and 132 n. 2.

D1311.9. Coconut shell answers questions. D1505.18.1. Coconut shoots restore sight.

D985.2. *Magic chestnut.* Italian: Basile Pentamerone introduction.

H1333.5. Quest for magic chestnut.

D985.3. *Magic hazel-nut.* Irish myth: *Cross; Italian: Basile introduction.

D950.1. Magic hazel tree.

D985.4. *Magic acorn.* Irish myth: Cross.

D1667.2. Magic acorns grow at once.

D985.5. *Magic betel-nut.* Philippine (Tinguian): Cole 93.

D1524.11. Magic betel-nut comes to one over water.

D990—D1029. MAGIC BODILY MEMBERS

D990. Magic bodily members — human. N. A. Indian: Thompson Tales 318 n. 150.

A1262. Man created from sweat. D1312.1. Bodily members as advisers. D1318.7. Flesh reveals guilt. D1472.1.34. Part of human body furnishes food. D1500.1.7. Parts or products of human body cure disease. D1645.10. Man's body emits light. D1685. Interred body of saint performs signs and miracles.

D991. *Magic hair.* *Fb "guld" I 512a, "hår" I 771ab, "styrke" III 630a; *Hdwb. d. Abergl. III 1274; Köhler-Bolte I 126, 573; *Penzer VIII 59 n. 3; MacCulloch Childhood 211; Chauvin V 230 No. 130; *Wesselski Märchen 196; *Pauli (ed. Bolte) No. 150. — Irish myth: Cross; French Canadian: Barbeau JAFL XXIX 12; Spanish: Boggs FFC XC 67 No. 508A*; Greek: Frazer Apollodorus II 117 n. 3, Fox 69, 77; Jewish: *Neuman; India: Thompson-Balys. — N. A. Indian (Mohegan): Speck JAFL XVI 106; (Micmac): Rand 356, 369 Nos 67, 71, Leland 83, (Skidi Pawnee): Dorsey MAFLS VII 102, 113 Nos. 28, 31, (Wichita): Dorsey CI XXI No. 19, (Modoc): Curtin Myths of the Modocs (Boston 1912) 32, 46, (Ojibwa): Radin GSCan II 51; Eskimo (Greenland): Rasmussen I 97; Africa (Kaffir): Theal 131.

C912. Hair turns to gold as punishment in forbidden chamber. D466. Transformation: hair to another object. D499.1. Transformation: hair to animal. D771.1. Disenchantment by burning magic hair. D1323.11. Hair gives clairvoyance. D1335.3.5. Boiling lock of lover's hair draws him to sweetheart. D1355.5. Magic hair produces love. D1355.14. Eaten fruit causes sexual desire. D1402.2. Magic hair in man's eyebrow kills all who see it. D1421.0.3. Magic hair when thrown into fire summons supernatural helper. D1421.1.9. Magic hair (when burned) summons genie. D1421.4.1. Magic hair summons giant. D1425.2. Magic hairs summon husband. D1428.1. Magic hair draws back quiver from which it has been taken. D1436. Magic hair stretches after fugitive. D1454.1 Hair furnishes treasure. D1470.1.36. Magic wishing hair. D1475.5. Magic hair produces soldiers. D1520.3. Magic transportation by hairs. D1564.4.2. Magic hair cuts down iron tree. D1611.2. Magic hair answers for fugitive. D1831. Magic strength resides in hair.

D991.1. *Magic beard.* Fb "styrke" III 630a.

D991.2. *Magic pubic hair.* *Fb "kusse" II 334a; India: Thompson-Balys; N. A. Indian: *Thompson Tales 290 n. 65, (Tlingit): Golder JAFL XX 292.

B1311.20. Oracular pubic hair.

D991.3. *Magic ball of hair.* North Carolina: Brown Collection I 667.

D2070.2. Magic hair-ball used for bewitching.

D992. *Magic head.* Irish myth: *Cross; Welsh: MacCulloch Celtic 105; Breton: Sébillot Incidents s.v. "tête"; Jewish: Neuman.

D1311.8. Human head (skull) used for divination. D1311.8.2. Cut-off head prophesies fight. D1380.3. Head of divinity as protection of land. D1400.1.20. Magic (human) head defeats enemy. D1402.23. Killing with head of fallen enemy. D1472.1.34.2. Stream flows from man's head. D1500.1.7.1.1. Magic head (of saint) heals diseases. D1549.7. Murdered man's head will cause earth to burn up or sea to boil: must be carried about. D1602.12. Self-returning head. D1610.5. Speaking head. D1615.7. Singing head. D1641.7. Severed head moves from place to place. D1654.14. Severed head cannot be moved from helmet. R261.1. Pursuit by rolling head.

D992.1. *Magic horns (grow on person's forehead).* (Cf. D1011.1.) *Type 566; Penzer III 187. — Irish myth: *Cross; Icelandic: Boberg; Jewish: *Neuman; bin Gorion Born Judas[2] IV 122; N. A. Indian (Mohegan): Speck JAFL XVII 184.

A131.6. Horned god. B23.3. Man with (two) horns on his head. D1375.1.3. Charm causes horns to grow on person. D1500.1.7.1. Powdered skull as remedy. D1610.5.1. Magic speaking tongue. F545.2.2. Horns on forehead. H425.2. Horns grow on cuckold.

D992.2. *Magic lips.* Type 403; Köhler-Bolte I 126. — French Canadian: Barbeau JAFL XXIX 10.

D1454.2. Treasure falls from mouth. D1454.2.1. Roses fall from lips. F544.1. Remarkable lips.

D992.3. *Magic face.* Jewish: *Neuman.

D992.4. *Magic skull.*

D1500.1.7.1. Powdered skull as remedy.

D992.5. *Magic tongue.* Jewish: Neuman.
D1610.5.1. Magic speaking tongue.

D993. *Magic eye.* See references to D2071. Jewish: Neuman.

D995. *Magic foot.*
D1273.0.4. Spell chanted standing on one foot with one eye shut, etc.

D995.1. *Magic toe.* Africa (Basuto): Jacottet 56 No. 9.
D1470.2.4. Supplies from toe of old woman.

D996. *Magic hand.* *Penzer III 150; *Baker AA o.s. I 51ff.; Irish myth: *Cross; Jewish: Neuman.
D1162.2.1. Hand-of-glory. Magic candle made of criminal's hand. D1478.1. Saint's hand illumines darkness. D1500.1.6.1. Corpse's hand as remedy. D1503.9. Magic hand heals wounds. D1810.3. Magic knowledge from touching "knowledge tooth" with thumb. D1811.1.1. Thumb of knowledge.

D996.0.1. *Magic right hand.*

D996.0.1.1. *Magic power of right hand for good.* Irish myth: *Cross.
D1791.1. Dextrorsum (sunwise) circuit (for good luck). V52.15. Prayer said by saint into his right hand restores displaced eye of opponent.

D996.0.2. *Magic left hand.* Irish myth: Cross.

D996.0.2.1. *Magic power of left hand for evil.* Irish myth: *Cross.
D1791.2. Withershins (countersunwise) circuit (for ill luck).

D996.1. *Magic finger.* Irish myth: Cross; Jewish: Neuman.
D1472.1.34.1. Magic finger provides food. D1810.4. Magic knowledge from sucking finger of knowledge. D1811.1.1. Thumb of knowledge.

D997. *Magic internal organs — human.*
D1505.6.1. Gall of slain giant restores sight.

D997.1. *Magic heart — human.*
F559.7. Remarkable heart.

D997.1.1. *Magic heart of unborn child.* *Fb "hjærte" I 631b.
D1361.8. Heart of unborn child renders person invisible.

D997.2. *Magic brain.* Irish myth: Cross.
D1588.1. Magic brain assures heaven for man who dies upon it. F557.1. Removable brain.

D997.3. *Magic liver.* Cheremis: Sebeok-Nyerges.
D1652.19. Inexhaustible human liver.

D998. *Magic private parts — human.* Taylor MLN XXXI (1916) 249 n. 2; Gaster Thespis 327. — N. A. Indian: *Thompson Tales 296 nn. 83a, 83b.
D1355.2.3. Semen in love philtre. D1610.6. Speaking privates. D1610.6.1. Speaking vulva. D1610.6.2. Mentula loquens.

D1001. *Magic spittle.* *Type 313; *BP II 527 n. 1; *Fb "spytte" III 514b, 515a; Penzer VIII 59 n. 3. — Irish: Plummer clxxxiii, *Cross; Icelandic: Boberg; Jewish: Neuman; India: Thompson-Balys; Maori: Dixon 59; N. A. Indian: *Thompson Tales 329 n. 190, 331 n. 196a; Africa (Zulu): Callaway 64, 234, (Upoto): Einstein 125; Jamaica: Beckwith MAFLS XVII 263 No. 67.
A1211.3. Man from spittle of creator. A1718. Animals from spittle of deity (saint). D475.1.4. Transformation: spittle to gold. D483. Sea formed from giant's spittle. D1316.3. Speaking spittle reveals truth. D1337.1.6. Beautification by use of saint's spittle. D1381.2. Saint's spittle protects

fugitive from attack. D1402.14. Magic circle of saliva kills dragon. D1454.3. Treasure from spittle. D1500.1.7.2. Magic healing spittle. D1505.2. Spittle restores sight. D1506.1. Spittle restores hearing. D1541.1.9. Magic spittle causes storm. D1542.1.2. Magic spittle controls rain. D1564.2. Saint's spittle splits rocks. D1611.5. Magic spittle impersonates fugitive. D1776. Magic results from spitting. E114. Resuscitation by spittle. F235.4.5. Fairies made visible through the use of saliva. G272.5. Protection from witch by spitting. M201.3. Spitting into vessel to seal bargain. T533. Conception from spittle. T579.4. Mother of saint has healing spittle during pregnancy.

D1002. *Magic excrements.* Hindu: Keith 145; India: Thompson-Balys; Chinese: Eberhard FFC CXX 161; N. A. Indian: Thompson Tales 296 n. 83c, 329 n. 190a, (Takelma): Sapir UPa II 65 No. 4.

D1312.1.1. Excrements as advisers. D1402.18. Excrements cause approaching animals to fall dead. D1454.5. Treasure from excrements. D1502.10.1. Magic excrement as cure for cancer.

D1002.1. *Magic urine.*

D1500.1.36 Urine used in medicine. F964.3.1. Enchanted lamp burns with urine.

D1003. *Magic blood — human.* *Fb "blod" IV 46—48; *BP II 527 n. 1; Hdwb. d. Märchens s.v. "Blut". — Irish: Plummer cl, clxxxi, *Cross; English: Child I 172, II 39b; Italian: Basile II 5, III 9, Italian Novella: Rotunda; Jewish: Neuman, Gaster Thespis 296; India: Thompson-Balys, Penzer I 98.

D766.2. Disenchantment by application of blood. D1273.0.1. Charm written in blood has magic power. D1318.5. Blood indicates guilt or innocence. D1338.1.3. Magic blood rejuvenates. D1347.2. Blood as remedy for barrenness in woman. D1349.1.6.1. One drop of blood when licked satisfies hunger. D1355.2.2. Blood as love-philtre. D1500.1.7.3. Magic healing blood. D1502.4.2. Blood as cure for leprosy. D1503.15. Wound healed with own blood. D1505.8. Blood restores sight. D1507.6. Saint's blood restores speech. D1563.1.5. Blood makes soil fertile. D1567.1. Saint's blood produces fountain. D1594.2. God's blood vitalizes image. D1610.16. Blood speaks. D1610.16.1. Speaking blood drops. D1611.6. Magic blood-drops impersonate fugitive. D1652.20. Inexhaustible sacrificial blood. D1654.3. Indelible blood. D1741.6. Magic power lost with loss of blood. E113. Resuscitation by blood. E761.1. Blood as life token. F554. Person remarkable as to his blood. F979.12. Trees spring up from blood spilled on ground. S268. Child sacrificed to provide blood for cure of friend. T534. Conception from blood. T541.1. Birth from blood.

D1003.1. *Magic menstrual blood.* India: Thompson-Balys.

D1003.2. *Magic blood of circumcision.* Jewish: Neuman.

D1003.3. *Magic blood of unborn child.* Jewish: Neuman.

D1004. *Magic tears.* Hartland Science 238. — Irish: Plummer cl, *Cross; Norse: De la Saussaye 277; Jewish: *Neuman; N. A. Indian: *Thompson Tales 329 n. 190b.

A1012. Flood from tears. D766.2. Disenchantment by tears. D1454.4. Treasure from tears. D1454.4.2. Jewels from tears. D1567.2. Saint's tears produce fountain. T512.4. Conception from drinking saint's tears. T541.3. Birth from tears.

D1005. *Magic breath.* Irish: Plummer clxxii, *Cross; Jewish: Neuman.

D588. Transformation by blowing. D1364.5. Saint's breath causes magic sleep. D1365.7. Breath causes magic forgetfulness. D1402.8. Magic breath kills. D1442.7. Magic breath subdues animals. D1500.4.2. Magic breath causes disease. D1500.4.2.1. Saint's breath makes men drunk. D1500.4.2.2. Saint's breath causes death. D1505.10. Saint's breath restores sight. D1507.4. Saint's breath restores speech. D1518.3. Hero's breath returns head to headless horseman. D1565.4. Saint's breath restores shattered vessel. D1566.1.4. Saint's breath kindles lamps. D1566.1.4.1. Saint's breath kindles coals. D1566.1.4.2. Saint's (man's) breath makes icicles (snow, water) burn. D2091.11. Black cloud magically blown upon enemy. D2176.3.3.4. Saint's breath drives away the devil.

D1006. *Magic buttocks.* N. A. Indian: *Thompson Tales 296 n. 83.

D1317.1. Buttocks as magic watcher. D1610.6.3. Speaking buttocks.

D1007. *Magic bone (human).* (Cf. D1013.) Jewish: Neuman.

D1317.14. Bones (human) warn of danger. D1401.9. Magic bone beats king's face. D1611.17. Magic bone answers for fugitive.

D1008. *Magic human flesh.* Eskimo (Greenland): Rink 329.

D1500.1.46. Human flesh as cure.

D1009. *Magic bodily members (human) — miscellaneous.*

D1009.1. *Magic scab (from skin).* Tsimshian: Boas BBAE XXVII 190.

D1454.6. Treasure from scab.

D1009.2. *Magic tooth.* Irish myth: Cross.

D1810.3. Magic knowledge from touching "knowledge tooth" with thumb. D1810.3.1. Future revealed by "knowledge tooth". F513.1. Person unusual as to his teeth.

D1009.2.1. *Magic dead man's tooth.* Kittredge Witchcraft 142, 460 nn. *11, 13.

D1502.2.1. Dead man's tooth as cure for toothache.

D1009.3. *Magic breasts of woman.*

D1514.4.1. Maid cuts off pap to heal man's serpent wound.

D1010. Magic bodily members — animal. Jewish: *Neuman.

B100—B199. Magic animals. B110 Treasure-producing parts of animals. B171. Demi-coq. A cock is cut in two and made magic. B501. Animal gives part of body as talisman for summoning its aid. D532. Transformation by putting on claw, feather, etc. of helpful animal. D1472.1.24.4. Body of tortoise provides food. D1500.1.33. Parts or products of animal cure disease. D1502.9. Viper body cures skin disease. D1515.4.4. Body of gnat as antidote for snakebite. D1517.1 Body of housefly as remedy for hornet sting.

D1011. *Magic animal head.*

B107.2. Fish with silver and gold heads. B108.2. Serpent with jewel in head. B112. Treasure-producing serpent's crown. B133.4. Speaking horse-head. D1311.8.1. Dog's head used for divination. D1380.3.1. Magic head of horse as protection of land. D1500.1.33.5. Fish head cures disease.

D1011.0.1. *Magic bird head.* *Aarne MSFO XXV 175; *Type 567; India: Thompson-Balys.

D1301.4. Bird's head (when eaten) teaches animal languages.

D1011.0.2. *Magic ass's head.* Spanish: Boggs FFC XC No. 425.

D1470.1.7. Magic ass's head fulfills wishes.

D1011.0.3. *Magic serpent head.* Jewish: Neuman; Chinese: Eberhard FFC CXX 33.

D1561.1.1.3. Snake's head (when eaten) brings man to kingship.

D1011.1. *Magic animal horn.* (Cf. D992.1.) Cross MPh X 289; Icelandic: Boberg; Greek: Fox 93; Jewish: Neuman; India: Thompson-Balys; Africa (Basuto): Jacottet 160 No. 23, 242 No. 35, (Kaffir): Theal 169f; N. A. Indian (Micmac): Rand 196 No. 25.

B115. Animal with horn of plenty. D1375.1. Magic object causes horns to grow on person. D1402.3.3. Magic animal horn kills. D1470.2.3. Horn of plenty. D1515.4.3. Hind's horns as antidote for snakebite. D1520.32. Magic transportation on antlers.

D1011.2. *Magic ear of animal.* See references to B115.1.

D1472.1.24.3. Food and drink from elk's ears. E115. Resuscitation by wax from deer's ear.

D1011.3. *Magic animal's crown.*

D1011.3.1. *Magic serpent's crown.* (Cf. B112.) Cox Cinderella 517.

D1361.9. Serpent's crown renders invisible.

D1011.4. *Magic tooth of animal.* Jewish: Neuman.

D1364.30. Tooth of fox causes magic sleep. D1508.3. Jackal-tooth as cure for madness.

D1011.5. *Magic lips of animal.*

D1552.9. When enchanted deer touches rock with her muzzle it flies asunder and reveals entrance to caves.

D1011.6. *Magic tongue of animal.* Jewish: Neuman.

D1316.13. Magic bird's tongue reveals truth.

D1011.7. *Magic brain of animal.*

D1502.8.1. Magic dog brain cures boils.

D1012. *Magic limbs of animal.*

D1012.1. *Magic legs of animal.*

D1012.1.1. *Magic legs of bull.* India: Thompson-Balys.

D1013. *Magic bone of animal.* Breton: Sébillot Incidents s.v. "os"; cf. Type 780. — India: Thompson-Balys; Africa (Basuto): Jacottet 180 No. 26, 190 No. 28.

B172.4. Bird with magic bones and feathers. D1311.10.1. Divination by shoulder-bone of sheep. D1312.2. Magic bone gives advice. D1318.6. Divining bones reveal guilt. D1402.3.4. Magic jaw bone of ass kills. D1472.1.24.2. Jawbone of ass supplies water. D1549.3.5. Fish bone holds back water in river. D1594.0.2. Vivification by hitting with bone. K113.1. Alleged resuscitating bone sold.

D1013.1. *Magic chicken-thigh.* India: Thompson-Balys.

D1015. *Magic internal organs of animal.*

D1015.1. *Magic heart of animal.*

D1357.1. Eating ferocious animal's heart makes person cruel. D1361.29. Magic animal's heart renders invisible. D1500.1.9.3. Dragon's heart-blood as remedy.

D1015.1.1. *Magic bird heart.* *Type 567; *BP I 528, III 3ff.; *Aarne MSFO XXV 176; Penzer I 19 n. 2; *Fb "hjærte" I 631b. — Breton: Sébillot Incidents s.v. "mendiant".

B113.1. Treasure-producing bird heart. D1561.1. Magic bird heart (when eaten) brings man to kingship. M312.3. Eater of magic bird heart will become rich (or king).

D1015.1.2. *Magic dragon heart.* (Cf. B11.2.9.) Icelandic: Völsunga Saga 66.

D1358.1.1. Eating dragon's heart makes courageous.

D1015.1.3. *Magic serpent heart.* Spanish: Boggs FFC XC 43 No. 302 A*.

D1402.3.1. Magic serpent heart kills giant.

D1015.1.4. *Magic wolf heart.* Icelandic: Boberg.

D1015.1.5. *Magic fox heart.* Jewish: Neuman.

D1300.7. Fox heart gives magic wisdom.

D1015.2. *Magic gall-bladder of animal.* Africa (Basuto): Jacottet 214 No. 32; (Ekoi): Talbot 27.

D1311.10.2. Divination from gall and liver of pig. D1317.2. Magic gall-bladder warns of danger. D1402.3.2. Magic leopard gall causes death.

D1015.3. *Magic entrails of animal.*

D1015.3.1. *Magic entrails of bird.* Aarne MSFO XXV 176.

D1335.3.4. Entrails of live pigeon placed above house door fetches lover to the spot.

D1015.3.2. *Magic entrails of goat.* German: Grimm No. 130.

D1015.4. *Magic liver of animal.* Chinese-Persian: Coyajee JPASB XXIV 187.

D1500.2.8. Snake liver prevents disease. D1505.14. Animal liver cures blindness. D1542.1.7. Blood and liver of black dog sacrificed to bring rain. D1694.0.1. Liver of deer vitalize.

D1015.4.1. *Magic bird liver.* *Aarne MSFO XXV 176; Type 567.

D1015.5. *Magic stomach of animal.*

D1015.5.1. *Magic stomach of hare.* Jewish: Neuman.

D1347.6. Hare's stomach causes fecundity.

D1016. *Magic blood of animal.* Jewish: Neuman; Africa (Ekoi): Talbot 187.

B11.2.13. Blood of dragon. D449.9. Transformation: blood drops to serpents. D1003. Magic blood — human. D1335.3.8. Person burns dragon's blood (plant) and says charm to bring lover to spot. D1344.12. Blood smeared on body renders invulnerable. D1355.2.2.1. Blood of wounded centaur as love philtre. D1382.13. Blood of salamander protects against fire. D1500.1.7.3.3. Dragon's heart-blood as remedy. D1542.1.7. Blood and liver of black dog sacrificed to bring rain. D1563.2.2. Monster's blood makes tree and surroundings poisonous. D1566.2.6. Salamander's blood quenches fire. D1594.4. Blood of twelve buffaloes vitalizes tiger. D1846.4. Invulnerability through bathing in dragon's blood. E761.1.4. Life token: blood of fish calls out. F872.3.1. Bath of blood of dragons, lions, adders, etc.

D1017. *Magic flesh of animal.* Irish: Cross.

B635.2. Eaten meat of bear lover causes unborn son to have bear characteristics. D1032. Magic meat. D1318.7. Flesh of animal reveals guilt. D1318.7.1.1. Flesh of stolen animal cannot be cooked.

D1017.1. *Magic fat of animal.*

D1017.1.1. *Magic fat of crow.* Fb "fedt" I 278b.

B1382.2. Fat of crow prevents burning.

D1018. *Magic milk of animal.* *Köhler-Bolte I 468; Dh II 154. — Irish myth: *Cross; Jewish: Neuman; India: Thompson-Balys; Africa (Kaffir): Theal 70.

B109.4.3. Cow gives milk without cessation. B182.1. Magic cow gives red milk. D921.3.1. Lake of milk created through merit of saint. D1043. Milk as magic drink. D1063. Magic dairy products. D1337.1.3. Milk gives magic beauty. D1337.1.3.1. Bathing hair in buffalo milk makes it unusually long. D1338.4. Bath in magic milk rejuvenates. D1349.1.3.1. Magic milk produces immunity from hunger and thirst. D1500.1.33.1. Magic healing milk. D1503.7.1. Magic pool of milk heals wounds. D1515.3. Bath in milk of white, hornless cows as antidote for poison. D1652.3.1. Cow with inexhaustible milk. D2083. Evil magic in the dairy. D2161.4.14.1. Magic cure by bathing in milk. E80.1.1. Resuscitation by bathing in milk. E102.1. Resuscitation by magic milk. F241.2.5. Woman lives only on milk from fairy cow. F989.9. Milk from saint's cows forms lake. F1094. Milk has taste of wine and honey. T601. Infant bathed in milk. V229.2.3. Saint will drink only milk of cow milked by faithful woman.

D1021. *Magic feather.* *Types 552, 534*; BP III 18ff.; 424ff. — Breton: Sébillot Incidents s.v. "plume"; English: Child V 496 s.v. "sleep"; Persian: Carnoy 290, 331; India: Thompson-Balys; Eskimo (Greenland): Rasmussen III 304; Africa (Kaffir): Theal 126.

B101.1. Golden bird. Bird with golden feathers. B172.4. Bird with magic bones and feathers. B501. Animal gives part of its body as talisman for summoning its aid. D275. Transformation man to feather. D532. Transformation by putting on claw, feather, etc. of helpful animal.

D1313.10. Magic feather indicates road. D1323.16. Magic feather gives clairvoyance. D1338.12. Magic feather transforms one into much younger person. D1341.4. Magic feather brings supernatural old age. D1355.23. Love-producing magic feather. D1361.10. Magic feather renders invisible. D1364.6. Feather causes magic sleep. D1375.6. Magic object causes feathers to grow on person. D1380.22. Magic feather protects. D1400.1.19. Magic feather defeats enemy. D1505.3. Magic feather restores sight. D1565.1. Magic feather causes chips from tree to return as fast as cut. D1645.6. Self-luminous feather. E64.9. Resuscitation by magic feather. F61.2. Ascent to sky on feather.

D1021.1. *Magic bird's power in one feather.* India: Thompson-Balys.

D1022. *Magic wings.* Aarne MSFO XXV 176; Jewish: Neuman.

D1481.1. Magic chicken wing keeps one warm in cold weather.

D1022.0.1. *Wings grown by magic.* Breton: Sébillot Incidents s.v. "ailes".

B115.2. Wing cornucopia. D150. Transformation: man to bird.

D1023. *Magic hair of animal.* Fb "hår" I 771b.

B501. Animal gives part of its body as talisman for summoning its aid. D532. Transformation by putting on claw, feather (hair), etc. of helpful animal. D1361.35. Magic tiger's hair renders invisible. D1390.1. Hairs of lion, when burnt, get owner out of difficulties. D1427.3. Magic horse hairs (when rubbed) compel horse to follow.

D1023.1. *Magic hair of bear.* *Fb "hår" I 771b.

D1023.2. *Magic hair of fox.* *Fb "hår" I 771b.

D1562.2. Hair from fox's tail opens all doors.

D1023.3. *Magic hair of lion's tail.* French Canadian: Sister Marie Ursule.

D1023.4. *Magic hair of ant's beard.* French Canadian: Sister Marie Ursule.

D1024. *Magic egg.* Irish myth: Cross (D1019); Breton: Sébillot Incidents s.v. "œuf"; Jewish: Neuman; Chinese: Eberhard FFC CXX 104f., 151; Jamaica: Beckwith MAFLS XVII 269 No. 81, 277 No. 89.

B101.2. Treasure-laying bird. D1375.6.1. Magic egg causes feathers to grow on person. D1470.1.8. Magic wishing-eggs. D1470.2.9. Supplies from magic skin worn by man. D1472.1.26. Magic egg supplies food. D1502.7.1. Magic locust egg cures earache. D1599.3.1. Magic egg multiplies objects. D1599.4.1. Magic egg produces house. D1610.29. Speaking eggs. E711.1. Soul in egg.

D1025. *Magic skin of animal.*

B105. Ram with golden fleece. B182.3.1. Magic bull to be flayed. D530. Transformation by putting on skin. D1337.2.5. Magic skin makes person appear ugly. D1381.3.2. Magic unpierceable skin protects against attack. D1532.1. Magic flying skin. K114.1. Alleged oracular cowhide sold. K114.2. Alleged oracular bird-skin sold.

D1025.1. *Magic pigskin.* Irish: MacCulloch Celtic 40; *Cross.

B104. Treasure-hog. B183.9. Skin of magic pig heals wound. D1503.2. Magic pigskin heals wounds. H1332.5. Quest for magic pigskin.

D1025.2. *Magic fishskin.* *Chauvin V 230 No. 130.

D1520.5. Magic transportation by skin of fish.

D1025.3. *Magic mouseskin.* Africa (Zulu): Callaway 97.

B185.1. Magic mouse to be flayed. D1532.1. Magic mouseskin bears person aloft.

D1025.4. *Magic skin of swallow.* Africa (Zulu): Callaway 53.

D1317.3. Magic swallow-skin warns of danger.

D1025.5. *Magic cowhide.* Irish myth: Cross.

D1588.2. Magic cowhide assures heaven for man who dies upon it.

D1025.6. *Magic dogskin.* Irish myth: Cross.

D565.7. Transformation at touch of magic dogskin. D1520.5.2. Magic transportation by dogskin.

D1025.7. *Magic horseskin.* French Canadian: Sister Marie Ursule; Chinese: Eberhard FFC CXX 79.

D1520.5.4. Magic transportation by horseskin.

D1025.8. *Magic sheepskin.* Jewish: Neuman; India: Thompson-Balys.

D1469.1.1. Magic sheepskin, shaken inside and outside shed, showers gold and silver. D1472.1.29. Magic sheepskin supplies food. D1500.1.33.4. Hide of sheep or goat as cure.

D1025.9. *Magic sealskin.*

D1520.5.3. Magic transportation by sealskin.

D1026. *Magic dung of animal.* Irish myth: Cross; India: Thompson-Balys.

B102. Gold producing ass. D1338.11. Rejuvenation by magic manure dust. D1500.1.33.3. Magic animal dung. D1505.13. Animal excreta cures blindness. D1610.6.4. Speaking excrements. D1649.4. Dung and wood burst into flames of their own accord.

D1026.1. *Magic bird dung.* Africa (Yoruba): Ellis 256 No. 4.

D1500.1.33.3.1. Magic bird dung cures. D1505.13. Bird dung restores sight. E64.20. Resuscitation from bird dung.

D1026.2. *Magic cow-dung.* BP II 527 n. 1.

D1470.2.7. Supplies from bull's dung. D1611.3. Magic cow-dung answers for fugitive.

D1027. *Magic urine of animal.* Irish myth: Cross.

D1331.2.7. Dog's urine makes tiger blind.

D1027.1. *Magic urine of serpent.* Africa (Zanzibar): Bateman 204 No. 10.

D1345.1. Serpent's water gives longevity.

D1028. *Magic shell of animal.*

D1028.1. *Magic conch shell.* India: Thompson-Balys.

D1452.4. Magic conch shell furnishes money.

D1028.2. *Magic tortoise shell.*

D1469.14. Magic tortoise shell produces pearls.

D1029. *Other bodily members of animals — magic.*

D1029.0.1. *Other bodily members of bird — magic.* Aarne MSFO XXV 176.

D1029.1. *Magic breath of animal.* Irish myth: Cross.

D1337.11. Dragon's breath renders hideous. D1566.1.6. Magic dog's breath burns dead bodies.

D1029.2. *Magic tail of animal.* Jewish: Neuman.

D1400.1.21. Bull's tail becomes a stick.

D1029.2.1. *Magic yak tail.* India: Thompson-Balys.

D1029.2.2. *Magic goat tail.* India: Thompson-Balys.

D1029.2.3. *Magic snake tail.* Jewish: Neuman.

D1029.3. *Magic animal feet.*

D1469.7. Wealth from drawing cow's feet over money box.

D1029.4. *Magic sex organs of animal.*

D1469.5. Worshipped sex organ of horse provides money, etc.

D1029.5. *Magic spittle of animal.* (Cf. D1001.) Jewish: Neuman.

D1029.6. *Magic shell of animal.* Chinese: Eberhard FFC CXX 107.

D1452.4. Magic conch-shell furnishes money. D1470.1.41. Magic wishing conch-shell.

D1030. **Magic food.** *Fb "tønde" III 934b, "mad" II 525a, "styrke" III 630a. — Irish: Plummer clxxxv, *Cross, O'Suilleabhain 57, Béal XXI 322; Icelandic: De la Saussaye 254, Boberg; French Canadian: Barbeau JAFL XXIX 11; Arabic: Burton Nights II 212; India: Thompson-Balys; Philippines: Dixon 221ff.; Melanesian: ibid. 224 n. 28; Indonesian: ibid. 238 n. 51; Java: ibid. 209; Eskimo (Greenland): Rink 446, Rasmussen I 202; N. A. Indian: *Thompson Tales 335 n. 210.

A153.2. Magic food gives immortality to gods. D1318.7.1.2. Food sticks in thief's throat and betrays him. D1335.1. Magic strength-giving food. D1336.2. Magic food gives weakness. D1346.3. Food of immortality. D1349.1.6. Tiny amount of food magically satisfies. D1359.4. Magic food causes intoxication and sobriety. D1365.3. Food causes magic forgetfulness. D1419.4. Magic food brings eater into sender's power. D1472. Food and drink from magic object. D1500.1.30. Magic healing banquet. D1601.25. Self-cooking food. D1610.31. Speaking food. D1665. Food has taste of any dainty desired. D1982.4. Food and drink appear and disappear in otherworld.

D1030.1. *Food supplied by magic.* Most of the references in D1030 also belong here. *Types 563, 564. — Irish: *Cross, O'Suilleabhain 38, Beal XXI 314; Welsh: MacCulloch Celtic 192; Breton: Sébillot Incidents s.v. "repas"; Jewish: *Neuman; India: Thompson-Balys; Indonesian: Dixon 238 n. 51; Jamaican: *Beckwith MAFLS XVII 248 No. 25; Eskimo (Cumberland Sound): Boas BAM XV 248; S. A. Indian (Toba): Métraux MAFLS XL 44, 88.

B101.4. Magic bird produces unlimited food. D1171. Magic vessel. D1472. Food and drink from magic object. D1472.1.21. Magic chest supplies food. D1652.1 Inexhaustible food. D1982.4. Food and drink appear and disappear in otherworld. D2106. Provisions magically furnished. J2411.3. Unsuccessful imitation of magic production of food.

D1030.1.1. *Food supplied by means of prayer.* Irish myth: Cross.

D2106. Magic multiplication of objects by saints.

D1030.2. *Magic banquet.* Irish myth: *Cross.

D1500.1.30. Magic healing banquet.

D1030.3. *Magic food from herbs.* India: Thompson-Balys.

D1031. *Magic pastry (bread, cake, etc.).*

D1031.0.1. *Manna.* Food from skies in basket each morning. Jewish: *Neuman; India: Thompson-Balys; N. A. Indian (Maidu): Dixon BAM XVII 39ff. No. 1.

D1318.19. Manna reveals guilt. D1335.1.4. Manna produces magic strength. D1472.2.8. Magic musical pipe causes food to fall from sky. D1665.4. Manna tastes bitter to gentiles. D1676.1. Manna does not fall on Sabbath.

D1031.1. *Magic bread.* *Type 310C*; *Fb "brød" IV 74b. — Breton: Sébillot Incidents s.v. "pain"; Spanish: Boggs FFC XC 60 No. 438*; Jewish: Neuman; Babylonian: Gilgamesch-Epos XI 220ff., cf. p. 141ff.

D1314.6. Loaf of bread locates drowned man. D1373.2. Two loaves of bread — one to excite, the other to appease hunger. D1385.15. Bread keeps off evil spirits. D1465.1. Magic bread furnishes treasure. D1487.2. Consecrated bread makes vegetables grow. D1610.31.2. Speaking bread. D1652.1.1. Inexhaustible bread. E501.17.5.6. Wild hunt avoided by holding bread.

D1031.1.1. *Consecrated bread as magic object.* *Kittredge Witchcraft 149f., 469 nn. 103—116; Irish: *Cross, O'Suilleabhain 25, 48f., Beal XXI 307, 317f.

D1355.10.1. Consecrated bread produces love. D1465.1.1. Consecrated bread brings wealth. D1487.2. Consecrated bread makes vegetables grow.

D1500.1.10.1. Consecrated bread as cure. G281. Consecrated wafer kept in mouth in order to be a witch. H1292.4.1. Question (propounded on quest): How can the princess be cured? — Answer: She must recover consecrated wafer which rat has stolen from her first communion. V363. Jewish child thrown into oven by father for taking eucharist.

D1031.2. *Magic cake.* *Type 751; *BP II 527 n. 1. — Chinese: Werner 186.

D1313.1.2. Magic cake indicates road. D1382.3. Magic cake protects from heat. D1507.5. Magic cake restores speech. D1611.8. Magic cakes answer for fugitive. D1652.1.2. Cake magically increases.

D1031.2.1. *Cake made by rubbing flour on griddle.* Irish myth: Cross.

D1031.2.2. *Magic cake of figs.* Jewish: *Neuman.

D1032. *Magic meat.* Type 301C*; Irish myth: Cross; *Frazer Apollodorus II 70 n. 2; Africa (Benga): Nassau 227 No. 34.

B161.3. Wisdom from eating serpent. D444.2. Transformation: meat to toad. D1017. Magic flesh of animal. D1017.1. Magic fat of animal. D1335.1.3. Fighting animals eaten produce magic strength. D1358.1.2. Eating worm's and wolf's flesh makes courageous and impeduous. D1442.9. Magic meat pacifies animal guardians. D1500.1.33.2. Flesh of white cow with red ears as only cure for mysterious illness. D1561.1.1.1. Bird (when eaten) brings man to kingship. D1561.2.1. Magic bird (when eaten) gives power of excreting jewels. D1601.25.1. Self-cooking fowls. D1610.7. Speaking loin of goat meat. D1619.2.2. Eaten goat bleats from eater's stomach. D1652.1.9. Inexhaustible meat. D1652.1.9.1.1. Inexhaustible boar's flesh. D1652.1.9.2. Inexhaustible sheep.

D1032.1. *Magic meal of fishes.* Mark 6: 41—44.

B162.1. Supernatural knowledge from eating magic fish. D1347.5. Magic fish (eaten) causes fecundity. D1385.27. Meal of fishes protects against demons. D1561.1.1.2. Magic fish (when eaten) brings man to kingship. D1652.1.10. Inexhaustible fish. P1601.25.2. Self-cooking fish.

D1032.2. *Flesh of cat when chewed has magic results.* Irish myth: *Cross.

B184. Magic cat

D1032.3. *Flesh of dog when chewed has magic results.* Irish myth: *Cross.

B187. Magic dog. D1508.4. Soup made of black dog's head cures madness.

D1032.4. *Flesh of pig when chewed has magic results.* Irish myth: *Cross.

B183. Magic boar (pig). D1359.3.2. Happiness from eating magic pig.

D1033. *Magic cereal (food).*

D2157. Magic control of soil and crops. D1610.31.1. Speaking porridge.

D1033.0.1. *Cereal from man's body.* India: Thompson-Balys.

D1033.1. *Magic rice.* Indonesian: DeVries's list No. 206; Chinese: Graham.

D1652.1.3.1 Inexhaustible rice. D1652.5.10. Inexhaustible ricestores.

D1033.2. *Magic wheat.* Irish myth: Cross.

D1652.1.3.3. Inexhaustible wheat. F962.6. Shower of wheat.

D1034. *Magic vegetable (as food).* (Cf. D983.) Icelandic: Ragnars saga 112.

D1472.1.4. Vegetable supporting life without other food.

D1035. *Magic nuts (as food).* (Cf. D985.)

D1035.1. *Magic chestnut (as food).* Seneca: Curtin-Hewitt RBAE XXXII 148, 187, 199, 503.

D1652.1.5. Inexhaustible chestnut.

D1035.2. *Magic coconut (as food).* Leper's Island: Dixon 127.

D1652.1.6. Inexhaustible coconut.

D1036. *Magic dairy products.* Irish myth: *Cross.

D1018. Magic milk of animal. D1043. Milk as magic drink. D1573.1. Much butter made from little milk by power of saint. D2083. Evil magic in the dairy.

D1036.1. *Magic cheese.* Swiss: Jegerlehner Oberwallis 318 No. 3, 321 No. 59.

D1652.1.4. Ever-renewing cheese.

D1037. *Magic honey.* Irish myth: *Cross, Beal XXI 337; Gaster Thespis 364; Jewish: Neuman; Hindu: Keith 158.

D479.4.4. Transformation: water to honey. D1338.9. Rejuvenation by magic honey. D1346.3.1. Magic honey gives immortality. D1385.28. Magic honey protects against demons. D1500.1.29. Magic healing honey. D1505.4. Magic honey restores sight. F962.7. Shower of honey.

D1038. *Magic sweets.*

D1349.1.5. Magic sweets: one can quench thirst and the other can allay hunger.

D1039. *Magic food — miscellaneous.*

D1039.1. *Magic vermicelli.* Chinese: Werner 222.

D1039.2. *Magic salt.* Jewish: Neuman; Cape Verde Islands: Parsons MAFLS XV (1) 282 No. 92.

D456.3. Transformation: stone to salt. D471.5. Transformation: salt to stone. D1402.31. Magic salt kills. D1551.1. Magic salt causes waters to divide. F384.1. Salt powerful against fairies.

D1040. Magic drink. *MacCulloch Childhood 70—72; *Fb "drikke" I 204b, "styrke" III 630a. — Greek: Frazer Apollodorus II 287 n. 2; Irish: Plummer clxxii, *Cross; Icelandic: De la Saussaye 143, *Boberg; English: Child I 363 n. 364; Swiss: Jegerlehner Oberwallis 328 No. 24; Italian Novella: Rotunda; Hindu: Keith 46; Eskimo (Greenland): Rink 453.

A154. Drink of the gods. D555. Transformation by drinking. D1242. Magic fluid. D1242.1. Magic water. D1242.2. Magic potion. D1335.2. Magic strength-giving drink. D1336.7. Magic drink gives weakness. D1338.1. Magic drink rejuvenates. D1364.7. Drink causes magic sleep. D1364.7.1. Liquor blessed by saint causes magic sleep. D1364.12. Contents of bottle cause magic sleep. D1365.2. Drink causes magic forgetfulness. D1365.6. Magic cup causes forgetfulness. D1366.1. Magic drink causes memory. D1367.2. Magic drink causes insanity. D1403.3. Magic drink causes arms to fall from shoulders. D1472. Food and drink from magic object. D1500.1.11. Magic healing drink. D1518.1. Magic drink restores arms. D1652.2. Inexhaustible drink. D1665.1. Drink has taste of any liquor desired. D1982.4. Food and drink appear and disappear in otherworld.

D1040.1. *Drink supplied by magic.* Irish myth: *Cross.

D1041. *Blood as magic drink.* Frazer Golden Bough XII 189 s.v. "blood"; Zs. f. deutsche Philologie XXVI (1894) 9; Irish myth: Cross; Icelandic: Hrolfs saga Kraka 62, 69, Völsungasaga 45, *Boberg; Eskimo (Cumberland Sound): Boas BAM XV 248.

D1003. Magic blood — human. D1301.2. Drinking blood teaches animal language. D1335.2.1. Blood as magic strengthening drink. P312.1. Drinking mixture of blood, milk, and wine as pledge of covenant.

D1043. *Milk as magic drink.* Irish myth: *Cross; Swiss: Jegerlehner Oberwallis 310 No. 30; Jewish: Neuman; Hindu: Keith 134.

B182.1. Magic cow gives red milk. D1018. Magic milk of animal. D1036. Magic dairy products. D1335.2.3. Milk as magic strengthening drink. D1385.14. Milk of two king's children protects hero in dragon fight. D2083. Evil magic in the dairy. P312.1. Drinking mixture of blood, milk, and wine as pledge of covenant.

D1045. *Magic beer.*

E761.6.4. Life token: beer foams.

D1045.0.1. *Beer brewed by means of magic song.* Finnish: Kalevala rune 20.

D1275. Magic song.

D1045.1. *Magic ale.* Irish myth: *Cross; Icelandic: MacCulloch Eddic 172.

D1500.1.10.5. Consecrated ale as magic cure. D1601.23. Ale serves itself.

D1046. *Magic wine.* Irish myth: *Cross; Jewish: *Neuman.

E761.6.5. Life token: wine turns to vinegar.

D1046.1. *Consecrated wine as magic object.* *Kittredge Witchcraft 148, 468f. nn. 97—101; Irish myth: Cross.

D1500.1.10.2. Consecrated wine as magic cure. D1652.13. Everlasting wine-odor. V30. Sacrament.

D1050. Magic clothes. BP II 527 n. 1. — Breton: Sébillot Incidents s.v. "habit", "évêque"; India: Thompson-Balys; N. A. Indian (Seneca): Curtin-Hewitt RBAE XXXII 128, 131 No. 20, 264 No. 50.

D1355.11. Magic clothes produce love. D1385.19. Clothing protects from evil spirit. D1610.26. Speaking clothes. D1611.7. Magic clothes answer for fugitive. F166.3.1. Otherworld clothes never wear out. F820. Extraordinary clothing and ornaments.

D1050.1. *Clothes produced by magic.* *Type 510; *Cox Cinderella passim; Saintyves Perrault 151; Irish myth: Cross.

D1051. *Magic cloth.* Icelandic: *Boberg; India: Thompson-Balys, Penzer I 26; Chinese: Eberhard FFC CXX 221; Africa (Ekoi): Talbot 226; (Ibo, Nigeria): Thomas 124.

D1314.9. Magic cloth leads owner to lost horses. D1318.8. Magic cloth reveals guilt. D1361.40. Magic cloth renders invisible. D1380.18. Magic cloth protects. D1409.2. Magic roll of cloth pacifies demon. D1410.8. Magic cloth renders girls helpless against lovers. D1421.1.10. Magic roll of cloth summons demon. D1470.1.9. Magic wishing-cloth. D1500.1.36. Magic healing handkerchief. D1601.31. Magic towel wipes person. D1612.4.1. Magic cloth tells where it is hidden. D1652.8. Inexhaustible cloth. E64.10. Resuscitation by piece of felt.

D1052. *Magic garment (robe, tunic).* *Fb "ønske" III 1178b. — Irish: Plummer clxxx, clxxxi, *Cross; Breton: Sébillot Incidents s.v. "robe"; Icelandic: *Boberg; Jewish: Neuman; India: Thompson-Balys; Chinese: Eberhard FFC CXX 165; Hawaii: Beckwith Myth *491, 499f.; N. A. Indian: *Thompson Tales 303 n. 109i.

D930.1.0.2. Robe sent to saint on stream not wet. D1335.17. Garment gives bearer magic strength. D1344.6. Saint's tunic renders invulnerable. D1361.12.1. Saint's tunic renders invisible. D1381.3. Magic garment protects against attack. D1381.3.3. Protective garment which spears cannot penetrate. D1382.6.1. Magic garment protects from fire. D1382.10. Magic garment prevents burning. D1383.1. Magic garment protects from poison. D1388.0.4. Magic garment protects from drowning. D1400.1.18. Thread from jogi's garment when pulled makes fort fall to ground. D1402.30. Magic coat kills. D1414.5. Magic garment makes weapons useless. D1442.12. Magic garment tames animals. D1445.5. Magic garment kills animals. D1447.2. Magic garment protects against wild animals. D1470.1.10. Magic wishing-smock. D1500.1.25. Magic garment as remedy. D1532.6. Magic robe bears person aloft. D1602.3. Self-returning robe. D1608. Object automatically clothes nude person. D1721.0.1. Magic power from donning magician's clothes. D2182. Flow of cow's milk increased by licking saint's garment. E64.11. Resuscitation by magic robe (blanket). F964.2. Fire spares saint's tunic, though wearer is burned.

D1052.1. *Magic uniform.* *Fb "guldmundering".

D1520.7. Magic transportation by gold uniform.

D1053. *Magic mantle (cloak).* *Types 328, 400, 566; *Chauvin V 230; Pauli (ed. Bolte) No. 323; *Cross MPh XVI 649; Köhler-Bolte II 409. — Irish: *Cross, Beal XXI 328, O'Suilleabhain 85; Icelandic: *Boberg; French Canadian: Barbeau JAFL XXIX 10; Hindu: Penzer I 25ff.;

Japanese: Mitford 185ff.; Easter Island: Métraux Ethnology 367; N.A. Indian: *Thompson Tales 339 n. 221a.

D682.4.1. Magic mantle changes color hourly. D1317.19. Cloak warns. D1329.1. Putting head under saint's cloak reveals rewards of heaven. D1341.2. Magic cloak makes person old. D1361.12. Magic cloak of invisibility. D1368.3. Magic cloak causes illusion. D1402.0.1.2. Holy man's cloak burns person up. D1410.8. When spying follower accidentally touches holy man's cloak he loses his eyesight and falls down senseless. D1455.1. Magic mantle provides treasure. D1470.1.11. Magic wishing-cloak. D1520.6. Magic transportation by cloak (cape). D1524.1.3. Saint spreads his cloak (or other clothes) upon the water and rides to his desired destination. D1543.6. Wind carried in mantle. D1610.26.1. Speaking cloak. D1652.12. Mantle ever new. D1692. Cloak (and shirt) fit person of any size. H411.7. Mantle as chastity test.

D1055. *Magic trousers (breeches).* Fb "lærredsbukser" II 501a, *"bukser" IV 77b. — Chinese: Werner 307, 309, 313.

D1344.9.2. Magic trousers render invulnerable. D1361.36. Magic trousers render invisible. D1400.1.1. Magic trousers conquer enemy. D1532.2. Magic breeches bear person aloft. D1549.3.3. Magic trousers make river boil. D1657.1. Magic untiring breeches.

D1056. *Magic shirt.* *BP I 42; Fb "skjorte" III 285b, W. S. Johnsson Om Sejrsskjorten (Danske Studier 1929 97ff.); Irish myth: *Cross; Icelandic: *Boberg; Greek: Fox 94; Jamaica: Beckwith MAFLS XVII 241 No. 15.

D1344.9.1. Magic shirt gives invulnerability. D1361.37. Magic shirt renders invisible. D1381.5. Magic shirt protects against attack. D1382.6. Magic shirt protects from cold and burning. D1384.4.1. Magic shirt prevents fatigue during swimming. D1389.7. Magic shirt protects against opposition. D1402.5. Nessus-shirt. Magic shirt burns wearer up. D1541.1.4. Shirt laid upon altar raises storm. D1612.5.1. Magic shirt tells owner when it is stolen. D1692. Shirt fits person of any size. F343.5.1. Fairy gives magic cloak and shirt. H431.1. Shirt as chastity index. H1022.4.1. Task: making shirt derived from a single flaxseed.

D1057. *Magic belt.* *Type 590; *Fb "ønske" III 1178b, "træ" III 868a, "bælte" IV 84a; Hdwb. d. Märchens II s.v. "Gürtel". — Irish myth: Cross; Breton: Sébillot Incidents s.v. "ceinture"; Icelandic: De la Saussaye 286 *Boberg. — N.A. Indian (Passamaquoddy): Prince PAES X 31 No. 5, (Chipewyan [European borrowing]): Thompson CColl II 392, (Micmac): Rand 274, 369 Nos 46, 71, Leland 31, (Ojibwa): Schoolcraft Indian in his Wigwam (Buffalo, 1848) 106, (Quinault): Farrand JE II 114 No. 10.

D469.6. Transformation: belt to bridge. D1335.4. Magic belt gives strength. D1349.1.4. Magic belt produces immunity from hunger. D1355.9. Magic belt produces love. D1361.13. Magic belt renders invisible. D1381.18. Magic belt assures victory. D1387.3. Magic belt protects against husband. D1410.4. Possession of mermaid's belt gives power over her. D1470.1.12. Magic wishing-belt. D1501.5. Magic belt assists in childbirth. D1524.2.2. Belt carries owner over water. D1539.2. Magic belt carries tree away. F302.5.5. Fairy mistress tries to destroy mortal's wife (mother) by sending her a magic belt.

D1057.1. *Magic girdle.* Herbert III 207; Oesterley No. 10. — Middle English: Wells 55 (Sir Gawayne and the Green Knight), 85 (Sowdone of Babylone); Irish: Plummer clxxxi, *Cross; Jewish: *Neuman; Chinese: Werner 218; Tuamotu: Stimson MS (z-G. 13/152, 221, z-G. 3/1146, 1301.).

D1323.17. Magic clairvoyant girdle. D1344.7. Saint's girdle renders invulnerable. D1356.2. Saint's girdle represses lust. D1365.4. Girdle causes forgetfulness. D1381.14. Magic girdle protects from all wounds. D1389.16. Magic girdle protects from pain. D1472.2.1. Magic wishing-girdle supplies food. D1500.1.13.1. Saint's girdle as magic cure. D1500.2.6. Magic girdle prevents disease. D1514.2. Magic girdle relieves pain. D1549.2. Saint's girdle causes tree to fall in right direction. D1566.2.7. Magic girdle produces stream of water to quench fire.

D1058. *Magic underclothing.*

D1058.1. *Magic shift.* Ward II 603.

D1331.2.3. Virgin Mary's shift as banner causes blindness to opposing army.

D1061. *Magic veil.* Greek: Fox 262; Africa (Zulu): Callaway 201.

D1351.3. Magic veil changes enmity into peacefulness. D1361.33. Magic veil renders invisible. D1381.26. Magic veil protects from attack. D1388.0.2. Magic veil keeps man from sinking in water. D1549.6. Saint's veil quells volcano.

D1062. *Magic stockings.* Breton: Sébillot Incidents s.v. "bas"; Eskimo (Greenland): Rink 173.

D1364.8. Enchanted stockings cause magic sleep. D1380.26. Reindeer hose from corpse protect women. D1385.19.1. Saint's hose protects woman from devil.

D1063. *Magic garter.* *Fb "hosebånd" I 650b; *Chauvin V 230 No. 130.

D1520.9. Magic transportation by garter.

D1064. *Magic pocket.* Chauvin VI 104 No. 270 n. 2.

D1451.1. Inexhaustible pocket furnishes money.

D1065. *Magic footwear.*

D1065.1. *Magic boots.* *Type 328; Saintyves Perrault 283, 286; Fb "stövle" III 642a. — Irish myth: Cross; Breton: Sébillot Incidents s.v. "bottes"; French Canadian: Barbeau JAFL XXIX 10; Russian: Andrejev No. 515**; Hindu: Penzer I 25ff.; N. A. Indian: cf. Thompson Tales 315 n. 145.

D1361.38. Magic boots render invisible. D1521.1. Seven-league boots. D1524.2.1. Boots carry owner on sea.

D1065.1.1. *Boots produced by magic.* Welsh: MacCulloch Celtic 96f.

D1065.2. *Magic shoes.* Type 515**; *Chauvin V 229 No. 130; Penzer I 24 n. 1; Fb "sko" III 288a; Icelandic: Boberg.

D1313.13. Magic shoe points out road. D1520.10. Magic transportation by shoes. D1532.3. Magic shoes bear person aloft. D1532.3.1. Special shoes enable hero to climb a stone pillar. D1601.36. Self-going shoes. F823. Extraordinary shoes.

D1065.3. *Magic snowshoes.* N. A. Indian (Menomini): Skinner JAFL XXVII 98.

D1615.5. Singing snowshoes.

D1065.4. *Magic moccasins.* N. A. Indian: *Thompson Tales 303 n. 109i, 322 n. 164, (Zuñi): Parsons JAFL XXXI 242 No. 16.

D1355.11. Magic moccasins produce love. D1566.1.2. Magic fire-moccasins. D1602.4. Self-returning moccasins.

D1065.5. *Magic sandals.* Irish myth: Cross; Greek: Fox 34, Frazer Apollodorus I 153 n. 3 (Perseus); India: Thompson-Balys, Penzer 28, III 56, VII 235.

D1520.10.1. Magic transportation by sandals. D1521.1.1. Sandals with magic speed. D1532.4. Magic sandals bear person aloft.

D1065.6. *Magic gaiters.* Penzer I 27.

D1065.7. *Magic slippers.*

D1326.1. Magic slippers approve or disapprove judicial decisions. D1401.7. Magic slipper beats person.

D1066. *Magic glove.* Fb "styrke" III 630a. — Icelandic: *Boberg.

D1335.3. Magic iron glove gives strength. D1364.29. Touch of glove and ring causes sleep. D1500.4.5. Gloves thrown after ship cause disease. D1605.3. Magic thieving glove. D1653.1.2.1. Gloves make spear-cast infallible.

D1067. *Magic head-wear.*

D1520.11. Magic transportation by cap (hat). D1532.8. Magic headdress bears person aloft.

D1067.1. *Magic hat.* *Fb "hat" I 563b, "usynlig" III 985b; Mt. 581*; Saintyves Perrault 291. — Irish myth: Cross; Icelandic: Herrmann Saxo II 596; Greek: Fox 195 (Hermes); Breton: Sébillot Incidents s.v. "chapeau"; N. A. Indian (Haida): Alexander N. Am. 261, (Lkuñgen): Hill-Tout JAI XXXVII 342.

D1300.1. Hat gives magic wisdom. D1313.2. Hat thrown in air indicates road. D1323.10. Hat gives clairvoyance. D1361.14. Magic hat renders invisible. D1470.1.13. Magic wishing-hat. D1475.4. Magic soldier-producing hat. D1542.9.3. Magic hat brings flood. D1546.1.1. Hat which turns the sun. D1601.3. Magic hat works independently. D1610.26.2. Speaking hat.

D1067.2. *Magic cap.* *Types 328, 566; *BP I 470ff.; *Aarne MSFO XXV 116; *Chauvin V 229 No. 130; *Fb "kappe" II 89a, "ønske" III 1178b. — Icelandic: Bosa saga 38, Boberg; Greek: Frazer Apollodorus I 153 n. 3 (Perseus), Fox 34; Chinese: Eberhard FFC CXX 253; Korean: Zong in-Sob 152ff.; Japanese: Mitford 185ff; N. A. Indian: *Thompson Tales 339 n. 221a.

D1300.2. Cap gives magic wisdom. D1361.15. Magic cap renders invisible: tarnkappe. D1470.1.14. Magic wishing-cap. D1531.5. Witch flies with aid of magic cap or hood.

D1067.3. *Magic hood.* Irish myth: *Cross; Eskimo (Greenland): Rink 470.

D537.1. Transformation by donning hood. D568. Transformation by turning magic hood. D1344.8.1. Hood renders invulnerable. D1525.1. Magic hood enables person to pass under water.

D1067.3.1. *Magic cowl.* Irish: Plummer clxxxi, *Cross.

D1344.8. Saint's cowl renders invulnerable. D1361.16. Saint's cowl renders invisible. D1382.9. Magic cowl protects from fire. D1447.2.10. Saint's cowl protects fox from hounds. D1500.1.13.2. Saint's cowl as magic cure. F930.1.0.1. Dashing sea does not touch saint's cowl. Q552.18.1.1. Cowl demanded as ransom from saint bursts into flames.

D1067.4. *Magic mask.* Irish myth: Cross.

D1361.32. Magic mask renders invisible.

D1068. *Magic collar.* Irish myth: Cross.

D1316.8. Magic collar indicates falsehood by squeezing throat, truth by falling to ground. D1810.8. Magic knowledge from dream.

D1068.1. *Magic hunting collar.* Irish myth: Cross.

D1449.2. Magic hunting collar insures death of game.

D1069. *Magic clothes — miscellaneous.*

D1069.1. *Magic handkerchief.* Korean: Zong in-Sob 91f.

D1402.28. Handkerchief whirled vs. advancing army stretches them lifeless. D1500.1.35. Magic healing handkerchief.

D1069.2. *Magic feather dress.*

D1520.35. Magic transportation by feather-dress.

D1070. Magic ornaments. Tawney I 300, II 150; De Cock Studien 156; Encyc. Rel. Ethics III 392—472. — Jewish: *Neuman; India: Thompson-Balys.

D1342.5. Amulet guarantees health. D1344.3. Amulet renders invulnerable. D1355.20. Green stone causes women to love the possessor. D1383.6. Magic red stone protects from poison. D1384.4.2. Magic blue stone prevents fatigue during swimming. D1385.24. Amulet guards against sorcery. D1387.1. Amulet preserves chastity. D1389.9.1. Magic red stone protects against poverty. D1392.1. Amulet saves one from death. D1400.1.6. Magic amulet in mouth conquers enemies. D1427.2. Woman's arm-tassel lent to ogre compels her to follow him. D1500.1.8. Magic amulet cures disease. D1501.6. Amulet assists in childbirth. D1504.2. Amulet cures nosebleed. D1548.0.1. Amulet has control over weather. D1577.2. Charm renders amulet efficacious. D1587.1. Magic amulet expels person from land. D1611.18. Magic buckle answers for fugitive. D1651.13. Jewel responds to owner's voice. F820. Extraordinary clothing and ornaments. H422.1. Crown exposes infidelity of husbands. V152. Rosary.

D1071. *Magic jewel (jewels).* **J. Evans Magic Jewels of the Middle Ages and Renaissance (Oxford, 1922); **G. F. Kunz The Magic of Jewels and Charms (Philadelphia, 1915); **R. Grötzinger Das Geheimnis der Amulette und Talismane (Leipzig, 1919); **R. H. Laarsz Talismanische Magie (Leipzig, 1920); **E. A. W. Budge Amulets and Superstitions (Oxford, 1930); *Hdwb. d. Abergl. I 374; *Penzer III 167, VIII 172ff., 195 n. 1; *Chauvin V 4, 293 No. 443; *Reinhard PMLA XXXVIII 434 n. 32. — Irish myth: *Cross; Icelandic: *Boberg; Italian Novella: Rotunda; Jewish: *Neuman; India: Thompson-Balys; Chinese: Ferguson 149, Eberhard FFC CXX 25, 67, 105.

D861. Magic object stolen. D1301.3. Marvelous ruby teaches bird speech. D1314.8. Jewels aid in search for treasure. D1331.1.5. Jewel gives magic sight. D1337.1.12. Magic jewel beautifies. D1349.3. Magic stone makes water like wine. D1349.4. Magic jewel makes owner fat. D1358.3. Magic crystal makes owner courageous. D1361.19. Magic jewel renders invisible. D1364.32. Jewel causes magic sleep. D1380.11. Magic jewel protects. D1400.1.5. Magic jewel conquers enemies. D1400.1.14. Magic stone (jewel) gives victory. D1442.11. Diamond charms serpents into harmlessness. D1456.3. Magic jewel provides wealth. D1470.1.42. Magic wishing-jewel. D1500.1.9. Magic jewel cures disease. D1503.6. Magic jewel heals wounds. D1520.29.1. Transportation by magic pearl. D1521.5. Jewel gives miraculous speed. D1531.11. Gem gives power of flying. D1541.2.2. Magic pearl draws storm away. D1545.1. Magic jewel controls tides. D1549.3.4. Magic gem causes river waters to recede. D1551.7.1. Diamond in snake king's forehead in hero's pocket opens lake waters to reveal pathway to underground palace. D1557.3. Magic diamond provides ingress to subterranean palace. D1561.12. Jewel brings good luck. D1610.27. Speaking jewel. D1641.14. Jewelry intended by groom for prospective bride strangely disappears and a slip of paper alone is left in box. D1645.1. Incandescent jewel. D1662.3. Diamond works by being pressed. D1682. Magic jewel which outweighs many heavy objects in the scale. E711.4. Soul in necklace.

D1071.0.1. *Jewels produced by magic.* *Type 403. — Irish myth: *Cross; India: Thompson-Balys; N. A. Indian: *Thompson Tales 329 nn. 190, 190a, 190b.

B722. Magic stone in animal's head. D1469.3. Shower of gems from magic anvil.

D1071.1. *Magic beads.* Breton: Sébillot Incidents s.v. "chapelet".

D1456.1. Magic beads produce treasure. D1549.11. Magic beads break ice jam.

D1072. *Magic hair ornaments.*

D1072.1. *Magic comb.* See references to D672; in a large proportion of the occurrences of that motif (Obstacle flight) the comb is one of the magic objects thrown. Köhler-Bolte I 177.

D1364.9. Comb causes magic sleep. D1377.1. Magic comb changes person's size at will. D1500.1.32. Magic comb as cure.

D1072.2. *Magic hairpin.* Chinese: Werner 264.

D1364.16. Hairpin causes magic sleep.

D1072.3. *Magic brooch.* Penzer I 26.

D1073. *Magic necklace.* Irish myth: Cross; Icelandic: MacCulloch Eddic 261, 263, *Boberg; India: Thompson-Balys, Penzer III 30f.

D1366.2. Lack of magic necklace causes forgetfulness. D1381.6. Stone necklace protects from attack. D1520.34. Transportation by means of necklace. D1561.11. Necklace brings good luck. D1610.27.1. Speaking necklace.

D1074. *Magic bracelet.* *Chauvin VI 107 No. 272 n. 4; Chinese: Werner 308f.

D1317.4. Magic bracelet warns of poison. D1402.6. Magic bracelet kills man. D1470.1.39. Magic wishing bracelet.

D1075. *Magic bangle.* India: Thompson-Balys; Africa (Vai): Ellis 235 No. 36.

D1602.5. Self-returning bangle. D1651.13. Jewel responds to owner's voice.

D1076. *Magic ring.* *Types 400, 554*, 560, 665; *Aarne MSFO XXV 43; *Bolte Reise der Söhne Giaffers 214; *Kittredge Witchcraft 111, 439f. nn. 49—58; *Bolte Zs. f. Vksk. XX 66; Köhler-Bolte I 110f., 308ff.; *Fb "ring" III 60ab, "ønske" III 1178b; **A. Stern Hessische Blätter für Volkskunde XXX 106; *Chauvin V 229 No. 130, VI 108 Nos. 272, 273; Penzer I 26, VI 73; Bédier Fabliaux 442; Herbert III 207; *Oesterley No. 10. — Irish: MacCulloch Celtic 172, *Cross; English: Wells (King Horn) 9, 11 (Horne Childe and Maiden Rimnild), 65 (Ywain and Gawain), Child I 189f.; Icelandic: *Boberg; Italian Novella: Rotunda; Breton: *Sébillot Incidents s.v. "bague"; Jewish: Neuman; India: Thompson-Balys; Arabian: Burton Nights VI 243, VII 283, X 1—54, S III 51, 72, 136ff., S V 245; Chinese: Werner 331, Eberhard FFC CXX 67; Sumatran: Dixon 163; Africa (Wakweli): Bender 106.

B548.1. Animal recovers lost wishing ring. D771.10. Disenchantment by ring. D1310.4.1. Magic ring tells how another fares. D1311.18. Oracular ring. D1316.4. Magic ring permits owner to learn person's secret thoughts. D1316.4.1. Magic ring shows the true nature of its possessor. D1317.5. Magic ring gives warning. D1317.5.1. Magic ring warns of poison. D1317.5.2. Magic ring awakens in the morning. D1318.9. Ring reveals guilt. D1335.5. Magic ring gives strength. D1338.5. Rejuvenation by ring. D1342.1. Magic ring gives health. D1344.1. Magic ring renders invulnerable.. D1355.4. Ring produces love. D1361.17. Magic ring renders invisible. D1364.0.1. Ring wakes from sleep. D1365.5. Ring causes forgetfulness. D1368.2. Magic ring causes illusion. D1372.1. Magic ring causes continued sneezing. D1376.1.2. Magic ring makes nose grow long (restores it). D1380.23. Magic ring protects. D1382.11. Magic ring protects against fire. D1383.3. Magic ring protects against poison. D1384.1. Magic ring prevents discomfort. D1384.7. Magic ring prevents losing one's way. D1385.3. Marriage ring protects from devil. D1388.0.1. Magic ring protects from drowning. D1389.9.2. Magic ring prevents poverty. D1395.5. Magic ring enables captive to escape. D1400.1.2. Magic ring conquers enemy. D1402.0.2.3. Magic ring causes person to be drowned. D1402.12. Magic ring kills. D1405.1. Magic ring causes person to disappear. D1407.1. Magic ring helps gambler win. D1413.2. Ring prevents person from rising from chair. D1425.2 Magic ring causes woman to come to man. D1431.3. Pursuit by magic ring. D1456.2. Magic ring provides money. D1470.1.15. Magic wishing ring. D1477.2. Magic ring furnishes livestock. D1487.1. Magic ring makes sea-weeds grow. D1500.1.15. Magic healing ring. D1507.1. Magic ring restores speech. D1520.12. Magic transportation by ring. D1549.3.6. Ring of hay thrown into empty lake fills it up with water. D1561.1.2. Magic ring brings good luck. D1566.2.5. Ring makes boiling water cold. D1567.9. Ring brings forth water from dry soil. D1592.1. Magic ring cools boiling water. D1602.17.1. Magic ring when sold returns to original owner. D1610.8. Speaking ring. D1612.2.1. Magic ring compels would-be fugitive to keep calling out, "Here I am." D1662.1. Magic ring works by being stroked. D1821.3.5. Magic sight by looking through ring. E761.4.4. Life token: ring rusts. E761.5.3. Life token: ring springs asunder. E761.7.1. Life token: ring pressed finger. H433.1. Ring as chastity index. T85.4.1. Ring of Fastrada.

D1077. *Magic fan.* India: Thompson-Balys; Chinese: Werner 242, 245, 359, 361f., Graham; Japanese: Ikeda.

D1331.1.3. Fan gives magic sight. D1381.21. Magic fan protects against attack. D1400.1.3. Magic fan conquers enemy. D1425.3. Magic fan summons prince for heroine. D1431.2. Pursuit by magic fan. D1532.10. Magic fan bears person aloft. D1542.4.1. Magic fan produces rain. D1543.3. Magic fan produces wind. D1566.2.2. Magic fan quenches fire.

D1078. *Magic chain (ornament).* Wesselski Märchen 174 No. 64; Irish myth: *Cross.

D536.1. Transformation to swans by taking chains off neck. D723.1. Disenchantment by putting chains around neck. D1251. Magic chain (iron). D1381.19. Magic chain protects from attack. D1388.0.3. Magic chain protects from drowning. D1561.2.3. Magic power in chain, lost when chain is stolen. D1563.2.1. Magic chain renders orchard barren. D1671. Silver in chain increases in fire. H251.3.6. Chain around neck tests truth. Tightens when wearer speaks falsehood.

D1078.1. *Magic blue ribbon.* (Cf. D1835.4.) French Canadian: Sister Marie Ursule.

D1079. *Magic ornaments — miscellaneous.*

D1079.1. *Magic crown.* French Canadian: Sister Marie Ursule.

D1079.2. *Magic diadem.* Jewish: Neuman.

D1079.3. *Magic ornamental breastplate.* (Cf. D1101.3.) Jewish: Neuman.

D1080. Magic weapons. Irish: *Cross, Plummer clxxxv; Icelandic: *Boberg; English: Wells 132 (Sir Launfal); Jewish: Neuman; India: Thompson-Balys; Hindu: Keith 152; Chinese: Werner 161.

D1311.17. Divination by magic weapon. D1381.8. Arms that protect from attack. D1400.1.4. Magic weapon conquers enemy. D1402.7. Magic weapon kills. D1402.19. Weapons magically venomous. **D1438. Magic weapon** pursues victim. D1442.10. Magic whip makes docile animal-guardians of wonderful birds. D1500.1.17. Magic weapon cures disease. D1503.14. Wound healed by wounding weapon. D1542.2.1. Sacred weapon thrown into sky causes drought. D1564.7. Magic weapon (sword, axe) cuts hair (on water, in wind). D1601.4. Automatic weapon. D1601.14.3. Magic axe cuts off enemy's head. D1610.9. Speaking weapon. D1618.4. Weapons weep as warning to master. D1645.8. Magic flaming arms. D1653.1.8. Magic mirror as infallible weapon. D1655.1. Invisible weapons. D1674. Iron blessed by saint incapable of wounding. D2163.1. Broken weapons magically restored. F830. Extraordinary weapon.

D1081. *Magic sword.* **Burton Sword; *Types 328, 611, 665; *Fb "sværd" III 690ab; *MacCulloch Childhood 202; *Chauvin VI 66 No. 233; Gaster FL II 57; Penzer I 109 n. 1, IV 235f., VI 28 n. 2, 72 n. 1, VIII 154 n. 2. — Welsh: MacCulloch Celtic 191, 197f.; Irish: O'Suilleabhain 63, Beal XXI 324, Plummer clxxxv, *Cross; Icelandic: *Boberg; Finnish: Kalevala runes 12, 36, 39; Breton: Sébillot Incidents s.v. "épée"; French Canadian: Barbeau JAFL XXIX 10; Spanish: Boggs FFC XC 67 No. 508*; Scotch: Macdougall and Calder 197; English: Wells 115 (Sir Eglamour of Artois); Greek: Frazer Apollodorus II 63 n. 4; Jewish: *Neuman; India: Thompson-Balys; Arabian: Burton Nights IV 176, VI 221f., 230, VII 41, 44, S VI 221f., 426, S VII 257; Indo-Chinese: Scott Indo-Chinese 303; Chinese: Werner 121, 236; Korean: Zong in-Sob 59; Cape Verde Islands: Parsons MAFLS XV (1) 354; S. A. Indian (Mataco): Métraux MAFLS XL 132.

D631.3.3. Sword large or small at will. D771.8. Disenchantment by sword. D1316.11. Sword turns upon owner when untruth is uttered. D1336.1. Magic sword gives weakness. D1344.11. Magic sword gives invulnerability. D1346.9. Magic sword gives immortality. D1361.18. Magic sword renders invisible. D1364.27. Sword causes magic sleep. D1386.1. Magic sword protects woman from fairy lover in husband's absence. D1389.14. Sword puts to flight evil passions. D1400.1.4.1. Magic sword conquers enemy. D1400.1.4.1.1. Sacred sword of saint repulses army of heretics. D1402.7.1. Magic sword kills man. D1402.7.1.1. Magic sword slays a man daily. D1402.7.1.2. Magic sword always inflicts mortal wounds D1404.2. Drop of hound's blood from magic spear (lance) pierces owner's foot (head). D1421.1.8. Magic sword (rubbed) summons genie. D1500.1.17.1. Magic sword cures disease. D1520.8.1. Magic transportation by sword. D1531.3. Magic sword gives power of flying. D1532.12. Magic sword carries person through air. D1543.4. Magic sword produces wind. D1564.6. Magic sword cuts stone and fells trees. D1566.1.3. Magic sword causes fire and smoke. D1601.4.1. Automatic sword. D1610.9.1. Speaking sword. D1601.5.1. Stick turns into automatic magic sword. D1645.4. Incandescent sword. D1645.8.4. Magic flaming sword. D1652.9. Monkey cut in two by magic sword becomes two monkeys. D1653.1.1. Infallible sword. D1654.4.1. Sword can be moved only by right person. D1666. Sword leaves no trace of blow behind it. D1766.6.2. Sign of the cross made over sword endows it with magic powers. E163. Man kept alive by consecrated sword. F343.3. Fairy smith gives knight magic sword. F405.1. Priest bans spirit with sword. F833. Extraordinary sword. F1087. Hero's marvelous sword falls and cuts off hand of enemy. H435.1. Sword as chastity index.

D1081.1. *Sword of magic origin.* Welsh: MacCulloch Celtic 197; Irish myth: Cross; Indo-Chinese: Scott Indo-Chinese 303.

A523.1. Giant sword of culture hero. D813.1.1. Magic sword received from Lady of Lake. D878.1. Magic sword returned to lake whence it was received. F244.1. "The Four Jewels of the Tuatha Dé Danann." F343.10.1. Fairy gives hero magic sword.

D1082. *Magic saber.* Type 308*, 576***; *Chauvin V 230 No. 130, 259 No. 154 n. 1. — Breton: Sébillot Incidents s.v. "sabre".

D1400.1.4.2. Magic saber conquers enemy. D1520.8. Magic transportation by saber.

D1083. *Magic knife.* *Type 576**, 576******. — Icelandic: *Boberg; Jewish: Neuman; Eskimo (Greenland): Holm 68, Rasmussen I 230; Africa (Ekoi): Talbot 127, 211.

D1173. Magic carving knife. D1313.8. Magic two-edged knife indicates direction. D1317.17. Knife sings as warning of fraud. D1400.1.4.3. Magic knife conquers enemy. E761.4.1. Life token: knife stuck in tree rusts (becomes bloody). K113.6. Alleged resuscitating knife sold.

D1083.1. *Magic poignard (dagger).* *Basset 1001 Contes I 143; Breton: Sébillot Incidents s.v. "poignard".

D1335.6. Magic dagger gives strength. D1364.10. Dagger causes magic sleep. D1381.9. Dagger protects owner from attack. D1653.1.9. Infallible dagger. D1654.4.5. Dagger sticks to killer's hand.

D1084. *Magic spear.* (Cf. D1086.) MacCulloch Childhood 203; Greek: Fox 72 (Prokris); Irish myth: *Cross; Icelandic: *Boberg; Gaster Thespis 158; Hindu: Keith 140; India: Thompson-Balys; Chinese: Werner 316, 355; Hawaii: Beckwith Myth 492; Eskimo (Greenland): Rasmussen III 192; Africa (Benga): Nassau 177 No. 24, (Duala): Lederbogen Märchen V 138.

A941.3.1. Spring breaks forth where magic spear strikes ground. D1311.17.1. Magic spear gives omen of victory. D1317.16. Magic spear warns of danger. D1355.0.1. Magic spear produces love-sickness. D1337.5. Magic spear gives beauty. Also gives ugliness at will. D1381.17. Spear in ground pointed toward ferocious animal protects. D1389.5. Magic spear protects against spell. D1400.1.4.4. Magic spear conquers enemy. D1402.7.2. Magic spear kills. D1402.8. Magic spear always inflicts mortal wounds. D1438. Spell causes spear to pursue and slay man. D1445.2. Magic spear kills animals. D1549.3.8. Spear stuck in river bed stops water. D1549.5.1. Fountain of clear water appears when spear is driven into earth. D1601.4.2. Automatic spear. D1602.6. Self-returning spear. D1610.9.3. Speaking spear. D1645.8.1. Magic flaming spear. D1651.1.1. Spear can be wielded by only one person. D1653.1.2. Unerring spear. D1654.4.4. Magic spear cannot be pulled out of ground.

D1084.1. *Magic spear-head.* Welsh: MacCulloch Celtic 198f.; Africa (Benga): Nassau 177 No. 24 (version 1).

D1402.8.1. Magic all-killing spear-head. D1564.4.1. Magic spear-head cuts down trees. D1602.6.1. Self-returning spear-head.

D1085. *Magic javelin.* Hindu: Tawney I 166.

D1086. *Magic lance.* *Gaster FL II 57; Irish myth: *Cross; Welsh MacCulloch Celtic 202; Jewish: Neuman.

C855.1. Tabu: failing to make gift to magic lance. The lance kills. D1311.17.3. Lance sounds when knocked on shield, except when its owner will be defeated. D1402.7.3 Magic lance kills. D1645.8.3. Magic flaming lance. D1654.4.3. Lance imbedded in earth cannot be moved. F832.1.1. Gaí bulga. F991.1. Bleeding lance.

D1087. *Magic sling.* Irish myth: *Cross.

D1653.1.3. Infallible sling.

D1091. *Magic bow.* *Type 592; Icelandic: *Boberg; Greek: Fox 139 (Odysseus); Hindu: Penzer IV 55; Chinese: Werner 312; Eskimo (Greenland): Rasmussen II 213; S. A. Indian (Mataco): Métraux MAFLS XL 99.

D1338.10. When bow is taken away from owner he loses all strength. D1400.1.4.5. Hercules' bow and arrow essential to capture Troy. D1421.4.2. Magic bow summons giant. D1470.1.34. Magic wishing-bow. D1651.1. Only master able to bend bow. D1653.1.4. Unerring bow. F65. Giant shot into upper world by means of magic bow.

D1092. *Magic arrow.* *Chauvin V 230 No. 130; Köhler-Bolte I 554. — Irish myth: Cross; Icelandic: *Boberg; Breton: Sébillot Incidents s.v. "flèches"; Greek: Pauly-Wissowa s.v. "Anaphe", Fox 84, 131; Jewish: *Neuman; Hindu: Tawney I 166, 358, 438; Chinese: Werner 182, 312; Chinese-Persian: Coyajee JPASB XXIV 185; Hawaii: Dixon 75; N. A. Indian: *Thompson Tales 315 n. 145a, 333 n. 203, 356 n. 287b, (Seneca): Curtin-Hewitt RBAE XXXII 318 No. 58, 514 No. 109, (Cree, Menominee): Skinner JAFL XXVII 98; Eskimo (Greenland): Holm 37, Rink 316; S. A. Indian (Jibaro, Eastern Equador): Boas JAFL XXXII 446 (from Karsten Myths of the Jibaros), (Mataco): Métraux MAFLS XL 99, 132, (Toba): ibid. 77; Africa (Fang): Einstein 71, (Vai): Ellis 191 No. 8; Jamaica: Beckwith MAFLS XVII 277 No. 89.

A955.2. Island created by shooting arrow. D1311.17.2. Divination by magic arrow. D1314.1. Magic arrow indicates desired place. D1327.1. Magic arrow locates fish. D1400.1.4.5. Hercules' bow and arrow essential to capture Troy. D1400.1.4.7. Magic arrows annihilate army. D1402.7.5. Magic arrow kills. D1438.2. Magic arrow pursues victim. D1421.2.1. Magic arrow summons water-spirit. D1520.13. Magic transportation by arrow. D1549.1. Magic arrow shakes heavens. D1566.1.1. Magic arrow sets fire to whatever it hits. D1601.30. Automatic arrows. D1602.16. Arrow shot at bull returns to shooter. D1610.9.2. Speaking arrow. D1612.6.2. Arrows shake when master is disturbed. D1653.1.5. Unerring arrow. D1654.4.2. Arrow can be moved only by owner. D1655.1.1. Invisible arrows. F53. Ascent to upper world on arrow chain. F831. Extraordinary arrow. Q566.10. Demons shoot fiery arrows at souls in hell.

D1092.0.1. *Magic arrow makes five wounds.* India: Thompson-Balys.

D1092.1. *Magic quiver.* Hindu: Penzer IV 54.

D1093. *Magic missile.* Hindu: Meyer Hindu 75 n.; Fuegian: Alexander Lat. Am. 340; N. A. Indian: *Thompson Tales 356 n. 287b.

D1653.1.6. Unerring stone missile.

D1093.1. *Boomerang effect of hurled missiles caused by a saint.* *Loomis White Magic 131.

D1093.1.1. *Arrows returned upon those who shoot saint.* *Loomis White Magic 114.

D1094. *Magic cudgel (club).* *Types 563, 534*; BP I 349ff.; *MacCulloch Childhood 214; Aarne MSFO XXVII 1—96; Gaster Thespis 158, Oldest Stories 231; Spanish: Boggs FFC XC 49 No. 330; French Canadian: Barbeau JAFL XXIX 9; India: Thompson-Balys; Chinese: Werner 196; Tonga: Gifford 178; N. A. Indian: *Thompson Tales 336 n. 214; S. A. Indian (Toba): Métraux MAFLS XL 75; Africa (Gold Coast): Barker and Sinclair 44 No. 4; Jamaica: Beckwith MAFLS XVII 248 No. 25.

D881.2. Recovery of magic object by use of magic cudgel. D1380.19. Magic club protects ten men. D1400.1.7.1. Magic club (staff) gives victory. D1401.1. Magic club beats person. D1402.10.1. Stick becomes a sword, flies through air to kill ferocious animal-guardians of extraordinary lotus. D1427.6. Magic club brings thieves to master. D1438.3. Magic club flies through air after victim. D1472.1.31. Magic food-providing pair of sticks. D1520.27.1. Magic transportation by club. D1601.5. Automatic cudgel. K1605. Thief catcher caught by his magic club.

D1651.2. Magic cudgel works only for master. D1663.1.1. Magic club kills and revives. F835.1. Winking club. Z312.2. Giant ogre can be killed only with iron club he carries (with own sword).

D1095. *Magic hammer (Mjölnir).* Icelandic: MacCulloch Eddic 78ff.

D1096. *Magic firearms.*

D1402.7.4. Magic cartridge kills.

D1096.1. *Magic gun.* *Type 304, 594*; *Fb "bøsse" IV 86b, "skyde" III 345b. — Breton: Sébillot Incidents s.v. "fusil"; Spanish: Boggs FFC XC 49 No. 330.

D1651.11. Stolen gun works only for master. D1652.4. Magic gun is always loaded. D1653.1.7. Infallible gun.

D1096.2. *Magic pistol.* Breton: Sébillot Incidents s.v. "pistolet".

D1526.3. Magic pistol forces one to run behind the ball.

D1096.3. *Magic bullet.* Fb "sølvknap", "sølvkugle" III 737a; Japanese: Ikeda.

D1385.4.1. Witch shot dead with a bullet of salt.

D1097. *Magic battle-axe.* Chinese: Werner 196.

D1400.1.4.6. Magic stone axe conquers enemies.

D1101. *Magic armor.* Irish myth: *Cross; Icelandic: *Boberg; Korean: Zong in-Sob 64; Eskimo (Greenland): Holm 16.

D1080. Magic weapons. D1381.8. Arms protect from attack. D1381.10. Magic armor protects from attack. D1389.11. Magic armature protects soul from hurt. D1400.1.15. Armor gives victory. D1610.24. Speaking armor. K1563. Husband (god) traps wife and paramour with magic armor.

D1101.1. *Magic shield.* Andrews MPh. IX 27, 32. — Irish myth: *Cross; Icelandic: Boberg; Spanish: Boggs FFC XC 67 No. 508*A; Jewish: Neuman; N. A. Indian (Seneca): Curtin 5.

D44. Transformation to likeness of the person whose shield one carries. D1317.13. Magic shield roars when bearer is in danger. D1336.4. Magic shield gives weakness. D1382.5.1. Flaming shield does not burn owner. D1402.0.1.1. Magic shield shoots balls of fire among enemies. D1549.10. Waves answer roar of magic shield. D1610.24.1. Magic shield roars. D1645.8.2. Magic flaming shield. D1672.1. Flaming shield unquenchable. D1812.5.1.25. Falling of shield as evil omen. D1812.5.1.17.3. Roaring shields as evil omen. E761.7.9. Life token: flaming shield goes out. F343.10.3. Fairy gives person invulnerable shield. F824.2. Extraordinarily painted shield. F839.2.1. Gigantic shield. F839.2.2. Edge of shield sharp enough to cut hair on water. F995. Shield shrieks in battle.

D1101.2. *Magic cuirass.* Spanish: Boggs FFC XC 67 No. 508A*

D1381.10.2. Magic unpierceable cuirass.

D1101.3. *Magic breastplate.* Irish myth: Cross.

D1381.10.1. Magic inpenetrable breastplate. D1079.3. Magic ornamented breastplate.

D1101.4. *Magic helmet.* Irish myth: *Cross; Icelandic: *Boberg; Greek: Frazer Apollodorus I 47 n. 3.

D1344.13. Magic golden helmet renders invulnerable. D1361.20. Helmet renders invisible. D1381.10.3. Magic unpierceable helmet. D1388.0.6. By means of magic helmet it is possible to stay on the bottom of the sea as long as one wants. D1389.8. Magic helmet prevents baldness. D1400.1.17. Magic helmet gives victory. D1610.24.2. Helmet shrieks.

D1101.5. *Magic scabbard.* Jewish: *Neuman.

D1413.25. Magic scabbard causes sword to stick to it.

D1101.6. *Magic yoke.*

D1381.10.4. Magic impenetrable yoke.

D1102. *Magic trident.* India: Thompson-Balys.

D1110. Magic conveyances.

D1523.2.6. Bundle of wood magically acts as riding-horse. F861. Extraordinary wagon (cart, carriage, etc.)

D1111. *Magic carriage.* *Chauvin V 229 No. 130.

D1520.14. Transportation in magic carriage.

D1111.1. *Carriage produced by magic.* Saintyves Perrault 151ff.; Type 510.

D315.1. Transformation rat to person. D411.6.1. Transformation mouse to horse. D452.1. Transformation pumpkin to carriage. D1521.4. Carriage as swift as thought.

D1112. *Magic cart.* Breton: Sébillot Incidents s.v. "charette".

D1113. *Magic wagon.* *Type 675; *Fb "vogn" III 1078a.

D1317.10. Wagon refuses to move because ghost is sitting in it. D1523.1. Self-propelling wagon. D1654.5. Wagon refuses to move.

D1114. *Magic chariot.* *Chauvin V 229; Loomis White Magic 35f.; Jones PMLA XXIII 574; *Fb "guldkaret" I 513b. — Irish myth: *Cross; Greek: Fox 115, 119, 213, *Frazer Apollodorus I 38 n. 2; Jewish: *Neuman; Hindu: Keith 108, Penzer IV 3ff., 8ff.

D1532.5. Magic chariot bears person aloft. D1533.1.2. Magic land and water chariot. D1601.33. Chariot collects flowers by itself. D1654.5.1. Chariot refuses to move.

D1115. *Magic sleigh.* Fb "kane".

D1413.3. Sleigh makes person magically hold on. D1521.3. Sleigh as swift as thought.

D1118. *Magic airships.* *BP III 273. — Irish myth: *Cross; India: Thompson-Balys; N. A. Indian: *Thompson Tales 275 n. 14d.

D1520.19. Magic transportation by carpet. D1532. Magic object bears person aloft. D2135. Magic air journey. F841.3.1. Winged ship. F861.2. Winged chariot. F1021.1. Flight on artificial wings.

D1118.1. *Magic air-riding basket.* Cox Cinderella 323; N. A. Indian (Atsina): Curtis N. A. Indian V 123.

D1121. *Magic boat.* (Cf. D1123.) *Barry JAFL XXVIII 195. — Irish myth: *Cross; Icelandic: Boberg; Jewish: Neuman; Arabian: Burton Nights I 242f.; India: Thompson-Balys; Chinese: Eberhard FFC CXX 150; Eskimo (Greenland): Rink 154, 300, 417, Holm 43, Rasmussen III 102, 294, (Smith Sound): Kroeber JAFL XII 26, 171, (Bering Strait): Nelson RBAE XVIII 500, (Kodiak): Golder JAFL XXII 17, (Mackenzie Area): Jenness 41, (Cumberland Sound): Boas BAM XV 181, (Central Eskimo): Boas RBAE VI 628; N. A. Indian: *Thompson Tales 275 n. 14a.

D1470.1.43. Magic wishing-boat. D1502.4.3. Touching magic boat with exposed child in it cures leprosy. D1523.2. Self-propelling boat. D1523.2.7.1. Self-guiding rudderless boat. D1525. Magic submarine boat. F841.1.1. Stone boat (ship). K14.1. Rowing contest won by deception: magic boat.

D1121.0.1. *Boat made by magic.* Breton: Sébillot Incidents s.v. "bateau"; Finnish: Kalevala rune 16.

D632. Boat transforms self at will of master. D632.1. Island canoe.

D1121.1. *Magic hollow-log boat.* N. A. Indian: Thompson Tales 275 n. 14e.

D1122. *Magic canoe.* (Cf. D1121.) Marquesas: Handy 46; N. A. Indian: *Thompson Tales 275 n. 14e.

D631.3.1. Compressible canoe. D632.1. Island canoe. D1523.2. Self-propelling (ship) boat. D1524.3.1. Stone canoe.

D1122.1. *Canoe made by magic.* Polynesian, Melanesian, Indonesian: Dixon 68 nn. *39, *40; N. A. Indian: *Thompson Tales 275 n. 14b; Eskimo (Cumberland Sound): Boas BAM XV 192.

D1123. *Magic ship.* (Cf. D1121.) *Fb "skib" III 242b, 243ab; *Chauvin V 201 No. 117 n. 1; cf. Cox Cinderella 159, 480 n. 11. — Irish myth: Cross; Welsh: MacCulloch Celtic 192; Breton: Sébillot Incidents s.v. "navire"; English: Child IV 376—380, V 275f., 484 s.v. "Jonah"; Icelandic: *Boberg; Finnish: Kalevala rune 30, 39; Greek: Fox 138, *Frazer Apollodorus I 109 n. 4.

D631.3.1.1. Compressible ship. D1310.3. Intelligent ship. D1318.10. Ship reveals guilt. D1361.21. Ship becomes invisible. D1469.15. Magic ship furnishes treasure. D1520.15. Transportation in magic ship. D1521.2. Ship with miraculous speed. D1523.2. Self-propelling ship. D1525. Magic submarine ship. D1532.11. Magic journey in flying boat. D1533.1.1. Magic land and water ship. D1610.11. Speaking ship. D1654.6. Ship refuses to move. D1982.2. Ship made invisible. F841. Extraordinary boat (ship).

D1124. *Magic oar.* Breton: Sébillot Incidents s.v. "aviron"; Eskimo (Greenland): Rasmussen II 153, 157.

D1343.1. Magic oars give skill. D1523.2.1. Automatic oar.

D1124.1. *Magic paddle.* India: Thompson-Balys.

D1130. Magic buildings and parts.

D1675. Garden wall that cannot be overleapt.

D1131. *Magic castle.* Breton: Sébillot Incidents s.v. "château"; English: Wells 17 (Reinbrun, Gy sone of Warwike); Spanish: Boggs FFC XC 56 No. 408A*.

D6. Enchanted castle (building). D1457.1. Magic castle provides treasure. D1645.3. Magic castle shines from afar. F636.4. Remarkable stone-thrower. Makes castle. F771. Extraordinary castle.

D1131.1. *Castle produced by magic.* *Type 554, 560, 561, 675, 512*; *Aarne MSFO XXV 44; *BP II 455ff., 547ff.; India: Thompson-Balys.

D6. Enchanted castle. H1133. Task: Building castle.

D1132. *Magic palace.* Irish myth: *Cross; Spanish: Boggs FFC XC 56 No. 408*A; English: Wells 145 (Parthenope of Blois); India: Thompson-Balys Tawney I 257.

B572. Animals build palace (home) for hero. D1472.1.5. Magic palace supplies food and drink.

D1132.1. *Palace produced by magic.* *Chauvin V 63 No. 19. India: Thompson-Balys; Chinese: Werner 183.

D1483.1. Palace arises from bull's legs buried in soil.

D1133. *Magic house.* *Fb "hus" I 686b. — Irish myth: *Cross.

D1133.1. *House created by magic.* India: Thompson-Balys; Chinese: Graham; N. A. Indian (Seneca): Curtin-Hewitt RBAE XXXII 349 No. 60, 392 No. 70; Africa (Kaffir): Theal 77.

D1133.1.1. *Magic house made by prayer.* India: Thompson-Balys.

D1766.1. Magic results produced by prayer.

D1134. *Magic church (temple).*

D1557.4. Gate of temple opens and shuts by magic.

D1134.1. *Church produced by magic.* Cheremis: Sebeok-Nyerges.

D1136. *Magic fort.*

A179. God as rath-builder. A538. Culture hero builds raths. A1435.2. Origin of raths. D2031.13. Magic rath always seems distant, never near. F163.5. Fortress in otherworld. F163.6. Stronghold in otherworld. F531.6.3.1.

Giants live in castles (raths, duns) (ruins of which may still be seen). F531.6.6. Giants as builders of great structures. F770. Extraordinary buildings and furnishings. H1133. Task: building castle (fort, rath). P427.6.3. Druids as rath-builders. P447.2. Smith as rath-builder.

D1136.1. *Fort produced by magic.* Irish myth: *Cross; Breton: Sébillot Incidents s.v. "fort".

A179. God as rath-builder. A538. Culture hero builds raths. A1435.2. Origin of raths. D2031. Magic illusion. F221.1. Fairy house disappears at dawn F222. Fairy castle. F531.6.6. Giants as builders of great structures. K1870. Illusions. P427.6.3. Druids as rath-builders. P447.2. Smith as rath-builder.

D1138. *Magic tent.* *Chauvin VI 135 No. 286 n. 1; Icelandic: Hjalmþers Saga ok Ölvis 468; Indonesian: DeVries Volksverhalen II 365, No. 114.

D631.3.2. Compressible tent. D1380.4. Magic tent protects occupant.

D1141. *Magic room.*

F165.3. Rooms in otherworld dwellings. F223. Fairy hall. F781. Extraordinary rooms.

D1141.1. *Magic kitchen.* Hindu: Tawney II 226.

D1472.1.6. Magic kitchen supplies food and drink.

D1144. *Magic stairs.* Spanish: Boggs FFC XC 49 No. 330.

D1413.4. Stairs to which person sticks.

D1145. *Magic windows.* Type 329; BP III 366.

D1323.3. Magic clairvoyant windows.

D1146. *Magic door (gate).* Jewish: *Neuman; N. A. Indian (Shasta): Farrand-Frachtenberg JAFL XXVIII 216 No. 6.

D1381.30. Magic gate swallows axes trying to force it open. D1402.9. Magic door catches bear so that he is burned to death. D1557.1. Door (lock) magically opens for saint. D1601.37. Self-opening door. D1651.8. Door will open only for hero. D1654.15. Door stuck by witchcraft so that it cannot be opened. D1658.1.4. Continually slamming doors grateful for being fastened. D1982.1. Magic door invisible to women. F91.1. Slamming door on exit from mountain otherworld. F782.2. Door of precious stones.

D1146.1. *Magic doorstep.* Chinese: Graham.

D1413.16.1. Magic doorstep will not let person pass over.

D1147. *Magic hearth.* Irish myth: Cross.

D1683. Hearth cleaned by angel always free of ashes.

D1148. *Magic tomb.* Jewish: Neuman.

D1149. *Magic buildings and parts — miscellaneous.*

D1149.1. *Store, fully supplied, produced by magic.* Cheremis: Sebeok-Nyerges.

D1149.2. *Magic tower.* Jewish: Neuman.

D1365.9. Tower causes magic forgetfulness.

D1149.3. *Magic house-pillars.* Eskimo (Greenland): Rink 442.

D1317.21. House-pillars warn. D1610.30.1. Speaking house-post.

D1150. Magic furniture. BP II 527.

E761.4.2. Life token: picture burns black.

D1151. *Magic seat.* *BP II 188. — Icelandic: De la Saussaye 286, Hrólfs saga Kraka ch. 33, *Boberg.

D1310.1. Magic seat gives omniscience. H41.9. King recognized by unique ability to occupy certain seat.

D1151.1. *Magic bench.* *Type 330.

D1413.5. Bench to which person sticks.

D1151.2. *Magic chair.* *BP II 188; *Chauvin V 229 No. 130. — Breton: Sébillot Incidents s.v. "chaise"; Swiss: Jegerlehner Oberwallis 322 No. 92; Greek: Fox 206, Frazer Apollodorus II 152 No. 4; Jewish: Neuman.

D1413.6. Chair to which person sticks. D1520.16. Magic transportation by chair. D1601.28. Self-rocking chair. H411.6. Magic chair as chastity test.

D1153. *Magic table.* *Types 563, 564; BP I 346ff.; *Aarne JSFO XXVII 1—96 passim, MSFO XXV 118; *Köhler-Bolte I 109; *Chauvin V 272 No. 154. — Irish myth: *Cross; Icelandic: Boberg; English: Wells 32 (Layamon's Brut); Swiss: Jegerlehner Oberwallis 297 No. 28.

D1415.3. Magic table causes the persons who look at it to dance. D1470.2.5. Supplies from magic table. D1472.1.7. Magic table supplies food and drink.

D1153.1. *Magic tablecloth.* *Type 569, 851, 853; BP I 464ff.; *Aarne MSFO XXV 118; Penzer I 25f. — Breton: Sébillot Incidents s.v. "serviette".

D1395.2. Escape from prison by use of tablecloth. D1472.1.8. Magic tablecloth supplies food.

D1154. *Magic couch.*

D1520.17.2. Transportation on magic couch.

D1154.1. *Magic bed.* German: Grimm No. 4; Irish: O'Suilleabhain 57; Jewish: Neuman.

D631.6. Bed large or small at will. D1317.11. Bedstead warns of danger of snake. D1380.12. Magic bedstead protects from harm. D1385.22. Bedstead at doorway prevents spirit from entering. D1500.4.7. Magic bed causes disease. D1520.17.1. Magic transformation on flying bedstead. D1610.17. Speaking bed.

D1154.1.1. *Magic bed-legs.*

D1402.17. Magic bedstead-legs kill dangerous animals. D1610.17.1. Talking bed-legs.

D1154.2. *Magic sofa.* *Chauvin V 230 No. 130.

D1520.17. Magic transportation by sofa.

D1154.3. *Magic hammock.* Africa (Vai): Ellis 200 No. 18.

D1520.18. Magic transportation by hammock.

D1154.3.1. *Magic swing.*

D1530.18.1. Transportation on magic swing.

D1154.3.2. *Magic palanquin.*

D1520.18.2. Transportation in magic palanquin.

D1154.4. *Magic divan.* (Cf. D1310.8.) India: Thompson-Balys.

D1310.8. Speaking and walking divan brings supernatural information.

D1154.5. *Magic pillow.* Papua: Ker 109.

D1364.11. Pillow causes magic sleep. H411.10. Magic bed and pillows as chastity test.

D1155. *Magic carpet.* *Chauvin V 230 No. 130; Fb "luftrejse" II 457a. — Cape Verde Islands: Parsons MAFLS XV (1) 111 No. 39; Chinese: Werner 192; Eskimo (Greenland): Rasmussen III 62.

D1511.1. Magic carpet cures drunkenness. D1520.19. Magic transportation by carpet D1658.2.2. Grateful carpets.

D1156. *Magic throne.* Chauvin V 230 No. 130.

A661.0.2.1. Heavenly music caused by four columns under Lord's chair.

D1520.20. Transportation by magic throne. D1654.17. Throne of goddess's idol is lifted only after goat has been sacrificed. F785. Extraordinary throne.

D1157. *Magic platform.* *Chauvin V 230 No. 130.

D1520.21. Transportation by magic platform.

D1158. *Magic key.* *Type 531.

D1161. *Magic stove.* *Fb "ovn" II 774a.

D1601.6. Oven heats without fire. D1610.12. Speaking stove. D1658.2.1. Grateful stove. D1641.3. Stove runs over hill.

D1162. *Magic light.* *Types 328, 562; *Thompson CColl II 361ff.; *Fb "lys"; Irish myth: *Cross.

A124.0.1. God with luminous countenance. A661.0.7. Self-illuminating precious stones in heaven. B15.7.12. Eel with fiery mane. B15.7.13. Bird with fiery beak. B19.4. Glowing animals. D1271. Magic fire. D1318.11. Light reveals guilt. D1322.2. Light moving toward cemetery as sign of death. D1361.27. Magic light renders invisible. D1381.29. Speaking lamp prevents king from killing queen. D1421.1.4. Magic light summons genie. D1478. Magic object provides light. D1500.4.4. Ray of sunlight causes leprosy. D1503.5. Magic lantern heals wounds. D1470.1.17. Magic wishing-lantern. E761.7.4. Life token: light goes out. F552.2. Fingers of saint give light. F574. Luminous person. F969.3.2. Hero's light. F969.3.1. Marvelous light reveals man hiding from saint. H71.6.1. Luminous face as sign of royalty. H1341. Quest for magic lantern. V211.1.3.1. Vast intolerable light on night of Christ's Nativity. V222.0.1.3. Dazzling heavenly light by day and night marks place of saint's birth. V222.1. Marvelous light accompanying saint. V241.2.1. Angels shed light upon saint's tomb.

D1162.1. *Magic lamp.* *Types 561, 301C*; *BP II 544ff. — Jewish: Neuman; India: Thompson-Balys; Chinese: Graham; Africa (Angola): Chatelain 45.

D1316.2. Magic lamp indicates falsehood by lighting. D1323.19. Lamp gives him who looks into its flame a vision of the Most High. D1373.0.1.3. Magic lamp (eaten, causes thirst). D1385.29. Magic lamp protects against demons. D1470.1.16. Magic wishing-lamp. D1601.7. Lamp lights self. D1652.6. Ever-burning lamp. D1662.2. Magic lamp works by being stroked. H411.13. Magic lamp as chastity test.

D1162.2. *Magic candle.* Type 301C*; Icelandic: Boberg.

D1652.11. Ever-burning candle. E64.6. Resuscitation by candle. E765.1.1. Life bound up with candle. H41.3. Test of king (pope): his candle lights itself.

D1162.2.1. *Hand-of-glory.* Magic candle made of criminal's hand. *Kittredge Witchcraft 144f., 463 nn. 50, 55; Penzer III 150; Baker AA old ser. I 51ff.; *Fb "tyvefinger"; *Taylor JAFL XXXI 561. — Irish myth: Cross; England, Ireland, Wales: *Baughman.

D996. Magic hand. D1314.5. Hand-of-glory indicates location of treasure. D1361.7. Hand-of-glory renders light invisible. D1410.2. Light from hand-of-glory renders persons helpless. D1575.1. Hand-of-glory does not awaken sleepers.

D1163. *Magic mirror.* *Type 709; *BP I 450, 463; *Bolte Reise der Söhne Giaffers 202f.; *Chauvin VIII 191 No. 228; Köhler-Bolte I 334; *Handwb. d. Abergl. IX Nachträge 565—577; *Fb "spejl" III 481a; *MacCulloch Childhood 34—37; *Cox Cinderella 483; Pauli (ed. Bolte) No. 232. — Icelandic: *Boberg; India: Thompson-Balys; Chinese: Werner 244, 331; Cape Verde Islands: Parsons MAFLS XV (1) 111 No. 39; Aztec: Alexander Lat. Am. 62; Africa (Vai): Ellis 200 No. 18, (Fjort): Dennett 60 No. 12, (Angola): Chatelain 43, (Mpongwe): Nassau 15 No. 1.

D579. Transformation by looking in a mirror. D1311.2. Mirror answers questions. D1323.1. Magic clairvoyant mirror. D1331.2.6. Magic mirror causes blindness. D1361.28. Magic mirror renders invisible. D1400.1.13. Magic mirror kills enemy soldier. D1470.1.38. Magic wishing mirror. D1653.1.18. Magic mirror as infallible weapon. D1889.2. Rejuvenation by looking into mirror. E761.4.3. Life token: mirror becomes black (misty).

D1164. *Magic lock.*

D1557.1. Door (lock) magically opens for saint. D2088.0.1. All locks opened on the night of Christ's Nativity.

D1166. *Magic altar.* Jewish: Neuman.

D1618.3. Magic weeping altar.

D1167. *Magic quilt.*

D1365.23. Magic quilt protects wearer from demons and human weapons. D1469.12. Magic quilt: gold coins shake out of it. D1470.1.44. Magic wishing-quilt.

D1170. Magic utensils and implements. Penzer IV 248.

D1601.9. Household articles act at command. D1602.19. Equipment of slain hunter returns alone. D1610.14. Speaking implement. D1611.9. Magic household articles answer for fugitive.

D1171. *Magic vessel.* Fb "tønde" III 934b. — Irish: Plummer clxxxv, *Cross.

D771.5. Disenchantment by drinking from golden vessel. D953.1.1. Magic twigs grow from buried magic vessel. D1318.12. Vessels reveal guilt. D1601.10. Self-cooking vessel. D1652.5. Inexhaustible vessel.

D1171.1. *Magic pot.* *Types 565, 591; *Fb "potte" II 866f.; Jewish: Neuman; India: Thompson-Balys, Penzer I 26ff; Chinese: Eberhard FFC CXX 107, 272; Africa (Basuto): Jacottet 220 No. 33, (Gold Coast): Barker and Sinclair 40f. No. 4.

D1401.4. Magic pot with demons who beat owner's enemy. D1412.2. Magic pot draws person into it. D1452.2. Magic pot furnishes money. D1470.1.19. Magic wishing-pot. D1472.1.9. Magic pot supplies food and drink. D1472.1.12.1. Food-providing frying pan. D1601.10.1. Self-cooking pot. D1605.1. Magic thieving pot. D1615.6. Singing rice-pot. D1651.3. Magic cooking-pot obeys only master. D1652.5.7. Inexhaustible cooking pot. D1654.16. Pot cannot be lifted. E761.5.1. Life token: pot breaks.

D1171.1.1. *Magic coffee-pot.* Fb "tønde" III 934b.

D1472.1.10. Magic coffee-pot supplies drink.

D1171.2. *Magic cauldron.* Brown MPh XIV 385. — Irish: Plummer clxxxvi, *Cross; Welsh: MacCulloch Celtic 95, 101, 110; Hindu: Penzer VII 224f.

D1310.2. Drop from magic cauldron gives supernatural information. D1335.8. Bathing in magic cauldron gives strength. D1337.1.4. Bathing in magic cauldron gives beauty. D1413.14. Magic cauldron to which one sticks. D1472.1.11. Magic cauldron supplies food. D1601.10.2. Magic cauldron boils a year. D1601.10.2.1. Magic cauldron boils only enough of its contents to satisfy immediate need. E64.2. Resuscitation by magic cauldron. F686.1. Cauldron warmed by breath of nine maidens. H1336. Quest for magic cauldron.

D1171.3. *Magic kettle.* *Fb "gryde" I 494b. — Japanese: Mitford 175ff.; N. A. Indian: *Thompson Tales 349 n. 257.

D1452.1. Magic kettle furnishes money. D1472.1.12. Magic kettle supplies food. D1601.10.3. Self-boiling kettle. D1610.13.1. Speaking kettle. D1646.3. Dancing kettle.

D1171.4. *Magic pitcher.* *Chauvin V 230 No. 130; Penzer V 3 n. 1; Chinese: Graham.

D1469.9. Silver leaps into wine pitcher. D1472.1.13. Magic pitcher supplies drink. D1520.22. Transportation by magic pitcher. D1651.4. Inexhaustible pitcher stops pouring only at owner's command. D1652.5.4. Inexhaustible pitcher.

D1171.5. *Magic can.* Fb "kande".

D1171.6. *Magic cup.* Type 301C*; *Fb "sølvbæger" III 736b, "tønde" III 934b, "ønske" III 1178b, "bæger" IV 83a; *Loomis and Lindsay Magic Horn and Cup in Celtic and Grail Tradition (Romanische Forschungen XLV [1931] 66); *Boberg Des Knaben Wunderhorn-Oldenburgerhornet (Festskrift til L. L. Hammerich [København, 1952] 53). — Irish: *Cross, MacCulloch Celtic 171; Welsh: ibid. 202f.; Manx: Hartland Science 156f.; Greek: Fox 86; Icelandic: *Boberg; Jewish: *Neuman; Hindu: Penzer I 25.

D491.1.1. Herd of cattle put into magic cup. D1311.21. Divination by cup. D1346.14. Magic cup gives immortality. D1365.6. Magic cup causes forgetfulmess. D1380.17. Magic cup protects. D1389.3. Magic cup protects against loss of strength. D1400.1.8. Magic cup gives victory. D1410.6. Drink from magic cup deprives man of legs. D1472.1.14. Magic cup supplies drink. D1472.1.14.1. Magic food-providing cup. D1645.2. Incandescent cup. D1665.1. Drink has taste of any liquor desired. E64.5. Resuscitation by magic cup. E761.5.4. Life token: cup springs asunder. F866.1. Cup of three hundred colors. H411.4. Magic drinking horn (cup) as chastity test.

D1171.6.1. *Magic tankard.* Chinese: Werner 382.

D1472.1.15. Magic tankard supplies drink.

D1171.6.2. *Magic goblet (glass).* *Fb "tønde" III 934b. — Irish myth: *Cross; Greek: *Frazer Apollodorus I 213 n. 2.

D1316.6. Magic goblet indicates falsehood by breaking, truth by reassembling. D1396.1. Magic goblet breaks spells. D1472.16. Magic glass supplies drink. D1503.8. Magic goblet heals wounds. D1520.23. Transportation by magic goblet. D1652.5.1. Magic goblet cannot be filled.

D1171.6.3. *Magic drinking horn.* Irish myth: *Cross; Icelandic: Herrmann Saxo II 593, 596, *Boberg.

D1317.18. Magic drinking horn gives warning. D1472.1.24.1. Magic drinking horn supplies wine. D1610.25. Magic drinking horn with a man's head speaks. D1652.17. Inexhaustible horn. H411.4. Magic drinking horn (cup) as chastity test. N223. Man must have drinking horn: stumble reveals one as he departs on search.

D1171.6.4. *Magic chalice.* Jewish: Neuman.

D1171.7. *Magic vase:* *Chauvin V 259 No. 154; India: Thompson-Balys; Chinese: Werner 348.

D1323.2. Magic clairvoyant vase. D1610.13.2. Speaking jar. D1652.5.5. Inexhaustible vase of bonbons.

D1171.7.1. *Magic jar.* Philippine (Tinguian): Cole 50f.

D1171.8. *Magic bottle.* *Köhler-Bolte II 471; *Fb "flaske" I 309a; Hartland Science 142. — Breton: Sébillot Incidents s.v. "bouteille", "flacon"; Chinese: Werner 202.

D1335.7. Flask imparts magic strength to drinker. D1364.12. Contents of bottle cause magic sleep. D1500.1.16. Magic healing bottle. D1601.35. Magic water bottle brings water.

D1171.8.1. *Magic cruet.* Irish myth: Cross.

D1602.13. Self-returning cruet.

D1171.9. *Magic barrel (cask).* *Fb "styrke" III 630a, "tønde" III 934b. — Swiss: Jegerlehner Oberwallis 297 No. 6.

D1652.5.2. Inexhaustible barrel.

D1171.10. *Magic bucket.* Chinese: Werner 221, 233.

D1431.4. Pursuit by magic bucket.

D1171.11. *Magic basket.* Irish myth: *Cross; Welsh: MacCulloch Celtic 192; Chinese: Werner 233; Tonga: Gifford 113.

A137.4. God (goddess) with basket. D1472.1.23. Magic basket supplies food. D1476.3. Magic basket (box) furnishes slaves. D1477.4. Magic basket (box) furnishes livestock. D1652.5.8. Inexhaustible food basket.

D1171.12. *Magic basin.* *BP II 40 n. 2.

D1413.7. Basin to which one sticks.

D1171.13. *Magic chamber-pot.* *BP II 40 n. 2; Eskimo (Greenland): Rink 452.

D1413.8. Chamber-pot to which one sticks.

D1171.14. *Magic tub.* Irish myth: Cross.

D1324.1.1. Magic tub drips at high tide, is watertight at ebb tide. D1338.10. Rejuvenation by magic tub. F1081. Tub of water dropped neither breaks nor spills.

D1171.15. *Magic urn.* Irish myth: Cross.

D1472.1.25. Magic urn supplies drink.

D1172. *Magic dish.* English: Child I 126.

D1610.13. Speaking dish.

D1172.1. *Magic plate.* *Fb "tønde" III 934b.

D1472.1.20. Magic plate supplies food.

D1172.2. *Magic bowl.* Irish myth: Cross.

D1349.2.2. Washing in magic bowl produces immunity from old age. D1472.1.33. Magic bowl supplies food. D1519.1.1. Magic bowl restores strength.

D1173. *Magic carving knife.* (Cf. D1083.) Magic knife (weapon). English: Child I 266; Swiss: Jegerlehner Oberwallis 293 n. 1.

D1472.2.11 Magic knife stuck in tree causes wine to flow. D1583. Magic carving knife serves twenty-four men at meat simultaneously. E434.7. Knives as protection against revenants.

D1173.1. *Magic razor.* Chinese: Werner 366; Africa (Angola): Chatelain 45 (version B).

D1364.13. Razor causes magic sleep. D1601.8. Razor whets itself.

D1174. *Magic box.* *Type 561; Cox Cinderella 484 n. 19, 489; *Chauvin V 230 No. 130. — Breton: Sébillot Incidents s.v. "boîte", "coffre"; Scotch: Macdougall and Calder 161; India: Thompson-Balys; Chinese: Eberhard FFC CXX 67; Japanese: Ikeda; N. A. Indian (Micmac, Maliseet): Thompson CColl II 398f.; Africa (Ekoi): Talbot 185, (Angola): Chatelain 45.

D1400.1.23.2. Lightning in magic box kills an army sent by king to conquer hero. D1452.3. Lid of casket furnishes money. D1470.1.20. Magic wishing-box. D1470.2.2. Supplies received from magic box. D1472.1.21. Magic chest supplies food. D1520.24. Transportation by magic box. D1533.2.1. Box which travels above or below ground. D1541.1.5. Tempest box raises storm. D1651.12. Box can be opened only by right person.

D1174.1. *Magic box containing castle.* Lithuanian: Balys Index No. *320.

D1131. Magic castle. D1132. Magic palace.

D1175. *Magic match.* Breton: Sébillot Incidents s.v. "briquet".

D1175.1. *Magic tinder.* Fb. "fyrtøj" I 390b. — Breton: Sébillot Incidents s.v. "amadou".

D1421.1.1. Magic tinder summons genie.

D1175.2. *Magic fire-steel (flint, strike-a-light).* *Type 562.

D1421.1.2. Magic fire-steel summons genie.

D1176. *Magic key.* Fb "nøgle"; Irish: O'Suilleabhain 27, 29, Beal XXI 309; Jewish: Neuman; Chinese: Eberhard FFC CXX 221.

C913. Bloody key as sign of disobedience. D1552.12. Magic key opens treasure mountain. D1810.0.8.1. Druid's "keys of wisdom". E434.6. Keys as protection against revenants.

D1177. *Magic spoon.*

D1601.34. Self-serving spoon.

D1181. *Magic needle.* *Type 585; Fb "synål"; Köhler-Bolte I 187. — Irish myth: Cross; Icelandic: Boberg; Breton: Sébillot Incidents s.v. "aiguille"; Jewish: Neuman.

D1337.1.7. Magic needle transforms a room from plainness to beauty. D1364.14. Needle causes magic sleep. D1562.4. Magic needle makes everything fall to pieces. D1601.11. Self-sewing needle.

D1182. *Magic pin.* *Type 400; *Basset 1001 Contes I 143.

D582. Transformation by sticking magic pin into head. D1364.15. Pin causes magic sleep. H411.5. Magic pin as chastity test.

D1183. *Magic scissors (shears).* Köhler-Bolte I 187; Fb "saks" III 143a. — Irish myth: *Cross; Chinese: Werner 158; Africa (Angola): Chatelain 45 (Version B).

D1355.15. Magic shears produce love. D1601.12. Self-cutting shears.

D1184. *Magic thread.* Köhler-Bolte I 187; Jewish: Neuman; Chinese: Eberhard FFC CXX 152.

D1385.18. Magic thread protects against demons. D1601.13.1. Selftying thread.

D1184.1. *Magic ball of thread.* *Köhler-Bolte I 407; Fb "nøgle".

D1313.1.1. Magic ball of thread indicates road. D1610.28. Speaking ball of thread.

D1184.2. *Magic string.* Penzer VI 59ff.

D1380.10. Magic string protects. D1413.18. Magic ball of string to which one sticks.

D1185. *Magic shuttle.* *Type 585.

D1484.1. Magic shuttle makes road. D1485.1. Magic shuttle makes carpet.

D1186. *Magic spindle.* *Types 410, 585; Saintyves Perrault 62.

D1364.17. Spindle causes magic sleep. D1425.1. Magic spindle brings back prince for heroine.

D1187. *Magic awl.* BP II 527. — Icelandic: MacCulloch Eddic 267; Breton: Sébillot Incidents s.v. "alène".

D1523.2.2. Boat propelled by magic awl. D1611.10. Magic awl answers for fugitive.

D1187.1. *Magic auger.* Icelandic: Snorra Edda Skaldsk. II, Boberg.

D1188. *Magic hone.* Icelandic: Snorra Edda Skaldsk. II, Boberg.

D1192. *Magic purse.* *Types 564, 566, 580*; *Aarne MSFO XXV 116; *Fb "pung", "Fortunatus". — Breton: Sébillot Incidents s.v. "bourse", Hartland Science 174; Arabian: Burton Nights I 215; Hindu: Penzer I 20 n, 25ff.

D1364.28. Smoke from magic purse makes man sleep. D1395.3. Escape from prison by use of magic purse. D1413.9.1. Wallet from which one cannot escape. D1451. Inexhaustible purse furnishes money.

D1193. *Magic bag (sack).* *Types 330, 563, 564; *Chauvin V 272 No. 154; Fb "ransel", "pose". — Icelandic: *Boberg; Breton: Sébillot Incidents s.v. "blague"; Spanish: Boggs FFC XC 49 No. 330; Swiss: Jegerlehner Oberwallis 314f. No. 114, 322 No. 92; India: Thompson-Balys, Penzer I 28. — N. A. Indian (Ojibwa, Potawatomi): Skinner JAFL XXVII 98.

D1318.14. Sack of gold retains at will any hand thrust in it. D1324.1. Magic bag full at high tide, empty at ebb tide. D1388.0.5. By means of magic bag it is possible to stay so long on the bottom of the sea as one wants. D1401.2. Magic sack furnishes mannikin who cudgels owner's enemies. D1410.7. Magic bag shaken against enemies renders them helpless in face of mist or poison. D1412.1. Magic sack draws person into it. D1413.9. Sack holds person who puts hand into it. D1421.5.3. Magic sack contains soldiers which appear when it is struck. D1451.2. Inexhaustible sack furnishes treasure. D1472.1.22. Magic bag supplies food. D1483.2. Magic bag builds palaces of gold and gems. D1520.25. Transportation by magic bag. D1540.1. Magic bag controls storm, mist, darkness, etc. D1605.2. Magic bag sucks milk from cows. D1652.5.9. Inexhaustible food bag. D1652.5.11. Inexhaustible meal sack.

D1193.1. *Magic bag made from skin of crane (transformed woman).* Irish myth: *Cross.

D350. Transformation: bird to person.

D1194. *Magic umbrella.* Chinese: Werner 12, 242.

D1546.1.3. Magic umbrella makes sun stand still.

D1195. *Magic soap.* Scotch: Macdougall and Calder 277.

D1323.6. Magic soap gives clairvoyance.

D1196. *Magic net.* Africa (Benga): Nassau 186 No. 24 version 2.

D1352.1. Magic net has prenatal influence.

D1202. *Magic anvil.* Irish myth: *Cross; Breton: Sébillot Incidents s.v. "enclume"; Chinese: Graham.

A966.2. Hill from anvil cast by supernatural smith. D1413.10. Anvil to which one sticks. D1469.3. Shower of gems from magic anvil. D1566.1.5. Shower of fire from magic anvil. D2143.1.6. Shower (of water) from magic anvil.

D1203. *Magic rope.* *Type 559; *BP II 539; Chinese: Werner 348; Eskimo (Greenland): Rasmussen III 216; Africa (Ekoi): Talbot 402.

D1314.12.1. Rope breaks at proper burial place. D1411.1. Magic rope binds person. D1520.31. Magic transportation by rope. D1582. Climbing into air on magic rope.

D1204. *Magic hoe.* Africa (Zulu): Callaway 363.

D1601.16.1. Self-digging hoe. D1610.14. Speaking hoe.

D1205. *Magic shovel.* Fb "skovl", "redskab".

D1601.15. Automatic shovel.

D1205.1. *Magic spade.* Fb "redskab", "spade"; S. A. Indian (Toba): Métraux MAFLS XL 3.

D1601.16. Self-digging spade.

D1206. *Magic axe.* *Fb "styrke" III 630a, "redskab" III 30a, "økse" III 1171b. — Icelandic: Bósa Saga 58; Irish myth: Cross; Jewish: Neuman; India: Thompson-Balys; Buddhist myth: Malalasekera I 1055; Chinese: Eberhard FFC CXX 107; Tahiti: Beckwith Myth 468.

D1302.1. Magic axe teaches magic. D1335.9. Magic axe gives strength. D1364.0.2. Hero can only wake when a certain axe falls down. D1385.5.2. Axe driven into house entrance keeps werwolf out. D1472.1.35. Water flows from axe. D1524.12. Magic handaxe comes to one over water. D1601.14. Self-chopping axe.

D1206.1. *Magic sickle.* India: Thompson-Balys.

D1207. *Magic wheel.* *Fb "hjul"; Irish myth: Cross; Jewish: Neuman.

D1313.15. Magic wheel indicates road. D1331.2.5. Sight of magic wheel causes blindness. D1332.1.2. Sound of magic wheel causes deafness. D1385.10. Wheel buried in doorstep to prevent deviltry. D1389.4. Magic wheel prevents entrance to fortress. D1402.20. Magic wheel kills all upon whom it falls. D1562.5. Hero crosses impassable plain in path of magic object. D1602.7. Self-returning wheel.

D1207.1. *Destructive "rolling wheel" of druid.* Irish myth: *Cross.

M341.2.20. Prophecy: wholesale slaughter to be inflicted by colossal wheel rolling over Europe. P427. Druid (magus).

D1208. *Magic whip.* Fb "pisk". — Chinese: Werner 161.

D1401.3. Magic whip beats person. D1411.2. Magic whip holds person fast. D1442.10. Magic whip makes docile animal-guardians of wonderful bird. D1470.1.31. Magic wishing whip. D1601.17. Automatic whip.

D1209. *Miscellaneous utensils and implements.*

D1209.1. *Magic bridle.* Greek: Fox 40.

C837. Tabu: loosing bridle in selling man transformed to horse. D535. Transformation to horse by putting on bridle. D722. Disenchantment by taking off bridle. D1442.1. Magic bridle restrains all horses.

D1209.2. *Magic saddle.* *Fb "guldsadel" I 514b, "ønske" III 1178b.

D1470.1.21. Magic wishing-saddle. F868. Extraordinary saddle.

D1209.3. *Magic plow.* Fb "plov"; Irish myth: Cross.

D1209.4. *Magic hammer.* Type 308*; Jewish: Neuman; Korean: Zong in-Sob 144.

D631.3.5. Compressible hammer. D1322.1.1. Hammer in coffin-maker's shop makes noise to announce a death. D1335.13. Magic hammer gives strength. D1401.6. Magic hammer beats person. D1472.2.9. Magic mallet produces provisions. D1500.1.14. Saint's mallet cures disease. D1601.5.2. Automatic hammer kills enemy. D1602.15. Self-returning hammer. D1610.14.3. Speaking hammer.

D1209.5. *Magic fish-hook.*

D1653.2. Infallible fish-hook.

D1209.6. *Magic thong.* Icelandic: MacCulloch Eddic 267.

D1209.7. *Magic game board (chessboard).* Icelandic: *Boberg.

D1601.29. Self-playing game board. D1311.23. Divination with chessboard.

D1209.8. *Magic broom.* India: Thompson-Balys; Chinese: Eberhard FFC CXX 152.

D1601.9.1. Automatic broom.

D1210. **Magic musical instruments.** Finnish: Kalevala rune 41; India: Thompson-Balys; Africa (Basuto): Jacottet 176 No. 25.

D1275. Magic song. D1275.1. Magic music. D1275.2. Magic melody. D1364.25. Musical instrument causes magic sleep. D1415.2. Magic musical instrument causes person to dance. D1441.1. Magic musical instrument calls animals together. D1442.13. Magic musical instrument tames animals. D1500.1.27. Magic musical instrument as cure for disease. D1601.18. Self-playing musical instruments. D1601.18.0.1. Magic musical instrument reproduces songs sung in heaven. D1610.34. Speaking musical instrument. D1651.7. Magic musical instrument plays only for owner. F803. Musical rock in fairyland.

D1211. *Magic drum.* India: Thompson-Balys; Indo-Chinese: Scott 283; Eskimo (Greenland): Rasmussen III 96; Africa (Ekoi): Talbot 47, (Gold Coast): Barker and Sinclair 90 No. 16, (Benga): Nassau 113 No. 11.

C811.1. Tabu: heeding persuasion of drum. D1364.25.2. Drum causes magic sleep. D1402.29. Magic drum enters enemy's body and kills him. D1470.1.22. Magic wishing-drum. D1472.2.3. Magic wishing-drum supplies food. D1601.18.3. Self-beating drum. D1609.1. Drum flies about room. D1651.7.2. Magic wishing-drum works only for owner.

D1212. *Magic rattle.* Ibo (Nigeria): Thomas 119.

D1213. *Magic bell.* Fb "kirkeklokke"; *Thompson CColl II 348, 358, 363. — Irish: Plummer clxxvi—clxxvii, *Cross, Beal XXI 328, O'Suilleabhain 88; English: Child I 173, 231, III 235, 244, 519f.; Breton: Sébillot Incidents s.v. "cloche"; Jewish: *Neuman; Thompson River: Teit JAFL XXIX 320 No. 11.

D1311.12. Oracular bell. D1314.4. Bell indicates place for settlement. D1317.7. Magic bell gives alarm. D1323.4.1. Salvatio Romae. Image of land showing by means of magic bell outbreak of rebellion in any province. D1336.5. Saint's bell gives weakness. D1389.6. Saint's bell carried around tribe averts all danger. D1385.12. Saint's bell disperses demons. D1400.1.9. Saint's bell conquers enemies. D1419.2.1. Magic bell paralyzes perjurer. D1421.0.1. Magic bell summons helper. D1446.1. Saint's bell keeps cattle from straying. D1470.1.30. Magic wishing-bell. D1500.1.27.2. Magic healing bell. D1500.2.1. Saint's bell wards off disease. D1500.3.2. Disease transferred to saint's bell. D1500.1.13.3. Saint's bell cures disease. D1507.3. Saint's bell restores speech. D1508.1. Saint's bell restores reason. D1524.3.2. Saint's bell carried on floating stone. D1563.1.4. Saint's bell starts crops growing. D1601.18.1. Self-ringing bell. D1602.8. Saint's bell, when stolen, miraculously returns. D1602.8.0.1. Self-returning bell. D1654.10. Bell refuses to be moved. D2131.1.1. Church bell rung as protection against storm. To thwart devil. D2175.4. Saint's bell used in cursing. E64.3. Resuscitation by magic bell. E434.1. Hiding from ghosts under church bell. E545.14. The dead hear saint's bell. F933. Sunken bell sounds. F933.1.1. Spring bursts forth where saint spills water from his bell. K1887.3.1. (Saint's) bell heard but never found. M411.8.1. Saint's curse by ringing bells against offenders. V115. Church bells. V222.6. Bell sounds at approach of saint.

D1213.1. *Magic gong.* India: Thompson-Balys.

D1221. *Magic trumpet.* *Aarne MSFO XXV 117; Jewish: Neuman; Africa (Ekoi): Talbot 62.

D1470.1.33. Magic wishing-trumpet. D1475.2. Magic soldier-producing trumpet. E55.3. Resuscitation by blowing trumpet.

D1222. *Magic horn (musical).* *Types 566, 569, 592; *BP I 464ff., 470ff., II 470ff.; *Aarne MSFO XXV 117. — Icelandic: *Boberg; English: Child I 15—17, 23, 55, 367; Italian Novella: Rotunda.

D1355.1.3. Magic love-producing horn. D1359.3.1.1. Magic horn relieves hearers of sorrow. D1415.2.1. Magic horn causes dancing. D1421.5.1. Magic horn summons army for rescue. D1440.1. Magic horn has power over animals. D1470.1.32. Magic wishing-horn. D1475.1. Magic soldier-producing horn. D1562.3. Magic horn blows down wall.

D1223. *Magic clarinet.* Breton: Sébillot Incidents s.v. "clarinette".

D1415.2.2. Magic clarinet causes dancing.

D1223.1. *Magic flute.* (Cf. D1224.) *Type 780; *Fb "fløjte". — Icelandic: Boberg; India: Thompson-Balys; Chinese: Graham; Ibo (Nigeria): Thomas 146.

D1313.7. Magic flute indicates road. D1337.1.11. Playing of magic flute beautifies. D1364.25.1. Flute causes magic sleep. D1415.2.3. Magic flute causes dancing. D1421.6.1. Flute to summon fairy to hero's aid. D1421.3.2. Magic flute summons dwarfs. D1426.1. Magic flute compels woman to come to man. D1441.1.1. Magic flute calls animals together. D1610.34.2. Speaking flute. E55.2. Resuscitation by playing flute.

D1224. *Magic pipe (musical).* *Aarne MSFO XXV 117; *Fb "rotte" III 83a, "ønske" III 1178b; *Type 570, 515*; Penzer III 187. — English: Child I 47; Breton: Sébillot Incidents s.v. "pipe"; N. A. Indian (Central Algonquin): Skinner JAFL XXVII 98.

D1355.1.2. Magic love-producing pipe (musical). D1364.25.3. Pipe (musical) causes magic sleep. D1415.2.4. Magic pipe causes dancing. D1421.1.12. Magic pipe summons genie. D1426.3. Magic pipe compels woman to come to man. D1427.1. Magic pipe compels one to follow. D1441.1.2. Magic pipe calls animals together. D1470.1.23. Magic wishing-pipe. D1472.2.4. Magic wishing-pipe supplies game. D1472.2.8. Magic musical pipe causes food to fall from sky. D1475.3. Magic soldier-producing pipe. D1643.4. Magic pipe travels about.

D1224.1. *Magic flageolet.* Spanish: Boggs FFC XC 75 No. 594*.

D1651.7.3. Magic flageolet stolen but loses its magic power.

D1225. *Magic whistle.* Breton: Sébillot Incidents s.v. "sifflet"; French Canadian: Barbeau JAFL XXIX 10; Missouri French: Carrière.

D1594.6. Magic whistle gives life to cockroach.

D1225.1. *Magic mouth harp.* Chinese: Graham.

D1231. *Magic harp.* Hertz Spielmannsbuch 71, 363; *Fb "harpe" IV 201b; Irish myth: *Cross; Icelandic: *Boberg; English: Child V 482 s.v. "harp"; Greek: Grote I 214; Jewish: Neuman.

D1311.1. Harp struck for divination. D1359.2.1. Magic music causes mourning. D1402.22. Magic harp kills. D1427.5. Magic harp compels one to follow. D1441.1.4. Magic harp calls animals together. D1449.3. Swine summoned out of magic harp. D1500.1.27.1. Magic healing harp. D1507.7. Magic harp restores speech. D1612.5.2. Magic harp gives alarm when it is stolen. D1649.2.1. Harp comes at owner's call. D1651.7.1. Magic harp plays only for owner. F81.1. Orpheus. H411.12. Magic harp as chastity test.

D1231.1. *Magic lyre.* Greek: Fox 44 (Amphion).

D1232. *Magic lute.* Hindu: Tawney I 338 n; Buddhist myth: Malalasekera I 192, II 859.

D1415.2.6. Magic lute causes dancing. D1427.4. Lute (rubbed) compels one to follow. D1441.1.3.1. Magic lute calls animals together.

D1233. *Magic violin (fiddle).* *Types 559, 577, 592, 851, 853; Fb "fiol" I 293b, "spille" III 488a; Basset RTP XXVI 266; Breton: Sébillot Incidents s.v. "violon"; Jewish: Neuman; India: Thompson-Balys, Penzer III 187 n. 3; Cape Verde Islands: Parsons MAFLS XV (1) 280 No. 91; Africa (Gold Coast): Barker and Sinclair 97, 100 No. 18.

D1395.1. Escape from prison by use of magic fiddle. D1415.2.5. Magic fiddle causes dancing. D1423.3.1. Magic fiddle summons dwarfs. D1441.1.3. Magic fiddle calls animals together. D1472.1.32. Magic fiddle provides food. D1531.9. Magic flying by means of magic fiddle. D1601.18.2. Self-playing violin. D1610.34.1. Fiddle made from wood secret has been confided to reveals it. E55.4. Resuscitation by playing violin. K113.5. Alleged resuscitating fiddle sold.

D1233.1. *Magic musical bow.* India: Thompson-Balys.

D1520.33. Magic transportation on musical bow.

D1234. *Magic guitar.* Chinese: Werner 121; Philippine: Fansler MAFLS XII 231, 278.

D1420.3. Guitar charms all who hear it. D1599.1. Pillars dance when ogre plays guitar. E55.5. Resuscitation by playing guitar. E761.5.2. Life token: zither string breaks. K113.8. Alleged resuscitating guitar sold.

D1239. *Magic musical instruments — miscellaneous.*

D1610.34.2. Speaking jew's harp.

D1240. Magic waters and medicines. *Types 331, 513, 551, 576****; *Penzer III 60ff. — Irish myth: *Cross; Breton: Sébillot Incidents s.v. "guérison"; Greek: Fox 72 (Minos), 112 (Medea and Jason); Arabian: Burton Nights I 124, III 259, V 394, IX 204, S VI 328; Hindu: Tawney I 265, 360, 534, 554, II 4ff., 208, 211; Chinese: Werner 275ff.; Africa (Benga): Nassau 208 No. 33.

A454. God of healing. D1344.2 Magic drug renders invulnerable. D1344.2.1. Magic drug gives immunity from fire and iron. D1346.11. Medicine gives immortality. D1355. Love-producing magic object. E100. Resuscitation by medicines. F344. Fairies heal mortals. F379.2.1. Book (medical) brought back from otherworld. H1324. Quest for marvelous remedy. P424. Physician. P427.5. Druid as physician.

D1241. *Magic medicine* (= charm). Hindu: Tawney II 165; India: Thompson-Balys; Africa (Benga): Nassau 100, 139, 178, 208 Nos. 7, 15, 24 (version 1), 33, (Ekoi): Talbot 34, 178, 344, 359, (Hottentot): Bleek 55 No. 24, (Zanzibar): Bateman 204 No. 10, (Fang): Nassau 242 No. 9, (Basuto): Jacottet 212 No. 31.

D771.6. Disenchantment by medicine. D1273. Magic formula (charm). D1313.9. Charm (medicine) indicates direction. D1335.10. Magic medicine (charm) gives strength. D1331.1.2. Medicine gives magic sight. D1346.11. Medicine gives immortality. D1347.3. Magic medicine makes sterile fertile. D1361.22. Magic medicine (charm) renders invisible. D1365.8. Magic medicine (sprinkled on head) causes loss of memory. D1373.1. Fetish medicine causes constant hunger. D1379.5. "Milk-medicine" causes milk to appear in woman's breast. D1413.11. Magic medicine causes person to stick to seat. D1501.8. Medicine causes woman to bear twins. D1524.1.1. Medicine on feet permits man to walk on water. D1542.3.1. Magic medicine causes streams to dry up. D1543.5. Magic medicine produces wind. D1561.1.4. Magic medicine brings success.

D1242. *Magic fluid.* See references for D1040. — Chinese: Werner 216.

D1337.1.8. Magic liquid gives beauty. D1364.7. Sleeping potion: drink causes magic sleep. D1364.12. Contents of bottle cause magic sleep. D1410.3. Magic fluid takes away magic powers. D1500.1.11. Magic healing drink. E102. Resuscitation by magic liquid. E761.6. Life token: troubled liquid.

D1242.1. *Magic water.* (Note: here are included all references to magic water, whether as a remedy or as another type of magic agent). *Types 590, 613; *Christiansen FFC XXIV 79; *Chauvin VI 202; *Fb "vand", "livets vand"; *Pauli (ed. Bolte) Nos. 34, 328; Köhler-Bolte I 118, 143; Morgan MPh. VI 331; Nitze MPh. VII 145; *MacCulloch Childhood 67ff. — Irish: Plummer cl, clxxviii, clxxx, *Cross, O'Suilleabhain 69, Beal XXI 325; Icelandic: Göngu Hrolfs Saga 309, Boberg; Italian Novella: Rotunda; Jewish: *Neuman; Babylonian: Spence 178; Arabian: Burton Nights S VI 213; India: Thompson-Balys, Penzer I 28, III 227f., VI 5, 8, 62; Chinese: Werner 205. — N. A. Indian: *Thompson Tales 354 n. 279; Eskimo (Mackenzie Area): Jenness 47.

A910. Origin of water features. A427.1. Goddesses of springs and wells. D902. Magic rain. D910. Magic body of water. D925. Magic fountain (well, spring). D926.3. Drinking from well prevents sadness and grief. D1040. Magic drink. D1305.1. Drop of water from Paradise gives power of prophecy. D1310.9. Magic water gives knowledge. D1311.3.1.1. Divination by water. D1317.22. Water rages by boat of would-be murderer. D1335.2.2. Water as magic strengthening drink. D1337.1.2. Water gives magic beauty. D1337.2.4. Magic water makes ugly. D1338.1. Magic drink rejuvenates. D1338.1.2. Water of youth. D1346.10. Magic water (sprinkled) gives immortality. D1355.2.1. Water blessed by saint as love-philtre. D1347.3. Impotent king becomes normal after drink of magic elixir. D1375.2.4. Magic water removes horns from person. D1380.5. Magic water protects. D1402.24.1. Giant kills people by sprinkling water on their heads. D1467. Magic water furnishes treasure. D1500.1.1.1. Magic healing well dug by saint. D1500.1.18. Magic healing water. D1502.11. Magic water cures stomach trouble. D1503.16. Wound healed by water from place wounded man's heel dragged. D1505.5. Magic water restores sight. D1567.3. Water poured from saint's bell produces fountain. D1567.7. Fountain produced from drop of water. D1610.36. Speaking water. D1615.4. Singing water. D1646.2. Dancing water. D1658.1.3. Bitter water grateful for being praised. D1811.1.2. Magic wisdom from drinking of well. D2143. Precipitation produced by magic. D2143.1.1. Rain produced by pouring water. D2143.1.6. Shower from magic anvil. D2151. Magic control of waters. D2151.6.1. Saint causes wells to fail. D2151.7.1. Saint causes lakes to dry up. E80. Water of Life. Resuscitation by water. F235.4.4. Fairies made visible through use of magic water. F930. Extraordinary occurrences concerning seas and waters. F933.1. Miraculous spring bursts forth for holy person. H222. Ordeal by water. H1321. Quest for marvelous water. V132. Holy water. V134. Sacred wells.

D1242.1.1. *Baptismal water as magic object.* *Kittredge Witchcraft 150f., 470 nn. 117—125; England: Baughman.

D1355.2.1.1. Baptismal water as love philtre. D1500.1.18.2. Baptismal water as remedy. V81. Baptism.

D1242.1.2. *Holy water as magic object.* Kittredge Witchcraft 124ff., 449f. nn. 1—33 passim; Irish myth: *Cross; England: Baughman.

D1385.15. Holy water and mass prevent demons alighting on grave. D1500.1.18.3. Holy water as remedy. D1562.6. Holy water destroys veil over well. D1810.6. Magic knowledge from bathing in holy water. D1819.4.1. Man enabled to read baptismal service by washing in holy water. E80.4. Resuscitation by holy water. G271.2.2. Witch exorcised by holy water. G303.16.7. Devil is chased by holy water. H222.2. Ordeal by holy water. T512.3. Conception from drinking holy water.

D1242.2. *Magic potion.* Irish myth: *Cross; Icelandic: Þorsteinssaga Vikingssona (FAS II) 394, Flateyarbók I 279, *Boberg; English: Wells 80 (Sir Tristrem), 145 (Parthenope of Blois), Child V 305b; Greek: Fox 200 (Phaon), *Grote I 219; Africa (Hottentot): Bleek 55 No. 24.

D1355.2. Magic love-philtre. D1364.7. Sleeping potion: drink causes magic sleep. D1500.4.1. Magic drink causes disease. D1502.4.1. Magic potion cures leprosy. D1503.13. Magic potion heals wounds. T548.3. Magic elixir to produce a child.

D1242.3. *Magic drops.* Type 576*****; India: Thompson-Balys.

D1338.0.1.1. Elixir retards aging.

D1242.4. *Magic oil.* India: Thompson-Balys; Jewish: *Neuman.

D1361.24. Magic drops render invisible. D1542.1.6. Oil poured in left. Ear of black dog brings rain.

D1243. *Magic pill.* *Chauvin VIII 133 No. 126; India: Thompson-Balys, Meyer Hindu 193, Penzer II 183 n. 1, III 75f, VII 40 n. 1, 41ff., 222f.; Chinese: Werner 134, 159, 184f., 275ff., Eberhard FFC CXX 162.

D551.4.1. Transformation by placing pill in mouth. D765.1.1. Disenchantment by removal of enchanting pill from mouth. D1346.7. Pill of immortality. D1347.1.1. Magic pills insure birth of twin sons. D1347.3. Magic pill makes sterile fertile. D1361.22.1. Magic pills render invisible. D1402.25. Magic pill kills. D1531.2. Magic pill gives power of flying. D1585.1. Magic pill saves corpse from corruption. D1652.1.8. Magic pill on which one feeds self for years. E107. Resuscitation by magic pill.

D1244. *Magic salve (ointment).* *Type 611: *Fb "salve" III 150b, "øje" III 1166b; Chauvin V 41 No. 388, 146 No. 72; Penzer IV 90 n. 1, IX 45 n. 1; Griffith MLN XXV 102. — Irish myth: *Cross; Breton: Sébillot Incidents s.v. "onguent"; Greek: Roscher Lexikon s.v. "Achilleus" I 24, *Grote I 219; Chinese: Werner 276f., 281f; Cape Verde Islands: Parsons MAFLS XV (1) 219 No. 73.

D101. Resuscitation by salve (oil). D771.2. Disenchantment by rubbing with magic grease. D1323.5. Magic salve gives clairvoyance. D1331.2.2. Magic salve causes blindness. D1331.3.1. Salve causes magic sight and blindness. D1338.8. Rejuvenation by magic oil. D1344.5. Magic ointment renders invulnerable. D1341.3. Magic ointment makes person old. D1346.8.1. Magic ointment gives immortality. D1361.22.2. Magic salve renders invisible. D1368.1. Magic snakeoil causes illusions. D1368.1.1. Ointment applied to eyes makes night seem day. D1375.3.1. Magic ointment causes wings to grow on person. D1375.2.3. Magic salve removes horns from person. D1380.21. Magic ointment protects. D1382.4. Magic oil prevents burning. D1384.6. Ointment gives protection on journey. D1385.6. Magic salve protects from enchantment. D1500.1.19.1. Magic healing salve. D1503.4. Magic balm heals wounds. D1505.6. Magic ointment restores sight. D1512.1. Magic ointment cures ulcers. D1520.26. Transportation by putting magic ointment on feet. D1663.1. Ointment cures left cheek. not right. D1821.4. Magic sight by putting ointment into eye. D1846.1. Invulnerability by being burns and anointed with magic ointments. E101. Resuscitation by salve (oil). G224.2. Witch's salve. Source of magic power.

D1245. *Magic perfume.* *Chauvin V 10 No. 7, 60 No. 19 n. 1.

D575. Transformation by fumigations. D1349.1.2. Magic perfume produces immunity from hunger and thirst. E64.8. Resuscitation by perfume.

D1246. *Magic powder.* Type 726*; Chauvin VI 8 No. 273. — India: Thompson-Balys, Tawney I 378; Chinese: Werner 375; Cape Verde Islands: Parsons MAFLS XV (1) 214 No. 73; Africa (Basuto): Jacottet 142 No. 20.

D712.3. Disenchantment by striking. D771.3. Disenchantment by using powder. D1323.13. Magic powder gives clairvoyance. D1331.3.2. Powder causes magic sight and blindness. D1335.11. Powder gives magic strength. D1470.1.40. Magic wishing-powder. D1500.1.20. Magic healing powder. D1551.4. Magic powder causes waters to divide. D1555.2. Magic powder causes earth to open up. D1610.0.1. Magic powder makes objects speak what owner wants them to.

D1248. *Human liver as medicine.* India: Thompson-Balys.

D1250. Miscellaneous magic objects.

D1251. *Magic chain (iron).*

D1078. Magic chain (ornament). D1421.1.11. Magic chain summons genie. D1470.1.40. Magic wishing-chain. F863. Extraordinary chain. F169.6. Gold chain as support in otherworld.

D1251.1. *Iron chain made by magic.* Breton: Sébillot Incidents s.v. "chaine".

D1252. *Magic metal.* Irish myth: *Cross.

F384.3. Iron powerful against fairies.

D1252.1. *Magic steel.* Fb "stål" III 647b; Penzer II 106 n. 4.

E434.5. Steel as protection against revenants. F384.2. Steel powerful against fairies. G272.1. Steel powerful against witches.

D1252.1.1. *Magic iron.* India: Thompson-Balys.

D1252.1.2. *Magic nails.* India: Thompson-Balys.

D1252.2. *Magic copper.* *Zingerle 589.

D1385.5. Copper as defense against ghosts and magic.

D1252.3. *Magic gold.*

A1252.4. Magic gold head. D1507.8. Magic gold taken from hill restores speech when it is laid under the tongue of dumb person. E64.15. Resuscitation by magic gold.

D1254. *Magic staff.* (Cf. D1277.) *Fb "kjæp" II 150—151, "stav" III 541b. — Irish myth: *Cross; Icelandic: MacCulloch Eddic 84, 111, *Boberg; Swiss: Jegerlehner Oberwallis 302 No. 6; Jewish: bin Gorion Born Judas[2] III 19, *Neuman; India: Thompson-Balys, Penzer I 22ff., IX 68f.; Chinese: Graham; Hawaii: Dixon 90; Marquesas: Handy 134; Africa (Kaffir): Theal 145, (Upoto): Einstein 142f., (Bakuba): ibid. 100.

D565.2 Transformation by touching with rod. D1277. Magic bachall. D1300.5. Staff gives magic wisdom. D1310.5. Magic staff gives supernatural information. D1313.5. Magic stick indicates road. D1314.2.5. Saint's staff becomes tree to indicate building site. D1314.2.6. Golden staff stuck into ground finds site for city. D1335.14. Magic strengthening staff. D1361.25.1. Magic staff renders invisible. D1364.18. Staff causes magic sleep. D1381.32. Staff protects from attack. D1400.1.7. Magic staff defeats enemies. D1413.13. Magic stick holds person fast. D1442.4. Magic staff thrown causes wild animals to stand still. D1446.3. Shepherd's consecrated staff keeps cow from straying. D1446.4. Saint's staff serves as a shepherd. D1524.1.2.1. Saint casts staff to distant island. Staff that reaches owner shall have island. D1524.10. Magic staff comes to one over water. D1539.3. Magic staves enable man to gain precipitous height. D1549.5. Magic staff draws water from stone. D1562.1. Magic staff destroys obstacles. D1567.6. Stroke of staff brings water from rock. D1611.12. Magic stick of wood answers for fugitive. D1651.5. Dead beggar's stick will not stay still until back in beggar's service. D1673. Magic staff blossoms. E64.1. Resuscitation by staff. E761.2. Life token: staff stuck in ground.

D1254.1. *Magic wand.* *MacCulloch Childhood 205ff.; *Bolte Reise der Söhne Giaffers 221; Saintyves Perrault 63; *Cox Cinderella 485. — Irish myth: *Cross; Icelandic: Corpus Poeticum Boreale I 115; Breton: Sébillot Incidents s.v. "baguette", "sommeil", "navigation"; Spanish: Boggs FFC XC 67 No. 510; French Canadian: Barbeau JAFL XXIX 9; India: Thompson-Balys; Chinese: Werner 324, 326. — N. A. Indian (Passamaquoddy): Leland 127, (Chilcotin): Farrand JE II 44 No. 30, (Bella Coola): Boas JE I 54, 57, (Kwakiutl): Boas and Hunt JE III 356, (Mandan): Curtis N. A. Indian V 39ff., (Salishan): Boas Proc. Am. Philosophical Soc. XXXIV 38.

D565.2. Transformation by touching with rod. D467.1. Transformation wand to bridge. D771.4. Disenchantment by using wand. D1337.1.9. Magic wand beautifies. D1342.0.1. Quest for magic wand. D1342.4. Magic wand gives health. D1361.25. Magic wand renders invisible. D1364.18. Wand causes magic sleep. D1402.10. Magic wand kills. D1414.1. Magic wand breaks enemy's sword. D1409.1.1. Magic wand brings evil upon person. D1470.1.24. Magic wishing-wand. D1473.1. Magic wand furnishes clothes. D1500.1.21. Magic healing wand. D1505.7. Magic wand restores sight. D1520.27. Magic transportation by means of wand. D1523.2.3. Boat propelled by magic wand. D1542.4. Magic wand keeps outdoor sleeping place dry. D1555.1. Magic wand opens underground passage. D1663.1. Wands of life and death. K113.4. Alleged resuscitating wand sold.

D1254.1.1. *Magic pair of sticks.* India: Thompson-Balys.

D1254.2. *Magic rod.* (Cf. D1254.1.) Fb "pilegren"; Krappe MLN LVIII (1943) 515ff. — Irish myth: *Cross; Jewish: *Neuman; Hindu: Penzer I 22ff.; Chinese: Eberhard FFC CXX 87, 107; Hawaii: *Beckwith Myth 466; Africa (Kaffir): Theal 129, (Zulu): Callaway 307.

D1311.4.0.1. Oracular twig. D1311.15. Magic rod used for divination. D1314.2. Magic wand locates hidden treasure. D1355.16. Magic rod produces love. D1364.26. Silver rods cause magic sleep. D1399.1. Magic spinning rod pulls horse out of the earth. D1404.1. Magic rod pierces whatever diverted against. D1442.4.1. Magic rod tames lions. D1470.1.25. Magic wishing-rod. D1472.2.10. Magic rod provides water. D1549.9. Magic rod causes all waters to turn to blood. D1551.2. Magic iron rod causes waters to divide and close. D1552.1. Mountain opens at blow of divining rod. D1557.2.1. Magic rod causes door to open. D1693. Magic rod swallows other rods. F971.1. Dry rod blossoms. H412.1. Chastity ordeal: passing under magic rod. H1342. Quest for magic iron rod. Z312.2. Giant ogre can be killed only with iron club he carries.

D1254.3. *Magic pestle.* Chinese: Eberhard 221; Africa (Tim): Frobenius Atlantis XI 224ff. No. 38, (Fang): Einstein 151.

D1541.2.1. Magic pestle draws storm away.

D1254.4. *Magic trident.* Greek: *Grote I 180.

D1255. *Magic tube.* *Chauvin VI 133 No. 286 n. 2.

D1323.9. Clairvoyant tube. D1413.23. Magic drinking-tube holds person fast. Z323. Vessel from which nothing can be drunk save through certain tube.

D1256. *Magic ball.* *Chauvin V 87 No. 27 n. 2, VII 98 No. 375 n. 3. — Irish myth: Cross; Breton: Sébillot Incidents s.v. "boule"; N. A. Indian: *Thompson Tales 315 n. 145b, Thompson CColl II 331 (Osage).

D1313.1. Magic ball indicates road. D1314.14. Four balls given to each of four impoverished men point out places where they should dig. D1470.1.29. Magic wishing-ball. D1526.2. Magic ball flight. D1610.23. Speaking muirlan (ball). D1641.5. Muirlan (ball) removes itself. E711.9. Soul in golden ball.

D1257. *Magic fishhook.* Breton: Sébillot Incidents s.v. "hameçon"; Maori: Dixon 43, Clark 153; Hawaii: Beckwith Myth 420.

D1444.3. Magic fishhook catches cats.

D1258. *Magic bridge.* Irish myth: Cross; India: Thompson-Balys.

D1642.1. Self-folding bridge prevents pursuit. F152. Bridge to otherworld. F842. Extraordinary bridge. H411.8. Magic bridge as chastity test.

D1258.1. *Bridge made by magic.* *Types 313, 314; Köhler-Bolte I 195. — Irish myth: *Cross; Breton: Sébillot Incidents s.v. "pont"; Chinese: Werner 213; Japanese: Ikeda; N. A. Indian (Cherokee): Mooney RBAE XIX 319 No. 67, (Quinault): Farrand JE II 115 No. 10.

D466.3. Transformation hair to bridge. D467.1. Transformation wand to bridge. D469.5. Transformation wisp of hay to bridge. D469.6. Transformation belt to bridge. D469.7. Transformation thread to bridge. D469.8. Transformation smoke to bridge. D469.9. Transformation chain of arrows to bridge. H13.2.1. Recognition by overheard conversation with bridge.

D1261. *Magic cigar.* Spanish: Boggs FFC XC 56 No. 408*A.

D1364.19. Cigar causes magic sleep.

D1262. *Magic grinding-stone.* Gold Coast: Barker and Sinclair 81 No. 13.

D931. Magic stone.

D1262.1. *Magic millstone.* Chinese: Eberhard 107.

D1601.20. Self-grinding millstone.

D1263. *Magic mill.* *Type 565; BP II 439; Fb "salt", "havet", "kværn"; *Dh II 155; Gering Festschrift für Eugen Mogh 37. — Irish: Plummer clxxxvi, *Cross.

D1318.15. Mill will not grind stolen wheat. D1338.6. Rejuvenation in magic mill. D1601.21. Self-grinding mill. Grinds whatever owner wishes. D1601.21.1. Self-grinding salt mill. D1601.27. Automatic mill. D1676. Mill refuses to work on Sunday. D1677. Mill refuses to work when saint is mistreated.

D1264. *Magic sphere.* *Chauvin V 259 No. 154.

D1408.1. Magic sphere burns up country.

D1266. *Magic book.* *Chauvin V 135, 262, 295; Type 611; *Fb "Cyprianus" I 166—7, "bog", "Cyprian" IV 88f.; Hartland Science 199. — Irish: Plummer clxxviii, *Cross; Swiss: Jegerlehner Oberwallis 297 No. 29, 314 No. 102; Norwegian: Christiansen Norske Eventyr 90; Italian Novella: Rotunda; Jewish: *Neuman; Hindu: Penzer I 37 n. 2, 129f.

D1311.14. Divination from chance reading of sacred (magic) book. D1312.4. Magic book gives advice. D1325.1. Magic book wherein is written family's destiny. D1331.4.1. Saint's gospel-book causes sight-shifting. D1381.25. Carrying saint's book around army (righthandwise) insures victory. D1385.25. Magic book disperses demons. D1421.1.3. Magic book summons genie. D1446.2. Saint's gospel-book keeps cattle from straying. D1469.6. Magic book furnishes wealth. D1470.1.26. Magic wishing-book. D1484.2. Reading from magic book causes road to appear. D1500.0.1. Magic book controls disease. D1500.1.22. Magic healing book. D1507.2. Saint's gospel-book restores speech. D1542.3.2. Reading book causes river to dry up. D1505.12. Man cured of blindness by touching book of St. Oswin's life. D1602.10. Self-returning magic book. D1641.11.1. Magic book removes itself. D1656.1. Incombustible book. D1678. Magic book, once used, compels person to do evil. D1889.1. Rejuvenation by reading in book. E64.7. Resuscitation by book. E383. Ghosts summoned by opening sacred book. E434.8. Ghost cannot pass cross or prayerbook. F721.2.3. Sorcerer and books in mountain. Opens only for short periods. F883. Extraordinary writings (book, letter). K113.3. Alleged resuscitating book sold. K218.2. Devil cheated of his victim by boy having a bible under his arm.

D1266.1. *Magic writings (gramerye, runes).* Child I 28, 48, 362, 391f., II 53ff., 506a; *Hdwb d. Abergl. I 1225; Krappe The Sending (Scandinavian Studies XVII [1943] 297—304). — Irish myth: *Cross, Beal XXI 311, O'Suilleabhain 33; Icelandic: MacCulloch Eddic 46f., 295ff., *Boberg; Jewish: Neuman.

A465.3.1.1. God of eloquence and learning as inventor of ogum alphabet. A1469.2. Origin of ogam inscriptions. D1273. Magic charm. D1316.9. Magic epistle (brought from apostle) assures wearer will utter truth. D1355.19. Magic writings produce love. D1364.20. Magic runes cause sleep. D1367.5. Runes cause frenzy. D1379.1.1. Magic runes control person's will. D1379.3. Magic writings (human) cause enmity. D1380.20. Runes protect. D1381.16. Magic letters (amulets) guard against attack by wild animals or men. D1381.24. Magic letter protects against attack. D1382.7.1.1. Runes (magic writing) protect from frost and cold. D1385.20. Runes protect from the curse of a dead Christian woman. D1387.2. Magic charm (writings) preserve chastity. D1388.1.3. Runes protect from storm and shipwreck. D1400.1.11. Magic runes give power over enemy. D1414.2. Magic writings on sword render it harmless. D1500.1.34. Magic writings heal. D1541.1.6. Magic writings raise storms. D1545.0.1. Magic runes control sea. D1549.3.7. Written charm causes river to flow quietly. D1561.1.8. Runes bring luck. D1566.2.4. Runes quench fire. D1601.32. Letter delivers self. D1611.16 Magic writings on stone cause corpse to answer for absent man. D1641.11. Sacred scroll returns to heaven. D1654.3.1.1. Indelible writing: the scraped word found written as before. D1654.11. Paper in hand which none but king can remove. K115.1. Alleged healing letter sold. P273.2.4. Magic writings make foster-brothers enemies. V211.10. Letter (message) of Christ. V221.7. Woman relieved of an incurable malady by kissing letter from saint. V246.0.1. Angel leaves letter (book) with instructions for saint. V283. Testament of Virgin Mary.

D1266.1.1. *Magic ogam writing.* Irish myth: *Cross.

A1469.2. Origin of ogam inscriptions.

D1266.2. *Magic picture.* Hdwb. d. Abergl. I 1282 s.v. "Bild"; Hdwb. d. Märchens s.v. "Bild". — Irish: O'Suilleabhain 33; Italian Novella: Rotunda; Jewish: Neuman; Chinese: Werner 139, Graham, Eberhard FFC CXX 233f.

D435.2. Transformation picture to person. D1379.4. Magic picture causes people to wet the bed. D1500.2.3. Magic picture prevents disease. D1586.1. Magic image of animal relieves from plague (of that animal). D1654.8. Picture that cannot be removed in ship. H439.1. Picture as chastity index.

D1266.3. *Magic story.* Irish myth: Cross.

D1380.13. Magic story protects.

D1267. *Magic card.* *Köhler-Bolte Zs f. Vksk. VI 62 (to Gonzenbach No. 10); — German Grimm No. 82.

D1364.21. Magic card causes sleep. D1470.1.48. Magic rubber card for wishing.

D1268. *Magic statue (doll).* Basset RTP XXVI 22 (and following numbers passim). — Irish: Beal XXI 312; Italian Novella: Rotunda (D1295); Jewish: *Neuman; Chinese: Eberhard FFC CXX 152; Eskimo (Bering Strait): Nelson RBAE XVIII 494.

D435.1.1. Transformation statue comes to life. D1311.7. Oracular image. D1311.7.1. Oracular artificial head. D1313.3. Copper horseman indicates route. D1317.9.1. Brass (copper) statue at city gates blows on trumpet at stranger's approach. D1327.2. Magic doll consulted for hunting. D1345.2. Magic statue of dragon gives longevity. D1347.4. Magic statue gives fecundity. D1380.0.1.1. Palladium. City impregnable while statue remains. D1402.19. Magic statue kills. D1444.1.2. Magic wooden fish attracts live fish to fisherman's net. D1469.2. Magic doll furnishes treasure. Excreta of gold. D1469.13. Treasure falls from stone lion's mouth. D1500.1.12. Magic statue cures disease. D1505.16. Magic statue (when kissed) restores sight. D1515.4.5. Sight of brass serpent as antidote for snakebite. D1595.1. Image of love grants man wife. D1610.21. Speaking image. D1611.11. Magic doll answers for fugitive. D1620. Magic automata. D1620.0.1. Automatic doll. D1620.1.5.1. Magic statue of archer put into action by picking up precious object from ground. D1620.1.6. Magic statue of man labors for owner. D1620.1.6.1. Magic statue of man fights for master. D1620.2 Automatic statue of animal. D1633. Image eats or drinks. D1639.5. Calf of gold moves. D1639.6. Carved image jumps at maker's command. D1654.7. Statues that cannot be removed. D1661.1. Talking statue, when destroyed, cannot be replaced for thirty thousand years. H251.1. Bocca della Verità. Person swearing oath places hand in mouth of image. If oath is false the hand is bitten off. H411.9. Magic statue as chastity test. Moves eyes in presence of unchaste woman. V120. Images.

D1271. *Magic fire.* *BP I 440; *Hdwb. d. Märchens s. v. "Waberlohe"; Panzer Sigfrid 281 s.v. "Waberlohe"; Fb "ild" II 10a. — Irish: Plummer clxvi, cxxxviii, *Cross; Icelandic: Herrmann Saxo II 601, *Boberg; Breton: Sébillot Incidents s.v. "feu"; Jewish: *Neuman; Africa (Fang): Tessman 104.

D1162. Magic light. D1311.5. Oracular flame. D1313.16. Magic pillar of fire indicates direction. D1314.10. Fiery pillar guides person to church. D1336.6. Magic fire gives weakness. D1380.1. Waberlohe. Magic fire surrounds and protects. D1380.1.1. Pillar of fire protects in desert. D1382.5. Magic fire does not harm one. D1402.4. Magic fire kills. D1412.3. Flames draw person into them. D1445.6.2. Magic heavenly fire burns animals. D1555.4. Fairy music causes earth to open. D1566.1.5. Shower of fire from magic anvil. D1572. Magic smoke carries power of saint. D1609.2. Self-generated flame. D1641.10. Magic fire removes itself. D1643.1. Stick of fire comes to river bank of itself. D1672. Unquenchable fire. D1836.1. Ghost's strength waxes and wanes with height of fire. D2064.2. Sickness of princess dependent on witch's fire. D2065.4. Insanity of princess dependent on height of fire. D2091.1. Magic fire drawn down on foe. F882. Extraordinary fire. F964.0.1. Pillar of fire in sky. V211.2.1. Fiery pillar is sign of Christ's birth. V222.0.1.1. Pillar of fire rises over woman pregnant with future saint.

D1272. *Magic circle.* *Types 810, 815; *Chauvin VII 104 No. 378; *Penzer II 98f., III 201, VI 167 n. 3; Saintyves RTP XXV 113; MacCartney Classical Weekly XXII 175 f.; *Loomis White Magic 100; Harou RTP XXV 294. — Icelandic: Boberg; Jewish: *Neuman; Chinese: Eberhard FFC CXX 237.

D787. Disenchantment by encircling. D1380. Magic circle protects. D1381.11. Magic circle protects from devil. D1385.7. Magic circle averts sorcery. D1384.3.1. Turning right-handwise insures safe journey. D1402.14. Magic circle of saliva kills dragon. D1417.1. Magic circle prevents escape. D1446.5. Magic circle keeps herd within. D1500.2.4. Magic circle prevents disease. D1791. Magic power by circumambulation. E501.17.5.5. Wild hunt avoided by staying within circle. N131.2. Turning righthandwise in certain place brings luck.

D1272.1. *Magic line.* Irish: Plummer clxxv, *Cross; India: Thompson-Balys; Koryak: Jochelson JE VI 364; Eskimo (Mackenzie Area): Jenness 79, (Cumberland Sound): Boas BAM XV 177f., (West Hudson Bay): ibid. 308f.

D1574. Line drawn by saint's bachall separates calves from their mothers.

D1273. *Magic formula (charm).* *Types 676, 677; DeCock Studien 156; Encyc. Religion and Ethics III 392; *Chauvin V 10 No. 7, 60 No. 19 n. 1; *Grendon JAFL XXII 105ff.; *Ohrt Danmarks Trylleformler, ibid. Trylleord Fremmede og Danske; *Hestesko FFC XIX; *Kittredge Witchcraft 31f., 386ff. nn. 71, 72, 90, 104; *Fb "læsning" II 502f.; Penzer I 138ff. — Irish: Plummer cl, clxxix, *Cross; Breton: Sébillot Incidents s.v. "charme", "blessure"; English: Child I 28, 48, 55, 391f., II 441, 445, 450; French Canadian: Barbeau JAFL XXIX 16; Spanish: Boggs FFC XC 84 No. 746; Finnish: Kalevala runes 16, 26; Estonian: Loorits Grundzüge I 288f; Swiss: Jegerlehner Oberwallis 300 No. 10; Jewish: *Neuman; India: Thompson-Balys. — Cape Verde Islands: Parsons MAFLS XV (1) 9, 61; Africa (Zulu): Callaway 101, 143, (Kaffir): Theal 41 No. 2, 45 No. 2, 30 No. 1, 125, (Ekoi): Talbot 401, (Yoruba): Ellis 253 No. 4, 271, (Basuto): Jacottet 100 No. 15, (Angola): Chatelain 183ff. No. 22. — Eskimo: Rink 107 No. 3.

B501.2. Kite teaches rhyme by which he may be summoned for help. D522. Transformation through magic word. D789.6. Disenchantment by repeating magic formula. D886. Magic object recovered through recitation of magic formula. D1310.6. Magic charm gives knowledge. D1335.13.1. Charm placed on cheeks of hag causes love. D1336.8. Magic spell gives weakness. D1337.1.1. Charm gives magic beauty. D1344.4. Charm (written) renders invulnerable. D1351.4. Charm which makes all inhabitants of city faint-hearted. D1355.18. Love charm (words). D1358.2. Magic spell makes person courageous. D1361.26. Magic formula renders invisible. D1364.22. Sleep-charm. D1380.24. Spell overcomes all danger. D1381.23. Magic spell causes fortress to revolve, preventing entrance. D1383.2. Charms protect against poison. D1384.3. Charm gives safety on journey. D1384.4. Charms prevent fatigue. D1385.13. Charm prevents witchcraft. D1389.2. Charms against theft. D1395.6. Escape from prison by use of charm (formula). D1396. Magic object breaks spell. D1400.1.10. Charm gives victory in fight. D1402.13. Druid's spells kill Christian king. D1402.13.3. Charm used to kill. D1402.0.2.2. Magic spell causes person to be drowned. D1402.13.1. Druid's spells kill enemies. D1402.14.1. Magic charmed spittle kills. D1406.1. Charm to win cases in law court. D1407.4. Charm gives victory in game of dice. D1410.5. Serpent charmed into helplessness by magic formula. D1411.4. Magic charm binds deer so that it cannot move. D1413.0.1.1. Magic formula causes persons to stick together. D1420.1. Person drawn by magic spell. D1421.3.3. Magic charm summons dwarfs. D1421.5.2. Magic charm summons army. D1428.2. Charm causes spearhead to return. D1438. Spell causes spear to pursue and slay man. D1441.2. Charm calls down swarm of bees. D1442.6. Magic spell tames animals. D1443.1. Charm expels flies from city. D1444.1.4. Magic charm allows person to hook mythical eel. D1444.2. Charm to catch hare and money. D1447.1. Charm protects against wild animal. D1449.1. Charm makes cows give plenty of milk. D1449.4. Charm prevents fish being caught. D1469.17. Charm makes treasure rain from sky. D1472.2.5. Charm prepares feast. D1473.2. Rubbing charm provides garments. D1487.3. Magic spell makes tree grow. D1500.1.23. Magic healing charm. D1500.2.2. Charm against sickness. D1500.3.1. Charm shifts disease to another person. D1501.1. Charms prevent barrenness or miscarriage.

D1501.2. Charms make childbirth easy. D1502.1.1. Charm for headache. D1502.2.2. Charm for toothache. D1502.3.1. Charm for fever. D1502.6.1. Charm for urinary disease. D1503.3. Charm for wounds. D1503.3.1. Charm for burns or scalds. D1504.1. Charm stanches blood. D1505.11. Charm for diseased eye. D1513. Charm removes thorn. D1514.3. Charm for pain. D1515.1. Charms as antidote for poison. D1515.1.1. Charms as antidote for snakebite. D1516. Charms against elfshot. D1523.2.7. Boat guided by magic sea-charm. D1524.5. River crossed by means of charm. D1531.8. Witch flies with aid of word charm. D1541.0.1. Charms control storms. D1542.3.4. Magic spell dries up lake. D1544.1. Magic spell controls earthquake. D1546.1.2. Magic spell controls sun. D1549.9. Magic spell dries up lake. D1551.9. Magic formula causes sea to open up. D1552.2. Mountain opens to magic formula. D1555.3. Magic formula causes silver to hide itself in mountain. D1556. Magic formula causes tree to open. D1557. Magic charm causes door to open. D1561.2.4. Charm gives invisibility and power of moving everywhere. D1563.1.1. Charms make soil fertile. D1563.2.4. Magic spell destroys crops. D1573. Charms to make butter come. D1577.1. Charm renders medicinal herbs efficacious. D1577.2. Charm renders amulet efficacious. D1584.1. Charm induces dreams. D1591. Magic spell causes vessel to burst. D1599.2. Air made fragrant with odors of flowers by spell. D1599.5. Magic charm uproots mandrake. D1681. Charm incorrectly uttered will not work. D1686. Magic object departs and returns at formulistic command. D1822.1. Magic sight overcome by incantation. D2061.2.2.2. Spell chanted over person's shadow brings death. E52. Resuscitation by magic charm. E501.17.4.2. Power of wild hunt evaded by formula. G272.15. Witch controlled by means of magic spells. H1382.1. Quest for unknown magic words. V50. Prayer.

D1273.0.1. *Charm written in blood has magic power.* (Cf. D1003.) Fb "blod" IV 47b.

M201.1. Blood covenant. Contract written (or signed) with blood.

D1273.0.2. *Magic spells mixed with Christian prayers.* *Kittredge Witchcraft 146, 465 n. 64; *Fb "Fader Vor" I 260. — Irish myth: *Cross.

V50. Prayer.

D1273.0.3. *Charm sung over flesh chewed by wizard has magic power.* Irish myth: Cross.

D1799.4. Magic results from chewing. P427. Druid (magus).

D1273.0.4. *Charm chanted standing on one foot with one eye shut, etc.* Irish myth: *Cross.

D1273.0.5. *Charm containing name of God.* Jewish: Neuman.

C431. Tabu: uttering name of god.

D1273.1. *Magic numbers.* (Cf. Z71.) Irish myth: Cross; Jewish: Neuman.

D1273.1.1. *Three as magic number.* *Hdwb. d. Abergl. s. v. "Drei"; Irish myth: *Cross; French Canadian: Barbeau JAFL XXIX 8f.; Jewish: Neuman.

D1273.1.1.1. *Three on a match (lighting cigarettes or cigars).* England, U.S.: *Baughman.

D1273.1.1.2. *Breakage of glass or crockery occurs in threes.* One breakage is followed by two more. England, U.S.: *Baughman.

D1273.1.1.3. *Deaths in a community come in threes.* One death is shortly followed by two more. England, U.S.: *Baughman.

D1273.1.1.4. *Three meditations on death which prevent laughter.* Irish myth: Cross.

D1273.1.2. *Four as magic number.* Irish myth: *Cross; French Canadian: Barbeau JAFL XXIX 9.

D1273.1.2.1. *Five as magic number.* Irish myth: *Cross.

D1273.1.3. *Seven as magic number.* *Fb "syv"; Irish myth: *Cross; England: Baughman; French Canadian: Barbeau JAFL XXIX 9; Jewish: Neuman; Siberian: Holmberg Siberian 338.

D1273.1.3.1. *Nine as magic number.* Irish myth: *Cross.

D1273.1.4. *Ten as magic number.* Jewish: Neuman.

D1273.1.5. *Twelve as magic number.* Fb "tolv"; Gaster Thespis 369; Jewish: Neuman.

D1273.1.6. *Thirteen as magic number.* Jewish: Neuman; England, U.S.: *Baughman.

N135.1. Thirteen as unlucky number.

D1273.1.7. *Magic numbers — miscellaneous.*

D1273.1.7.1. *101 as magic number.* French Canadian: Barbeau JAFL XXIX 9.

D1273.1.7.2. *9999 as magic number.* Persian: Carnoy 327.

D1273.2. *Magic secret.* Finnish: Kalevala rune 20.

D1445.1. Revelation of magic secret permits animal to be killed.

D1273.3. *Bible texts as magic spells.* *Kittredge Witchcraft 146, 465 nn. 66, 67, 70; Jewish: *Neuman.

D1273.4. *Magic measurement (height of Christ).* Irish myth: Cross.

D1385.17. Magic measurement protects against devil. D1389.10. Magic measurement protects against sudden death. F950.3. Measuring the sick as means of cure.

D1273.5. *Magic oath.* India: Thompson-Balys.

D1400.1.11.1. Magic oath stops killer and sends invading army back. M100. Vows and oaths.

D1273.6. *Magic alphabet.* Jewish: Neuman.

D1274. *Magic fetish.* *Seligmann 39. — English: Child I 28, 48, 55, 57, 391; Eskimo (Greenland): Rink 56, 148, 433, Rasmussen III 100, Holm 56; Africa (Fjort): Dennett 96, (Bushmen, South of Zambesi): Theal 56; S. A. Indian (Toba): Métraux MAFLS XL 38.

D1318.3. Charms indicate guilt. D1355.3. Love charm. D1601.22. Fetish clears forest. E53. Resuscitation by fetish. G613. Ogre's charm stolen. V14. Fetish worship.

D1274.1. *Magic conjuring bag.* Filled with nail parings, human hair, feet of toads, and the like. *Kittredge Witchcraft 48ff., 401f. nn. 197—208. — Africa (Ekoi): Talbot 403.

D1470.1.27. Magic wishing-bag.

D1275. *Magic song.* Fb "synge" III 706b, "Kanariefugle" II 85; Hdwb. d. Abergl. IX Nachträge 424ff.; Köhler-Bolte I 125. — Irish: Plummer clxxix, *Cross; Icelandic: *Boberg; Finnish: Kalevala runes 8, 10, 12, 14, 15, 24, 40; Greek: Grote I 242; Jewish: Neuman; India: Thompson-Balys; Chinese: Graham; Eskimo (Greenland): Rink 125; Africa (Kaffir): Theal 85, 125, (Angola): Chatelain 110ff. No. 7.

D523. Transformation through song. D786.1. Disenchantment by song. D1045.1. Beer brewed by means of magic song. D1335.12. Magic song gives strength. D1361.31. Magic song renders invisible. D1364.23. Song causes magic sleep. D1380.14. Magic poems protect. D1381.27. Magic song stops spears. D1384.5. Song as protection on journey. D1372.7. Song protects from fire. D1383.4. Song protects against poison. D1402.11. Magic song kills person. D1402.15.1. Magic poem (satire) causes man to melt. D1403.1. Magic poem (satire) raises blotches on face. D1414.4. Magic song dulls enemy's sword. D1441.1.4. Magic song calls animals together. D1442.5. Saint's song silences hound. D1444.4. Magic song to catch animals. D1445.3. Saint's chant kills animal. D1445.4. Magic poem (satire) kills animals. D1500.1.24. Magic healing song. D1503.1. Magic song heals wound. D1523.2.6. Boat guided by magic songs. D1541.3. Magic song causes storm. D1549.8. Magic song drives back flooding sea. D1563.5. Magic song makes barren land fruitful. D1563.7. Magic poem (satire) makes land sterile. D1565.1.1. Magic song causes chips from tree to return. D1565.3. Magic song causes plowed ground to become unplowed. D1566.2.3. Magic song quenches fire. D1576.1. Magic song causes tree to rise to sky. D1731.1. Magic song learned in dream. D1889.3. Rejuvenation by song of pelican. D2011.1. Years seem moments while man listens to song of bird. D2143.1.2. Rain produced by singing. E55.1. Resuscitation by song. J672.1. Ears stopped with wax to avoid enchanting song. Odysseus and the Sirens.

D1275.1. *Magic music.* *Krappe Classical Journal XXI 21ff.; *Fb "spille" III 488ab; Gaster Oldest Stories 131. — Irish: *Cross; Plummer clxxii, O'Suilleabhain 54, Beal XXI 320; English: Child V 489 s.v. "music"; Greek: Fox 193 (Hermes and Argos), Frazer Apollodorus I 17 (Orpheus) .

B172.2.1. Magic bird's song brings sleep. B767.1. Snakes got to sleep by music on harp. D786. Disenchantment by music. D1210. Magic musical instrument. D1336.3. Magic music gives weakness. D1355.1. Love-producing music. D1359.2.1. Magic music causes mourning. D1359.3.1. Magic music causes joy. D1374.1. Magic music causes longing. D1402.11.1. Magic music kills person. D1441.1. Musical instrument calls animals together. D1508.2. Music restores reason. D1514.1. Magic music relieves pain. D2143.4.1. Hail produced by whistling tune. E55. Resuscitation by music. F262.5. Fairy music — person listening is without food or sleep for a year.

D1275.2. *Magic melody.* (Cf. D1275.1.) *BP II 502.

D1275.3. *Magic hymn.* (Cf. D1275.) Irish myth: *Cross.

D1380.14.1. Magic hymn protects. D1382.7.1. Magic hymn protects from fire. D1383.4.1. Magic hymn protects against poison. D1385.16. Magic hymn protects against demons and evils. D1389.9. Magic hymn protects against poverty, death, and dishonor. D1395.7. Escape from prison by use of magic hymn. D1541.1.9. Singing magic hymn raises storm. D1588.3. Magic hymn assures heaven for person who sings it. D1766.9. Magic results from singing hymn. Q172.5. Numerous sinners to go to heaven as reward for man's writing hymn. V83. Hymns.

D1275.4. *Magic poem (satire).*

D1318.12.1.1. Poet's spell causes ale vessels to burst when request for ale is refused. D1336.9. Druids' (poets') spells bind. D1380.14. Magic poems protect. D1402.15. Magic poem (satire) causes king to waste away. D1403.1. Magic poem (satire) raises blotches on face. D1445.4. Magic poem (satire) kills animals. D1449.4.1. Poet's incantations drive away fish. D1563.2.3. Magic poem (satire) makes land sterile.

D1276. *Magic straw.* *Fb "hest" I 598b; Irish: O'Suilleabhain 98, Beal XXI 331.

D469.5. Transformation wisp of hay to bridge. D1442.2. Straw on horse's back restrains him. D1549.3.6. Ring of hay thrown into empty lake fills it up with water.

D1277. *Magic bachall.* (Cf. D1254.) Irish: Plummer cl, clxxv, *Cross, O'Suilleabhain 85, Beal XXI 328.

D1314.3. Saint's bachall discovers gold. D1351.1. Saint's bachall makes person peaceful. D1381.12. Saint's bachall keeps off enemies. D1385.8. Saint's bachall keeps off monsters and ghosts. D1388.1.1. Saint's bachall protects from shipwreck. D1391.2. Saint's bachall saves prisoner from execution. D1395.4. Saint's bachall enables captive to escape. D1400.1.12. Saint's bachall defeats enemies. D1419.3.1. Saint's bachall prevents ship from moving. D1442.3. Saint's bachall subdues wild animals. D1444.1.1. Saint's bachall catches fish. D1500.1.13.4. Saint's bachall as remedy. D1524.1.2. Saint's bachall permits him to walk on sea. D1549.3.1. Saint's bachall drives back flooding river. D1549.3.2. Saint's bachall leads stream through mountain (up hill). D1549.4. Saint's bachall brings down mountain on heads of enemies. D1551.5. Saint's bachall causes sea to divide. D1564.3. Saint's bachall splits rock, cuts stone, and cleaves ground. D1566.2.1. Saint's bachall quenches fire. D1567.4. Saint's bachall produces fountain. D1602.9. Saint's bachall when lost returns. E64.4.1. Resuscitation by saint's bachall. V211.2.2. Christ leaves bachall after visit. V227.1.

God gives staff of Christ to saint. V353. Saint's bachall pointed at idol defaces it.

D1277.1. *Magic crozier.* Irish: Plummer cl, *Cross.

D1567.5. Saint's crozier produces fountain. D1610.20. Speaking crozier. F962.13.1. Crozier falls from heaven for saint.

D1278. *Ghoulish charm.* Charm made from parts of corpse or things associated with corpse. *Kittredge Witchcraft 141ff., 458ff. nn. 1—55; Eskimo (Greenland): Rink 148, 173, 347, Rasmussen II 233, III 105, Holm 15, (Bering Strait): Nelson RBAE XVIII 495.

D1384.2. Noose used by suicide as protection from accident. D1407.2. Hangman's noose gives luck in gambling. D1500.1.6. Ghoulish magic object cures disease. D1500.1.26. Fragment of gibbet as cure. D1502.1.1. Hangman's noose cures headache. D1502.3.1. Hangman's noose cures scrofula. D1549.7. Murdered man's head will cause earth to burn up or sea to boil: must be carried about. E595. Cure by transferring disease to dead. Ghoulish charm used for this purpose. N1.2.2. Dice made from bones from graveyard always win.

D1278.1. *Magic churchyard mould.* *Fb "kirkegaardsmuld", "grav"; Hdwb. d. Abergl. III 95; Irish myth: *Cross.

B217.4. Animal languages learned from carrying churchyard mould in hat. D935. Magic earth (soil). D1323.8. Churchyard mould gives clairvoyance. D1355.6. Churchyard mould produces love. D1385.11. Churchyard mould in hat prevents witchery. D1500.1.6.2. Churchyard mould as remedy.

D1278.2. *Sorcerers use marrow of corpses' bones.* Irish myth: Cross.

G260. Evil deeds of witches.

D1281. *Magic dead fish.* Hindu: *Penzer I 46ff.

B107. Treasure fish. B124. Wise fish. B175. Magic fish. D1318.2.1. Laughing fish reveals unjust judgment.

D1281.1. *Magic dead pig.*

B183. Magic boar. D1316.10. Pig cooked when true story is told.

D1282. *Magic coil.* Chinese: Werner 358.

D1282.1. *Magic knot.* *Fb "vindknude"; Penzer II 189 n. 1; Jewish: Neuman.

D468.1. Transformation: handkerchief with three knots to clod, potsherd and charcoal. D2142.0.2. Wind raised by loosing certain knots.

D1282.1.1. *Druid's knot: magic defense.* Irish myth: Cross.

D1381.1. Druid's hedge prevents attack.

D1282.1.2. *Magic phylactery.* Jewish: Neuman.

D1282.2. *Magic wisp.* Irish myth: Cross.

D1367.4. Magic wisp causes insanity.

D1283. *Magic packet.* Chinese: Werner 230.

D1284. *Magic dice.* Pauli (ed. Bolte) No. 379; India: Thompson-Balys; Chinese: Eberhard FFC CXX 151.

D1317.8. Magic dice give warning.

D1285. *Magic spike.* Chinese: Werner 123.

D1331.2.1. Magic spike causes blindness. D2061.2.6. Person killed by spike magically made to appear on chair.

D1285.1. *Spike produced by magic.* Irish myth: Cross.

D1286. *Magic horseshoe.* *Fb "hestesko" I 603b, IV 213b; Frazer Golden

Bough XII 309 s.v. "horseshoes"; **Means-Lawrence Magic of the Horseshoe.

D1385.9. Magic horseshoe keeps off devils, trolls, and witches. D1561.1.3. Horseshoe brings good luck. G272.11. Horseshoes powerful against witches.

D1287. *Magic fly-whisk.* Chinese: Werner 322.

D1381.13 Magic fly-whisk stops sword-thrusts. E64.18. Resuscitation by fly-whisk.

D1288. *Magic coin.* *Type 745; *Fb "vekseldaler"; Chinese: Eberhard FFC CXX 107, 152, 222; Japanese: Ikeda; N. A. Indian (Skaulitz): Hill-Tout JAI XXXIV 374.

D1452.5. Coin put in huge bell fills it with rupees. D1470.1.28. Magic coin fulfills wishes. D1500.1.10.3. Money from offertory as cure. D1602.11. Self-returning magic coin.

D1291. *Heavenly body as magic object.*

D1311.6. Divination by heavenly bodies.

D1291.1. *Sun as magic object.* Cox Cinderella 483.

D1311.6.3. Sun answers questions.

D1291.1.1. *Magic sun-ray.* Jewish: Neuman.

D1291.2. *Star as magic object.* Irish myth: Cross; Jewish: Neuman.

D1311.6.4. Divination by stars.

D1291.2.1. *Sign in stars as portent.* Irish myth: Cross.

D1291.2.2. *Magic star later resolves into its elements.* Irish myth: Cross.

D1292. *Magic bird nest.* Cox Cinderella 517.

D1361.30. Magic bird nest renders invisible.

D1293. *Magic color.*

Z65. Color formulas. Z130. Color symbolism.

D1293.1. *Red as magic color.* Swiss: Jegerlehner Oberwallis 300 No. 6; Irish myth: *Cross; Jewish: Neuman; Gaster Oldest Stories 69; India: Thompson-Balys.

B183.3. Magic red swine. D1381.15. Red wards off danger. D1385.26. Red color protects against demons.

D1293.2. *Green as magic color.* Irish myth: *Cross.

D1293.3. *White as magic color.* Irish myth: *Cross.

D1293.4. *Black as magic color.* Irish myth: *Cross.

D1294. *Magic footprint.* *Seligmann 153; Boberg.

D578. Transformation by stepping into footprint. D1454.7. Treasure from footprints.

D1295. *Magic incense.* Jewish: Neuman (D1297).

D1346.12. Incense gives immortality. D1389.15. Magic incense protects from plague.

D1296. *Sacred relic as magic object.* Irish myth: *Cross.

D1381.20 Sacred relics protect against attack. E64.12. Resuscitation by sacred relics. V140. Sacred relics.

D1297. *Magic dye.* Irish myth: Cross.

D1684. Dye blessed by saint colors animals, trees.

D1298. *Magic firewood.* Irish myth: Cross.

D1652.10.1. Inexhaustible firewood.

D1299. *Other magic objects.* Irish myth: Cross.

D1299.1. *Magic sign (symbol, insignia).* Irish myth: Cross.
D1359.5. Magic sign assures warriors will not flee from battle.

D1299.2. *Magic sepulchre (grave).* Irish myth: Cross.
D484. Stretching sepulchre. Magically becomes longer. D1413.24. Grave holds person fast. D1419.1.1. Magic grave compels person to laugh (shriek). D1641.8. Grave removes itself.

D1299.3. *Magic cross.* Irish myth: Cross.
D1361.41. Cross renders invisible. D1641.9. Magic cross removes itself. D1766.6. Magic results from sign of the cross.

D1299.4. *Magic cotton-wool.*
D1505.16. Magic cure for blindness by using magic cotton-wool.

D1299.5. *Magic pair of spectacles.* India: Thompson-Balys.
D1316.4.2. Magic spectacles allow wearer to read others' thoughts.

D1300—D1599. Function of magic objects.

D1300—D1379. MAGIC OBJECTS EFFECT CHANGES IN PERSONS

D1300. Magic object gives supernatural wisdom.
B120—B169. Animals with magic wisdom. B160. Wisdom-giving animals. D1811. Magic wisdom.

D1300.1. *Hat gives magic wisdom.* (Cf. D1067.1.) *Type 328.

D1300.2. *Cap gives magic wisdom.* (Cf. D1067.3.) *Type 328.

D1300.3. *Magic well of wisdom.* (Cf. D926.) Irish myth: *Cross; Icelandic: MacCulloch Eddic 49, Boberg.
D925. Magic fountain. D927. Magic spring. D1811.1.2. Magic wisdom from drinking of well. V134.1. Oracles and auguries from holy well.

D1300.3.1. *Streams of wisdom flow from magic well.* (Cf. D915.) Irish myth: Cross.

D1300.4. *Stone gives magic wisdom.* (Cf. D931.) Jewish: Neuman; Icelandic: Boberg.

D1300.5. *Staff gives magic wisdom.* (Cf. D1254.) Jewish: Neuman.

D1300.6. *Charm gives magic wisdom.* (Cf. D1273.) Jewish: Neuman.

D1300.7. *Fox-heart gives magic wisdom.* (Cf. D1015.1.5.) Jewish: Neuman.

D1301. *Magic object teaches animal languages.* (Cf. D1268.) India: Thompson-Balys.
B216. Knowledge of animal languages. B217. Animal languages learned. B217.1.2. Animal languages learned from eating dragon's heart. B217.2. Animal languages learned from eating plant. B217.4. Animal languages learned from carrying churchyard mould in hat. B217.5. Bird language learned by having ears magically cleansed. D1815. Magic knowledge of strange tongues.

D1301.1. *Magic turf from church-roof teaches animal languages.* (Cf. D934.) *Fb "græstørv".

D1301.2. *Drinking blood teaches animal languages.* (Cf. D1041.) — **Scott Thumb; Panzer Sigfrid 281 s.v. "Vogelsprache". — Icelandic: Völsungasaga 45, Boberg.

D1301.3. *Marvelous ruby teaches bird's speech.* (Cf. D1071.) — India: Thompson-Balys.

D1301.4. *Bird's head (when eaten) teaches animal languages.* India: Thompson-Balys.

B217. Child taught crow's language. D1011.0.1. Magic bird head. D1561.1. Magic bird heart (when eaten) brings man to kingship.

D1302. *Magic object teaches magic.*

B1720. Acquisition of magic powers.

D1302.1. *Magic axe teaches magic.* (Cf. D1206) India: Thompson-Balys.

D1305. *Magic object gives power of prophecy.*

M300. Prophecies.

D1305.1. *Drop of water from Paradise gives power of prophecy.* (Cf. D1242.1.) Jewish: Neuman.

D1310. Magic object gives supernatural information.

B162.1. Supernatural knowledge from eating magic fish. D1810. Magic knowledge. F1061. Flame as miraculous index.

D1310.1. *Magic seat gives omniscience.* (Cf. D1151.) Icelandic: Boberg.

D1310.2. *Drop from magic cauldron gives supernatural information.* (Cf. D1171.2.) — Irish myth: *Cross; Welsh: MacCulloch Celtic 110.

D1310.3. *Intelligent ship.* (Cf. D1123.) — Icelandic: Boberg; English: Child IV 376—80, V 275f.

D1610.11 Speaking ship.

D1310.4. *Magic object tells how another fares.*

E761. Life token. H430. Chastity index.

D1310.4.1. *Magic ring tells how another fares.* (Cf. D1076.) — *Kittredge Witchcraft 111, 440 n. 55.

D1310.4.2. *Magic plant bears fruit to indicate that heroine is ready to marry.* (Cf. D965.) India: Thompson-Balys.

D760. Life index. T50. Wooing.

D1310.4.3. *Barley plant droops if prince is in trouble.* (Cf. D965.15.) India: Thompson-Balys.

D1310.5. *Magic staff gives supernatural information.* (Cf. D1254.) — — Irish myth: Cross.

D1799.3. Magic results from special rituals.

D1310.6. *Magic charm gives knowlcdge.* (Cf. D1273.) — Irish myth: Cross.

D1310.7. *Singing of wave gives supernatural information.* (Cf. D911.1.) — Irish myth: *Cross.

V220. Saints.

D1310.8. *Speaking and walking divan brings supernatural information.* India: Thompson-Balys.

D1154.4. Magic divan. D1600. Automatic object. D1610. Magic speaking objects.

D1310.9. *Magic water gives knowledge.* (Cf. D1242.1.) — India: Thompson-Balys.

D1310.10. *Magic fruit gives supernatural knowledge.*

D1310.10.1. *Magic apple gives supernatural knowledge.* (Cf. D981.1.) — Jewish: Neuman.

D1310.10.2. *Magic fig gives supernatural knowledge.* (Cf. D981.5.) — Jewish: Neuman.

D1310.10.3. *Magic grape gives supernatural knowledge.* (Cf. D981.8.) — Jewish: Neuman.

D1310.11. *Magic nut gives supernatural knowledge.* (Cf. D985.) — Jewish: Neuman.

D1311. *Magic object used for divination.* Irish myth: *Cross.

B140. Prophetic animal. B147. Animals furnish omens. B150. Oracular animal. D1266.1.1. Magic ogam writing. D1663.5. Well rises or sinks to indicate long or short life. D1799.3. Magic results from special rituals. D1933. Magic power of lighting empty lamp by breathing on it used for divination. H41.3. Test of king (pope): his candle lights itself. M300. Prophecies.

D1311.1. *Harp struck for divination.* (Cf. D1231.) — Africa (Mpongwe): Nassau 15 No. 1.

D1311.2. *Mirror answers questions.* (Cf. D1163, D1323.1.) — *Type 709; *Böklen Sneewittchenstudien 70 (Leipzig, 1915); *MacCulloch Childhood 34ff.; *BP I 463; *Cox Cinderella 483. — Africa (Angola): Chatelain 29.

D1311.3. *Oracular fountain.* (Cf. D925.) — Irish: Plummer cli, *Cross; Icelandic: *Boberg.

D926. Magic well. D927. Magic spring. F933.6. Spring miraculously breaks forth against wrongdoer. V134.1. Oracles and auguries from holy well.

D1311.3.1. *Spring gives omens.* (Cf. D927.) — Type 709; Böklen Sneewittchenstudien (Leipzig, 1915) 73; *Kittredge Witchcraft 34, 394 n. 116.

D1311.3.1.1. *Divination by water.* Irish myth: *Cross.

D1242.1. Magic water. H222. Ordeal by water.

D1311.4. *Oracular tree.* (Cf. D950.) — Irish: Plummer cliii, *Cross; India: Thompson-Balys; Chinese: Graham.

C621.1. Tree of knowledge forbidden. D1610.2. Speaking tree. D1812.5.1.20. Withering of tree as bad omen. J165. Tree of knowledge. T589.3. Birth trees. V1.1. Worship of trees.

D1311.4.0.1. *Oracular twig.* (Cf. D953, D1254.2, D1311.15, D1314.2.) — Irish myth: Cross; Norse: MacCulloch Eddic 86; Tacitus Germania Ch. 10.

D1311.4.0.1.1. *Sight of magic twigs gives foreknowledge of day's events.* Irish myth: Cross.

D1311.4.0.2. *Falling of two trees reveals Savior's will as to separation of friends.* Irish myth: Cross.

D1311.4.1. *Tree appealed to as arbitrator.* Penzer V 60.

D1311.4.1.1. *Ash (quicken, rowan) used (by druids) for divinations.* Irish myth: *Cross.

D950.6. Magic ash tree. D1385.2.2. Ash protects against spells and enchantments.

D1311.4.1.2. *Hazel used by druids for divination.* (Cf. D950.1.) — Irish myth: *Cross.

D1311.4.2. *Speaking trees give prophecy.* Jewish: *bin Gorion Born Judas[2] III 140, 307.

D1311.5. *Oracular flame.* (Cf. D1271.) — Norwegian: Dasent Popular Tales from the Norse (New York, 1888) 261.

D1311.6. *Divination by heavenly bodies.* (Cf. D1291.) — Jewish: Neuman.

D1311.6.0.1. *Divination by looking upon astrolabe.* Jewish: Neuman.

D1311.6.1. *Moon (stars) answers questions.* Africa (Tonga): Junod 266ff., (Swahili): Baker FL XXXVII 299f. No. 16.

D1311.6.2. *Magic cloud answers questions.* (Cf. D901.) Chinese: Graham.

D1311.6.3. *Sun answers questions.* (Cf. D1291.1.) — Type 709; *Böklen Sneewittchenstudien (Leipzig, 1915) 72; Cox Cinderella 483.

H1284. Quest to sun for answers to questions.

D1311.6.4. *Divination by stars.* (Cf. D1291.2.) — Jewish: Neuman; Buddhist myth: Malalasekera I 828.

D1311.7. *Oracular image.* (Cf. D1268.) — *Dickson 193 (n. 75) ff.

D1610.21. Speaking image. D1620. Magic automata. D1651.6. Oracular image refuses information except to hero. K1972. Oracular images occupied by spirits or priests who give the answers. V120. Images.

D1311.7.1. *Oracular artificial head.* (Cf. D1268.) — *Dickson 200 n. 94, 213 n. 145.

B133.3. Speaking horse-head. D1621. Image renders judgments. F415. Demon occupies artificial oracular head and gives responses to questions. H251.1. Bocca della Verità. Person swearing oath places hand in mouth of image. If oath is false the hand is bitten off.

D1311.7.2. *Oracular brazen lion.* Dickson 197 n. 83.

D1311.8. *Divination by head (skull).* (Cf. D992, D1610.5, M118.) — *Dickson 201 n. 97; Icelandic: MacCulloch Eddic 46.

D1311.8.1. *Dog's head used for divination.* (Cf. D1011.) Irish myth: *Cross.

D1311.8.2. *Cut-off head prophesies fight.* Icelandic: Boberg.

E783. Head retains life after being cut off.

D1311.9. *Coconut shell answers questions.* Sinks for yes, floats for no. (Cf. D985.1.) — Sulka of New Britain: Dixon 132 and 132 n. 2.

D1311.10. *Divination by part of animal's body.*

D1311.10.1. *Divination by shoulder-bone of sheep.* (Cf. D1013.) — *Kittredge Witchcraft 144, 462 n. 44.

D1311.10.2. *Divination from gall and liver of pig.* (Cf. D1015.2.) Philippine (Tinguian): Cole 19 note 1, 91.

D1311.11. *Oracular river.* (Cf. D915.)

D1311.11.1. *River says, "The time has come but not the man".* Man thus induced to drown himself. — *Fb "tid" III 789b; *Lizbarski Am Urds-Brunnen IV 56. — England: Baughman; Finnish-Swedish: Wessman 54 No. 460; Netherlands: Sinninghe FFC CXXXII 52 No. 1; Lithuanian: Balys Index No. 3495; Livonian: Loorits in FFC LXVI 45 No. 44f.; Estonian: Aarne in FFC XXV 136 No. 95.

D1610. Magic speaking objects. F420.1.5.2. Mysterious voice — water-spirit — is calling from sea. F420.5.2.6.1. Water-spirits take revenge if yearly tribute is not given. M219.2.3. Man contracted to the devil responds to call by voice: "The hour has come but not the man"; the man dies or kills himself. N101. Inexorable fate. S264. Sacrifice to rivers and seas.

D1311.12. *Oracular bell.* (Cf. D1213.)

D1311.12.1. *Bell sounds to designate pope.* (Cf. D1213.) — Breton: Sébillot Incidents s.v. "cloche".

H171. Animal or object indicates election of ruler.

D1311.13. *Plant used for divination.* (Cf. D965.)

D1311.13.1. *Mandrake as magic forecaster.* (Cf. D965.1, D1314.7.1.) — *Starck; *Taylor JAFL XXXI 561f.

D1311.13.2. *Weeds used for divination.* Africa (Fang): Einstein 51.

D1311.14. *Divination from chance reading of sacred (magic) book.* Jewish: Neuman; India: Thompson-Balys.

D1266. Magic book. D1816.3. Location of fort determined by reading in book.

D1311.15. *Magic rod used for divination.* (Cf. D1311.4.0.1.) — Irish myth: *Cross.

D1254.2. Magic rod. D1314.2. Magic wand (twig) locates hidden treasure.

D1311.15.1. *Magic yew rod used by druid to discover whereabouts of woman carried off by fairies to underground retreat.* Irish myth: *Cross.

D950.14. Magic yew tree. D1711.4. Druid as magician. D1816.5. Druid divines whereabouts of missing person.

D1311.16. *Oracular stone.* (Cf. D931.) Irish myth: *Cross; Icelandic: *Boberg; India: Thompson-Balys; Hawaii: Beckwith Myth 89.

D1311.16.0.1. *Saint's blessing makes stone oracular.* Irish myth: Cross.

D1713. Magic power of hermit (saint).

D1311.16.1. *Number of screams from stone indicates number of kings to descend from man standing upon it.* Irish myth: Cross.

H171.5. Stone of Destiny.

D1311.17. *Divination by magic weapon.* (Cf. D1080.)

D1311.17.1. *Magic spear gives omen of victory.* (Cf. D1084.) — Irish myth: *Cross.

D1311.17.2. *Divination by magic arrow.* (Cf. D1092.) Jewish: Neuman.

D1311.17.3. *Lance sounds when knocked on shield, except when its owner will be defeated.* Icelandic: Boberg.

D1311.18. *Oracular ring.* (Cf. D1076.) Icelandic: Boberg.

D1311.19. *Divination by water.* (Cf. D1242.1.) Jewish: Neuman.

D1311.20. *Oracular pubic hair.* (Cf. D991.2.) — India: Thompson-Balys.

D1311.21. *Divination by cup.* (Cf. D1171.6.) Jewish: Neuman.

D1311.22. *Divination from (sound of) wind.* (Cf. D906.) Irish myth: *Cross.

D1311.23. *Divination with chessboard.* (Cf. D1209.7.) Irish myth: *Cross.

D1312. *Magic object gives advice.* *Huet 94. — N. A. Indian: *Thompson Tales 297 n. 86b.; Africa (Bankon): Ittman 97.

B560. Animals advise men. D1814. Magic advice.

D1312.1. *Bodily members as advisers.* (Cf. D990.) — N. A. Indian: *Thompson Tales 318 n. 150.

D1312.1.1. *Excrements as advisers.* (Cf. D1002.) — N. A. Indian: *Thompson Tales 296 n. 83c.

D1610.6. Speaking privates. Man given advice by his private parts. D1610.6.4. Speaking excrements.

D1312.2. *Magic bone gives advice.* (Cf. D1013.) — Africa (Basuto): Jacottet 192 No. 28.

D1312.3. *Speaking grass gives advice.* (Cf. D965.12.) India: Thompson-Balys.

D1610. Magic speaking objects. F810. Extraordinary trees, plants, fruit, etc.

D1312.4. *Magic book gives advice.* (Cf. D1266.) Jewish: Neuman.

D1313. *Magic object points out road.* *BP I 434. — Irish myth: Cross; N. A. Indian: *Thompson Tales 297 n. 86c.

B151. Horses determine road to be taken. B563. Animals direct man on journey.

D1313.1. *Magic ball indicates road.* Rolls ahead. (Cf. D1256.) — Type 425; Tegethoff 43; *Chauvin V 87 No. 27 n. 2, VII 98 No. 375 n. 3; *Kittredge Gawain 170 n. 2. — Irish myth: Cross; Breton: Sébillot Incidents s.v. "boule"; India: Thompson-Balys; U. S. (Ozarks): Randolph Who Blowed Up the Church House (New York, 1953) 59.

D1526.2. Magic ball flight. N777. Dropped ball (basket) leads to adventures when recovery is attempted.

D1313.1.1. *Magic ball of thread indicates road.* Rolls ahead. (Cf. D1184.1) — *Köhler-Bolte I 407; BP I 434; Fb "nøgle".

D1313.1.2. *Magic rolling cake indicates road.* (Cf. D1031.2.) BP III 458f.; Hdwb. d. März. I 335a.

D1313.2. *Hat thrown in air indicates road.* (Cf. D1067.1.) — Breton: Sébillot Incidents s.v. "chapeau".

D1313.3. *Copper horseman indicates road.* By striking his hand one makes him turn and indicate the proper road for travelers. (Cf. D1268, D1620.) — Chauvin V 33 No. 16.

D1620.1.2. Automatic statue of horseman.

D1313.4. *Blinded trickster directed by trees.* He asks them their names and by their answers he can tell where he is. (Cf. D950.) — N. A. Indian: *Thompson Tales 297 n. 86a.

D1393.4. Tree points way to fugitive but misdirects enemy. D1610.2. Speaking tree.

D1313.5. *Magic stick indicates road.* (Cf. D1254.) — Fb "kjæp" II 151a.

D1313.5.1. *Saint's staff as an excellent pilot at sea.* *Loomis White Magic 90.

D1313.5.2. *Reed as direction finder.* (Cf. D953) India: Thompson-Balys.

D1313.6. *Magic apple indicates road.* Rolls ahead. (Cf. D981.1.) — Irish myth: *Cross.

D1313.7. *Magic flute indicates road.* (Cf. D1223.1.) — Africa (Ibo of Nigeria): Thomas 146.

D1313.8. *Magic two-edged knife indicates direction.* Points in proper direction; bends downward to indicate wrong direction. (Cf. D1083.) — Africa (Ekoi): Talbot 127.

D1313.9. *Charm (medicine) indicates direction.* (Cf. D1241.) — Africa (Ekoi): Talbot 34.

D1313.10. *Magic feather indicates road.* (Cf. D1021.) — *BP II 37.

D1313.11. *Magic fountain indicates road for saint by removing itself.* (Cf. D925.) — Irish: Plummer cli, *Cross.

D1641.1. Fountain removes self. D1641.13. Well removes itself. V220. Saints.

D1313.12. *Magic cake indicates road.* Rolls ahead. (Cf. D1031.2.) — *Hdwb. d. Märchens s.v. "Ariadnefaden" n. 12.

D1313.13. *Magic shoe points out road.* (Cf. D1065.2.) — Scottish: Campbell-McKay No. 22.

D1313.14. *Magic thornbush points out road.* (Cf. D958.) — India: Thompson-Balys.

D1313.15. *Magic wheel indicates road.* (Cf. D1207.) — Irish myth: *Cross.

D1313.16. *Magic pillar of fire indicates direction.* (Cf. D1271.) — Jewish: Neuman.

D1314. *Magic object indicates desired place.* Irish myth: Cross; Finnish-Swedish: Wessman 70f. Nos 598—604; Jewish: Neuman; Chinese: Werner 197.

B153. Dog's barking indicates hidden treasure. B155.1. Building site determined by halting of animal. D1620. Magic automata. D1816. Magic discovery of desired place. D2101. Treasure magically discovered. F990. Inanimate objects act as if living.

D1314.0.1. *Magic object shows place where person has been killed.* India: Thompson-Balys.

D1314.1. *Magic arrow indicates desired place.* (Cf. D1092.)

D1314.1.1. *Magic arrow shot to determine place to lodge for night.* Köhler-Bolte I 554.

D1314.1.2. *Magic arrow shot to determine where to build city.* (Cf. D1314.4.) *Köhler-Bolte I 554.

D1314.1.3. *Magic arrow shot to determine where to seek bride.* Köhler-Bolte I 419, 554. — English: Child II 499; India: Thompson-Balys; Hawaii: Dixon 75f. n. 65.

H1381.3.2. Quest for bride for oneself. T10. Falling in love. T50. Wooing.

D1314.1.4. *Magic arrow indicates place to build church.* Fb "kirke" II 125a.

V111. Churches.

D1314.1.5. *Arrow shot to determine burial place.* English: Child I 185, III 106.

D1314.1.6. *Arrow shot into air discovers iron pit.* — India: Thompson-Balys.

D1314.1.7. *Arrov shot to discover direction of attacking army.* Jewish: Neuman.

D1314.2. *Magic wand (twig) locates hidden treasure.* (Cf. D954, D1254, D1254.2.) — *Barrett and Besterman The Divining Rod (London 1926); Encyc. Religion and Ethics II 832a; Fb "finkelrut", "skat", "pilegren"; *Norlind Skattsägner 28. — Icelandic: MacCulloch Eddic 86; Eng., U.S.; *Baughman; Finnish-Swedish: Wessman 77 No. 650.

D954. Magic bough. D1254.2. Magic rod. D1311.15. Magic rod used for divination. D1311.4.0.1. Oracular twig. N533. Treasure discovered by magic object.

D1314.2.1. *Divining rod sinks at place where tribe shall settle.* S. A. Indian (Inca): Alexander Lat. Am. 249.

D1314.2.2. *Divining rod (twig) locates underground water supply.* Ireland, England, U. S.: *Baughman.

D1314.2.3. *Divining rod points to house of thief.* England: Baughman.

D1314.2.4. *Divining rod (twig) points out spot where unwed mother had drowned child.* U.S.: Baughman.

D1314.2.5. *Saint's staff becomes tree to indicate building site.* England: Baughman.

D1314.2.6. *Golden staff stuck into ground finds site for city.* S. A. Indian (Inca): Rowe BBAE CXLIII (2) 317.

D1314.3. *Saint's bachall discovers gold.* (Cf. D1277.) — Irish: Plummer clxxv, Cross.

N533. Treasure discovered by magic object.

D1314.4. *Bell indicates place for settlement.* Remains dumb until place destined for saint's final settlement is reached. (Cf. D1213, D1314.1.2, D1314.2.1.) — Irish: Plummer clxxvii, *Cross.

D1314.4.0.1. *Saint's bell lands at place where monastery is to be founded.* Irish myth: *Cross.

D1213. Magic bell. V118. Monasteries.

D1314.4.1. *Bell rings to indicate location of well.* Irish myth: Cross.

D1314.5. *Hand-of-glory indicates location of treasure.* (Cf. D1162.2.1.) — *Kittredge Witchcraft 144, 463 n. 50.

D1314.6. *Loaf of bread locates drowned man.* Floated on water comes to rest directly over corpse. (Cf. D1031.1.) — *Kittredge Witchcraft 48, 400 n. 194; England: *Baughman.

D1314.7. *Magic plant (flower) shows location of treasure.* (Cf. D965, D975.) — *Norlind Skattsägner 19ff. — Lithuanian: Balys Index No. 3646.

D1314.7.1. *Mandrake shows location of treasure.* (Cf. D965.1, D1311.13.) — *Norlind Skattsägner 23ff.; Penzer III 153.

D1314.8. *Jewels aid in search for treasure.* (Cf. D1071.) — *Norlind Skattsägner 29.

D1314.9. *Magic cloth leads owner to lost horses.* (Cf. D1051.) Irish myth: Cross.

D1314.10. *Fiery pillar guides person* (to church). (Cf. D1271.) Irish myth: *Cross.

D1162. Magic light. F964.0.1. Pillar of fire in sky.

D1314.11. *Seat-pillars thrown in the sea (with god's image) indicate where to settle.* Icelandic: *Boberg.

D1314.12. *Coffin lands where the dead is to be buried, and his son to settle.* Icelandic: *Boberg.

D1314.12.1. *Rope breaks at proper burial place* (Cf. D1203.) Chinese: Graham.

D1314.13. *Star indicates location of newborn hero.* Irish myth: Cross.

F961.2.1. Bright star (indicates birth of holy person).

D1314.13.1. *Star of Bethlehem.* Irish myth: Cross.

V211. Christ.

D1314.14. *Four balls given to each of four impoverished men point out places where they should dig.* (Cf. 1256.) India: Thompson-Balys.

D1314.15. *Dried root sprouts when planted to indicate spot where holy man should set up his abode.* (Cf. D967.) India: Thompson-Balys.

D1315. *Magic object locates lost person.*

D1315.1. *Magic arrow locates lost person.* (Cf. D1314.1.ff.) S. A. Indian (Toba): Métraux MAFLS XL 147.

D1316. *Magic object reveals truth.* (Cf. D1318.) Irish myth: *Cross; Icelandic: Boberg.

B130. Truth-telling animals. B131. Bird of Truth. B133.4. Speaking horse-head. B134. Truth-telling dog. D1419.2.1. Magic bell paralyzes perjurer. G64. Speaking human flesh. H251. Test of truth by magic object. H410. Chastity test by magic object or ordeals.

D1316.1. *Stone reveals truth.* (Cf. D931.) Icelandic: *Boberg; Africa (Angola): Chatelain 29ff., 43ff.

H171.5. Stone of Destiny. H251.2. Stone of truth.

D1316.2. *Magic lamp indicates falsehood by lighting.* (Cf. D1162.1.) India: Thompson-Balys; Africa (Angola): Chatelain 43ff. (Version B.)

D1316.3. *Speaking spittle reveals truth.* (Cf. D1001.) Africa (Zulu): Callaway 64.

R135.0.1. Stolen wife makes trail of speaking spittle for husband.

D1316.4. *Magic ring permits owner to learn person's secret thoughts.* (Cf. D1076.) — Chauvin VI 108 No. 272.

D1316.4.1. *Magic ring shows the true nature of its possessor.* (Cf. D1076.) Icelandic: *Boberg.

D1316.4.2. *Magic spectacles allow wearer to read others' thoughts.* (Cf. D1299.5.) India: Thompson-Balys.

D1316.5. *Magic speaking reed (tree) betrays secret.* King has whispered secret to hole in the ground. Reed growing from this hole tells the secret. — *Köhler-Bolte I 383 n. 1, 511, 587; Sébillot RTP I 327, VII 356; *Zs. d. deutschen morgenland. Gesel. XL 549; Crooke FL XXII 183; *BP IV 147 n. 7 (Celtic): *Basset 1001 Contes II 258; Irish myth: *Cross; India: Thompson-Balys.

D950. Magic tree. D1610. Magic speaking objects. D1610.2. Speaking tree. D1610.34. Fiddle made from wood secret has been confided to reveals it. F511.2.2. Person with ass's (horse's) ears. N440. Secrets overheard. N465. Secret physical peculiarity discovered by barber.

D1316.5.1. *Voice comes forth from tree, revealing truth.* India: Thompson-Balys.

D1316.6. *Magic goblet (cup) indicates truth or falsehood.* (Cf. D1171.6.2.) Irish myth: *Cross; Jewish: Neuman.

D1565.4. Saint's breath restores shattered vessel.

D1316.7. *Magic sod indicates falsehood by turning grassy surface downward, truth by turning it upward.* (Cf. D934.1.) Irish myth: *Cross.

D1316.8. *Magic collar indicates falsehood by squeezing throat (hand, foot), truth by falling to ground.* (Cf. D1068.) Irish myth: *Cross.

H251.3.6. Chain (collar) around neck tests truth.

D1316.9. *Magic epistle (brought from apostle) assures wearer will utter truth.* (Cf. D1266.1.) Irish myth: *Cross.

V151. Sacred writings.

D1316.10. *Pig cooked when true story is told.* (Cf. D1281.1.) Irish myth: *Cross.

H252.0.1. Test: telling true stories.

D1316.11. *Sword turns upon owner when untruth is uttered.* (Cf. D1081.) Irish myth: Cross.

D1610.9. Speaking sword. F408.1. Demon occupies sword. M113.1. Oath taken on arms.

D1316.12. *Magic root reveals truth when water is poured over it.* (Cf. D967.) India: Thompson-Balys.

D1316.13. *Magic bird's tongue reveals truth.* (Cf. D1011.6.) Jewish: Neuman.

D1317. *Magic object warns of danger.* Irish myth: Cross.

B133.1. Horse warns hero of danger. B143.1. Bird gives warning. B521.3. Animal warns against attack. D1380. Magic object protects. D1813.1.1. Dream warns emperor of wife's unfaithfulness. K500. Escape from death or danger by deception.

D1317.0.1. *Magic object detects poison.* (Cf. D1317.4.) — *Penzer I 110, IV 228 n. 1, IX 143; Dickson 228 n. 25.

B521.1. Animals warns against poison. D1383. Magic object protects from poison. D1820.1.1. Magic sight of holy man enables him to recognize the king even though he is blind. He also sees that a man is about to poison him. H1515.2. Poisoned drink test. V229.6.2. Ale poisoned by druid miraculously purified by saint.

D1317.1. *Buttocks as magic watcher.* (Cf. D999.) — N. A. Indian: *Thompson Tales 296 n. 83.

D1610.6.3. Speaking buttocks.

D1317.2. *Magic gall-bladder warns of danger.* (Cf. D1015.2.) — Africa (Basuto): Jacottet 214 No. 32.

D1317.3. *Magic swallow-skin warns of danger.* (Cf. D1025.4.) — Africa (Zulu): Callaway 53.

D1317.4. *Magic bracelet warns of poison.* (Cf. D1074, D1317.0.1.) — *Chauvin VI 107 No. 272 n. 4.

D1317.4.1. *Truth-telling voice in wall warns against poisoned food.* India: Thompson-Balys.

D1317.5. *Magic ring gives warning.* (Cf. D1076.) — Type 425; Tegethoff 34f. — Icelandic: *Boberg; English: Wells II (Horn Childe and Maiden Rimnild).

D1317.5.1. *Magic ring warns of poison.* (Cf. D1076, D1317.4, D1317.0.1.) — Kittredge Witchcraft III, 440 n. 58.

D1317.5.2. *Magic ring awakens person in morning.* (Cf. D1076.) — *Fb "ring" III 60b.

D1317.6. *Magic sword gives warning.* (Cf. 1081.)

D1610.9. Speaking sword.

D1317.6.1. *Sword bursts in son's hand when he is about to kill his father.* *Fb "sværd" III 690b.

N731.2. Father-son combat. Neither knows who the other is.

D1317.7. *Magic bell gives alarm.* (Cf. D1213.) — French Canadian: Barbeau JAFL XXIX 73; cf. Types 327A, 328. — Thompson River: Teit JAFL XXIX 320 No. 11.

D1601.18.1. Self-ringing bell. D1612.1. Magic object betrays fugitive.

D1317.8. *Magic dice give warning.* Tell their master, a thief, when to seek safety (Cf. D1284.) — Pauli (ed. Bolte) No. 379.

D1317.9. *Statue gives warning.* (Cf. D1268.)

D1317.9.1. *Brass (copper) statue at city gates blows on trumpet at stranger's approach.* *Chauvin V 30 No. 13 n. 1, 265 No. 154.

D1620.1.1. Automatic statue of trumpeter.

D1317.10. *Wagon refuses to move because ghost is sitting in it.* (Cf. D1113, D1654.5.) — Fb "vogn" III 1078a.

E411.9.3. Horse unable to draw evil dead man.

D1317.11. *Bedstead warns of danger of snake.* (Cf. D1154.1.) India: Thompson-Balys.

D1317.12. *Magic stone gives warning.* (Cf. D931.) Irish myth: Cross; Icelandic: *Boberg; Eskimo (Greenland): Rasmussen III 300.

D1317.12.1. *Stone bleeds three days before church is plundered.* Irish myth: Cross.

D474. Transformation: object becomes bloody. F991. Object bleeds.

D1317.13. *Magic shield roars when bearer is in danger.* (Cf. D1101.1.) Irish myth: *Cross.

D1549.10. Waves answer roar of magic shield. D1610.24. Magic shield roars. D1812.5.1.17.3. Roaring of shield as evil omen.

D1317.14. *Bones (human) warn of danger.* (Cf. D1007.) Eskimo (Greenland): Rink 265.

D1317.15. *Golden cock on tent warns against danger.* Norse: *Boberg.

D1317.16. *Magic spear warns of danger.* (Cf. D1084.) Icelandic: Boberg.

D1317.17. *Knife sings as warning of fraud.* (Cf. D1083.) Icelandic: Boberg.

D1317.18. *Magic drinking horn gives warning.* (Cf. D1171.6.3.) Icelandic: *Boberg.

F866. Extraordinary cup.

D1317.19. *Cloak warns.* (Cf. D1053) Icelandic: *Boberg.

D1317.20. *Tree warns of danger.* India: *Thompson-Balys.

D950. Magic tree. D1610.2. Speaking tree.

D1317.21. *House-pillars warn.* Eskimo (Greenland): Rink 442.

D1317.22. *Water rages by boat of would-be murderer.* (Cf. D1242.) Eskimo (Greenland): Rasmussen II 317, 321, III 300, Holm 45, Rink 147.

D1318. *Magic object reveals guilt.*

B130. Truth-telling animals. B131.1. Bird reveals murder. B131.2. Bird reveals treachery. B131.3. Bird betrays woman's infidelity. B133.2.

Horse reveals treachery. B134.1. Dog betrays woman's infidelity. D1316. Magic object reveals truth. D1817. Magic detection of crime. E631.0.5. Tree from innocent man's blood. F961.1.1. Sun refuses to shine when murder is done. H210. Test of guilt or innocence. H251.1. Bocca della Verità. Person swearing oath places hand in mouth of image. If oath is false the hand is bitten off. H410. Chastity test by magic objects and ordeals. H411. Magic object points out unchaste woman. H430. Chastity index. Objects indicate faithfulness or unfaithfulness of separated lovers (husband or wife). J1142. Pseudo-scientific methods of detecting. K425. King's daughter put into brothel to catch thief. M359.1. Prophecy: weapons with which man is killed will recount deed to his son. N270. Crime inevitably comes to light. N271.1. The sun brings all to light. N271.3. The Cranes of Ibycus. T575.1.1. Child in mother's womb reveals crime.

D1318.0.1. *Magic object picks out guilty man.* Basset RTP VII 621.

D1318.1. *Stone reveals guilt.*

D931. Magic stone. H251.2. Stone of truth.

D1318.1.1. *Stone bursts as sign of unjust judgment.* *Fb "sten" III 554a.

M0. Judgments and decrees.

D1318.2. *Dead fish reveals guilt.*

D1318.2.1. *Laughing fish reveals unjust judgment.* A severe judgment is rendered for a small offence. As the convicted man is being led away, a dead (dried) fish is heard to laugh. The fish reveals that he has laughed at the foolishness of the judge who, while he punishes minor offences severely, is unable to see the capital crimes in his own household. (Cf. D1281.) *Bolte Reise der Söhne Giaffers 216. — India: Thompson-Balys, *Penzer I 46ff., VII 254, IX 142. — Cf. Child I 241, II 501b, IV 452a, V 288b.

B124. Wise fish. B144. Prophetic fish. B175. Magic fish. B211.11. Speaking fish. C460. Laughing tabu. D1639.4. Statue laughs and reveals crime. J130. Wisdom (knowledge) acquired from animals. K2000. Hypocrites. M0. Judgments and decrees. N456. Enigmatical smile (laugh) reveals secret knowledge. S261.1. Child as foundation sacrifice smiles and wins freedom.

D1318.3. *Charms indicate guilt.* (Cf. D1274.) — Africa (Bushman): Theal Zambesi 56.

D1318.4. *Magic seed indicates guilt.* (Cf. D971.)

D1318.5. *Blood indicates guilt or innocence.* (Cf. D1003.) Hdwb. d. Märchens s.v. "Blut"; Icelandic: Boberg.

D1610.16. Blood speaks.

D1318.5.1. *Blood springs from murderer's finger when he touches victim.* Fb "blod" IV 47a.

D1318.5.2. *Corpse bleeds when murderer touches it.* **Christensen (C. V.) Baareprøven (1900); Fb "blod" IV 47a; Knudsen (H.) En Baareprøve (Danske Studier 1932 69ff.); Von Künssberg Jahrb. f. historische Volksk. I (1925) 94, 120; Jobbé-Duval Essais de folklore juridique[2] (Paris, 1920); English: Child II 143, 146, 148, 153, IV 468a, *Baughman; North Carolina: Brown Coll. I 639; Jewish: Neuman.

D1318.5.3. *Each drop of innocent blood turns to burning candle.* English: Child I 172, II 39b.

D1318.5.4. *Speaking blood reveals murder.* Frazer Old Testament I 101; Fb "blod" IV 47ab; Hdwb. d. Märchens s.v. "Blut".

D1318.5.5. *Blood drops from stone to indicate girl's innocence.* Finnish: Aarne FFC XXXIII 47 No. 87**.

D1318.5.6. *Blood bubbles at place of murder.* Jewish: Neuman.

E761.1.5. Life token: blood boils.

D1318.6. *Divining bones reveal guilt.* (Cf. D1013.) — Africa (Basuto): Jacottet 180 No. 26.

D1318.7. *Flesh reveals guilt.*

D1318.7.0.1. *Speaking flesh reveals murder.* Molucca: Dixon 230.

D1318.7.1. *Flesh of animal reveals guilt.* (Cf. D1017.) India: Thompson-Balys.

E784. Flesh regrows.

D1318.7.1.1. *Flesh of stolen animal cannot be cooked* (turns putrid). Irish: Plummer cxliii, Cross.

C841. Tabu: killing certain animals. V134.3. Fish in water from certain well: water refuses to boil till fish are returned to well.

D1318.7.1.2. *Food sticks in thief's throat and betrays him.* (Cf. D1030.) India: Thompson-Balys.

D1318.8. *Magic cloth reveals guilt.* (Cf. D1051.)

D1318.8.1. *Magic cloth betrays thief.* Calls out, telling who is wearing it. Ibo of Nigeria: Thomas 124.

D1318.9. *Ring reveals guilt.* (Cf. D1076.)

D1318.9.1. *Ring springs asunder when faithlessness of lover is learned* *Bolte Zs. f. Vksk. XX 66.

E761.5.3. Life token: ring springs asunder. H433.1. Ring as chastity index. Indicates faithlessness by color.

D1318.10. *Ship reveals guilt.* (Cf. D1123.)

D1318.10.1. *Ship refuses to move with guilty man aboard.* *BP IV 196f.; Fb "skib" III 242b. — English: Child V 484 s.v. "Jonah"; U. S.: Baughman.

D1318.11. *Light reveals guilt.* (Cf. D1162).

D1318.11.1. *Light where murder is committed.* Fb "lys" II 481b.

D1318.12. *Vessels reveal guilt.* (Cf. D1171.)

D1318.12.1. *Vessels burst and reveal disobedience.* Irish: Plummer clxxxvi, Cross.

D1318.12.1.1. *Poet's spell causes ale vessels to burst when request for ale is refused.* (Cf. D1275.4.) Irish myth: Cross.

P427.4. Poet (druid) as satirist. Q499.3. Satirizing as punishment for refusal to grant request.

D1318.13. *Magic cauldron reveals guilt.* (Cf. D1171.2.) — Welsh: Mac Culloch Celtic 95, Plummer clxxxvi, *Cross.

D1318.14. *Sack of gold retains at will any hand thrust in it.* (Cf. D1193.) — Spanish: Boggs FFC XC 49 No. 330.

D1318.15. *Mill will not grind stolen wheat.* (Cf. D1263.) Irish: Plummer clxxxvi, *Cross.

D1318.16. *Speaking earth reveals murder.* (Cf. D935, D1610.19.) Irish myth: Cross.

D1318.17. *River rises to drown liars.* (Cf. D1316, D915) Irish myth: Cross.

Q263. Lying (perjury) punished.

D1318.18. *Apples which grow from tree under which murder was done have red centers.* (Cf. D981.1.) U.S.: Baughman.

D1318.19. *Manna reveals guilt.* (Cf. D1031.0.1.) Jewish: Neuman.

D1322. *Magic object warns of death.*

D1812. Magic power of prophecy.

D1322.1. *Saw for coffin-making sounds to announce death.* North Carolina: Brown Collection I 641.

D1322.1.1. *Hammer in coffin maker's shop makes noise to announce a death.* (Cf. D1209.4.) North Carolina: Brown Collection I 640.

D1322.1.2. *Boards for coffin making mysteriously moved announces death.* North Carolina: Brown Collection I 641.

E723.5. Wraith selects lumber for coffin.

D1322.2. *Light moving toward cemetery as sign of death.* (Cf. D1162.) North Carolina: Brown Collection I 641.

D1323. *Magic object gives clairvoyance.* (Cf. D1331.1, D1825.) Jewish: Neuman.

D1323.1. *Magic clairvoyant mirror.* Type 425; Tegethoff 32; **Róheim Spiegelzauber; *Liebrecht 85, 88; *BP III 366ff.; *Kittredge Witchcraft 503 n. 1; MacCulloch Childhood 36f.; *Chauvin VIII 191 No. 228; *Handwb. d. Abergl. IX Nachträge 547—565; Fb "spejl" III 481a; *Bolte Reise der Söhne Giaffers 202f.; Pauli (ed. Bolte) No. 232. — England, U.S., Wales: *Baughman; Irish: Beal XXI 323; Icelandic: *Boberg; Chinese: Werner 244, 331; Japanese: Anesaki 325; Cape Verde Islands: Parsons MAFLS XV (1) 111 No. 39; S. A. Indian (Aztec): Alexander Lat. Am. 62; Africa (Fjort): Dennett 61 No. 12, (Vai): Ellis 200 No. 18, (Mpongwe): Nassau 15 No. 1.

D1163. Magic mirror. D1311.2. Mirror answers questions. D1821.3.7. Magic sight by looking into glass of water. N533.2. Treasure found by clairvoyant mirror.

D1323.1.1. *Magic mirror reflects the face of whoever dies.* India: Thompson-Balys.

D1323.2. *Magic clairvoyant vase.* (Cf. D1171.7.) — *Chauvin V 259 No. 154.

N533.1. Treasure discovered by clairvoyant vase.

D1323.3. *Magic clairvoyant windows.* Twelve, each more powerful than the next. (Cf. D1145.) — *Type 329; *BP III 365.

D1323.4. *Magic clairvoyant sphere.* Shows all that passes on earth by looking at that part of globe. (Cf. D1264.) — *Chauvin V 259 No. 154.

D1821.3.7.3. Crystal gazing.

D1323.4.1. *Salvatio Romae.* Image of land showing by means of magic bell outbreak of rebellion in any province. (Cf. D1213.) *Spargo 496b s.v. "Salvatio Romae".

D1323.5. *Magic salve gives clairvoyance* (Cf. 1244.) — *Fb "salve" III 150b; Chauvin V 146 No. 72.

D1331.2.2. Magic salve causes blindness. D1331.3.1. Salve causes magic sight and blindness. F235.4.1. Fairies made visible through use of ointment.

D1323.6. *Magic soap gives clairvoyance.* (Cf. D1195.) — Scotch: Macdougall and Calder 277.

F235.4.2. Fairies made visible through use of magic soap.

D1323.7. *Turf from church roof gives clairvoyance.* Placed on head in order to see witches. (Cf. D934.) — Fb "græstørv"; *De Vries Acta Philologica Scandinavica III 106ff.

D1981.4. Magic invisibility of witches. G250. Recognition of witches.

D1323.8. *Churchyard mould gives clairvoyance.* Placed in pocket in order to see witches. (Cf. D1278, G250.) — Fb. "kirkegaardsmuld".

D1323.9. *Clairvoyant tube.* (Cf. D1255.) — *Chauvin VI 133 No. 286 n. 2.

D1323.10. *Hat gives clairvoyance.* (Cf. D1067.1.) — Fb "hat" I 563b; Saintyves Perrault 291.

D1323.11. *Hair gives clairvoyance.* (Cf. D991.) — Modoc: Curtin Myths of the Modocs (Boston, 1912) 32.

D1323.12. *Clairvoyance by looking at object filled with water.* Marquesas: Handy 109, 118; Hawaii: Beckwith Myth 528; Tuamotu: Stimson MS (z-G. 13/420).

D1323.12.1. *Clairvoyant spring.* Lady whose lover is absent to look in spring each day. If she sees his shadow, he is about to marry another. (Cf. D927.) — English: Child I 192.

H430. Chastity index.

D1323.13. *Magic powder gives clairvoyance.* (Cf. D1246.) — Type 726.

D1331.3.2. Powder causes magic sight and blindness.

D1323.14. *Four-leaf clover gives clairvoyance.* (Cf. D965.7.) — *BP III 201.

F235.4.6. Fairies made visible when one carries four-leaf clover.

D1323.15. *Magic clairvoyant telescope.* Shows distant events. — *Fb "kikkert" IV 257a.

D1323.16. *Magic feather gives clairvoyance.* (Cf. D1021.) India: Thompson-Balys.

D1323.17. *Magic clairvoyant girdle.* (Cf. D1057.) Jewish: Neuman.

D1323.18. *Clairvoyance from prayer.* India: Thompson-Balys.

D1323.19. *Lamp gives him who looks into its flame a vision of the Most High.* (Cf. D1162.1.) India: Thompson-Balys.

D1324. *Magic object indicates tides.*

D1324.1. *Magic bag full at high tide, empty at ebb tide.* (Cf. D1193.) Irish myth: Cross.

D1663. Magic object works in contrary fashions.

D1324.1.1. *Magic tub drips at high tide, is watertight at ebb tide.* (Cf. D1171.14.) Irish myth: *Cross.

D1324.2. *Magic faggot drips to indicate rising tide.* (Cf. D957.) Irish myth: Cross.

D1325. *Magic object reveals future history.* (Cf. D1812.3.)

D1325.1. *Magic book wherein is written family's destiny.* (Cf. D1266.) India: Thompson-Balys.

D1326. *Magic object renders judgment.*

D1326.1. *Magic slippers approve or disapprove judicial decisions.* (Cf. D1065.7.) Buddhist myth: Malalasekera I 1066.

D1327. *Magic object locates fish (game).*

D1327.1. *Magic arrow locates fish.* (Cf. D1092.) S. A. Indian (Mataco): Métraux MAFLS XL 132.

D1327.2. *Magic doll consulted for hunting.* (Cf. D1268.) Eskimo (Bering Strait): Nelson RBAE XVIII 494.

D1329. *Magic object gives supernatural information — miscellaneous.*

D1329.1. *Putting head under saint's cloak reveals rewards of heaven.* Irish myth: *Cross.

D1053. Magic mantle (cloak). V511.1. Visions of heaven.

D1330. Magic object works physical change.

D685. Transformation by magic object.

D1331. *Magic object affects eyesight.*

D1820. Magic sight. F642. Person of remarkable sight. V52.15. Prayer said by saint into his right hand restores displaced eye of opponent.

D1331.1. *Object gives magic sight.* (Cf. D1323, D1825.)

F235.4. Fairies made visible through use of magic object.

D1331.1.1. *Hempseed sown to acquire magic sight.* (Cf. D971.2.) England, Wales: *Baughman; English: Child V 59, 286a.

D1331.1.2. *Medicine gives magic sight.* (Cf. D1240.) — India: Thompson-Balys; Africa (Benga): Nassau 215 No. 33.

D1331.1.3. *Fan gives magic sight.* (Cf. D1077.) Irish myth: Cross.

D1331.1.4. *Stone gives magic sight.* (Cf. D931.) Jewish: Neuman; Icelandic: *Boberg.

D1331.1.5. *Jewel gives magic sight.* (Cf. D1071.)

D1331.1.5.1. *Sapphire gives magic sight.* Jewish: Neuman.

D1331.2. *Magic object blinds.*

C943. Loss of sight for breaking tabu. D2062.2. Blinding by magic. D2066. Elfshot. Q451.7.0.2. Miraculous blindness as punishment.

D1331.2.1. *Magic spike causes blindness.* Throws such a strong ray of light. (Cf. D1285.) — Chinese: Werner 123.

D1331.2.2. *Magic salve causes blindness.* (Cf. D1244, D1331.3.1.) — *Fb "öje" III 1166b.

D1331.2.2.1. *Magic salve from underworld causes blindness.* Fb "öje".

D1331.2.3. *Virgin Mary's shift as banner causes blindness to opposing army.* (Cf. D1058.1.) — *Ward II 603.

V250. The Virgin Mary.

D1331.2.4. *Magic stone causes blindness.* (Cf. D931.) Irish myth: Cross.

D1331.2.5. *Sight of magic wheel causes blindness.* (Cf. D1207.) Irish myth: Cross.

D1331.2.6. *Magic mirror causes blindness.* (Cf. D1163.) Icelandic: Boberg.

D1331.2.7. *Dog's urine makes tiger blind.* (Cf. D1027.) India: Thompson-Balys.

D1331.2.8. *Magic storm blinds enemy troops.* (Cf. D905.) Jewish: Neuman.

K2350. Military strategy.

D1331.2.9. *Magic wind blinds.* (Cf. D906.) Jewish: Neuman.

D1331.3. *Magic object causes both supernatural sight and blindness.*

D1331.3.1. *Salve causes magic sight and blindness.* (Cf. D1244, D1323.5, D1331.2.2.) Put on left eye causes one to see all treasure of earth; on the right, makes blind. Chauvin V 146 No. 72.

N533. Treasure discovered by magic object.

D1331.3.2. *Powder causes magic sight and blindness.* (Cf. D1246, D1323.13.) Type 726*.

D1331.3.3. *Magic antimony, rubbed on hero's eyes, will make whatever he looks at become far or near, as he desires it.* (Cf. D1246.) India: Thompson-Balys.

D1331.4. *Magic object causes sight-shifting.* Irish myth: *Cross.

D1368. Magic object causes illusions.

D1331.4.1. *Saint's gospel-book causes sight-shifting.* (Cf. D1266.) Irish: Plummer clxxviii, Cross.

D1332. *Magic object affects hearing.*

D1332.1. *Magic object deafens.*

D1332.1.1. *Magic stone causes deafness.* (Cf. D931.) Irish myth: Cross.

D1332.1.2. *Sound of magic wheel causes deafness.* (Cf. D1207.) Irish myth: Cross.

D1335. *Object gives magic strength.* Irish myth: Cross.

D1389.3. Magic cup protects against loss of strength. D1830. Magic strength. D1836.1. Magic waxing and waning of strength. F531.1.6.13. Giant's strength in hair. F611.3. Strong hero acquires his strength.

D1335.1. *Magic strength-giving food.* (Cf. D1030.) — Fb "mad" II 525a, "styrke" III 630a. — Norse: Boberg; French Canadian: Barbeau JAFL XXIX 11; Greek: Frazer Apollodorus II 70 n. 2; Chinese: Graham; N. A. Indian (Thompson River): Hill-Tout BAAS LXIX 540.

G304.2.2.1. Troll's food gives man strength.

D1335.1.1. *Magic strength-giving rice-grain.* (Cf. D973.1.) — Japanese: Anesaki 358.

D1335.1.2. *Heart of enemy eaten produces magic strength.* Finnish: Holmberg Finno-Ugric 5.

D1335.1.3. *Fighting animals eaten produce magic strength.* (Cf. D1032.) India: Thompson-Balys.

D1335.1.4. *Manna produces magic strength.* (Cf. D1031.0.1.) Jewish: Neuman.

D1335.2. *Magic strength-giving drink.* (Cf. D1040.) — *Fb "styrke". — Icelandic: Sveinsson FFC LXXXIII xxxiii, Boberg*; Korean: Zong in-Sob 167 No. 72.

F833.1. Sword so heavy that hero must take drink of strength before swinging it.

D1335.2.1. *Blood as magic strengthening drink.* (Cf. D1041.) — Hdwb. d. Märchens s.v. "Blut". — Icelandic: *Boberg; Finnish: Holmberg Finno-Ugric 5.

E714.1. Soul (life) in the blood. M257. Dying monster's request and promise. Hero is to drink his blood, suck his eyes and brains, and give his heart to his loved one to eat. He will become marvelously strong and his wife will have three sons and four daughters with great powers.

D1335.2.2. *Water as magic strengthening drink.* (Cf. D1242.2.) *MacCulloch Childhood 70ff. — Irish myth: Cross.

D1335.2.3. *Milk as magic strengthening drink.* (Cf. D1043.) — Irish myth: Cross; Hindu: Keith 134; India: Thompson-Balys.

D1335.3. *Magic (iron) glove gives strength.* (Cf. D1066.1.) — Fb "styrke" III 630a, "handske" IV 199b. — Icelandic: *Boberg.

D1335.4. *Magic belt gives strength.* (Cf. D1057.) — *Type 590; *Fb "bælte" IV 84a; A. Haberlandt Gurtel als Heiltum in Volkskunde (Otto Lauffer zum 60. Geburtstage [1934] 83—96); Von der Hagen Gesammtabenteuer I 455ff. — Icelandic: *Boberg. — N. A. Indian (Chippewyan [European borrowing]): Thompson CColl II 392, (Micmac): Rand 274, 369, (Passamaquoddy): Leland 31.

F451.3.1. Power of dwarf in his belt. K975. Secret of magic strength treacherously discovered.

D1335.5. *Magic ring gives strength.* (Cf. D1076.) — *Dickson 135 n. 118; *Kittredge Witchcraft 111, 440 n. 53.

D1335.5.1. *Magic ring gives remarkable sexual prowess.* Cheremis: Sebeok-Nyerges.

D1335.5.2. *Solomon's power to hold kingdom dependent on ring; drops it in water.* Jewish: Neuman.

A2275.5.4. Dolphins seek King Solomon's ring.

D1335.6. *Magic dagger gives strength.* (Cf. D1083.1.) — Malone PMLA XLIII 409.

D1335.7. *Flask imparts magic strength to drinker.* (Cf. D1171.8.) — *Fb "flaske". — Norwegian: Dasent 204, 223.

D1335.8. *Bathing in magic cauldron gives strength.* (Cf. D1171.2.) — Norwegian: Dasent 281. — S. A. Indian (Kwakiutl): Boas and Hunt JE III 104 (certain wash-basin); cf. Haida: Swanton JE X 365.

D1832. Magic strength by bathing.

D1335.9. *Magic axe gives strength.* (Cf. D1206.) — Fb "styrke" III 630a.

D1335.10. *Magic medicine (charm) gives strength.* (Cf. D1241.) — Africa (Benga): Nassau 100 No. 7.

D1335.11. *Powder gives magic strength.* (Cf. D1246.) — Africa (Basuto): Jacottet 142 No. 20.

D1335.12. *Magic song gives strength.* (Cf. D1275.) — Icelandic: Boberg.

D1335.13. *Magic hammer gives strength.* (Cf. D1209.4.) — Icelandic: MacCulloch Eddic 22 (Thor).

D1335.14. *Magic strengthening staff.* (Cf. D1254.) Icelandic: *Boberg.

D1349.2. Magic object produces immunity from old age.

D1335.15. *Magic strength-giving apple.* (Cf. D981.) Cheremis: Sebeok-Nyerges.

D1335.16. *Image of lion gives magic strength.* (Cf. D468.) Jewish: Neuman.

D1335.17. *Garment gives bearer magic strength.* (Cf. D1052.) Jewish: Neuman.

D1336. *Magic object gives weakness.*

C942. Loss of strength from broken tabu. D1410. Magic object renders helpless. D1837. Magic weakness.

D1336.1. *Magic sword gives weakness.* (Cf. D1081.) — Irish myth: *Cross.

D1336.2. *Magic food gives weakness.* (Cf. D1030.) Irish myth: *Cross.

D1336.2.1. *Magic apple gives weakness.* (Cf. D981.1.) Icelandic: Boberg.

D1336.3. *Magic music gives weakness.* (Cf. D1275.1.) Irish myth: *Cross.

F262.3.7. Fairy music causes weakness.

D1336.4. *Magic shield gives weakness.* (Cf. D1101.1.) Irish myth: *Cross.

D1336.5. *Saint's bell gives weakness.* (Cf. D1213.) Irish myth: Cross.

D1336.6. *Magic fire gives weakness.* (Cf. D1271.) Irish myth: Cross.

D1336.7. *Magic drink gives weakness.* (Cf. D1040.) Irish myth: Cross.

D1336.8. *Magic spell gives weakness.* (Cf. D1273.) Irish myth: *Cross.

D1336.9. *Druids' (poets') spells bind.* (Cf. D1275.4.) Irish myth: *Cross.

D1411. Magic object binds person.

D1336.10. *When bow is taken away from owner, he loses all strength.* (Cf. D1091.) India: Thompson-Balys.

D1337. *Magic object makes beautiful or hideous.* Irish myth: Cross; Jewish: Neuman; Japanese: Ikeda.

D1860. Magic beautification. D1870. Magic hideousness.

D1337.1. *Magic object beautifies.* Chinese: Eberhard FFC CXX 121.

D1337.1.1. *Charm gives magic beauty.* (Cf. D1273.) — Breton: Sébillot Incidents s.v. "charme".

D1337.1.2. *Water gives magic beauty.* (Cf. D1242.1.) — Fb "livets vand" II 439b. — Jewish: Neuman; India: Thompson-Balys.

D1337.1.3. *Milk gives magic beauty.* When magic milk touches ugly girl she turns beautiful. (Cf. D1018.) — Italian Novella: Rotunda; Africa (Kaffir): Theal 70.

D1337.1.3.1. *Bathing hair in buffalo milk makes it unusually long.* India: Thompson-Balys.

D1337.1.4. *Bathing in magic cauldron gives beauty.* (Cf. D1171.2.) — Norwegian: Dasent 281.

D1866. Beautification by bathing.

D1337.1.5. *Magic spear gives beauty.* (Cf. D1084.) — Also gives ugliness at will. Icelandic: Ritterhaus 227f. No. 54.

D1337.1.6. *Beautification by use of saint's spittle.* (Cf. D1001.) — Irish: Plummer clxxviii, *Cross.

D1337.1.7. *Magic needle transforms a room from plainness to beauty.* (Cf. D1181.) — *Type 585; BP III 355.

D1337.1.8. *Magic liquid gives beauty.* (Cf. D1242.) — Penzer VII 61.

D1337.1.8.1. *Rose water gives magic beauty.* Italian Novella: Rotunda.

D1337.1.9. *Magic wand beautifies.* (Cf. D1254.1.) — Irish myth: Cross.

D1337.1.10. *Magic apple makes beautiful.* (Cf. D981.1.) Cheremis: Sebeok-Nyerges.

D1337.1.11. *Playing of magic flute beautifies.* (Cf. D1223.1.) — Chinese: Graham.

D1337.1.12. *Magic jewel beautifies.* (Cf. D1071.) — Jewish: Neuman.

D1337.2. *Magic object makes hideous.*

A2402. Cause of animal's ugliness.

D1337.2.1. *Magic leaves turn white bird black.* (Cf. D955, A2411.2.6.) — Africa (Ibo of Nigeria): Basden 280.

D1337.2.2. *Magic herbs render hideous.* (Cf. D965.) — Greek: Fox 263 (Skylla).

D1337.2.3. *Dragon's breath renders hideous.* (Cf. D1029.1.) — Irish myth: Cross.

B11.2.11. Fire-breathing dragon.

D1337.2.4. *Magic water makes ugly.* (Cf. D1242.1.) — Jewish: Neuman.

D1337.2.5. *Magic skin makes person appear ugly.* (Cf. D1005.) German: Grimm No. 179.

D1338. *Magic object rejuvenates.* (Cf. D1880.) Irish myth: *Cross.

B594. Animal rejuvenates person. D1889.1. Rejuvenation by reading in book. D1889.2. Rejuvenation by looking into mirror. E670. Repeated reincarnation. F167.9. Otherworld people ever young, ever beautiful.

D1338.0.1. *Magic object retards aging.*

D1338.0.1.1. *Elixir retards aging.* (Cf. D1242.3.) — India: Thompson-Balys.

D1338.1. *Magic drink rejuvenates.* (Cf. D1040.) — Irish myth: *Cross; India: Thompson-Balys.

A154. Magic drink gives immortality to gods.

D1338.1.1. *Fountain of youth.* (Cf. D925, D926, D927, D1341.1.) Water from certain fountain rejuvenates. — **Hopkins JAOS XXVI 1—67, 411—415; Penzer Ocean IV 145; DeCock Studien 16ff.; *Fb "ungdom" III 979b. — Irish myth: *Cross; Icelandic: Boberg; Breton: Sébillot Incidents s.v. "fontaine"; French Canadian: Barbeau JAFL XXIX 11; U.S.: *Baughman; Greek: Rohde Der griechische Roman 222; Japanese: Ikeda. — Alexander Lat. Am. 20 n. 6, 349. — N. A. Indian: *Thompson Tales 284 n. 50a.

K116. Betrayal through pretended fountain of youth.

D1338.1.1.1. *Magic lake rejuvenates.* (Cf. D921.) — Irish myth: *Cross.

D1338.1.2. *Water of youth.* (Cf. D1242.1.) — Type 551; *BP II 394ff.; *Wünsche Die Sagen vom Lebensbaum und Lebenswasser (Leipzig, 1905); *Dh II 154; *Chauvin VI 73f. Nos. 239, 202.

E80. Water of life. H1321.3. Quest for the water of youth.

D1338.1.3. *Magic blood rejuvenates.* (Cf. D1003.) — Fb "blod" IV 47a.

D1338.2. *Rejuvenation by plant.* (Cf. D965.) — *Chauvin VI 74 No. 239. — Babylonian: Gilgamesh-epos XI 282ff. (eaten by serpent); Gaster Oldest Stories 51.

D1338.2.1. *Rejuvenation by juice of plant.* (Cf. D974). — *Dh II 154. — Irish myth: Cross.

D1338.2.2. *Root of eternal youth.* India: Thompson-Balys.

D1338.3. *Rejuvenation by fruit.* (Cf. D981.) — *Chauvin VI 74 No. 239; BP II 147. — India: Thompson-Balys, Penzer VI 216.

D1338.3.1. *Rejuvenation by apple.* Golden apples of youth. (Cf. D981.1.) — *Chauvin VI 74 No. 239. — Icelandic: Boberg (Idhunn).

D1338.3.2. *Magic peach gives immunity from age.* (Cf. D981.2.) — Chinese: Werner 270.

D1338.3.3. *Rejuvenation by fruit of magic tree.* (Cf. D950.) — Irish myth: Cross.

D981. Magic fruit.

D1338.3.3.1. *Year added to life by eating fruit of magic tree.* (Cf. D950.) Irish myth: Cross.

D1793. Magic results from eating or drinking.

D1338.4. *Bath in magic milk rejuvenates.* (Cf. D1080.) — Köhler-Bolte I 468 (boiling milk); Dh II 154.

D1886.1. Rejuvenation by burning and throwing bones into tub of milk. D1887. Rejuvenation by bathing. E80.1.1. Resuscitation by bathing in milk.

D1338.5. *Rejuvenation by ring.* (Cf. D1076.) — Hartland Science 204; Fb "ungdom" III 979b.

D1338.6. *Rejuvenation in magic mill.* (Cf. D1263.) — Dh II 155.

D1338.7. *Land of youth.* Land which keeps off old age. — Fb "ungdom" III 979b; Hartland Science 196f. — Irish: MacCulloch Celtic 181, *Cross; Icelandic: Boberg.

F111. Journey to earthly paradise.

D1338.8. *Rejuvenation by magic oil.* (Cf. D1244.) — Pauli (ed. Bolte) No. 328.

D1338.9. *Rejuvenation by magic honey.* (Cf. D1037.) Hindu: Keith 158.

D1338.10. *Rejuvenation by magic tub.* (Cf. D1171.14.) — Irish myth: Cross.

D1338.11. *Rejuvenation by magic manure dust.* (Cf. D1026.) Chinese: Graham.

D1338.12. *Rejuvenation by magic feather* (Cf. D1021.) — India: Thompson-Balys.

D1338.13. *Rejuvenation by magic rice.* (Cf. D973.1.) — India: Thompson-Balys.

D1341. *Magic object makes person old.*

D1890. Magic aging. K1072. Fairy induces hero to dive into lake which makes person old.

D1341.0.1. *Magic well makes person's hair gray.* (Cf. D926.) — Irish myth: Cross.

D1341.1. *Magic fountain makes person old.* (Cf. D925, D1338.1.1.) — *Fb "ungdom" III 979b; Boberg.

D1341.2. *Magic cloak makes person old.* (Cf. D1053.) — Irish myth: Cross.

D1341.3. *Magic ointment makes person old.* (Cf. D1244.) Cheremis: Sebeok-Nyerges.

D1341.4. *Magic feather brings supernatural old age.* (Cf. D1021.) — India: Thompson-Balys.

D1342. *Magic object gives health.* Irish myth: Cross.

A1438. Origin of medicine (healing). B510. Healing by animals. D1500. Magic object controls disease. D2161. Magic healing power. F950. Marvelous cures. V221. Magic healing by saints.

D1342.1. *Magic ring gives health.* (Cf. D1076.) — Kittredge Witchcraft III, 440 n. 54.

D1342.2. *Magic apple gives health.* (Cf. D981.1.) — *Fb "æble" III 1135b.

F343.15. Magic apple as fairy gift.

D1342.3. *Magic wood gives health.* (Cf. D956.) — Jewish: Neuman.

D1342.4. *Magic wand gives health.* (Cf. D1254.1.) — India: Thompson-Balys.

D1342.5. *Amulet guarantees health.* (Cf. D1070.) Eskimo (Greenland): Rink 424.

D1343. *Magic object gives skill.*

D1343.1. *Magic oars give skill.* (Cf. D1124.) — Eskimo (Greenland): Rasmussen II 153, 157.

D1344. *Magic object gives invulnerability.* *Kittredge Witchcraft *405 nn. 238—9. — Irish myth: *Cross.

D1840. Magic invulnerability.

D1344.1. *Magic ring renders invulnerable.* (Cf. D1076.) — *Kittredge Witchcraft 111, 440 n. 52; *Fb "ring" III 60b. — English: Child I 189f., Wells 9 (King Horn), II (Horn Childe and Maiden Rimnild); Icelandic: Boberg.

D1344.2. *Magic drug renders invulnerable.* (Cf. D1240.) — Greek: Frazer Apollodorus I 110 n. 1.

D1344.2.1. *Magic drug gives immunity from fire and iron.* Greek: Fox 112.

D1344.3. *Amulet renders invulnerable.* (Cf. D1070.) — De Cock Studien 156.

D1344.4. *Charm (written) renders invulnerable.* (Cf. D1273.) — De Cock Studien 161; Irish myth: Cross.

D1344.5. *Magic ointment renders invulnerable.* (Cf. D1244.) — Greek: Roscher Lexikon I 24 s.v. "Achilleus"; Boberg.

D1344.6. *Saint's tunic renders invulnerable.* (Cf. D1052.) — Irish: Plummer clxxx, Cross.

V220. Saints.

D1344.7. *Saint's girdle renders invulnerable.* (Cf. D1057.1.) — Irish: Plummer clxxx, Cross.

D1344.8. *Saint's cowl renders invulnerable.* (Cf. D1067.3.1.) — Irish: Plummer clxxx, *Cross.

N339.6. Man forgets to wear magic cowl and is killed.

D1344.8.1. *Hood renders invulnerable.* Eskimo (Greenland): Holm 17, Rasmussen II 70, III 304, Rink 344.

D1344.9. *Magic garment renders invulnerable.* (Cf. D1052.) — Icelandic: *Boberg; Jewish: Neuman; Eskimo (Greenland): Rasmussen II 210, III 105, 117, 153.

D1344.9.1. *Magic shirt gives invulnerability.* (Cf. D1056.) — *Fb "skjorte" III 268a; *Hdwb. d. Abergl. III 1712; Icelandic: *Boberg; Eskimo (Greenland): Rasmussen I 187.

F343.5.1. Fairy gives magic cloak (and shirt).

D1344.9.2. *Magic trousers render invulnerable.* (Cf. D1055.) — Irish myth: Cross.

D1344.10. *Magic mandrake gives invulnerability.* (Cf. D965.1.) — Penzer III 153.

D1344.11. *Magic sword gives invulnerability.* (Cf. D1081.) — Irish myth: *Cross.

D1344.12. *Blood smeared on body renders invulnerable.* (Cf. D1016.) — Jewish: Neuman.

D1344.13. *Magic (golden) helmet renders invulnerable.* (Cf. D1101.4.) — Icelandic: *Boberg.

D1345. *Magic object gives longevity.* Penzer VI 6 n. 1.

A191.1. Great age of gods. B841. Long-lived animals. D1857. Magic longevity.

D1345.1. *Serpent's water gives longevity.* (Cf. D1027.1.) — Africa (Zanzibar): Bateman 204 No. 10.

D1345.2. *Magic statue of dragon gives longevity.* (Cf. B11, D1268.) — Jewish: Neuman.

D1346. *Magic object gives immortality.*

D1850. Immortality. E700. The Soul. V311. Belief in the life to come.

D1346.1. *Magic drink gives immortality.* (Cf. D1040.) — Irish: MacCulloch Celtic 31, 54; Greek: Grote I 219; Jewish: Neuman; Hindu: Keith 41, Penzer III 253f.; Chinese: Giles 316.

A154.1. Magic drink gives immortality to gods.

D1346.1.1. *Water of life destroyed to prevent immortality: too long life would become tiresome.* India: Thompson-Balys.

E80. Water of life.

D1346.1.2. *Nectar of immortality.* (Cf. A154.) — India: Thompson-Balys.

D1346.2. *Fountain of immortality.* (Cf. D925, D926, D927, D1341.1, D1338.1.1.) — Hindu: Tawney I 499.

D1346.3. *Food of immortality.* (Cf. D1030.) — **G. Dumézil Le festin d'Immortalité (Paris, 1924). — Irish myth: *Cross.

A153.2. Magic food gives immortality to gods. F243.5. Fairies' food gives immortality.

D1346.3.1. *Magic honey gives immortality.* (Cf. D1037.) — Jewish: Neuman; Hindu: Keith 158.

D1346.4. *Tree of immortality.* (Cf. D950.) — Jewish: Neuman; Persian: Carnoy 281; S. A. Indian (Tiatinagua): Métraux BBAE CXLIII (3) 449.

E90. Tree of Life. Resuscitation by touching its branches. F162.3.1. Tree of Life in otherworld. Nourishes mankind.

D1346.5. *Plant of immortality.* (Cf. D965.) — Babylonian: Spence 158, 160, 178; Chinese: Eberhard FFC CXX 215.

H1333.2. Quest for plant of immortality.

D1346.6. *Fruit of immortality.* (Cf. D981.) — Jewish: Neuman; India: Thompson-Balys, Penzer VI 216.

C621. Forbidden fruit.

D1346.6.1. *Magic peach gives immortality.* (Cf. D981.2.) — Chinese: Werner 270, Eberhard FFC CXX 210.

D1346.6.2. *Apple of immortality.* (Cf. D981.1.) — India: Thompson-Balys.

D1346.7. *Pill of immortality.* (Cf. D1243.) — Chinese: Werner 184f., 330.

D1346.8. *Magic ointment gives immortality.* Burning at night and anointment with magic ointment by day. (Cf. D1244.) — Greek: Roscher Lexikon s.v. "Achilleus".

D1851.1. Immortality by burning.

D1346.8.1. *Oil of immortality.* (Cf. D1244.) — Jewish: Neuman.

D1346.9. *Magic sword gives immortality.* (Cf. D1081.) India: Thompson-Balys.

D1081. Magic sword.

D1346.10. *Magic water (sprinkled) gives immortality.* (Cf. D1242.) India: Thompson-Balys.

D1346.11. *Medicine gives immortality.* (Cf. D1241.) — India: Thompson-Balys.

D1346.12. *Incense gives immortality.* (Cf. D1295.) — Jewish: Neuman.

D1346.13. *Filth (dirt, excrements) eaten gives immortality.* (Cf. D1002.) — Chinese: Eberhard FFC CXX 161f.

D1346.14. *Magic cup gives immortality.* (Cf. D1171.6.) — Jewish: Neuman.

D1347. *Magic object produces fecundity.*

D1925. Fecundity magically induced. H1572. Test of fertility. T591.1. Magic remedies for barrenness or impotence.

D1347.1. *Magic apple produces fecundity.* (Cf. D981.1.) — Icelandic: Völsunga Saga 4.

T511.1.1. Conception from eating apple.

D1347.2. *Blood as remedy for barrenness in woman.* (Cf. D1003.) — *Fb "blod" IV 47a.

D1347.3. *Magic medicine makes sterile fertile.* (Cf. D1241.) — India: Thompson-Balys.

D1347.3.1. *Magic pills insure birth of twin sons.* (Cf. D1243.) India: Thompson-Balys.

D1347.4. *Magic statue gives fecundity.* (Cf. D1268.) — Jewish: Neuman.

D1347.5. *Magic fish (eaten) causes fecundity.* (Cf. D1032.1.) — Jewish: Neuman; S. A. Indian (Tupinamba): Métraux RMLP XXXIII 169.

D1347.6. *Hare's stomach causes fecundity.* (Cf. D1015.5.1.) — Jewish: Neuman.

D1349. *Magic object produces miscellaneous physical changes in persons or things.*

D1349.1. *Magic object produces immunity from hunger and thirst.* Irish myth: Cross.

D2033. Thirst magically caused to disappear.

D1349.1.1. *Magic peach produces immunity from hunger and thirst.* (Cf. D981.2.) — Chinese: Werner 270.

D1349.1.2. *Magic perfume produces immunity from hunger and thirst.* (Cf. D1245.) Irish myth: *Cross.

D1349.1.3. *Magic milk produces immunity from hunger and thirst.* (Cf. D1018.) — Irish myth: Cross.

D1349.1.4. *Magic belt produces immunity from hunger.* (Cf. D1057.) Icelandic: *Boberg.

D1349.1.5. *Magic sweets: one can quench thirst and the other can allay hunger.* (Cf. D1038.) India: Thompson-Balys.

D1349.1.6. *Tiny amount of food magically satisfies.* (Cf. D1030.) India: Thompson-Balys.

D1349.1.6.1. *One drop of blood when licked satisfies hunger.* (Cf. D1003.) — India: Thompson-Balys.

D1349.2. *Magic object produces immunity from old age.* Irish myth: Cross.

D1338. Magic object rejuvenates. F167.9. Otherworld people ever young, ever beautiful. F172. No time, no birth, no death in otherworld.

D1349.2.1. *Magic peach produces immunity from old age.* (Cf. D981.1.) — Chinese: Werner 270.

D1349.2.2. *Washing in magic bowl produces immunity from old age.* (Cf. D1172.2.) — Irish myth: *Cross.

D1788. Magic results from bathing.

D1349.2.3. *Magic apple produces immunity from old age.* (Cf. D981.1.) — Irish myth: Cross.

D1349.3. *Magic stone makes water like wine.* (Cf. D1071.) — Icelandic: Boberg.

D477.1. Water becomes wine. D1472.1.23. Rock produces wine.

D1349.4. *Magic jewel makes owner fat.* (Cf. D1071.) — Jewish: Neuman.

D1350. Magic object changes person's disposition.

D1351. *Magic object makes person peaceful.* Icelandic: *Boberg.

D1351.1. *Saint's bachall makes person peaceful.* (Cf. D1277.) — Irish: Plummer clxxv, Cross.

D1351.2. *Magic branch of peace.* Warfare ceases when it is shaken. (Cf. D954.) — Irish myth: *Cross.

D1359.3.1.2. Magic musical branch soothes listeners. P19.4.0.1. King's wand (rod).

D1351.3. *Magic veil changes enmity into peacefulness.* (Cf. D1061.) — Icelandic: Boberg.

D1351.4. *Charm which makes inhabitants of city faint-hearted.* (Cf. D1273.) — India: Thompson-Balys.

D1352. *Magic object has pre-natal influence.*

B635.2. Eaten meat of bear lover causes unborn son to have bear characteristics. D1925. Fecundity magically induced. T597. Ambitions of father transferred to child at moment of conception.

D1352.1. *Magic net has prenatal influence.* (Cf. D1196.) — Africa (Benga): Nassau No. 24, version 2.

D1353. *Magic object makes person foolish.*

D1367. Magic object causes insanity.

D1353.1. *Magic rain makes people foolish.* All on whom it falls act like fools. (Cf. D902.) — Pauli (ed. Bolte) No. 34.

J1714.2. The wise man and the rain of fools.

D1354. *Magic object makes person kind.* Italian Novella: Rotunda.

D1355. *Love-producing magic object.* *Hdwb. d. Abergl. I 775, 1007, II 1506, 1589, 1616, III 1279. — Breton: Sébillot Incidents s.v. "aimer".

B722.1. Magic love-working stone in swallow's head. C922. Death by smothering for breaking tabu. Man given secret box conveying power of making women love him. D1374. Magic object causes longing. D1425. Magic object draws lover (husband) to woman. D1426. Magic object draws woman to man. D1900. Love induced by magic. D2064.0.1. Magic love-sickness. H1213.1.1. Quest for man caused by sight of one of his hairs dropped by bird (or floating on river.)

D1355.0.1. *Magic spear produces love-sickness.* (Cf. D1084.) — Irish myth: Cross.

T24.1. Love-sickness.

D1355.1. *Love-producing music.* (Cf. D1275.1.) — English: Child V 489 s.v. "music".

D1355.1.1. *Love-producing song.* (Cf. D1275.) — Icelandic: *Boberg; Breton: Sébillot Incidents s.v. "chant". — N. A. Indian (Wichita): Barbeau GSCan XI 162f. Nos. 50, 51, (Micmac): Leland 82.

B53. Siren.

D1355.1.2. *Magic love-producing pipe (musical).* (Cf. D1224.) — English: Child I 47; N. A. Indian (Arikara): Dorsey CI XVII 85 No. 25, 90 No. 27.

D1355.1.3. *Magic love-producing horn.* (Cf. D1222.) — English: Child I 15—17, 23, 55, 367.

F301.2.1. Elf-knight produces love-longing by blowing on horn.

D1355.2. *Magic love-philtre.* (Cf. 1242.2.) — *Schoepperle Tristan and Isolt 401ff.; *Kittredge Witchcraft 107f., 436 nn. 26—31, 30, 383 n. 54. — Greek: Fox 72 (Minos), 200 (Phaon); Icelandic: *Boberg; English: Child V 305b, Wells 80 (Sir Tristrem), 145 (Parthenope of Blois); England, U.S.: *Baughman; India: *Thompson-Balys.

T21. Mutual love through accidental drinking of love-philtre.

D1355.2.1. *Water blessed by saint as love-philtre.* (Cf. D1242.1.) — Irish: Plummer clxxxviii, *Cross.

T53.3. Saint as matchmaker. V220. Saints.

D1355.2.1.1. *Baptismal water as love-philtre.* (Cf. D1242.1.1.) — Kittredge Witchcraft 470 nn. 123—125.

D1355.2.1.2. *Magic water causes sexual desire.* (Cf. D1242.1.) — Jewish: Neuman.

D1355.2.2. *Blood as love-philtre.* (Cf. D1003). — *Fb "blod" IV 46b; *Kittredge Witchcraft 30, 382 n. 53.

D1355.2.2.1. *Blood of wounded centaur as love philtre.* (Cf. D1016.) Greek: Grote I 139.

B21. Centaur.

D1355.2.3. *Semen in love-philtre.* — Kittredge Witchcraft 30, 382 n. 53.

D1355.3. *Love charm.* (Cf. D1274.) — Kittredge Witchcraft 30, 111, 382 n. 52, 440 nn. 61—70 passim. — Irish myth: *Cross; Icelandic: *Boberg; *English: Child I 57; India: *Thompson-Balys, Penzer I 137f.; Am. Negro (Georgia): Harris Nights 198 No. 34.

C192. Tabu: refusing to elope with woman who desires it. C929. "Destruction" threatened for refusing love of forthputting woman. D1273. Magic formula (charm). D1355.13. Love spot. D1782. Sympathetic magic. D1900. Love induced by magic. P535.0.4. Eric fine for seduction of means of love-charm. T55. Girl as wooer.

D1355.3.1. *Seed mixed with blood as love charm.* (Cf. D971.) — Greek: Frazer Apollodorus I 261 n. 1.

D1355.3.2. *Image (animal) pierced with pins as love charm.* Kittredge Witchcraft 100, *431f. nn. 202—211; England: Baughman.

D2063.1. Tormenting by sympathetic magic.

D1355.3.3. *Fruit pierced with pins as love charm.* (Cf. D981.) Kittredge Witchcraft 102, 433 n. 226.

D1355.3.4. *Entrails of live pigeon placed above house door fetch lover to the spot.* England: Baughman.

D1355.3.5. *Boiling lock of lover's hair draws him to sweetheart.* England: Baughman.

D1355.3.6. *Burning candle stuck with pins fetches lover.* England: *Baughman.

D1355.3.7. *Person burns salt and says charm to bring lover to spot.* England, U. S.: *Baughman.

D1355.3.8. *Person burns dragonsblood (plant) and says charm to bring lover to spot.* England: *Baughman.

D1355.4. *Ring produces love.* (Cf. D1076.) — *Kittredge Witchcraft 109, 436ff. nn. 38—48 passim; Fb "ring" III 60b. — Icelandic: *Boberg; Italian Novella: Rotunda.

D1355.5. *Magic hair produces love.* (Cf. D991.) — Wesselski Märchen 196; Frazer Golden Bough III 270. — N. A. Indian (Thompson River): Teit MAFLS VI 73 No. 23, (Shuswap): Teit JE II 708 No. 34 (in the last two named references, the hair is a woman's pubic hair); India: Thompson-Balys.

T11.4.1. Love through sight of hair of unknown princess.

D1355.6. *Churchyard mould produces love.* Girl takes three handfuls and passes it over churn. (Cf. D1278.1.) — Fb "kirkegaardsmuld" II 129b.

D1355.7. *Apple produces love.* (Cf. D981.1.) — *Fb "æble" III 1135a. — English: Child I 364; Irish myth: *Cross; Icelandic: *Boberg.

D1905.2. Apple divided and eaten as love charm. H316. Suitor test: apple thrown indicates princess's choice.

D1355.8. *Olive branch insures fidelity of husband.* Wife to beat him with it. (Cf. D954.) — Spanish: Boggs FFC XC 51 No. 340.

D1355.9. *Magic belt produces love.* (Cf. D1057.) — *Fb "bælte" IV 84a; Icelandic: *Boberg.

D1355.10. *Consecrated bread produces love.* (Cf. D1031.1.1.) *Kittredge Witchcraft 149, 469 nn. 107, 108.

D1355.10.1. *Consecrated bread kept in mouth and fed to toad produces love.* Kittredge Witchcraft 149, 469 n. 104; England: Baughman.

D1355.11. *Magic clothes produce love.* (Cf. D1050.) — Jewish: bin Gorion Born Judas[2] I 274.

D1355.11.1. *Magic moccasins produce love.* (Cf. D1065.4.) — N. A. Indian (Arapaho): Dorsey and Kroeber FM V 15 No. 6.

D1355.12. *Magic nuts (eaten) produce love.* (Cf. D985.) — Irish myth: *Cross.

F243.2. Fairies eat nuts.

D1355.13. *Love-spot.* Mark which makes man irresistible to any woman who sees it. — *Schoepperle Tristan and Isolt 401f.; Irish myth: *Cross.

A526.3. Culture hero has irresistible beauty spot.

D1355.13.1. *Charm placed on cheeks of hag causes love.* Irish myth: *Cross.

D1355.14. *Eaten fruit causes sexual desire.* (Cf. D981.) India: Thompson-Balys; Jewish: Neuman.

D1355.15. *Magic shears produce love.* (Cf. D1183.) — Irish myth: *Cross.

D1355.16. *Magic rod produces love.* (Cf. D1254.1, D1254.2.) Irish myth: Cross.

D1355.17. *Herb bath produces love.* (Cf. D965.) Irish myth: *Cross.

D1788. Magic results from bathing.

D1355.18. *Love charm (words).* (Cf. D1273.) India: Thompson-Balys.

D1355.18.1. *Word charms woven in clothing produce love.* England: Baughman.

D1355.19. *Magic writings produce love.* (Cf. D1266.1.) Icelandic: *Boberg.

D1355.20. *Green stone causes women to love the possessor.* (Cf. D1070.) Icelandic: *Boberg.

D1355.21. *Magic grass produces love when girl sleeps on it.* (Cf. D965.12) Icelandic: Boberg.

D1355.21.1. *Love charm from tuber.* S. A. Indian (Toba): Métraux MAFLS XL 28.

D1355.22. *Love-producing magic plant.* (Cf. D965.) Cheremis: Sebeok-Nyerges.

D1355.23. *Love-producing magic feather.* (Cf. D1021.) India: Thompson-Balys.

D1356. *Magic object represses lust.*

T317. The repression of lust.

D1356.1. *Magic girdle represses lust.* (Cf. D1057.1.) Icelandic: Boberg.

D1356.1.1. *Saint's girdle represses lust.* (Cf V220.) — Irish: Plummer clxxxi, Cross.

D1356.3. *Magic stone represses lust.* (Cf. D930.) Icelandic: Boberg.

D1357. *Magic object makes person cruel.*

S. Unnatural cruelty.

D1357.1. *Eating ferocious animal's heart makes person cruel.* (Cf. D1015.1, D1335.1.2.) — Icelandic: Boberg.

D1782. Sympathetic magic. E714.4.1. Eaten heart gives one the owner's qualities.

D1358. *Magic object makes person courageous.*

D1358.1. *Eating courageous animal's heart makes courageous.* (Cf. E714.4.1.)

D1782. Sympathetic magic.

D1358.1.1. *Eating dragon's heart makes courageous.* (Cf. B11, D1015.1.2.) — Icelandic: Völsunga Saga 79, Boberg.

D1358.1.2. *Eating serpent's and wolf's flesh makes courageous and impetuous.* (Cf. D1032.) Icelandic: Boberg.

D1358.2. *Magic spell makes person courageous.* (Cf. D1273, D1359.5.) — Irish myth: Cross.

D1358.3. *Magic crystal makes owner courageous.* (Cf. D1071.) — Jewish: Neuman.

D1359. *Magic object changes person's disposition — miscellaneous.*

D1359.1. *Magic object makes woman masterful.*

D1359.1.1. *Magic olive branch makes woman master in household.* (Cf. D954.) — Spanish: Boggs FFC XC 51 No. 340.

D1359.2. *Magic object causes mourning.*

D1273.1.1.1. Three meditations on death which prevent laughter.

D1359.2.1. *Magic music causes mourning.* (Cf. 1275.1.) — *BP II 502f.; Irish myth: *Cross; England: Baughman.

D1359.3. *Magic object causes joy.*

D1359.3.1. *Magic music causes joy.* (Cf. D1275.1.) — Irish myth: *Cross.

B172.2.2. Magic bird's song dispels grief.

D1359.3.1.1. *Magic (musical) horn (bell) relieves hearers of sorrow.* (Cf. D1213, D1222.) — *Krappe Balor 159.

D1359.3.1.2. *Magic musical branch soothes listeners.* (Cf. D1615.2.) — *Schoepperle Tristan and Isolt II 325. — Irish myth: *Cross.

D954. Magic bough. D1275.1. Magic music. D1351.2. Magic branch of peace. D1364.25.0.1. Musical branch causes magic sleep. F811.6. Tree with musical branches.

D1359.3.1.3. *Grief dispelled by sound of bell attached to magic fairy dog.* Irish myth: *Cross.

B731.6.0.1. Polychromatic dogs. D1275.2. Magic melody. F241.6. Fairy dogs.

D1359.3.2. *Happiness from eating magic pig.* (Cf. D1032.4.) Irish myth: Cross.

B183. Magic boar. F241.3.1. Fairy swine.

D1359.3.3. *Fruit of magic tree exhilarating.* (Cf. D950, D981.) Irish myth: Cross.

D1359.3.4. *Stone blessed by saint banishes sorrow.* (Cf. D931.) — Irish myth: *Cross.

D1359.4. *Magic food causes intoxication and sobriety.* (Cf. D1030.) — Irish myth: *Cross.

F243. Fairies' food.

D1359.5. *Magic sign assures that warriors will not flee from battle.* (Cf. D1299.1, D1358.2.) Irish myth: Cross.

D2350. Military strategy. P550. Military affairs.

D1359.6. *Magic object destroys pride.* German: Grimm No. 17.

D1360. Magic object effects temporary change in person.

D1361. *Magic object renders invisible.* *Aarne MSFO XXV 117; *Cox Cinderella 518; *Fb "usynlig". — Irish myth: *Cross; Breton: Sébillot Incidents s.v. "invisibilité".

B11.5.2. Dragon's power of magic invisibility. D1980. Magic invisibility. E421.1. Invisible ghosts.

D1361.1. *Magic mist of invisibility.* (Cf. D902.1.) — *Cox Cinderella 477. — Irish myth: *Cross; N. A. Indian: *Thompson Tales 339 n. 221b.

K532.1. Escape in mist of invisibility. R236. Fugitive aided by magic mist.

D1361.1.0.4. *Demons cause inpenetrable fog.* Irish myth: Cross.

D1361.1.1. *Magic mist separates person from his companions.* Irish myth: *Cross.

D1361.2. *Magic stone gives invisibility.* (Cf. D931.) — Köhler-Bolte I 114; Kittredge Witchcraft 176 n. 17. — Icelandic: *Boberg.

D1361.3. *Magic ash-tree renders invisible.* (Cf. D950.6.) — *Fb "usynlig".

D1361.4. *Magic calabash renders invisible.* (Cf. D965.2.) — Africa (Ekoi): Talbot 34.

D1361.5. *Magic seed renders invisible.*

D1361.5.1. *Magic fernseed renders invisible.* (Cf. D971.3.) — *Cox Cinderella 517; *Hdwb. d. Abergl. II 1215ff. — Irish myth: Cross; Scotland: Baughman.

D1361.6. *Magic flower renders invisible.* (Cf. D975.) — Cox Cinderella 518; Scottish: Baughman.

D1361.7. *"Hand of glory" renders light invisible.* Candles of human fat from dead man's hand make light invisible except to man holding it. (Cf. D1162.2.1.) — Penzer III 150; *Fb "tyvefinger" III 917b.

D1361.8. *Heart of unborn child renders person invisible.* (Cf. D997.1.1.) *Fb "hjærte" I 631b, IV 218b. — Swiss: Jegerlehner Oberwallis 293 No. 1.

D1985. Means of acquiring invisibility.

D1361.9. *Serpent's crown renders invisible.* (Cf. D1011.3.1, B112.)

D1361.10. *Magic feather renders invisible.* (Cf. D1021.) — Cox Cinderella 517.

D1361.11. *Magic herb renders invisible.* (Cf. D965.) Africa (Fang): Trilles 269.

D1361.12. *Magic cloak of invisibility.* (Cf. D1053.) — *Types 328, 400; Cox Cinderella 517; Penzer I 26; Dickson 134 n. 113; *Loomis White Magic 51. — English: Wells 59 (The Turke and Gawin); Irish: Krappe Balor 2 n. 9, *Cross, MacCulloch Celtic 55; Welsh: ibid. 106, 190; French Canadian: Barbeau JAFL XXIX 10. — Chinese: Graham; Japanese: Mitford 185ff., Ikeda; Philippine: Fansler MAFLS XII 177, (Tinguian): Cole 201 n. 1.; N. A. Indian: *Thompson Tales 339 n. 221a.

K532. Escape under mantle of invisibility.

D1361.12.1. *Saint's tunic renders invisible.* (Cf. D1052.) — Irish: Plummer clxxx, *Cross. (D1361.11.); Icelandic: Boberg.

V220. Saints.

D1361.13. *Magic belt renders invisible.* (Cf. D1057.) — *Fb "bælte" IV 84a; *Loomis White Magic 51. — French Canadian: Barbeau JAFL XXIX 10; Irish: Plummer clxxx, Cross.

D1361.14. *Magic hat renders invisible.* (Cf. D1067.1.) — Fb "usynlig" III 985b, "hat" I 563b, IV 202b. — Breton: Sébillot Incidents s. v. "chapeau".

D1361.15. *Magic cap renders invisible: tarnkappe.* (Cf. D1067.2, D1361.16.) *Penzer VI 149 n. 1; *Fb "usynlig" III 985b, "kappe" II 89, IV 253a; Cox Cinderella 517; Thien 30. — Greek: Fox 34, *Frazer Apollodorus I 153 n. 3 (Perseus); Icelandic: Dehmer Primitives' Erzählungsgut in den Islendingasögur 97, *Panzer Sigfrid 281 s.v. "Tarnkappe"; India: *Thompson-Balys; Chinese: Graham, Eberhard FFC CXX 109, 253. — N. A. Indian: *Thompson Tales 339 n. 221a.

D1067.2. Magic cap. K1349.10. Admission to woman's room by means of cap of invisibility.

D1361.16. *Saint's cowl renders invisible.* (Cf. D1067.3.1.) — Irish: Plummer clxxx, Cross.

D1361.17. *Magic ring renders invisible.* (Cf. D1076.) — *Fb "ring" III 60b; *Dickson 133f.; Cox Cinderella 518; *Kittredge Witchcraft 111, 440 n. 50; Brown Iwain 14 and passim; Günter 64. — Icelandic: *Boberg; Irish myth: Cross; Greek: Roscher Lexikon s.v. "Gyges"; India: *Thompson-Balys.

D1361.18. *Magic sword renders invisible.* (Cf. D1081.) — *Chauvin VI 66 No. 233.

D1361.19. *Magic jewel renders invisible.* (Cf. D1071.) — Cox Cinderella 517; Italian Novella: Rotunda.

H501.1. Test of wisdom: wise man sends ruler magic jewel.

D1361.20. *Helmet renders invisible.* (Cf. D1101.4.) — Greek: *Frazer Apollodorus I 47 n. 3; Icelandic: *Boberg.

D1361.21. *Ship becomes invisible.* (Cf. D1123.) — Breton: Sébillot Incidents s.v. "navire".

D1982.2. Ship made invisible.

D1361.22. *Magic medicine renders invisible.* (Cf. D1240.) — Type 576****.

D1361.22.1. *Magic pills render invisible.* (Cf. D1243.) — India: Thompson-Balys.

D1361.22.2. *Magic salve renders invisible.* (Cf. D1244.) — India: Thompson-Balys.

D1361.23. *Magic charm renders invisible.* (Cf. D1241.) — Jewish: Neuman; Africa (Ekoi): Talbot 34, 178.

D1361.24. *Magic drops render invisible.* (Cf. D1242.3.) — Type 576*****.

D1361.25. *Magic wand renders invisible.* (Cf. D1254.1.) — Fb "usynlig" III 985b. — Irish myth: Cross; German: MacCulloch Eddic 260; Chinese: Werner 326.

D1361.25.1. *Magic staff renders invisible.* (Cf. D1254.) Icelandic: MacCulloch Eddic 301, Boberg.

D1361.26. *Magic formula renders invisible.* (Cf. D1273.) — Irish myth: *Cross; Chinese: Werner 310.

D1985.2. Invisibility by reciting formula backwards.

D1361.27. *Magic light renders invisible.* (Cf. D1162.) — *Fb "usynlig" III 985b. — Icelandic: Boberg.

D1361.28. *Magic mirror renders invisible.* Does so when owner looks into it. (Cf. D1163.) — Fb "usynlig" III 985b.

D1361.29. *Magic animal's heart renders invisible.* (Cf. D1015.1.) — Fb "usynlig" III 985b.

D1361.30. *Magic bird-nest renders invisible.* (Cf. D1292.) — Cox Cinderella 517.

D1361.31. *Magic song renders invisible.* (Cf. D1275.) — Irish: Plummer clxxix, Cross; Eskimo (Greenland): Rasmussen III 293.

D1361.32. *Magic mask renders invisible.* (Cf. D1067.4.) — Irish myth: Cross; Chinese: Eberhard FFC CXX 110.

R23. Abduction with aid of magic mask which makes invisible.

D1361.33. *Magic veil renders invisible.* (Cf. D1061.) — Irish myth: Cross.

D1361.34. *Magic bag renders invisible.* (Cf. D902.1.1.) Icelandic: *Boberg.

D1361.35. *Magic tiger's hair renders invisible.* (Cf. D1023.) India: Thompson-Balys.

D1023. Magic hair of animal.

D1361.36. *Magic trousers render invisible.* (Cf. D1055.) Cheremis: Sebeok-Nyerges.

D1361.37. *Magic shirt renders invisible.* (Cf. D1056.) Cheremis: Sebeok-Nyerges.

D1361.38. *Magic boots render invisible* (Cf. D1065.1.) Cheremis: Sebeok-Nyerges.

D1361.39. *Fact that woman bears future saint in womb renders her invisible.* Irish myth: Cross.

D1361.40. *Magic cloth renders invisible.* (Cf. D1051.) Icelandic: Boberg.

D1361.41. *Cross renders invisible.* Icelandic: Boberg.

D1361.42. *Magic lampblack renders invisible.* (Cf. D931.1.3.) India: Thompson-Balys.

D1361.43. *Magic mark on forehead renders invisible.* India: Thompson-Balys.

D1361.44. *Magic ashes render invisible.* (Cf. D931.1.2.) India: Thompson-Balys.

D1364. *Object causes magic sleep.* *Schoepperle Tristan and Isolt I 257 n. 1; Irish myth: *Cross; India: Thompson-Balys.

B172.9. Magic birds cause hosts to sleep by shaking wings. D1960. Magic sleep.

D1364.0.1. *Ring wakes from magic sleep.* (Cf. D1076.) — *Fb "ring" III 60a

D1364.0.2. *Hero can only wake when a certain axe falls down.* (Cf. D1206.) Icelandic: Boberg.

D1364.1. *Fountain causes magic sleep.* (Cf. D925.) — Hdwb. d. Märchens s.v. "Brunnen" nn. 108—110. — Breton: Sébillot Incidents s.v. "fontaine"; Irish: Plummer cli, clxxii, *Cross.

D1364.2. *Sleep-thorn.* Thorn causes magic sleep. (Cf. D958.) — *Köhler-Bolte I 261; *BP I 440; *Panzer Sigfrid 281 s.v. "Schlafdorn"; **Cosquin Études 95ff., Contes indiens 59ff. — English: Child V 495 s.v. "sleep"; Icelandic: *Boberg.

B511.3. Faithful horse pushes sleep-thorn out of its master's head, so that he awakes.

D1364.3. *Flowers cause magic sleep.* (Cf. D975.) — *Basset 1001 Contes I 143.

D1364.4. *Fruit causes magic sleep.* (Cf. D980.) — *Basset 1001 Contes I 143e.

D1364.4.1. *Apple causes magic sleep.* (Cf. D981.1.) — *Types 400, 590, 709; *BP I 463, II 346, III 1; Icelandic: Boberg.

D1364.4.2. *Figs cause magic sleep.* (Cf. D981.5.) — Spanish: Boggs FFC XC 56, 116 Nos. 408*A, 970.

J585.1. Clever girl refrains from eating figs which would bring on magic sleep.

D1364.5. *Saint's breath causes magic sleep.* (Cf. D1005.) — Irish: Plummer clxxii, Cross.

D1364.6. *Feather causes magic sleep.* (Cf. D1021.) — English: Child V 496 s.v. "sleep".

D1364.7. *Sleeping potion: drink causes magic sleep.* (Cf. D1040, D1242.2, D1364.12.) — Dickson 63; Cox Cinderella 483; Irish myth: *Cross; Icelandic: *Boberg.

D1364.7.1. *Liquor blessed by saint causes magic sleep.* Irish: Plummer clxxii, Cross.

D1040. Magic drink.

D1364.8. *Enchanted stockings cause magic sleep.* (Cf. D1062.) — Breton: Sébillot Incidents s.v. "bas."

D1364.9. *Comb causes magic sleep.* (Cf. D1072.1.) — *BP I 463; cf. Type 709.

D1364.10. *Dagger causes magic sleep.* (Cf. D1083.1.) — *Basset 1001 Contes I 143.

D1364.11. *Pillow causes magic sleep.* (Cf. D1154.5.) *Schoepperle Tristan and Isolt I 257 n. 1. — English: Child V 496 s.v. "sleep"; Irish myth: *Cross; Icelandic: Boberg.

D1364.12. *Contents of bottle cause magic sleep.* (Cf. D1040, D1171.8, D1242.) — Breton: Sébillot Incidents s.v. "flacon".

D1364.13. *Cloth causes magic sleep.* (Cf. D1051.) — BP I 463.

D1364.14. *Needle causes magic sleep.* (Cf. D1181.) — Köhler-Bolte I 261.

D1364.15. *Pin causes magic sleep.* (Cf. D1182.) — *Type 400; *Cosquin Contes indiens 95ff.; *BP II 346; Cox Cinderella 483; *Basset 1001 Contes I 143. — English: Child V 496 s.v. "sleep"; Irish myth: Cross; Missouri French: Carrière.

D1364.16. *Hairpin causes magic sleep.* (Cf. D1072.2.) — *Type 709; *BP I 463.

D1364.17. *Spindle causes magic sleep.* (Cf. D1186.) — *Type 410; *BP I 434ff., 440; *Saintyves Perrault 62.

D1364.18. *Wand causes magic sleep.* (Cf. D1254.1.) — Saintyves Perrault 63; Cox Cinderella 483. — Icelandic: Corpus Poeticum Boreale I 158, Boberg; Breton: Sébillot Incidents s.v. "baguette", "sommeil"; India: Thompson-Balys.

D1364.19. *Cigar causes magic sleep.* (Cf. D1261.) — Spanish: Boggs FFC XC 56 No. 408*A.

D1364.20. *Magic runes cause sleep.* (Cf. D1266.1.) — Fb "sove" III 472b. — English: Child I 28, 48, 55, 391f, Wimberly 355.

D1364.21. *Magic card causes sleep.* (Cf. D1267.) — Köhler-Bolte Zs. f. Vksk. VI 62 (to Gonzenbach No. 10); Basile Pentamerone III Nos. 1, 9; Italian Novella: Rotunda.

D1364.22. *Sleep-charm.* Charm causes magic sleep. (Cf. D1273.) — Dickson 62 n. 6. — English: Child I 28, 48, 55, 391f; Irish myth: *Cross; India: Thompson-Balys; Chinese: Werner 366.

D1364.23. *Song causes magic sleep.* (Cf. D1275, D1364.24.) — Irish myth: *Cross; Breton: Sébillot Incidents s.v. "chant".

B81.11. Mermaid's singing causes sleep. B172.2.1. Magic bird song brings sleep.

D1364.24. *Music causes magic sleep.* (Cf. D1275.1.) — Greek: Fox 193 (Argos); Irish: Plummer clxxii, *Cross; English: Child V 489 s.v. "music"; Finnish: Kalevala rune 42.

F156.1. Door to otherworld island sounds sleep-bringing music. F512.2.2. Argos. K606.1.2. Escape by playing sleep-bringing music. K776.1 Capture with aid of sleep-bringing music.

D1364.25. *Musical instrument causes magic sleep.* (Cf. D1210.) Irish myth: Cross.

D1364.25.0.1. *Musical branch causes magic sleep.* (Cf. D1615.2.) Irish myth: *Cross.

D954. Magic bough. D1359.2.1.2. Magic musical branch soothes listener.

D1364.25.1. *Flute causes magic sleep.* (Cf. D1223.1.) Irish myth: Cross.

D1364.25.2. *Drum causes magic sleep.* (Cf. D1211.) Irish myth: Cross.

D1364.25.3. *Pipe (musical) causes magic sleep.* (Cf. D1224.) Irish myth: Cross.

D1364.26. *Silver rods cause magic sleep.* (Cf. D1254.2.) Irish myth: Cross.

D1364.27. *Sword causes magic sleep.* (Cf. D1081.) Irish myth: Cross.

D1364.28. *Smoke from magic purse makes man sleep.* (Cf. D1192.) Icelandic: Boberg.

D1364.29. *Touch of glove and ring causes sleep.* Icelandic: Boberg.

D1364.30. *Tooth of fox causes magic sleep.* (Cf. D1011.4.) Jewish: Neuman.

D1364.31. *Plant produces sleep.* (Cf. D965.) India: Thompson-Balys.

D1364.32. *Jewel causes magic sleep.* (Cf. D1071.) Jewish: Neuman.

D1365. *Object causes magic forgetfulness.*

C945. Magic forgetfulness for breaking tabu. D1366.2. Lack of magic necklace causes forgetfulness. D2000. Magic forgetfulness. D2004.2. Kiss of forgetfulness. D2004.3. Forgetfulness by eating. D2004.6. Magic forgetting of wife when husband removes shirt she has given him. D2011.1. Years seem moments while man listens to song of bird.

D1365.1. *Plant causes magic forgetfulness.* (Cf. D965.) Breton: Sébillot Incidents s.v. "herbe".

D1365.1.1. *Lotus causes forgetfulness.* (Cf. D965.6, D2004.3.) Greek: *Frazer Apollodorus II 280 n. 2.

F111.3. Voyage to land of Lotus Eaters.

D1365.1.2. *Myrtle causes forgetfulness.* (Cf. D965.10.) Hartland Science 204.

D1365.1.3. *Laurel causes forgetfulness.* (Cf. D965.9.) — Hartland Science 204.

D1365.2. *Drink causes magic forgetfulness.* (Cf. D1040, D2004.3.1.) — Jiriczek "Der Vergessenheitstrank in der Nibelungensage" Zs. f. vgl. Litgsch. N. F. VII 49ff.; Cox Cinderella 512; Wimberly 278f. — Irish myth: *Cross; English: Child I 363 and note, 364; Norse: Herrmann II 590; Icelandic: *Boberg; Greek: Odyssey IV line 220 et passim; India: Thompson-Balys.

D1365.3. *Food causes magic forgetfulness.* (Cf. D1030.) — Icelandic: *Boberg; Eskimo (Greenland): Rink 446.

C200. Tabu: eating.

D1365.4. *Girdle causes forgetfulness.* (Cf. D1057.1.) English: Herbert III 207.

D1365.5. *Ring causes forgetfulness.* (Cf. D1076.) — *Oesterley No. 10. — English: Wells 66 (Ywain and Gawain).

D1365.6. *Magic cup causes forgetfulness.* (Cf. D1171.6, D1365.2.) — *Fb "bæger" IV 83a.

D1365.7. *Breath causes magic forgetfulness.* (Cf. D1005.) Irish myth: Cross.

D1365.8. *Magic medicine causes loss of memory.* (Sprinkled on head.) (Cf. D1241, D1242.) India: Thompson-Balys.

D1365.8.1. *Medicines of forgetfulness and remembering.* India: Thompson-Balys.

E82. Water of life and death.

D1365.9. *Tower causes magic forgetfulness.* (Cf. D1149.) Jewish: Neuman.

D1365.10. *Magic writings on drinking horn cause forgetfulness.* (Cf. D1365.2.) Icelandic: Boberg.

D1365.11. *"Brain of forgetfulness" lost by person in battle.* Irish myth: *Cross.

D1366. *Magic object causes memory.*

D1910. Magic memory. D2006. Magic reawakening of memory. F692. Person with remarkable memory.

D1366.1. *Magic drink causes memory.* (Cf. D1040.) — Icelandic: *Boberg; Irish myth: Cross.

D1366.2. *Lack of magic necklace causes forgetfulness.* (Cf. D1365.) — India: Thompson-Balys.

D1073. Magic necklace.

D1367. *Magic object causes insanity.*

C949.1. Insanity from breaking tabu. D1508. Magic object restores reason. D2065. Magic insanity. D1353. Magic object makes person foolish. F362.2. Fairies cause insanity. F1041.8.6. Men go mad in battle. P192. Madmen. P427.2.1.1. Poets and fools (madmen) closely allied. T24.3. Madness from love.

D1367.1. *Magic plant causes insanity.* (Cf. D965.) — Chauvin VII 19 No. 373D n. 1; Fb "vild" III 1052b.

D1367.2. *Magic drink causes insanity.* (Cf. D1040.) — *Kittredge Witchcraft 128, 450 n. 25. — Irish myth: *Cross.

D1367.3. *Magic spell causes insanity.* (Cf. D1273.) — *Kittredge Witchcraft 128, 450 n. 24.

D1367.4. *Magic wisp (withe) causes insanity.* (Cf. D1282.2.) Irish myth: *Cross.

D1367.5. *Runes cause frenzy.* (Cf. D1266.1.) Norse: MacCulloch Eddic 298, Herrmann Saxo Gr. II 239, *Boberg; India: Thompson-Balys.

D1367.6. *Magic food causes insanity.* (Cf. D1030.) India: Thompson-Balys.

D1368. *Magic object causes illusions.* Irish myth: Cross.

D1331.4. Magic object causes sight-shifting. D2031. Magic illusion. K1870. Illusions.

D1368.1. *Magic snake-oil causes illusions.* (Cf. D1244.) — Kittredge Witchcraft 144, 463 nn. 51—54.

D1368.1.1. *Ointment applied to eyes makes night seem day.* India: Thompson-Balys.

D1368.2. *Magic ring causes illusion.* (Cf. D1076.) Icelandic: Boberg.

D1368.3. *Magic cloak causes illusion.* (Cf. D1053.) Icelandic: Boberg.

D1368.4. *Tree of delusion.* (Cf. D950.) Indian: Thompson-Balys.

D1368.5. *Magic forest seems to stretch farther as mortals travel within.* (Cf. D941.) India: Thompson-Balys.

D1372. *Magic object causes continued sneezing.*

D2063. Magic discomfort.

D1372.1. *Magic ring causes continued sneezing.* (Cf. D1076.) — Bédier Fabliaux 442.

D1373. *Magic object causes constant hunger.*
D2063. Magic discomfort.

D1373.0.1. *Magic object causes constant thirst.*
D2063.3. Magic insatiable thirst.

D1373.0.1.1. *Magic lamp (eaten, causes thirst.)* (Cf. D1162.1) India: Thompson-Balys.

D1373.1. *Fetish medicine causes constant hunger.* (Cf. D1241.) Africa (Benga): Nassau 177 No. 24 version I.

D1373.2. *Two loaves of bread* — one to excite, the other to appease hunger. (Cf. D1031.1.) India: Thompson-Balys.

D1374. *Magic object causes longing.*

D1374.1. *Magic music causes longing.* (Cf. D1275.1.) Irish myth: Cross.
D1355. Love-producing magic object.

D1375. *Magic object causes (or removes) temporary growths.*
D51. Magic appearance of human limbs.

D1375.1. *Magic object causes horns to grow on person.* Irish myth: Cross.
B23.3. Man with (two) horns on his head. D881.1. Recovery of magic object by use of magic apples. These apples cause horns to grow. D895. Magic object returned in payment for removal of magic horns. D1011.1. Magic animal horn. F545.2.2. Horns on forehead. H425.2. Horns grow on cuckold.

D1375.1.1. *Magic fruit causes horns to grow on person.* (Cf. D981.) — Philippine: *Fansler MAFLS XII 17.
D551.1. Transformation by eating fruit.

D1375.1.1.1. *Magic apples cause horns to grow on person.* (Cf. D981.1) — *Type 566; *BP I 470ff., 482; *Aarne MSFO XXV 121. — Breton: Sébillot Incidents s.v. "cornes"; N. A. Indian (European borrowings): *Thompson CColl II 399ff.

D1375.1.1.2. *Magic peaches cause horns to grow on person.* (Cf. D981.2.) Breton: Sébillot Incidents s.v. "cornes".

D1375.1.1.3. *Magic orange causes horns to grow on person.* (Cf. D981.3.) Breton: Sébillot Incidents s.v. "orange", "cornes".

D1375.1.1.4. *Magic cherries cause horns to grow on person.* (Cf. D981.4.) *Aarne MSFO XXV 121.

D1375.1.1.5. *Magic figs cause horns to grow on person.* (Cf. D981.5.) — *Aarne MSFO XXV 121.

D1375.1.1.6. *Magic pear causes horns to grow on person.* (Cf. D981.6.) *Aarne MSFO XXV 121.

D1375.1.1.7. *Magic plums cause horns to grow on person.* (Cf. D981.7.) *Aarne MSFO XXV 121.

D1375.1.1.8. *Magic grapes cause horns to grow on person.* (Cf. D981.8.) *Aarne MSFO XXV 121.

D1375.1.1.9. *Magic dates cause horns to grow on person.* (Cf. D981.9.) *Aarne MSFO XXV 122.

D1375.1.1.10. *Magic berries cause horns to grow on person.* (Cf. D981.10.) *Aarne MSFO XXV 122.

D1375.1.2. *Magic vegetable causes horns to grow on person.* (Cf. D983.) *Aarne MSFO XXV 122.

D1375.1.3. *Charm causes horns to grow on person.* (Cf. D992.1.) Penzer III 187.

D1375.1.4. *Blossom causes horns to grow on person.* (Cf. D975.) — Philippine: Fansler MAFLS XII 16.

D1375.1.5. *Magic drink causes horns to grow on person.* (Cf. D1040.) Icelandic: Boberg.

D1375.2. *Magic object removes horns from person.*

D1375.2.1. *Magic fruit removes horns from person.* (Cf. D1375.1.1, D981.)

D1375.2.1.1. *Magic apple removes horns from person.* (Cf. D981.1.) — *Aarne MSFO XXV 121.

D1375.2.1.2. *Magic orange removes horns from person.* (Cf. D981.3.) Breton: Sébillot Incidents s.v. "orange".

D1375.2.1.3. *Magic pear removes horns from person.* (Cf. D981.6.) Aarne MSFO XXV 121.

D1375.2.2. *Magic nut removes horns from person.* (Cf. D985.) Aarne MSFO XXV 121.

D1375.2.3. *Magic salve removes horns from person.* (Cf. D1244.) — Aarne MSFO XXV 121.

D1375.2.4. *Magic water removes horns from person.* (Cf. D1242.1.) Aarne MSFO XXV 121.

D1375.2.5. *Blossoms remove horns from person.* (Cf. D975.) Philippine: Fansler MAFLS XII 16.

D1375.3. *Magic object causes wings to grow on person.* Aarne MSFO XXV 123.

D1375.3.1. *Magic ointment causes wings to grow on person.* (Cf. D1244.) Chauvin V 41 No. 388; India: Thompson-Balys.

D1375.4. *Magic object causes tail to grow.*

D1375.4.1. *Magic plant causes tail to grow.*

D1375.4.1.1. *Magic plantain causes four tails to grow.* (Cf. D965.11.) — Africa (Ibo, Nigeria): Thomas 126.

D1375.4.2. *Magic fruit causes tail to grow.* (Cf. D981.) Aarne MSFO XXV 123. — Philippine: Fansler MAFLS XII 16.

D1375.5. *Magic object causes humps to appear on back.* (Cf. F344.1.) Aarne MSFO XXV 123.

D1375.6. *Magic object causes feathers to grow on person.* Irish myth: Cross.

D1021. Magic feather. F521.2. Feathered people.

D1375.6.1. *Magic egg causes feathers to grow on person.* (Cf. D1024.) Irish myth: Cross.

D1793. Magic results from eating or drinking.

D1376. *Magic object causes members to grow long or short.*

D1376.1. *Magic object makes nose long (restores it.)* *Aarne MSFO XXV 123; Type 566; *BP I 470ff.; *Fb "næse" II 716b. — Japanese: Ikeda.

Q551. Magic manifestations as punishments.

D1376.1.1. *Magic fruit makes nose long (restores it.)*

D1376.1.1.1. *Magic apple makes nose long (restores it).* (Cf. D981.1.) *Fb "æble" III 1136a; Hdwb. d. Märchens s.v. "Apfel" n. 10.

D1376.1.1.2. *Magic cherry makes nose long (restores it).* (Cf. D981.4.) Fb "kirsebær" II 133a.

D1376.1.2. *Magic ring makes nose grow long (restores it).* (Cf. D1076.) Köhler-Bolte I 110f.

D1377. *Magic object changes person's size.*

D631.1 Person changes size at will.

D1377.1. *Magic comb changes person's size at will.* (Cf. D1072.1.) Köhler-Bolte I 177.

D1379. *Magic object produces miscellaneous temporary changes in persons, animals, or objects.*

D1379.1. *Magic object controls person's will.*

D1379.1.1. *Magic runes control person's will.* (Cf. D1266.1.) English: Child I 362.

D1379.2. *Magic writings (runes) cause dead to speak.* Icelandic: Boberg.

E164. Dead body caused to speak by setting door ajar. E443. Ghost exorcised and laid.

D1379.3. *Magic writings (runes) produce enmity.* (Cf. D1266.1.) Icelandic: Boberg.

D1379.4. *Magic picture causes people to wet the bed.* (Cf. D1379.4.) Chinese: Graham.

D1379.5. *"Milk-medicine" causes milk to appear in woman's breast.* (Cf. D1241.) India: Thompson-Balys.

T592. Milk suddenly appears in woman's dry breast.

D1380. Magic object protects. **Seligmann 72ff. — Irish myth: *Cross.

D1317. Magic object warns of danger. D1344. Magic object gives invulnerability. D1447. Magic object protects against wild animals. D1500.2. Magic object wards off disease. D1578. Magic object keeps off enchantment. D2064.0.1. Magic sickness (discomfort) prevents lover from raping woman. D2163. Magic defense in battle. V52.7. Prayer at saint's flagstone averts trouble.

D1380.0.1. *Magic object protects a city.* *Chauvin VIII 191 No. 228.

A412. City-god.

D1380.0.1.1. *Palladium. City impregnable while statue remains.* (Cf. D1268.) Greek: Grote I 276.

D1380.1. *Waberlohe. Magic fire surrounds and protects.* (Cf. D1271.) BP I 440; *Panzer Sigfrid 281 s.v. "Waberlohe"; Seligmann 110ff., *122, 123ff., *130; Krappe Archiv für das Studium der Neueren Sprachen 1937, 1938. — Icelandic: Boberg.

D1967. Person in magic sleep surrounded by protecting fire.

D1380.1.1. *Pillar of fire protects in desert.* (Cf. D1271.) Jewish: Neuman.

D1380.2. *Tree (plant) protects.*

D1380.2.1. *Calabash as guardian of girl.* (Cf. D965.2.) Africa (Ekoi): Talbot 27.

D1380.2.2. *Tree as guardian of girl.* India: Thompson-Balys.
D950.15. Magic bamboo tree.

D1380.3. *Head of divinity as protection of land.* Buried. (Cf. D992.) *Kittredge Gawain 180 n. 1. — Welsh: MacCulloch Celtic 105.

D1380.3.1. *Magic head of horse as protection of land.* (Cf. D1011.) Hdwb. d. Abergl. VI 996. — Icelandic: *Boberg.
F494.1. Guardian spirit of land.

D1380.4. *Magic tent protects occupant.* (Cf. D1138.) Icelandic: Boberg.

D1380.5. *Magic water protects.* (Cf. D1242.1.) Seligmann 73ff, *106. — Irish myth: *Cross; Cheremis: Sebeok-Nyerges.

D1380.6. *Magic coal protects.* (Cf. D931.1.) Seligmann 131, *133; India: Thompson-Balys.

D1380.7. *Magic soot protects.* (Cf. D931.1.1.) Seligmann 137, *138.

D1380.8. *Magic ashes protect.* (Cf. D1271.1.) Seligmann 134, *137.

D1380.9. *Magic earth (dirt) protects.* (Cf. D935.) Seligmann *154.

D1380.10. *Magic string protects.* (Cf. D1184.2.) Penzer VI 59.

D1380.11. *Magic jewel protects* (Cf. D1071.) Seligmann *205, *285; Icelandic: *Boberg.

D1380.12. *Magic bedstead protects from harm.* (Cf. D1154.1.) India: Thompson-Balys.

D1380.13. *Magic story protects.* (Cf. D1266.3.) Irish myth: *Cross.

D1380.14. *Magic poems protect.* (Cf. D1275.4.) Irish myth: *Cross; Icelandic: Boberg.

D1380.14.1. *Magic hymn protects.* (Cf. D1275.3, D1382.7.1, D1383.4.1, D1385.16, D1389.9.) Irish myth: Cross.

D1380.15. *Magic well protects.* (Cf. D926.) Irish myth: *Cross.

D1380.16. *Magic dog protects.* Irish myth: *Cross.
B182.1. Magic dog. B576.1. Animal as guard of person or house.

D1380.16.1. *Magic statue of dog protects.* (Cf. D1268.1.) Jewish: Neuman.

D1380.17. *Magic cup protects.* (Cf. D1171.6.) Irish myth: Cross.

D1380.18. *Magic cloth protects.* (Cf. D1051.) Icelandic: *Boberg; India: Thompson-Balys.

D1380.19. *Magic club protects ten men.* (Cf. D1094.) Irish myth: Cross.

D1380.20. *Runes protect.* (Cf. D1266.1.) Icelandic: MacCulloch Eddic 298, Boberg.

D1380.21. *Magic ointment protects.* (Cf. D1244.) India: Thompson-Balys.

D1380.22. *Magic feather protects.* (Cf. D1021.) India: Thompson-Balys.

D1380.23. *Magic ring protects.* (Cf. D1076.) India: *Thompson-Balys.

D1380.24. *Spell overcomes all danger.* (Cf. D1273.) India: Thompson-Balys.

D1380.25. *Magic cloud protects.* (Cf. D901.) Jewish: Neuman.

D1380.26. *Reindeer hose from corpse protect women.* (Cf. D1062, D1278.) Eskimo (Greenland): Rink 173.

D1381. *Magic object protects from attack.* *Kittredge Witchcraft 54, 404 nn. 231—234. — Irish myth: Cross; India: Thompson-Balys.

D1381.1. *Druid's hedge prevents attack.* (Cf. D945, D1282.1.1, D1361.1.) Irish: Plummer clxi, *Cross.

D1381.2. *Saint's spittle protects fugitive from attack.* (Cf. D1001.) Irish: Plummer clxxviii, Cross.

D1381.3. *Magic garment protects against attack.* (Cf. D1052, D1053.) *Thien Motive 30; *Hdwb. d. Abergl. III 1712. — Icelandic: Corpus Poeticum Boreale II 354, Möbius Háttatal II 130, *Boberg; Irish myth: *Cross.

D1381.3.1. *Garment proof against all but man's own sword.* Icelandic: Boberg.

D1381.3.2. *Magic unpierceable (horn) skin protects against attack.* (Cf. D1025.) Irish myth: *Cross; Icelandic: Boberg.

A1292. First man covered with horny substance. D1840. Magic invulnerability. F558. Man covered with horn.

D1381.3.3. *A protective garment which spears could not penetrate.* (Cf. D1052.) *Loomis White Magic 123.

D1381.4. *Magic coat protects against attack.* (Cf. D1053.)

D1381.4.1. *Christ's coat of mercy protects Pilate from punishment.* Pauli (ed. Bolte) No. 323.

D1381.5. *Magic shirt protects against attack.* (Cf. D1056, D1344.9, D1389.7.) Ǫrvar Odds Saga 75, 109 (will not protect when in flight). — Hawaii: Beckwith Myth 499.

D1381.6. *Stone necklace protects from attack.* (Cf. D1073.) Icelandic: *Boberg.

D1381.7. *Magic ring protects from attack.* (Cf. D1076.) English: Wells 9 (King Horn); Icelandic: *Boberg.

D1381.8. *Arms that protect from attack.* (Cf. D1080.) English: Wells 132 (Sir Launfal); Irish myth: *Cross.

D1381.9. *Dagger protects owner from attack.* (Cf. D1083.1.) Malone PMLA XLIII 402.

D1381.10. *Magic armor protects from attack.* (Cf. D1101.) Thien Motive 30. — Icelandic: *Boberg.

D1381.10.1. *Magic impenetrable breastplate.* (Cf. D1101.3.) Irish myth: *Cross.

D1381.10.2. *Magic unpierceable cuirass.* (Cf. D1101.2.) Spanish: Boggs FFC XC 67 No. 508*A.

D1381.10.3. *Magic unpierceable helmet.* (Cf. D1101.4.) Irish myth: Cross; Icelandic: *Boberg.

D1381.10.4. *Magic impenetrable yoke.* (Cf. D1101.5.) Irish myth: Cross.

D1381.11. *Magic circle protects from devil.* (Cf. D1272.) *Types 810, 815, Fb "kreds" II 293. — Irish: Beal XXI 316; Lithuanian: Balys Legends Nos. 693—697, 700; India: Thompson-Balys, Penzer II 99 n.

K218.1. Devil cheated by having priest draw a sacred circle about the intended victim.

D1381.11.1. *Magic circle protects from wild animals.* Chinese: Graham.

D1381.11.2. *Magic circle protects from ghosts.* (Cf. D1272.) India: Thompson-Balys.

E434. Magic protection against revenants.

D1381.12. *Saint's bachall keeps off enemies.* (Cf. D1277.) Irish: Plummer clxxv, *Cross. — *Loomis White Magic 123.

D1381.13. *Magic fly-whisk stops sword-thrusts.* (Cf. D1287.) Chinese: Werner 322.

D1381.14. *Magic girdle protects from all wounds.* (Cf. D1057.1.) English: Wells 55 (Gawayne and the Grene Knight.).

D1381.15. *Red wards off danger.* (Cf. D1293.1.) Swiss: Jegerlehner Oberwallis 300 No. 6.

D1381.16. *Magic letters (amulets) guard against attack by wild animals or men.* (Cf. D1266.1.) Hdwb. d. Abergl. III 1.

D1381.17. *Spear in ground pointed toward ferocious animal protects.* (Cf. D1084.) India: Thompson-Balys.

D1782. Sympathetic magic.

D1381.18. *Magic belt assures victory.* (Cf. D1057.) Irish myth: Cross; Icelandic: Boberg.

D1381.19. *Magic chain protects from attack.* (Cf. D1078.) Irish myth: Cross.

D1381.20. *Sacred relics protect against attack.* (Cf. D1296.) Irish myth: Cross.

D1381.21. *Magic fan protects against attack.* (Cf. D1077.) Irish myth: Cross.

D1381.22. *Magic mist protects against attack.* (Cf. D902.1.) Irish myth: *Cross.

D1361.1. Magic mist of invisibility. D1380.25. Magic cloud protects. K2369.11. Fairy mist mistaken for smoke of enemy's burning ships.

D1381.23. *Magic spell causes fortress to revolve, preventing entrance.* (Cf. D1273.) Irish myth: *Cross.

F771.2.6. Revolving castle.

D1381.24. *Magic letter protects against attack.* (Cf. D1266.1.) *Fb I 609 "himmelbrev". — Irish myth: Cross.

D1381.24.1. *Reading letter written by Christ protects against attack.* Irish myth: Cross.

V151. Sacred writings. V211.10. Letter (message) of Christ.

D1381.25. *Carrying saint's book around army right-handwise insures victory.* (Cf. D1266.) Irish myth: *Cross.

D1791. Magic power by circumambulation.

D1381.25.1. *Dextrorsum circuit (around sacred stone) insures victory.* Irish myth: *Cross.

D931. Magic rock (stone). D1791.1. Dextrorsum circuit.

D1381.26. *Magic veil protects from attack.* (Cf. D1061.) Icelandic: Boberg.

D1381.27. *Magic song stops spears.* (Cf. D1275.) Icelandic: *Boberg.

D1381.28. *Magic tree protects from attack.* India: Thompson-Balys.
D950. Magic tree.

D1381.29. *Speaking lamp prevents king from killing queen.* (Cf. D1162.) India: Thompson-Balys.

D1381.30. *Rider on magic horse immune to harm or danger.* (Cf. B181.) India: Thompson-Balys.

D1381.31. *Magic gate swallows axes trying to force it open.* (Cf. D1146.) Jewish: Neuman.

D1381.32. *Staff protects from attack.* (Cf. D1254.) Jewish: Neuman.

D1382. *Magic object protects against cold or burning.*
B526. Animal saves man from death by burning. D1592. Magic object heats or cools water. D1841.3. Burning magically evaded. D2144.4. Burning by magic. F222.1.1. Fairies' underground palace cannot be burned by fire or destroyed by water.

D1382.1. *Magic pebble prevents burning.* (Cf. D931.) Southern Paiute: Lowie JAFL XXXVII 144.
D1273. Magic formula (charm).

D1382.1.0.1. *Magic stones from holy well protect against loss by fire or water.* Irish myth: Cross.
D926. Magic well. D931. Magic rock (stone).

D1382.2. *Fat of crow prevents burning.* (Cf. D1017.1.1.) *Fb "fedt" I 278b.

D1382.3. *Magic cake protects from heat.* (Cf. D1031.2.) Chinese: Werner 186.

D1382.4. *Magic oil prevents burning.* (Cf. D1244.) Malone PMLA XLIII 406.

D1382.5. *Magic fire does not burn one.* (Cf. D1271.) Irish myth:*Cross, Plummer cxxxviii; Breton: Sébillot Incidents s.v. "feu".
D1841.3. Burning magically evaded.

D1382.5.1. *Flaming shield does not burn owner.* (Cf. D1101.1.) Irish myth: Cross.

D1382.6. *Magic shirt protects from cold and burning.* (Cf. D1056.) Icelandic: *Boberg; Hawaii: Beckwith Myth 491.

D1382.6.1. *Magic garment protects from fire.* (Cf. D1052.) Icelandic: *Boberg; Jewish: Neuman; Chinese: Eberhard FFC CXX 210 No. 159.

D1382.7. *Song protects from fire.* (Cf. D1275.) Irish: Plummer clxxix, Cross.

D1382.7.1. *Magic hymn protects from fire.* (Cf. D1275.3, D1380.14.1.) Irish myth: *Cross.

D1382.7.1.1. *Magic song protects from frost and cold.* (Cf. D1275.) Icelandic: MacCulloch Eddic 298, Boberg.

D1382.8. *Magic stream quenches fire.* (Cf. D915.2.) *Type 715; *BP I 258.
K481. Demi-coq by means of his magic animals and magic water collects money.

D1382.9. *Magic cowl protects from fire.* (Cf. D1067.3.1.) Irish myth: Cross.

D1382.9.1. *Magic cowl protects from cold.* Icelandic: Boberg.

D1382.10. *Magic garment prevents burning.* (Cf. D1052.) Irish myth: Cross; Icelandic: *Boberg; Jewish: Neuman; Chinese: Eberhard FFC CXX 210 No. 159.

D1382.11. *Magic ring protects against fire.* (Cf. D1076.) Icelandic: *Boberg.

D1382.12. *Magic blue stone protects against frost.* (Cf. D931.) Icelandic: *Boberg.

D1382.13. *Blood of salamander protects against fire.* (Cf. D1016.) Jewish: Neuman.

D1383. *Magic object protects from poison.*

B514.3. Snake gives man antidote for poison. B521.1. Animal warns against poison. D1317.0.1. Magic object detects poison. D1515. Magic antidote for poison.

D1383.1. *Magic garment protects from poison.* (Cf. D1052.) Icelandic: *Boberg..

D1383.2. *Charms protect from poison.* (Cf. D1273.) *Kittredge Witchcraft 32, 387 n. 82; Irish myth: *Cross; India: Penzer I 113.

D1515.1. Charms as antidote for poison.

D1383.3. *Magic ring protects against poison.* (Cf. D1076.) *Kittredge Witchcraft 111, 440 n. 57; Icelandic: *Boberg; India: Penzer I 110 n. 1.

D1383.4. *Song protects against poison.* (Cf. D1275.) Irish: Plummer clxxix, Cross.

D1383.4.1. *Magic hymn protects against poison.* (Cf. D1275.3, D1380.14.1.) Irish myth: *Cross.

D1383.5. *Leek in beer protects against poison.* (Cf. D983.3.) Icelandic: *Boberg.

D1383.6. *Magic red stone protects from poison.* (Cf. D1070.) Icelandic: *Boberg.

D1384. *Magic object protects from discomfort or from accident on journey.*

V111.1. Visit to certain church protects from drowning on pilgrimage.

D1384.1. *Magic ring prevents discomfiture.* (Cf. D1076.) Kittredge Witchcraft 111, 440 n. 51.

D1384.2. *Noose used by suicide as protection from accident.* (Cf. D1278.) Kittredge Witchcraft 142, 461 n. 24.

D1384.3. *Charm gives safety on journey.* (Cf. D1273.) Kittredge Witchcraft 32, 388 n. 93; Hälsig Der Zauberspruch bei den Germanen 48ff. — Irish myth: *Cross.

D1384.3.1. *Turning right-handwise insures safe journey.* (Cf. D1272.) Irish myth: Cross.

D1791. Magic power by circumambulation.

D1384.4. *Charms prevent fatigue.* (Cf. D1273.) Kittredge Witchcraft 32, 388 n. 93.

D1384.4.1. *Magic shirt prevents fatigue during swimming.* (Cf. D1056.) Icelandic: *Boberg.

D1384.4.2. *Magic blue stone prevents fatigue during swimming.* (Cf. D1072.) Icelandic: *Boberg.

D1384.5. *Song as protection on journey.* (Cf. D1275.) Irish: Plummer clxxix, *Cross; Icelandic: Boberg.

D1384.6. *Ointment gives protection on journey.* (Cf. D1244.) India: Thompson-Balys.

D1384.7. *Magic ring prevents losing one's way.* (Cf. D1076.) Icelandic: *Boberg.

D1385. *Magic object protects from evil spirits.* Irish myth: *Cross; Jewish: Neuman.

D712.10. Disenchantment by driving stake through body. D1586.2. Prayer to Virgin protects against plague. D1766.7.1. Evil spirits conjured away in name of deity. D2176. Magic exorcising. E434. Magic protection against revenants. E444. Ghost laid by talisman. F405. Means of combating spirits. F471.1.2. Protection against Nightmare (Alp). F493.3.3. Magic protection against pestilence spirit. G270. Witch overcome or escaped. G272. Protection against witches. G303.16. How the devil's power may be escaped or avoided.

D1385.1. *Earth from saint's grave expels demons.* (Cf. D935, V220.) Seligmann 149. — Irish: Plummer clxxx, Cross.

D1385.2. *Plant as antidote to spells and enchantments.* (Cf. D965.) Greek: Frazer Apollodorus II 288 n. 1 (moly); Jewish: Neuman.

D1385.2.1. *Herbs worn in ears keep off power of evil spirits.* (Cf. D965.) India: Thompson-Balys.

D1385.2.2. *Rue, when burned, keeps evil spirits at a distance.* (Cf. D965.16.) India: Thompson-Balys.

D1385.2.3. *Hawthorn protects travelers.* (Cf. D950.13.) Irish myth: Cross.

D1385.2.4. *Witch will never visit a house where pipal is strewn.* India: Thompson-Balys.

D1385.2.5. *Ash (quicken, rowan) protects against spells and enchantment.* (Cf. D950.6, D1311.4.1.1.)

D1385.2.6. *Roots protect from evil spirits.* (Cf. D967.) Jewish: Neuman.

D1385.2.7. *Mandrake protects from evil spirits.* (Cf. D965.1.) Jewish: Neuman.

D1385.2.8. *Garlic protects from evil spirits.* (Cf. D1383.5.) Jewish: Neuman.

D1385.3. *Marriage ring protects from devil.* (Cf. D1076.) Breton: Sébillot Incidents s.v. "bague".

T320. Escape from undesired lover.

D1385.3.1. *Magic ring protects from spirit.* Swiss: Jegerlehner Oberwallis 309 No. 17.

D1385.4. *Silver bullet protects against giants, ghosts, and witches.* (Cf. D1096.3.) Fb "sølvknap", "sølvkugle". — Japanese: Ikeda; North Carolina: Brown Collection I 644.

G100. Giant ogre. G271.4.2. Exorcism by injuring image of witch. G271.4.8. Breaking spell by shooting bewitched object.

D1385.4.1. *Witch shot dead with bullet of salt.* (Cf. D1096.3.) Lithuanian: Balys Historical.

D1385.5. *Metal as defense against spirits.* (Cf. D1252.) *Seligmann *178; Penzer II 161ff.

D1385.5.1. *Copper as defense against ghosts and magic.* (Cf. D1252.2.) *Zingerle Sagen aus Tirol 589. — N. A. Indian (Ojibwa): Skinner PaAM XII 84.

D1385.5.2. *Axe driven into house entrance keeps werwolf out.* (Cf. D1206.) Jijena Sanchez 35.

D1385.6. *Magic salve protects from enchantment.* (Cf. D1244.) Fb "salve".

D1385.7. *Magic circle averts sorcery.* (Cf. D1272.) *Chauvin VII 104 No. 378. — Scotland: Baughman.

G303.16.19.15. Devil cannot enter magic circle made to keep him out.

D1385.8. *Saint's bachall keeps off monsters and ghosts.* (Cf. D1277.) Irish: Plummer clxxv, Cross.

D1385.9. *Magic horseshoe keeps off devils, trolls, and witches.* (Cf. D1286.) *Fb "hestesko"; Hdwb. d. Abergl. III 437ff.

G272.11. Horseshoes powerful against witches.

D1385.10. *Wheel buried in doorstep to prevent deviltry.* (Cf. D1207.) Fb "hjul".

D1385.11. *Churchyard mould in hat prevents witchery.* (Cf. D1278.1.) Fb "kirkegaardsmuld".

D1385.12. *Magic bell disperses demons.* (Cf. D1213.) *Frazer Old Testament III 446ff. — Irish: Plummer clxxvi, *Cross; Jewish: Neuman.

G304.2.4.1. Trolls cannot endure churchbells. V115. Churchbells.

D1385.12.1. *Saint's bell rung against black birds (demons).* Irish myth: *Cross.

B172.10. Black birds. V229.5. Saint banishes demons.

D1385.13. *Charm prevents witchcraft.* (Cf. D1273.) *Kittredge Witchcraft 32, 388 nn. 87, 98, 99; ibid. 133, 453ff. nn. 62—82 passim; *Fb "læse", "læsning", "Fader Vor"; Penzer III 137.

D1385.13.1. *Ineffable Name subjugates demons.* (Cf. D807, G302.) Jewish: Neuman.

D1385.14. *Milk of two king's children protects hero in dragon fight.* (Cf. B11.11, D1043.) Dickson 135 n. 117.

D1385.15. *Holy water and mass prevent demons alighting on grave.* (Cf. D1242.1.2.) Irish myth: *Cross.

D1766.5. Magic produced by saying mass. F402.1.5.1. Demons seek to carry off king's soul.

D1385.15.1. *Holy water dispels demons.* Irish myth: Cross.

D1385.16. *Magic hymn protects against demons and vices.* (Cf. D1275.3.) Irish myth: *Cross.

D1380.14.1. Magic hymn protects.

D1385.16.1. *Magic hymn protects against spells of druids.* Irish myth: *Cross.

D1385.16.2. *Magic hymn protects against spells of smiths.* Irish myth: *Cross.

D1385.16.3. *Magic hymn protects against spells of women.* Irish myth: *Cross.

K778. Capture through the wiles of a woman.

D1385.17. *Magic measurement protects against devil.* (Cf. D1273.4, D1389.10, F950.3.) Irish myth: Cross.

D1385.18. *Magic thread protects against demons.* (Cf. D1184.) Jewish: Neuman.

D1385.19. *Clothing protects from evil spirit.* (Cf. D1050.)

D1385.19.1. *Saint's hose protects woman from devil.* Spanish Exempla: Keller.

G303.16. How the devil's power may be escaped or avoided. V220. Saints.

D1385.20. *Runes protect from the curse of a dead Christian woman.* (Cf. D1266.1.) Icelandic: MacCulloch Eddic 298, cf. Boberg.

D1385.21. *Magic stone makes demons despair.* Irish myth: Cross.

D931. Magic rock (stone).

D1385.22. *Bedstead at doorway prevents spirit from entering.* (Cf. D1154.1.) India: Thompson-Balys.

F480. House spirits.

D1385.23. *Magic quilt protects wearer from demons and human weapons.* (Cf. D1167.) India: Thompson-Balys.

D1385.24. *Amulet guards against sorcery.* (Cf. D1070.) India: Thompson-Balys; Eskimo (Greenland): Holm 54, Rink 151, (Bering Strait): Nelson RBAE XVIII 511.

D1385.25. *Magic book disperses demons.* (Cf. D1266.) Jewish: Neuman.

D1385.26. *Red color protects against demons.* (Cf. D1293.1.) Jewish: Neuman.

D1385.27. *Meal of fishes protects against demons.* (D1032.1.) Jewish: Neuman.

D1385.28. *Magic honey protects against demons.* (Cf. D1037.) Jewish: Neuman.

D1385.29. *Magic lamp protects against demons.* (Cf. D1162.1.) Eskimo (Cumberland Sound): Boas BAM XV 239.

D1386. *Magic object protects from unwelcome lover.*

T320. Escape from undesired lover.

D1386.1. *Magic sword protects woman from fairy lover in husband's absence.* (Cf. D1081, F301.) — Scotch: Macdougall and Calder 197.

D1386.2. *Magic herb keeps off demon lover.* (Cf. D965.) Kittredge Witchcraft 120ff., 446ff. nn. 136—152 passim. — England, Scotland: *Baughman.

F405. Means of combating spirits. F471.2.0.1. Demon lover.

D1386.2.1. *Clever woman and devil as paramour.* Devil betrays means by which he can be driven out. Lithuanian: Balys Index Nos. *368, 3682, Legends No. 390.

D834. Magic objects acquired by tricking devil.

D1387. *Magic object preserves chastity.* Schoepperle Tristan and Isolt I 123; *Boje 106ff. — Irish myth: Cross; Jewish: Neuman.

T313. Ravished girl's virginity restored by Virgin Mary.

D1387.1. *Amulet preserves chastity.* (Cf. D1070.) Dickson 53 n. 62.

D1387.2. *Magic charm (writings) preserves chastity.* (Cf. D1266.1.) English: Child II 506a; Wells 22 (Sir Beues of Hamtoun).

D1387.3. *Magic belt protects against husband.* (Cf. D1057.) Icelandic: FSS 225, Boberg.

D1388. *Magic object protects from drowning.* Irish myth: *Cross, Beal XXI 328.

D1384.4.1. Magic shirt prevents fatigue during swimming. D2151.3.2. Dashing waves do not touch saint. F1088.3. Extraordinary escape from drowning. V111.1. Visit to certain church protects from drowning on pilgrimage.

D1388.0.1. *Magic ring protects from drowning.* (Cf. D1076.) *Dickson 189 n. 65.

D1388.0.2. *Magic veil keeps man from sinking in water.* (Cf. D1061.) Greek: Fox 262.

D1388.0.3. *Magic chain protects from drowning.* Irish myth: Cross.

D1078. Magic chain.

D1388.0.4. *Magic garment protects from drowning.* (Cf. D1052.) Irish myth: *Cross.

D1388.0.5. *By means of magic bag it is possible to stay as long on the bottom of the sea as one wants.* (Cf. D1193.) Icelandic: Boberg.

D1388.0.6. *By means of magic helmet it is possible to stay on the bottom of the sea as long as one wants.* (Cf. D1101.4.) Icelandic: Boberg.

D1388.1. *Magic object protects from shipwreck.*

D1388.1.1. *Saint's bachall protects from shipwreck.* (Cf. D1277.) Irish: Plummer clxxv, Cross.

D1388.1.2. *Herb protects from storms at sea.* (Cf. D965.) Kittredge Witchcraft 153, 474 n. 10.

D1388.1.3. *Runes protect from storm and shipwreck.* (Cf. D1266.1.) Norse: MacCulloch Eddic 298.

D1388.2. *Magic stone keeps flood from overflowing earth.* (Cf. A1010, D931, D1389.1.) Jewish: Neuman.

D1389. *Magic object affords miscellaneous protection.*

D1447. Magic object protects against wild animals.

D1389.1. *Magic stone protects church from oppression.* (Cf. D931, V111.) Irish: Plummer clvii, Cross.

D1389.2. *Charms against theft.* (Cf. D1273.) *Kittredge Witchcraft 32, 190f., 388 n. 96, 508 nn. 34—43.

D1389.2.1. *Theft from church prevented by apparent heat.* *Loomis White Magic 98.

D1389.2.2. *Thieves cannot cross a river because the water suddenly becomes too hot for them.* *Loomis White Magic 98.

D1389.3. *Magic cup protects against loss of strength.* (Cf. D1171.6.) Irish myth: Cross.

D1335. Object gives magic strength.

D1389.4. *Magic wheel prevents entrance to fortress.* (Cf. D1207.) Irish myth: *Cross.

F165.1.0.2. Magic revolving wheel at door of otherworld dun.

D1389.5. *Magic spear protects against spell.* (Cf. D1084.) Irish myth: Cross.

D1389.6. *Saint's bell carried around tribe averts all danger.* (Cf. D1213.) Irish myth: Cross.

D1791. Magic power by circumambulation.

D1389.7. *Magic shirt protects against opposition.* (Cf. D1056.) Irish myth: Cross.

D1389.8. *Magic helmet prevents baldness.* (Cf. D1101.4.) Irish myth: *Cross.

D1389.9. *Magic hymn protects against poverty, death and dishonor.* (Cf. D1275.3, D1380.14.1.) Irish myth: *Cross.

D1389.9.1. *Magic red stone protects against poverty.* (Cf. D1070.) Icelandic: Boberg.

D1389.9.2. *Magic ring prevents poverty.* (Cf. D1076.) Icelandic: Boberg.

D1389.10. *Magic measurement protects against sudden death.* (Cf. D1273.4.) Irish myth: Cross.

D1389.11. *Magic armature protects soul from hurt.* (Cf. D1101.) Irish myth: *Cross.

D1585. Magic object saves corpse from corruption. E750. Perils of the soul.

D1389.12. *Leek put under the tongue of supposed dead person preserves him from harm by burial.* (Cf. D983.3.) Icelandic: Boberg.

D1389.13. *Magic plant banishes fear.* (Cf. D965.) Cheremis: Sebeok-Nyerges.

D1389.14. *Sword puts to flight five evil passions.* (Cf. D1081.) India: Thompson-Balys.

D1389.15. *Magic incense protects from plague.* (Cf. D1295.) Jewish: Neuman.

D1389.16. *Magic girdle protects from pain.* (Cf. D1057.1.) Jewish: Neuman.

D1390. Magic object rescues person. Missouri French: Carrière.

B540. Animal rescuer or retriever. D672. Obstacle flight. D1421.5.1. Magic horn summons army for rescue. D1564.5. Magic cranberry opens wedge and frees hero. R100. Rescues. R150. Rescuers.

D1390.1. *Hairs of lion, when burnt, get owner out of difficulties.* (Cf. D1023.) Malone PMLA XLIII 409.

D1391. *Magic object saves person from execution.* Type 562. — Irish myth: *Cross; Missouri French: Carrière.

D2086.1.1. Execution sword turned to wood. D2165. Escapes by magic. K510. Death order evaded. R175. Rescue at the stake.

D1391.1. *Miraculous rain extinguishes fire used at stake.* (Cf. D902.) *Basset RTP XXIII 167; Irish myth: *Cross.

B526.1. Helpful animals quench execution fire. D2141.0.7. Storm raised by incantation. Extinguishes execution fire. D2158.2. Magic extinguishing of fires. J1180. Clever means of avoiding legal punishment.

D1391.2. *Saint's bachall saves prisoner from execution.* (Cf. D1277, V220.) Irish: Plummer clxxv, Cross.

D1392. *Magic object saves owner from death.* *Kittredge Witchcraft 54f., 405 nn. 235—237. — Irish myth: *Cross.

Q145. Miraculously long life as reward.

D1392.1. *Amulet saves one from death.* (Cf. D1070.) Eskimo (Greenland): Rasmussen I 187, III 114, 211, 216, Rink 168.

D1393. *Magic object helps fugitive.* Irish myth: *Cross.

B523. Animal saves man from pursuer. D1611. Magic object answers for fugitive. D1658.3.4. Grateful objects help fugitive. V211.1.8.3. Christ as infant in mother's arms causes bare hillside to become field of wheat as protection.

D1393.1. *Tree opens and conceals fugitive.* (Cf. D950.) Irish: Plummer cliii, Cross; India: Thompson-Balys; Eskimo (Greenland): Rasmussen II 90.

D1556. Self-opening tree trunk. F979.2. Leaves of tree open and close to give saint passage.

D1393.1.1. *Woman charms stick of wood so she can hide inside it.* (Cf. D956.) Eskimo (Greenland): Rink 107.

D1393.2. *Magic object maintains quiet so that fugitive may escape.* Africa (Hottentot): Bleek 54 No. 24, 63 No. 27.

D1393.3. *Magic storm protects hidden children.* (Cf. D905.) Icelandic: Boberg.

D1393.4. *Tree points way to fugitive but misdirects enemy.* (Cf. D950.) Hdwb. d. Märchens s.v. "Baum".

D1313.4. Blinded trickster directed by trees. K646. Fugitives' confederate misdirects pursuer. R243.1. Pursuer misdirected by animal to help fugitive.

D1393.5. *Magic thorn-tree attacks pursuer and helps fugitive.* India: Thompson-Balys.

D1394. *Magic object helps hero in trial.*

D1394.1. *Trial by ordeal subverted by carrying magic object.* *Kittredge Witchcraft 54, 404 nn. 227—229.

H220. Ordeals.

D1394.2. *Magic object enables one to withstand inquisitorial torture.* Kittredge Witchcraft 405 n. 235.

D1395. *Magic object frees person from prison.* *Type 559. — Irish myth: Cross.

D2165. Escapes by magic. R211. Escape from prison.

D1395.1. *Escape from prison by use of magic fiddle.* (Cf. D1233.) *Types 851, 853.

K606.1.1. Escape by playing magic music. Captor is compelled to dance while victims escape.

D1395.2. *Escape from prison by use of magic tablecloth.* (Cf. D1153.1.) *Types 851, 853.

D1395.3. *Escape from prison by use of magic purse.* (Cf. D1192.) *Types 851, 853.

D1395.4. *Saint's bachall enables captive to escape.* (Cf. D1277, V220.) Irish: Plummer clxxv, Cross.

D1395.5. *Magic ring enables captive to escape.* (Cf. D1076.) English: Wells 65 (Ywain and Gawain); Icelandic: Boberg.

D1395.6. *Escape from prison by use of charm (formula).* (Cf. D1273.) Penzer I 136f.; Dickson 220 n. 12. — Icelandic: MacCulloch Eddic 298, *Boberg.

D1395.7. *Escape from prison by use of magic hymn.* (Cf. D1275.3.) Irish myth: *Cross.

D1395.8. *All fetters loosed on the night of Christ's Nativity.* Irish myth: Cross.

V211.1. The Nativity of Christ.

D1395.9. *Magic centipede enables captive to make hole in wall.* Chinese: Graham.

D1396. *Magic object breaks spells.* Irish myth: Cross.

D1273. Magic formula charm.

D1396.1. *Magic goblet breaks spells.* (Cf. D1171.6.2.) Irish myth: Cross.

D1399. *Rescue by magic object — miscellaneous.*

D1399.1. *Magic spinning rod pulls horse out of the earth.* (Cf. D1254.2.) India: Thompson-Balys.

D1400—D1439. MAGIC OBJECT GIVES POWER OVER OTHER PERSONS

D1400. Magic object overcomes person.

D1663.4. Fountains poison and cure. D2060. Death or bodily injury by magic.

D1400.1. *Magic object conquers enemies.*

D1400.1.1. *Magic trousers conquer enemy.* Hero spreads them in air and balls of fire fall from them on enemy. (Cf. D1055.) Chinese: Werner 309.

D1400.1.2. *Magic ring conquers enemy.* (Cf. D1076.) *Fb "ring" III 60b.

D1400.1.3. *Magic fan conquers enemy.* (Cf. D1077.) Chinese: Werner 242, Eberhard FFC CXX 232.

D1400.1.4. *Magic weapon conquers enemy.* (Cf. D1080.)

D1400.1.4.1. *Magic sword conquers enemy.* (Cf. D1081, D1601.4.) *Type 328; MacCulloch Childhood 202. — Irish myth: *Cross; Norse: MacCulloch Eddic 268 (Tyrfing); Finnish: Kalevala rune 36; French Canadian: Barbeau JAFL XXIX 10; India: *Thompson-Balys; Indo-Chinese: Scott Indo-Chinese 303.

D1400.1.4.1.1. *Sacred sword of saint repulses army of heretics.* *Loomis White Magic 123.

D1400.1.4.2. *Magic saber conquers enemy.* (Cf. D1082.) *Chauvin V 259 No. 154 n. 1; Type 576***.

D1400.1.4.3. *Magic knife conquers enemy.* (Cf. D1083.) Type 576******. — Africa (Ekoi): Talbot 211, (Fang): Tessman 93, 94,

D1400.1.4.4. *Magic spear conquers enemy.* (Cf. D1084, D1601.4.0.1.) Irish myth: *Cross (D1400.1.7); Chinese: Werner 355.

D1400.1.4.5. *Hercules' bow and arrow essential to capture Troy.* Greek: Grote I 275. (Cf. D1091, D1092.)
Z312. Unique deadly weapon.

D1400.1.4.6. *Magic stone axe conquers enemies.* (Cf. D1097.) Hawaii: Beckwith Myth 395.

D1400.1.4.7. *Magic arrows annihilate army.* (Cf. D1092.) India: Thompson-Balys.

D1400.1.5. *Magic jewel conquers enemies.* (Cf. D1071.) Jewish: Neuman.

D1400.1.6. *Magic amulet in mouth conquers enemies.* (Cf. D1270.). Eskimo (Greenland): Rasmussen II 175, III 291, (Central Eskimo): Boas RBAE VI 628.

D1400.1.7. *Magic staff defeats enemies.* (Cf. D1254.) German: Grimm Nos. 90, 166.

D1400.1.7.1. *Magic club (stick) gives victory.* (Cf. D1094.) India: *Thompson-Balys.

D1400.1.8. *Magic cup gives victory.* (Cf. D1171.6.) Irish: MacCulloch Celtic 171, Cross.

D1400.1.9. *Saint's bell conquers enemies.* (Cf. D1213.) Irish: Plummer clxxvi, *Cross.
V220. Saints.

D1400.1.9.1. *Saint rings the church bells, and enemies flee in dismay.* *Loomis White Magic 53.

D1400.1.10. *Charm gives victory in fight.* (Cf. D1273.) *Kittredge Witchcraft 32, 388 n. 97.

D1400.1.11. *Magic runes give power over enemy.* (Cf. D1266.1.) *Kittredge Witchcraft 31, 387 n. 77. — Icelandic: Boberg.

D1400.1.11.1. *Magic oath stops killer and sends invading army back.* India: Thompson-Balys.

D1400.1.12. *Saint's bachall defeats enemies.* (Cf. D1277.) Irish: Plummer clxxv, *Cross.

D1400.1.12.1. *Saint's bachall overcomes beast in hell.* Irish myth: Cross.
A671.2. Horrible sights in hell.

D1400.1.13. *Magic mirror kills enemy soldiers.* (Cf. D1163.) Africa (Quelimane): Torrend Zs. f. afrikan. u. ozean. Spr. I 247ff.

D1400.1.14. *Magic stone (jewel) gives victory.* (Cf. D931.) Icelandic: *Boberg.

D1400.1.15. *Armor gives victory.* (Cf. D1101.) Icelandic: Boberg.

D1400.1.16. *Magic banner gives victory.* Icelandic: *Boberg.

D1400.1.17. *Magic helmet gives victory.* (Cf. D1101.4.) Icelandic: *Boberg.

D1400.1.18. *Thread from jogi's garment when pulled makes fort fall to ground.* (Cf. D1052.) India: Thompson-Balys.

D1400.1.19. *Magic feather defeats enemy.* (Cf. D1021.) India: Thompson-Balys.

D1400.1.20. *Magic (human) head defeats enemy.* (Cf. D992.)

D1400.1.20.1. *Magic (human) head causes fortress to crumble.* India: Thompson-Balys.

D1400.1.21. *Bull's tail becomes a stick that lashes hero's enemies and exterminates an army.* (Cf. D1029.2.) India: Thompson-Balys.

D1400.1.22. *Raja's guards magically transform stones and dry bones rained upon him by army of witches and turn them back.* India: Thompson-Balys.

A1245.1. New race from stones thrown over head.

D1400.1.23. *Magic storm conquers enemies.* (Cf. D905.) Jewish: Neuman.

D1400.1.23.1. *Magic wind sinks five pursuing demons in sea.* (Cf. D906.) India: Thompson-Balys.

D1400.1.23.2. *Lightning in magic box kills an army sent by king to conquer hero.* (Cf. D1174.) India: Thompson-Balys.

D1540. Magic object controls the elements.

D1401. *Magic object cudgels person.*

D1401.1. *Magic club (stick) beats person.* (Cf. D1094.) **Aarne JSFO XXVII 1—96; *Types 563, 534*; *BP I 349ff.; Dickson 133f. nn. 110—116; Spanish: Boggs FFC XC 49 No. 330; Missouri French: Carrière; India: *Thompson-Balys; N. A. Indian (Jicarilla Apache): Goddard PaAM VIII 225 No. 27, (Tsimshian): Boas BBAE XXVII 225; S. A. Indian (Toba): Métraux MAFLS XL 70.

D831. Magic object acquired by trick exchange.

D1401.1.1. *Magic cudgel beats animals to death for owner.* S. A. Indian (Toba): Métraux MAFLS XL 70.

D1401.2. *Magic sack furnishes mannikin who cudgels owner's enemies.* (Cf. D1193.) *Type 564; *Aarne JSFO XXVII 48.

D1401.3. *Magic whip beats person.* (Cf. D1208.) Africa (Ekoi): Talbot 47, (Benga): Nassau 119 No. 11.

D1401.4. *Magic pot with demons who beat owner's enemy.* (Cf. D1171.1.) India: Thompson-Balys.

D1401.5. *Magic stone hits everything and returns by itself.* (Cf. D931.) Icelandic: Boberg.

D1401.6. *Magic hammer beats person.* (Cf. D1209.4.) India: Thompson-Balys.

D1401.7. *Magic slipper beats person.* (Cf. D1065.2) India: Thompson-Balys.

D1401.8. *Log of wood animated by spirit of malignant holy man strikes left and right to kill offending villagers.* (Cf. D956.) India: Thompson-Balys.

D1401.9. *Magic bone beats king's face.* (Cf. D1007.) Jewish: Neuman.

D1402. *Magic object kills.*

D1663.3. Well of life and death. Situated on one hand, kills; on the other protects against disease. D2061. Magic murder. G303.16.2.3.5. Blessing reveals seemingly pure stream to be devil's trap which kills whoever drinks from it. Q410. Capital punishment.

D1402.0.1. *Magic object burns person up.* Chinese: Werner 318.

D1402.0.1.1. *Magic shield shoots balls of fire among enemies.* (Cf. D1101.1.) Irish myth: Cross.

D1402.0.1.2. *Holy man's cloak burns person up.* (Cf. D1053.) India: Thompson-Balys.

D1402.0.2. *Magic object causes person to be drowned.* (Cf. D1402.13.2.) Irish myth: Cross.

F933.6. Spring miraculously breaks forth against wrongdoers. Q428. Punishment: drowning. S131. Murder by drowning.

D1402.0.2.1. *Magic well causes person to be drowned.* (Cf. D926). Irish myth: *Cross.

D1402.0.2.2. *Magic spell causes person to be drowned.* (Cf. D1273.) Irish myth: Cross.

D1402.0.2.3. *Magic ring causes person to be drowned.* (Cf. D1076.) India: Thompson-Balys.

D1402.1. *Magic plant kills.* (Cf. D965.) Jewish: Neuman.

D1402.2. *Magic hair in man's eyebrow kills all who see it.* (Cf. D991.) Irish: Plummer cxl, Cross.

D1402.3. *Magic part of animal kills.*

D1402.3.1. *Magic serpent heart kills giant.* (Cf. D1015.1.3.) Spanish: Boggs FFC XC 43 No. 302*A.

D1402.3.2. *Magic leopard gall causes death.* (Cf. D1015.2.) Africa (Ekoi): Talbot 27.

D1402.3.3. *Magic animal horn kills.* (Cf. D1011.1.) Africa (Fang): Trilles 268.

D1402.3.4. *Magic jaw bone of ass kills.* (Cf. D1011.) Jewish: Neuman.

D1402.4. *Magic fire kills.* (Cf. D1271.) Jewish: Neuman.

D1402.5 *Nessus-shirt.* Magic shirt burns wearer up. (Cf. D1056.) *BP I 42 n. 1; Fb "skjorte" III 268b.; Greek: Fox 94; Icelandic: *Boberg.

D1402.6. *Magic bracelet kills man.* (Cf. D1074.) Chinese: Werner 308.

D1402.7. *Magic weapon kills.* (Cf. D1080.)

D1402.7.0.1. *Weapons magically venomous.* (Cf. D1080.) Irish myth: Cross (D1402.19).

D1402.7.1. *Magic sword kills man.* (Cf. D1081.) Malone PMLA XLIII 403; Jewish: Neuman.

D1402.7.1.1. *Magic sword slays a man daily.* Fb "sværd" III 690b; Icelandic: *Boberg.

D1402.7.1.2. *Magic sword always inflicts mortal wounds.* Irish myth: *Cross (D1402.7.2.)

D1402.7.2. *Magic spear kills.* (Cf. D1084.)

D1402.7.2.1. *Magic spear always inflicts mortal wounds.* (Cf. D1084.) Irish myth: *Cross (D1402.8).

D1402.7.2.2. *Magic all-killing spear-head.* (Cf. D1084.1.) Hawaii: Beckwith Myth 418; Africa (Benga): Nassau 178 No. 24, version 1, (Duala): Lederbogen Märchen 138.

D1402.7.2.3. *Magic spear's point harmless, while its shaft inflicts mortal blow.* Irish myth: Cross (D1402.8.2).

D1402.7.2.4. *Magic spear kills man.* (Cf. D1084.) Irish myth: Cross (D1402.8.3).

D1402.7.3. *Magic lance kills.*

C835.2.1. Tabu: failing to make gift to magic lance. The lance kills.

D1402.7.4. *Magic cartridge kills.* (Cf. D1096.) Jijena Sanchez 32.

D1385.4. Silver bullet protects against giants, ghosts, etc.

D1402.7.5. *Magic arrow kills.* (Cf. D1092.) Chinese: Graham.

D1402.7.5.1. *Arrows rubbed with black chicken fatal.* Chinese: Graham.

D1402.8. *Magic breath kills.* (Cf. D1005.) Jewish: Neuman.

D1402.9. *Magic door catches bear so that he is burned to death.* (Cf. D1146.) Shasta: Farrand-Frachtenberg JAFL XXVIII 216 No. 6.

D1402.10. *Magic wand kills.* (Cf. D1254.1.) MacCulloch Childhood 205; N. A. Indian (Passamaquoddy): Leland 127, (Chilcotin): Farrand JE II 44 No. 30, (Kwakiutl): Boas and Hunt JE III 356, (Bella Coola): Boas JE I 54.

D1663.1. Wands of life and death.

D1402.10.1. *Stick, become a sword, flies through air to kill ferocious animal-guardians of extraordinary lotus.* (Cf. D1094, D1254.) India: *Thompson-Balys.

D1402.10.2. *Rod from magic hazel-tree kills snake immediately.* (Cf. D956.) (Cf. D950.1, A2711.4.1.) BP III 477.

G512.1.1. Giant killed with magic knife.

D1402.11. *Magic song kills person.* (Cf. D1275.) Finnish: Kalevala rune 12; Jewish: Neuman.

D1402.11.1. *Magic music kills person.* (Cf. D1275.1.) Irish myth: *Cross.

D1402.12. *Magic ring kills.* (Cf. D1076.) *Fb "ring" III 60b.

D1402.13. *Druid's spells kill Christian king.* (Cf. D1273.) Irish: Plummer clix, Cross.

F363.1. Fairies, directed by druid, bring about death of king by causing fish-bone to stick in his throat. M400. Curses. P427. Druid (Magus).

D1402.13.1. *Druid's spells kill enemies.* (Cf. D1273.) Irish myth: *Cross.

D1402.13.2. *Druid's spells cause drowning.* (Cf. D1402.0.2.) Irish myth: *Cross.

D1402.13.2.1. *Druidess' spell causes drowning.* Irish myth: Cross.

P427.0.3. Women druids. Q466.3.1. Punishment: sea-spell chanted by druidess causes rival to drown.

D1402.13.3. *Charm used to kill.* (Cf. D1273.) S. A. Indian (Toba): Métraux MAFLS XL 126f.

D1402.14. *Magic circle of saliva kills dragon.* (Cf. D1001, D1272.) Wesselski Mönchslatein 171 No. 136.

D1402.14.1. *Magic charmed spittle kills.* Irish myth: *Cross.

D1402.15. *Magic poem (satire) causes king to waste away.* (Cf. D1275.4.) Irish myth: *Cross.

M400.1. Satire.

D1402.15.1. *Magic poem (satire) causes man to melt.* Irish myth: Cross.

F1041.4. Person melts away from heat.

D1402.15.2. *Magic poem (satire) causes death.* Irish myth: *Cross.

D1402.15.3. *Satire causes ulcers on face.* Irish myth: *Cross.

D1402.16. *Magic mustard-seed causes man to turn to ashes.* India: Thompson-Balys.

D971.1. Magic mustard-seed. D2061.1.1. Person magically reduced to ashes.

D1402.16.1. *Magic mustard seed causes man to be dead for an hour.* India: Thompson-Balys.

D1402.17. *Magic bedstead-legs kill dangerous animals.* (Cf. D1154.1.) India: Thompson-Balys.

D1402.18. *Excrements cause approaching animals to fall dead.* (Cf. D1002.) India: Thompson-Balys.

D1402.19. *Magic statue kills.* (Cf. D1268.)

D1402.19.1. *Magic statue of animal kills.* Chinese: Eberhard FFC CXX 152.

D1402.20. *Magic wheel kills all upon whom it falls.* (Cf. D1207.) Irish myth: Cross.

D1402.21. *Magic stone kills person whom it strikes.* (Cf. D931.) Irish myth: Cross.

D1402.22. *Magic harp kills.* (Cf. D1231.) Irish myth: Cross.

D1402.23. *Killing with head of fallen enemy.* Irish myth: Cross.

F839.4. Human head as weapon.

D1402.24. *Water from magic fountain kills.* (Cf. D925.)

D1402.24.1. *Giant kills people by sprinkling water on their heads.* (Cf. D1242.1.) India: Thompson-Balys.

D1402.25. *Magic pills kill.* (Cf. D1243.)

D1402.25.1. *Magic pills reduce snake to ashes.* India: Thompson-Balys.

D2061.1.1. Person magically reduced to ashes.

D1402.26. *Magic wind kills.* (Cf. D906.) Jewish: Neuman.

D1402.27. *Magic dust kills snake.* (Cf. D935.3.) India: Thompson-Balys.

D1402.28. *Handkerchief whirled against advancing army stretches them lifeless.* (Cf. D1069.1.) India: Thompson-Balys.

D1402.29. *Magic drum enters enemy's body and kills him.* (Cf. D1211.) India: Thompson-Balys.

D1402.30. *Magic coat kills.* (Cf. D1052.) Africa: Bouveignes 44.

D1402.31. *Magic salt kills.* (Cf. D1039.2.) Jewish: Neuman.

D1402.32. *Magic tomb kills.* Jewish: Neuman.

D1403. *Magic object maims.* Irish myth: Cross.

D2062. Maiming by magic. H251.3.9. Magic spring detects perjury. Disfigures perjurer. Q551.8. Deformity as punishment.

D1403.1. *Magic poem (satire) raises blotches on face.* (Cf. D1275.4.) Irish myth: *Cross.

D1273. Magic formula (charm). D1402.15. Magic poem (satire) causes king to waste away. D2175.3. Magic satire as curse. M400.1. Satire. Q265.2.1. Blotches on face of satirist (judge) as punishment for wrongful satire (judgment).

D1403.1.1. *Magic poem causes deformity.* Irish myth: Cross.

D1403.2. *Magic well maims.* (Cf. D926.) Irish myth: *Cross.

C623.1. Well upon which no one can look without losing his eyes.

D1403.3. *Magic drink causes arms to fall from shoulders.* (Cf. D1040.) Irish myth: Cross.

D1404. *Magic object pierces.*

D1653.1. Infallible weapon.

D1404.1. *Magic rod pierces whatever directed against.* (Cf. D1254.2.) India: Thompson-Balys.

D1404.2. *Drop of hound's blood from magic spear (lance) pierces owner's foot (head).* (Cf. D1081.) Irish myth: *Cross (D1403.4).

D1645.8.1.1. Flaming spear must be cooled in noxious blood.

D1405. *Magic object causes person to disappear.*

D1987.1. Magic disappearance of witch. D2095. Magic disappearance.

D1405.1. *Magic ring causes person to disappear.* Breton: Sébillot Incidents s.v. "bague".

D1406. *Magic object helps win in law court.*

P510. Law courts.

D1406.1. *Charm to win cases in law court.* (Cf. D1273.) Kittredge Witchcraft 55, *406 nn. 240—3.

D1407. *Magic object helps gambler win.*

N0. Wagers and gambling. N1.2.2. Dice made from bones from graveyard always win.

D1407.1. *Magic ring helps gambler win.* (Cf. D1076.) Kittredge Witchcraft 67, *410 n. 302.

D1407.2. *Hangman's noose gives luck in gambling.* (Cf. D1278.) *Kittredge Witchcraft 142, 461 n. 23.

D1407.3. *Magic game board helps win.* Icelandic: Boberg.

D1407.4. *Charm gives victory in game of dice.* (Cf. D1273.) India: Thompson-Balys.

D1408. *Magic object devastates country.*

D1408.1. *Magic sphere burns up country.* By turning that part of the globe to the sun, one can make any place on earth burn up. (Cf. D1264.) *Chauvin V 259 No. 154.

D1408.1.1. *Magic bark sets creek on fire and burns it up.* (Cf. D952.) Chinese: Graham.

D1566. Magic object controls fire. D2144.4. Burning by magic. D2158.1.4. Magician opens his eyes and forest burns for twenty-four miles in front of him.

D1408.2. *Magic red wind devastates country.* (Cf. D906.) Irish myth: Cross.

B16. Devastating animals.

D1409. *Magic object overcomes person — miscellaneous.* Irish myth: Cross.

D1409.1. *Magic object brings evil (bad luck) upon person.* Irish myth: Cross.

N135. Objects effect change of luck. N250. Persistent bad luck.

D1409.1.1. *Magic wand brings evil upon person.* (Cf. D1254.1, D1254.2.) Irish myth: *Cross.

D1409.2. *Magic roll of cloth pacifies demon.* India: Thompson-Balys.

D1051. Magic cloth. D1442. Magic object tames or restrains animal. F402. Evil spirits. Demons.

D1410. Magic object renders person helpless.

C942. Loss of strength from broken tabu. D1336. Magic object gives weakness. D1837. Magic weakness. D2072.5. Robber-proof house: thieves are petrified when they enter house for unlawful purposes; are fed and welcomed, otherwise.

D1410.1. *Seeds cast on lions and tigers render them helpless.* (Cf. D971.) Fb "frø" I 378b.

D1410.2. *Light from hand-of-glory renders person helpless.* (Cf. D1162.2.1.) Baker Am. Anthropologist o.s. I 55f.

D1410.3. *Magic fluid takes away magic powers.* Fluid is to be sprinkled with a willow branch. (Cf. D1242.) Chinese: Werner 216.

D1410.4. *Possession of mermaid's belt gives power over her.* (Cf. D1057.) *Fb "bælte" IV 84a.

B81. Mermaid.

D1410.5. *Serpent charmed into helplessness by magic formula.* (Cf. D1273.) Finnish: Kalevala rune 26; India: Thompson-Balys.

D1410.6. *Drink from magic cup deprives man of legs.* (Cf. D1040, D1171.6.) Irish myth: Cross.

D1410.7. *Magic bag shaken against enemies renders them helpless in face of mist or poison.* (Cf. D1193.) Icelandic: *Boberg.

D1410.8. *When spying follower accidentally touches holy man's cloak he loses his eyesight and falls down senseless.* (Cf. D1053.) India: Thompson-Balys.

D1411 *Magic object binds person (animal).* Irish myth: Cross; India: *Thompson-Balys.

D1203. Magic rope. D1336.9. Druids' (poets') spells bind. D2074. Attracting by magic. K1563. Husband (god) traps wife and paramour with magic armor.

D1411.1. *Magic rope binds person.* (Cf. D1203.) Irish myth: Cross.

D1411.2. *Magic whip holds person fast.* (Cf. D1208.) Fb "pisk".

D1411.3. *Magic grass holds person fast.* (Cf. D965.12.) Irish myth: Cross.

D1411.4. *Magic charm binds deer so that it cannot move.* (Cf. D1273.) India: Thompson-Balys.

D1412. *Magic object pulls person into it.*

K730. Victim trapped.

D1412.1. *Magic bag draws person into it.* (Cf. D1193.) Fb "pose"; *Type 330. — Swiss: Jegerlehner Oberwallis 314f. No. 114.

D1412.2. *Magic pot draws person into it.* (Cf. D1171.1.) N. A. Indian: *Thompson Tales 321 n. 157.

G331. Pot-tilter. Ogre who tilts a pot so that victims are drawn into it.

D1412.3. *Flames draw person into them.* (Cf. D1271.) Jewish: Neuman.

D1413. *Magic object holds person fast.* *Type 571. — Icelandic: Boberg; Irish myth: Cross; Chinese: Graham; Japanese: Ikeda.

D2171. Magic adhesion. F61.2.1. Ascent to sky by sticking to magic feather. F155. Journey to otherworld by clinging magically to an object. K741. Capture by tarbaby.

D1413.0.1. *Magic object causes persons to stick together.*

D1413.0.1.1. *Magic formula causes persons to stick together.* (Cf. D1273.) India: Thompson-Balys.

D1413.1. *Tree from which one cannot descend.* (Cf. D950.) *Type 330; BP II 163ff, *188.

G303.16. How the devil may be overcome or avoided.

D1413.1.1. *Cherry tree from which one cannot descend.* (Cf. D950.4.) Breton: Sébillot s.v. "cerisier".

D1413.1.2. *Pear tree from which one cannot descend.* (Cf. D950.5.) Fb "pæretræ" II 905b.

D1413.1.3. *Fig tree from which one cannot descend.* (Cf. D950.8.) Italian Novella: Rotunda.

D1413.2. *Ring prevents person from rising from chair.* (Cf. D1076.) *Fb "ring" III 60b, 61a. — Icelandic: Boberg.

G254.1. Witch cannot rise if ring lies under her chair.

D1413.3. *Sleigh makes person magically hold on.* (Cf. D1115.) Fb "kane".

D1413.4. *Stairs to which person sticks.* (Cf. D1144.) Spanish: Boggs FFC XC 49 No. 330.

D1413.5. *Bench to which person sticks.* (Cf. D1151.1.) *Type 330. — Irish myth: *Cross.

D1413.6. *Chair to which person sticks.* (Cf. D1151.2.) *Kittredge Witchcraft 202, 515 n. 107. — Greek: Fox 206; Irish myth: Cross; Breton: Sébillot Incidents s.v. "chaise"; Swiss: Jegerlehner Oberwallis 322 No. 92; U.S.: *Baughman; India: Thompson-Balys.

D1413.7. *Basin to which one sticks.* (Cf. D1171.12.) *BP II 40 n. 2.

K1217. Tale of the basin. Lover caught on magic basin and left in embarrassing position.

D1413.8. *Chamber-pot to which one sticks.* (Cf. D1171.13.) *BP II 40 n. 2.

D1413.9. *Sack holds person who puts hand into it.* (Cf. D1193.) Swiss: Jegerlehner Oberwallis 322 No. 92; Breton: Sebillot Incidents s.v. "blague".

K420. Thief loses his goods or is detected.

D1413.9.1. *Wallet (sack) from which one cannot escape.* (Cf. D1192.) *Fb "pung" II 897b, "pose" II 864a. — Spanish: Boggs FFC XC 49 No. 330.

K711.1. Deception into magic bag which closes on prisoner.

D1413.10. *Anvil to which one sticks.* (Cf. D1202.) Breton: Sébillot Incidents s.v. "enclume".

D1413.11. *Magic medicine causes person to stick to seat (pot).* (Cf. D1241.) Africa (Benga): Nassau 138 No. 15, (Ekoi): Talbot 115.

D1413.12. *Magic hand causes sword to stick to it.* (Cf. D996.) Jewish: Neuman.

D1413.13. *Magic stick holds person fast.* (Cf. D1254.) Fb "kjæp". — Icelandic: Boberg.

D1413.14. *Magic cauldron (cup) to which one sticks.* (Cf. D1171.2.) Irish: Plummer clxviii, *Cross.

D1146. Magic door. D1171.6. Magic cup. D2006.1.1. Forgotten fiancée reawakens husband's memory by detaining lovers through magic. D2171.5. Cauldron magically sticks to wall. H251.3.8. Magic object clings to hand of guilty person. H411.4.2. Magic cup as chastity test: sticks to hands of adulterer.

D1413.15. *Magic window holds person fast.* (Cf. D1145.) *Cosquin Lorraine II 28.

D1413.16. *Magic door holds person fast.* (Cf. D1146.) *Cosquin Lorraine II 28. — Icelandic: Boberg.

D1413.16.1. *Magic doorstep will not let person pass over.* (Cf. D1146.1.) Chinese: Graham.

D1413.17. *Magic adhesive stone.* Makes all who poke in fire stick and say "Fiddevav." (Cf. D931.) Type 593*.

D1413.18. *Magic ball of string to which one sticks.* (Cf. D1184.2.) Irish myth: *Cross.

D1413.19. *Magic plain to which one sticks.* (Cf. D937.) Irish myth: *Cross.

D1413.20. *Magic earth-mould holds person fast.* (Cf. D935.) Irish myth: Cross.

D1413.21. *Magic grass holds person fast.* (Cf. D965.12.) Irish myth: *Cross.

D1413.22. *Magic cloth holds person fast.* (Cf. D1413.0.1.) India: Thompson-Balys.

D1413.23. *Magic drinking-tube holds person fast.* (Cf. D1255.) India: Thompson-Balys.

D1413.24. *Grave holds person fast.* (Cf. D1299.1.) Eskimo (Greenland): Rink 270.

D1413.25. *Magic scabbard causes sword to stick to it.* (Cf. D1101.5.) Jewish: Neuman.

D1414. *Magic object renders weapon useless.*

D2072.0.1. Sword made magically helpless. D2086.1. Sword magically dulled.

D1414.0.1. *Magic object makes fortifications useless.* German: Grimm No. 54.

D1414.1. *Magic wand breaks enemy's sword.* (Cf. D1254.1.) Chinese: Werner 324.

D1414.2. *Magic writings on sword render it harmless.* (Cf. D1266.1.) Kittredge Witchcraft 31, 387 n. 78. — Icelandic: Boberg.

D1414.3. *Magic wind causes arms to fall from warrior's hands.* (Cf. D906.) Irish myth: Cross.

D1414.4. *Magic song dulls enemy's sword.* (Cf. D1275.) Icelandic: Boberg.

D1414.5. *Magic garment makes weapons useless.* (Cf. D1052.) Jewish: Neuman.

D1415. *Magic object compels person to dance.* England, Wales, U.S.: *Baughman; Icelandic: Boberg.

D2061.1.2. Persons magically caused to dance themselves to death. D2174. Magic dancing.

D1415.1. *Water from magic well causes person to dance.* (Cf. D926, D1353.1.) Pauli (ed. Bolte) No. 54.

D1415.2. *Magic musical instrument causes person to dance.* (Cf. D1210.) *Fb "spille" III 488b.

D1415.2.1. *Magic horn causes dancing.* (Cf. D1222.) Type 592; *BP II 501.

D1415.2.2. *Magic clarinet causes dancing.* (Cf. D1223.) Breton: Sébillot Incidents s.v. "clarinette".

D1415.2.3. *Magic flute causes dancing.* (Cf. D1223.1.) *BP II 490—503 passim; *Fb "flöjte".

D1415.2.4. *Magic pipe causes dancing.* (Cf. D1224.) Penzer III 187.

D1415.2.5. *Magic fiddle causes dancing.* (Cf. D1233.) *Types 559, 592, 853; *Basset RTP XXVI 266; *Fb "Jøde" II 66b, "fiol" I 292b. — Breton: Sébillot Incidents s.v. "violon"; Africa (Gold Coast): Barker and Sinclair 97ff. No. 18.

D1415.2.6. *Magic lute causes dancing.* (Cf. D1232.)

D1415.2.6.1. *Magic lute causes animals to dance.* India: Thompson-Balys.

D1440. Magic object gives power over animals.

D1417. *Magic object imprisons person.*

D1601. Deceiver falls into his own trap (literally).

D1417.1. *Magic circle prevents escape.* (Cf. D1272.) Fb "kreds" II 293.

D1446. Magic object prevents animals from straying.

D1418. *Magic object causes person to become lost.* Irish myth: Cross.

D1418.1. *Magic mist causes person to become lost.* (Cf. D902.1.) Irish myth: *Cross.

D1419. *Magic object renders person helpless — miscellaneous.* Irish myth: Cross.

D1419.1. *Magic object compels person to laugh (shriek).* Irish myth: Cross.

D1419.1.1. *Magic grave compels person to laugh (shriek).* (Cf. D1299.2.) Irish myth: Cross.

D1419.2. *Magic object paralyzes.* Irish myth: Cross.
D2072. Magic paralysis.

D1419.2.1. *Magic bell paralyzes perjurer.* (Cf. D1213.) Irish myth: Cross.
Q263. Lying (perjury) punished.

D1419.3. *Magic object prevents ship from moving.* Irish myth: Cross.
D1654.6. Ship refuses to move. D2072.0.3. Ship held back by magic.

D1419.3.1. *Saint's bachall prevents ship from moving.* (Cf. D1277.) Irish myth: Cross.

D1419.4. *Magic food brings eater into sender's power.* (Cf. D1031.1, D1273.) Jewish: Neuman.

D1420. Magic object draws person (thing) to it.
D1649.2. Magic object comes at owner's call. D2074. Attracting by magic.

D1420.1. *Person drawn by magic spell.* (Cf. D1273.) Tawney II 571.

D1420.2. *Person follows magic receding well.* (Cf. D926.) Irish myth: Cross.
D1641.13. Well removes itself.

D1420.3. *Guitar charming all who hear it.* (Cf. D1234.) India: Thompson-Balys.

D1420.4. *Helper summoned by calling his name.* India: Thompson-Balys.
C430. Name tabu.

D1421. *Magic object summons helper.*
B501. Animal gives part of body as talisman for summoning its aid.

D1421.0.1. *Magic bell summons helper.* India: Thompson-Balys.
D1213. Magic bell.

D1421.0.2. *Magic ashes summon helper.* (Cf. D931.1.2.) India: Thompson-Balys.

D1421.0.3. *Magic hair when thrown into fire summons supernatural helper.* (Cf. D991.) India: Thompson-Balys.

D1421.1. *Magic object summons genie.*
D2074.2.4. Genie called by writing his name on papers and burning them. F403.2. Spirits help mortal. Familiar spirits. F404. Means of summoning spirits. N813. Helpful genie. N800. Helpers.

D1421.1.1. *Magic tinder summons genie.* (Cf. D1175.1.) Fb "fyrtøj".

D1421.1.2. *Magic fire-steel summons genie.* (Cf. D1175.2.) *Type 562.

D1421.1.3. *Magic book summons genie.* (Cf. D1266.) Chauvin V 262 No. 154; *Fb "bog" IV 54a; Lithuanian: Balys Index No. 3315, Legends Nos. 597ff., 716; Icelandic: Boberg.
E383. Ghosts summoned by opening sacred book.

D1421.1.4. *Magic light summons genie.* (Cf. D1162.) *Type 562; *BP II 535; *Fb "lys" II 483a.

D1421.1.5. *Magic lamp summons genie.* (Cf. D1162.1.) *Type 561; *BP II 544ff.

D1421.1.6. *Magic ring summons genie.* (Cf. D1076.) *Bolte Reise der Söhne Giaffers 214; India: Thompson-Balys.

D1421.1.7. *Magic incense (when burned) summons genie.* Africa (Swahili): Baker FL XXXVIII 183ff. No. 1.

D1787. Magic results from burning.

D1421.1.8. *Magic sword (rubbed) summons genie.* (Cf. D1081.) India: Thompson-Balys.

D1421.1.9. *Magic hair summons demon.* (Cf. D991.) India: Thompson-Balys.

D1421.1.10. *Magic roll of cloth summons demon.* (Cf. D1051.) India: Thompson-Balys.

D1421.1.11. *Magic chain summons genie.* (Cf. D1251.) India: Thompson-Balys.

D1421.1.12. *Magic pipe summons genie.* (Cf. D1224.) India: Thompson-Balys.

D1421.1.13. *Magic ring summons air spirits.* (Cf. D1076.) German: Grimm No. 166.

D1421.1.14. *Opening bottle summons genie.* (Cf. D1171.8.) German: Grimm No. 99.

D1421.2. *Magic object summons water-spirit.*

F420. Water-spirits.

D1421.2.1. *Magic arrow summons water-spirit.* (Cf. D1092.) Chinese: Werner 182.

D1421.3. *Magic object summons dwarfs.* (Cf. F451.)

D1421.3.1. *Magic fiddle summons dwarfs.* (Cf. D1233.) *Fb "fiol" I 292b.

D1421.3.2. *Magic flute summons dwarfs.* (Cf. D1223.1.) German: Grimm No. 91.

D1421.3.3. *Magic charm summons dwarfs.* (Cf. D1273.) German: Grimm No. 113.

D1421.4. *Magic object summons giant.* India: Thompson-Balys.

G100. Giant ogre. N812. Giant or ogre as helper.

D1421.4.1. *Magic hairs summon giant.* He gives hero some hairs from his own beard. (Cf. D991.) Malone PMLA XLIII 412; India: Thompson-Balys.

D1421.4.2. *Magic bow summons giant.* (Cf. D1091.) India: Thompson-Balys.

D1421.5. *Magic object summons army for rescue.*

D1421.5.1. *Magic horn summons army for rescue.* (Cf. D1222.) *BP II 501.

B501.1. Buffaloes give hero horns to blow for summoning them. D1390. Magic object rescues person. R100. Rescues.

D1421.5.2. *Magic charm summons army.* (Cf. D1273.) German: Grimm No. 136.

D1421.5.3. *Magic sack contains soldiers which appear when it is struck.* (Cf. D1193.) German: Grimm No. 54.

D1421.6. *Magic object summons fairy.*

F340. Gifts from fairies. N815. Fairy as helper.

D1421.6.1. *Magic flute summons fairy.* (Cf. D1223.1.) India: Thompson-Balys.

D1425. *Magic object draws lover (husband) to woman.*

D1355. Love-producing magic object.

D1425.1. *Magic spindle brings back prince for heroine.* (Cf. D1186.) India: Thompson-Balys.

D1425.2. *Magic hairs summon husband.* (Cf. D991.) Pauli (ed. Bolte) No. 150.

K1281. Woman draws a pelt to her instead of her husband.

D1425.3. *Magic fan summons prince for heroine.* (Cf. D1077.) India: *Thompson-Balys.

D1426. *Magic object draws woman to man.* *Type 562; *BP II 538.

D1426.0.1. *Magic objects help hero win princess.* India: Thompson-Balys.

D1426.1. *Magic flute compels woman to come to man.* (Cf. D1223.1.) Arikara: Dorsey CI XVII 90 No. 27; India: *Thompson-Balys.

T111.1. Marriage of a mortal and a god.

D1426.2. *Magic ring causes woman to come to man.* (Cf. D1076.) India: Thompson-Balys.

D1426.3. *Magic pipe compels woman to come to man.* (Cf. D1224, D1427.1.) India: Thompson-Balys.

D1427. *Magic object compels one to follow.*

D1427.1. *Magic pipe compels one to follow.* Pied Piper of Hamelin. (Cf. D1224.) *Fb "rotte" III 83a; *Chauvin VIII 155 No. 157; *Wehrhan Die Sage 51; *Dickson Studies in Philology XXIII (1926) 327f.; Zs. f. Vksk. XXIV 78; Solymossy Hongaarsche Sagen (Zutphen, 1929) 32, 375 No. 11; England, U.S.: *Baughman.

D1427.2. *Woman's arm-tassel lent to ogre compels her to follow him.* India: Thompson-Balys.

D1427.3. *Magic horsehairs (when rubbed) compel horse to follow.* (Cf. D1023.) Africa (Kordofan): Frobenius Atlantis IV 134ff. No. 13, (Swahili): Büttner 113ff.

D1427.4. *Lute (rubbed) compels one to follow.* (Cf. D1232.) India: Thompson-Balys.

D1427.5. *Harp compels one to follow.* (Cf. D1231.) India: Thompson-Balys.

D1427.6. *Magic club brings thieves to master.* (Cf. D1094.) India: Thompson-Balys.

K420. Thief loses his goods or is detected. B501. Animal gives part of body as talisman for summoning its aid. D1425.2 Magic hair summons husband.

D1428. *Magic object fetches another object.*

D1428.1. *Magic hair draws back quiver from which it has been taken.* (Cf. D991.) Pauli (ed. Bolte) No. 150.

D1428.2. *Charm causes spearhead to return.* (Cf. D1273.) Africa (Benga): Nassau 178 No. 24 version 1.

D1429. *Magic object draws person (thing) to it — miscellaneous.*

D1429.1. *Magic stone turned thrice compels person to return to it.* (Cf. D931.) Irish myth: Cross.

D1430. Magic object pursues or captures.

D1413. Magic object holds person fast. R260. Pursuits.

D1431. *Magic object pursues.*

D1431.1. *Rock (stone) pursues person.* (Cf. D931.) Africa (Kaffir): Theal 161; Eskimo (Greenland): Rasmussen III 99.

C91.1. Tabu: stealing garment from rock. The rock pursues. R261. Pursuit by rolling object.

D1431.2. *Pursuit by magic fan.* (Cf. D1077.) Chinese: Werner 242.

D1431.3. *Pursuit by magic ring.* (Cf. D1076.) Chinese: Werner 331.

D1431.4. *Pursuit by magic buckets.* (Cf. D1171.10.) Chinese: Werner 233.

D1431.5. *Pursuit by magic calabash.* (Cf. D965.2.) Africa (Nago): Bouche Mélusine II 123f. No. 9.

D1432. *Waters magically pursue man.* (Cf. D910.) Irish myth: *Cross; Greek: Iliad XXI lines 234ff. — N. A. Indian (Menomini): Skinner and Satterlee PaAM XIII 257.

A425. River-god. F932.1. River pursues fugitive. R260. Pursuits.

D1432.1. *Water gradually envelops girl filling pitcher and drowns her.* Work of malevolent rice-spirit. India: Thompson-Balys.

A432.1.1. God of rice fields. C41. Tabu: offending water-spirit. D2151.3.1. Magic tidal wave. Q501.2. Punishment of Tantalus.

D1436. *Magic hair stretches after fugitive.* (Cf. D991.) Molucca: Dixon 231.

R220. Flights.

D1438. *Magic weapon pursues victim.* (Cf. D1080.)

D1438.1. *Spell causes spear to pursue and slay man.* Irish myth: Cross.

D1273. Magic formula (charm). D1402.8.3. Magic spear kills man.

D1438.2. *Magic arrow pursues victim.* (Cf. D1092.) S. A. Indian (Toba): Métraux MAFLS XL 77.

D1438.3. *Magic club flies through air after victim.* (Cf. D1094.) S. A. Indian (Toba): Métraux MAFLS XL 75.

D1440. Magic object gives power over animals.

D1586.1. Magic image of animal relieves from plague (of that animal). D2074.1. Animals magically called.

D1440.1. *Magic horn has power over animals.* (Cf. D1222.) Italian Novella: Rotunda; Cheremis: Sebeok-Nyerges.

D1441. *Magic object calls animals together.*

D1427.3. Magic horsehairs compel horse to follow.

D1441.1. *Magic musical instrument calls animals together.* (Cf. D1210.) Finnish: Kalevala rune 41; India: Thompson-Balys.

D1275.1. Magic music.

D1441.1.1. *Magic flute calls animals together.* (Cf. D1223.1.) *Fb "flöjte"; India: *Thompson-Balys.

D1441.1.2. *Magic pipe calls animals together.* (Cf. D1224.) *Types 515*, 570; *Fb "rotte"; India: *Thompson-Balys.

D1441.1.3. *Magic fiddle calls animals together.* (Cf. D1233.) Type 650***.

D1441.1.3.1. *Magic lute calls animals together.* (Cf. D1232.) India: *Thompson-Balys; Buddhist myth: Malalasekera II 859.

D1441.1.3.2. *Magic harp calls animals together.* (Cf. D1231.) India: Thompson-Balys.

D1441.1.4. *Magic song calls animals together.* (Cf. D1275) Africa (Ba Ronga): Einstein 266.

D1441.2. *Charm calls down swarm of bees.* (Cf. D1273.) Kittredge Witchcraft 32, 388 n. 92.

D1442. *Magic object tames or restrains animal.*

B771. Animal tamed by maiden's beauty. B771.1. Animal tamed by holiness of saint. F618. Strong man tames animals. G224.11. Witch power from bone.

D1442.1. *Magic bridle restrains all horses.* (Cf. D1209.1.) Type 594*. — Greek: Fox 40 (Bellerophon and Pegasus).

D1442.1.1. *Mad horse becomes tame when girl's voice reaches his ears.* India: Thompson-Balys.

D1442.2. *Straw on horse's back restrains him.* (Cf. D1276.) *Fb "hest" I 598b.

D1442.3. *Saint's bachall subdues wild animals.* (Cf. D1277, V220.) Irish: Plummer clxxv, Cross.

D1442.4. *Magic staff thrown causes wild animals to stand still.* (Cf. D1254.) Jewish: bin Gorion Born Judas^2 III 19, *Neuman.

D1442.4.1. *Magic rod tames lions.* (Cf. D1254.2.) Jewish: Neuman.

D1442.5. *Saint's song silences hound.* (Cf. D1275.) Irish myth: Cross.

D1442.6. *Magic spell tames animals.* (Cf. D1273.) Buddhist myth: Malalasekera I 120, 379, II 389, 917.

D1442.6.1. *Spell tames horse.* India: Thompson-Balys.

D1442.6.2. *Magic spell causes birds to roost.* Irish myth: Cross. (D1442.6.)

D1442.7. *Magic breath subdues animals.* (Cf. D1005.) Irish myth: Cross.

D1442.8. *"Witch bone" enables possessor to control animals in any way he wishes.* England: Baughman.

G224.11. Witch power from bone.

D1442.9. *Magic meat pacifies animal guardians.* (Cf. D1032.) India: Thompson-Balys.

K330. Means of hoodwinking guardian or owner.

D1442.10. *Magic whip makes docile animal-guardians of wonderful birds.* (Cf. D1208.) India: Thompson-Balys.

D1442.11. *Diamond charms serpents into harmlessness.* (Cf. D1071.) India: Thompson-Balys.

D1442.12. *Magic garment tames animals.* (Cf. D1052.) Jewish: Neuman.

D1442.13. *Magic musical instrument tames animals.* (Cf. D1210.) Buddhist myth: Malalasekera I 192, 1055.

D1443. *Magic object expels animals.*

D1443.1. *Charm expels flies from city.* (Cf. D1273.) India: Thompson-Balys.

D1444. *Magic object catches animal.*

B845. Wild animals herded (captured).

D1444.1. *Magic object catches fish.* Hawaii: Beckwith Myth 19.

D1653.2. Infallible fish-hook.

D1444.1.1. *Saint's bachall catches fish.* (Cf. D1277, V220.) Irish: Plummer clxxv, Cross.

D1444.1.2. *Magic wooden fish attracts live fish to fisherman's net.* (Cf. D1268.) Italian Novella: Rotunda.

D1444.1.3. *Magic branch catches fish.* (Cf. D954.) Hawaii: Beckwith Myth 276.

D1444.1.4. *Magic charm allows person to hook mythical eel.* (Cf. D1273.) Cook Islands: Bechwith Myth 104.

D1444.2. *Charm to catch hare and monkey.* (Cf. D1273.) Africa (Angola): Chatelain 183 No. 22.

D1444.3. *Magic fishhook catches cats.* (Cf. D1257.) Breton: Sébillot Incidents s.v. "hameçon".

D1444.4. *Magic song to catch animals.* (Cf. D1275.) Finnish: Kalevala rune 14; India: Thompson-Balys.

D1445. *Magic object kills animal.*

D2061.2.3. Death by pointing.

D1445.1. *Relevation of magic secret permits animal to be killed.* (Cf. D1273.2.) Finnish: Kalevala rune 20.

D1445.2. *Magic spear kills animals.* (Cf. D1084.) Africa (Benga): Nassau 184 No. 24 version 2.

D1445.3. *Saint's chant kills animal.* (Cf. D1275, V220.) Irish myth: *Cross.

D1445.4. *Magic poem (satire) kills animals.* (Cf. D1275.4.) Irish myth: *Cross.

D1445.5. *Magic garment kills animals.* (Cf. D1052.) Jewish: Neuman.

D1445.6. *Magic object burns animals.*

D1445.6.1. *Magic clouds burn animals.* (Cf. D901.) Jewish: Neuman.

D1445.6.2. *Magic heavenly fire burns animals.* (Cf. D1271.) Jewish: Neuman.

D1446. *Magic object prevents animal from straying.*

D1446.1. *Saint's bell keeps cattle from straying.* (Cf. D1213.) Irish: Plummer clxxvi, Cross.

D1446.2. *Saint's gospel-book keeps cattle from straying.* (Cf. D1266.) Irish: Plummer clxxviii, Cross.

D1446.3. *Shepherd's consecrated staff keeps cow from straying.* (Cf. D1254.) Swiss: Jegerlehner Oberwallis 302 No. 6.

D1446.4. *Saint's staff serves as a shepherd.* (Cf. D1254.) *Loomis White Magic 100.

D1446.5. *Magic circle keeps herd within it.* (Cf. D1272.) Chinese: Eberhard FFC CXX 237.

D1447. *Magic object protects against wild animals.*

D1380. Magic object protects.

D1447.1. *Charm protects against wild animals.* (Cf. D1273.) *Kittredge Witchcraft 32, 388 n. 84. — Irish: Plummer clxxix, Cross.

D1447.2. *Magic garment protects against wild animals.* (Cf. D1052.) Jewish: Neuman.

D1447.2.1. *Saint's cowl protects fox from hounds.* (Cf. D1067.3.1.) Irish myth: Cross.

D1447.3. *White ash stick held before snakes causes them to flee.* U.S.: *Baughman.

D1449. *Magic object gives miscellaneous powers over animals.*

D1449.1. *Charm makes cows give plenty of milk.* (Cf. D1273.) *Kittredge Witchcraft 164, 483 n. 12.

D1449.2. *Magic hunting collar insures death of game.* (Cf. D1068.1.) Irish myth: Cross.

D1449.3. *Swine summoned out of magic harp.* (Cf. D1231.) Irish myth: Cross.

B184.3. Magic swine.

D1449.4. *Charm prevents fish being caught.* (Cf. D1273.) Irish myth: Cross.

D2085.1. Curse makes river barren of fish.

D1449.4.1. *Poet's incantations drive away fish.* (Cf. D1275.4.) Irish myth: Cross.

D1449.5. *Magic sand causes crocodile to go ashore.* (Cf. D935.1.) India: Thompson-Balys.

D1450. Magic object furnishes treasure. Handwb. d. Abergl. II "Geldzauber"; Chinese: Eberhard FFC CXX 106, 108.

B100. Treasure animal. B100.2. Magic animal supplies treasure. B110. Treasure-producing parts of animals. D475.1. Transformation: objects to gold. D2100. Magic wealth. F731. Island covered with treasure. F752. Mountain of treasure. K111. Pseudo-treasure-producing objects sold. N500. Treasure trove.

D1451. *Inexhaustible purse furnishes money.* (Cf. D1192.) *Aarne MSFO XXV 116; *Types 564, 566, 580*; *BP I 470ff.; *Fb "pung" II 897b; *Chauvin VI 136 No. 286; *Loomis White Magic 87. — Breton: Sébillot Incidents s.v. "bourse"; English: (Romance) Sir Launfal (Ritson ed.) lines 320ff.; India: Thompson-Balys; Philippine: Fansler MAFLS XII 16, 177.

D1451.1. *Inexhaustible pocket furnishes money.* (Cf. D1064.) Chauvin VI 104 No. 270 n. 2. — India: *Thompson-Balys; German: Grimm No. 101.

D1451.2. *Inexhaustible bag (sack) furnishes money.* (Cf. D1193.) *Fb "pose" II 864a.

D1452. *Magic vessel (box) furnishes money.* (Cf. D1171.) India: Thompson-Balys.

D1452.1. *Magic kettle furnishes money.* (Cf. D1171.3.) *Fb "gryde" I 494b.

D1452.2. *Magic pot furnishes money.* (Cf. D1171.1.) Chinese: Eberhard FFC CXX 151; Ibo (Nigeria): Thomas 119.

D1452.3. *Lid of casket furnishes money.* (Cf. D1174.) India: Thompson-Balys.

D1452.4. *Magic conch shell furnishes money.* (Cf. D1029.6, D1470.1.41.) India: Thompson-Balys.

D1452.5. *Coin put in huge bell fills it with rupees.* (Cf. D1288.) India: Thompson-Balys.

D1454. *Parts of human body furnish treasure.*

C911. Golden finger as sign of opening forbidden chamber. D457.1.1. Transformation: blood to rubies.

D1454.1. *Hair furnishes treasure.* (Cf. D991.)

C912. Hair turns to gold as punishment in forbidden chamber. H71.3. Pearls from hair as sign of royalty.

D1454.1.1. *Gold and silver combed from hair.* Fb "hår" I 771b, "guld" I 512a.

D1454.1.1.1. *The devil runs hands through his hair; coins fall to the floor.* U.S.: *Baughman.

D1454.1.2. *Jewels from hair.* *Type 403; Köhler-Bolte I 126; *Penzer VIII 59 n. 3; *BP I 100 n. 1; Italian Novella: Rotunda; India: Thompson-Balys.

F826. Extraordinary jewels. Q2. Kind and unkind.

D1454.2. *Treasure falls from mouth.* (Cf. D992.2, D1454.3.) *Type 403; *BP I 100 n. 1; Fb "spytte" III 515a. — Icelandic: Snorra Edda Skaldsk. XXXII and XXXVIII; French Canadian: Barbeau JAFL XXIX 10; India: *Thompson-Balys.

D1773. Magic results from laughing. D1774. Magic results from speaking. M431.2. Curse: toads from mouth.

D1454.2.1. *Flowers fall from lips.* *BP I 100 n. 1; Köhler-Bolte I 126. — Malone PMLA XLIII 405; India: *Thompson-Balys.

H71.4. Roses from lips as sign of royalty. Princess laughs roses.

D1454.3. *Treasure from spittle.* (Cf. D1454.2, D1001.) *Penzer VIII 59 n. 3. — Irish: Plummer clxxviii, Cross; India: Thompson-Balys; N. A. Indian: *Thompson Tales 329 n. 190.

D475.1.4. Transformation: spittle to gold.

D1454.4. *Treasure from tears.* (Cf. D1004.)

D1454.4.1. *Tears of gold.* Icelandic: Boberg; India: Thompson-Balys.

D1454.4.2. *Jewels from tears.* Malone PMLA XLIII 405. — Finnish: Kalevala rune 41; Irish myth: *Cross; India: *Thompson-Balys; Jewish: Neuman; N. A. Indian: *Thompson Tales 329 n. 190b.

D1071. Magic jewel. F826. Extraordinary jewels.

D1454.4.3. *Flowers from tears.* Hartland Science 238.

A2612. Plants from tears. A2621.1. Flowers from under the feet of Virgin Mary.

D1454.5. *Treasure from excrements.* (Cf. D1002.) India: Thompson-Balys; Hindu: Keith 145; N. A. Indian: *Thompson Tales 329 n. 190a; Africa (Yoruba): Ellis 256 No. 4.

B102.1. Cow with droppings of gold. B113.1. Treasure-producing bird heart. D1561.1.0.2. Magic bird (when eaten) gives power of excreting jewels.

D1454.6. *Treasure from scab.* (Cf. D1009.1.) N. A. Indian (Tsimshian): Boas BBAE XXVII 190.

D1454.7. *Treasure from footprints.* (Cf. D1294.) India: Thompson-Balys.

D1454.8. *Treasure issues from girl's head.* India: *Thompson-Balys.

D1454.9. *Treasure from nose (with sneezing).* India: Thompson-Balys.

D1455. *Magic clothing furnishes treasure.*

K111.2. Alleged bill-paying hat sold.

D1455.1. *Magic mantle provides treasure.* (Cf. D1053.) *Type 566; *BP I 470; Aarne MSFO XXV 116. — India: Thompson-Balys.

D1456. *Magic ornament provides treasure.*

D1456.1. *Magic beads produce treasure.* (Cf. D1071.1.) Breton: Sébillot Incidents s.v. "chapelet".

D1456.2. *Magic ring provides money.* (Cf. D1076.) *Fb "ring" III 60b; India: *Thompson-Balys; Icelandic: Boberg.

D1456.2.1. *Magic ring multiplies wealth.* Icelandic: MacCulloch Eddic 66 (Draupnir); Snorra Edda Skaldsk. XXXIX (Andvari's), *Boberg.

D1456.3. *Magic jewel provides wealth.* (Cf. D1071.) Pauli (ed. Bolte) No. 328; India: Thompson-Balys.

D1457. *Magic building provides treasure.*

D1457.1. *Magic castle (palace) provides treasure.* (Cf. D1131, F771.) Hartland Science 174; Spanish: Boggs FFC XC 56 No. 408*A.

D1461. *Magic tree furnishes treasure.* (Cf. D950.) *Type 511; *BP III 60ff.; *Penzer VIII 69 n. 1. — Spanish: Boggs FFC XC 56 No. 412; Indonesian: Dixon 238 n. 51, DeVries Volksverhalen Nos. 116, 174.

F811.2.1.2. Tree with golden leaves.

D1461.0.1. *Tree with golden fruit.* *Hdwb. d. Märchens s.v. "Baum mit goldenen Früchten".

D1461.0.2. *Tree with silver branches.* (Cf. D950, F811.1.2.) Irish myth: Cross.

D1461.1. *Magic fruit furnishes treasure.* (Cf. D981.) Indonesian: DeVries's list No. 195.

D1463. *Magic plant furnishes treasure.* Africa (Bulu): Krug 120.

D1463.1. *Magic mandrake furnishes treasure.* (Cf. D965.1.) **Starck Der Alraun; *Taylor JAFL XXXI 561f.

D1463.2. *Magic calabash furnishes treasure.* (Cf. D965.2.) Africa (Yoruba): Ellis 246.

D1463.2.1. *Magic pumpkin furnishes treasure.* Chinese: Eberhard FFC CXX 35, 37.

D1463.3. *Magic seed produces golden gourd seed.* Chinese: Graham, Eberhard FFC CXX 36f.

D1463.4. *Magic tobacco plant hides treasure.* (Cf. D965.17.) Chinese: Graham.

D1463.5. *Treasure-giving magic flower (gold and silver).* (Cf. D975.) India: Thompson-Balys.

D1463.6. *Magic grass furnishes treasure.* (Cf. D965.) Jewish: Neuman.

D1465. *Magic food furnishes treasure.*

D1465.1. *Magic bread furnishes treasure.* (Cf. D1031.1.)

D1465.1.1. *Consecrated bread brings wealth.* (Cf. D1031.1.1.) *Kittredge Witchcraft 150, 469 n. 111. — India: Thompson-Balys.

D1466. *Magic stone furnishes wealth.* (Cf. D931.) Penzer III 161 n. 1, 162 n. — India: Thompson-Balys: Chinese: Werner 383; Eskimo (Greenland): Holm 47.

D1466.1. *Magic stone turns everything to gold.* (Cf. D1470.1.1., D931.) India: *Thompson-Balys.

D475.1. Transformation: objects to gold. D565.1. Midas' golden touch.

D1467. *Magic water furnishes treasure.* Everything it touches turns to gold. (Cf. D1242.1.) Pauli (ed. Bolte) No. 328.

D1467.1. *Magic fountain produces gold.* (Cf. D925.) French Canadian: Barbeau JAFL XXIX 10.

D1467.2. *Rubies found in whirlpool in sea.* India: Thompson-Balys.

F710. Extraordinary bodies of water. F826. Extraordinary jewels.

D1469. *Miscellaneous objects furnish treasure.*

D1314.3. Saint's bachall discovers gold.

D1469.1. *Magic flower pot bears plants with gold letters and leaves.* (Cf. D965.) Chinese: Werner 299.

D1469.2. *Magic doll furnishes treasure.* Excreta of gold. (Cf. D1268.) Italian Novella: Rotunda.

D1469.3. *Shower of gems from magic anvil.* Irish myth: *Cross.

D1202. Magic anvil. F243.4. Fairies' treasure.

D1469.4. *Magic hail on lake causes treasure to spring from it.* Cf. D902.3.) Irish myth: Cross.

D1469.5. *Worshipped sex organ of horse provides money, etc.* (Cf. D1029.4.) Icelandic: *Boberg.

D1469.6. *Magic book furnishes wealth.* (Cf. D1266.) India: Thompson-Balys.

D1469.7. *Wealth from drawing cow's feet over money box.* (Cf. D1029.3.) India: Thompson-Balys.

D1469.8. *Treasure from magic stick.* (Cf. D956, D1254.) Chinese: Graham.

D1469.9. *Silver leaps into wine pitcher.* (Cf. D1171.4.) Chinese: Graham.

D1469.10. *Magic ashes produce jewelry.* (Cf. D931.1.2.) India: Thompson-Balys.

D1469.10.1. *Ashes from burned snake-woman's body will turn anything into gold.* India: Thompson-Balys.

D1469.11. *Magic sheepskin, shaken inside and outside shed, showers gold and silver.* (Cf. D1225.8.) India: Thompson-Balys.

D1469.12. *Magic quilt: gold coins shake out of it.* (Cf. D1167.) India: Thompson-Balys.

D1469.13. *Treasure falls from stone lion's mouth.* (Cf. D1268.) India: Thompson-Balys.

D1469.13.1. *Statue of eagle gives wealth.* Jewish: Neuman.

D1469.14. *Magic tortoise shell produces pearls.* (Cf. D1029.6.) Chinese: Eberhard FFC CXX 222.

D1469.15. *Magic ship furnishes treasure.* (Cf. D1123.) German: Grimm No. 125.

D1469.16. *Clouds fetch previous stones.* (Cf. D901.) Jewish: Neuman.

D1469.17. *Charm makes treasure rain from sky.* (Cf. D1273.) Buddhist myth: Malalasekera II 920.

D1470. Magic object as provider.

B100. Treasure animals. D1601.21. Self-grinding mill. Grinds whatever owner wishes. D2100. Magic wealth.

D1470.1. *Magic wishing-object.* Object causes wishes to be fulfilled. — *Types 560, 561, 562, 563, 564, 565, 566, 567, 569; **Aarne MSFO XXV; *Cox Cinderella 484 n. 19; *Chauvin VI 136 No. 286.

D1472.2. Magic object causes food and drink to be furnished. D1720.1. Man given power of wishing. D1761. Magic results produced by wishing. D2172.2. Magic gift: power to continue all day what one starts. F341. Fairies give fulfillment of wishes.

D1470.1.1. *Magic wishing-stone.* (Cf. D931.) Fb "ønske" III 1178b. — Irish myth: Cross; Italian: Basile IV No. 1; India: Thompson-Balys.

D1470.1.2. *Magic wishing-tree.* (Cf. D950.) *Cox Cinderella 477; Fb "træ" III 866a; India: *Thompson-Balys, Penzer I 144; BP I 165ff.

D1470.1.3. *Magic wishing-laurel.* (Cf. D965.9.) Cox Cinderella 484 n. 19.

D1470.1.4. *Magic wishing-calabash.* (Cf. D965.2.) Africa (Yoruba): Ellis 246.

C324.1. Tabu: looking into magic calabash. D1475.6. Magic soldier-producing calabash.

D1470.1.5. *Magic wishing-apple.* (Cf. D981.1.) Fb "ønske" III 1178b.

D1470.1.6. *Magic wishing-nut.* (Cf. D985.) Spanish: Boggs FFC XC 53 No. 400B*.

D1470.1.7. *Magic ass's head fulfills wishes.* (Cf. D1011.0.2.) Spanish: Boggs FFC XC 57 No. 425.

D1470.1.8. *Magic wishing-eggs.* (Cf. D1019.) Jamaica: *Beckwith MAFLS XVII 269 No. 81.

D1475.7. Magic soldier-producing egg. D1476.2. Magic egg furnishes slaves (subjects for chief or king, etc.). D1477.3. Magic egg furnishes livestock.

D1470.1.9. *Magic wishing-cloth.* (Cf. D1051.) German: Grimm No. 54; Icelandic: Boberg; Philippine: Fansler MAFLS XII 230; S. A. Indian (Yuracare): Métraux BBAE CXLIII (3) 503.

D1470.1.10. *Magic wishing-smock.* (Cf. D1052.) Fb "ønske" III 1178b.

D1470.1.11. *Magic wishing-cloak (mantle).* (Cf. D1053.) Cox Cinderella 485.

D1470.1.12. *Magic wishing-belt.* (Cf. D1057.) Fb "ønske" III 1178b.

D1470.1.13. *Magic wishing-hat.* (Cf. D1067.1.) Type 581*; Cox Cinderella 485; Irish myth: Cross.

D1470.1.14. *Magic wishing-cap.* (Cf. D1067.2.) Fb "ønske" III 1178b, "kappe" II 89a; India: Thompson-Balys.

D1470.1.15. *Magic wishing-ring.* (Cf. D1076.) *Type 560, 665; *Aarne MSFO XXV 43; *Fb "ønske" III 1178b, "ring" III 60b; Cox Cinderella 484f. n. 19. — Irish myth: Cross; India: *Thompson-Balys; Africa (Thonga): Junod 231.

D877.1. Magic wishing-ring loses power by touching water.

D1470.1.16. *Magic wishing-lamp.* (Cf. D1162.1.) *Type 561; *Aarne MSFO XXV 3—82; BP II 544ff. — Missouri-French: Carrière.

D1470.1.17. *Magic wishing-lantern.* (Cf. D1162.) Cox Cinderella 484 n. 19.

D1470.1.18. *Magic wishing-cup.* (Cf. D1171.6.) Fb "ønske" III 1178b.; India: Thompson-Balys; Buddhist myth: Malalasekera II 361.

D1470.1.19. *Magic wishing-pot.* (Cf. D1171.1.) Fb "potte" II 867a.

D1470.1.20. *Magic wishing-box.* (Cf. D1174.) Cox Cinderella 484 n. 19; Thompson CColl II 398 (Micmac, Maliseet). — Africa (Ekoi): Talbot 18, (Angola): Chatelain 29.

D1470.1.21. *Magic wishing-saddle.* (Cf. D1209.2.) Fb "ønske" III 1178b.

D1470.1.22. *Magic wishing-drum.* (Cf. D1211.) Indo-Chinese: Scott Indo-Chinese 283. — Africa (Benga): Nassau 113 No. 11.

D1470.1.23. *Magic wishing-pipe.* (Cf. D1224.) Fb "ønske" III 1178b; Cox Cinderella 484 n. 19.

D1470.1.24. *Magic wishing-wand.* (Cf. D1254.1.) *Cox Cinderella 484f. n. 19; Missouri French: Carrière.

D1470.1.25. *Magic wishing-rod.* (Cf. D1254.2.) *MacCulloch Childhood 206. — India: Thompson-Balys; Africa (Zulu): Callaway 307.

D1470.1.26. *Magic wishing-book.* (Cf. D1266.) Fb "Cyprianus" I 167a.

D1470.1.27. *Magic wishing-bag.* (Cf. D1193, D1274.1.) India: *Thompson-Balys; N. A. Indian (Ojibwa, Potawatomi): Skinner JAFL XXVII 98.

D1470.1.28. *Magic coin fulfills wishes.* (Cf. D1288.) N. A. Indian (Skaulitz): Hill-Tout JAI XXXIV 374.

D1470.1.29. *Magic wishing-ball.* (Cf. D1256.) Cox Cinderella 484 n. 19.

D1470.1.30. *Magic wishing-bell.* (Cf. D1213.) Cox Cinderella 484 n. 19.

D1470.1.31. *Magic wishing-whip.* (Cf. D1208.) Cox Cinderella 484 n. 19.

D1470.1.32. *Magic wishing-horn.* (Cf. D1222.) Cox Cinderella 484 n. 19.

D1470.1.33. *Magic wishing-trumpet.* (Cf. D1221.) Cox Cinderella 485.

D1470.1.34. *Magic wishing-bow.* (Cf. D1091.) Çox Cinderella 485.

D1470.1.35. *Magic wishing-well.* (Cf. D926.) Kittredge Witchcraft 34, 394 n. 114; Irish myth: Cross.

D1470.1.36. *Magic wishing hair.* (Cf. D991.) India: *Thompson-Balys.

D1470.1.37. *Magic wishing ivory tusk.* When struck on ground (only once) provides treasure. Africa (Bulu): Krug JAFL XXV 113 No. 9.
D806.1. Magic object effective when struck on ground once only.

D1470.1.38. *Magic wishing mirror.* (Cf. D1163.) Africa (Quelimane): Torrend Zs. f. afrikan. u. ozean. Spr. I 247ff.

D1470.1.39. *Magic wishing bracelet.* (Cf. D1074.) Western Sudan: Tauxier Le Noir du Yatenga (Paris, 1917) 473 No. 74.

D1470.1.40. *Magic wishing-powder.* (Cf. D1251.) India: *Thompson-Balys.
D1246. Magic powder.

D1470.1.41. *Magic wishing conch shell* (Cf. D1029.6, D1452.4.) India: Thompson-Balys.

D1470.1.42. *Magic wishing-jewel* (Cf. D1071.) India: Thompson-Balys; Buddhist myth: Malalasekera I 289, II 422, 1355, 1369.

D1470.1.43. *Magic wishing-boat.* (Cf. D1121.) India: Thompson-Balys.

D1470.1.44. *Magic wishing-quilt.* (Cf. D1167.) India: Thompson-Balys.

D1470.1.45. *Magic lake: whoever dies in it will have his desires fulfilled in future birth.* (Cf. D921.) India: Thompson-Balys.

D1470.1.46. *Magic wishing-hammer.* (Cf. D1209.4.) Japanese: Ikeda.

D1470.1.47. *Magic iron measure for wishing.* Korean: Zong in-Sob 27.

D1470.1.48. *Magic rubber card for wishing.* (Cf. D1267) Africa (Luba): DeClerq Zs. f. Kolonialsprachen IV 202.

D1470.1.49. *Moon provides by magic.* Eskimo (Greenland): Holm 47.

D1470.2. *Provisions received from magic object.*
D2105. Provisions magically furnished.

D1470.2.1. *Provisions received from magic tree.* (Cf. D950.) Irish myth: *Cross; German: Grimm No. 123 (food and beds in tree); India: Thompson-Balys; Africa (Zulu): Callaway 217 (cattle emerge from tree when it is cut).

D1470.2.1.1. *Leaves turn into fish to feed family.* (Cf. D955.) Chinese: Graham.

D1470.2.2. *Supplies received from magic box.* (Cf. D1174.) India: Thompson-Balys; Africa (Ekoi): Talbot 185.

D1470.2.3. *Horn of plenty (cornucopia.)* (Cf. D1011.1, B115, D1475.1.) Cox Cinderella 473; Greek: Grote I 137; Icelandic: Boberg; India: Thompson-Balys; *Cosquin Contes indiens 517. See also references to B115 and D1475.1.

D1470.2.4. *Supplies from toe of old woman.* (Cf. D995.1.) Africa (Basuto): Jacottet 56 No. 9.

D1470.2.5. *Supplies from magic table.* (Cf. D1153.) Icelandic: *Boberg.

D1470.2.6. *Supplies from bull's belly.* India: Thompson-Balys.

D1470.2.7. *Supplies from bull's dung.* (Cf. D1026.2.) India: Thompson-Balys.

D1470.2.8. *Supplies from magic ashes.* (Cf. D931.1.2.) India: Thompson-Balys.

D1470.2.9. *Supplies from magic skin worn by man.* (Cf. D1024.) S. A. Indian (Toba): Métraux MAFLS XL 93.

D1472. *Food and drink from magic object.* India: *Thompson-Balys; N. A. Indian: *Thompson Tales 335 n. 210; Jamaica: *Beckwith MAFLS XVII 248 No. 25.

D1030.1. Food supplied by magic. D1601. Automatic objects. D2105. Provisions magically furnished. K112. Pseudo-magic food-producing object sold.

D1472.1. *Food or drink received directly from magic object.* Cox Cinderella 473; Chinese: Eberhard FFC CXX 106ff.

D1652.5. Inexhaustible vessel.

D1472.1.1. *Fountain miraculously supports life.* (Cf. D925.) Irish: Plummer cl, *Cross.

D1472.1.2. *Stone provides food.* (Cf. D931.) Jewish: Neuman; India: Thompson-Balys.

D1472.1.2.1. *Man strikes stone: wine flows.* (Cf. D1472.1.23, D1567.6.) Swiss: Jegerlehner Oberwallis 309 No. 9.

D1472.1.2.2. *Rock produces wine.* Herder sees resemblance of stone to wine cask. He strikes it and wine flows. (Cf. D931, D1472.1.2.) Swiss: Jegerlehner Oberwallis 327 No. 21.

D1349.3. Magic stone makes water like wine. D1576.6. Stroke of staff brings water from rock.

D1472.1.2.3. *Magic pebble provides food.* (Cf. D930.) Jewish: Neuman.

D1472.1.2.4. *Magic rock supplies water.* (Cf. D930.) Jewish: Neuman.

D1472.1.3. *Magic tree supplies food.* German: Grimm No. 82; Jewish: Neuman; Buddhist myth: Malalasekera II 555; Hawaii: Beckwith Myth 287.

A878.4. Earth tree furnishes health-giving and hunger-satisfying sap.

D1472.1.3.1. *Magic lime tree distills sustenance for saint.* (Cf. D950.7.) Irish: Plummer cliii, Cross.

D1472.1.3.2. *Food-providing leaf.* (Cf. D955.) Hawaii: Beckwith Myth 491.

D1472.1.4. *Vegetable supporting life without other food.* (Cf. D1034.) Icelandic: Boberg.

D1472.1.5. *Magic palace supplies food and drink.* (Cf. D1132.) Irish: Beal XXI 311; Spanish: Boggs FFC XC 56 No. 408*A.

D1472.1.6. *Magic kitchen supplies food and drink.* (Cf. D1141.1.) Hindu: Tawney II 226.

D1472.1.7. *Magic table supplies food and drink.* (Cf. D1153.) *Types 563, 564, 569; BP I 349ff., 464ff.; **Aarne JSFO XXVII 1—96; *Chauvin V 259, 272 No. 154. — Swiss: Jegerlehner Oberwallis 297 No. 28; Icelandic: Boberg.

D1472.1.8. *Magic table-cloth supplies food and drink.* (Cf. D1153.1.) *Type 569; Irish myth: Cross; Icelandic: *Boberg; Breton: Sébillot Incidents s.v. "serviette"; Missouri French: Carrière; Italian: Basile I No. 1.

D1472.1.9. *Magic pot supplies food and drink.* (Cf. D1171.1.) *Types 565; BP II 438; *Fb "potte" II 867a. — India: *Thompson-Balys; Chinese: Eberhard FFC CXX 106; Africa (Gold Coast): Barker and Sinclair 40f. No. 4.

J2411.3. Unsuccessful imitation of magic production of food.

D1472.1.10. *Magic coffee-pot supplies drink.* (Cf. D1171.1.1.) Fb "tønde" III 934b.

D1472.1.11. *Magic cauldron supplies food.* (Cf. D1171.2.) Brown MPh XIV 585; Irish myth: *Cross.

D1472.1.11.1. *Magic kettle (cauldron) turns stones to excellent food.* Irish myth: Cross.

D1472.1.12. *Magic kettle supplies food.* (Cf. D1171.3.) *Fb "gryde" I 494; India: *Thompson-Balys; Chinese: Graham.

D1472.1.12.1. *Food-providing frying pan.* (Cf. D1171.1.) India: Thompson-Balys.

D1472.1.13. *Magic pitcher supplies drink.* (Cf. D1171.4.) Penzer V 3 n. 1; India: Thompson-Balys.

D1472.1.14. *Magic cup supplies drink.* (Cf. D1171.6.) Fb "tønde" III 934b. — Irish myth: *Cross; Welsh: MacCulloch Celtic 202f. (gives any taste drinker desires); India: Thompson-Balys; Chinese: Graham.

D1410.6. Drink from magic cup deprives man of legs. D1665. Food has taste of any dainty desired.

D1472.1.14.1. *Magic food-providing cup.* (Cf. D1171.6.) India: Thompson-Balys.

D1472.1.15. *Magic tankard supplies drink.* (Cf. D1171.6.1.) Chinese: Werner 382.

D1472.1.16. *Magic glass supplies drink.* (Cf. D1171.6.2.) Fb "tønde" III 934b.

D1472.1.17. *Magic bottle supplies drink.* (Cf. D1171.8.) *Fb "flaske" I 309; Hartland Science 142; Icelandic: Boberg.

D1472.1.18. *Magic barrel supplies drink.* (Cf. D1171.9.) Fb "tønde" III 934b. — Swiss: Jegerlehner Oberwallis 297 No. 6; U.S.: Baughman.

D1472.1.19. *Magic food-basket (vessel) supplies food.* (Cf. D1171.11.) Irish myth: *Cross; Welsh: MacCulloch Celtic 192.

D1472.1.20. *Magic plate supplies food.* (Cf. D1172.1.) Fb "tønde" III 934b; India: *Thompson-Balys.

D1472.1.21. *Magic chest supplies food.* (Cf. D1174.) Scotch: Macdougall and Calder 160; India: Thompson-Balys.

D1472.1.22. *Magic bag (sack) supplies food.* (Cf. D1193.) *Types 563, 564; *Aarne JSFO XXVII 1—96 passim; BP I 349ff.; *Chauvin V 259, 272 No. 154; *Kittredge Witchcraft 165, 483 nn. 14—16. — India: *Thompson-Balys; Chinese: Eberhard FFC CXX 106; Eskimo (Greenland): Rasmussen I 368, III 247, Rink 401.

D1472.1.22.1. *Man compels food to enter magic sack.* Spanish: Boggs FFC XC Type 330.

D1472.1.22.2. *Saint's inexhaustible sack of wheat.* Irish myth: Cross.

D1652. Inexhaustible object.

D1472.1.23. *Magic basket supplies food.* (Cf. D1171.11.) Tonga: Gifford 113.

D1472.1.24. *Part of animal's body supplies food or drink.*

B19.2. Nectar-yielding cow.

D1472.1.24.1. *Magic drinking horn supplies drink.* (Cf. D1171.6.3.) Irish myth: Cross.

B115. Animal with horn of plenty.

D1472.1.24.2. *Jawbone of ass supplies water.* (Cf. D1013.) Jewish: Neuman.

D1472.1.24.3. *Food and drink from elk's ears.* (Cf. D1011.2.) Klikitat: Jacobs CU XIX 3.

D1472.1.24.4. *Body of tortoise provides food.* (Cf. D1010.) Chinese: Eberhard FFC CXX 106.

D1472.1.25. *Magic urn supplies drink.* (Cf. D1171.15.) Irish myth: Cross.

D1472.1.26. *Magic egg supplies food.* (Cf. D1024.) Chinese: Eberhard FFC CXX 105.

D1472.1.27. *Magic well supplies food.* (Cf. D926.) Irish myth: Cross; Chinese: Eberhard FFC CXX 106.

D1472.1.28. *Magic stump supplies drink.* (Cf. D950.) England, U.S.: Baughman.

D1472.1.29. *Magic sheepskin supplies food.* (Cf. D1025.8.) India: Thompson-Balys.

D1472.1.30. *Magic ashes produce food.* (Cf. D931.1.2.) India: Thompson-Balys.

D1472.1.31. *Magic food-providing sticks.* (Cf. D1094.) India: Thompson-Balys.

D1472.1.32. *Magic fiddle provides food.* (Cf. D1233.) India: Thompson-Balys.

D1472.1.33. *Magic bowl furnishes food.* (Cf. D1172.2.) India: *Thompson-Balys; Buddhist myth: Malalasekera I 1025, 1055.

D1472.1.34. *Part of human body furnishes food.*

D1472.1.34.1. *Magic finger provides food.* (Cf. D996.1.) Jewish: Neuman.

D1472.1.34.2. *Stream flows from man's head.* (Cf. D992.) Jewish: Neuman.

D1472.1.35. *Water flows from axe.* (Cf. D1206.) Philippine (Tinguian): Cole 91.

D1472.1.36. *Magic apple satisfies hunger.* (Cf. D981.1.) Irish myth: *Cross.

D1472.2. *Magic object causes food and drink to be furnished.* (Cf. D1470.1.) Chinese: Graham.

D1472.2.1. *Magic wishing-girdle supplies food.* (Cf. D1057.1.) English: Wells 85 (The Sowdone of Babylone).

D1472.2.2. *Magic wishing-drum supplies food.* (Cf. D1211.) Africa (Gold Coast): Barker and Sinclair 90 No. 16; (Ekoi): Talbot 47.

D1472.2.3. *Magic wishing-pipe supplies game.* (Cf. D1224.) Central Algonquin: Skinner JAFL XXVII 98.

D1472.2.4. *Charm prepares feast.* (Cf. D1273.) India: Thompson-Balys; Jewish: Neuman; Marquesas: Handy 114; Africa (Fjort): Dennett 60 No. 9.

D1472.2.5. *Magic song produces food.* (Cf. D1275.) Chinese: Graham. — N. A. Indian: *Boas RBAE XXXI 696, 712, 943 (Kwakiutl, Nootka, Comox, Tsimshian, Nass, Haida, Bella Coola, Chilcotin, Quinault, Lkuñgen, Squamish).

D1472.2.6. *Magic pumpkin yields year's supply of rice.* (Cf. D981.11.) India: Thompson-Balys.

D1472.2.7. *Magic calabash causes food to be furnished.* (Cf. D965.2.) Korean: Zong in-Sob 228; Africa (Lamba): Doke MAFLS XX 32 No. 15, (Yoruba): Frobenius Atlantis X 310ff. No. 53, (Bassari): ibid. XI 100ff. No. 13, (Tim): ibid. XI 233 No. 46.

D1472.2.8. *Magic musical pipe causes food to fall from sky.* (Cf. D1031.1.1, D1224.) India: Thompson-Balys.

D1472.2.9. *Magic mallet produces provisions.* (Cf. D1209.4.) Korean: Zong in-Sob 144.

D1472.2.10. *Magic rod provides water.* (Cf. D1254.2.) Chinese: Eberhard FFC CXX 109.

D1472.2.11. *Magic knife stuck in tree causes wine to flow.* (Cf. D1173.) Swiss: Jegerlehner Oberwallis 293 No. 1.

D1473. *Magic object furnishes clothes.* (Cf. D1470.)

D1473.1. *Magic wand furnishes clothes.* (Cf. D1254.1.) *Type 510; Africa (Kaffir): Theal 145.

D1473.2. *Rubbing charm provides garments.* (Cf. D1273.) Africa (Loango): Pechuël-Loesche 109.

D1475. *Magic object furnishes soldiers.*

B184.2.1.2. Magic soldier-producing cow.

D1475.1. *Magic soldier-producing horn.* (Cf. D1222, D1470.2.3.) *Aarne MSFO XXV 117; *Types 566, 569; *BP I 470ff.

D1475.2. *Magic soldier-producing trumpet.* (Cf. D1221.) *Aarne MSFO XXV 117.

D1475.3. *Magic soldier-producing pipe.* (Cf. D1224.) *Aarne MSFO XXV 117.

D1475.4. *Magic soldier-producing hat.* (Cf. D1067.1.) *Fb "hat" I 563b. — Breton: Sébillot Incidents s.v. "chapeau".

D1475.5. *Magic hair produces soldiers.* (Cf. D991.) India: Thompson-Balys; Africa (Tosa): Equilbecq III 291ff.

D1475.6. *Magic soldier-producing calabash.* (Cf. D965.2, D1470.1.4.) Africa (Wolof): Equilbecq III 19ff.

D1475.7. *Magic soldier-producing egg.* (Cf. D1470.1.8.) Africa (Hausa): Equilbecq III 291ff.

D1476. *Magic object furnishes slaves (subjects).* (Cf. D1025.8.) India: Thompson-Balys.

D491.2.1.1. Compressible magic box containing many people and objects.

D1476.1. *Magic calabash furnishes slaves.* (Cf. D965.2.) Africa (Yoruba): Frobenius Atlantis X 232f. No. 16.

D1476.2. *Magic egg furnishes slaves (subjects for chief or king, etc.).* (Cf. D1470.1.8.) Africa (Mossi): Frobenius Atlantis VIII 274ff. No. 120, (Hausa): Equilbecq III 291ff.

D1476.3. *Magic basket (box) furnishes slaves.* (Cf. D1171.11.) Africa (Hausa): Tremearne Hausa Superstitions (London, 1913) 424ff. No. 93.

D1477. *Magic object furnishes livestock (oxen, horses, etc.).*

D491.2.1.1. Compressible magic box containing many people and objects.

D1477.1. *Magic calabash furnishes livestock.* (Cf. D965.2.) Africa (Wolof): Equilbecq III 19ff.

D1477.2. *Magic ring furnishes livestock.* (Cf. D1076.) Africa (Bambara): Travélé 205ff. No. 66.

D1477.3. *Magic egg furnishes livestock.* (Cf. D1470.1.8.) Africa (Mossi): Frobenius Atlantis VIII 274ff. No. 120, (Hausa): Equilbecq III 291ff.

D1477.4. *Magic basket (box) furnishes livestock.* (Cf. D1171.11.) Africa (Hausa): Tremearne Hausa Superstitions (London, 1913) 424ff. No. 93.

D1478. *Magic object provides light.* (Cf. D1162.) Irish myth: Cross.

D1478.1. *Saint's hand illumines darkness.* (Cf. D996.) Irish myth: Cross.

F552.2. Fingers of saint give light or fire.

D1478.2. *Magic light illuminates bottom of lake.* Irish myth: Cross.

D1481. *Magic object furnishes warmth.* Chinese: Graham.

D1382. Magic object protects against cold or burning. D2144. Magic control of cold and heat.

D1481.1. *Magic chicken wing keeps one warm in cold weather.* (Cf. D1022.) Chinese: Graham.

D1481.2. *Magic object provides fire.* Chinese: Eberhard FFC CXX 108.

D1482. *Magic object produces oil.*

D1482.1. *Oil comes out of sacred white stone.* (Cf. D931.) India: Thompson-Balys.

D1482.2. *Magic pumpkin holds streams of oil.* (Cf. D981.11.) India: Thompson-Balys.

D1483. *Magic object produces building.*

D1483.1. *Palace arises from bull's legs buried in soil.* (Cf. D1012.1, D1132.1.) India: Thompson-Balys.

D1483.2. *Magic bag builds palaces of gold and gems.* (Cf. D1193.) India: Thompson-Balys.

D1483.3. *Magic stick: when planted in ground, palace rises.* (Cf. D956.) India: Thompson-Balys.

D1484. *Magic object makes road.*

D1313. Magic object points out road.

D1484.1. *Magic shuttle makes road.* (Cf. D1185.) *Type 585; BP III 355.

D1484.2. *Reading from magic book causes road to appear.* (Cf. D1266.) Chinese: Graham.

D1485. *Magic object makes carpet.*

D1485.1. *Magic shuttle makes carpet.* (Cf. D1185.) *Type 585; BP III 355.

D1486. *Magic object makes rivers and lakes.*

D1486.1. *Magic stone makes rivers and lakes.* (Cf. D931.) Africa (Ekoi): Talbot 366.

A920.1. Origin of lakes. A930. Origin of streams.

D1487. *Magic object makes plants grow.*

D1487.1. *Magic ring makes seaweeds grow.* (Cf. D1076.) Breton: Sébillot Incidents s.v. "bague".

D1487.2. *Consecrated bread makes vegetables grow.* (Cf. D1031.1.) Kittredge Witchcraft 149, 469 n. 109.

D1487.3. *Magic spell makes tree grow.* (Cf. D1273.) Irish myth: *Cross.

D2157. Magic control of soil and crops.

D1488. *Magic object provides wood.* Chinese: Eberhard FFC CXX 108.

D1500. Magic object controls disease. Irish myth: Cross.

B512. Medicine shown by animals. D1273. Magic formula (charm). D1342. Magic object gives health. P424. Physician.

D1500.0.1. *Magic book controls disease.* (Cf. D1266.) Jewish: Neuman.

D1500.1. *Magic object heals diseases.* **Seligmann; *De Cock Volksgeneeskunde; Brown Iwain 44; Irish myth: *Cross.

D1577.1. Charm renders medicinal herbs efficacious. D2161. Magic healing power. F950. Marvelous cures. H1324. Quest for marvelous remedy. K551.15. Respite from death until person is healed by magic object. V221. Magic healing by saints.

D1500.1.1. *Magic healing fountain.* (Cf. D925, V134.) Irish: Plummer cl, *Cross; Breton: Sébillot Incidents s.v. "fontaine"; Jewish: Neuman.

D1500.1.1.1. *Magic (healing) well dug by saint.* (Cf. V220.) Irish myth: *Cross.

D1500.1.1.2. *The water of spring which a saint caused to flow has curative powers.* *Loomis White Magic 104.

D1500.1.2. *Sacred healing stone.* (Cf. D931.) Irish: Plummer clvii, *Cross; Icelandic: *Boberg; Jewish: Neuman.

D1500.1.2.1. *Magic healing coal.* (Cf. D931.1.) Seligmann 131, *133.

D1500.1.2.2. *Magic healing ashes.* (Cf. D1271.1.) Seligmann 134, *137. — India: Thompson-Balys.

D1500.1.2.3. *Magic healing soot.* (Cf. D931.1.1.) Seligmann 137, *138.

D1500.1.2.4. *Magic healing lime.* (Cf. D931.1.4.) Irish myth: Cross.

D1500.1.3. *Magic tree heals.* (Cf. D950.)

D1500.1.3.1. *Magic healing hazel tree.* (Cf. D950.1.) — BP III 477; Irish: Plummer cliii, Cross.

D1500.1.4. *Magic healing plant.* (Cf. D965.) *Fb "blad" IV 44a; Type 612; Irish myth: *Cross; Breton: Sébillot Incidents s.v. "herbe"; Icelandic: *Boberg; Italian Novella: Rotunda; India: Thompson-Balys.

D1503.10. Magic plant heals wounds. D1505.1. Herbs restore sight. D1519.1.1. Magic plant heals broken bone.

D1500.1.4.1. *Magic healing grass.* Chinese: Graham.

D1500.1.4.2. *Magic healing leaves.* (Cf. D955.) Tonga: Gifford 28.

D1500.1.4.3. *Magic healing herb.* (Cf. D965.) Korean: Zong ín-Sob 220.

D1500.1.5. *Magic healing fruit.* (Cf. D980.)

D1500.1.5.1. *Magic healing apple.* (Cf. D981.1, H1333.3.1.5.) *Chauvin VI 133 No. 286; Hdwb. d. Märchens s.v. "Apfel" n. 2; Irish myth: *Cross; Chinese: Eberhard FFC CXX 253 No. 196.

D1500.1.6. *Ghoulish magic object cures disease.* (Cf. D1278.)

D1500.1.6.1. *Corpse's hand as remedy.* (Cf. D996.) Kittredge Witchcraft 142, 459f. nn. 8, 9; England: Baughman.

D1500.1.6.2. *Churchyard mould as remedy.* (Cf. D1278.1.) Seligmann 148; *Fb "grav" IV 184a; Irish myth: *Cross (D1500.1.28.1).

D1500.1.6.2.1. *Consecrated clay as remedy.* (Cf. D935.2.) Irish myth: *Cross (D1500.1.28.2).

D1500.1.7. *Parts or products of human body cure disease.*

D1500.1.7.1. *Powdered skull as remedy.* (Cf. D992.) Kittredge Witchcraft 142, 460 nn. 14, 15; England: Baughman.

D1500.1.7.1.1. *Magic head (of saint) heals diseases.* (Cf. D992, D1500.1.13.) Irish myth: Cross (D1500.1.6.1).

D1685. Interred body of saint performs signs and miracles.

D1500.1.7.2. *Magic healing spittle.* (Cf. D1001, D1505.2.) *Fb "spytte" III 514b, 515a; Irish: Plummer clxxvii, *Cross (D1500.1.8); Jewish: Neuman.

D1500.1.7.2.1. *Healing power of saint's spittle.* *Loomis White Magic 103f.

T579.4. Mother of saint has healing spittle during pregnancy. V256.1. Magic healing spittle of Virgin Mary.

D1500.1.7.3. *Magic healing blood.* (Cf. D1003.) *Fb "blod" IV 46b; Penzer I 98; *Kittredge Witchcraft 31, 386 n. 67; Irish myth: *Cross (D1500.1.9); Italian Novella: Rotunda.

F872.3. Bath of blood. F955.1. Blood-bath as cure for leprosy. T82. Bath of blood of beloved to cure lovesick empress.

D1500.1.7.3.1. *Blood of executed man as remedy.* *Fb "blod" IV 47a.

D1500.1.7.3.2. *Blood of saint as cure.* Irish: Plummer clxxxi, *Cross (D1500.1.9.2); *Loomis White Magic 104; Icelandic: Boberg (D1500.1.9.2).

D1500.1.7.3.3. *Dragon's heart-blood as remedy.* (Cf. B11.2.9, D1015.1.2, D1016) *Type 305*.

D1846.4. Invulnerability through bathing in dragon's blood.

D1500.1.7.3.4. *Bath in blood of king as remedy.* Irish myth: *Cross (D1500.1.9.4).

D1502.5.1. Bath in blood of king as cure for mange. D1788. Magic results from bathing. F872.3. Bath of blood.

D1500.1.8. *Magic amulet cures disease.* (Cf. D1070.) Jewish: Neuman.

D1500.1.9. *Magic jewel cures disease.* (Cf. D1071.) Jewish: Neuman.

D1500.1.9.1. *Magic sapphire cures disease.* Jewish: Neuman.

D1500.1.9.2. *Magic pearls cure disease.* Africa (Dahome): Einstein 31.

D1500.1.10. *Sacred objects cure disease.* (Cf. V150.)

D1500.1.10.1. *Consecrated bread as cure.* (Cf. D1031.1.1.) Kittredge Witchcraft 149, 469 nn. 110, 112; *Loomis White Magic 105; Irish myth: Cross.

D1500.1.10.2. *Consecrated wine as magic cure.* (Cf. D1046.1.) Kittredge Witchcraft 148, 469 nn. 97—101.

D1500.1.10.2.1. *Wine blessed by saint or received from the saint's hand cures various ills.* *Loomis White Magic 104.

D1500.1.10.3. *Money from offertory as cure.* (Cf. D1288.) Kittredge Witchcraft 151, 470f, n. 126; England: Baughman.

D1500.1.10.4. *Consecrated grain as remedy.* (Cf. D973.) Irish myth: Cross.

D1500.1.10.5. *Consecrated ale as magic cure.* (Cf. D1045.1.) Irish myth: Cross (D1500.1.34).

D1500.1.10.6. *Lime used in building church as cure.* (Cf. D931.1.4.) Irish myth: Cross (D1500.1.35).

D1500.1.11. *Magic healing drink.* (Cf. D1040, D1242.) Icelandic: *Boberg; Irish myth: *Cross.

D1500.1.12. *Magic statue cures disease.* (Cf. D1268.) Jewish: Neuman.

D1500.1.12.1. *Magic statue of brazen serpent cures disease.* Jewish: Neuman.

D1500.1.13. *Saint's possessions cure disease.* (Cf. V221.)

D1500.1.13.1. *Saint's girdle as magic cure.* (Cf. D1057.1.) Loomis White Magic 105; Irish: Plummer clxxxi, *Cross. Cf. Dh II 26f.

D1500.1.13.2. *Saint's cowl as magic cure.* (Cf. D1067.3.1.) Irish: Plummer clxxxi, Cross.

D1500.1.13.3. *Saint's bell cures disease.* (Cf. D1213.) Irish: .Plummer clxxvi, Cross.

D1500.1.13.4. *Saint's bachall as remedy.* (Cf. D1277.) *Loomis White Magic 105; Irish: Plummer clxxv, Cross.

D1500.1.14. *Saint's mallet cures disease.* (Cf. D1209.4.) Korean: Zong in-Sob 145.

D1500.1.15. *Magic healing ring.* (Cf. D1076.) *Kittredge Witchcraft 151, 470f. nn. 126—129; Irish myth: *Cross.

D1500.1.15.1. *Consecrated healing ring.* Kittredge Witchcraft 151, 471 n. 134; England: Baughman.

D1500.1.15.2. *Ring made of coffin-hinge as remedy.* Kittredge Witchcraft 142, 461 n. 33; England: Baughman.

D1500.1.16. *Magic healing bottle.* (Cf. D1171.8.) Chinese: Werner 202.

D1500.1.17. *Magic weapon cures disease.* (Cf. D1080.)

D1500.1.17.1. *Magic sword cures disease.* (Cf. D1081.) Greek: Grote I 268.

D1500.1.18. *Magic healing water.* (Cf. D1242.1.) *Type 590; Seligmann 13ff., *106; Fb "vand" III 1001b, "livets vand" II 439b; MacCulloch Childhood 67f. — Irish myth: *Cross; Babylonian: Spence 178; Jewish: Neuman; Arabian: Burton Nights S VI 213; India: Thompson-Balys; Buddhist myth: Malalasekera I 23; N. A. Indian: *Thompson Tales 354 nn. 279, 279a.

B512. Medicine shown by animal. E80. Water of Life. H1321.2. Quest for healing water.

D1500.1.18.1. *Dew from saint's grave as cure.* (Cf. D1500.1.10.) Irish: Plummer clxxx, Cross.

D1500.1.18.1.1. *Water which had contact with the tombs of holy men proved curative.* *Loomis White Magic 104.

D1500.1.18.1.2. *Water from saint's washing as remedy.* Loomis White Magic 104; Irish myth: *Cross.

D1500.1.18.2. *Baptismal water as remedy.* (Cf. D1242.1.1.) Kittredge Witchcraft 150f., 470 nn. 117—122; England: Baughman.

D1500.1.18.3. *Holy water as remedy.* (Cf. D1242.1.2.) Kittredge Witchcraft 124ff., 449f. nn. 1—33 passim; *Loomis White Magic 104; Irish myth: *Cross; Icelandic: *Boberg; England, U.S.: Baughman; India: Thompson-Balys.

D1500.1.18.4. *Magic healing lake.* (Cf. D921.) Irish myth: Cross.

D2161.4.14.2. Magic cure by bathing in consecrated water (lake, etc.).

D1500.1.18.5. *Water from bullaun (hollowed-out stone) as remedy.* (Cf. D931.) Irish myth: Cross.

D1500.1.18.6. *Magic healing river.* (Cf. D915.) Jewish: Neuman.

D1500.1.19. *Magic healing salve.* (Cf. D1244.) Type 611; Irish myth: *Cross; Icelandic: *Boberg; India: Thompson-Balys.

X1787.1. Lies about remarkable healing salve.

D1500.1.19.1. *Magic healing salve restores severed feet.* (Cf. D1240.) Icelandic: Boberg.

E782. Limbs successfully replaced.

D1500.1.19.2. *Magic healing oil from saints (sacred places).* (Cf. D1500.1.10.) Loomis White Magic 79, 104, 115.

D1500.1.20. *Magic healing powder.* (Cf. D1246.) Chinese: Werner 375.

D1500.1.21. *Magic healing wand.* (Cf. D1254.1.) Breton: Sébillot Incidents s.v. "baguette".

D1500.1.22. *Magic healing book.* (Cf. D1266.) Type 611; Kittredge Witchcraft 146, 465 nn. 68—73 passim.

D1500.1.23. *Magic healing charm (spell).* (Cf. D1273.) Kittredge Witchcraft 31f., 387f. nn. 75; Icelandic: *Boberg; Irish myth: *Cross; England, Wales, U.S.: *Baughman; India: Thompson-Balys.

D1500.1.24. *Magic healing song.* (Cf. D1275.) Fb. "kanariefugl" II 85; H. C. Andersen "Nattergalen". — Icelandic: Boberg.

D1500.1.25. *Magic garment as remedy.* (Cf. D1052.) Jewish: Neuman.

D1500.1.26. *Fragments of gibbet as cure.* (Cf. D1278.) Kittredge Witchcraft 142, 461 nn. 25, 26.

D1500.1.27. *Magic musical instrument as cure for disease.* (Cf. D1210.)

D1500.1.27.1. *Magic healing harp.* (Cf. D1231.) India: Thompson-Balys.

D1500.1.27.2. *Magic healing bell.* (Cf. D1213.) Irish myth: *Cross (D1500.1.32).

D1500.1.28. *Earth as remedy.* (Cf. D935, D1503.12.) Seligmann 144ff., *154; England: Baughman.

D1500.1.29. *Magic healing honey.* (Cf. D1037.) Irish myth: *Cross.

D479.4.4. Transformation: water to honey.

D1500.1.30. *Magic healing banquet.* (Cf. D1030.2.) Irish myth: Cross.

D1500.1.31. *Gold used in medicine.* Irish myth: Cross.

D1500.1.32. *Magic comb as cure.* (Cf. D1072.1.) India: Thompson-Balys.

D1500.1.33. *Parts or products of animal cure disease.*

D1500.1.33.1. *Magic healing milk.* (Cf. D1018.) Irish myth: Cross.

D1500.1.33.1.1. *Cures by the milk of the mothers of saints.* (Cf. D1500.1.10.) *Loomis White Magic 104.

D1500.1.33.1.2. *Magic healing milk of lioness.* (Cf. D1018.) Jewish: Neuman.

D1500.1.33.2. *Flesh of white cow with red ears as only cure for mysterious illness.* (Cf. D1032.) Irish myth: Cross.

B182. Magic cow. B182.0.1. White cow. B182.2.0.3. Magic white cow with red ears. B731.4.2. Cow with red ears. D1515.3. Bath in milk of white hornless cows as antidote for poison.

D1500.1.33.3. *Magic animal dung.* (Cf. D1026.)

D1500.1.33.3.1. *Magic bird dung cures.* (Cf. D1026.1.) India: Thompson-Balys.

D1500.1.33.4. *Hide of sheep or goat as cure.* (Cf. D1025.8.) India: Thompson-Balys.

D1500.1.33.5. *Fish head cures disease.* (Cf. D1011.) Chinese: Eberhard FFC CXX 42.

D1500.1.34. *Magic writings heal.* (Cf. D1266.1.) Icelandic: *Boberg.

D1500.1.35. *Magic healing handkerchief.* (Cf. D1056.1.) S. A. Indian (Chiriguano): Métraux RMLP XXXIII 182.

D1500.1.36. *Sweat used in medicine.* Irish myth: Cross.

D1500.1.37. *Urine used in medicine.* (Cf. D1002.1.1.) Irish myth: Cross.

D1500.1.38. *M. healing mountain.* (Cf. D932.) Icelandic: Boberg.

D1500.2. *Magic object wards off disease.* Irish myth: *Cross.

D1380. Magic object protects. D1663.3. Well of life and death. Situated on one hand kills; on the other, protects against disease. S276. Sacrifice as protection against disease.

D1500.2.1. *Saint's bell wards off disease.* (Cf. D1213, V221.) Irish: Plummer clxxvi, Cross.

V221. Miraculous healing by saints.

D1500.2.2. *Charm against sickness.* (Cf. D1273.) Kittredge Witchcraft 40, *396 n. 145, 146; England: Baughman.

D1500.2.3. *Magic picture prevents disease.* (Cf. D1266.2, D1586.1.) Alphabet No. 471; Chinese: Werner 139.

D1500.2.4. *Magic circle prevents disease.* (Cf. D1272.) Fb "kreds" II 293.

D1500.2.5. *Eating magic pig prevents disease.* (Cf. B184.3.) Irish myth: Cross.

D1500.2.6. *Magic girdle prevents disease.* (Cf. D1057.1.) Irish myth: *Cross.

D1500.2.7. *Magic tree bears prophylactic fruit.* (Cf. D950.) Irish myth: Cross.

D1500.2.8. *Snake liver prevents disease.* (Cf. D1015.4.) Chinese: Eberhard FFC CXX 32.

D1500.3. *Magic object transfers disease to another person or thing.* Kristensen Danske Sagn VI (1891) 345ff., (1936) 299ff., Icelandic: *Boberg.

D2064.3. Sickness transferred to animal. D2161.4.1. Cure by transferring disease to animal.

D1500.3.1. *Charm shifts diseases to another person.* (Cf. D1273.) Kittredge Witchcraft 32, 388 n. 86.

D1500.3.1.1. *Saint causes pain of sick man to be transferred to himself.* *Loomis White Magic 106.

D1500.3.2. *Disease transferred to saint's bell.* (Cf. D1213.) Irish: Plummer clxxvi, *Cross.

D2161.4.2.1. Saint transfers disease to his bell. V220. Saints.

D1500.4. *Magic object causes disease.* Chinese: Werner 245.

B177.1. Magic toad under king's bed causes magic sickness. D2064. Magic sickness. F362. Fairies cause disease.

D1500.4.1. *Magic drink causes disease.* (Cf. D1242.2.) Icelandic: *Boberg; Japanese: Ikeda.

D1783.2. Cure for leprosy by drinking from opposite lip of horn from that which caused it.

D1500.4.2. *Magic breath causes disease.* (Cf. D1005.) Irish myth: Cross.

B33.1.1. Devastating birds wither everything with their breath.

D1500.4.2.1. *Saint's breath makes men drunk.* *Loomis White Magic 46.

D1500.4.2.2. *Saint's breath causes death.* (Cf. D1005.) *Loomis White Magic 46f.

D1500.4.3. *Magic pond causes disease.* (Cf. D921.) Irish myth: Cross.

D1500.4.3.1. *Magic tank causes disease.* (Cf. D921.4.) India: Thompson-Balys.

D1500.4.4. *Ray of sunlight causes leprosy.* (Cf. D1162.) Jewish: Neuman.

D1500.4.5. *Gloves thrown after ship cause disease.* (Cf. D1066.) Icelandic: Flateyjarbók 144—45.

D1500.4.6. *Ashes cause leprosy.* (Cf. D931.1.2.) Jewish: Neuman.

D1500.4.7. *Magic bed causes disease.* (Cf. D1154.1.) Jewish: Neuman.

D1501. *Magic object assists woman in childbearing.* Irish myth: *Cross.

T584.0.1. Childbirth assisted by magic.

D1501.1. *Charms prevent barrenness or miscarriage.* (Cf. D1273.) Kittredge Witchcraft 32, 388 n. 89; Irish myth: *Cross; India: Thompson-Balys.

D1925. Fecundity magically induced. T591.1. Magic remedies for barrenness or impotence.

D1501.1.1. *Mistletoe used by druids to prevent barrenness.* Irish myth: *Cross.

D965.4.1. Mistletoe used by druids. P427.5. Druid as physician.

D1501.2. *Charms make childbirth easy.* (Cf. D1273.) Kittredge Witchcraft 32, 388 n. 88; Icelandic: MacCulloch Eddic 296, *Boberg.

D1501.3. *Magic plant makes childbirth easy.* (Cf. D965.) Icelandic: MacCulloch Eddic 331.

D1501.4. *Magic fruit from Yggdrasil placed in fire makes childbirth easy.* (Cf. D981.) Icelandic: MacCulloch Eddic 331, Boberg (D1501.2).

D1501.5. *Magic belt assists in childbirth.* (Cf. D1057.) Icelandic: *Boberg.

D1501.6. *Amulet assists in childbearing.* (Cf. D1070.) Jewish: Neuman.

D1501.7. *Leaves assist in childbearing.* (Cf. D955.) Marquesas: Handy 58.

D1501.8. *Medicine causes woman to bear twins.* (Cf. D1241.) Africa (Fang): Tessman 90.

D1502. *Magic object cures particular diseases.* Irish myth: *Cross.

D1586. Magic object relieves from plague. D2161. Magic healing power. F950. Marvelous cures.

D1502.1. *Magic object cures headache.*

D1502.1.1. *Charm for headache* (Cf. D1273.) Irish myth: *Cross.

D1502.2. *Magic object cures toothache.* England: Baughman.

D1502.2.1. *Dead man's tooth as cure for toothache.* (Cf. D1009.2.1.) Kittredge Witchcraft 142, 460 nn. *11, 13.

D1502.2.2. *Charm for toothache.* (Cf. D1273.) Kittredge Witchcraft 33, 389 n. *105. — England: Baughman.

D1502.2.3. *Magic object cures scrofula.*

D1502.2.3.1. *Hangman's noose cures scrofula.* (Cf. D1278.) Kittredge Witchcraft 461 n. 22; England: Baughman.

D1502.3. *Magic object cures fever.* (Cf. D2161.1.2.)

D1502.3.1. *Charm for fever.* (Cf. D1273.) *Kittredge Witchcraft 392 n. 105. — Jewish: Neuman; Hindu: Tawney II 165.

D1502.4. *Magic object cures leprosy.*

D1783.2. Cure for leprosy by drinking from opposite lip of horn from that which caused it. D2161.1.1. Magic cure of leprosy. F955. Miraculous cure for leprosy. Rage at hearing for first time of Christ's passion causes cure. V221.3. Saint cures leprosy.

D1502.4.1. *Magic potion cures leprosy.* (Cf. D1242.2.) Icelandic: *Boberg.

D1502.4.2. *Blood as cure for leprosy.* (Cf. D1003.) *Chauvin VIII 195 No. 235 n. 1; Herbert Catalogue of Romances III 202; Jewish: Neuman.

D1502.4.2.1. *Blood of children (innocent maidens) as cure for leprosy.* Child I 47, 50 n., IV 441b, V 285; Penzer I 98 n.; Alphabet No. 713.

D1502.4.3. *Touching magic boat with exposed child in it cures leprosy.* (Cf. D1121.) Jewish: Neuman.

S141. Exposure in boat.

D1502.5. *Magic object cures mange.* Irish myth: Cross.

D1502.5.1. *Bath in blood of king as cure for mange.* (Cf. D1500.1.9.4, F872.3.) Irish myth: Cross.

D1502.6. *Magic object cures urinary disease.*

D1502.6.1. *Charm for urinary disease.* (Cf. D1273.) Irish myth: *Cross.

D1502.7. *Magic object cures earache.*

D1502.7.1. *Magic locust egg cures earache.* (Cf. D1024.) Jewish: Neuman.

D1502.8. *Magic object cures boils (tumors).*

D1502.8.1. *Magic-dog brain cures boils.* (Cf. D1010.) Jijena Sanchez 136.

D1502.8.2. *Magic snail body cures boils.* (Cf. D1010.1.) Jewish: Neuman.

D1502.8.3. *Magic figs cure boils.* (Cf. D1031.2.) Jewish: Neuman.

D1502.9. *Viper body cures skin disease.* (Cf. D1010.1) Jewish: Neuman.

D1502.10. *Magic cure for cancer.*

D1502.10.1. *Magic excrement as cure for cancer.* (Cf. D1002.) India: Thompson-Balys.

D1502.11. *Magic water cures stomach trouble.* (Cf. D1242.1.) Buddhist myth: Malalasekera I 98.

D1503. *Magic object heals wound.* Irish myth: *Cross.

D2161.2. Magic cure of wound. F959.3. Miraculous cure of wound.

D1503.1. *Magic song heals wound.* (Cf. D1275.) Icelandic: De la Saussaye 241; cf. Finnish: Kalevala rune 8; Eskimo (Mackenzie Area): Jenness 89.

D1503.2. *Magic pigskin heals wounds.* (Cf. D1025.1.) Irish myth: *Cross.
B183.9. Skin of magic pig heals wounds. H1151.13.1. Task: stealing pigskin from a king.

D1503.3. *Charm for wounds.* (Cf. D1273.) Kittredge Witchcraft 32, 387 n. 80. — Irish myth: *Cross; England: *Baughman; Breton: Sébillot Incidents s.v. "blessure".

D1503.3.1. *Charm for burns or scalds.* (Cf. D1273.) England, U.S.: Baughman (D1500.1.23.1).

D1503.4. *Magic balm heals wounds.* (Cf. D1244.) Dickson 187 nn. 61, 62.

D1503.5. *Magic lantern heals wounds.* (Cf. D1162.) Irish myth: Cross.

D1503.6. *Magic jewel heals wounds.* (Cf. D1071.) Irish myth: Cross.

D1503.7. *Magic well heals (wounds).* (Cf. D926.) Irish myth: *Cross.
D1788. Magic results from bathing.

D1503.7.1. *Magic pool of milk heals wounds.* Irish myth: Cross.
D1018. Magic milk of animal. D1500.1.33. Magic healing milk. E80.1.1. Resuscitation by bathing in milk.

D1503.8. *Magic goblet heals wounds.* (Cf. D1171.6.2.) Irish myth: Cross.

D1503.9. *Magic hand heals wounds.* (Cf. D996.) Irish myth: Cross.
V52.15. Prayer said by saint into his right hand restores displaced eye of opponent.

D1503.10. *Magic plant heals wounds.* (Cf. D965.) Irish myth: *Cross.

D1503.10.1. *Grass and flowers which grew upon a saint's grave are good for cures.* (Cf. D975.) *Loomis White Magic 105.

D1503.11. *Wounds healed by eating fruit of magic tree.* (Cf. D950.) Irish myth: Cross.
D1793. Magic results from eating or drinking.

D1503.12. *Magic earth heals wounds.* (Cf. D935.) Irish myth: Cross.

D1503.12.1. *Earth receives curative powers from contact with saint.* *Loomis White Magic 104f.

D1503.13. *Magic potion heals wounds.* (Cf. D1242.2.) Irish myth: Cross.

D1503.14. *Wound healed by wounding weapon.* (Cf. D1080.) Greek: Grote I 268.

D1503.14.1. *Wounds caused by sword can only be healed by a certain stone.* Icelandic: MacCulloch Eddic 267., *Boberg.

D1503.15. *Wound healed with own blood.* (Cf. D1003.) Hawaii: Beckwith Myth 118.

D1503.16. *Wound healed by water from place wounded man's heel dragged.* (Cf. D1240.) Marquesas: Handy 117.

D1503.17. *Magic gloves heal wound.* Icelandic: Boberg.

D1504. *Magic object stanches blood.*
D2161.2.2. Flow of blood magically stopped.

D1504.1. *Charm stanches blood.* (Cf. D1273.) Kittredge Witchcraft 32, 387 n. 81; Irish myth: Cross; English: Child II 441, 445, 450; England, Wales, U.S.: *Baughman.

D1504.2. *Amulet cures nosebleed.* (Cf. D1070.) Jewish: Neuman.

D1505. *Magic object cures blindness.* *Type 550.

D2161.3.1. Blindness magically cured. F952. Blindness miraculously cured. K115.1. Alleged healing letter sold. Woman sold a letter to wear around her neck which will prevent eye trouble. It helps only so long as she believes in it.

D1505.1. *Herbs restore sight.* (Cf. D965.) *Chauvin II 193 No. 12, V 14 No. 9. — India: *Thompson-Balys.

D1505.2. *Spittle restores sight.* (Cf. D1001, D1500.1.8.) India: *Thompson-Balys; Chinese: Graham; Maori: Dixon 59. Cf. Mark 8:23.

D1505.3. *Magic feather restores sight.* (Cf. D1021.) Spanish: Boggs FFC XC 59 No. 425D*.

D1505.4. *Magic honey restores sight.* (Cf. D1037.) Hindu: Keith 158.

D1505.5. *Magic water restores sight.* (Cf. D1242.1.) *Types 590, 613; *Christiansen FFC XXIV 79. — India: *Thompson-Balys; Irish myth: Cross; Missouri French: Carrière.

E80. Water of Life. Resuscitation by water. F952.7. Eyes restored by bathing in spring. H1321.2. Quest for healing water.

D1505.5.1. *Bird's tears restore sight.* (Cf. B736.) Spanish: Boggs FFC XC 59 No. 425D.

D1505.5.2. *Dew restores sight.* (Cf. D902.2.) Christiansen FFC XXIV 78.

D1505.5.2.1. *Dew falling on St. John's Night restores sight.* (Cf. D902.2.) *Fb "Sankt Hansdag" III 161a.

V70. Religious feasts and fasts.

D1505.5.3. *Magic fountain restores sight.* (Cf. D925.) Breton: Sébillot Incidents s.v. "fontaine"; Icelandic: Boberg.

D1505.5.4. *Holy spring restores sight.* (Cf. D927, V134.) *Fb "blind" IV 45b; Irish myth: *Cross.

D1505.5.5. *Magic coconut water restores sight.* Marquesas: Beckwith Myth 485.

D1505.6. *Magic ointment restores sight.* (Cf. D1244.) Malone PMLA XLIII 410; India: Thompson-Balys.

D1505.7. *Magic wand restores sight.* (Cf. D1254.1.) India: Thompson-Balys; Spanish: Boggs FFC XC 67 No. 510.

D1505.8. *Blood restores sight.* (Cf. D1003.) India: *Thompson-Balys.

D1505.8.1. *Blood from Christ's wounds restores sight.* Longinus. Paris Légendes du moyen âge 151.

D1505.9. *Magic flower restores sight.* (Cf. D975.) India: *Thompson-Balys.

D1505.10. *Saint's breath restores sight.* (Cf. D1005.) Irish myth: Cross.

D1505.10.1. *Hero's breath restores sight.* India: Thompson-Balys.

D1505.11. *Charm for diseased eye.* (Cf. D1273.) Irish myth: Cross.

D1505.11.1. *Charm for removing object from eye.* U.S.: *Baughman (D1500.1.23.3.)

D1505.12. *Man who touches book of St. Oswin's life is cured of blindness.* (Cf. D1266.) India: Thompson-Balys.

D1505.13. *Animal excreta cures blindness.* (Cf. D1026.1.) India: Thompson-Balys.

D1505.14. *Animal liver cures blindness.* (Cf. D1015.4.) Chinese-Persian: *Coyajee JPASB XXIV 187.

D1505.14.1. *Liver of shining goat heals blindness of raja.* India: Thompson-Balys.

D1505.15. *Magic cotton-wool restores sight.* (Cf. D1299.4.) India: Thompson-Balys.

D1505.16. *Magic statue (when kissed) restores sight.* (Cf. D1268, D1794.) Jewish: Neuman.

D1505.17. *Magic stone restores sight.* (Cf. D931.) Jewish: Neuman.

D1505.18. *Tree restores sight.* (Cf. D950.)

D1505.18.1. *Coconut shoots restore sight.* Hawaii: Beckwith Myth 492.

D1505.19. *Gall of slain giant restores sight.* Cheremis: Sebeok-Nyerges.

D1506. *Magic object cures deafness.* Jewish: Neuman.

D2161.3.5. Deafness magically cured.

D1506.1. *Spittle restores hearing.* (Cf. D1001.) Mark 7:33.

D1507. *Magic object restores speech.*

D2020. Magic dumbness. D2025. Magic recovery of speech. D2161.3.6. Dumbness magically cured. F954. Dumb person brought to speak.

D1507.1. *Magic ring restores speech.* (Cf. D1076.) Fb "ring" III 60b.

D1507.2. *Saint's gospel-book restores speech.* (Cf. D1266.) Irish: Plummer clxxviii, Cross.

D1507.3. *Saint's bell restores speech.* (Cf. D1213.) Irish: Plummer clxxvi, Cross.

D1507.4. *Saint's breath restores speech.* (Cf. D1005.) *Loomis White Magic 105; Irish: Plummer clxxviii, Cross.

D1507.5. *Magic cake restores speech.* (Cf. D1031.2.) BP II 473; Hdwb. d. Märchen I 335b.

D1507.6. *Saint's blood restores speech.* (Cf. D1003.) Irish myth: Cross.

D1507.7. *Magic harp restores speech.* (Cf. D1231.) Irish myth: Cross.

D1507.8. *Magic gold taken from hill restores speech when it is laid under the tongue of dumb person.* Icelandic: Flateyjarbók I 250, Boberg.

D1252.3. Magic gold. E52. Resuscitation by magic charm. E64.15. Resuscitation by magic gold.

D1508. *Magic object restores reason.*

D1367. Magic object causes insanity. D2065. Magic insanity.

D1508.1. *Saint's bell restores reason.* (Cf. D1213.) Irish: Plummer clxxvi, Cross.

D1508.2. *Music restores reason.* (Cf. D1275.1.) Dickson 121.

D1508.3. *Jackal-tooth as cure for madness.* (Cf. D1011.) India: Thompson-Balys.

D1508.4. *Soup made of black dog's head cures madness.* (Cf. D1032.3.) Chile: Jijena Sanchez 137.

D1511. *Magic object cures drunkenness.*

D1511.1. *Magic carpet cures drunkenness.* (Cf. D1155.) Chinese: Werner 192.

D1512. *Magic object cures ulcers.*

D1512.1. *Magic ointment cures ulcers.* (Cf. D1244.) Chinese: Werner 276, 281f.

D1513. *Charm removes thorn.* (Cf. D1273.) Irish myth: Cross.

D1514. *Magic object relieves pain.* Irish myth: Cross.

D1514.1. *Magic music relieves pain.* (Cf. D1275.1.) Irish myth: *Cross.

D1514.2. *Magic girdle relieves pain.* (Cf. D1057.1.) Jewish: Neuman.

D1514.3. *Charm for pain.* (Cf. D1273.) England, U.S.: Baughman (D1500.1.23.2).

D1515. *Magic antidote for poison.* *Penzer II 303 n.; *Gimlette Malay Poisons and Charm Cures; Irish myth: Cross.

B514.3. Snake gives man antidote for poison. B521.1. Animal warns against poison. D1317.0.1. Magic object detects poison. D1383. Magic object protects from poison. D2168. Magic used against poison.

D1515.1. *Remedies for poison.* Irish myth: Cross.

D1515.2. *Charms as antidote for poison.* (Cf. D1273.) Kittredge Witchcraft 32, 387 nn. 82, 83; England: Baughman.

D1515.2.1. *Charms as antidote for snakebite.* (Cf. D1273, D1515.4.) Kittredge Witchcraft 32, 389 n. 101; India: Thompson-Balys.

D1515.3. *Bath in milk of white, hornless cows as antidote for poison.* Irish myth: Cross.

B15.3.0.1. Hornless cow. B184.2.0.1. White cow. D1018. Magic milk of animal. D1788. Magic results from bathing.

D1515.4. *Antidote for snakebite.* (Cf. D1515.2.1.) Jewish: Neuman.

D1515.4.1. *Maid cuts off pap to heal man's serpent wound.* (Cf. D1009.3.) English: Child V 177.

D1515.4.2. *Snake stone applied to snakebite absorbs poison.* (Cf. D930.) Scotland: Baughman.

D1515.4.3. *Hind's horns as antidote for snakebite.* (Cf. D1011.1.) Jewish: Neuman.

D1515.4.4. *Body of gnat as antidote for snakebite.* (Cf. D1010.) Jewish: Neuman.

D1515.4.5. *Sight of brass serpent as antidote for snakebite.* (Cf. D1268.3.) Jewish: Neuman.

D1515.4.6. *Magic potion mixed with brains of deceitful person as cure for snakebite.* (Cf. D1242.2.) Africa (Timne): Schlenker Collection of

Timne Traditions (London, 1861) 87ff., (Hausa): Tremearne FL XXII 464ff. No. 50.

D1515.5. *Remedy for mad dog bite.* Irish myth: Cross (D1519.3).

D1515.5.1. *Stone as antidote for mad dog bite.* (Cf. D930.) U.S.: *Baughman.

D1516. *Charms against elfshot.* (Cf. D2066, D1273.) Kittredge Witchcraft 133, 453ff. nn. 62—82 passim; Irish myth: Cross; Icelandic: MacCulloch Eddic 83, Snorra Edda Skaldsk. XVII; England: *Baughman.

F380. Defeating or ridding oneself of fairies. F405. Means of combatting spirits.

D1517. *Cure for insect's sting.*

D1517.1. *Body of housefly as remedy for hornet sting.* (Cf. D1010.) Jewish: Neuman.

D1518. *Magic object restores bodily members.* Irish myth: Cross.

D1518.1. *Magic drink restores arms.* (Cf. D1040.) Irish myth: Cross.

D1518.2. *Root restores amputated hands and feet.* (Cf. D967.) India: Thompson-Balys.

D1518.3. *Hero's breath returns head to headless horseman.* (Cf. D1005.) India: Thompson-Balys.

D1518.4. *Magic object heals broken bone.* Irish myth: Cross.

D1518.4.1. *Magic plant heals broken bone.* (Cf. D1500.1.4.) Irish myth: Cross.

D1519. *Magic object controls disease — miscellaneous.* Irish myth: Cross.

D1519.1. *Magic object restores strength.* Irish myth: Cross.

D1519.1.1. *Magic bowl restores strength.* (Cf. D1172.2.) Irish myth: Cross.

D1520. Magic object affords miraculous transportation. *Aarne MSFO XXV 116; *Types 560, 566; Irish myth: Cross; India: Thompson-Balys.

D1641. Object removes itself. D2120. Magic transportation. D2121. Magic journey. D2186. Magician carries woman in glass coffin.

D1520.1. *Magic transportation by bough.* (Cf. D954.) *Chauvin V 229 No. 130; India: Thompson-Balys.

D1520.1.1. *Transportation by stretching and swaying tree.* The tree stretches and bends over so as to land hero in a distant country. (Cf. D482.) Tahiti, Melanesia, Indonesia: Dixon 66.

D1520.1.2. *Transportation by hollow tree.* (Cf. D950, D1532.7.) India: Thompson-Balys.

D1520.2. *Magic transportation by cloud.* (Cf. D901.) Chauvin V 230 No. 130; Irish myth: Cross.

D2121.7. Magic journey in cloud. D2135. Magic air journey. F61.1. Ascent to sky on cloud. F61.3. Transportation from heaven in mist.

D1520.3. *Magic transportation by hairs.* (Cf. D991.) Chauvin V 230 No. 130.

D1520.4. *Magic transportation by golden apple.* (Cf. D981.1, F813.1.1.) *Fb "guldæble" I 516a.

D1520.5. *Magic transportation by animal skin.*

D1520.5.1. *Magic transportation by skin of fish.* (Cf. D1025.2.) Chauvin V 230 No. 130.

D1520.5.2. *Magic transportation by dog skin.* (Cf. D1025.6.) Eskimo (Greenland): Rasmussen III 54.

D1520.5.3. *Magic transportation by seal skin.* (Cf. D1025.9.) Eskimo (Bering Strait): Nelson RBAE XVIII 512.

D1520.5.4. *Magic transportation by horse skin.* (Cf. D1025.7.) Chinese: Eberhard FFC CXX 79.

D1520.6. *Magic transportation by cloak (cape).* (Cf. D1053.) *Chauvin V 230 No. 130; Penzer I 27; Spanish: Boggs FFC XC 91 No. 771*.

D1520.7. *Magic transportation by gold uniform.* (Cf. D1052.1.) *Fb "guldmundering".

D1520.8. *Magic transportation by saber.* (Cf. D1082.) Chauvin V 230 No. 130.

D1520.8.1. *Magic transportation by sword.* (Cf. D1081.) Korean: Zong in-Sob 59.

D1520.9. *Magic transportation by garter.* (Cf. D1063.) Chauvin V 230 No. 130.

D1520.10. *Magic transportation by shoes.* (Cf. D1065.2, D1521.1.) Chauvin V 229 No. 130; Icelandic: MacCulloch Eddic 267; India: *Thompson-Balys.

D1520.10.1. *Magic transportation by sandals.* (Cf. D1065.5.) India: Thompson-Balys.

D1520.11. *Magic transportation by cap (hat).* (Cf. D1067.1, D1067.2.) *Type 566; Chauvin V 229 No. 130; Greek: Fox 195.

D1520.12. *Magic transportation by ring.* (Cf. D1076.) Chauvin V 229 No. 130; India: *Thompson-Balys; Icelandic: Boberg.

D1520.13. *Magic transportation by arrow.* (Cf. D1092, D1526.1.) Chauvin V 230 No. 130.

D1520.14. *Transportation in magic carriage.* (Cf. D1111.) Chauvin V 229 No. 130.

D1520.15. *Transportation in magic ship.* (Cf. D1123, D1521.2, D1525, D1533.1.) Finnish: Kalevala rune 39; Greek: Fox 138; Irish myth: Cross.

F242.2. Fairy boat.

D1520.15.1. *Sailing against a contrary wind, current and tide.* *Loomis White Magic 90.

D1520.16. *Magic transportation by chair.* (Cf. D1151.2.) Chauvin V 229 No. 130; India: Thompson-Balys.

D1520.17. *Magic transportation by sofa.* (Cf. D1154.2.) Chauvin V 230 No. 130; India: Thompson-Balys.

D1520.17.1. *Magic transportation on flying bedstead.* (Cf. D1154.1.) India: *Thompson-Balys.

D1520.17.2. *Transportation on magic couch.* (Cf. D1154.) India: Thompson-Balys.

D1520.18. *Magic transportation by hammock.* (Cf. D1154.3.) Africa (Vai): Ellis 200 No. 18 (Type 653).

D1520.18.1. *Transportation on magic swing.* (Cf. D1154.3.1.) India: Thompson-Balys.

D1520.18.2. *Transportation in magic palanquin.* (Cf. D1154.3.2.) India: Thompson-Balys.

D1520.19. *Magic transportation by carpet.* (Cf. D1155, D1118, D1118.1.) *Chauvin V 230 No. 130; Fb "luftrejse" II 457; Icelandic: *Boberg; India: *Thompson-Balys; Cape Verde Islands: Parsons MAFLS XV (1) 111 No. 39; Philippine: Fansler MAFLS XII 137.

D1532. Magic object bears person aloft. D2135. Magic air journey.

D1520.20. *Transportation by magic throne.* (Cf. D1156.) Chauvin V 230 No. 130; India: Thompson-Balys.

D1520.21. *Transportation by magic platform.* (Cf. D1157.) Chauvin V 230 No. 130.

D1520.22. *Transportation by magic pitcher.* (Cf. D1171.4.) Chauvin V 230 No. 130.

D1520.23. *Transportation by magic goblet.* (Cf. D1171.6.2.) Greek: *Frazer Apollodorus I 213 n. 2.

D1520.24. *Transportation by magic box.* (Cf. D1174.) Chauvin V 230 No. 130.

D1520.25. *Transportation by magic bag.* (Cf. D1193.) Fb "rænsel".

D1520.26. *Transportation by putting magic ointment on feet.* (Cf. D1244.) Penzer IV 90 n. 1.

D1520.27. *Magic transportation by means of wand.* (Cf. D1254.1.) Breton: Sébillot Incidents s.v. "baguette"; India: *Thompson-Balys.

D1520.27.1. *Magic transportation by club.* (Cf. D1094.) India: Thompson-Balys.

D1520.28. *Magic transportation in whirlwind.* (Cf. D906.) *Taylor FFC LXX 24 n. 1; Jewish: Neuman.

D2121.8. Magic journey by throwing knife into whirlwind. F411.1. Demon travels in whirlwind. R17. Abduction by whirlwind.

D1520.29. *Transportation by magic jewel.* Italian Novella: Rotunda; Icelandic: Boberg.

D1520.29.1. *Transportation by magic pearl.* (Cf. D1071.) Jewish: bin Gorion Born Judas[2] III 159.

D1520.30. *Magic transportation on piece of rock.* (Cf. D971.4.) India: Thompson-Balys.

D1520.31. *Magic transportation by rope.* (Cf. D1203.) India: Thompson-Balys.

D1520.32. *Magic transportation on antlers.* (Cf. D1011.1.) N. A. Indian (Calif.): Gayton and Newman 75.

D1520.33. *Magic transportation on musical bow.* (Cf. D1210.) N. A. Indian (Calif.): Gayton and Newman 79; India: Thompson-Balys.

D1233.1. Magic musical bow.

D1520.34. *Transportation by means of necklace.* (Cf. D1073.) German: MacCulloch Eddic 261.

D1520.35. *Magic transportation by feather-dress.* (Cf. D1069.2.) Icelandic: MacCulloch Eddic 259, *Boberg.

D1520.36. *Transportation by magic stone.* (Cf. D931.) India: Thompson-Balys.

D1520.37. *Magic journey by reading book.* Chinese: Graham.

D1521. *Miraculous speed from magic object.*

D2122. Journey with magic speed.

D1521.1. *Seven-league boots.* Boots with miraculous speed. (Cf. D1065.1.) *Type 328; *Saintyves Perrault 283, 286; *Fb "sko" III 288a, "støvle" III 642a. — Breton: Sébillot Incidents s.v. "bottes"; French Canadian: Barbeau JAFL XXIX 10; England: *Baughman; India: Thompson-Balys; Chinese: Eberhard FFC CXX 253; Philippine: Fansler MAFLS XII 177.

D1520.10. Magic transportation by shoes. D2122.2. Hundred-league stride.

D1521.1.1. *Sandals with magic speed.* India: Thompson-Balys.

D1521.2. *Ship with miraculous speed.* (Cf. D1123, D1520.15.) Fb "skib" III 243ab; Welsh: MacCulloch Celtic 192; Irish myth: *Cross.

F242.2. Fairy boat.

D1521.2.1. *Ship as swift as a bird.* Icelandic: Boberg.

D1521.3. *Sleigh as swift as thought.* (Cf. D1115.) *Taylor FFC LXX 45ff.

D2122.3. Magic journey as swift as thought. F681.3. Marvelous runner swift as thought.

D1521.4. *Carriage as swift as thought.* (Cf. D1111.) Hindu: Keith 108; Japanese: Anesaki 359.

F681.3. Marvelous runner swift as thought.

D1521.5. *Jewel gives miraculous speed.* (Cf. D1071.)

D1521.5.1. *Turquoise gives miraculous speed.* Jewish: Neuman.

D1523. *Magic self-moving vehicle.* Irish myth: *Cross.

D1600. Automatic objects.

D1523.1. *Self-propelling wagon.* (Cf. D1113.) *Type 675; Fb "vogn" III 1078a.

D1523.2. *Self-propelling (ship) boat.* (Cf. D1121, D1123, D1520.15.) *Barry JAFL XXVIII 195; Irish myth: *Cross; Breton: Sébillot Incidents s.v. "bateau"; India: *Thompson-Balys; Marquesas: Handy 46; N. A. Indian: *Thompson Tales 275 n. 14a; Africa (Fang): Trilles 137. See also references to D1520.15.

D1523.2.1. *Automatic oar.* (Cf. D1124.) Breton: Sébillot Incidents s.v. "aviron".

D1523.2.2. *Boat propelled by magic awl.* (Cf. D1187.) Breton: Sébillot Incidents s.v. "alène".

D1523.2.3. *Boat propelled by magic wand.* (Cf. D1254.1.) Breton: Sébillot Incidents s.v. "navigation".

D1523.2.4. *Boat obeys master's will.* *Kittredge Witchcraft 16; Irish myth: *Cross; England: Baughman.

D1523.2.5. *Boat guides self.* *Kittredge Witchcraft 16; *Loomis White Magic 90; Irish myth: *Cross.

D1523.2.6. *Boat guided by magic songs.* (Cf. D1275.) Finnish: Kalevala rune 40.

D1523.2.7. *Boat guided by magic sea-charm.* (Cf. D1273.) Irish myth: *Cross.

D1523.2.7.1. *Self-guiding rudderless boat.* Irish myth: *Cross.
N781. Hero embarks in rudderless boat. S141. Exposure in boat.

D1523.2.8. *Magic boat is rowed by two wooden figures as soon as it is put on water.* (Cf. D1524, D1620.) India: Thompson-Balys.

D1523.3. *Bundle of wood magically acts as riding horse.* Italian: Basile I No. 3.

D1524. *Magic object enables person to cross water.*
B175.1. Magic salmon carries hero over water. B541.1. Escape from sea on fish's back. B551. Fish carries man across water. F911.3.2. Winged serpent as boat: passengers within.

D1524.1. *Magic object permits man to walk on water.* Irish myth: Cross.
D2125. Magic power to walk on water.

D1524.1.1. *Medicine on feet permits man to walk on water.* (Cf. D1241.) Zanzibar: Bateman 207 No. 10.

D1524.1.2. *Saint's bachall permits him to walk on sea.* (Cf. D1277.) Irish: Plummer clxxv, Cross.

D1524.1.2.1. *Saint casts staffs to distant island.* Staff that reaches owner shall have island. (Cf. D1254.) Irish myth: Cross.

D1524.1.3. *Saint spreads his cloak (or other clothes) upon the water and rides to his desired destination.* (Cf. D1053.) *Loomis White Magic 91.
D1520.6. Magic transportation by cloak (cape).

D1524.1.4. *Sand permits man to walk on water.* (Cf. D935.1.) India: Thompson-Balys.

D1524.2. *Clothes carry owner over water.*

D1524.2.1. *Boots carry owner on sea.* (Cf. D1065.1.) Irish myth: *Cross (D1524.2); Breton: Sébillot Incidents s.v. "bottes".

D1524.2.2. *Belt carries owner over water.* (Cf. D1057.) Philippine (Tinguian): Cole 43, 55.

D1524.3. *Magic stone serves as boat.* (Cf. D931.) *Loomis White Magic 90; Irish: Plummer clv, *Cross; England: *Baughman.

D1524.3.1. *Stone canoe.* (Cf. D1122.) N. A. Indian (Ojibwa): Schoolcraft Hiawatha 223.

D1524.3.2. *Saint's bell carried on floating stone.* (Cf. D1213.) Irish myth: *Cross.

D1524.4. *Island canoe.* Magic island acts as canoe or boat. (Cf. D936, D1122.) N. A. Indian: *Thompson Tales 275 n. 14.
F737. Wandering island.

D1524.5. *River crossed by means of charm.* (Cf. D1273.) India: Thompson-Balys.

D1524.6. *River crossed by means of magic stone.* (Cf. D930.) Congo: Pratt-Chadwick and Lamprey The Alo Man (New York, 1927) 17ff.

D1524.7. *Magic sod serves as boat.* (Cf. D934.1.) Irish myth: *Cross.

D1524.8. *Leaf serves as boat.* (Cf. D955, D1121.)

D1524.8.1. *Leaf serves as boat for saint.* England: Baughman.

D1524.9. *Magic wind catches hero up and transports him across immense sea.* (Cf. D906.) India: Thompson-Balys.

D1524.10. *Magic staff comes to one over water.* (Cf. D1254.) Marquesas: Handy 134.

D1524.11. *Magic betelnut comes to one over water.* Philippine (Tinguian): Cole 63.

D1524.12. *Magic handaxe comes to one over water* (Cf. D1206.) Philippine (Tinguian): Cole 84ff., 101.

D1525. *Magic submarine ship (boat).* (Cf. D1123.) Breton: Sébillot Incidents s.v. "navire", "bateau". — Eskimo (Kodiak): Golder JAFL XXII 18.

D1525.1. *Magic hood enables person to pass under water.* (Cf. D1067.3.) Irish myth: Cross.

D1526. *Magic object thrown ahead carries owner with it.*

D1526.1. *Magic arrow flight.* Man keeps ahead of arrow which he shoots. (Cf. D1092.) N. A. Indian: *Thompson Tales 315 n. 145a.

H1226.2. Pursuit of magic arrow leads to adventure.

D1526.2. *Magic ball flight.* Man throws ball and is carried along with it. (Cf. D1256.) N. A. Indian: *Thompson Tales 315 n. 145b.

D1313.1. Magic ball indicates road. Rolls ahead.

D1526.3. *Magic pistol forces one to run behind the ball.* (Cf. D1096.2.) Breton: Sébillot Incidents s.v. "pistolet".

D1531. *Magic object gives power of flying.*

D2135. Magic air journey.

D1531.1. *Mustard seeds give power of flying.* (Cf. D971.1.) Penzer II 63f.

D1531.2. *Magic pill gives power of flying.* (Cf. D1243.) Chinese: Werner 185.

D1531.3. *Magic sword gives power of flying.* (Cf. D1081.) *Penzer IV 235f.

D1531.4. *Magic stone under tongue gives power of flying.* (Cf. D931.) India: Thompson-Balys.

D1531.5. *Witch flies with aid of magic cap or hood.* Scotland, U.S.: *Baughman.

D1531.6. *Witch flies with aid of magic stick.* (Cf. D956.) England: Baughman.

G242.1. Witch flies through air on broomstick.

D1531.7. *Witch flies with aid of magic juice.* (Cf. D981.0.1.) U.S.: Baughman.

D1531.8. *Witch flies with aid of word charm.* (Cf. D1273.) England, Scotland, U.S.: *Baughman.

D1531.9. *Magic flying by means of magic fiddle.* (Cf. D1233.) India: Thompson-Balys.

D1531.10. *Palmetto leaves give power of flying.* (Cf. D955.) Marquesas: Handy 53.

D1531.11. *Gem gives power of flying.* (Cf. D951.) Buddhist myth: Malalasekera I 1056.

D1532. *Magic object bears person aloft.*

B31.1. Roc. B41.2. Flying horse. B45. Air-going elephant. B552. Man carried by birds. D1118. Magic airships. D1118.1. Magic air-riding basket. D1520.19. Magic transportation by carpet. D1626. Image flies through air. D1626.1. Artificial flying horse. D2135. Magic air journey. F61.2.1. Ascent to sky by sticking to feather. G242. Witch flies through air.

D1532.1. *Magic flying skin.* (Cf. D1025.) India: Thompson-Balys.

D1532.1.1. *Magic mouse-skin bears person aloft.* (Cf. B183.1.1, D1025.3.) Africa (Zulu): Callaway 98.

D1532.2. *Magic breeches bear person aloft.* (Cf. D1055.) *Fb "bukser". IV 77b.

D1532.3. *Magic shoes bear person aloft.* (Cf. D1065.2.) Penzer I 24 n. 1, III 56; Fb "sko" III 288a; India: Thompson-Balys.

D1532.3.1. *Special shoes enable hero to climb a stone pillar.* Chinese: Graham.

D1532.4. *Magic sandals bear person aloft.* (Cf. D1065.5.) Greek: *Frazer Apollodorus I 153 n. 3.

D1532.5. *Magic chariot bears person aloft.* (Cf. D1114.) Jones PMLA XXIII 574. — Greek: *Frazer Apollodorus I 38 n. 2, Fox 115, 213; Irish: Plummer xxvii, *Cross; Jewish: Neuman; India: *Thompson-Balys, Penzer VI 21f., 201ff.

D1532.6. *Magic robe bears person aloft.* (Cf. D1052.) Pauli (ed. Bolte). No. 668.

D1532.7. *Magic tree bears person through air.* India: Thompson-Balys.

D950. Magic tree. D1520.1.1. Transportation by stretching and swaying tree.

D1532.8. *Magic head-dress bears person aloft.* (Cf. D1067.) Irish myth: Cross.

D1532.9. *Magic leaf bears person aloft.* (Cf. D955.) Irish myth: Cross.

G242.3. Witch flies through air on leaf.

D1532.10. *Magic fan bears person aloft.* Chinese: Graham.

D1532.11. *Magic journey in flying boat.* (Cf. D1123.) India: Thompson-Balys.

D1532.12. *Magic sword carries person through air.* (Cf. D1081.) India: Thompson-Balys.

D1532.13. *Magic brick bears person to moon.* (Cf. D935.4.) Chinese: Eberhard FFC CXX 221.

D1533. *Magic amphibian vehicle.*

B181.4. Magic horse travels on sea or land.

D1533.1. *Magic land and water vehicle.*

D1533.1.1. *Magic land and water ship.* (Cf. D1123.) *Type 513B; *BP II 79ff., III 272; *Fb "skib" III 242b; *Cosquin Contes indiens 452ff.; *Brown Iwain 112; Köhler-Bolte I 134, 192f. — Irish myth: *Cross; Norse: MacCulloch Eddic 108—09; Breton: Sébillot Incidents s.v. "bateau".

B184.1.4. Magic horse travels on sea or land. F841. Extraordinary boat (ship).

D1533.1.2. *Magic land and water chariot.* (Cf. D1114.) Fb "guldkaret". — Irish myth: *Cross.

A171.0.1. God drives chariot over waves. F242.1.2. Fairy chariots ride waves.

D1533.2. *Vehicle travels above and below ground.*

B181.2. Magic horse goes underground. D2131. Magic underground journey. F721.1. Underground passages. Journey made through natural subways.

D1533.2.1. *Box which travels above or below ground.* (Cf. D1174.) Breton: Sébillot Incidents s.v. "coffre".

B181.2. Magic horse goes underground.

D1539. *Miscellaneous forms of magic transportation.*

D1539.1. *Magic elevator.* Stone on which one steps carries one underground. (Cf. D931.) German: Grimm No. 163.

D1539.2. *Magic belt carries tree away.* (Cf. D1057.) *Fb "træ" III 868a.

D1539.3. *Magic staves enable man to gain precipitous height.* (Cf. D1254.) Irish myth: Cross.

F1071. Prodigious jump.

D1540. Magic object controls the elements. Chinese: Graham.

A1130. Establishment of present order: weather. D900. Magic weather phenomena. D2140. Magic control of the elements. F790. Extraordinary sky and weather phenomena. F960. Extraordinary nature phenomena.

D1540.1. *Magic bag controls storm, mist, darkness, etc.* (Cf. D1193.) Icelandic: *Boberg.

D1540.2. *Magic white, red and yellow stone causes hail, sunshine or fire, according to which side is scratched.* (Cf. D931.) Icelandic: Boberg.

D1540.3. *Magic stone controls water.* (Cf. D931.) Jewish: Neuman.

D1541. *Magic object controls storms.* Irish myth: Cross.

D905. Magic storm. D2141. Storm produced by magic.

D1541.0.1. *Charms control storms.* (Cf. D1273.) Kittredge Witchcraft 32, 388 n. 94.

D1541.0.2. *Magic song controls storm.* (Cf. D1275.) Icelandic: *Boberg.

D1541.1. *Magic object raises storm.*

D1541.1.1. *Magic spittle causes storm.* (Cf. D1001.) Africa (Zulu): Callaway 228.

D1541.1.2. *Magic song causes storm.* (Cf. D1275.) Africa (Kaffir): Theal 83.

D1541.1.3. *Magic fountain causes storm (rain).* (Cf. D925, D926, D2143.1.) *Hamilton Romanic Review II 355ff., V 213ff.; *Brown Iwain 13ff.,

*126f.; Hdwb. d. Abergl. III 1307; Holmberg Die Wassergottheiten 181ff. — Irish myth: *Cross; Icelandic: *Boberg; English: Wells 65; French: Chretien de Troyes Iwain (ed. Foerster) lines 380ff.

D905. Magic storm. D927. Magic spring.

D1541.1.4. *Shirt laid upon altar raises storm.* (Cf. D1056.) Hawaii: Beckwith Myth 531.

D1541.1.5. *Tempest box raises storm.* (Cf. D1174.) India: Thompson-Balys.

D1541.1.6. *Magic writings raise storm.* (Cf. D1266.1.) Korean: Zong in-Sob 170.

D1541.1.7. *Magic calabash holding bones raises storm.* (Cf. D965.2) Hawaii: Beckwith Myth 449.

D1541.1.8. *Singing magic hymn raises storm.* (Cf. D1275.3) Korean: Zong in-Sob 66.

D1541.2. *Magic object draws storm away.*

D1541.2.1. *Magic pestle draws storm away.* (Cf. D1254.3.) Chinese: Eberhard FFC CXX 221.

D1541.2.2. *Magic pearl draws storm away.* (Cf. D1071.) Chinese: Eberhard FFC CXX 221.

D1542. *Magic object controls rain.* (Cf. D1541.4.) Irish myth: *Cross.

D902. Magic rain. D2143.1. Rain produced by magic.

D1542.1. *Magic object produces rain.*

D1542.1.1. *Magic stone produces rain.* (Cf. D931, D1541.4.) Irish: Plummer clvii, Cross.

D1542.1.2. *Magic spittle controls rain.* Makes rain on everyone but possessor of spittle himself. (Cf. D1001.) Africa (Zulu): Callaway 228.

D1542.1.3. *Magic hat brings flood.* (Cf. D1067.1.) N. A. Indian (Haida): Alexander N. Am. 261.

D1542.1.4. *Magic fan produces rain.* Must be waved three times. (Cf. D1077.) Chinese: Werner 359, 362.

D1542.1.5. *Magic song brings rain.* (Cf. D1275.) Chinese: Graham.

D1542.1.6. *Oil poured in left ear of black dog brings rain.* (Cf. D1242.2.) Jijena Sanchez 134.

D1542.1.7. *Blood and liver of black dog sacrificed to bring rain.* (Cf. D1016., D1015.4.) Jijena Sanchez 134.

D1766.2. Magic results produced by sacrifice.

D1542.2. *Magic object causes drought.*

D1542.2.1. *Sacred weapon thrown into sky causes drought.* (Cf. D1080.) Buddhist myth: Malalasekera I 293.

D1542.3. *Magic object causes streams to dry up.*

D1542.3.1. *Magic medicine causes streams to dry up.* (Cf. D1241.) Africa (Ekoi): Talbot 115.

D1542.3.2. *Reading book causes river to dry up.* (Cf. D1266.) Chinese: Graham.

D1542.3.3. *Branch which dries up water in great river so person can cross.* (Cf. D954.) India: Thompson-Balys.

D1542.3.4. *Magic spell dries up lake.* (Cf. D1273.) Irish myth: Cross (D1549.9).

D1542.3.5. *Not a drop of water will remain in tank no matter how hard laborers work.* (Cf. D921.2.) India: Thompson-Balys.

D1542.4. *Magic wand keeps outdoor sleeping place dry.* (Cf. D1254.1.) South Africa: Bourhill and Drake 237ff. No. 20.

D1543. *Magic object controls wind.*

A1120. Establishment of present order: winds. D906. Magic wind. D2142. Wind produced by magic.

D1543.1. *Fountain insures favorable wind when drained.* (Cf. D925.) Irish: Plummer cli, Cross.

D1543.2. *Magic stone causes favorable wind.* (Cf. D931.) Irish: Plummer clvii, Cross.

D1543.3. *Magic fan produces wind.* (Cf. D1077.) Chinese: Werner 359, 362.

D1543.4. *Magic sword produces wind.* (Cf. D1081.) Chinese: Werner 121.

D1543.5. *Magic medicine produces wind.* (Cf. D1241.) Africa (Ekoi): Talbot 344.

D1543.6. *Wind carried in mantle.* (Cf. D1053.) Irish myth: Cross.

H1020. Tasks contrary to laws of nature.

D1543.7. *Magic calabash (gourd) controls winds.* (Cf. D965.2.) Hawaii: Beckwith Myth 86, 405.

D1544. *Magic object controls earthquakes.*

D1544.1. *Magic spell controls earthquake.* (Cf. D1273.) Penzer VI 29.

D1545. *Magic object controls sea.*

D1545.0.1. *Magic runes control sea.* (Cf. D1266.2.) Icelandic: Boberg.

D1545.1. *Magic object controls tides.*

D1545.1.1. *Magic jewel controls tides.* (Cf. D1071.) Japanese: Anesaki 305.

D1546. *Magic object controls heavenly bodies.* Irish myth: Cross.

A700. Creation of the heavenly bodies. F961. Extraordinary behavior of heavenly bodies.

D1546.1. *Magic object controls sun.*

A725. Rising and setting of the sun controlled by a man. D2146. Magic control of day and night. F961.1. Extraordinary behavior of sun. H1023.16. Task: making sun and moon shine in the north.

D1546.1.1. *Hat which turns the sun.* (Cf. D1067.1.) Breton: Sébillot Incidents s.v. "chapeau". — Danish: Boberg.

D1546.1.2. *Magic spell controls sun.* (Cf. D1273.) Irish myth: *Cross (D1546.2).

D1546.1.2.1. *Magic spell darkens sun.* Irish myth: *Cross (D1546.2.1).

D1546.1.3. *Magic umbrella makes sun stand still.* (Cf. D1194.) Chinese: Eberhard FFC CXX 237.

D1547. *Magic object reverses gravitation.*

D1547.1. *Magic root floats against the current.* (Cf. D967.) India: Thompson-Balys.

T255.2. The obstinate wife sought for up-stream.

D1547.2. *Magic flower thrown into lake causes waters to follow in the footsteps of the one who throws it in.* (Cf. D975.) India: Thompson-Balys.

D1547.3. *Magic object lifts heavy object from river bottom.* Jewish: Neuman.

D1548. *Magic object controls weather.*

A1130. Establishment of present order: weather phenomena. D900. Magic weather phenomena. F790. Extraordinary sky and weather phenomena. F960. Extraordinary nature phenomena.

D1548.0.1. *Amulet has control over weather.* (Cf. D1070.) Eskimo (Greenland): Rink 459, Rasmussen II 175.

D1548.1. *Magic object assures good weather.*

D1548.1.1. *Magic stalk assures good weather.* (Cf. D977.) Eskimo (Greenland): Rink 429.

D1549. *Magic object controls elements: miscellaneous.*

D1549.1. *Magic arrow shakes heavens.* (Cf. D1092.) Chinese: Werner 312.

D1549.2. *Saint's girdle causes tree to fall in right direction.* (Cf. D1057.1.) Irish: Plummer clxxxi, Cross.

D1549.3. *Magic object controls river (lake).* Icelandic: Boberg.

A930. Origin of streams. D915. Magic river. D2151.2. Magic control of rivers.

D1549.3.1. *Saint's bachall drives back flooding river.* (Cf. D1277.) Irish: Plummer clxxv, Cross.

D1549.3.2. *Saint's bachall leads stream through mountain* (or up hill.) (Cf. D1277.) Irish: Plummer clxxv, *Cross.

D1549.3.3. *Magic trousers make river boil.* (Cf. D1055.) Chinese: Werner 307.

D1549.3.4. *Magic gem causes river waters to recede.* (Cf. D1071, D1551.) India: Thompson-Balys.

D1549.3.5. *Fish bone holds back water in river.* (Cf. D1013.) India: Thompson-Balys.

D1549.3.6. *Ring of hay thrown into empty lake fills it up with water.* (Cf. D1276.) India: Thompson-Balys.

D1549.3.7. *Written charm causes river to flow quietly.* (Cf. D1266.1.) Korean: Zong in-Sob 57.

D1549.3.8. *Spear stuck in river bed stops water.* (Cf. D1084.) S. A. Indian (Mataco): Métraux MAFLS XL 132.

D1549.4. *Saint's bachall brings down mountain on heads of enemies.* (Cf. D1277.) Irish: Plummer clxxv, *Cross.

A960. Creation of mountains. D932. Magic mountain. D2152. Magic control of mountains.

D1549.5. *Magic staff draws water from stone.* (Cf. D925.1, D1254, D1567.6.) Spanish Exempla: Keller; Jewish: bin Gorion Born Judas[2] III 19, *Neuman: India: Thompson-Balys.

D1549.5.1. *Rock beaten by sword provides water.* (Cf. D930.) Chinese: Eberhard FFC CXX 114.

D1549.6. *Saint's veil quells volcano.* (Cf. D1061.) Acta Sanctorum February I 635.

D1549.7. *Murdered man's head will cause earth to burn up or sea to boil: must be carried about.* (Cf. D1278.) India: Thompson-Balys.

D992. Magic head. D1278. Ghoulish charm. Q520.1. Murderer does penance.

D1549.8. *Magic song drives back flooding sea.* (Cf. D1275.) Irish myth: Cross.

D1549.9. *Magic rod causes all waters to turn to blood.* (Cf. D1254.2.) Jewish: Neuman.

D1549.10. *Waves answer roar of magic shield.* (Cf. D1101.1, D1610.24.) Irish myth: *Cross.

D1549.11. *Magic beads break ice jam.* (Cf. D1071.1.) Eskimo (Greenland): Rink 150.

D1550. Magic object miraculously opens and closes.

D1600. Automatic object. F979.2. Leaves of tree open and close to give saint passage. V211.7.3. Three bolts left on hell by Christ.

D1551. *Waters magically divide and close.* *Frazer Old Testament II 456ff.; Breton: Sébillot Incidents s. v. "rivière"; Irish: Plummer cxlviii, Cross; Icelandic: Boberg; England: Baughman; Spanish Exempla: Keller; India: *Thompson-Balys; N. A. Indian: *Thompson Tales 276 n. 15b; Africa (Zulu): Callaway 82, 93; (Hottentot): Bleek 75 No. 36.

D1549.3. Magic object controls rivers (lake). D2151. Magic control of waters. F930. Extraordinary occurrences concerning seas or waters. R220. Flights.

D1551.0.1. *Water becomes shallow so man is able to cross the river.* India: Thompson-Balys.

D1551.1. *Magic salt causes waters to divide.* (Cf. D1039.2.) Cape Verde Islands: Parsons MAFLS XV (1) 282 No. 92.

D1551.2. *Magic rod causes waters to divide and close.* (Cf. D1254.2.) Spanish Exempla: Keller; Jewish: Neuman; Africa (Kaffir): Theal 129.

D1551.3. *Magic root causes waters to divide and close.* (Cf. D967.) Ila (Rhodesia): Smith and Dale II 416.

D1551.4. *Magic powder causes waters to divide.* (Cf. D1246.) Cape Verde Islands: Parsons MAFLS XV (1) 214 No. 73.

D1551.5. *Saint's bachall causes sea to divide.* (Cf. D1277.) Irish: Plummer clxxv, Cross.

D1551.6. *Magic stick causes waters to divide.* (Cf. D956.) India: Thompson-Balys.

D1551.7. *Magic diamond on ogre's waist opens passage in tank by its reflection on water.* India: Thompson-Balys.

D1551.7.1. *Diamond in snake king's forehead in hero's pocket opens lake waters to reveal a pathway to underground palace.* (Cf. D1071.) India: Thompson-Balys.

D1551.8. *Magic brick causes waters to divide.* (Cf. D935.4.) India: Thompson-Balys.

D1551.9. *Magic formula causes sea to open up.* (Cf. D1273.) Korean: Zong in-Sob 26, 170.

D1552. *Mountains or rocks open and close.* (Cf. D931, D932.) *Cox Cinderella 499; Fb "rundt" III 96b; India: Thompson-Balys; Buddhist myth: Malalasekera I 319; Calif. Indian: Gayton and Newman 73; Eskimo (Greenland): Rink 156, 278, 299, Holm 52, Rasmussen III 53; (Central Eskimo): Boas RBAE VI 798, (Cumberland Sound): Boas BAM XV 180, 232.

C652. Compulsion: taking back talisman which opened treasure mountain. F92.3. Visit to lower world through opening rocks. Rocks open with a charm. F721.4. Underground treasure chambers. F750. Extraordinary mountains and valleys. N552. Treasure opens itself.

D1552.0.1. *Door opens in mountain.* (Cf. D932.) India: Thompson-Balys.

D1552.1. *Mountain opens at blow of divining rod.* (Cf. D1254.2.) Fb "pilegren".

D1552.2. *Mountain opens to magic formula (Open Sesame).* (Cf. D1273.) *Type 676; BP III 137.—Jewish: Neuman; Gaster Oldest Stories 132; Icelandic: Boberg; Chinese: Eberhard FFC CXX 108, 226; Tahiti: Dixon 63; New Zealand, Samoa, Mongaia (Cook Group), Tahiti, British New Guinea, Halmahera: ibid., 48 nn. 37—41; Am. Negro (Georgia): Harris Friends 81 No. 11; Africa (Zulu): Callaway 143.

N455.3. Secret formula for opening treasure mountain overheard from robbers (Open Sesame). N471. Foolish attempt of second man to overhear secrets (from animals, demons, etc.).

D1552.3. *Mountain pass magically closes.* South Africa: Bourhill and Drake 237ff. No. 20.

D1552.4. *Mountain opens and lets ship on wheels out, permitting magician's escape.* Icelandic: Boberg.

D1552.5. *Cave opens and hides fugitives.* *Loomis White Magic 89, 119.

D2152.5. Rock at cave's entrance falls on pursuer. R315. Cave as refuge.

D1552.6. *Gate or wall opens and closes, letting saint through.* (Cf. D1554.) *Loomis White Magic 89.

D1552.7. *Mountain opens and furnishes stones for church.* Icelandic: *Boberg.

D1552.8. *Hill opens and closes to let fugitives pass.* (Cf. D938.1.) India: Thompson-Balys.

D1552.9. *When enchanted deer touches rock with her muzzle it flies asunder and reveals entrance to cave.* (Cf. D1011.5.) India: Thompson-Balys.

D1552.10. *Magic soot causes mountain to open.* (Cf. D931.1.) Africa (Washaga): Gutman 137.

D1552.11. *Magic stone opens treasure mountain.* (Cf. D930.) Chinese: Eberhard FFC CXX 221.

F721.4. Underground treasure chambers.

D1552.12. *Magic key opens treasure mountain.* (Cf. D1176.) Chinese: Eberhard FFC CXX 221; Icelandic: Boberg.

D1553. *Symplegades.* Rocks that clash together at intervals. (Cf. D931.) *Reinhard PMLA XXXVIII 458 n. 108; *Krappe Balor 111 n. 11a; Köhler-Bolte I 572. — Greek: Fox 111, 137; *Frazer Apollodorus I 106 n. 2; Euripides Iphegenia in Taurica lines 123ff.; Herodotus 4:85; Janet Bacon Voyage of the Argonauts 79f.; India: Thompson-Balys; N. A. Indian: *Thompson Tales 275 n. 15, (Calif.): Gayton and Newman 102; S. A. Indian (Tupinamba): Métraux BBAE CXLIII (3) 132. Maori: Clark 36ff.

D1554. *Magic forest opens and closes for hero to pass.* (Cf. D941.) Saintyves Perrault 65.

D1554.1. *Woods opens and hides fugitive.* (Cf. D941.) India: Thompson-Balys.

D1555. *Underground passage magically opens.* Chinese: Graham.

D1555.1. *Magic wand opens underground passage.* (Cf. D1254.1.) *Bolte Reise der Söhne Giaffers 221; MacCulloch Childhood 207.

D1555.2. *Magic powder causes earth to open up.* India: Thompson-Balys.

D1246. Magic powder. F942.1. Ground opens and swallows up person.

D1555.3. *Magic formula causes silver to hide itself in mountain.* (Cf. D1273.) Chinese: Graham.

D1555.4. *Fairy music causes earth to open (burst).* (Cf. D1275.1, F262.) Irish myth: Cross (D1558).

D1556. *Self-opening tree-trunk.* (Cf. D950.) Jewish: Neuman; India: Thompson-Balys.

D1556.1. *Magic formula causes tree to open.* (Cf. D1273.) *Hdwb. d. Märchens s.v. "Baum"; BP III 139f.

D1556.2. *Tree opens its trunk to give shelter to abandoned girls.* (Cf. D950.) India: Thompson-Balys.

D1557. *Magic charm causes door to open.* (Cf. D1273.) India: *Thompson-Balys; Africa (Venda): Stayt The Bavenda (London, 1931) 351ff. No. 16, (Nubia): Rochemonteix Quelques Contes Nubiens (Cairo, 1888) 112ff. No. 11, (Fang): Trilles XVI 212ff. No. 14, (Gouro): Tauxier Nègres Gouro et Gagou (Paris, 1924) 277f. No. 12, (Mossi): Frobenius Atlantis VIII 239ff. No. 103.

D2088. Locks opened by magic. V211.7.3. The three bolts left on hell by Christ.

D1557.1. *Door (lock) magically opens (for saint).* (Cf. D1146, D1164.) Irish myth: *Cross.

D2088.0.1. All locks opened on the night of Christ's Nativity.

D1557.2. *Magic herb causes door to open.* (Cf. D965.) Cheremis: Sebeok-Nyerges; India: Thompson-Balys.

D1557.2.1. *Magic rod causes door to open.* (Cf. D1254.2.) India: Thompson-Balys.

D1557.3. *Magic diamond provides ingress to subterranean palace.* (Cf. D1071.) India: Thompson-Balys.

D1557.4. *Gate of temple opens and shuts by magic.* (Cf. D1131.) Jewish: Neuman.

D1560. Magic object performs other services for owner.
E64. Resuscitation by magic object.

D1561. *Magic object confers miraculous powers (luck).*
D1720. Acquisition of magic powers.

D1561.1. *Magic object brings luck.*
N135. Object effects change of luck.

D1561.1.1. *Magic bird-heart (when eaten) brings man to kingship.* (Cf. D1015.1.1, B113.1.) *Type 567; BP I 528, III 3; *Aarne MSFO XXV 176; Breton: Sébillot Incidents s.v. "oiseau".
M312.3. Eater of magic bird-heart will become rich (or king).

D1561.1.1.1. *Bird (when eaten) brings man to kingship.* (Cf. D932.) India: Thompson-Balys.

D1561.1.1.2. *Magic fish (when eaten) brings man to kingship.* (Cf. D1032.1.) India: Thompson-Balys.

D1561.1.1.3. *Snake's head (when eaten) brings man to kingship.* (Cf. D1011.0.3.) India: Thompson-Balys.

D1561.1.2. *Magic ring brings good luck.* (Cf. D1076.) *Fb "ring" III 60b.

D1561.1.3. *Horseshoe brings good luck.* (Cf. D1286.) *Howey 102ff.; **Means-Lawrence Magic of the Horseshoe; *Fb "hestesko" I 603b. — England: Baughman.

D1561.1.4. *Magic medicine brings success.* (Cf. D1241.) Africa (Ekoi): Talbot 359.

D1561.1.5. *Four-leaf clover brings good luck.* (Cf. D965.7.) *BP III 201; *Fb "firkløver".

D1561.1.6. *Food left on magic stone brings good luck thereafter.* (Cf. D931.) Irish myth: Cross (D1561.8).

D1561.1.7. *Magic stone brings good luck.* (Cf. D930.) Icelandic: Boberg.

D1561.1.8. *Runes bring luck.* (Cf. D1266.1.) Icelandic: Boberg.

D1561.1.9. *Lucky places for grave.* (Cf. D1073.) India: Thompson-Balys; Chinese: Graham.

D1561.1.10. *Jewel brings good luck.* (Cf. D1071.) India: Thompson-Balys.

D1561.1.11. *Magic song brings luck.* (Cf. D1275.) Icelandic: Boberg.

D1561.2. *Magic object confers miraculous powers.*

D1561.2.1. *Magic bird (when eaten) gives power of excreting jewels.* (Cf. D1032.) India: Thompson-Balys.

D1561.2.2. *Magic treasure gives miraculous powers.* Spanish Exempla: Keller; Penzer V 76 n. 1; Busk Sagas from the Far East (London, 1878) 257, 263

D1561.2.3. *Magic power in chain.* Lost when chain is stolen. (Cf. D1078.) Wesselski Märchen 174 No. 64.

D1561.2.4. *Charm gives invisibility and power of moving everywhere.* (Cf. D1273.) Buddhist myth: Malalasekera I 750.

D1562. *Magic object removes obstacles.*

D1562.1. *Magic staff destroys obstacles.* (Cf. D1254.) Hawaii: Dixon 90.

D1562.2. *Hair from fox's tail opens all doors.* (Cf. D1023.2, D1557.) *Fb "hår" I 771b.

D1562.3. *Magic horn blows down wall.* (Cf. D1222.) *Type 569; BP I 464ff. Cf. Joshua 6:20; Jewish: Neuman.

D1562.4. *Magic needle makes everything fall to pieces.* (Cf. D1181.) *Type 594.

D1562.5. *Hero crosses impassable plain in path of magic object.* Irish myth: *Cross.

D1313.1. Magic ball indicates road. D1313.6. Magic apple indicates road.

D1562.6. *Holy water destroys veil over well.* (Cf. D1242.1.2.) Irish myth: Cross.

D1562.7. *Magic root snaps bars of iron in two.* (Cf. D1564.) India: Thompson-Balys.

D1563. *Magic object controls condition of soil.*

D2081. Land made magically sterile. D2157.1. Land made magically fertile.

D1563.0.1. *Magic springs fertilize or sterilize earth.* (Cf. D927.) *Herbert III 238; *Oesterley No. 253.

D1563.1. *Magic object makes soil fertile.*

D1563.1.1. *Charms make soil fertile.* (Cf. D1273.) Kittredge Witchcraft 32, 388 n. 91.

D1563.1.2. *Magic song makes barren land fruitful.* (Cf. D1275.) Irish: Plummer clxxix, Cross.

D1563.1.3. *Sign of the cross makes barren land fruitful.* Irish myth: Cross.

D1766.6. Magic results from sign of the cross.

D1563.1.4. *Saint's bell starts crops growing.* (Cf. D1213.) Irish myth: Cross.

D1563.1.5. *Blood makes soil fertile.* (Cf. D1003.) Icelandic: *Boberg.

D1563.1.6. *Magic branch when used as a threshing pole produces marvelous harvest of rice.* (Cf. D954.) India: Thompson-Balys.

D1563.2. *Magic object makes soil sterile.*

D1563.2.1. *Magic chain renders orchard barren.* (Cf. D1078.) Norwegian: Christiansen 91 No. 613, Asbjørnsen og Moe (3d ed.) 240 No. 48.

D1563.2.2. *Blood makes tree (and surroundings) poisonous.* (Cf. D1016.) Irish myth: *Cross; Gaster Thespis 296.

G346. Devastating monster.

D1563.2.2.1. *Well (river) polluted by blood shed in battle.* (Cf. D926.) Irish myth: *Cross.

D1563.2.2.2. *Snake's venom poisons tree.* India: Thompson-Balys.

D1563.2.3. *Magic poem (satire) makes land sterile.* (Cf. D1275.4.) Irish myth: Cross (D1563.7).

M411.6.1. Druid's curse makes land sterile.

D1563.2.4. *Magic spell destroys crops.* (Cf. D1273.) Irish myth: Cross.

D1564. *Magic object splits or cuts things.* Jewish: Neuman.

D1564.1. *Magic pebble splits wood.* (Cf. D931.) Southern Paiute: Lowie JAFL XXXVII 143 No. 15.

D1564.2. *Saint's spittle splits rocks.* (Cf. D1001.) *Loomis White Magic 131; Irish: Plummer clxxviii, *Cross.

D1564.3. *Saint's bachall splits rock, cuts stone, and cleaves ground.* (Cf. D1277.) Irish: Plummer clxxv, *Cross.

D1564.4. *Magic object cuts down trees.*

D1564.4.1. *Magic spear-head cuts down trees.* (Cf. D1084.1.) Africa (Benga): Nassau 187 No. 24, Version 1.

D1564.4.2. *Magic hair cuts down iron tree.* (Cf. D991.) India: Thompson-Balys.

D1564.5. *Magic cranberry opens wedge and frees hero.* (Cf. D981.10.1.) Eskimo (Kodiak): Golder JAFL XVI 91.

H1532. Wedge test. Hero is caught in cleft of tree.

D1564.6. *Magic sword cuts stone and fells trees.* (Cf. D1081.) Irish myth: *Cross.

D1564.7. *Magic weapon (sword, axe) cuts hair (on water, in wind).* Irish myth: *Cross.

D1080. Magic weapons. F839.2.2. Edge of shield sharp enough to cut hair on water.

D1565. *Magic object causes things to seek their proper place.*

D1565.1. *Magic feather causes chips from tree to return as cut.* Thus the tree remains uncut. (Cf. D1021.) Africa (Kaffir): Theal 126.

D1602.2. Felled tree raises itself again at night. D1602.2.2. Chips from tree return to their places as cut.

D1565.1.1. *Magic song causes chips from tree to return.* (Cf. D1275, A2426.4.1.) Africa (Kaffir): Theal 125, cf. (Angola): Chatelain 110.

D1565.2. *Magic lyre charms stones into their place in building.* (Cf. D1231.1.) Greek: Fox 44 (Amphion), *Grote I 242.

D1565.3. *Magic song causes plowed ground to become unplowed.* (Cf. D1275.) Africa (Kaffir): Theal 30 No. 1, 41 No. 2, (Basuto): Jacottet 100 No. 15, (Yoruba): Ellis 253 No. 4.

D1565.4. *Saint's breath restores shattered vessel.* (Cf. D1005.) Irish myth: Cross.

D1316.6. Magic goblet indicates falsehood by breaking, truth by reassembling. V52.5. Prayer restores shattered vessel.

D1566. *Magic object controls fire.* Irish myth: Cross.

D1408.1.1. Magic bark sets a creek on fire. D2158. Magic control of fires.

D1566.1. *Magic object sets things afire.*

D1566.1.1. *Magic arrow sets fire to whatever it hits.* (Cf. D1092.) N. A. Indian (Cree, Menomini): Skinner JAFL XXVII 98.

D1566.1.2. *Magic fire-moccasins.* Set fire to surroundings. (Cf. D1065.4.) N. A. Indian: *Thompson Tales 322 n. 164.

D1566.1.3. *Magic sword causes fire and smoke.* (Cf. D1081.) Chinese: Werner 121.

D1566.1.4. *Saint's breath kindles lamps.* (Cf. D1005.) *Loomis White Magic 46f.; Irish: Plummer clxxviii, *Cross.

D1566.1.4.1. *Saint's breath kindles coals.* Irish myth: Cross.

D1566.1.4.2. *Saint's (man's) breath makes icicles (snow, water) burn.* Irish myth: *Cross.

F962.9. Icicles gathered by saint as firewood burn.

D1566.1.5. *Shower of fire from magic anvil.* (Cf. D1202.) Irish myth: *Cross.

D1566.1.6. *Magic dog's breath burns dead bodies.* (Cf. B182.1, D1029.1.) Irish myth: Cross.

D1566.1.7. *Holy water procures fire or light.* (Cf. V132.) Icelandic: *Boberg.

D1566.2. *Magic object quenches fire.*

D1271. Magic fires. D1656. Incombustible objects. D1841.3. Burning magically evaded.

D1566.2.1. *Saint's bachall quenches fire.* (Cf. D1277.) Irish: Plummer clxxv, Cross.

D1566.2.2. *Magic fan quenches fire.* (Cf. D1077.) Chinese: Werner 359, 362.

D1566.2.3. *Magic song quenches fire.* (Cf. D1275.) Icelandic: *Boberg.

D1566.2.4. *Runes quench fire* (D1266.1.) Icelandic: *Boberg.

D1566.2.5. *Ring makes boiling water cold.* (Cf. D1076.) India: Thompson-Balys.

D1566.2.6. *Salamander's blood quenches fire.* (Cf. D1016.) Jewish: Neuman.

D1566.2.7. *Magic girdle produces stream of water to quench fire.* (Cf. D1057.1.) Tuamotu: Stimson MS (z-G 13/221).

D1567. *Magic object produces fountain.* (Cf. D925.1.) Jewish: Neuman.

A941.5. Spring breaks forth through power of saint. D1549.5. Magic staff draws water from stone. D2151.6. Magic control of wells.

D1567.1. *Saint's blood produces fountain.* (Cf. D1003, V220.) Irish: Plummer cl, Cross; Icelandic: *Boberg.

D1567.2. *Saint's tears produce fountain.* (Cf. D1004.) Irish: Plummer cl, Cross; Jewish: Neuman.

A911. Bodies of water from tears. A1012.1. Flood from tears. F1051. Prodigious weeping. V462.3. Ascetic weeping.

D1567.3. *Water poured from saint's bell produces fountain.* (Cf. D1242.1.) Irish: Plummer cl.

F933.1.1. Spring bursts forth where saint spills water from his bell.

D1567.4. *Saint's bachall produces fountain.* (Cf. D1277.) *Loomis White Magic 37; Irish: Plummer cl, *Cross.

D1567.5. *Saint's crozier produces fountain.* (Cf. D1277.1.) Irish: Plummer cl, *Cross.

D1567.6. *Stroke of staff brings water from rock.* (Cf. D927.1, D1254.) *Saintyves Essais 139ff; Irish myth: Cross; Jewish: Neuman.

A941.3. Spring from striking earth with sword. A941.5.1. Spring breaks forth where saint smites rock. D1472.1.2. Man strikes stone: wine flows. D1472.1.23. Rock produces wine. F933.1. Miraculous spring bursts forth for holy person. F971.6. Flowers spring up when saint strikes ground.

D1567.7. *Fountain produced from drop of water.* (Cf. D1242.1.) Irish myth: Cross.

D1567.8. *Sign of cross brings water from rock.* (Cf. D1766.6.) Irish myth: Cross.

D1567.9. *Ring brings forth water from dry soil.* (Cf. D1076.) India: Thompson-Balys.

D1571. *Magic object revivifies trees.*

D1571.1. *Magic ashes revivify trees.* (Cf. D1271.1.) Japanese: Mitford 182.

E2. Dead tree comes to life.

D1571.2. *Presence of a person revivifies trees.* India: Thompson-Balys.

D1571.3. *Reading from a book makes fallen tree stand up.* Chinese: Graham.

D1572. *Magic smoke carries power of saint.* (Cf. D1271, V220.) Irish: Plummer clxvi, Cross.

D1573. *Charms to make butter come.* (Cf. D1273, D2084.2.5.) Kittredge Witchcraft 169, 487f. nn. 46, 47; Irish myth: Cross; England, Scotland: *Baughman.

D1573.1. *Much butter made from little milk by power of saint.* Irish myth: *Cross.

D1036. Magic dairy products. D2106. Magic multiplication of objects by saints.

D1574. *Line drawn by saint's bachall separates calves from their mothers.* (Cf. D1272.1, D1277.) Irish: Plummer clxxv, *Cross.

D1575. *Magic object does not awaken sleepers.*

D1575.1. *Hand-of-glory does not awaken sleepers.* The hand is lighted as a candle. See references for D1162.2.1.

D1576. *Magic object causes tree to spring up.*

D1576.1. *Magic song causes tree to rise to sky.* Has moon and Great Bear in its branches. (Cf. D1275.) Finnish: Kalevala rune 10.

A652. World-tree. A714.2. Sun and moon placed in top of tree. A771. Origin of Great Bear. D482. Transformation: stretching tree. A tree magically shoots upward.

D1577. *Charm renders magic efficacious.*

D1577.1. *Charm renders medicinal herbs efficacious.* (Cf. D1273, D1500.) *Kittredge Witchcraft 31f., 386, 388, nn. *71, 90; England: Baughman.

D1577.2. *Charm renders amulet efficacious.* (Cf. D1070, D1273.) *Kittredge Witchcraft 31, 386f. n. 72; England: Baughman.

D1581. *Tasks performed by use of magic object.* *Types 576, 577; Christiansen 87; Chinese: Graham.

H970. Help in performing tasks.

D1582. *Climbing into air on magic rope.* (Cf. D1203.) *BP II 539.

D1583. *Magic carving knife serves twenty-four men at meat simultaneously.* (Cf. D1173.) English: Child I 266.

D1584. *Magic object induces dreams.*

D1812.3.3.6. Prophetic dream induced by eating meat of bull.

D1584.1. *Charm induces dreams.* Penzer VI 76ff.

D1585. *Magic object saves corpse from corruption.*

D1389.11. Leek put under the tongue of supposed dead person prevents him from harm by the burial. D2167. Corpse magically saved from corruption. T84.5.1. Ring of Fastrada.

D1585.1. *Magic pill saves corpse from corruption.* (Cf. D1243.) Chinese: Werner 266.

D1585.2. *Magic plant saves cut-off limbs from corruption.* (Cf. D965.) Icelandic: *Boberg.

D1586. *Magic object relieves from plague.* Irish myth: Cross.

D911.1.1. Magic virtue of nine waves. D1385. Magic object protects from evil spirits. D1502. Magic object cures particular diseases. D2162. Magic control of disease. F493. Spirit of plague. M356.2. Prophecy of a plague which can be prevented by fasting, etc. V73.1. Fast to prevent pestilence.

D1586.1. *Magic image of animal relieves from plague (of that animal).* (Cf. D1266.2, D1500.2.3.) Liebrecht Germania X (1865) 408, Zur Volkskunde 85 No. 9, 88 No. 2. — Hebrew: I Samuel 6:4—5, *Neuman.

D1586.2. *Prayer to Virgin protects against plague.* (Cf. V250.) Irish myth: Cross.

D1586.3. *Incense relieves from plague.* Jewish: Neuman.

D1587. *Magic object expels person from land.*

D1587.1. *Magic amulet expels person from land.* (Cf. D1070.) Africa (Hausa): Mischlich 179ff. No. 24.

D1588. *Magic object assures going to heaven.* Irish myth: Cross.

E754.3. Burial in certain ground assures going to heaven. Q172. Reward: admission to heaven.

D1588.1. *Magic brain assures heaven for man who dies upon it.* (Cf. D997.2.) Irish myth: Cross.

D1588.2. *Magic cowhide assures heaven for man who dies upon it.* (Cf. D1025.5.) Irish myth: Cross.

D1588.3. *Magic hymn assures heaven for person who sings it.* (Cf. D1275.3.) Irish myth: *Cross.

D1591. *Magic spell causes vessel to burst.* (Cf. D1273.) Irish myth: Cross.

D1592. *Magic object heats or cools water.* (Cf. D1382.)

D1592.1. *Magic ring cools boiling water.* (Cf. D1076.) India: Thompson-Balys.

D1594. *Magic object vitalizes.* (Cf. D445.) India: Thompson-Balys.

D1594.0.1. *Liver of deer vitalizes.* (Cf. D1015.4.) India: Thompson-Balys.

D1594.0.2. *Vivification by hitting with bone.* (Cf. D1013.) India: Thompson-Balys.

D1594.1. *Magic dust vitalizes seeds and they become insects.* (Cf. D935.1.) India: Thompson-Balys.

D1594.2. *God's blood vitalizes image.* (Cf. D1003.) India: Thompson-Balys.

D1594.3. *Bee in its belly vitalizes tiger.* India: Thompson-Balys.

D1594.4. *Blood of twelve buffaloes vitalizes tiger.* (Cf. D1016.) India: Thompson-Balys.

D1594.5. *Girl's blood vitalizes axe and it becomes a tiger.* (Cf. D444.) India: Thompson-Balys.

D1594.6. *Magic whistle gives life to cockroach.* (Cf. D1225.) India: Thompson-Balys.

D1595. *Magic object provides beautiful bride for hero.* India: Thompson-Balys.

D1595.1. *Image of love grants man wife.* (Cf. D1268.) Jewish: Neuman.

D1599. *Magic object performs services—miscellaneous.*

D1599.1. *Pillars dance when ogre plays guitar.* (Cf. D1234.) India: Thompson-Balys.

D1599.2. *Air made fragrant with odors of flowers by spell.* (Cf. D1273.) India: Thompson-Balys.

D1599.3. *Magic object multiplies objects.* (Cf. D2106.)

D1599.3.1. *Magic egg multiplies objects.* (Cf. D1024.) Chinese: Eberhard FFC CXX 104f.

D1599.4. *Magic object produces house.*

D1599.4.1. *Magic egg produces house.* (Cf. D1024.) Africa (Duala): Lederbogen Fable 66.

D1599.5. *Magic charm uproots mandrake.* (Cf. D1273.) Jewish: Neuman.

D1599.6. *Magic dew destroys enemy's books.* (Cf. D902.2.) Jewish: Neuman.

D1600—D1699. Characteristics of magic objects.

D1600—D1649. AUTOMATIC MAGIC OBJECTS

D1600. Automatic object.

D1313.6. Magic apple indicates road. Rolls ahead. D1314. Magic object indicates desired place. D1550. Magic object marvelously opens and closes. D1812.5.1.17.3. Roaring of shields as evil omen. D1620. Magic automata. D2091.12. Plants and animals magically caused to shriek. F931.4.2. Waves moan (shriek) during battle. F990. Inanimate objects act as if living.

D1601. *Object labors automatically.* Irish: Plummer clxxxvi, *Cross.

D1472. Food and drink from magic object. D1472.1.7. Magic table supplies food and drink. D1472.1.8. Magic tablecloth supplies food and drink. D1523. Magic self-moving vehicle.

D1601.1. *Magic calabash cooks and cares for child.* (Cf. D965.2.) Africa (Ekoi): Talbot 27.

D1601.2. *Self-growing and self-gathering corn.* (Cf. D965.8.) Irish myth: *Cross.

D1601.3. *Magic hat works independently.* (Cf. D1067.1.) Lkuñgen: Hill-Tout JAI XXXVII 342.

D1601.4. *Automatic weapon.* (Cf. D1081.) India: Thompson-Balys.

D1601.4.1. *Automatic sword.* (Cf. D1081, D1400.1.4.) MacCulloch Childhood 202; Icelandic: Boberg; Cape Verde Islands: Parsons MAFLS XV (1) 354.

D1601.4.2. *Automatic spear.* (Cf. D1084, D1400.1.7.) Irish myth: *Cross; India: Thompson-Balys.

D1601.4.2.1. *Spear rushes out of joking raja's hand and pierces his visitor's chest; it is hungry for blood and has had no food for twelve years.* India: Thompson-Balys.

D1601.5. *Automatic cudgel.* (Cf. D1094.) *Type 563; BP I 349ff.; Aarne JSFO XXVII 1—96 passim; India: Thompson-Balys.

D1601.5.1. *Stick turns into automatic magic sword.* (Cf. D1081.) India: Thompson-Balys.

D1601.5.2. *Automatic hammer kills enemy.* (Cf. D1209.4.) Africa (Fang): Trilles Proverbes 202.

D1601.6. *Oven heats without fire.* (Cf. D1161, D1649.5.) Fb "ovn" II 774a.

D1601.7. *Lamp (fire) lights itself.* (Cf. D1162, D1275, D1781.) Zs. f. Vksk. VI 70 (to Gonzenbach No. 28); Crane Italian Popular Tales No. 30; India: *Thompson-Balys, Tawney I 567; Africa (Angola): Chatelain 45.

H41.3. Test of king (pope): his candle lights itself.

D1601.8. *Razor whets itself.* (Cf. D1173.1) Africa (Angola): Chatelain 45.

D1601.9. *Household articles act at command.* (Cf. D1170.) Penzer IV 248.

D1601.9.1. *Automatic broom.* (Cf. D1209.8.) German: Grimm No. 42.

D1601.10. *Self-cooking vessel.* (Cf. D1171.) Philippine: Fansler MAFLS XII 196.

D1601.10.1. *Self-cooking pot.* (Cf. D1171.1.) *Type 565; BP II 438; India: Thompson-Balys; Africa (Basuto): Jacottet 220 No. 33.

D1651.3. Magic cooking-pot obeys only master.

D1601.10.2. *Magic cauldron boils a year.* (Cf. D1171.2.) Welsh: MacCulloch Celtic 110.

D1601.10.2.1. *Magic cauldron boils only enough of its contents to satisfy immediate need.* (Cf. D1171.2.) Irish myth: *Cross.

D1601.10.3. *Self-boiling kettle.* (Cf. D1171.3.) *Fb "gryde"; N. A. Indian: *Thompson Tales 349 n. 257; Eskimo (Greenland): Rink 118, 448, (Smith Sound): Kroeber JAFL XII 171.

D1601.11. *Self-sewing needle.* (Cf. D1181.) Fb "synål" III 710b; Köhler-Bolte I 187.

D1601.12. *Self-cutting shears.* (Cf. D1183.) Fb "saks" III 143a; Köhler-Bolte I 187. — Africa (Angola): Chatelain 45.

D1601.12.1. *Magic shears clip garments from air.* Fb "saks" III 143a.

D1601.13. *Self-tying thread.* (Cf. D1184.) Köhler-Bolte I 187.

D1601.13.1. *Self-weaving threads.* (Cf. D1184.) Africa (Bambara): Travélé 205ff. No. 65.

D1601.13.2. *Self-fastening line.* (Cf. D1272.1.) Eskimo (Greenland): Rasmussen III 216.

D1601.14. *Self-chopping axe.* (Cf. D1206.) Fb "økse" III 1171b, "redskab" III 30a; India: Thompson-Balys.

D1601.14.1. *Magic axe cuts thousands of trees at a single blow.* India: Thompson-Balys.

D1601.14.2. *Magic adze cuts down tree.* Marquesas: Handy 70.

D1601.14.3. *Magic axe cuts off enemy's head.* (Cf. D1080, D1402.) Philippine (Tinguian): Cole 65f., 75.

D1601.15. *Automatic shovel.* (Cf. D1205.) Fb "redskab" III 30a, "skovl" III 301b.

D1601.16. *Self-digging spade.* (Cf. D1205.1.) Fb "redskab" III 30a. — S.A. Indian (Toba): Métraux MAFLS XL 3.

D1601.16.1. *Self-digging hoe.* (Cf. D1204.) Africa (Hausa): Rattray I 74ff. No. 4, Best Black Folk Tales (New York, 1928) 23ff.; Chinese: Graham.

D1601.17. *Automatic whip.* (Cf. D1208.) Africa (Benga): Nassau No. 11, (Cameroon): Rosenhuber 52.

D1601.18. *Self-playing musical instruments.* (Cf. D1210.) Irish myth: *Cross; Africa (Basuto): Jacottet 176 No. 25.

D1601.18.0.1. *Magic musical instrument reproduces songs sung in heaven.* (Cf. D1210.) India: Thompson-Balys.

D1601.18.1. *Self-ringing bell.* (Cf. D1213.) Fb "kirkeklokke"; *Thompson CColl II 348, 358, 363. — English: Wells 97 (Chevalere Assigne), Child I 173, 231, III 235, 244, 519f.; Irish myth: *Cross; U.S.: Baughman.

D1311.12.1. Bell sounds to designate pope. D1314.4. Bell indicates place for settlement. D1317.7. Magic bell gives alarm. V222.6. Bell sounds at approach of saint.

D1601.18.1.1. *Cleric's tongueless bell rings.* Irish myth: Cross.

D1601.18.1.2. *Sounding bell silenced by a gesture by a saint.* *Loomis White Magic 53.

D1601.18.2. *Self-playing violin.* (Cf. D1233.) Type 577; Christiansen 87; Fb "spille" III 488a; *Loomis White Magic 52. — Breton: Sébillot Incidents s.v. "violon"; Jewish: Neuman.

D1601.18.3. *Self-beating drum.* (Cf. 1211.) Eskimo (Greenland): Holm 70; Africa (Fang): Trilles 249.

D1601.19. *Fetish-medicine automatically punishes.* (Cf. D1241.) Africa (Fang): Nassau 243 No. 9.

D1601.20. *Self-grinding millstone.* (Cf. D1262.) Africa (Gold Coast): Barker and Sinclair 81 No. 13.

D1601.21. *Self-grinding mill.* Grinds whatever owner wishes. (Cf. D1263, D1470.) Gering Festschrift für Eugen Mogk (1925) 37; Fb "kværn" II 345b; Irish myth: *Cross (D1601.27).

Z185. Mill turned by water of Grace of God as a symbol of a saint.

D1601.21.1. *Self-grinding salt-mill.* (Cf. D1263.) *Type 565; *BP II 439; Fb "kværn" II 345b, "salt" III 148b, "hav" I 565b; *Krappe Modern Language Review XIX (1924) 325—334.

A1115. Why the sea is salt. Magic salt mill is stolen by seacaptain, who takes it aboard and orders it to grind. It will stop only for its master; ship sinks and mill keeps grinding salt.

D1601.22. *Fetish clears forest.* (Cf. D1274.) Africa (Benga): Nassau 187 No. 24 version 2.

D1601.23. *Ale serves itself.* (Cf. D1045.1.) Icelandic: Boberg.

D1601.24. *Automatic fire tongs.* Scotland: Campbell-McKay No. 22.

D1601.25. *Self-cooking food.*

F989.22.2. Tiger lives on self-cooking food.

D1601.25.1. *Self-cooking fowls.* (Cf. D1032.) Africa (Hausa): Tremearne Hausa Superstitions and Customs (London, 1913) 424ff. No. 93.

D1601.25.2. *Self-cooking fish.* (Cf. D1032.1.) German: Grimm No. 42.

D1601.26. *Self-pouring horn.* (Cf. D1171.6.3.) Irish myth: Cross.

D1601.27. *Magic thorns make road through marsh.* (Cf. D976.) India: Thompson-Balys.

D1601.28. *Self-rocking chair.* North Carolina: Brown Collection I 640.

D1601.29. *Self-playing game-board.* (Cf. D1209.7.*) Icelandic: Boberg.

D1601.30. *Automatic arrows.* (Cf. D1092.) Icelandic: Boberg.

D1601.31. *Magic towel wipes person.* (Cf. D1051.) Cheremis: Sebeok-Nyerges.

D1601.32. *Letter delivers self.* (Cf. D1266.)

D1601.32.1. *Letter from captive prince asking for help flies through the air to addressee.* India: Thompson-Balys.

D1601.33. *Chariot collects flowers by itself.* (Cf. D1114.) India: Thompson-Balys.

D1601.34. *Self-serving spoon.* (Cf. D1177.) India: Thompson-Balys.

D1601.35. *Magic water bottle brings water.* (Cf. D1171.8.) Tonga: Gifford 178.

D1601.36. *Self-going shoes.* (Cf. D1065.2.) Chinese: Eberhard FFC CXX 230.

D1601.37. *Self-opening door.* (Cf. D1146.) Africa (Fang): Trilles 249.

D1602. *Self-returning magic object.* (Cf. D868.1.) *Plummer clxxxvi; Irish myth: *Cross.

D1686. Magic object departs and returns at formulistic command. K423. Stolen object magically returns to owner. V224. Miraculous replacement of objects (animals) for saint.

D1602.1. *Stones, being removed, return to their places.* (Cf. D931, D1401.5.) Irish: Plummer clvii, *Cross; England, Ireland: *Baughman.

D1641.2. Stones remove themselves. D2136.1. Rocks moved by magic.

D1602.2. *Felled tree raises itself again.* (Cf. D950.) Type 577; Christiansen 87. — India: Thompson-Balys; Cook Islands: Beckwith Myth 252, 269; Maori: ibid. 265; Quiché: Alexander Lat. Am. 172. Cf. Zulu: Callaway 146.

C43.3. Felled tree restored for failure to make proper offerings to tree spirit. C939.3. Felled tree (cut weeds) return to their places because of broken tabu. F970. Extraordinary behavior of trees and plants. H1115.1. Task: cutting down huge tree which magically regrows.

D1602.2.1. *Fallen trees upraised at saint's request.* *Loomis White Magic 49; Plummer cliii, *Cross.

D1602.2.2. *Chips from tree return to their places as cut.* (Cf. D950.) Irish myth: *Cross.

D1565.1. Magic feather causes chips from tree to return as cut.

D1602.3. *Self-returning robe.* (Cf. D1052.) Jewish: Neuman; N. A. Indian: Thompson Tales 303 n. 109; Eskimo (Greenland): Rink 277, Holm 94, (Mackenzie Area): Jenness 40.

D1602.4. *Self-returning moccasins.* (Cf. D1005.4.) N. A. Indian: Thompson Tales 303 n. 109i.

D1602.5. *Self-returning bangle.* (Cf. D1075.) Africa (Vai): Ellis 235 No. 36.

D1602.6. *Self-returning spear.* (Cf. D1084.) Irish myth: *Cross; Icelandic: Boberg; Gaster Thespis 158; Hindu: Keith 140; Africa (Duala): Lederbogen Märchen 138.

D1602.6.1. *Self-returning spear-head.* (Cf. D1084.1.) Irish myth: Cross; Welsh: MacCulloch Celtic 198f.

D1602.7. *Self-returning wheel.* (Cf. D1207.) Cherokee: Mooney JAFL I 103.

D1602.8. *Saint's bell when stolen miraculously returns.* (Cf. D1213.) Irish: Plummer clxxvii, Cross.

D1602.8.0.1. *Self-returning bell.* (Cf. D1213.) *Loomis White Magic 53; Irish myth: Cross.

D1602.8.1. *Stolen bell refuses to make a sound.* *Loomis White Magic 53.

D1602.9. *Saint's bachall when lost returns.* (Cf. D1277.) Irish: Plummer clxxv, Cross.

D1602.10. *Self-returning magic book.* (Cf. D1266.) *Fb "Cyprianus" I 166b; Kristensen Danske Sagn VI (1900) 97ff.; Irish myth: Cross.

D1602.11. *Self-returning magic coin.* Keeps coming back. (Cf. D1288.) *Type 745; *Fb "vekseldaler"; *Liebrecht Zur Volkskunde 89; Irish: O'Suilleabhain 38, Beal XXI 314; Lithuanian: Balys Index No. 3650.

N212. Money cannot be kept from where it is destined to go.

D1602.12. *Self-returning head.* When head is cut off it returns to proper place without harm to owner. (Cf. D992.) *Kittredge Gawain 147ff. — Irish myth: *Cross; India: *Thompson-Balys.

B11.5.5. Self-returning dragon's head. D1610.5. Speaking head. E783 Vital head. Retains life after being cut off. F531.1.2.3. Giant's self-returning head.

D1602.12.1. *Self-returning body.* India: Thompson-Balys.

E783.6. Vital body.

D1602.13. *Self-returning cruet.* (Cf. D1171.8.1.) Irish myth: Cross.

D1602.14. *Self-returning magic apple.* (Cf. D981.1.) Irish myth: Cross.

D1602.15. *Self-returning hammer.* (Cf. D1209.4.) Icelandic: Boberg (Mjöllnir).

D1602.16. *Arrow shot at bull returns to shooter.* (Cf. D1092.) Irish myth: Cross.

D1602.17. *Magic object when sold always returns to original owner.* (Cf. D1605, D1602.11.) Irish myth: Cross.

K252. Selling oneself and escaping. K366.1.3. Self-returning cow.

D1602.17.1. *Magic ring when sold returns to original owner.* (Cf. D1076.) India: Thompson-Balys.

D1602.18. *Magic object given away returns to giver.* S. A. Indian: Métraux RMLP XXXIII 178.

D1602.19. *Equipment of slain hunter returns alone.* (Cf. D1170.) Eskimo Greenland): Rink 262, Rasmussen I 131.

D1605. *Magic thieving object.* Steals for master. (Cf. D1602.17.)

K366. Theft by trickster's trained animal.

D1605.1. *Magic thieving pot.* Boy sells pot to neighbors and when they have put things into it the pot returns to the boy. (Cf. D1171.1.) Type 591.

D1605.2. *Magic bag sucks milk from cows.* It is commanded by a witch. (Cf. D1193, D2083.3.) Kittredge Witchcraft 165, 483 nn. 14—16. — England: Baughman.

K300. Thefts and cheats.

D1605.3. *Magic thieving glove.* (Cf. D1066.) Eskimo (Greenland): Holm 95, Rasmussen I 103.

D1606. *Magic objects automatically keep out of reach.* Eskimo (Greenland): Rink 264, (Central Eskimo): Boas RBAE VI 622, (Cumberland Sound): Boas BAM XV 183.

D1609. *Automatic magic objects—miscellaneous.*

D1609.1. *Drum flies about room.* (Cf. D1211.) Eskimo (Greenland): Rink 451, Rasmussen I 100.

D1609.2. *Self-generated flame.* (Cf. D1276.) Buddhist myth: Malalasekera II 502.

D1610. Magic speaking objects. *Günter 242 s.v. "redend"; *Fb "tale" III 766a; Jamaica: Beckwith MAFLS XVII 269 No. 81; Cape Verde Islands: Parsons MAFLS XV (1) 326 No. 111; Eskimo (Greenland): Rasmussen III 97, (West Hudson Bay): Boas BAM XV 313.

B210. Speaking animals. D1311.2. Mirror answers question. D1311.6. Sun answers questions. D1312. Magic object gives advice. D1316.3. Speaking spittle reveals truth. D1317.8. Magic dice give warning. D1318.2.1. Laughing (dead) fish reveals unjust judgment. D1318.7.0.1. Speaking flesh reveals murder.

D1610.0.1. *Magic powder makes objects speak what owner wants them to.* (Cf. D1246.) India: Thompson-Balys.

D1610.1. *Speaking sink-hole.* (Cf. D933.) Fb "grøft".

D1610.2. *Speaking tree.* (Cf. D950, D1317.20.) Köhler Aufsätze 19ff.; Irish myth: *Cross; Jewish: Neuman; India: *Thompson-Balys.

D1311.4. Oracular tree. D1313.4. Blinded trickster directed by tree. D1316.5.

Magic speaking reed (tree) betrays secret. E631.0.4. Speaking and bleeding trees. Reincarnated persons. E632. Reincarnation as musical instrument. A musical instrument made from the bones of a murdered person, or from a tree growing from the grave, speaks and tells of the crime. F811. Extraordinary tree.

D1610.2.0.1. *Tree asks to be shaken.* Fb "træ" III 867b, and references in D1658.1.5.

D1610.2.1. *Speaking oak.* (Cf. D950.2.) Greek: Fox 109 (oak at Dodona).

D1610.2.2. *Speaking bush.* (Cf. D964.) Moreno Esdras.

A182. God (angel) speaks to mortal.

D1610.3. *Speaking plant.* (Cf. D965, F815.) India: Thompson-Balys.

D1610.3.1. *Speaking gourd.* (Cf. D965.2.) Africa (Benga): Nassau 213 No. 33.

D1610.3.2. *Speaking bean.* (Cf. D983.1.) Breton: Sébillot Incidents s.v. "fève".

D1610.3.3. *Speaking pouka-herb.* India: Thompson-Balys.

D1610.3.4. *Speaking egg-plant.* (Cf. D983.5.) Africa (Luba): DeClerq Zs. f. Kolonialsprachen IV 226.

D1610.4. *Speaking flower.* (Cf. D975.) India: Thompson-Balys.

D1610.4.1. *Speaking lotus flower.* (Cf. D975.1.) India: Thompson-Balys.

D1610.5. *Speaking head.* (Cf. D992.) *Kittredge Gawain 177ff.; Breton: Sébillot Incidents s.v. "tête"; Icelandic: *Boberg (Mimir); Irish myth: *Cross; German: Grimm No. 42; India: *Thompson-Balys.

D1602.12. Self-returning head. D1615.2. Singing head. E545. The dead speak. E783. Vital head. F511.0.4. Man carries his head under his arm. N819.3.1. Helpful speaking skull.

D1610.5.1. *Magic speaking tongue.* Irish myth: Cross.

S163. Mutilation: cutting (tearing) out tongue.

D1610.6. *Speaking privates.* Man given advice by his private parts. (Cf. D998.) N. A. Indian: *Thompson Tales 296 n. 83a, (Calif.): Gayton and Newman 84.

D1312.1. Bodily members as advisers.

D1610.6.1. *Speaking vulva.* Man has power to make vulvas speak. This is used as a chastity test. *Taylor MLN XXXI (1916) 249 n. 2; Von der Hagen III *v, 17; Italian Novella: Rotunda.

H451. Talking private parts betray unchastity.

D1610.6.2. *Mentula loquens.* A man's member speaks and can be silenced only by his mother-in-law. N. A. Indian: *Thompson Tales 296 n. 83b.

D1610.6.3. *Speaking buttocks.* (Cf. D999, D1317.1.) N. A. Indian: *Thompson Tales 296 n. 83.

D1610.6.4. *Speaking excrements.* (Cf. D1022, D1026.) S. A. Indian (Mataco, Amazon, Guiana, Tembé): Métraux MAFLS XL 122; Africa (Nigeria): Herskovits JAFL XLIV 466 No. 7. See also many references to D1611.

D1312.1.1. Excrements as advisers.

D1610.7. *Speaking loin of goat meat.* (Cf. D1032.) Africa (Benga): Nassau 227 No. 34.

D1610.8. *Speaking ring.* (Cf. D1076.) Breton: Sébillot Incidents s.v. "bague"; English Romance: Bevis of Hampton, line 2320.

D1610.9. *Speaking weapon.* (Cf. D1080.)

D1610.9.1. *Speaking sword.* (Cf. D1081.) Irish myth: *Cross.
F408.1. Demon occupies (speaks from) lance (sword).

D1610.9.1.1. *Sword shrieks when it feels the bone.* Icelandic: Hrolfs saga Kraka 100, Boberg.
F995. Sword shrieks in battle.

D1610.9.2. *Speaking arrow* (Cf. D1092.) Hawaii: Dixon 75.

D1610.9.3. *Speaking spear.* (Cf. D1084.) Philippine (Tinguian): Cole 102.

D1610.10. *Speaking fruit.* (Cf. D981.)

D1610.10.1. *Speaking grapes.* (Cf. D981.8.) Jewish: Neuman.

D1610.10.2. *Speaking bananas.* (Cf. D981.13.) Easter Island: Métraux Ethnology 375.

D1610.10.3. *Speaking fig.* (Cf. D981.5.) Jewish: Neuman.

D1610.11. *Speaking ship.* (Cf. D1123.) Fb "skib" III 243a; Greek: Frazer Apollodorus I 109 n. 4; English: Child IV 376—80, V 275f.; Irish: O'Suilleabhain 33, Beal XXI 311.

D1610.12. *Speaking stove.* (Cf. D1161.) Fb "ovn" II 774a.

D1610.13. *Speaking dish.* (Cf. D1172.) English: Child I 126.

D1610.13.1. *Speaking kettle.* (Cf. D1171.3.) Eskimo (Greenland): Rasmussen III 75.

D1610.13.2. *Speaking jar.* (Cf. D1171.7.) Philippine (Tinguian): Cole 192.

D1610.14. *Speaking implement.*

D1610.14.1. *Speaking hoe.* (Cf. D1204.) Africa (Zulu): Callaway 363.

D1610.14.2. *Speaking axe.* (Cf. D1206.) Jewish: Neuman.

D1610.14.3. *Speaking hammer.* (Cf. D1209.4.) Jewish: Neuman.

D1610.15. *Speaking bell.* (Cf. D1213.)
F993. Sunken bell sounds.

D1610.15.1. *Church bell speaks.* (Cf. V115.) Fb "kirkeklokke" II 130a; *Sartori Das Buch von deutschen Glocken (Berlin, 1932).

D1610.15.2. *Saint's bell speaks.* Irish: Plummer clxxvi, Cross.

D1610.16. *Blood speaks.* (Cf. D1003, D1318.5.) *Chauvin V 13 No. 8.

D1610.16.1. *Speaking blood drops.* (Cf. D1003.) German: Grimm Nos. 56, 89.

D1610.17. *Speaking bed.* (Cf. D1154.1.) India: Thompson-Balys.
H411.10. Magic bed and pillows as chastity test. N617. Impostor accidentally gives king talking bed, which reveals his identity.

D1610.17.1. *Legs of bedstead talk.* (Cf. D1154.1.1.) India: *Thompson-Balys.
N454. Conversation of objects overheard: speaking bed-legs.

D1610.18. *Speaking rock (stone).* (Cf. D931.) Jewish: Neuman; India: *Thompson-Balys; Chinese: Graham.

D1610.19. *Earth speaks.* (Cf. D935, D1318.16.) Irish myth: *Cross.

D1610.19.1. *Speaking island.* (Cf. D936.) Marquesas: Handy 128.

D1610.20. *Speaking crozier.* (Cf. D1277.1.) Irish myth: Cross.

D1610.21. *Speaking image.* (Cf. D1266.)
D1311.7. Oracular image. V120. Images.

D1610.21.1. *Image of the Virgin Mary speaks.* (Cf. V250.) Irish myth: Cross.

D1610.21.2. *Speaking idol.* India: Thompson-Balys.

D1610.22. *Speaking nut.* (Cf. D985.) Jewish: Neuman.

D1610.23. *Speaking muirlan (ball).* (Cf. D1256.) Irish myth: Cross.

D1610.24. *Speaking armor.* (Cf. D1101.)

D1610.24.1. *Magic shield roars.* (Cf. D1101.1.) Irish myth: Cross.
D1317.13. Magic shield roars when bearer is in danger. D1549.10. Waves answer roar of shield. D1812.5.1.17.3. Roaring of shields as evil omen.

D1610.24.2. *Helmet shrieks.* (Cf. D1101.4.) Irish myth: *Cross.

D1610.25. *Magic drinking horn with a man's head speaks.* (Cf. D1171.6.3.) Icelandic: *Boberg.

D1610.26. *Speaking clothes.* (Cf. D1050.)

D1610.26.1. *Speaking cloak.* (Cf. D1053.) Icelandic: Boberg.

D1610.26.2. *Speaking hat.* (Cf. D1067.1.) Philippine (Tinguian): Cole 48.

D1610.27. *Speaking jewel.* (Cf. D1071.)

D1610.27.1. *Speaking necklace.* (Cf. D1073.) India: Thompson-Balys.

D1610.27.2. *Voice issues from ruby.* (Cf. D1071.) India: Thompson-Balys.

D1610.27.3. *Diamond speaks from inside statue.* (Cf. D1071.) Jewish: Neuman.

D1610.28. *Speaking ball of thread.* (Cf. D1256.) India: Thompson-Balys.

D1610.29. *Speaking eggs.* (Cf. D1024.) India: Thompson-Balys; Africa (Duala): Lederbogen Märchen 84.

D1610.30. *Speaking timber.* (Cf. D956.) Greek: Grote I 214, 229; Jewish: Neuman.

D1610.30.1. *Speaking house-post.* Tuamotu: Stimson MS (z-G. 13/276).

D1610.31. *Speaking food.* (Cf. D1030.) India: Thompson-Balys.

D1610.31.1. *Speaking porridge.* (Cf. D1033.) Chinese: Graham.

D1610.31.2. *Speaking bread.* (Cf. 1031.1.) German: Grimm No. 24.

D1610.32. *Transformed bird reveals its identity by speaking out.* (Cf. D150.) India: Thompson-Balys.

D1610.33. *Speaking cliffs* (Cf. D938, D932.8.) India: Thompson-Balys.

D1610.34. *Speaking musical instrument.* (Cf. D1210.)

D1610.34.1. *Fiddle made from wood secret has been confided to reveals it* (Cf. D1233.) India: Thompson-Balys.

D1610.34.2. *Speaking flute.* (Cf. D1223.1.) Philippine: Cole 152.

D1610.34.3. *Speaking Jew's harp.* (Cf. D1239.) Philippine: Cole 163.

D1610.35. *Speaking river.* (Cf. D915.) India: Thompson-Balys.

D1610.36. *Speaking water.* (Cf. D1242.1.) Jewish: Neuman.

D1611. *Magic object answers for fugitive.* Left behind to impersonate fugitive and delay pursuit. *Type 313; *Aarne Die Magische Flucht (FFC XCIII); *BP II 527; *Fb "spytte" III 515a; India: Thompson-Balys; Japanese: Ikeda; Indonesian: Dixon 85 n. *91, 225 n. 32; Melanesian, Maori: ibid. 85 n. 91; N. A. Indian: *Thompson Tales 331 n. 196.

D1658.3.4. Grateful objects help fugitive. K525. Escape by use of substituted object. The object is attacked rather than the intended victim. K643. Confederate sings and delays pursuers so that fugitive escapes. K1840. Deception by substitution. R121.2. Rescuer impersonates captive and deceives blind guardian while captive escapes. R220. Flights.

D1611.1. *Magic rosebush answers for fugitives.* (Cf. D965.3.) BP II 527.

D1611.2. *Magic hair answers for fugitive.* (Cf. D991.) *BP II 527; Africa (Kaffir): Theal 129ff.

D1611.3. *Magic cow-dung answers for fugitive.* (Cf. D1026.2.) BP II 527.

D1611.4. *Magic beans answer for fugitive.* (Cf. D983.1.) BP II 527.

D1611.5. *Magic spittle impersonates fugitives.* (Cf. D1001.) *BP II 527; *Fb "spytte" III 515a. — Jamaica: *Beckwith MAFLS XVII 263 No. 67; N. A. Indian: *Thompson Tales 331 n. 196a.

D1611.6. *Magic blood-drops impersonate fugitive.* (Cf. D1003.) Fb "blod" IV 47b.

D1611.7. *Magic clothes answer for fugitive.* (Cf. D1050.) BP II 527; Eskimo (Greenland): Holm 12.

D1611.8. *Magic cakes answer for fugitive.* (Cf. D1031.2.) BP II 527.

D1611.9. *Magic household articles answer for fugitive.* (Cf. D1170.) BP II 527.

D1611.10. *Magic awl answers for fugitive.* (Cf. D1187.) BP II 527.

D1611.11. *Magic doll answers for fugitive.* (Cf. D1268.) BP II 527; Eskimo (Greenland): Holm 33.

D1611.12. *Magic stick of wood answers for fugitive.* (Cf. D1254.) BP 527.

D1611.12.1. *Magic log answers for fugitive.* (Cf. D956.) Koryak: Jochelson JE VI 206.

D1611.13. *Magic louse answers for fugitive.* Indonesian: Dixon 229.

B100—B199. Magic animals.

D1611.14. *Magic apple answers for fugitives.* (Cf. D981.1.) MacCulloch Childhood 193; Hdwb. d. Märchens s. v. "Apfel" n. 23.

D1611.15. *Magic echo answers for fugitive.* Calif. Indian: Gayton and Newman 92.

D1611.16. *Magic writings on stone cause corpse to answer for absent man.* (Cf. D1266.1.) Icelandic: FSS 38, Boberg.

D1611.17. *Magic bone answers for fugitive.* (Cf. D1007.) Jewish: Neuman.

D1611.18. *Magic buckle answers for fugitive.* (Cf. D1070.) Eskimo (West Hudson Bay): Boas BAM XV 318.

D1612. *Tell-tale magic objects.*
B141.1. Bird gives warning.

D1612.1. *Magic objects betray fugitive.* Give alarm when fugitive escapes. Wesselski Theorie 34; N. A. Indian: *Thompson Tales 331 n. 196b.
D1317.7. Magic bell gives alarm. R220. Flights.

D1612.1.1. *Horns call out when girl tries to escape.* (Cf. D1011.1.) Africa (Basuto): Jacottet 160 No. 23.

D1612.1.2. *Banana tree tells who cut its branches.* (Cf. D950.) Easter Island: Métraux Ethnologie 364.

D1612.1.3. *Fetish betrays fugitive.* (Cf. D1241.) Africa (Fang): Trilles 160.

D1612.2. *Magic object compels fugitive to betray himself.*

D1612.2.1. *Magic ring compels would-be fugitive to keep calling out, "Here I am".* (Cf. D1076.) BP III 372.

D1612.3. *Hiding place speaks and betrays hider.* *Beckwith MAFLS XVII 247 No. 23.

D1612.4. *Magic object tells where it is hidden.* MacCulloch Childhood 195f.

D1612.4.1. *Magic cloth tells where it is hidden.* (Cf. D1051.) Africa (Ekoi): Talbot 226.

D1612.5. *Magic object raises alarm when stolen.* Icelandic: Boberg.

D1612.5.1. *Magic shirt tells owner when it is stolen.* (Cf. D1056.) *Beckwith MAFLS XVII 241 No. 15.

D1612.5.2. *Magic harp gives alarm when it is stolen.* (Cf. D1231.) Japanese: Anesaki 229.

D1612.6. *Magic object gives alarm when touched.*

D1612.6.1. *Singing tree when touched wakes master.* (Cf. D950, D1615.1.) India: Thompson-Balys.

D1612.6.2. *Arrows shake when master is disturbed.* (Cf. D1092.) Eskimo (Greenland): Rasmussen III 105.

D1613. *Magic object helps overawe captor.*

D1613.1. *Magic fish talk so that ogre thinks hero has many brothers with him.* (Cf. B175.) German New Guinea: Dixon 134.

D1615. *Magic singing object.*
D1275. Magic song. D1620.0.1.2. Automatic singing doll. F811.6. Tree with musical branches.

D1615.1. *Singing tree.* (Cf. D950.) *Type 707; *BP II 380ff.; Fb "træ" III 867a; Chauvin VII 98 No. 375; Irish: MacCulloch Celtic 120, *Cross.
H1333.1. Quest for singing tree.

D1615.2. *Magic musical branch.* (Cf. D954, F811.6.) Irish: MacCulloch Celtic 114f., *Cross.

D1351.2. Magic branch of peace. D1359.3.1.2. Magic musical branch soothes listeners. D1364.25.0.1. Musical branch causes magic sleep.

D1615.3. *Singing apple.* (Cf. D981.) *Köhler-Bolte I 143; Breton: Sébillot Incidents s.v. "pomme".

D1615.4. *Singing water.* (Cf. D1242.1.) *Type 707; *BP II 380; Köhler-Bolte I 118; Jewish: Neuman; India: Thompson-Balys.

H1321.5. Quest for singing water.

D1615.5. *Singing snowshoes.* (Cf. D1065.3.) Menomini: Skinner JAFL XXVII 98.

D1615.6. *Singing rice-pot.* (Cf. D1171.1.) Philippine: Fansler MAFLS XII 348.

D1615.7. *Singing head.* (Cf. D992.) Irish myth: *Cross.

D1610.5. Speaking head. E783. Vital head.

D1615.8. *Headless body sings.* Irish myth: Cross.

D1615.9. *Singing heavens and earth.* Jewish: Neuman.

A659.1. Music of spheres.

D1617. *Magic laughing object.*

D1617.1. *Magic laughing stone.* (Cf. D930.) Chinese: Graham.

D1618. *Magic weeping object.*

D1618.1. *Magic weeping waters.* (Cf. D910.) Jewish: Neuman.

D1618.2. *Magic weeping stone.* (Cf. D931.) Jewish: Neuman.

D1618.3. *Magic weeping altar.* (Cf. D1166.) Jewish: Neuman.

D1618.4. *Weapons weep as warning to master.* (Cf. D1080.) Philippine (Tinguian): Cole 43.

D1619. *Miscellaneous speaking objects.*

D1619.1. *Speaking beans rebuke wife for misdeed.* (Cf. D983.1.) Spanish: Boggs FFC XC 124 No. 1374A.

D1619.2. *Eaten object speaks from inside person's body.*

B171.1. Demi-coq crows in king's body when the king eats him. F915. Victim speaks from swallower's body.

D1619.2.1. *Eaten magic dog howls from eater's belly.* *Wesselski Theorie 34f; New Zealand: Dixon 86.

D1619.2.2. *Eaten goat bleats from eater's stomach.* (Cf. D1032.) Irish myth: *Cross.

D1619.3. *Fruits that laugh or cry.* Chauvin VII 56 No. 77.

D981. Magic fruit. F813. Extraordinary fruits.

D1620. Magic automata. Statues or images that act as if alive. (Cf. D1523.2.8.) **A. Chapuis and Ed. Gélis Le monde des automates (2 vols. Paris 1928); *E. Faral Recherches sur les sources latines des contes et romans courtois du moyen age (Paris, 1913) 328ff.; *M Hallauer Das wunderbare Element in den Chansons de Geste (Basel diss., 1918); *Dickson 193 n. 75, 197 n. 80; *Baum PMLA XXXIV 533; *Liebrecht 88; **Bruce Human Automata in Classical Tradition and Mediaeval Romance (MPh X 511); *Penzer III 56ff., 212 n. 1, IX 9 n., 149; *Reinhard PMLA XXXVIII 436 n. 41; Irish myth: *Cross.

A141.1. God makes automata and vivifies them. D435.1.1. Transformation: statue comes to life. D1268. Magic statue. D1311.7. Oracular image. D1311.7.1. Oracular artificial head. D1311.7.2. Oracular brazen lion. D1661.1. Talking statue, when destroyed, cannot be replaced for thirty thousand years. D2178. Objects produced by magic. F855.2. Statues animated by water or wind. F990. Inanimate objects act as if living. T376. Young man betrothed to statue.

D1620.0.1. *Automatic doll.* (Cf. D1268.) BP II 527. — Hindu: Tawney I 257.

D1620.0.1.1. *Automatic gold-spinning doll.* Italian: Basile introduction.

D1620.0.1.2. *Automatic singing doll.* (Cf. D1615.) Italian: Basile introduction.

D1620.1. *Automatic statue of man.* Icelandic: *Boberg; Jewish: Neuman; Chinese: Eberhard FFC CXX 230f.

D1620.1.1. *Automatic statue of trumpeter.* Jones PMLA XXIII 563.

D1317.9.1. Brass (copper) statue at city gates blows on trumpet at stranger's approach.

D1620.1.2. *Automatic statue of horseman.* Chauvin V 200 No. 117.

D1313.3. Copper horseman indicates route.

D1620.1.3. *Smith forges iron man, who helps him.* Fb "jærn" IV 249b.

D1620.1.4. *Statue of Virgin sews for suppliant.* Spanish: Boggs FFC XC 100 No. 849B.

D1620.1.5. *Magic statue of archer.*

N535. Treasure indicated by statue with inscription, "Dig here".

D1620.1.5.1. *Magic statue of archer put into action my picking up precious object from ground.* Oesterley No. 107.

D1620.1.6. *Magic statue of man labors for owner.* Chinese: Eberhard FFC CXX 236.

D1620.1.6.1. *Magic statue of man fights for master.* Jewish: Neuman; Hawaii: Beckwith Myth 428.

D1620.1.7. *Speaking statue of man.* (Cf. D1610.) Jewish: Neuman.

D1620.2. *Automatic statue of animal.* Jewish: Neuman; India: Thompson-Balys.

D1645.7. Self-luminous artificial boar. H326.1.1. Suitor test: constructing automatic peacock.

D1620.2.1. *Automatic statue of horse.* (Cf. D1626.1.) Chauvin V 200 No. 117; Jones PMLA XXIII 563; *Köhler-Bolte I 412. — India: Thompson-Balys.

D1620.2.2. *Automatic hen and chickens of gold.* Jones PMLA XXIII 563. — Italian: Basile introduction.

D1620.2.2.1. *Silver cock, sitting on a flower, crows.* India: Thompson-Balys.

D1620.2.3. *Deer of gold and jewels possessing life.* Penzer IX 9 n. 1, 28ff.

D1620.2.3.1. *Magic journey on back of flying golden deer.* (Cf. D1520.) India: Thompson-Balys.

D1620.2.4. *Automatic statue of lion.* Jewish: Gaster Exempla 209 No. 115, Neuman.

D1620.2.5. *Automatic figures on harp—birds, serpents, hounds.* Irish myth: *Cross.

D1620.2.6. *Automatic metal (jewel) fish.* India: *Thompson-Balys.

D1620.2.7. *Plough of gold and yoke of gold and pair of bullocks used by hero tills as much land as lies within a village boundary in one day.* India: Thompson-Balys.

D1620.2.8. *Automatic statue of dog.* Jewish: Neuman.

D1620.2.9. *Automatic brazen serpent.* Jewish: Neuman.

D1620.3. *Other automatic constructions.*

D1620.3.1. *Two automatic giants fight until separated.* India: Thompson-Balys.

D1620.3.2. *Magic carpenter constructs bed and stool that can become big or small, luxurious or otherwise.* India: Thompson-Balys.

D1621. *Image renders judgments.* *Chauvin VIII 191 No. 229.

D1311.7.1. Oracular artificial head. H251.1. Bocca della Verità. M0. Judgments and decrees.

D1622. *Image indicates favor to suppliant.* (Cf. D1639.3, V120.) *BP III 475.

D1622.1. *Crucifix bows as sign of favor.* Ward II 665 No. 24; *Pauli (ed. Bolte) No. 692; Alphabet No. 495; Loomis White Magic 124; English: Wells 177 (A Legend of the Crucifix); Spanish: Boggs FFC XC 100 No. 849A

D1622.2. *Image of Virgin bows to indicate favor.* Herbert III *26, 340; Crane Vitry 263 No. 296. — English: Child I 365b.

D1622.3. *Saint's image lets golden shoe (ring) fall as sign of favor to suppliant.* *Wesselski Erlesenes 64ff.; BP III 242.

D1623. *Image dresses self.* (Cf. D1268, V120.)

D1623.1. *Image of Virgin veils and unveils itself.* Ward II 616 No. 37; *Crane Miraculis 106 No. 43.

D1624. *Image bleeds.* Jewish: Neuman; India: Thompson-Balys; Eskimo (Greenland): Rink 459.

F991. Object bleeds. V120. Images.

D1624.1. *Image of Christ bleeds from thrown stone.* *Ward II 630 No. 24, 671; *Herbert III 364 No. 159; *Loomis White Magic 123f.

D1624.2. *Wounds of crucifix bleed.* Irish myth: Cross; Spanish Exempla: Keller.

V86. Sign of the Cross. V360. Christian traditions concerning Jews.

D1625. *Statue weeps.* *Loomis White Magic 124; Swiss: Jegerlehner Oberwallis 329 No. 41.

D1625.1. *Statue sheds tears of blood.* (Cf. D1624.) Jewish: Neuman.

D1626. *Image flies through air.* Jewish: Neuman.

D1118. Magic airships. D1118.1. Magic air-riding basket. D1520.19. Magic transportation by carpet. D1532. Magic object bears person aloft.

D1626.1. *Artificial flying horse.* (Cf. D1620.2.1.) *Jones PMLA XXIII 563; *Clouston Magical Elements in Squire's Tale (Chaucer Soc. Pub. 2d Ser. No. 26) 279ff. passim; Dickson 217; India: *Thompson-Balys.

B41.2. Flying horse. B45. Air-going elephant. B552. Man carried by birds. D1532. Magic object bears person aloft. D2135. Magic air journey. R215.3. Escape from execution on a flying wooden horse.

D1627. *Dancing automata.* (Cf. D1646.) *Liebrecht 90.

D1627.1. *Instrument's ornamental figures climb down and run about as harper plays.* Irish myth: *Cross.

D1628. *City populated by wooden automata.* Penzer III 58f., 281ff.

F760. Extraordinary cities.

D1631. *Images of animals ridden (driven).* Norse: MacCulloch Eddic 109 (Frey).

A136.1. Goddess rides boar.

D1632. *Images open and close eyes.* *Saintyves Les réliques et les images légendaires (Paris 1912) 84ff.; ibid. Les images qui ouvrent et ferment les yeux (Revue de psychothérapie XXV 316—324).

D1633. *Image eats or drinks.*

D1633.1. *Idol drinks up milk.* (Cf. D1268.) India: Thompson-Balys.

D1635. *Golem.* Automatic statue animated by insertion of written magic formula into an opening. *Penzer III 59; Jewish: Neuman.

D1639. *Automata: other motifs.*

D1639.1. *Automata as door-keepers.* Penzer IX 149; *Dickson 197 n. 84.

D1639.2. *Image of Virgin saves painter.* Stretches forth hand and keeps him from falling. Ward II 628 No. 17; *Wesselski Mönchslatein 162 No. 124; Spanish Exempla: Keller.

D1639.3. *Images at church turn backs as mark of disfavor.* Done when abandoned woman or merman enters. (Cf. B82, D1622.) English: Child I 231, 365a.

D1639.4. *Statue laughs and reveals crime.* *Bolte Reise der Söhne Giaffers 216; Penzer VII 211.

D1318.2.1. Laughing fish reveals unjust judgment. N456. Enigmatical laugh reveals secret knowledge.

D1639.5. *Calf of gold moves.* Irish myth: Cross.

D1639.6. *Carved image jumps at maker's command.* Easter Island: Métraux Ethnology 262.

D1640. Other automatic objects.

D1641. *Object removes itself.* Irish myth: Cross.

D1686. Magic object departs and returns at formulistic command. E631.0.1.2. Tablets made of trees from lovers' graves magically unite. N562. Treasure removes itself from time to time. V143.1. Saint's bones miraculously removed from reliquary broken in pillage.

D1641.1. *Fountain (well) removes itself.* (Cf. D925, D926, D927, D941.) Irish: Plummer cli, *Cross (D1641.1, D1641.13); Jewish: Neuman.

D1313.11. Magic fountain indicates road for saint by removing itself. D1420.2. Person follows magic receding well.

D1641.2. *Stones remove themselves.* (Cf. D931.) Fb "sten" III 553a; Irish:

O'Suilleabhain 85, Beal XXI 328, *Cross; England: *Baughman; Jewish: Neuman.

D1602.1. Stones, being removed, return to their places. D2136.1. Rocks moved by magic.

D1641.2.1. *Saint's flagstone follows him.* Irish myth: *Cross.

D1641.2.2. *Mountain moved by prayer so as to make room for church.* (Cf. D932.) Irish myth: Cross.

D1641.2.3. *Stone moves at cock-crow.* (Cf. E452, N555.1.) England: *Baughman.

D1641.2.4. *Stone moves at midnight.* England: *Baughman.

D1641.2.5. *Stones go down to stream to drink.* England: Baughman.

D1641.3. *Stove runs over hill.* (Cf. D1161.) Fb "ovn" II 774a.

D1641.4. *Forest cleared by magic.* (Cf. D950.) India: Thompson-Balys.

H1095. Task: felling a forest in one night.

D1641.5. *Muirlan (ball) removes itself.* (Cf. D1256.) Irish myth: Cross.

D1641.6. *Branch leaps from hand to hand.* (Cf. D954.) Irish myth: Cross.

D1641.7. *Severed head moves from place to place.* (Cf. D992.) Irish myth: Cross; Jewish: Neuman.

D1641.7.1. *Self-rolling head.* Jewish: Neuman.

R261.1. Pursuit by rolling head.

D1641.8. *Grave removes itself.* (Cf. D1299.2.) Irish myth: Cross.

D1641.9. *Magic cross removes itself.* (Cf. D1299.3.) Irish myth: Cross.

D1641.10. *Magic fire removes itself.* (Cf. D1271.) Irish myth: Cross.

D1641.11. *Sacred scroll returns to heaven.* (Cf. D1266.1, V151.) Irish myth: Cross.

D1641.11.1. *Magic book removes itself.* (Cf. D1266.) Irish myth: Cross.

F994.1. Books show sorrow for owner's death by falling from shelf.

D1641.12. *Lake removes itself.* (Cf. D921.) Irish myth: *Cross; Lithuanian: Balys Index No. 3605; Livonian: Loorits FFC LXVI 75 No. 243; Estonian: Aarne FFC XXV 135 No. 89.

D2136.4. Lake magically transported. F934.4. Lake disappears.

D1641.12.1. *Lake is drunk dry.* Irish myth: Cross.

D1641.13. *Coffin moves itself.* Chinese: Eberhard FFC CXX 122.

D1641.14. *Jewelry intended by groom for prospective bride strangely disappears and a slip of paper alone is left in box.* (Cf. D1071.) India: Thompson-Balys.

D1641.14.1. *Ruby shatters into half-dozen pieces when it is acquired by greedy lapidary.* India: Thompson-Balys.

D1641.15. *Lotus disappears whenever anyone tries to pluck it.* (Cf. D975.1.) India: Thompson-Balys.

D1641.16. *Bananas run and hide when stone is thrown at them.* (Cf. D981.13.) Easter Island: Métraux Ethnology 375.

D1642. *Self-folding object.*

D1642.1. *Self-folding bridge prevents pursuit.* (Cf. D1268.) Type 313.

D1643. *Object travels by itself.* (Cf. D1641.)

D1643.1. *Stick of fire comes to river bank of itself.* (Cf. D1271.) India: Thompson-Balys.

D1643.2. *Rock travels.* (Cf. D931) Jewish: Neuman; India: Thompson-Balys.

D1643.3. *Magic island moves about as owner wishes.* (Cf. D936.) Cook Islands: Beckwith Myth 467.

F737. Wandering island.

D1643.4. *Magic pipe travels about.* (Cf. D1224.) Hawaii: Beckwith Myth 540.

D1645. *Self-luminous objects.* Irish myth: *Cross.

A124. Luminous god. B19.4. Glowing animals. B721. Cat's luminous eye. D1009.2.2. Luminous tooth of saint. D1652.6. Ever-burning lamp. E421.3. Luminous ghosts. F541.1. Flashing eyes. F574. Luminous person.

D1645.1. *Incandescent jewel.* (Cf. D1071.) *Chauvin V 4 No. 443; *Penzer III 167; *Reinhard PMLA XXXVIII 434 n. 32; *Cosquin indiens 246ff.; Fb "edelsten"; *Boje 81; Irish myth: *Cross; Icelandic: *Boberg; Jewish: bin Gorion Born Judas[2] I 217, 375, Neuman; India: Thompson-Balys; Chinese: Werner 274.

A661.0.7. Self-illuminating precious stones in heaven. B722.3. Luminous jewel in animal's head. F162.0.1.2. Luminous precious stones in other-world dwelling. F826. Extraordinary jewels.

D1645.2. *Incandescent cup.* (Cf. D1171.6.) Irish myth: *Cross; Welsh: MacCulloch Celtic 203 (Grail).

D1645.3. *Magic castle shines from afar.* (Cf. D1131, F771.) Breton: Sébillot Incidents s.v. "château"; *Fb "slot" III 377a.

D1645.4. *Incandescent sword.* (Cf. D1081, D1645.8.4.) Malone PMLA XLIII 433; Irish myth: Cross.

H1337. Quest for sword of light.

D1645.5. *Magic dazzling shield.* (Cf. D1101.1.) Spanish: Boggs FFC XC 67 No. 508A*.

D1645.6. *Self-luminous feather.* (Cf. D1021.) Hdwb. d. Märchens s.v. "Baum bewacht".

D1645.7. *Self-luminous artificial boar.* (Cf. D1620.2.) Icelandic: MacCulloch Eddic 109.

D1645.8. *Magic flaming arms.* (Cf. D1080.) Irish myth: Cross.

D1645.8.1. *Magic flaming spear.* (Cf. D1084.) Irish myth: *Cross.

F834.3. Extraordinary gleaming spear.

D1645.8.1.1. *Flaming spear must be cooled in noxious blood.* Irish myth: *Cross.

D1003. Magic blood — human. D1084. Magic spear. F834.1. Remarkably hot spear must be kept in bath of blood (poison). F834.3. Extraordinary gleaming spear.

D1645.8.2. *Magic flaming shield.* (Cf. D1101.1.) Irish myth: Cross.

D1645.8.3. *Magic flaming lance.* (Cf. D1086, D1645.8.1.) Irish myth: Cross.

C835.2.1. Tabu: failing to make gift to magic lance. The lance kills offender.

D1645.8.4. *Magic flaming sword.* (Cf. D1081, D1645.4.) Irish myth: *Cross.

H1337. Quest for sword of light.

D1645.9. *Well shines at night.* (Cf. D926.) Irish myth: Cross.

D1645.10. *Man's body emits light.* Chinese: Graham.

D1645.11. *Extraordinary flower; rays of golden light fall from it.* (Cf. D975.) India: Thompson-Balys.

D1646. *Magic dancing object.* (Cf. D1627.)

D1646.1. *Dancing apple.* (Cf. D981.) *Köhler-Bolte I 118; cf. Type 707.

H1333.3.1.1. Quest for dancing apple.

D1646.2. *Dancing water.* (Cf. D1242.1.) *Köhler-Bolte I 143; cf. Type 707; Italian Novella: Rotunda.

H1321.4. Quest for dancing water.

D1646.3. *Dancing kettle.* (Cf. D1171.3.) Japanese: Mitford 175ff.

D1646.4. *Dancing stones.* (Cf. D931.) England, Wales: Baughman (D1641.2.5).

D1647. *Fountain magically dries up.* (Cf. D925.) Irish: Plummer cli, *Cross.

D927.5. Spring runs dry (as result of fratricide). D1641.13. Well removes itself.

D1647.1. *Water vanishes from water hole when man tries to drink.* Eskimo (Greenland): Rasmussen I 180.

D1648. *Magic object bows before certain person.*

D1648.1. *Tree bends to certain person.* (Cf. D950.) N. A. Indian (Seneca): Curtin-Hewitt RBAE XXXII 391 No. 70; India: Thompson-Balys; Philippine (Tinguian): Cole 100.

F979.16. Magic tree will allow person to take only two of its fruits. H31.12. Only one man is able to pluck fruits from tree. H71.10.1. Tree bows before prince.

D1648.1.1. *Tree bends only to heroine.* *Type 511; India: Thompson-Balys.

D1648.1.2. *Tree (forest) bows down to holy person (saint).* Dh II 30ff.; Irish: *Cross, O'Suilleabhain 108, Beal XXI 334; Spanish Exempla: Keller.

V222. Miraculous manifestation acclaims saint.

D1648.1.2.1. *Tree bows to help Virgin Mary in childbirth.* (Cf. V250.) *Dh II 10; Irish: O'Suilleabhain 1(a), Beal XXI 304.

D1648.1.2.2. *Twig of a tree bows down and releases a bag with relics when the man makes a promise.* *Loomis White Magic 129f.

D1648.2. *Flower bends only to certain person.* (Cf. D975.) India: Thompson-Balys.

D1648.3. *Stones prostrate themselves before certain persons.* (Cf. D931.) Jewish: Neuman.

D1649. *Miscellaneous automatic objects.*

D1649.1. *Magic object keeps falling down.*
Q501.1. Punishment of Sisyphus.

D1649.1.1. *Magic elk's head keeps falling down.* (Cf. D1011.) N. A. Indian (Tillamook): Boas JAFL XI 135.

D1649.1.2. *Magic birds keep falling off perch.* *Type 313; Thompson River: Thompson CColl II 372.

D1649.2. *Magic object comes at owner's call.* (Cf. D1651.) Irish myth: Cross.
D1420. Magic object draws person (thing) to it.

D1649.2.1. *Harp comes at owner's call.* (Cf. D1231.) Irish myth: *Cross.
D1651.7.1. Magic harp plays only for owner.

D1649.3. *Stones for heating water heated automatically in other world.* (Cf. D931.) Irish myth: *Cross.

D1649.4. *Dung and wood burst into flames of their own accord.* (Cf. D956, D1026.) India: Thompson-Balys.

D1649.5. *Magic crystals automatically heat for cooking.* (Cf. D1601.6.) Buddhist myth: Malalasekera I 972.

D1649.6. *Objects rebel against their owners.* American Indian (Maya, Andes, Chiriguano): Métraux BBAE CXLIII (3) 484.

D1649.7. *Magic wood stick makes noise at night.* (Cf. D956.) Chinese: Eberhard FFC CXX 151.

D1650. Other characteristics of magic objects.
D481. Transformation: stretching cliff. D482. Transformation: stretching tree. D491. Compressible objects. D631.3. Size of object changed at will. D771. Disenchantment by use of magic object. E64. Resuscitation by magic object. E80. Water of life. Resuscitation by water. E100. Resuscitation by medicines.

D1651. *Magic object obeys master alone.* *Type 565; Penzer III 40. — Jewish: bin Gorion Born Judas[2] III 21, *Neuman; N. A. Indian (Micmac): Rand 34 No. 6, (Iroquois): Smith RBAE II 95, (Thompson River): Teit MAFLS VI 31, (Seneca): Curtin-Hewitt RBAE XXXII 264 No. 50.
A1115. Magic salt mill will stop only for its master. D445.1. Image of horse will be vivified only for one person. D1648.1.1. Tree bends only to heroine. H31. Recognition by unique ability. H41.9. Seat in which only fated king can sit. Z300. Unique exceptions.

D1651.1. *Only master is able to bend bow.* (Cf. D1091.) Greek: Fox 139 (Odysseus.)
D1654.4.1. Sword can be moved only by right persons. D1654.4.2. Arrow can be moved only by master. H31.2. Recognition by unique ability to bend bow Z310. Unique vulnerability.

D1651.1.1. *Spear can be wielded by only one person.* (Cf. D1084.) Irish myth: Cross.

D1651.2. *Magic cudgel works only for master.* (Cf. D1094.) *Type 563; *BP I 349ff.; *Aarne JSFO XXVII 1—96 passim; French Canadian: Barbeau JAFL XXIX 9.

D1651.3. *Magic cooking-pot obeys only master.* (Cf. D1601.10.1, D1171.1.) *Type 565; *BP II 438ff.; Lithuanian: Balys Index No. *568.
C916.3. Magic porridge-pot keeps cooking.

D1651.4. *Inexhaustible pitcher stops pouring only at owner's command.* (Cf. D1171.4, D1652.) Penzer V 3 n. 1.

D1651.5. *Dead beggar's stick will not stay still until back in beggar's service.* (Cf. D1254.) Fb "kjæp".

D1651.6. *Oracular image refuses information except to hero.* (Cf. D1311.7.) Dickson 194.

D1651.7. *Magic musical instrument plays only for owner.* (Cf. D1210.) Africa (Basuto): Jacottet 176 No. 25.

D1651.7.1. *Magic harp plays only for owner.* (Cf. D1231.) Irish myth: *Cross.

D1649.2.1. Harp comes at owner's call.

D1651.7.2. *Magic wishing-drum works only for owner.* (Cf. D1211.) Africa (Benga): Nassau 113 No. 11.

D1651.7.3. *Magic flageolet stolen but loses its magic power.* (Cf. D1224.1.) Spanish: Boggs FFC XC 75 No. 594*.

D1651.8. *Door will open only for hero.* (Cf. D1146.) India: Thompson-Balys.

D1651.9. *Bonds cannot be loosed save by man who tied them.* Irish myth: Cross.

D1651.9.1. *Bonds can be loosed only by comrades of man who tied them.* Irish myth: Cross.

D1651.10. *Apple (or ball) containing man's soul can be split only by man's own sword.* (Cf. D981.1.) Irish myth: Cross.

E711. Soul kept in object.

D1651.11. *Stolen gun works only for master.* (Cf. D838, D1096.1.) India: Thompson-Balys.

D1651.12. *Box can be opened only by right person.* (Cf. D1170.) India: Thompson-Balys.

D1651.13. *Jewel responds to owner's voice.* (Cf. D1070.) India: Thompson-Balys.

D1651.14. *Magic clock flies only at owner's command.* Easter Island: Métraux Ethnology 367.

D1652. *Inexhaustible object.* Keeps magically renewing itself or expanding. Breton: Sébillot Incidents s.v. "inépuisables".

D1451. Inexhaustible purse furnishes money. D1451.1. Inexhaustible pocket furnishes money. D1451.2. Inexhaustible bag furnishes money. D1470.2.3. Horn of plenty. D2100.1. Inexhaustible treasure.

D1652.0.1. *Magic object causes thing to become inexhaustible.* Chinese: Eberhard FFC CXX 107.

D1652.1. *Inexhaustible food.* (Cf. D1030, and in general D1470—D1499.) Fb "tønde" III 934b; Irish: *Cross, Plummer clxxxiv; India: *Thompson-Balys; Japanese: Anesaki 315; Java: Dixon 209; Philippine: ibid. 221ff.; Melanesia: ibid. 224 n. 28; N. A. Indian: *Thompson Tales 335 n. 210, (Calif.): Gayton and Newman 70, 100.

A1420.5. After Fall first parents fed and clothed from one palmtree. B101.4. Magic bird produces unlimited food. D1470.2.1. Provisions received from magic tree. D1470.2.2. Supplies received from magic box. D1472. Food and drink from magic objects. D1982.4. Food and drink appear and disappear in otherworld. D2105. Provisions magically furnished. E251.3.1.1. Ghosts toast girl daily in oven and devour her flesh. F531.5.6.2. Giant's present: magic loaf producing inexhaustible harvest. K81.3. Deceptive eating contest: inexhaustible food.

D1652.1.0.1. *Miraculous increasing of small quantity of victuals or drinks to feed a great number of people.* *Loomis White Magic 86.

D1652.1.1. *Inexhaustible bread.* (Cf. D1031.1.) *Saintyves Ēssais 231ff.; *Fb "brød" IV 74b; Breton: Sébillot Incidents s.v. "pain"; England: Baughman; Jewish: Neuman; India: Thompson-Balys. Cf. Mark 6:41ff.

D1472.1.22.1. Saint's inexhaustible sack of wheat. V412.2. The more bread (flour) the monks gave to the poor the more God places in their bins.

D1652.1.2. *Cake magically increases.* (Cf. D1031.2.) Type 751.

D1652.1.3. *Inexhaustible grain.* India: *Thompson-Balys.

D1652.1.3.1. *Inexhaustible rice.* Rice cooked from a single kernel. (Cf. D1033.1.) Chinese: Graham; Indonesian: DeVries' list No. 206.

D1652.1.3.2. *Inexhaustible corn.* (Cf. D965.8.) Jewish: Neuman.

D1652.1.3.3. *Inexhaustible wheat.* (Cf. D1033.2.) Irish myth: Cross.

D1472.1.22.2. Saint's inexhaustible sack of wheat.

D1652.1.4. *Ever-renewing cheese.* (Cf. D1036.1.) Swiss: Jegerlehner Oberwallis 318 No. 3, 321 No. 59.

D1652.1.5. *Inexhaustible chestnut.* (Cf. D1035.1.) N. A. Indian (Seneca): Curtin-Hewitt RBAE XXXII 148, 187, 199, 503.

D1652.1.6. *Inexhaustible coconut.* (Cf. D1035.2.) Leper's Island: Dixon 127.

D1652.1.7. *Inexhaustible fruit.*

D1652.1.7.1. *Inexhaustible apple.* (Cf. D981.1.) Irish myth: *Cross.

D1652.1.7.2. *Magic banana skin always full of fruit.* Hawaii: Beckwith Myth 493.

D1652.1.8. *Magic pill on which one feeds self for years.* (Cf. D1243.) *Chauvin VIII 133 No. 126.

D1652.1.9. *Inexhaustible meat.* (Cf. D1032.) India: Thompson-Balys.

F348.13. Mortal not to tell secret of gift of inexhaustible meat.

D1652.1.9.1. *Inexhaustible pig.* (Cf. B184.3.) Irish myth: *Cross.

E155.5. Slain pigs revive nightly.

D1652.1.9.1.1. *Inexhaustible boar's flesh.* Danish: Grundtvig Gamle danske Minder I (1854) No. 248; Icelandic: MacCulloch Eddic 313, Boberg.

D1652.1.9.2. *Inexhaustible sheep.* Jewish: Neuman.

D1652.1.10. *Inexhaustible fish.* Irish myth: Cross; Hawaii: Beckwith Myth 20.

B175. Magic fish.

D1652.1.10.1. *Loaves and fishes, eaten at night, restored next morning through power of saint.* Irish myth: Cross.

D2106. Magic multiplication of objects by saint. E155.5.1. Calf, slain at night, alive next day through power of saint. F243.4. Fairy food undiminished when eaten. V411.6. Food given away by saint miraculously restored.

D1652.2. *Inexhaustible drink.* (Cf. D1040, D1472.1.16.) *Fb "drikke". — Swiss: Jegerlehner Oberwallis 310 No. 30; India: *Thompson-Balys.

D1652.3. *Inexhaustible milk.* (Cf. D1018.) India: Thompson-Balys.

D1652.3.1. *Cow with inexhaustible milk.* Irish myth: *Cross; India: Thompson-Balys.

B109.4.3. Cow gives milk without cessation. B182.1. Magic cow gives red milk. B184.2. Magic cow (ox, bull). B251.2.10. Cow gives 12 measures of milk for the twelve Apostles of Ireland. B597. Cow gives marvelous supply of milk through virtue of saint. C241.1. Boy tasted the milk of "cow of plenty" which was only for the use of the gods. C918.1. Marvelous cow offended disappears.

D1652.3.2. *Goat with inexhaustible milk.* Norse: MacCulloch Eddic 313f.

D1652.4. *Magic gun is always loaded.* (Cf. D1096.1.) Spanish: Boggs FFC XC 49 No. 330.

D1652.5. *Inexhaustible vessel.* (Cf. D1171.) *BP I 361; *Aarne JSFO XXVII 1—96 passim; Irish myth: *Cross; Icelandic: *Boberg; India: *Thompson-Balys. See also all references to motifs D1470—D1475, as indicated below.

A920.1.1. Inexhaustible buckets as source of lakes. D1472.1.9. Magic pot supplies food and drink. D1472.1.10. Magic coffee-pot supplies drink. D1472.1.11. Magic cauldron supplies food. D1472.1.12. Magic kettle supplies food. D1472.1.13. Magic pitcher supplies drink. D1472.1.14. Magic cup supplies drink. D1472.1.15. Magic tankard supplies drink. D1472.1.16. Magic glass supplies drink. D1472.1.17. Magic bottle supplies drink. D1472.1.18. Magic barrel supplies drink. D1472.1.19. Magic food-basket supplies food. K117. Alleged inexhaustible bottle sold.

D1652.5.1. *Magic goblet (cup) cannot be filled.* (Cf. D1171.6.2, D1472.1.14.) Irish myth: Cross; England: Baughman; India: Thompson-Balys.

D1652.5.2. *Inexhaustible barrel.* (Cf. D1171.9.) England, U.S.: *Baughman.

D1652.5.3. *Inexhaustible measure (for meal or flour).* Canada, Scotland, U.S.: *Baughman.

D1652.5.4. *Inexhaustible pitcher.* (Cf. D1171.4.) India: Thompson-Balys.

D1652.5.4.1. *Inexhaustible pitcher of milk.* India: Thompson-Balys.

D1652.5.5. *Inexhaustible vase of bonbons.* (Cf. D1171.7.) India: Thompson-Balys.

D1652.5.6. *Inexhaustible bowl.* (Cf. 1170.) Buddhist myth: Malalasekera I 1026; Korean: Zong in-Sob 43.

D1652.5.7. *Inexhaustible pot.* (Cf. D1171.1.) Buddhist myth: Malalasekera I 849, 969, II 656.

D1652.5.8. *Inexhaustible food basket.* (Cf. D1171.11.) Buddhist myth: Malalasekera II 414.

D1652.5.9. *Inexhaustible food bag.* (Cf. D1193.) Africa (Fang): Tessman 157f.

D1652.5.10. *Inexhaustible rice-stores.* (Cf. D1033.1.) Buddhist myth: Malalasekera II 934.

D1652.5.11. *Inexhaustible meal sack.* (Cf. D1193.) U.S.: *Baughman.

D1652.6. *Ever-burning lamp.* (Cf. D1162.1, D1645.) Chauvin V 4 No. 443; Jewish: Gaster Exempla 220 No. 163, *Neuman; Fb "lys" II 483a.

D1652.7. *Unfading garlands.* (Cf. D975.) Penzer I 100, II 22ff., IX 53 n. 2; Irish myth: Cross.

D1652.8. *Inexhaustible cloth.* (Cf. D1051, D1052, D1652.12.) Irish: Plummer clxxxiv, *Cross; Japanese: Anesaki 315.

D1652.9. *Monkey cut in two by magic sword becomes two monkeys.* (Cf. D1081.) India: Thompson-Balys.

D1652.10. *Inexhaustible fuel.* India: Thompson-Balys.

D1652.10.1. *Inexhaustible firewood.* (Cf. D1298.) Irish myth: *Cross.

D1652.11. *Ever-burning candle.* (Cf. D1162.2.) Irish myth: Cross; *Loomis White Magic 32f., 87.

D1652.12. *Mantle ever new.* (Cf. D1053.) Irish myth: *Cross.
F166.3.1. Otherworld clothing never wears out.

D1652.13. *Everlasting wine-odor.* (Cf. D1046.1.) Irish myth: Cross.

D1652.14. *Sheep with inexhaustible wool.* (Cf. B184.6, B412.) Irish myth: Cross.
H1022.4.2. Task: weaving mantle from wool of a single sheep.

D1652.15. *Inexhaustible well.* (Cf. D926.) Irish myth: Cross.

D1652.15.1. *Inexhaustible spring.* (Cf. D927.) Jewish: Neuman.

D1652.15.2. *Inexhaustible water-hole.* (Cf. D928.) Eskimo (Greenland): Rasmussen I 180.

D1652.16. *Lime (for building church) miraculously renewed by power of saint.* Irish myth. Cross.
V220. Saints.

D1652.17. *Inexhaustible horn.* (Cf. D1171.6.3.) Cox 473.

D1652.18. *Inexhaustible larder.* U.S.: Baughman.

D1652.19. *Inexhaustible human liver.* (Cf. D1003.) Greek: Grote I 74 (Prometheus).

D1652.20. *Inexhaustible sacrificial blood.* (Cf. D1003.) Jewish: Neuman.

D1653. *Infallible article.*
B121.1. Infallible hunting dog.

D1653.1. *Infallible weapon.* *Hdwb. d. Abergl. III 2.
D1923. Power to hit whatever one aims at.

D1653.1.1. *Infallible sword.* (Cf. D1081.) Penzer I 109 n. 1, VI 72 n. 1, VIII 154 n. 2; *Thien 30; *Fb "sværd" III 690a; Welsh: MacCulloch Celtic 191, 198; Irish myth: *Cross; Icelandic: *Boberg; Spanish: Boggs FFC XC 67 No. 508A*; French Canadian: Barbeau JAFL XXIX 10.

D1653.1.1.1. *Sword causes a man's death every time it is drawn.* Icelandic: MacCulloch Eddic 267 (Dainslef), 268 (Tyrfing), *Boberg.

D1653.1.2. *Unerring spear.* (Cf. D1084.) Irish myth: *Cross; Icelandic: *Boberg; Greek: Fox 72 (Procris); Hindu: Keith 140.

D1653.1.2.1. *Gloves make spear-cast infallible.* (Cf. D1066.) Irish myth: Cross.

D1653.1.3. *Infallible sling.* (Cf. D1087.) Irish: MacCulloch Celtic 90.

D1653.1.4. *Unerring bow. Always hits mark.* (Cf. D1091). Type 592.

D1653.1.5. *Unerring arrow.* (Cf. D1092.) Icelandic: Ánssaga Bogsveigis 327; Breton: Sébillot Incidents s.v. "flèches"; Greek: Fox 84, 131; India: *Thompson-Balys; Calif. Indian: Gayton and Newman 70.

D1653.1.6. *Unerring stone missile.* (Cf. D1093.) S. A. Indian (Fuegian): Alexander Lat. Am. 340.

D1653.1.7. *Infallible gun.* (Cf. D1096.1.) Types *304, *594; *Fb "skyde" III 345b, "bøsse" IV 86b; Breton: Sébillot Incidents s.v. "fusil".

D1653.1.8. *Magic mirror as infallible weapon.* (Cf. D1080, D1163.) Chinese: Werner 161.

D1653.1.9. *Infallible dagger.* (Cf. D1083.1.) Irish myth: *Cross.

D1653.2. *Infallible fish-hook.* (Cf. D1209.5.) Irish myth: Cross.

D1444. Magic object catches animal.

D1654. *Immovable object.* *Fb "tung" III 893a; *Irish myth: Cross.

H251.2.1. Stone cannot be moved by one who speaks falsehood. X514. Only usurers can carry the corpse of the usurer. It refuses to be moved by anyone else. X521. Only prostitutes can carry the corpse of a prostitute.

D1654.0.1. *Magic immovability of saints (or their possessions).* *Toldo Studien zur vgl. Littgsch. IV 83; Loomis White Magic 56f.; Irish myth: Cross.

D1654.0.2. *Magic stone, hitting object, renders it immovable.* (Cf. D931.) India: Thompson-Balys.

D1654.1. *Stone (rock) refuses to be moved.* (Cf. D931.) *Fb "sten" III 553a; Irish: Plummer clvii, Cross; England, Ireland, Wales: *Baughman; Jewish: Neuman; Aztec: Alexander Lat. Am. 118.

D1654.1.1. *Immovable stone moved by saint.* (Cf. D930.) Irish myth: Cross.

D2136.1. Rocks moved by magic.

D1654.1.1.1. *Stone rolls off well-top after saint has prayed.* India: Thompson-Balys.

D1654.2. *Immovable apples.* (Cf. C981.1.) Fb "æble" III 1135b.

D1654.3. *Indelible blood.* (Cf. D1003.) *Type 312; BP I 404ff.; *Fb "blod" IV 48b.

D1654.3.1. *Indelible mark.* *Loomis White Magic 119.

F552.2.1. Finger of saint makes indelible cross.

D1654.3.1.1. *Indelible writing: the scraped word found written as before.* (Cf. D1266.1.) *Loomis White Magic 85.

D1654.4. *Immovable weapon.*

D1651.1. Only master able to bend bow. F833.1.2. Sword so heavy that only its owner can lift it. F835.2. Iron club so heavy that five men hardly can lift it. H1558.8.1. Sword too heavy to lift against a friend.

D1654.4.1. *Sword can be moved only by right person.* (Cf. D1081.) *Fb "sværd" III 690b. — Icelandic: Boberg.

F624.9. Little girl moves enormous bow which nobody could ever move before. H31.1. Recognition by unique ability to dislodge sword. H1313. Quest for person who can withdraw sword.

D1654.4.1.1. *Sword can only be used by strong hero.* Icelandic: Boberg.

D1654.4.2. *Arrow can be moved only by owner.* (Cf. D1092.) Seneca: Curtin-Hewitt RBAE XXXII 318 No. 58, 514 No. 109.

D1654.4.3. *Lance imbedded in earth cannot be moved.* (Cf. D1086.) Irish myth: Cross.

D1654.4.4. *Magic spear cannot be pulled out of ground.* (Cf. D1084.) India: *Thompson-Balys; Eskimo (Greenland): Rink 136.

D1654.4.5. *Dagger sticks to killer's hand.* (Cf. D1083.1.) India: Thompson-Balys.

D1654.5. *Wagon refuses to move.* (Cf. D1113.) *Fb "vogn" III 1078a.; Irish myth: Cross.

D1317.10. Wagon refuses to move because ghost is sitting in it.

D1654.5.1. *Chariot refuses to move.* (Cf. D1114.) India: Thompson-Balys.

D1654.6. *Ship refuses to move.* (Cf. D1123.) Type 425; Tegethoff 13; *Fb "skib" III 242b; Greek: Frazer Apollodorus I 101 n. 3, 109 n. 4; India: *Thompson-Balys; Icelandic: Boberg.

D1121. Magic boat. D1318.10.1. Ship refuses to move with guilty man aboard. D1419.3. Magic object prevents ship from moving. D2072.0.3. Ship held back by magic. Q569.10. Magic boat keeps thief at sea until he promises to throw ill-got gains into sea.

D1654.7. *Statues that cannot be removed.* (Cf. D1268.) Basset RTP XXVI 22 and succeeding numbers.

D1654.8. *Picture that cannot be removed in ship.* (Cf. D1266.2, D1654.6.) *Fb "skib" III 242b, "tung" III 893a.

D1654.8.1. *Sacred image impossible to remove from the spot.* India: Thompson-Balys.

D1654.9. *Corpse in coffin refuses to be moved in wagon.* (Cf. D1654.5, E272.1, E411.0.3.) *Fb "ligkiste" II 421b, "tung" III 893a, "vogn" III 1078a, "hest" I 599b.; U.S.: Baughman; Icelandic: Boberg.

D1654.9.1. *Corpse cannot be moved.* Irish myth: Cross.

D1654.10. *Bell refuses to be moved.* (Cf. D1213.) Fb "tung" III 893a; Finnish-Swedish: Wessman 72 No. 607.

D1654.10.1. *Bell sunk in sea can be raised only under certain conditions.* Norlind Skattsägner 60; Finnish-Swedish: Wessman 73 No. 614; England: *Baughman.

F993. Sunken bell sounds.

D1654.11. *Paper in hand which none but king can remove.* (Cf. D1266.1.) Spanish: Boggs FFC XC 86 No. 754*B.

D1654.12. *Horse magically becomes immovable.* (Cf. B181.) Wesselski Bebel II 80 No. 179.

D1654.13. *Woman can be lifted only by her lover.* India: Thompson-Balys.

D1654.14. *Severed head cannot be moved from helmet.* (Cf. D992.) Irish myth: Cross.

D1654.15. *Door stuck by witchcraft so that it cannot be opened.* (Cf. D1146.) England, U.S.: *Baughman.

D1654.16. *Pot cannot be lifted.* (Cf. D1171.1.) India: Thompson-Balys.

D1654.17. *Throne of goddess' idol is lifted only after goat has been sacrificed.* (Cf. D1156.) India: Thompson-Balys.
V10. Religious sacrifices.

D1655. *Invisible objects.* (Cf. D1981.3; F235.1.) Jewish: Neuman.

D1655.1. *Invisible weapons.* (Cf. D1080.) Hindu: Keith 152.

D1655.1.1. *Invisible arrows.* (Cf. D1092.) Visible to one person alone. N. A. Indian: *Thompson Tales 356 n. 287b.

D1656. *Incombustible objects.* (Cf. D1841.3; D2158.2; F979.5.) Breton: Sébillot Incidents s.v. "incombustible".

D1656.1. *Incombustible book.* (Cf. D1266.) Swiss: Jegerlehner Oberwallis 297 No. 29.

D1656.2. *Incombustible house (dwelling).* (Cf. F222.1.1.) Irish myth: Cross.

D1657. *Untiring object.*

D1657.1. *Magic untiring breeches.* (Cf. D1055.) *Fb "bukser" IV 77b.

D1658. *Grateful objects.* *Type 480, 510, BP I 207 ff., *227; *Toldo Studien zur vgl. Littgsch. VIII 48ff., 60ff.
B350. Grateful animals. E341. The grateful dead. W27. Gratitude.

D1658.1. *Objects repay kindness.* Lithuanian: Balys Index No. *314C; India: Thompson-Balys.

D1658.1.1. *River grateful for being praised even when ugly.* (Cf. D915.) Sicilian: Gonzenbach I 99 No. 15.

D1658.1.2. *Figs grateful for being praised even when ill-tasting.* (Cf. D981.5.) Type 480; *Köhler-Bolte Zs. f. Vksk. VI 63 (to Gonzenbach No. 13).

D1658.1.3. *Bitter water grateful for being praised.* (Cf. D1242.1.) Type 480; *Köhler-Bolte Zs. f. Vksk. VI 63 (to Gonzenbach No. 13).

D1658.1.4. *Continually slamming doors grateful for being fastened.* (Cf. D1146.) Type 480; *Köhler-Bolte Zs. f. Vksk. VI 63 (to Gonzenbach No. 13).

D1658.1.5. *Apple-tree grateful for being shaken.* (Cf. D950, D1610.2.0.1.) *Type 480, 510; *BP I 208ff., 227; Fb "træ" III 867b; Hdwb. d. Märchens s.v. "Baum".

D1658.1.5.1. *Tree grateful for having boughs trimmed.* India: Thompson-Balys.

D1658.1.5.2. *Tree grateful for having milk poured on roots.* India: Thompson-Balys.

D1658.1.6. *River grateful for being given color.* Africa (Tim): Frobenius Atlantis XI 184ff. No. 7.

D1658.2. *Kinds of grateful objects.* (See also D1658.1.)

D1658.2.1. *Grateful stove.* (Cf. D1161.) BP I 227 n. 1.

D1658.2.2. *Grateful carpets.* (Cf. D1155.) BP I 227 n. 1.

D1658.2.3. *Grateful plant.* Japanese: Anesaki 337.

D1658.3. *Services of grateful objects.*

D1658.3.1. *Grateful objects give advice.* (Cf. D1312.) BP I 227.

D1658.3.2. *Grateful objects help in choice of caskets.* BP I 227.

D859.5. Magic object to be chosen from among identical worthless objects. H511.1. Three caskets. Princess offered to man who chooses correctly from three caskets.

D1658.3.3. *Grateful objects give helper gifts.* BP I 227.

D1658.3.4. *Grateful objects help fugitive.* (Cf. D1393, D1611.) BP I 227.

D1661. *Magic object cannot be replaced.*

D1661.1. *Talking statue, when destroyed, cannot be replaced for thirty thousand years.* (Cf. D1268, D1620.) Dickson 214.

D1662. *Magic object works by being stroked.*

D1662.1. *Magic ring works by being stroked.* (Cf. D1076.) *Type 560; Breton: Sébillot Incidents s.v. "bague"; India: *Thompson-Balys.

D1662.1.1. *Magic ring works by having sun's rays flash upon gem.* India: Thompson-Balys.

D1662.2. *Magic lamp works by being stroked.* (Cf. D1162.1.) *Type 561; *BP II 544f.

D1662.3. *Diamond works by being pressed.* (Cf. D1070.) French Canadian: Sister Marie Ursule.

D1663. *Magic object works in contrary fashions.* Irish myth: Cross.

D1324.1. Magic bag full at high tide, empty at ebb tide.

D1663.1. *Wands of life and death.* Pointed with one end, kill; with the other, resuscitate. (Cf. D1254.1, D1402.10.) MacCulloch Childhood 205; N. A. Indian (Bella Coola): Boas JE I 54, (Chilcotin): Farrand JE II 44 No. 30.

E11.1. Second blow resuscitates. First kills. E64.1.1. Staff of life and death. E82. Water of life and death.

D1663.1.1. *Magic club kills and revives.* (Cf. D1094.) Irish myth: Cross.

D1663.2. *Ointment cures left cheek, not right.* (Cf. D1244.) Chinese: Werner 281.

D1663.3. *Well of life and death.* Situated on one hand, kills; on the other, protects against disease. (Cf. E82.) Irish myth: Cross.

D926. Magic well. D1402. Magic object kills. D1500.2. Magic object wards off disease.

D1663.4. *Fountains poison and cure.* One, with bronze vessel, tastes sweet and poisons; other, with iron vessel, tastes bitter and cures. Irish myth: Cross.

D925. Magic fountain. D1400. Magic object overcomes person. F162.1.2.1. Sweet and bitter fountains in otherworld garden.

D1663.5. *Well rises or sinks to indicate long or short life.* (Cf. D926.) Irish myth: Cross.

D1310. Magic object gives supernatural information. E765. Life dependent on external object or event.

D1663.6. *Magic tree gives money to good brother, poisonous animals to bad.* (Cf. D950.) Chinese: Eberhard FFC CXX 46.

Q2. Kind and unkind.

D1664. *Summer and winter garden.* Garden which blooms in winter. (Cf. D961.) *BP II 232; Köhler-Bolte I 215f. — N. A. Indian (Tsimshian): Boas RBAE XXXI 182.

D2145. Magic control of seasons. D2145.1.1. Local winter. D2145.2.2. Fruit magically grows in winter. F162.1. Garden in otherworld. F172. No time, etc., in otherworld. G112. Giant's fields fertile; others arid. H352. Suitor test: to make garden bloom in winter. H1023.3. Task: bringing berries (fruit, roses) in winter.

D1665. *Food has taste of any dainty desired.* (Cf. D1030, D1359.4.) Irish: Plummer clxxxv, *Cross; Jewish: Neuman; Buddhist myth: Malalasekera II 824, 930.

D1665.1. *Drink has taste of any liquor desired.* (Cf. D1040.) Irish myth: *Cross.

D1665.2. *Cow whose milk "tastes of honey and intoxicating wine and the satisfaction of good food."* (Cf. B19.2, B182, F241.2.) Irish myth: *Cross.

D1665.3. *Fruit has any taste desired.* (Cf. D980.) Jewish: Neuman.

D1665.4. *Manna tastes bitter to gentiles.* (Cf. D1031.0.1.) Jewish: Neuman.

D1666. *Sword leaves no trace of blow behind it.* (Cf. D1081, D1564.7, F833.) Irish: MacCulloch Celtic 65, Cross.

D1667. *Magic garden grows at once.* (Cf. D961.) Africa (Benga): Nassau 216 No. 33.

F971.7. Sowing and reaping same day.

D1667.1. *Magic tree shoots forth leaf, flower, and fruit at once.* (Cf. D950.) Irish myth: Cross.

D1667.2. *Magic acorns grow at once.* (Cf. D985.4.) Irish myth: Cross.

D1667.3. *Million-fold rice which ripens in one night.* (Cf. D965.8.1.) India: Thompson-Balys.

D1667.4. *Garden that has not bloomed for twelve years does so when girl steps into it.* (Cf. D961.) India: Thompson-Balys.

D1668. *Magic tree continually in fruit.* (Cf. D950.) Irish: MacCulloch Celtic 120, *Cross.

D1671. *Silver in chain increases in fire.* (Cf. D1078.) English: Wells 97 (Chevalere Assigne).

D1672. *Unquenchable fire.* (Cf. D1271.) Fb "ild" II 10a; Jewish: *Neuman.

D1672.0.1. *Magic fire burns for seven years.* (Cf. D1271.) Irish myth: Cross; Jewish: Neuman.

D1672.1. *Flaming shield unquenchable.* (Cf. D1101.1.) Irish myth: Cross.

D1672.2. *Self-burning bush.* (Cf. D964.) Jewish: *Neuman.

D1673. *Magic staff blossoms.* (Cf. D1254.)

D1673.1. *Tree grows from stick saint has used and thrown aside.* (Cf. D956.) India: Thompson-Balys.

D1674. *Iron blessed by saint incapable of wounding.* (Cf. D1080, V220.) *Loomis White Magic 105; Irish: Plummer clxxxv, *Cross.

D1675. *Garden wall that cannot be overleapt.* Malone PMLA XLIII 401.

D1676. *Mill refuses to work on Sunday.* (Cf. D1263.) Irish: Plummer clxxxvi, *Cross.

D915.4.1. Sabbatical river. V71. Sabbath.

D1676.1. *Manna does not fall on Sabbath.* (Cf. D1031.0.1.) Jewish: Neuman.

D1677. *Mill refuses to work when saint is ill-treated.* (Cf. D1263.) Irish: Plummer clxxxvi, Cross.

D1678. *Magic book, once used, compels person to do evil.* (Cf. D1266.) *Fb "Cyprianus".

D1681. *Charm incorrectly uttered will not work.* Spanish: Boggs FFC XC 84 No. 746.

G224.1. Witch's charm opposite of Christian. Must be "Without God and Holy Mary" instead of "With God, etc."

D1682. *Magic jewel which outweighs many heavy objects in the scale.* (Cf. D1071.) *Hertz Abhandlungen 73ff.

D1683. *Hearth cleaned by angel always free of ashes.* (Cf. D1147, V230.) Irish myth: *Cross.

D1684. *Dye blessed by saint colors animals, trees.* (Cf. D1297, V220.) Irish myth: Cross.

D1685. *Interred body of saint performs signs and miracles.* Irish myth: *Cross; Icelandic: Boberg.

D990. Magic bodily members — human. D1500.1.6.1. Magic head (of saint) heals diseases. V220. Saints.

D1686. *Magic object departs and returns at formulistic command.* Irish myth: Cross.

D1273. Magic formula (charm). D1602. Self-returning magic object. D1641. Object removes itself. D1765. Magic results produced by command.

D1687. *Object magically becomes heavy.* *Loomis White Magic 49; India: Thompson-Balys.

D1688. *Marvelous post wears down at top instead of rotting from bottom.* (Cf. D956. D1250.) India: Thompson-Balys.

D1691. *Magic suspension of weight.* *Loomis White Magic 49.

D1691.1. *Huge load easily carried by a saint.* (Cf. V220.) *Loomis White Magic 48.

D1692. *Cloak (and shirt) fit person of any size.* (Cf. D1053, D1056.) Irish myth: *Cross.

D1693. *Magic rod swallows other rods.* (Cf. D1254.2.) Jewish: Neuman.

D1694. *Sword that cannot be magically dulled.* (See D2086.1.) Icelandic: Göngu-Hrólfs saga 354, Bósa saga p. lxvi, *Boberg.

D1700—D2199. MAGIC POWERS AND MANIFESTATIONS

D1700. **Magic powers.** *Kittredge Witchcraft passim; Fb "kunst" II 331; Penzer VIII 36ff., 46ff., 79, 100n.; E. E. Evans-Prichard Witchcraft, Oracles and Magic among the Azande (Oxford, 1937); M. Summers Witchcraft and Black Magic (London, 1946); *Arne Runeberg Witches, Demons and Fertility Magic (Helsinki, 1947); *E. M. Butler Ritual Magic (Cambridge, Eng., 1949); Loomis White Magic; *Tibbals Elements of Magic in the Romance of William of Palerne (MPh I (1903) 355ff.); *Easter A Study of Magic Elements in the Romans d'Aventure (Dissertation, Baltimore 1906). — Estonian: *Loorits Grundzüge; Japanese: Anesaki 274.

D630. Transformation and disenchantment at will. F600. Person with extraordinary powers. H1576. Tests of possession of magic powers.

D1710—D1799. Possession and means of employment of magic powers.

D1710. **Possession of magic powers.** (Cf. D800.) Hdwb. d. Märchens II "Gegenzauber"; Irish myth: *Cross.

D801. Ownership of magic object. H1023.2.0.2. Task: carrying water in sieve. Pious child able to do so.

D1711. *Magician.* (Cf. D1721.) *Type 325; Dickson 121 n. 64; *Finnur Jónsson "Um galdra, seið, seiðmenn og völur," þyjár ritgjörðir (København, 1892) 5—28; *Seligmann 6f.; *Penzer IV 39 n. 1, 46ff.; *Fb "klog mand" II 187; Malone PMLA XLIII 400. — Irish myth: *Cross; Icelandic: MacCulloch Eddic 299, *Boberg; Italian Novella: Rotunda; Livonian: Loorits FFC LXVI 57ff. Nos. 128—159; Lappish: Qvigstad FFC LX 50ff. Nos. 90—119; Jewish: Neuman; India: *Thompson-Balys; S. A. Indian (Toba): Métraux MAFLS XL 162.

A527.3. Culture hero as magician. A1459.3. Acquisition of sorcery. B191. Animal as magician. B191.3. Tiger as magician. D683. Transformation by magician. D801.1. Magic object possessed by sorcerer. D1810.0.2. Magic knowledge of magician. D1812.3.3.0.1. Druid interprets prophetic dream D1814.1. Advice from magician. D2091.14. Magician shoots an arrow of each finger against enemy. D2135.0.1. Levitation. Person able to raise self in the air. D2142.0.1. Magician controls winds. D2144.1.1. Porcupine as controller of cold. D2152.2. Magician able to cast mountains upon enemies. E121.7. Resuscitation by magician. F451.3.3. Dwarf as magician. F531.6.5. Giant as magician. F721.2.3. Sorcerer and books in mountain. Opens only for short periods. G200. Witch. G225. Witch's familiar spirit. H1277. Quest to confines of hell for blood of sorceress. J2411.4. Imitation of magician unsuccessful. L142.2. Pupil surpasses magician. N845. Magician as helper. R111.1.7. Rescue of princess (maiden) from magician. S212. Child sold to magician.

D1711.0.1. *Magician's apprentice.* India: Thompson-Balys.

L142.1. Pupil surpasses thieves in stealing.

D1711.0.2. *Magician keeps magic power in tumor in back.* India: Thompson-Balys.

D1711.0.3. *Means of becoming magician.* Eskimo (Greenland): Holm 92, 94.

D1711.1. *Biblical worthy as magician.*

D1711.1.1. *Solomon as master of magicians.* **G. Weil Biblische Legenden der Musselmänner (Frankfurt, 1845); *C. C. MacCown Journal of the Palestine Oriental Society II (1922) 1—24; **C. Singer Salomosagen in Deutschland (Zs. f. deutsches Altertum XXXV (1891) 177ff.); *E. A. W. Budge The Queen of Sheba (London, 1922); *M. D. Conway Solomon and Solomonic Literature (Chicago, 1900); St. John D. Seymour Tales of King Solomon (Oxford, 1924); *H. A. Winkler Salomo und die Karina: eine orientalische Legende von der Bezwingung einer Kindbettdämonin (Stuttgart, 1931); *Fb "Salomon" III 146b; Jewish: Neuman.

D1711.1.2. *Esau as magician.* Jewish: Neuman.

D1711.1.3. *Baalam as master of magicians.* Jewish: Neuman.

D1711.2. *Virgil as magician.* **D. Comparetti Virgilio nel medio evo[2] (Florence, 1896) (Eng. trans. by E. F. M. Benecke, London, 1895); *Chauvin VIII 188ff. No. 228; *Penzer I 24 n. 1; *C. G. Leland Unpublished Legends of Virgil (London, 1899); *Otto Söhring Romanische Forschungen XII (1900) 580ff.; *Hertel Verzauberte Oertlichkeiten; J. D. Bruce MPh X (1913) 511ff.; **John W. Spargo Virgil the Necromancer (Cambridge, Mass., 1934).

D1711.3. *Sun as magician.* Chinese: Werner 361.

D1711.4. *Druid as magician.* Irish myth: *Cross.

C999.1.1.1. Tabu imposed by druid. D1810.0.8. Magic knowledge of druid. D1816.5. Druid divines whereabouts of missing person. D1964.4. Magic sleep induced by druid. D1981.3. Magic invisibility of druids. D2091.8. Druids dry up water in enemy camp. D2141.0.8. Storms raised by druids. D2142.0.3. Druid controls winds. F389.5. Fairy defeated by druid's magic. H561.7. Druid as solver of riddles. H1573.1.3. Druid attempts to shake king's faith by magic manifestation. M301.3. Druids as prophets. M411.6. Druid's curse. P427. Druid. T281.1. Sex hospitality given to druid.

D1711.5. *Fairy as magician.* (Cf. F234.0.2.) Irish myth: Cross.

D1719.5. Magic power of fairy.

D1711.6. *God or demigod as magician.*

D1711.6.1. *Odin as magician.* Icelandic: MacCulloch Eddic 45ff., 296; Herrmann Saxo Gr. II 239ff., *Boberg.

D1711.6.2. *Aesculapius as magician.* Jewish: Neuman.

D1711.7. *King as magician.* Icelandic: *Boberg.

D1711.7.1. *Pharaoh as magician.* Jewish: Neuman.

D1711.8. *Strong man as magician.* Icelandic: *Boberg.

F610. Remarkably strong man.

D1711.9. *Dark-haired people (with bowed nose) as magicians.* Icelandic: Boberg.

D1711.10. *People of certain place as magicians.*

D1711.10.1. *Finns as magicians.* Icelandic: Herrmann Saxo II 372, *Boberg.

D1711.10.2. *People of Gestrikland (Sweden) as magicians.* Icelandic: Göngu-Hrólfs saga 240.

D1711.10.3. *Egyptians as magicians.* Jewish: Neuman.

D1711.10.4. *People of Palmyra as magicians.* Jewish: Neuman.

D1711.10.5. *Amonites as magicians.* Jewish: Neuman.

D1711.10.6. *Amalekites as magicians.* Jewish: Neuman.

D1711.11. *Family of magicians.*

D1711.11.1. *Baalam's family as magicians.* Jewish: Neuman.

D1711.12. *People who come on ship with sickness accused as magicians.* Icelandic: Flateyjarbók III 435, Boberg.

D1711.13. *Reptile-men cure snake bites, and can summon together snakes (or mice) and lead them away anywhere.* Lithuanian: Balys Index No. 3666.

D1712. *Soothsayer (diviner, oracle, etc.)* (Cf. M301.) *Kittredge Witchcraft 383ff. nn. 61, 62; Irish myth: *Cross; Icelandic: MacCulloch Eddic 299, *Boberg; England: Baughman; Estonian: Aarne FFC XXV 138 No. 104; Finnish: Aarne FFC XXXIII 48; Jewish: Neuman; India: *Thompson-Balys; Buddhist myth: Malalasekera II 349; Chinese: Eberhard FFC CXX 254; Africa (Angola): Chatelain 57 No. 2, 139 No. 13, (Congo): Weeks 202 No. 1.

A1501. Tribe's custom established by diviner. A1654.2. Origin of diviners. B154. Oracular animal. Animal acts as soothsayer. D1812.5.2.8. The auspicious day. M302.4. Horoscope taken by means of stars. P481. Astrologer.

D1712.0.1. *Astrologer-magician.* India: Thompson-Balys.

D1712.1. *Soothsayer at work by various methods of divination.* Lithuanian: Balys Index No. 3667; India: Thompson-Balys.

D1712.2. *Blind man as soothsayer.* Icelandic: Boberg.

D1712.3. *Interpreter of dreams.* Jewish: Neuman.

D1713. *Magic power of hermit (saint, yogi).* (Cf. P426.2.) **Loomis White Magic; *Plummer passim; Dickson 121 n. 66; Penzer VI 201ff., VII 73, 113f.; *Barry JAFL XXVIII 195; **Toldo Studien zur vgl. Littgsch. I-IX passim; Günter; Irish: *Cross, Beal. XXI 328, O'Suilleabhain 85; Spanish Exempla: Keller; Jewish: Neuman; India: *Thompson-Balys (D1711.14, D1711.16.); Buddhist myth: Malalasekera II 210, 286. See V220 for cross-references concerning magic powers of saints.

D2141.0.2. Storms raised by druids. D2161.5.1. Cure by holy man. M411.8.2. Hermit curses men who kill his pet bear and all the men die.

D1714. *Magic power of person without sin.* Irish myth: *Cross (D1716).

D1714.1. *Magic power of chaste woman.* Penzer I 166, III 171 n. 1; India: *Thompson-Balys.

B522.3. Lions do not harm chaste woman. D2061.2.5. Hunter reduced to ashes by power of heroine's chastity. H413. Special powers of chaste woman. T300. Chastity and celibacy.

D1714.1.1. *Chaste maiden at prayer vanishes from would-be ravisher's embrace.* Italian Novella: Rotunda.

Q550. Miraculous punishments.

D1715. *Magic power of dying man's words.* *Type 960; BP II 531; Krappe Science 216—217. — Icelandic: Völsunga saga ch. 33 (31).

D1812.2.4. Dying man's power of prophecy. J154. Wise words of dying father. J155.5. Wise words of dying woman (queen). M251. Dying man's promise will be kept. M258. Promise to dying man sacred. M411.3. Dying man's curse. P17.3. Dying king names successor. P401. Son insists on following father's trade. This has been kept secret at request of dying father who was unsuccessful. Son learns from mother.

D1715.1. *Magic last wish at death becomes a reality (reincarnation).* India: Thompson-Balys.

D1715.2. *Dying peasant summons greedy bishop for heavenly funeral; the bishop dies hearing the message.* Icelandic: Boberg.

D1715.3. *Dying man commands cloud to bear message to man's wife.* India: Thompson-Balys.

D1716. *Magic power of the infirm.*

D1716.1. *Magic power of the idiot.* Eskimo (Greenland): Rink 111.

D1716.2. *Magic power of the lame.* Eskimo (Greenland): Rasmussen III 99.

D1716.3. *Magic power of sterile woman.* Jewish: Neuman.

D1717. *Magic power of children.* Jewish: Neuman.

D1717.1. *Magic power of monster child.* *Type 708; U.S.: Baughman.

D1718. *Special location of magic powers.*

D1718.1. *Magic power contained in stick and water.* India: Thompson-Balys.

D1719. *Possession of magic powers—miscellaneous.*

D1719.1. *Contest in magic.* (Cf. H1573.3.) Type 325. — Irish myth: *Cross; Jewish: Neuman; India: *Thompson-Balys; N. A. Indian: *Thompson Tales 327 n. 182; Eskimo (Greenland): Thalbitzer 7, Rasmussen II 334; S. A. Indian (Toba): Métraux MAFLS XL 139, (Chiriguano): Métraux BBAE CXLIII 3 484.

D615. Transformation combat. L142.2. Pupil surpasses magician.

D1719.1.1. *Contest in magic between druid and saint.* Irish myth: *Cross.

D2076. Saint magically causes druids to bless instead of curse. M400.0.1. Cursing match. V229.6. Saint in conflict with druid.

D1719.1.2. *Contest between druid and fairy personage.* Irish myth: *Cross.

F389. Fairy defeated by druid's magic.

D1719.1.3. *Magic contest, magician and giant: magician would make a dog's tail crooked, the giant would straighten it — and so on, ad infinitum.* India: Thompson-Balys.

D2076. Saint magically causes druids to bless instead of curse.

D1719.1.4. *Contest between carpenter and son to race wooden horses they had both made.* India: Thompson-Balys.

D1719.2. *Magic wisdom possessed by wild man.* (Cf. F567.) Dickson 120 n. 62; *Handwb. d. Abergl. IX Nachträge 968f.

D1719.3. *Magic power of superhuman race.* Irish myth: *Cross.

A1611.5.4.3. Origin of the Tuatha Dé Danann. A1659.1. Origin of the Fomorians. D1810.0.7. Magic knowledge of superman.

D1719.4. *Magic wisdom possessed by extraordinary companion.* Irish myth: *Cross.

F601. Extraordinary companions.

D1719.5. *Magic power of fairy.* (Cf. A1611.10.1.) Irish myth: *Cross.

D1711.5. Fairy as magician.

D1719.6. *Magic power of holy cross.* (Cf. V86.) Irish myth: Cross.

D1766.6. Magic results from sign of the cross.

D1719.7. *Magic power of mermaid.* Irish myth: *Cross.

B81. Mermaid.

D1719.8. *Man has magic servants who plow for him; he swallows them each day and keeps them secret.* India: Thompson-Balys.

D1719.9. *Magic power at certain time.*

D1719.9.1. *Magic power only at night.* Jewish: Neuman.

D1719.9.2. *Magic power at Passover.* Jewish: Neuman.

D1719.10. *Magic power only under certain conditions.*

D1719.10.1. *Magic power only when magician's feet touch ground.* Jewish: Neuman.

D1833. Magic strength by touching earth.

D1719.11. *Limited amount of magic in world.*

D1719.11.1. *Only ten measures of magic allotted to world.* Jewish: Neuman.

D1720. Acquisition of magic powers. (Cf. D810.) Eskimo (Greenland): Rink 461, Rasmussen II 222, III 111.

A575. Departed deity grants requests to visitors. B165. Animal languages learned from animal. B217.3. Animal languages learned from ghosts (spirits). B311. Congenital helpful animals. Born at same time as master and (usually) by same magic means. B500. Magic power from animal. B560. Animals advise men. C423.1. Tabu: disclosing source of magic power. D1301. Magic object teaches animal language. D1302. Magic object teaches magic. D1312. Magic object gives advice. D1317. Magic object warns of danger. D1561. Magic object confers miraculous powers. D1810.0.1. Omniscience of a god. D1811.2. Magic wisdom received from supernatural being. D1812.2. Power of prophecy induced. D1815.0.1. Gift of tongues received from ghosts. D1821.6. Magic sight given to abandoned child. D1846.2. Invulnerability bestowed by many-headed monster. D1851.2. Immortality given by many-headed monster. D1903. Power of inducing love given by animals. D1983.1. Invisibility conferred by a god. S233. Children given in return for being taught music.

D1720.1. *Man given power of wishing.* Fb "ønske" III 1179a; Irish myth: Cross; Italian: Rotunda, Basile Pentamerone I No. 3; India: *Thompson-Balys; Eskimo (Greenland): Rink 453, Holm 25.

D1470.1. Magic wishing-object. D1761. Magic results produced by wishing. D2172.2. Magic gift: power to continue all day what one starts. D341. Fairies give fulfillment of wishes. G665. Vanquished ogre grants hero's three wishes. Q338. Immoderate request punished.

D1720.1.1. *Devil gives man power of wishing.* England: *Baughman.

D1720.2. *Man receives divine "possession" (becomes a diviner).* India: Thompson-Balys.

D1721. *Magic power from magician.* *Type 325; *Chauvin II 151 No. 11; *Fb. "sorte skole" III 469a. — Icelandic: MacCulloch Eddic 49, 296; English: Wells 43 (Arthour and Merlin); Lappish: Qvigstad FFC LX 49 No. 87; Jewish: Neuman; India: *Thompson-Balys; Chinese: Werner 383.

D1711. Magician. D1814.1. Advice from magician (fortune-teller, etc.). D1817.1. Druids magically detect crime. D2142.0.1.1. Witch sells power to control winds.

D1721.0.1. *Magic power from donning magician's clothes.* (Cf. D1052.) N. A. Indian (Seneca): Curtin-Hewitt RBAE XXXII 131 No. 20.

D1721.0.2. *Magic power obtained secretly from magician's friends.* India: Thompson-Balys.

D1721.1. *Magic power from devil.* Kittredge Witchcraft 45, 399 n. 175; Dickson 213 n. 145. — Spanish: Boggs FFC XC 47 No. 325*A.

D1810.2. Magic knowledge from devil. D2141.0.1. Storm from calling on evil spirit. D2141.0.3. Storms produced by devil. D2142.1.3. Wind raised by calling on devil G303. The devil. M211. Man sells soul to devil.

D1721.1.1. *Magic arts learned in hell.* Irish myth: *Cross (D1738).

D1721.1.2. *Magic power from demon.* Eskimo (Greenland): Rasmussen II 51.

D1721.1.3. *Spirit gives man the power of exorcising him out of anyone he possesses.* (Cf. D2176.) India: Thompson-Balys.

D1721.1.4. *Magic power from rakshasi.* India: Thompson-Balys.

D1721.2. *Magic power acquired by eating fish which have eaten dead magician's flesh.* India: Thompson-Balys.

D1721.3. *Magician blows magic into disciples' ears.* India: Thompson-Balys.

D1721.4. *Disciples drink magician's urine.* India: Thompson-Balys.

D1721.5. *Magician's disciples eat magic iron.* India: Thompson-Balys.

D1721.6. *Magician's disciples acquire magic powers by study.* India: Thompson-Balys.

D1722. *Magic power from saint.* (Cf. D1713, V223.4.1.) Irish: Plummer clxxxv, Cross.

D1722.1. *Magic power from prophet.* Jewish: Neuman.

D1723. *Magic power from fairy.* Type 403; Irish myth: Cross; Scotch: Macdougall and Calder 251; Italian: Basile Pentamerone. I No. 3, Rotunda.

D1810.1. Magic knowledge from queen of other world. D1812.1.1. Power of prophecy from fairy. D1983.2. Invisibility conferred by fairy. F305.1.1. Fairy mother bestows magic powers upon half-mortal son. F340. Gifts from fairies. F341. Fairies give fulfillment of wishes.

D1724. *Magic power from Death. Death as godfather.* (Cf. D1725.1.) *Type 332; *BP I 377ff. — Italian Novella: Rotunda.

D1825.3.1. Magic power of seeing Death at head or foot of bed and thus forecasting progress of sickness. D1851.2. Immortality gained from bargain with Death. Z111. Death personified.

D1725. *Magic power obtained from angels.* Jewish: Neuman, Penzer VI 63.

D1810.5. Magic knowledge from angel. V230. Angels. V232 Angel as helper.

D1725.1. *Magic power from Angel of Death* (Cf. 1724.). Jewish: Neuman.

D1726. *Magic power from deity.* Irish myth: Cross; Greek: Grote I 105; Italian Novella: Rotunda; Jewish: Neuman; India: Thompson-Balys.

D1812.1.2. Power of prophecy from God.

D1726.0.1. *Soothsaying learned from a god.* India: Thompson-Balys.

D1726.1. *Magic power from celestial maiden.* India: Thompson-Balys.

D1726.2. *Magic power from stone idol.* India: Thompson-Balys.

D1727. *Magic power learned from giant (as foster-father).* Icelandic: Bárdar saga Snæfellsáss ch. 2 (ed. Vigfússon 1860) 2, Boberg.

D1728. *Magic power from superhuman race.* (Cf. D1719.3.) Irish myth: *Cross.

D1731. *Magic power received in dream.* Dickson 188; Jewish: Neuman; Calif. Indian: Gayton and Newman 58; Eskimo (Greenland): Rasmussen I 134.

D1812.2.3. Future revealed in dream. D1813.1.1. Dream warns emperor of wife's unfaithfulness. D1816.1. Location of fountain revealed in dream.

D1731.1. *Song learned in dream.* (Cf. D1275.) See story of Caedmon in Bede's Ecclesiastical History, as well as numerous biblical stories of "inspiration"; *Kittredge Witchcraft 222, 529 n. 89. — Pawnee: Dorsey CI LIX 241ff. Nos. 77—116 passim.

D1810. Magic knowledge. F403.2.3.3. Spirits teach boy how to sing.

D1731.2. *Marvels seen in dreams.* Irish myth: *Cross.

D1812.3.3. Future revealed in dream. D1976.2. Future spouse met during magic sleep. K2035. Personifications (in dreams) advise opposed kings how each can overcome the other. V235.0.1. Mortal visited by angel in vision. V510. Religious visions.

D1731.2.1. *Fairy seen in dream.* (Cf. F471.2, K2035.) Irish myth: *Cross.

D1731.2.2. *All nature composed of food in vision.* (Cf. V514, X1503.) Irish myth: Cross.

D1731.3. *(Dream of) rock-casting contest.* (Cf. A966.1, D931.) Irish myth: *Cross.

D1732. *Magic power obtained by meditation.* Penzer VI 2.

D1733. *Acts producing magic power.*

D1733.1. *Magic power by jumping into fire.* Africa (Mpongwe): Nassau 76 No. 15.

D1733.2. *Magic power by crawling through ear of magic horse.* (Cf. B181.) Köhler-Bolte I 406.

D1733.3. *Magic power through ascetic practices.* Penzer IV 46, V 109; India: *Thompson-Balys.

V462. Asceticism.

D1733.3.1. *Magic power by fasting.* (Cf. G224.16, P623.) Kittredge Witchcraft 128, 450f. nn. 26—27 passim; Irish myth: *Cross; England: Baughman.

D1766.8. Magic results from fasting.

D1733.3.1.1. *Oracular twigs work only if man has fasted.* (Cf. D1311.4.0.1.) Irish myth: Cross.

D1733.4. *Magic power by sitting in certain seat.* Icelandic: *Boberg.

D1733.5. *Magic power from swooning.* Eskimo (Greenland): Rink 400.

D1733.6. *Magic power by magic songs.* Icelandic: MacCulloch Eddic 299.

D1734. *Magic powers from rubbing.* Eskimo (Greenland): Rink 219, 455.

D1734.1. *Magic power by rubbing talisman.* *Type 561.

D1735. *Magic powers from swallowing.*

D1735.1. *Magic powers from swallowing a straw.* Eskimo (Greenland): Rasmussen II 158.

D1735.2. *Language acquired by swallowing its written characters.* Jewish: Neuman.

D1735.3. *Magic powers from swallowing magic drink.* (Cf. D1040.) Eskimo (Greenland): Rink 453.

D1735.4. *Possession of magic knowledge and witchcraft from having eaten of father-of-man's corpse.* India: Thompson-Balys.

D1736. *Magic power from great piety.* India: Thompson-Balys.

D1736.1. *Magic power acquired by sacrificing.* (Cf. D1766.2.) India: Thompson-Balys.

D1737. *Magic power inherited.* Irish myth: Cross.

D1737.1. *Magic power from mother.* Irish myth: Cross; Icelandic: Corpus Poeticum Boreale I 93.

D1738. *Magic arts studied.* Jewish: Neuman; Chinese: Graham.

D1739. *Acquisition of magic power—miscellaneous.*

D1739.1. *Magic power from overheard talk of spirits.* Jewish: Neuman.
N950. Secrets overheard.

D1739.2. *Magic power from heavenly voice.* Jewish: Neuman.

D1740. Loss of magic power.

D1741. *Magic powers lost.*
D947. Magic power lost by breaking tabu. D1812.4. Power of prophecy lost. D1822. Loss of magic sight.

D1741.1. *Magic power lost in sleep.* Penzer VIII 25 n. 2.

D1741.2. *Magic power lost with loss of blood.* India: Thompson-Balys.
D1003. Magic blood — human.

D1741.2.1. *Drawing witch's blood annuls her spells.* (Cf. G271.4.4., G273.6.) Kittredge Witchcraft 47, *399f. nn. 190, 191; *Fb "blod" IV 47b.
G273. Witch rendered powerless.

D1741.3. *Silence under punishment breaks power of enchantment.* Fb "prygle" II 881.
C400. Tabu: speaking. D758.1. Disenchantment by three nights' silence under punishment. D1410.3. Fluid takes away magic powers. D1561.6. Magic power in chain. Lost when chain is stolen. D1812.4.1. Power of prophecy lost by spitting.

D1741.4. *Magic powers fail because of lack of faith in them.* India: Thompson-Balys.

D1741.5. *Magic power lost by being frightened.* India: Thompson-Balys.

D1741.6. *Loss of magic power through incest.* (Cf. Q242.) Irish myth: Cross.
T410. Incest.

D1741.7. *Saint causes loss of magic power.* Irish myth: Cross.
D1713. Magic power of hermit (saint).

D1741.8. *Sorcerer's power lost when his teeth are knocked out.* India: Thompson-Balys.

D1741.9. *Conjurer's power lost by eating magic food.* Eskimo (Greenland): Rink 423.

D1745. *Magic power rendered ineffective.*

D1745.1. *Magic power not effective on men born on certain day.* Jewish: Neuman.

D1745.2. *Magic power rendered ineffective by pious deeds.* Jewish: Neuman.

D1749. *Loss of magic power—miscellaneous.*

D1749.1. *Sorceress to lose her magic power as soon as one of her transformed husbands seizes her and swallows her.* India: Thompson-Balys.

D1749.2. *Woman loses her magic power when she loses her simplicity and humility.* India: Thompson-Balys.

D1750. Other characteristics of magic power.

D1751. *Magic passes from body to body.* Jewish: Neuman; India: Tawney I 417.

D1760. Means of producing magic power.

D1266. Magic book. D1273. Magic charm (formula). D1275. Magic song.

D1761. *Magic results produced by wishing.* **Riklin Wuncherfüllung und Symbolik in Märchen. (1908); *Fb "ønske" III 1178a. — Irish myth: *Cross; German: Grimm Nos. 50, 76; Jewish: Neuman; India: *Thompson-Balys; Seneca: Curtin-Hewitt RBAE XXXII 122 No. 19; Eskimo (Greenland): Rasmussen III 151.

A575. Departed deity grants requests to visitors. C12.4.1. Mother wishes lazy daughter may marry devil. Devil appears and marries her. C15. Wish for supernatural husband realized. C21. "Ah me": ogre's name uttered. He appears. C26. Wish for animal husband realized. C758.1. Monster born because of hasty wish of parents. D521. Transformation through wish. D565.1. Midas' golden touch. D852. Magic object acquired by wishing. D1470.1. Magic wishing-object. D1720.1. Man given power of wishing. D2074.2.3. Summoning by wish. D2121.1. Magic journey by wishing. D2172.2. Magic gift: power to continue all day what one starts. E71. Resuscitation by wishing. F341. Fairies give fulfillment of wishes. J2071. Three foolish wishes. M400. Curses. N202. Wishes for good fortune realized.

D1761.0.1. *Wishes granted without limit.* *Types 555, 592, 652, 675; BP I 138, II 121ff., *124, 490.

Q338. Immoderate request punished.

D1761.0.2. *Limited number of wishes granted.* *Types 750A, 1173*, 1951*; *BP II 491; *Loomis White Magic 124, 130; Irish myth: Cross; Italian Novella: Rotunda; India: Thompson-Balys.

F341.1. Fairies give three gifts. J1181.1. Execution evaded by using three wishes. K175. Deceptive bargain: three wishes. Q338. Immoderate request punished.

D1761.0.2.1. *Man to have wishes if he can repeat them in one breath.* Irish myth: Cross.

D1761.0.2.2. *One wish granted.* India: Thompson-Balys.

J2073. Same wishes used wisely and foolishly.

D1761.1. *Wishing by stars.*

D1761.1.1. *Wishing by shooting star.* BP III 234 n. 1.

D1812.5.2.6. Shooting star as good omen.

D1765. *Magic results produced by command.* Italian Novella: Rotunda; Babylonian: Spence 76f.; Jewish: Neuman, Genesis 1:3, etc.

A611. Fiat creation. Universe is created at command of creator. C12. Devil invoked: appears unexpectedly. D766.1.1. Disenchantment by water and command. D1686. Magic object departs and returns at formulistic command. D2162.2. Epidemic does not cross river (sea) at saint's command. D2188. Garment appears and disappears in reply to command. E26.1. Resuscitation by command. M0. Judgments and decrees.

D1766. *Magic results produced by religious ceremony.* (Cf. G224.5, V70.)

*Kittredge Witchcraft 145, 465f. nn. 56, 57, 74, 75, 76—87 passim; England: Baughman.

D1296. Sacred relic as magic object. F382. Exorcising fairies. Fairies disappear when some name or ceremony of the Christian Church is used. V0. Religious services.

D1766.1. *Magic results produced by prayer.* Irish myth: *Cross; Spanish Exempla: Keller; India: *Thompson-Balys; Norse: Boberg.

A934.5. Rivers originate through saint's prayer during drought. A1017.2. Flood caused by prayer. B771.2.2. Animal tamed by saint's prayers. D1133.1.1. Magic house made by prayer. D1864. Magic beautification through prayer by saint. D1925.3. Barrenness removed by prayer. D2074.2.5. Summoning by prayer. D2105.1. Provisions provided in answer to prayer. D2143.1.3. Rain produced by prayer. D2143.6.2. Wall of snow around hut in answer to prayer. D2151.1.3. Sea calmed by saint's prayer. D2162.3. Locality sanctified against pestilence by angel as result of prayer and fasting. D2163.5. Saint's prayer wins battle. E63. Resuscitation by prayer. E501.17.4.1. Power of wild hunt evaded by prayer. E501.19.6. Effects of wild hunt remedied by prayer. F962.2. Fire from heaven. T548.1. Child born in answer to prayer. V52. Miraculous power of prayer.

D1766.1.1. *Magic fountain produced by prayer.* (Cf. D925.1.) Irish: Plummer cl, Cross.

D1766.1.2. *Prayers of nun cause Virgin Mary to show her the infant Jesus.* Spanish Exempla: Keller.

D1766.1.3. *Garment produced by prayer.* Spanish Exempla: Keller.

D1766.1.4. *Pain stopped by prayer.* India: Thompson-Balys.

D2161. Magic healing power.

D1766.1.5. *Upon praying of a saint, sea or pool is filled with sand so that people are able to cross with dry feet.* *Loomis White Magic 43.

D1766.1.6. *Mouse's prayer to gods about her children granted.* India: Thompson-Balys.

T548. Birth obtained through magic or prayer.

D1766.1.7. *Saint opens prison door by prayer.* Alphabet No. 280; Boberg.

R121.6. Rescue from prison by saint.

D1766.1.8. *Food produced by prayer.* Scala Celi 138a No. 774.

D1766.2. *Magic results produced by sacrifices.* Irish: O'Suilleabhain 89, Beal XXI 329; Jewish: Neuman.

C57.1.1. Tabu: fraudulent sacrifice. E382. Ghost summoned by pouring blood of sacrifices into trench. E501.17.4.3. Power of wild hunt evaded by sacrificing to huntsman's dogs. S260. Sacrifices. V10. Religious sacrifices.

D1766.2.1. *Magic results from sacrifices at trees and wells.* Kittredge Witchcraft 33, *393f. nn. 106—108.

A427.1. Goddesses of springs and wells. D925. Magic fountain. V1.1. Worship of trees. V134. Sacred wells.

D1766.2.2. *Magic power from sacrificing a cock.* Kittredge Witchcraft 94, *424 nn. 132, 133.

D1766.2.3. *Magic power from shedding blood.* (Cf. D2136.8.) India: Thompson-Balys.

D1766.3. *Magic powers from baptizing an animal.* Kittredge Witchcraft 94, *424 nn. 134—136.

D2161.4.9. Baptism as magic cure. V81. Baptism.

D1766.4. *Magic power from christening an animal.*

D1766.4.1. *Magic power from christening a cock.* Kittredge Witchcraft 148, 467 nn. 89—90.

D1766.5. *Magic produced by saying mass.* Irish myth: Cross.

D1385.15. Holy water and mass prevent demons alighting on grave. F933.7. Well floods when gazed upon until mass said over it. V41. Mass works miracles.

D1766.5.1. *Masses used along with other magic for cursing.* Kittredge Witchcraft 147, 466 n. 88.

M400. Curses.

D1766.5.2. *Magic articles made during mass.* Fb "messe" II 582a.

D1766.6. *Magic results from sign of the cross.* Irish myth: *Cross.

D1563.5.1. Sign of the cross makes barren land fruitful. D1567.8. Sign of cross brings water from rock. D1719.6. Magic power of holy cross. D1810.7. Magic knowledge from sign of the cross. D2031.0.3. Magic illusion dissipated by sign of the cross. G273. Witch powerless when one makes sign of cross. V86. Sign of the cross. V221.5. Saint purifies monk with sign of the cross.

D1766.6.1. *Fountain produced from sign of the cross.* (Cf. D925.1.) Irish: Plummer cl, Cross.

D1766.6.2. *Sign of the cross made over sword (knife) endows it with magic powers.* Irish myth: *Cross; Argentina: Jijena Sanchez 82, 87.

E163. Man kept alive by consecrated sword.

D1766.6.3. *Sign of the cross enables person to relate marvel.* Irish myth: Cross.

D1766.6.4. *Sign of the cross made over beer protects against poison.* Icelandic: *Boberg.

D1766.6.5. *Venomous dog killed by sign of cross.* Irish myth: Cross.

D1766.7. *Magic results from uttering powerful name.*

D1766.7.1. *Magic results produced in name of deity.* Jewish: *Neuman.

V91. Accidental calling on god's name held to outweigh a life of wickedness.

D1766.7.1.1. *Evil spirits conjured away in name of deity.* (Cf. D1385.) Fb "lygtemand" II 473 b. — Irish: O'Suilleabhain 31f., 66, Beal XXI 310, 325; Spanish Exempla: Keller.

F382. Exorcising fairies. Fairies disappear when some name or ceremony of the Christian Church is used. F460.4.6. Failure to bless mountains gives mountain-men power. F491.3. Will o' the Wisp exorcised. G304.2.4.1. Trolls cannot endure churchbells.

D1766.7.2. *Magic use of hero's name brings water.* India: Thompson-Balys.

D1766.7.3. *Magic results produced in name of saint.* (Cf. V220.) Irish myth: Cross.

B251.4.1. Beast invokes saint's protection. D1846.5.1. Invulnerability by invoking saint.

D1766.8. *Magic results from fasting.* Irish myth: Cross; India: Thompson-Balys.

C200. Tabu: eating. D1735.1. Magic power by fasting. D2162.1. Saint ends epidemic by fasting. D2162.3. Locality sanctified against pestilence by angel as result of prayer and fasting. V235.0.2. Angel invoked by fasting.

D1766.8.1. *Fasting a part of magic ritual.* Irish myth: *Cross.

C200. Tabu: eating (general).

D1766.9. *Magic results from singing hymn.* (Cf. D1275.3.) Irish myth: Cross.

D1766.10. *Magic results from worshiping god (goddess).* India: Thompson-Balys.

D1773. *Magic results from laughing.*

D1454.2. Treasure falls from lips. D1454.2.1. Roses fall from lips.

D1773.1. *Scent of flowers from laughter.* India: Thompson-Balys.

D1774. *Magic results from speaking.* Jewish: Neuman.

D1454.2. Treasure falls from lips. D1454.2.1. Roses fall from lips. D1766.7. Magic results from uttering powerful name. E451.4. Ghost laid when living man speaks to it. M400. Curses.

D1775. *Magic results from licking.* Irish myth: *Cross; Japanese: Ikeda; Eskimo (Cumberland Sound): Boas BAM XV 201.

B251.2.6. Deer lick saint's tomb daily at noon. B251.10. Animals lick Christ-child. B635.3.1. Culture hero licked by deer mother. D565.3. Transformation by licking. D2004.2.1. Dog's licking of man produces forgetfulness. D2182. Flow of cow's milk increased by licking saint's garment. E17. Resuscitation by licking corpse.

D1776. *Magic results from spitting.* Jewish: Neuman; Eskimo (Koryak): Jochelson JE VI 170.

D1001. Magic spittle. D2004.4. Forgetfulness by spitting. D2143.1.4. Rain produced by spitting blood toward sky.

D1777. *Magic results from power of thought.* Eskimo (Mackenzie Area): Jenness 64.

D2074.2.1. Person summoned by thinking of him. D2121.3. Magic journey through power of imagination.

D1778. *Magic results from contact with earth.*

D1812.3.1. Future learned by sitting on hide. D1821.1. Magic sight by treading another's foot. D1821.5. Magic sight by standing on certain stone. D1833. Magic strength by touching earth. D1854. Giant immortal so long as he touches land of his birth. D1896. Magic aging by contact with earth after otherworld journey.

D1781. *Magic results from singing.* (Cf. D1275, D1275.3.)

D1503.1. Magic song heals wound. D2141.0.6. Storm because of bird's singing. D2143.1.2. Rain produced by singing.

D1782. *Sympathetic magic.* Magic results obtained by imitating desired action. *Frazer Golden Bough XII 481 s.v. "Sympathetic magic"; *Andree Ethnographische 8ff. — Irish myth: *Cross; Jewish: Neuman; Hindu: Penzer III 38, VI 24 n., 133, IX 27 n. 1; N. A. Indian (Blackfoot): Wissler and Duvall PaAM II 128, (Maliseet): Mechling GSCan IV 100 No. 29, (Arapaho): Dorsey and Kroeber FM V 271 No. 120, (Pawnee): Dorsey CI LIX 160 No. 43, (Micmac): Parsons JAFL XXXVIII 78 No. 11, Rand 370 No. 71, (Seneca): Curtin-Hewitt RBAE XXXII 186 No. 35, 457 No. 94, 659 No. 127.

D454.2.2. Bread tree springs from crumb of bread. D1357.1. Eating ferocious animal's heart makes person cruel. D1358.1. Eating courageous animal's heart makes person courageous. D1358.1.2. Eating worm's and wolf's flesh makes person courageous and impetuous. D1836.1. Ghost's strength waxes and wanes with height of fire. D2061.2.2. Murder by sympathetic magic. D2061.2.2.1. Person whose shadow is pierced by spear falls dead. D2063.1.1. Tormenting by sympathetic magic. D2064.2. Sickness of princess dependent on witch's fire. D2065.4. Insanity of princess dependent on height of fire. D2083.3.1. Milk transferred from another's cow by squeezing axe handle (or the like). D2142.1.2. Wind raised by loosing certain knots. D2142.1.4. Wind raised by troubling vessel of water. D2142.1.6. Wind raised by whistling. D2143.1.1. Rain produced by pouring water. D2143.4.1. Hail produced by whistling tune. D2161.4.4. Person cured by repairing image that has same deformity. D2176.5. Burning cut hair to prevent witchcraft. E66. Resuscitation by breathing on corpse. E431.2. Water thrown on corpse to prevent return. E431.3. Mould thrown on corpse to prevent return. E431.5. Limbs of dead fettered to prevent return. E431.6. Turf laid on breast of dead to prevent return. G271.4. Exorcism by sympathetic magic. G275.3.1. Witch burned by burning bewitched animal.

D1782.1. *Magic results obtained by imitating desired action.*

D1782.1.1. *Opening mouth makes door open wider.* Eskimo (Cumberland Sound): Boas BAM XV 193.

D1782.2. *Curing wound by treating object which caused wound.* England, U.S.: *Baughman.

D1782.3. *Magic result from loosing knots.* (Cf. D2142.0.2.)

D1782.3.1. *Loosing sandals destroys fakir's power.* India: Thompson-Balys.

D1782.3.2. *Loosing knots permits horse to return home.* India: Thompson-Balys.

D1783. *Reverse magic.* Magic results obtained by imitating reverse of desired results.

D1812.3.3.10. Dream interpreted by opposites. D1985.2. Invisibility by reciting formula backwards. P653. Bells rung backward as alarm.

D1783.1. *Magic results of reversing a spell.* Formula said backward will sometimes undo the work performed by the formula. (Cf. D1273.) *Kittredge Witchcraft 167, 485 nn. 31—33; Penzer VI 149 n. 1, 150ff.

F385.1. Fairy spell averted by turning coat. G272.9. Reversing the poker protects from witch.

D1783.2. *Cure for leprosy by drinking from opposite lip of horn from that which caused it.* (Cf. D1500.4.1, D1502.4.1.) Icelandic: *Boberg.

D1783.3. *Faster one walks, longer the trail.* The slower, the shorter. N. A. Indian (Plains Cree): Skinner JAFL XXIX 356 No. 3.

L148.1. If you hasten you will not get there.

D1783.4. *Power over monster (wizard, king) obtained by reversing orders.* Hero does exact opposite of the command. Scottish: Campbell-McKay No. 2.

B316. Abused and pampered horses.

D1783.5. *Magic turned against the makers, so that they are bewildered and kill themselves.* Icelandic: Göngu-Hrólfs saga 319, *Boberg.

D1784. *Magic results from breathing.* (Cf. D1557.) Eskimo (Greenland): Rink 428.

D1785. *Magic telepathy.* Influence at a distance. Koryak: *Jochelson JE VI 380.

D1786. *Magic power at cross-roads.* *Fb "korsvej" II 277f; *Frazer Golden Bough XII 232 s.v. "cross roads"; *Penzer III 37f.; Finnish: Kalevala rune 8.

D935.1. Magic earth from cross-roads. D2161.4.3. Cure by passing through earth at cross-roads. E434.4. Ghosts cannot pass cross-roads. E501.12.3. Wild hunt appears at cross-roads. E501.17.3. Wild hunt powerless at cross-roads. F217.3. Fairies assemble at cross-roads. F383.1. Fairy unable to pass cross-roads. G273.5. Witches powerless at cross-roads.

D1787. *Magic results from burning.*

D576. Transformation by being burned. D771.1. Disenchantment by burning magic hair. D1421.1.7. Magic incense (when burned) summons genie. D1846.1. Invulnerability by being burned and anointed with magic ointments. D1851.1. Immortality by burning. D1865.2. Beautification by boiling and resuscitation. D1885. Rejuvenation by boiling. D1886. Rejuvenation by burning. D2074.2.2. Summoning by burning hair. D2144.4. Burning by magic. D2161.4.7. Animal burned to cure disease. D2161.4.8. Cure by burning grain where man has died. D2176.3. Evil spirit exorcised by burning fish. E15. Resuscitation by burning. E218. Spells to recall dead lover. Boiling dead man's head, bones, or carcass in a pot, or burning a piece of lover's clothing or cat in a hot oven. E446.2. Ghost laid by burning body. G271.4.1. Exorcism by burning object for sympathetic magic.

D1788. *Magic results from bathing.* (Cf. D562, D925, D2161.4.14.) Jewish: Neuman.

D1349.2.2. Washing in magic bowl produces immunity from old age. D1355.17. Herb bath produces love. D1500.1.1. Magic healing fountain. D1500.1.7.3.4. Bath in blood of king as remedy. D1503.7. Magic well heals wounds. D1515.3. Bath in milk of white, hornless cows as antidote for poison. D1810.6. Magic knowledge from bathing in holy water. D1832. Magic strength by bathing. D1846.4. Invulnerability through bathing in dragon's blood. D1866. Beautification by bathing. D1887. Rejuvenation by bathing. D1895. Magic aging by bathing. D1925.2. Barrenness removed by bathing. D2161.4.14.2. Magic cure by bathing in consecrated water (lake, etc.). E80.1.1. Resuscitation by bathing in milk. F872. Extraordinary bath. F952.7. Eyes restored by bathing in spring. K1072. Fairy induces hero to dive into lake which makes person old. T523. Conception from bathing.

D1788.1. *Magic results from contact with water.* Irish myth: Cross.

C532. Tabu: touching water. D565.6. Transformation by touching water. D877.1. Magic wishing ring loses power by touching water.

D1791. *Magic power by circumambulation.* (Cf. G224.8, D1272.) *Fb "rundt" III 96b; Frazer Golden Bough X 233ff.; *Penzer X 109 s.v. "circumambulation"; Cowell Jātaka index s.v. "rightwise"; Cosquin Études 356ff.; *Saintyves Essais 196ff. — Irish myth: *Cross; Icelandic: *Boberg; Jewish: Neuman.

C643. Tabu: turning left side of chariot toward certain place. D563. Transformation by encircling object thrice. D787. Disenchantment by encircling. D1272. Magic circle. D1381.25. Carrying saint's book around army (right-handwise) insures victory. D1384.3.1. Turning right-handwise insures safe journey. D1389.6. Saint's bell carried around tribe averts all danger. D1812.2.1. Power of prophecy induced by crawling backward around grave. N131.2. Turning right-handwise in certain place brings luck. R112.2. Riding three times around hill to free captive confined within.

D1791.1. *Dextrosum (sunwise) circuit (for good luck).* Irish myth: Cross.

D1791.1.1. *Druid performs circumambulation right-handwise to confer honor or bring good luck.* Irish myth: *Cross.

D1791.2. *Withershins (countersunwise) circuit (for ill luck).* Irish myth: *Cross.

D1791.2.1. *Druid performs circumambulation withershins to bring ill luck.* Irish myth: *Cross.

D1792. *Magic results from curse.* Irish myth: *Cross.

A1017.3. Flood caused by curse. D5.1.1. Stepson cursed to stick in grave mound till pretty girl wants to substitute for him. D525. Transformation through curse. D1837.3. Magic weakness as result of fairy's curse. D1905.3. Love by curse. D1962.1. Magic sleep through curse. D2004.1. Curse of forgetfulness. D2021.1. Dumbness as curse. D2061.2.4. Death by cursing. D2062.2.1. Blinding by curse D2064.5. Magic sickness from curse. D2065.7. Insanity from curse. D2072.2. Magic paralysis by curse. D2085.1. Curse makes river barren of fish. D2089.2. Curse makes stones useless. D2089.5. Books illegible as result of curse. D2091.13. Army stopped by saint's curse. D2144.4.1. Person burned through magic wishing (curse). M400. Curses. M430. Curses on persons. Q556. Curse as punishment. T154. Cruel stepmother enchants stepdaughter.

D1792.1. *Saint's curse splits rocks.* Irish myth: Cross.

M411.8. Saint's curse.

D1792.2. *Cursing wells.* Irish myth: Cross.

D2175.1. Cursing by means of a well. V134. Holy wells.

D1792.3. *Cursing stones.* (Cf. D931.) Irish myth: *Cross.

D1793. *Magic results from eating or drinking.*

B161.3 Wisdom from eating serpent. B162.1. Supernatural knowledge from eating magic fish. B217.1. Animal languages learned from eating animals. B217.2. Animal languages learned from eating plant. D1338.3.3.1. Year added to life by eating fruit of magic tree. D1359.3.2. Happiness from eating magic pig. D1375.6.1. Magic egg causes feathers to grow on person. D1500.2.5. Eating magic pig prevents disease. D1503.11. Wounds healed by eating fruit of magic tree. D1811.1. Magic wisdom from eating or drinking. D1812.2.3. Power of prophecy from accidental drinking of water from magic fountain. D1812.3.3.6. Prophetic dream induced by eating meat of bull. D1819.4.2. Alphabet written on cake learned by eating it. D1925.1. Barrenness removed by eating or drinking. D2004.3. Forgetfulness by eating. D2004.3.1. Forgetfulness by drinking. D2122.1. Magic speed by eating magic grains (medicine). D2135.1. Power of flying from eating children's hearts. T511. Conception from eating. T512. Conception from drinking.

D1793.1. *Characteristics of animal acquired by eating it.* Jewish: Neuman; Eskimo (Greenland): Rink 227.

D1794. *Magic results from kissing.* Irish myth: Cross; Jewish: Neuman.

C120. Tabu: kissing. Usually causes disenchantment or magic forgetfulness. D565.5. Transformation by kiss. D735. Disenchantment by kiss. D2004.2. Kiss of forgetfullness. E65. Resuscitation by kiss.

D1795. *Magic by creeping (running, pulling) through a hole.* *Hdwb. d. Abergl. II 477 s.v. "durchkriechen"; *Lowy Zs. f. Vksk. XXXVII—XXXVIII 85.

D2161.4.3. Cure by passing through earth at cross-roads. D2161.4.5. Cure by passing patient under cleft of tree (other loop).

D1796. *Magic from maiden walking naked in public.* Hartland Science 83.

D759.3. Disenchantment by naked virgin undergoing frightful journey at midnight.

D1796.1. *Power of nudity in magic.* India: Thompson-Balys.

D1799. *Magic results from other acts.* (Cf. D1469.7, F547.1.3.)

A636. New creation shouted away. B217.4. Animal languages learned from carrying churchyard mould in hat. B217.5. Bird language learned by having ears magically cleansed. C762.1. Tabu: using magic power too often. D583. Transformation by lousing. D712.10. Disenchantment by driving stake through body. D1812.3.2. Fortune told by cutting sand. D1812.5.0.7. Divination from first person met. D1821.2. Magic sight from thumb of knowledge. D1821.3. Magic sight by looking in certain place. D1821.4. Magic sight by putting ointment in eye. D1822.1. Magic sight overcome by incantation. D1863. Beautification by stroking (tapping). D1889.1. Rejuvenation by reading in book. D1889.2. Rejuvenation by looking into mirror. D1889.4. Rejuvenation by smelling apple. D1962.2. Magic sleep by lousing. D1985.1. Invisibility by scarification. D2004.5. Forgetting by stumbling. D2025.1. Speech magically recovered on execution stake. D2025.2. Speech magically recovered when certain bird is caught. D2025.3. Speech magically recovered when third person guesses secret transaction. D2025.4. Dumbness magically cured by astonishment. D2064.4. Magic sickness because of Evil Eye. D2065.2. Insanity from seeing strange sight. D2065.5. Insanity because of Evil Eye. D2071. Evil Eye. D2072.1. Magic paralysis by Evil Eye. D2121.2. Magic journey with closed eyes. D2121.6. Magic journey during which one must not think good or evil. D2121.8. Magic journey by throwing knife into whirlwind. D2135.2. Magic air journey from biting an ear. D2141.0.4. Storm at death of wizard. Devil comes for him. D2141.0.7. Storm raised by incantation. D2142.0.5. Wind raised by putting cat under bushel (barrel) (drowning cat). D2143.1.7. Rain produced by striking rock. D2161.4.6. Animal buried alive to cure disease. D2161.4.11. Cure by putting children on roof (in oven). D2176.4. Magic book conjured away by throwing it on stream. E18. Resuscitation by tickling. E72. Resuscitation by smelling of moss. E164. Dead body caused to speak by setting door ajar. E251.2.1. Vampire brought to life through endurance of punishment by her victim. E381. Ghost summoned by weeping. E403.2.1.1. Familiar spirit acquired by carrying egg under left arm-pit. E431.8. Dog buried alive to prevent ghosts from walking. E501.17.4.4. Power of wild hunt evaded by silence.

D1799.1. *Magic power from cleansing.* (Cf. D1081, D1610.9, V1.8.) Irish myth: Cross.

D1799.2. *Magic results from clapping the hands together.* Cheremis: Sebeok-Nyerges.

D1799.3. *Magic results from special rituals.* Irish myth: *Cross.

D1711.4. Druid as magician. D1810.0.2. Magic knowledge of magician. D1810.0.8. Magic knowledge of druid. D1812.3.1 Future learned by sitting on hide. D1812.3.3.6. Prophetic dream induced by eating meat of bull. M400.1. Satire. P427.4. Poet (druid) as satirist.

D1799.4. *Magic powers from touching.* (Cf. D565, D1032.2f., D1273.0.3., D1810.3, D1833., D1854.)

G221.2. Strength of witches depends on their touching earth.

D1799.5. *Magic results from chewing.* Irish myth: Cross.

D1799.6. *Magic results from performing good deeds.* Jewish: Neuman.

D1800—D2199. Manifestations of magic power.

D1800—D1949. LASTING MAGIC QUALITIES

D1810. Magic knowledge. (Cf. D1310.) India: Thompson-Balys; Eskimo (Greenland): Rink 456, Rasmussen I 78, III 123, (Cumberland Sound): Boas BAM XV 244, (Bering Strait): Nelson RBAE XVIII 490.

D1719.2. Magic wisdom possessed by wild man. D1731.1. Magic song received in dream. F256. Fairies read men's thoughts. F403.2.3.3. Spirits teach boy how to sing. F645. Marvelously wise man. F1103.3. King sleeps for 6 days and after that acquires magic wisdom. J157. Wisdom (knowledge) from dream.

D1810.0.1. *Omniscience of a god.* Irish myth: *Cross; Norse: De la Saussaye 280, Boberg; Greek: Aeschylus Prometheus Bound line 167, Grote I 6; Jewish: Neuman.

A102.1. Omniscient god.

D1810.0.2. *Magic knowledge of magician.* (Cf. D1711, D1814.1.) Irish myth: *Cross; Icelandic: Boberg; English: Wells 42 (Arthour and Merlin); India: Thompson-Balys.

D1711. Magician. D1712. Soothsayer. D1721. Magic power from magician. M301. Prophets. P427. Druid (magus).

D1810.0.2.1. *Magician rebukes secret usury.* Italian Novella: Rotunda.

Q273. Usury punished.

D1810.0.3. *Magic knowledge of saints and holy men.* *Toldo I 345ff.; Irish myth: *Cross; Jewish: Neuman.

V223. Saints have miraculous knowledge.

D1810.0.3.1. *Saint perceives cheat.* Irish myth: Cross; Spanish Exempla: Keller.

J1521. Swindler's plans foiled.

D1810.0.3.2. *Lost object or person found by holy man.* Icelandic: *Boberg.

D1810.0.4. *Magic knowledge of fairies.* Irish myth: *Cross.

D1813.0.2. Fairy has knowledge of how mortals fare. F256. Fairies read men's thoughts. F347. Fairy adviser. M301.6. Fairies as prophets.

D1810.0.5. *Magic knowledge of witches.* Irish myth: Cross; England, U.S., Wales: *Baughman.

G220. Characteristics of witches.

D1810.0.6. *Magic knowledge of angels.* (Cf. D1810.5.) Irish myth: *Cross.

M301.10. Angels as prophets.

D1810.0.7. *Magic knowledge of superman.* Irish myth: Cross.

D1719.3. Magic power of superhuman race.

D1810.0.8. *Magic knowledge of druid.* (Cf. D1711.4, D1816.5.) Irish myth: *Cross.

D1817.1. Druids magically detect crime.

D1810.0.8.1. *Druid's "keys of wisdom".* Irish myth: *Cross.

D1810.0.9. *Magic knowledge of the Pope.* Irish myth: Cross.

V294. The Pope.

D1810.0.10. *Magic knowledge (wisdom) of Solomon.* (Cf. L212.2.) Irish myth: Cross.

D1810.0.11. *Magic knowledge of poet.* Irish myth: *Cross.

D1810.0.12. *Magic knowledge about culprit's offense to deity.* India: Thompson-Balys.

D1810.0.13. *Magic knowledge of identity of stranger.* India: Thompson-Balys.

D1810.1. *Magic knowledge from queen of other world.* (Cf. D1723.) Hartland Science 197.

F315. Fairy predicts birth of child.

D1810.2. *Magic knowledge from devil.* (Cf. D1721.1.) Dickson 235 n. 34; Icelandic: Boberg.

G303. The devil. M211. Man sells soul to devil.

D1810.3. *Magic knowledge from touching "knowledge tooth" with thumb.* (Cf. D1009.2, D1811.1.1.) **Scott Thumb; Irish myth: Cross; English: Baughman.

A527.2. Culture hero has knowledge-giving member (tooth, thumb). B124.1.1. Salmon of knowledge. D1811.1.1. Thumb of knowledge. D1813.3. "Knowledge tooth" reveals events in distant place. D1817.3. Detection of crime through "knowledge tooth."

D1810.3.1. *Future revealed by "knowledge tooth".* (Cf. D1009.) Irish myth: *Cross.

D1821.2. Magic sight from Thumb of Knowledge. M315. Prophecy: man will eat magic salmon and gain knowledge.

D1810.4. *Magic knowledge learned from magician teacher.* India: Thompson-Balys.

D1810.5. *Magic knowledge from angel.* (Cf. D1725, D1810.0.6.) Irish myth: *Cross.

D812.10.0.1. Angel reveals location of magic object. V232. Angel as helper. V232.6. Angel reveals location of lost (buried) object.

D1810.6. *Magic knowledge from bathing in holy water.* Irish myth: Cross.

D1242.1.2. Holy water as magic object. D1788. Magic results from bathing. D1819.4.1. Man enabled to read baptismal service by washing in holy water.

D1810.7. *Magic knowledge from sign of the cross.* (Cf. D1766.6, V86.) Irish myth: Cross.

D1810.8. *Magic knowledge from dream.* (Cf. D1812.3.3, D1812.5.1.2, D1813.1, D1814.2, D1817.2.1, D1819.2.) Irish myth: *Cross; Icelandic: þidriks saga II 393—95 (n.), *Boberg.

F1068.1. Advice and information given in dream. J157. Wisdom (knowledge) from dream. N531.4. Grateful king advises merchant in dream to take treasure from his grave mound.

D1810.8.1. *Truth given in vision.* India: Thompson-Balys.

D1810.8.2. *Information received through dream.* India: Thompson-Balys.

D1810.8.2.1. *Dream shows where stolen girl is hidden.* India: Thompson-Balys.

D1810.8.2.2. *Person dreams of spot where drowned body lies.* England: Baughman.

D1810.8.2.3. *Murder made known in a dream.* Canada: Baughman.

D1810.8.2.4. *Dream tells of safety of absent person who has been in danger.* Scotland: Baughman.

D1810.8.2.5. *Raja told in a dream the stranger he seeks to destroy is his own son.* India: Thompson-Balys.

N731. Unexpected meeting of father and son.

D1810.8.3. *Warning in dreams.* Icelandic: *Boberg; India: Thompson-Balys.

D1812.5.1.2. Bad dream as evil omen. D1814.2. Advice received in dream.

D1810.8.3.1. *Warning in dream fulfilled.* India: Thompson-Balys.

D1810.8.3.1.1. *Dream warns of illness or injury.* The dream is fulfilled. England: *Baughman.

D1810.8.3.2. *Dream warns of danger which will happen in near future.* Because of advance knowledge, the danger is averted. England, Scotland, U.S.: *Baughman.

D1810.8.4. *Solution to problem is discovered in dream.* England: Baughman.

D1810.9. *Magic knowledge from God.* Irish myth: *Cross; Icelandic: MacCulloch Eddic 297—98 (Odin); India: Thompson-Balys.

P623.0.1.1. Clerics fast against God for revelation.

D1810.10. *Magic knowledge from goddess.* Icelandic: MacCulloch Eddic 296, 299; India: Thompson-Balys.

D1810.11. *Magic knowledge from mythical ancestor.* Icelandic: MacCulloch Eddic 297 (Rig), 311.

D1810.12. *Magic knowledge from guardian spirits.* (See E721.9.) Icelandic: Hrólfs saga Kraka II, Boberg.

D1810.13. *Magic knowledge from the dead.* Icelandic: MacCulloch Eddic 46, 298, 299—300, 311, Herrmann Saxo II 98—99.

D1811. *Magic wisdom.* (Cf. D1300.)

B121. Dog with magic wisdom. B122. Bird with magic wisdom. B123. Wise serpent. B160. Wisdom-giving animal.

D1811.0.1. *Seventy-two kinds of wisdom mastered by Adam.* Jewish: Neuman.

D1811.1. *Magic wisdom from eating or drinking.* Jewish: Neuman.

B161.3. Wisdom from eating serpent. B162.1. Supernatural knowledge from eating magic fish. B217.1. Animal languages learned from eating animal. D1793. Magic results from eating or drinking.

D1811.1.1. *Thumb of knowledge.* Man cooks magic animal and burns thumb. When he puts thumb in mouth he has magic knowledge. (Cf. D1810.3.) **Scott Thumb; Irish myth: *Cross.

A527.2. Culture hero has knowledge-giving member (tooth, thumb). B162.1. Supernatural knowledge from eating magic fish. D1821.2. Magic sight from thumb of knowledge. M315. Prophecy: man will eat magic salmon and gain knowledge.

D1811.1.1.1. *Thumb of knowledge from catching thumb in door of fairy.* (Cf. F211.1.) Irish myth: *Cross.

D1811.1.2. *Magic wisdom from drinking of well.* (Cf. D1242.1, D1300.3, V134.) Irish myth: Cross; Icelandic: Boberg.

D1811.2. *Magic wisdom received from supernatural being.* Dickson 120 nn. 61—63.

D1811.2.1. *Divine inspiration for writing sacred books.* Moreno Esdras.

D1812. *Magic power of prophecy.* (Cf. D1311.) Icelandic: *Boberg; English: Child III 418—422; Greek: Grote I 216, 249, 307; Jewish: Neuman; India: Thompson-Balys; Chinese: Ferguson 135. — N. A. Indian (Micmac): Parsons JAFL XXXVIII 75 No. 10.

B81.7.1. Mermaid prophesies. B140. Prophetic animal. F403.2.3.2. Spirit gives warning. M300. Prophecies.

D1812.0.1. *Foreknowledge of hour of death.* Irish myth: *Cross; England: *Baughman; Icelandic: *Boberg; Breton: Sébillot Incidents s.v. "mort"; Greek: Aeschylus Agamemnon line 1260; India: Thompson-Balys.

B141.2.1. Horse weeps for master's (saint's) approaching death. J216. Choice of deaths. M301.0.1. Prophet destined never to be believed. M341. Death prophesied.

D1812.0.1.1. *Cheek bitten as warning of approaching death.* (Cf. D1812.5.1.16.1.) Irish myth: Cross.

D1812.0.1.2. *Foreknowledge of means of death.* Irish myth: *Cross.

D1812.0.2. *Saints have foreknowledge of coming of guests.* Irish: Plummer clxx, *Cross.

D1713. Magic power of hermit (saint). V223. Saints have miraculous knowledge. V246.3. Angel informs saint of coming of guests.

D1812.0.2.1. *Foreknowledge of unwished guests.* Icelandic: *Boberg.

D1812.0.2.2. *Hero has foreknowledge of coming of guests.* Irish myth: Cross.

D1812.0.2.3. *Fakir has foreknowledge of coming of guests.* India: Thompson-Balys.

D1812.0.3. *Foreknowledge of wounding in battle (combat).* Irish myth: *Cross.

M341.2.18. Prophecy: death in battle.

D1812.0.4. *Foreknowledge of unhappiness of son or sons.* Icelandic: *Boberg.

D1813.0.3. Father feels that son is in danger. P233. Father and son.

D1812.0.5. *Magic knowledge of what is to happen to himself after death.* (Cf. G283.1.) India: Thompson-Balys.

D1812.1. *Power of prophecy a gift.* Greek: Frazer Apollodorus I 313 n. 3.

D1812.1.1. *Power of prophecy from fairy.* (Cf. D1723.) Hartland Science 203.

D1812.1.2. *Power of prophecy from God.* (Cf. D1726.) Irish myth: *Cross.

D1812.2. *Power of prophecy induced.*

D1812.2.1. *Power of prophecy induced by crawling backward around* grave. (Cf. D1791.) *Fb "grav" I 478.

D1812.2.2. *Power of prophecy induced by conjuring.* Irish myth: Cross.

D1812.2.3. *Power of prophecy from accidental drinking of water from magic fountain.* Irish myth: *Cross.

D925. Magic fountain. D1793. Magic results from eating or drinking. N400. Lucky accidents.

D1812.2.4. *Dying man's power of prophecy.* Icelandic: *Boberg.

D1715. Magic power of dying man's words.

D1812.3. *Means of learning future.* (Cf. D1810.8, D1976.2.)

D1325. Magic object reveals future. M302. Means of prophesying.

D1812.3.1. *Future learned by sitting on hide.* Kittredge Witchcraft 47, *399 nn. 181—186; Irish myth: *Cross.

D1778. Magic results from contact with earth.

D1812.3.2. *Fortune told by cutting sand.* Africa (Vai): Ellis 214 No. 29.

D1812.3.3. *Future revealed in dream.* (Cf. D1810.8, D1812.5.1.2, D1813.1.) *Type 725; *BP I 324; *Fb "sove" III 472b; *Hartland FLJ IV 321; *Pauli (ed. Bolte) Nos. 182, 183, 287, 328, 466, 826—830; *Gaster Exempla Nos. 215, 216, 218, 219, 242; Loomis White Magic; Alphabet Nos. 266, 305; Child V 477 s.v. "dreams"; *Encyc. Religion and Ethics s.v. "Dreams and sleep"; Loomis White Magic 17f.; Corpus Poeticum Boreale I 334, 347. — Irish myth: *Cross; Norse: Sofus Larsen Antik og Nordisk Drømmetro (Aarbøger for Nordisk Oldkyndighed 1917, 37ff.), G. D. Kelchner Dreams in Old Norse Literature and Their Affinities in Folklore (Cambridge, England, 1935); Icelandic: MacCulloch Eddic 311—12, *Boberg; England, Scotland, Wales, U.S.: *Baughman; Spanish Exempla: Keller; Greek: Frazer Apollodorus II 46 n. 1 (Hecuba); Jewish: Neuman; India: Thompson-Balys; Chinese: Werner 276, Graham. — S. A. Indian (Cherentes): Alexander Lat. Am. 308; Eskimo (Greenland): Rasmussen I 134; Africa (Angola): Chatelain 67, 249, (Fjort): Dennett 39 No. 5, (Kaffir): Theal 128, (Bushman): Bleek and Lloyd 17, (Zulu): Callaway 146, (Gold Coast): Barker and Sinclair 124.

C168.1. Woman marries in spite of warning dream. Bears blind child who soon dies. D1731. Magic power received in dream. D1976.2. Future spouse met during magic sleep. E361.0.1. Dead appears in dream and complains that she is burned by tears after which bones and a magician's wand are found under church floor and removed. F1068.1. Advice and information given in dream. J157. Wisdom (knowledge) from dream. M300. Prophecies. M312.0.1. Dream of future greatness. N531.4. Grateful king advises merchant in dream to take treasure from his grave mound. T311.0.1. Woman's aversion to marriage motivated through a dream.

D1812.3.3.0.1. *Druid interprets prophetic dream.* (Cf. D1711.4, D1812.3.3.5.) Irish myth: *Cross.

D1712. Soothsayer (diviner, oracle, etc.). M301.3. Druids as prophets.

D1812.3.3.0.2. *Poets interpret dreams.* (Cf. P427.7.) Irish myth: *Cross.

D1812.3.3.0.3. *Dream interpreter corrects dream.* Jewish: Neuman.

D1812.3.3.1. *Truest dreams at daybreak.* *Penzer VIII 99f.

D1812.3.3.2. *Fortune-telling dream induced by sleeping in extraordinary place (position).* *Fb "sove" III 472b, 473a.

D1812.3.3.3. *Prophetic dream induced by incantation.* (Cf. D1799.3.) Irish myth: *Cross.

D1812.3.3.4. *Prophetic dream loses force after a year.* Irish myth: *Cross.

D1812.3.3.5. *Prophetic dream allegorical.* (Cf. D1812.3.3.0.1., V515.) Irish myth: *Cross.

D1812.3.3.5.1. *Allegorical dream: ripe and unripe ears, fat and lean kine.* India: Thompson-Balys.

F171.1. Fat and lean kine in otherworld. Z100. Symbolism.

D1812.3.3.6. *Prophetic dream induced by eating meat of bull.* Irish myth: *Cross.

A132.9. Bull-god. D1793. Magic results from eating and drinking. D1799.3. Magic results from special rituals. P11. Choice of kings. P427. Druid.

D1812.3.3.7. *Eve in vision sees Cain drink Abel's blood.* Irish myth: Cross.

D1812.3.3.8. *Dream by a (pregnant) woman about fate of her unborn child.* Icelandic: *Boberg.

D1812.3.3.9. *Future husband (wife) revealed in dream.* India: Thompson-Balys.

T11.3. Love through dream.

D1812.3.3.10. *Dream interpreted by opposites.* India: Thompson-Balys.

D1783. Reverse magic.

D1812.3.3.11. *Death of another revealed in dream.* England, Scotland, U.S.: *Baughman.

D1812.4. *Future revealed by presentiment: "knowledge within".* Irish myth: Cross; England, U.S.: *Baughman; India: Thompson-Balys; S. A. Indian (Toba): Métraux MAFLS XL 88; Africa (Ekoi): Talbot 68, 227, (Zulu): Callaway 194.

D1812.4.1. *Woman cries out on beholding man her unborn child is destined to slay.* (Cf. T575.1.) Irish myth: Cross.

D1812.5. *Future learned through omens.* *Fb "varsel"; *Kittredge Witchcraft 398 n. 170; Irish: *Cross, O'Suilleabhain 110, Beal XXI 334; Icelandic: *Boberg; Spanish Exempla: Keller; Jewish: Neuman; India: Thompson-Balys, Cowell Jātaka index s.v. "Omens".

B11.4.2. Dragon as giver of omens. B147. Animals furnish omens. C493.1. Tabu: wishing good luck. D1311.3. Oracular fountain. D1311.3.1. Spring gives omens. D1317.12. Magic stone gives warning. D1812.5.0.15. Weather signs. D1812.5.0.7.3. Prognostications from day of week on which first of year falls. E501.20. Wild hunt as omen. E761. Life-token. M302. Means of prophesying. N131. Acts performed for changing luck. V134.1. Oracles and auguries from holy well.

D1812.5.0.1. *Omens from sneezing.* *Kittredge Witchcraft 44, 398 n. 170; *Pease Classical Philology VI (1911) 429ff; *Tylor Primitive Culture (First Am. ed.) I 97ff.; Knowlson Popular Superstitions (1910) 175ff.; Schweizer Volkskunde (1912) 20f.; Encyc. Rel. Ethics IX 398f.; Penzer III 303ff.; Gessler Bull. bib. et péd. du Musée belge XXX (1926) 193ff.; Saintyves L'Eternuement et le Baillement (Paris, 1921) 148; *Fb "nyse" II 704; Hdwb. d. Abergl. s.v. "niesen" VI 1076ff.; India: Thompson-Balys.

D1812.5.0.2. *Omens from flight of birds.* *Kittredge Witchcraft 44, 398 n. 170; India: Thompson-Balys.

D1812.5.0.3. *Behavior of fire as omen.* *Fb "ild" II 13a.; Virgil Aeneid II 680, V 525, VII 74; India: Thompson-Balys.

F1061. Flame as miraculous index.

D1812.5.0.4. *Rising smoke as omen.* N. A. Indian: Kroeber JAFL XXI 224.

D1812.5.0.4.1. *Divination from rising smoke.* Irish myth: *Cross.

H1582.2. Recognition of good health by smoke rising from chimney.

D1812.5.0.5. *Haruspices: divination by condition of animal's liver.* *Hdwb. d. Abergl. III 1494; *Frazer Pausanias IV 5.

D1812.5.0.6. *Divination by throwing objects into water.* If they swim the omen is bad; if not, good. *Frazer Pausanias III 388.

H222. Ordeal by water. J1931. Money tested by throwing it into stream to see if it will float.

D1812.5.0.7. *Divination from first person (thing) met.* *Hdwb. d. Märch. s.v. "Erstes"; Jewish: Neuman.

N125.2. Districts named from first person met in each. T62. Princess to marry first man who asks for her.

D1812.5.0.7.1. *First to partake of certain feast will be first to disobey the king (etc.).* Irish myth: *Cross.

D1812.5.0.7.2. *Saint declares that first man to come to certain place shall be his successor.* Young cleric comes and is chosen. Irish myth: Cross.

D1812.5.0.7.3. *Prognostications from day of week on which first day of year falls.* (Cf. D1812.5.0.16.) Irish myth: Cross.

D1812.5.0.8. *Divination from animal fight.* Irish myth: Cross.

B264. Single combat between animals.

D1812.5.0.8.1. *Auguries from movement of animal.* (Cf. B563.) Irish myth: Cross.

D1812.5.0.9. *Divination from howling of dog.* (Cf. D1812.5.1.12.1.) Irish myth: *Cross.

B141.4.1. Dog (transformed man) prophesies coming of enemy.

D1812.5.0.10. *Divination from clouds.* (Cf. D1812.5.1.11.) Irish myth: *Cross.

D1812.5.0.11. *Divination from sound of voice.* Irish myth: *Cross.

D1812.5.0.12. *Divination from sound of chariot wheels.* Irish myth: *Cross.

D1812.5.0.13. *Magic manifestation as omen.* Irish myth: Cross; Icelandic: *Boberg.

D1812.5.0.14. *Stone changes from red to green as auspicious sign.* (Cf. D1293.1, D1293.2, D1317.12.) Irish myth: Cross.

D1812.0.15. *Weather signs.* Irish myth: Cross.

D1812.5.0.15.1. *Divination from wind.* Icelandic: Egils saga einhenda, ed. Lagerholm 47.

D1812.5.0.16. *Prognostications for year from winds blowing on January 1.* (Cf. D1812.5.0.7.3.) Irish myth: *Cross.

D1812.5.0.17. *Divination by choice of roads: which son to be born first.* India: Thompson-Balys.

T500. Conception and birth.

D1812.5.1. *Bad omens.* *Penzer III 46, 86, X 251 s.v. "Omen, evil."; Irish myth: *Cross; Icelandic: *Boberg; India: Thompson-Balys.

D1812.5.1.1. *Prodigy as evil omen.* *Bolte Zs. f. Vksk. XX 69; *Penzer II 39 n. 2. — Irish myth: *Cross; Greek: Frazer Apollodorus II 185 n. 1, 232 n. 2.

D474. Object becomes bloody. D1322. Magic object warns of death. D1546. Magic object controls heavenly bodies. E761.1.1. Life token: water turns to blood. F493.5. Sign of great plague. M301.6.1. Banshees as portents of misfortune. M341. Death prophesied.

D1812.5.1.1.1. *Tears of blood as evil omen.* Irish myth: Cross.

F1041.29. Tears of blood from excessive grief.

D1812.5.1.1.2. *Two drops of blood in book mean that two have been killed.* Icelandic: Boberg.

D1812.5.1.1.3. *Blood (in dream) as omen of killing.* Icelandic: *Boberg.

D1812.0.4. Foreknowledge of unhappiness of son or sons. D1813.0.3. Father feels that son is in danger. P233. Father and son.

D1812.5.1.1.4. *Wave of blood as sign of death.* (Cf. D1003, E761.1.1.) Irish myth: *Cross.

D1812.5.1.1.5. *Drops of blood presage slaughter.* Irish myth: Cross.

D1812.5.1.1.6. *Washers at the ford.* Appearance of female figure washing bloody armor, chariot cushions, or human limb (at ford) as sign of coming disaster in battle. (Cf. A485.1, E761.1, M301.6.1, Z129.2.2.) Irish myth: *Cross .

D1812.5.1.2. *Bad dream as evil omen.* (Cf. D1810.8, D1812.3.3, D1813.1.) Dickson 74, 225. — Irish myth: *Cross; English: Wells 9 (King Horn), 31 (Geoffrey's life of Arthur), 33 (Layamon's Brut), 48 (Lancelot of the Laik), 89 (The Sege of Melayne), 92 (The Song of Roland), 122 (The King of Tars); Icelandic: Herrmann Saxo II 233, *Boberg; Italian Novella: Rotunda; India: Thompson-Balys.

D1810.8. Magic knowledge from dreams. F1068.1. Advice and information given in dream. J157. Wisdom (knowledge) from dream. N531.4. Grateful king advises merchant in dream to take treasure from his grave mound.

D1812.5.1.2.1. *Vision as evil omen.* Irish myth: *Cross.

D1812.5.1.3. *Breaking mirror as evil omen.* *Fb "spejl" III 481b; *Kittredge Witchcraft 93, 423 n. 124.

D1812.5.1.4. *Eclipse as evil omen.* (Cf. F961.1, F965.2.) Penzer II 82. — Icelandic: Boberg.

D1812.5.1.5. *Moon furnishes omen.*

D1812.5.1.5.1. *New moon with old moon in her arm a sign of storm.* Child II 20ff.

D1812.5.1.5.2. *Red or pale moon an evil omen.* Chinese: Werner 176.

D1812.5.1.6. *Stars furnish omens*

D1812.5.1.6.1. *Sirius as bad omen.* Greek: Homer Iliad XXII 30.

D1812.5.1.7. *Meeting certain persons (animals) a bad omen.* *Kittredge Witchcraft 44f., 398 nn. 169—173.

D1812.5.1.7.1. *Bad omen: greeting one before dawn.* India: Thompson-Balys.

D1812.5.1.8. *Bad omen for two bridal processions to meet.* Estonian: Aarne FFC XXV 135 No. 91.

T130. Marriage customs.

D1812.5.1.9. *Sight of mermaid bad omen.* Child V 488 s.v. "mermaid".

B81. Mermaid.

D1812.5.1.10. *Sight of phantom ship a bad omen.* Fb "skib".

E536. Phantom ship.

D1812.5.1.11. *Red (gray, etc.) clouds as evil omens.* (Cf. D1812.5.0.10.) Irish myth: *Cross.

D1812.5.1.12. *Animal behavior as bad omen.*

B147. Animals furnish omens.

D1812.5.1.12.1. *Howling of dog as bad omen.* (Cf. D1812.5.0.9.) Irish myth: *Cross.

D1812.5.1.12.2. *Bird calls as evil omen.* Korean: Zong in-Sob 210.

D1812.5.1.12.3. *Spider dropping on person's back as ill omen.* Samoa: Clark 117.

D1812.5.1.12.4. *Mice gnawing garments as bad omen.* Buddhist myth: Malalasekera II 410.

D1812.5.1.13. *Fairy music as evil omen.* Irish myth: Cross.

F262. Fairies make music.

D1812.5.1.14. *Holy man's fall from horse a bad omen.* Irish myth: *Cross.

D1812.5.1.15. *Hailstorm as bad omen.* Irish myth: Cross.

D1812.5.1.16. *Dry river bed as bad omen.* Irish myth: *Cross.

D1812.5.1.16.1. *Dry river bed as omen of approaching death.* (Cf. D1812.0.1.1.) Irish myth: Cross.

D1812.5.1.17. *Spectre as evil omen.* (Cf. D1812.5.1.1.6.) Irish myth: *Cross; North Carolina: Brown Collection I 678f.

E421. Spectral ghosts. F400. Spirits and demons. M301.6.1. Banshees as portents of misfortune.

D1812.5.1.17.1. *Spirit host fighting in air as evil omen.* Irish myth: Cross.

D1812.5.1.17.2. *Clashing shields in heavens as evil omen.* Irish myth: Cross.

D1812.5.1.17.3. *Roaring of shields as evil omen.* Irish myth: Cross.

D1812.5.1.18. *Snow on house omen of approaching death.* (Cf. D1812.0.1.) Irish myth: Cross.

D1812.5.1.19. *Plague as bad omen.* Irish myth: Cross.
F493. Spirit of plague.

D1812.5.1.20. *Withering of tree as bad omen.* Irish myth: Cross.

D1812.5.1.21. *Forgetting leashes of hounds as bad omen.* Irish myth: Cross.

D1812.5.1.22. *Bad omen: seeing unusual sight on road home.* India: Thompson-Balys.

D1812.5.1.23. *Man killed by accident when ship is pushed into the sea taken as an evil omen.* Icelandic: Ragnars saga ch. 10 (9), Boberg.
N330. Accidental killing or death.

D1812.5.1.24. *Roaring of waves augurs danger to king.* (Cf. D911.1, D1812.5.2.7.) Irish myth: *Cross.

D1812.5.1.25. *Falling of shields as evil omen.* (Cf. D1101.1.) Irish myth: Cross.

D1812.5.1.26. *Falling of book satchels as evil omen.* (Cf. D1266, D1641.11.1.) Irish myth: Cross.

D1812.5.1.27. *Croaking of raven as bad omen.* Irish myth: *Cross.
B147.2.2.3. Raven as bird of ill-omen.

D1812.5.1.27.1. *Hooting of owl a bad omen.* Virgil Aeneid IV 464; *Fb "ugle" IV 963.

D1812.5.1.28. *Stirrup leather breaking as bad omen.* India: Thompson-Balys.

D1812.5.1.29. *Evil omen: scavenger carrying headload of wood.* India: Thompson-Balys.

D1812.5.1.30. *Place of bad omen.* Jewish: Neuman.

D1812.5.1.31. *Stumping toe a bad omen.* Samoa: Clark 116.

D1812.5.2. *Favorable omens.* Irish myth: *Cross; India: Thompson-Balys, *Penzer I 116, IV 122 n. 1, 171 n. 1.
N127. The auspicious day.

D1812.5.2.1. *Throbbing of right eye as favorable omen.* Penzer V 200 n. 3.

D1812.5.2.2. *Meeting certain person (animal) a good omen.* *Kittredge Witchcraft 45, 398 n. 172.

D1812.5.2.2.1. *Good omen: meeting old woman with pot of newly drawn water.* India: Thompson-Balys.

D1812.5.2.3. *Hearing thunder on setting forth a good omen.* *Kittredge Witchcraft 45, 398 n. 172; *Frazer Pausanias III 417 (lightning on the right).

D1812.5.2.4. *Bird of prey catching quarry a good omen.* *Kittredge Witchcraft 45, 398 n. 173.

D1812.5.2.5. *Hearing bird cry a good omen.*

D1812.5.2.5.1. *Hearing cuckoo call a good omen.* Alphabet No. 727.

D1812.5.2.5.2. *Hearing heron's cry a good omen.* Greek: Homer Iliad X 275.

D1812.5.2.6. *Shooting star as good omen.* (Cf. D1761.1.1.) *BP III 234.

D1812.5.2.7. *Roaring wave augurs luck.* (Cf. D911.1, D1812.5.1.24, F931.4.) Irish myth: Cross.

D1812.5.2.8. *Omen at laying foundation of building.* India: Thompson-Balys.

S261. Foundation sacrifice.

D1812.5.2.9. *King who finds golden bow and arrow (spindle) knows an heir will be born to him.* India: Thompson-Balys.

D1812.5.2.10. *Black dog as good omen.* Argentina: Jijena Sanchez 121.

D1812.5.2.11. *Spider dropping on one's front a good omen.* (Cf. D1812.5.1.12.3.) Samoa: Clark 117.

D1812.6. *Power of prophecy lost.* (Cf. D1741.)

D1812.6.1. *Power of prophecy lost by spitting.* When possessor of power on request spits into mouth of man who has taught him, he loses the power. Greek: Frazer Apollodorus I 313 n. 3.

D1813. *Magic knowledge of events in distant place.* Irish: Plummer clxx, *Cross; Icelandic: Boberg; Jewish: Neuman; India: Thompson-Balys.

D1813.0.1. *Bear knows if person looks at his track.* N. A. Indian (Seneca): Curtin 2.

D1813.0.2. *Fairy has knowledge of how mortals fare.* (Cf. D1810.0.4.) Irish myth: Cross.

F315. Fairy predicts birth of child. M301.6. Fairies as prophets.

D1813.0.3. *Father feels that son is in danger.* (Cf. D1812.0.4, D1812.5.1.1.4.) Icelandic: Hrólfs saga Kraka ch. 14, Boberg.

P233. Father and son.

D1813.0.3.1. *Father knows of son's death from far away.* India: Thompson-Balys.

D1813.1. *Dream shows events in distant place.* (Cf. D1810.8, D1812.3.3, D1812.5.1.2.) India: Thompson-Balys; Irish myth: *Cross; Icelandic: *Boberg.

D1813.1.1. *Dream warns emperor of wife's unfaithfulness.* English: Wells 138 (The Earl of Toulous); Italian Novella: Rotunda; India: Thompson-Balys.

B521. Animal warns of fatal danger. D1317. Magic object warns of danger. D1731. Magic power received in dream. K1550.1. Husband discovers wife's adultery.

D1813.1.2. *Dream warns king of error in judgment.* Italian Novella: Rotunda.

D1813.1.3. *Dream warns king of danger to kingdom.* Africa (Temne): Schlenker 87ff. No. 7.

D1813.1.4. *Dream reveals death of brother.* (Cf. D1812.3.3, D1812.5.1.2.) Irish myth: Cross.

D1813.1.5. *Dream reveals to girl death of her lover.* Heptameron No. 13.

D1813.1.6. *Dream shows others in danger.* Icelandic: FSS 247, 258, *Boberg; Papua: Ker 127.

D1813.2. *Pursuit revealed by magic.* Irish myth: Cross; Icelandic: Hrólfs saga Kraka ch. 2, Boberg.

R260. Pursuits.

D1813.3. *"Knowledge tooth" reveals events in distant place.* (Cf. D1810.3.) Irish myth: Cross.

D1813.4. *Fugitives' way revealed by magic.* Icelandic: Hrólfs saga Kraka ch. 1; Egils saga einhenda ch. IX 8 p. 44, *Boberg.

R220. Flights.

D1814. *Magic advice.* Jewish: Neuman.

B560. Animals advise men. D1312. Magic object gives advice. F1068.1. Advice and information given in dream.

D1814.1. *Advice from magician (fortune-teller, etc.).* (Cf. D1711, D1810.0.2, D1817.) Irish myth: *Cross; English: Wells 39 (Nennius Historia Britonum); Greek: Grote I 249

D1711.4. Druid as magician. D1712. Soothsayer. D1721. Magic power from magician. M301. Prophets. P427.3. Advice (instruction) from druid.

D1814.1.1. *Wizard shows man likeness of cock which will win fight.* England: Baughman.

D1814.2. *Advice from dream.* (Cf. D1810.8.) Irish myth: *Cross; India: Thompson-Balys. Icelandic: *Boberg.

D1810.8.3. Warning in dream. F1068. Realistic dream.

D1814.3. *Advice from God (or gods).* Irish myth: *Cross.

A180. Gods in relation to mortals. G303.22. The devil helps people.

D1815. *Magic knowledge of strange tongues.* Irish myth: *Cross; English: Child III 418—422; Ward II 676 No. 68; Jewish: Neuman.

D1815.0.1. *Gift of tongues received from ghosts.* Africa (Ekoi): Talbot 99.

B217.3. Animal languages learned from ghosts. E373. Ghosts bestow gifts on living.

D1815.1. *Knowledge of ghost language.* Africa (Ekoi): Talbot 99.

E545. The dead speak.

D1815.2. *Magic knowledge of language of animals.* India: Thompson-Balys.

B165. Animal languages learned from animal. B217. Animal language learned. C425. Tabu: revealing knowledge of animal languages. D1301.1. Magic turf from churchyard teaches animal languages.

D1815.3. *Magic knowledge of demon language.* Jewish: Neuman.

D1815.4. *Magic knowledge of tree language.* Jewish: Neuman.

D1815.5. *Magic knowledge of vegetable language.* Jewish: Neuman.

D1815.6. *Magic knowledge of language of valleys.* Jewish: Neuman.

D1816. *Magic discovery of desired place.* (Cf. D1314.)

B153. Dog's barking indicates hidden treasure. B156. Location determined by halting of an animal. D812.10.0.1. Angel reveals location of magic object. D1314. Magic object indicates desired place. V232.6. Angel reveals location of lost (buried) object.

D1816.1. *Location of fountain revealed in dream.* (Cf. D925, D925.1, D1731.) Irish: Plummer cl, Cross.

D1816.2. *Lost object discovered by magic.* India: Thompson-Balys.

D1816.2.1. *Lost object found by throwing spade at ghost. Where spade sticks one will find the lost object.* *Fb "gjenganger" I 443b.

D1816.3. *Location of fort determined by reading in book.* India: Thompson-Balys.

D1311.14. Divination from chance reading of sacred (magic) book.

D1816.4. *Location of buried object (body) magically revealed.* Irish myth: *Cross.

D1816.4.1. *Location of corpse of drowned person detected by magic.* India: Thompson-Balys.

D1816.5. *Druid divines whereabouts of missing person.* (Cf. D1711.4.) Irish myth: *Cross.

D1816.5.1. *Druid by magic discovers whereabouts of abducted wife.* (Cf. F322.2.) Irish myth: *Cross.

D1816.6 *Magic discovery of place for (church) building.* Icelandic: Kristensen Danske Sagn III (1895) 156ff., (1931) 115ff.

D1817. *Magic detection of crime.* (Cf. D1318.)

D1619.2.2. Eaten goat bleats from eater's stomach. H210. Test of guilt or innocence. H220. Ordeals. K420. Thief loses his goods or is detected. N270. Crime inevitably comes to light. T575.1.1. Child in mother's womb reveals crime.

D1817.0.1. *Magic detection of theft.* *Kittredge Witchcraft 190ff., 505 nn. 28, 29—53; Irish myth: *Cross; Icelandic: Boberg.

K420. Thief loses his goods or is detected.

D1817.0.1.1. *Witch (wizard) reveals name of thief.* England, U.S.: *Baughman.

D1817.0.1.2. *Wizard tells location of stolen property.* England, U.S.: *Baughman.

D1817.0.1.3. *Wizard compels thief to return stolen property.* England: *Baughman.

D1817.0.1.3.1. *Wizard compels thief to deliver stolen property in person to the owner.* England: *Baughman.

D1817.0.1.4. *Wizard shows form or shadow or picture of thief.* (Cf. D1323.1, D1821.3.7.1.) England: *Baughman.

D1817.0.1.5. *Wizard detects thieves by placing leaf from Bible under doorstep.* The guilty ones stumble over doorstep. England: Baughman.

H251.3.2. Thief detected by psalter and key. H251.3.3. Thief detected by sieve and shears.

D1817.0.1.6. *Wizard detects thief by trance.* England, U.S.: Baughman.

D1817.0.2. *Magic detection of poison.* (Cf. D1317.0.1.) Irish myth: *Cross.

F1092. Vessel of poisoned ale inverted; only poison flows out.

D1817.0.3. *Magic detection of murder.* Irish myth: Cross.

N271. Murder will out.

D1817.0.4. *Magic detection of conspiracy.* Irish myth: Cross.

D1817.0.5. *Magic detection of sin.* Irish myth: Cross.

D1817.1. *Druids magically detect crime.* Irish: Plummer clx, *Cross.

D1721. Magic power from magician. D1810.0.8. Magic knowledge of druid.

D1817.2. *Saints magically detect crime.* Irish myth: *Cross.

D1810.0.3. Magic knowledge of saints.

D1817.2.1. *Dream reveals sin to saint.* (Cf. D1810.8.) Irish myth: Cross.

D1817.2.2. *Saint magically compels thief to return goods.* *Loomis White Magic 85.

D1817.3. *Detection of crime through "knowledge tooth".* (Cf. D1810.3, D1811.1.1.) Irish myth: Cross.

D1818. *Magic remedy learned by magic.* (Cf. D1500.) Type 516; Rösch FFC LXXVII 137.

D1819. *Magic knowledge—miscellaneous.* Irish myth: Cross.

D1819.1. *Magic knowledge of another's thoughts.* Irish myth: *Cross; India: Thompson-Balys.

F256. Fairies read men's thoughts.

D1819.1.1. *Chief reads visitor's thoughts.* California Indian: Gayton and Newman 101.

D1819.2. *Deception revealed in dream.* (Cf. D1810.8.) Irish myth: Cross.

D1819.3. *Magic knowledge enables man to identify headless body.* Irish myth: Cross.

D1819.4. *Learning to read by magic.* Irish myth: *Cross.

F695.3. Learning to read in extraordinarily short time.

D1819.4.1. *Man enabled to read baptismal service by washing in holy water.* Irish myth: Cross.

D1242.1.2. Holy water as magic object. D1810.6. Magic knowledge from bathing in holy water.

D1819.4.2. *Alphabet written on cake learned by eating it.* Irish myth: *Cross.

D1793. Magic results from eating or drinking.

D1819.5. *Identity of grave revealed by magic.* Irish myth: Cross.

D1819.6. *Identity of singers revealed by magic.* Irish myth: Cross.

D1819.7. *Man is able to tell king dream which king himself does not remember.* India: Thompson-Balys.

D1819.8. *Magic knowledge of unborn calf.* India: Thompson-Balys.

D1820. Magic sight and hearing. (Cf. D1331.) *Kittredge Witchcraft 185ff.; 503ff. — Irish: Plummer clxxi; England, U.S.: Baughman; Jewish: Neuman; Buddhist myth: Malalasekera II 102.

A199.2. God has magic vision only from his throne. F642. Person of remarkable sight.

D1820.1. *Magic sight of saints.* (Cf. D1810.0.3, V220.) *Toldo Studien I 347. — Irish: *Cross, O'Suilleabhain 109, 128, Beal XXI 334, 337.

D1820.1.1. *Magic sight of blind holy man.* Spanish Exempla: Keller.

D1820.2. *Saint gives king power of long distance sight.* *Loomis White Magic 73.

D1820.3. *Saint blesses brothers' eyes so that they see heaven.* *Loomis White Magic 73.

D1821. *Means of acquiring magic sight.*

D1821.1. *Magic sight by treading on another's foot.* *BP II 319, 518; *Bolte Zs. f. Vksk. VI 204; Hdwb. d. Abergl. III 243; *Fb "se" III 175a. — Scotch: Macdougall and Calder 255, 283; Swiss: Jegerlehner Oberwallis 297 No. 1, 298 No. 7, 302 No. 27, 309 No. 10.

D1778. Magic results from contact with earth. F235.5.1. Fairies made visible by standing on another's foot. F412.2. Spirit made visible by standing on another's foot.

D1821.2. *Magic sight from thumb of knowledge.* Man cooks magic animal and burns thumb. When he puts thumb into mouth he has magic sight. (Cf. D1810.3, D1811.1.1.) **Scott Thumb. — Irish myth: *Cross; Scotch: Macdougall and Calder 253.

D1821.3. *Magic sight by looking in certain place.* *Fb "se" III 174.

D1821.3.1. *Magic sight by looking under arm.* Jakob Grimm Kleinere Schriften VII 3; *Fb "øje" III 1168b, "se" III 174. — Icelandic: *Boberg; English: Child III 411, V 299b.

D1821.3.2. *Magic sight by looking over right shoulder.* *BP II 319, 518.

D1821.3.3. *Magic sight by looking under one's legs.* *Fb "se" III 174; Icelandic: *Boberg.

D1821.3.4. *Magic sight by looking between dog's ears.* *Fb "se" III 174.

E722.1.1. Soul as black or white spirit over coffin. Black if condemned. Can be seen by peeping between horse's ears.

D1821.3.5. *Magic sight by looking through ring.* (Cf. D1076.) Irish myth: *Cross; English: Child III 412.

F235.6. Fairies visible through magic ring.

D1821.3.5.1. *One becomes ghost-seer after looking through hole in coffin.* Lithuanian: Baly Ghosts.

D1821.3.6. *Magic sight by looking through keyhole.* Fb "kirkedør" II 127.

D1821.3.7. *Magic sight by looking at shining object.*

D1323.1. Magic clairvoyant mirror.

D1821.3.7.1. *Magic sight by looking into glass of water.* Fb "vand" III 1001a; Kittredge Witchcraft 185ff., 504, 508 nn. 6, 47. — Chinese: Graham.

D1821.3.7.2. *Magic sight by looking at polished fingernail.* *Kittredge Witchcraft 185ff., 503ff. nn. 1, 5.

D1821.3.7.3. *Crystal-gazing.* Clairvoyance by looking into crystal. Kittredge Witchcraft 185ff., 503ff. nn. *1—3, 10—24, 35, 47. — England, U.S.: Baughman; India: Thompson-Balys.

D1821.3.7.4. *Magic sight by looking at polished sword-blade.* Kittredge Witchcraft 185ff., 504, 508 nn. 6, 7, 47.

D1821.3.8. *Magic sight by looking at shoulder-bone of sheep.* *Kittredge Witchcraft 186, 504 n. 6.

D1821.3.9. *Magic sight by looking in the hollow of one's hand.* Icelandic: *Boberg.

D1821.3.10. *Magic sight by looking through feather.* India: Thompson-Balys.

D1821.4. *Magic sight by putting ointment into eye.* (Cf. D1244.) England: Lang English Fairy Tales 220.

F235.4.1. Fairies made visible through use of ointment.

D1821.5. *Magic sight by standing on certain stone.* Hartland Science 197.

D1778. Magic results from contact with earth. F235.5. Fairies made visible by stepping on certain spot.

D1821.6. *Magic sight given to abandoned child.* Scotland: Macdougall and Calder 183.

S350. Fate of abandoned child.

D1821.7. *Deaf and dumb man can see soul taken to happiness or punishment.* Fb "sjæl" III 214b; Spanish Exempla: Keller.

D1821.8. *Possession by spirit of dead person gives second sight.* India: Thompson-Balys.

D1821.9. *Magic sight by turning clothes inside out.* Cheremis: Sebeok-Nyerges.

D1821.10. *Magic sight by standing alone for three days.* Icelandic: Boberg.

D1821.11. *Magic sight gift of grateful animals.* India: Thompson-Balys.

B500. Magic power from animals.

D1822. *Loss of magic sight.* (Cf. D1741.)

D1822.1. *Magic sight overcome by incantation.* (Cf. D1273.) Irish myth: *Cross.

D1825. *Kinds of magic sight.*

D1323.1. Magic clairvoyant mirror.

D1825.1. *Second sight.* Power to see future happenings. (Cf. D1812.) *Chauvin V 90 No. 28 n. 2; *Fb "synsk", "spåkjælling", "spåmand", "gjenviser"; *RTP XXVII *145, 151, 284, 382. — Irish: Plummer clxx, *Cross; Scotland: Macdougall and Calder 183, 251, 255, 281; Icelandic: Snorra Edda Prol. V and Gylf. II, *Boberg; Jewish: *Neuman; India: Thompson-Balys; N. A. Indian (Seneca): Curtin-Hewitt RBAE XXXII 478 No. 103, (Plains Ojibwa): Skinner JAFL XXXII 300.

B120.0.1. Animals have second sight. D1331.4. Magic object causes sight shifting. D1811.1.1. Thumb of knowledge. F451.3.3.7. Dwarfs predict. K1870. Illusions. M300. Prophecies. M301. Prophets.

D1825.1.2. *Magic view of future lover.* *Fb "kjæreste" II 153; Type 737*. — England, U.S.: *Baughman; Jewish: Neuman; India: Thompson-Balys.

T22. Predestined lovers.

D1825.2. *Magic power to see distant objects.* (Cf. D1813.3, D1817.0.1, D1825.5.) *BP II 319; *Bolte Zs. f. Vksk. VI 204. — Celtic: Hartland Science 197; England: Child III 412; England, Scotland, U.S.: *Baughman; Icelandic: *Boberg; Lithuanian: Balys Index No. 3507; India: Thompson-Balys; Africa (Angola): Chatelain 91 No. 5.

D1825.2.1. *Magic sight of earthly objects from otherworld.* Irish myth: Cross.

F210. Fairyland.

D1825.2.2. *Magic power to see whole country at once.* Jewish: Neuman.

D1825.3. *Magic power to see invisible creatures.* Swiss. Jegerlehner

Oberwallis 297f. Nos. 1, 7; Scotch: Macdougall and Calder 183, Lang English Fairy Tales 220; Lithuanian: Balys Index No. 3510.

D1323.5. Magic salve gives clairvoyance. F235.3. Fairies visible to one person alone.

D1825.3.1. *Magic power of seeing Death at head or foot of bed and thus forecasting progress of sickness.* *Type 332; *BP I 377 ff. — Italian Novella: Rotunda; Jewish: Neuman.

D1724. Magic power from Death. Death as godfather. Z111. Death personified.

D1825.3.2. *Man sees angels over the heads of the good and black stars over the bad.* Spanish Exempla: Keller.

E722.1.1. Soul as black or white spirit over coffin.

D1825.3.3. *Magic sight: ability to see the soul (astral body).* India: Thompson-Balys.

D1825.3.3.1. *Magic power to see souls after death.* Cheremis: Sebeok-Nyerges; India: Thompson-Balys.

D1825.3.3.2. *Magic power to see soul leaving body.* India: Thompson-Balys.

D1825.3.4. *Ability to see heavenly beings.* Jewish: Neuman.

D1825.3.4.1. *Ability to see angel of God.* India: Thompson-Balys.

D1825.3.4.2. *Ability to see messengers of Pluto.* India: Thompson-Balys.

D1825.4. *Magic power to see concealed things.* (Cf. D1817.) Irish myth: *Cross; Icelandic: *Boberg.

D1825.4.1. *Magic power of seeing things underground.* Irish myth: Cross; Greek: Frazer Apollodorus II 12 n. 3.

D1825.4.2. *Magic power to see whether girl is virgin.* Type 592; Norwegian Christiansen 89.

H400. Chastity test. T300. Chastity and celibacy.

D1825.4.3. *Magic power to see lost things.* England, Scotland: *Baughman.

D1825.4.3.1. *Prophet locates lost child.* Greek: *Grote I 206.

D1825.5. *Magic power to see death circumstances of absent person.* Canada, England, Scotland, U.S., Wales: *Baughman.

D1825.6. *Magic power to "see" who will die during coming year.* England, U.S.: *Baughman.

D1825.7. *Magic sight of incident before it actually happens.* Scotland, Wales, U.S.: *Baughman.

D1825.7.1. *Person sees phantom funeral procession some time before the actual procession takes place.* England, Ireland, Scotland: *Baughman.

D1825.8. *What religious ascetic sees as gold, ordinary people see as scorpions.* India: Thompson-Balys.

D1825.9. *Witches have power to see distant sights.* England: Baughman (D1912.1.).

D1827. *Magic hearing.*

E402. Mysterious ghost-like noises heard.

D1827.1. *Magic hearing of noises which portend death.* (Cf. D1812.)

D1827.1.1. *Listening at church door on Halloween to hear the names of those to die in the coming year.* (Cf. D1825.6.) Wales: Baughman.

D1827.1.2. *Sounds heard before death; the sounds are later repeated in connection with the death or funeral.* England, Scotland, Wales, Canada, U.S.: *Baughman.

D1827.1.3. *Noise warns of approaching death.* Scotland, Wales, U.S.: *Baughman.

D1827.1.4. *Sounds heard from distance at time of death.* England, Wales, Scotland, U.S.: *Baughman.

D1827.2. *Person hears call for aid from great distance.* U.S.: Baughman.

D1830. Magic strength.. (Cf. D1335.) Irish myth: *Cross; Jewish: Neuman; Eskimo (Bering Strait): Nelson RBAE XVIII 491.

F610. Remarkably strong man (Strong John). F611.2.2. Strong hero suckled by mermaid. Gives him strength of twelve men. F611.3. Strong hero acquires his strength. F982. Animals carry extraordinary burden. K185.6. Deceptive land purchase: bounds fixed by throwing object (axe, spear). Thrower has extraordinary strength. G13.1. Ritual cannibalism: corpse of a hero (demi-god) eaten to acquire his strength.

D1830.1. *Man's strength made equal to that of angel.* Jewish: Neuman.

D1831. *Magic strength resides in hair.* (Cf. D991.) *Frazer Old Testament II 482ff., Jewish: *Neuman; *Frazer Golden Bough I 102, XI 158ff.; *Hdwb. d. Abergl. III 1258; *Wilken Verspreide Geschriften III 551ff.; *Fb "styrke" III 630a, "hår" IV 241b; Krappe "Samson" Revue Archéologique (1933) 195—211. — Greek: Fox 69 (Nisos), 77 (Pterelaos); Spanish: Boggs FFC XC 67 No. 508A*, Keller; N. A. Indian (Pawnee): Dorsey MAFLS VIII 113 No. 31; Hawaii: Beckwith Myth 466.

E714. Soul (or life) kept in special part of body. F531.1.6.13. Giant's strength in hair. G221.1. Strength of witches in hair. K975. Secret of strength treacherously discovered.

D1831.1. *Saint binds devil with one of the hairs of her head.* Irish myth: Cross.

D1831.2. *Magic strength resides in beard.* *Fb "styrke" III 630a. — Icelandic: *Boberg.

D1831.3. *Magic strength resides in semen.* (Cf. T541.10.) Gaster Thespis 327.

D1832. *Magic strength by bathing.* (Cf. D1242.1.) *MacCulloch Childhood 70ff. — N. A. Indian (Tsimshian, Tlingit, Haida): Boas RBAE XXXI 729.

D1335.8. Bathing in magic cauldron gives strength. D1788. Magic results from bathing.

D1833. *Magic strength by touching earth.* Greek: Apollodorus I 222 n. 2 (Antaeus).

D1778. Magic results from contact with earth. G221.2. Strength of witches depends on their touching earth. K12.3. Wrestling match: Antaeus. Giant invincible in wrestling because with each contact with earth his strength is renewed.

D1834. *Magic strength from helpful animal.* Fb "styrke".

B500. Magic power from animals.

D1835. *Other means of acquiring magic strength.*

D1835.1. *Magic strength acquired by looking at necklace.* Penzer V 76 n. 1.

D1835.2. *Magic strength given horse by combing hair right way and wrong way.* Scottish: Campbell-McKay No. 1 and note 2.

D1835.3. *Magic strength by stroking.* Icelandic: Sturlaugs saga St. 605, *Boberg.

D1835.4. *Magic strength obtained by wearing blue ribbon.* French Canadian: Sister Marie Ursule. (Cf. D1078.1.)

D1835.5. *Magic strength results from songs.* (Cf. D1781.) Eskimo (Greenland): Rasmussen I 277.

D1835.6. *Magic strength from demon.* Eskimo (Greenland): Rasmussen II 51.

D1836. *Magic waxing and waning of strength.* It waxes till noon and wanes thereafter. English: Wells 50 (Le Morte Arthur); Irish myth: *Cross.

D1836.1. *Ghost's strength waxes and wanes with height of fire.* N. A. Indian (Teton): Dorsey Am. Anth. o.s. II (1889) 150.

D1271. Magic fire. D2064.2. Sickness of princess dependent on witch's fire. D2065.4. Insanity of princess dependent on height of fire. F1061. Flame as miraculous index.

D1836.2. *Strength wanes at particular places.* Jewish: *Neuman.

D1836.3. *Magic waxing of strength at night.* Jewish: *Neuman.

D1837. *Magic weakness.* Irish myth: *Cross; Scotch: Campbell Tales II 47; Icelandic: Boberg.

C111. Tabu: loss of chastity. Hero loses power with loss of chastity. C940. Sickness or weakness for breaking tabu. C942. Loss of strength from broken tabu. D1336. Magic object gives weakness. D1410. Magic object renders helpless. D2061.1.4. Persons magically made to decay and die. D2064. Magic sickness. D2070. Bewitching. F362.3. Fairies cause weakness. F585.3. Phantom women cause weakness.

D1837.1. *Magic weakness during certain period.*

D1837.1.1. *Magic weakness for five days each year.* (Cf. D1837.3.) Irish: MacCulloch Celtic 73f., *Cross.

T581.8. Woman bears twins at end of footrace (with king's horses). T583.1. Couvade.

D1837.2. *Magic weakness never entirely removed.* Irish myth: Cross.

D1837.3. *Magic weakness as result of fairy's (goddess's) curse.* (Cf. D1837.1.1.) Irish myth: *Cross.

D1792. Magic results from curse. F362.3. Fairies cause weakness.

D1837.4. *Snake becomes powerless when his path is crossed by a pregnant woman.* India: Thompson-Balys.

D1837.5. *Magic weakness from eating sender's food.* Jewish: Neuman.

D1840. Magic invulnerability. **Otto Berthold Die Unverwundbarkeit in Sage und Aberglauben der Griechen (Giessen, 1911); cf. Zs. f. Vksk. XXI 415. — Irish myth: *Cross; Icelandic: Herrmann Saxo II 312, *Boberg; Greek: Frazer Apollodorus II 150 n. 1; Swiss: Jegerlehner Oberwallis 300 No. 5; Jewish: *Neuman; India: Thompson-Balys; Buddhist myth: Malalasekera II 287, 597. — Eskimo (Greenland): Rink 99, 417, Rasmussen II 260, III 105, 250; Teheulche (Patagonian): Alexander Lat. Am. 336; Africa (Zulu): Callaway 93, 233.

B181.11. Magic invulnerable horse. D1344. Magic object gives invulnerability. D1381.3.2. Magic unpierceable horn skin protects against attack.

F259.1.4.1. Fairies cannot be slain. F343.10.3. Fairy gives invulnerable shield. F558. Person covered with horn. G229.4. Invulnerability of witches. K2213.4.1. Secret of vulnerability disclosed by hero's wife. M367.1. Immunity from wet or dry. V228. Immunities of saints (holy men). Z310. Unique vulnerability. Z311. Achilles' heel. Invulnerability except in one spot. Z312. Unique deadly weapon. Only one thing will kill a certain man.

D1840.1. *Magic invulnerability of saints.* (Cf. Q162, V228.) *Toldo IV 84. — Irish myth: *Cross.

H1573.3.1. Saint drinks poison without injury as proof of power of Christianity.

D1840.1.1. *Magic invulnerability of saint enables him to break poisonous snakes in bare hands.* Spanish Exempla: Keller.

D1840.1.2. *Saint invulnerable to poison.* Spanish Exempla: Keller.

H1573.3.1. Saint drinks poison without injury as proof of power of Christianity.

D1840.1.2.1. *Poisoned drink or food made harmless by saint's blessing.* *Loomis White Magic 57.

D1840.1.3. *St. Cecilia withstands three blows of beheading sword and lives three days after.* *Loomis White Magic 116.

D1840.2. *Magic invulnerability of animals.* *Loomis White Magic 57; Irish myth: *Cross.

B11.12.1. Dragon cannot be killed with weapons. B15.7.10.1. Animal with horny skin. B100. Magic animals. B184.1.11. Magic invulnerable horse. D1025. Magic skin of animal.

D1840.2.1. *Invulnerable cat.* India: Thompson-Balys.

D1840.2.2. *Invulnerable stag.* Chinese and Persian: Coyajee JPASB XXIV 182.

D1840.3. *Magic invulnerability of ogres.* Irish myth: *Cross.

G630. Characteristics of ogres. Z312.2. Giant ogre can be killed only with iron club he carries.

D1841. *Invulnerability from certain things.*

D1841.1. *Man proof against iron, stone, and wood.* Hindu: Tawney I 444; Icelandic: Boberg.

D1841.2. *Man proof against boiling water.* Type 534.

H328.5. Suitor test: bathing in boiling water.

D1841.2.1. *Saint kept in boiling water for three days shows no signs of discomfort.* *Loomis White Magic 33.

D1841.2.2. *Bath in boiling oil, pitch, or melted lead does not hurt a saint.* *Loomis White Magic 33.

D1841.2.2.1. *Saint placed in boiling oil but uninjured.* Irish myth: *Cross.

R215.2. Escape from death by boiling oil.

D1841.3. *Burning magically evaded.* (Cf. D1656.) Chauvin VI 189 No. 356; Crane Liber de Miraculis 88 No. 15; Günter Christliche Legende 234 s.v. "Feuer"; Cosquin Indiens 439ff.; Toldo Studien VI 298; Alphabet No. 308; *Loomis White Magic 114. — Jewish: *Neuman, Spence 51f., Gaster Rabbis 191 No. 28, 185 No. 2B; Irish: *Cross, O'Suilleabhain 71, Beal XXI 326; Spanish Exempla: Keller; N. A. Indian: *Thompson Tales 311 n. 120.

B526. Animal saves man from death by burning. D1271. Magic fire. D1382.5. Magic fire does not harm one. D1566. Magic object controls fire. D2158. Magic control of fires. F222.1.1. Fairies' underground palace cannot be burned by fire or destroyed by water. H221. Ordeal by fire. H1511. Heat test. Attempt to kill hero by burning him in fire. H1542. Contest in enduring heat. K955. Murder by burning. V137. House of woman who launders clothes for church spared in great fire.

D1841.3.1. *Magic animal proof against burning.* Irish myth: *Cross.

D1841.3.2. *Fire does not injure a saint.*

S192. Torturing by fire. V222.8. Holy man passes through fire for his faith.

D1841.3.2.1. *Fiery furnace as a mean of torture for a saint remains ineffective.* *Loomis White Magic 33; India: Thompson-Balys.

D1841.3.2.2. *Saint walks through glowing coals without harm.* *Loomis White Magic 33.

Q414.1. Punishment: boiling in oil (lead, tar).

D1841.3.2.3. *Red hot iron carried with the bare hands without harm to the saint.* *Loomis White Magic 34.

H221.1.1. Test of sanctity: carrying of live coals in a robe or a cloak without harm to the garment or injury to the bearer.

D1841.3.2.3.1. *Saint carries fire in hand to warm guests.* Irish myth: Cross.

D1841.3.2.4. *Holy maidens carry glowing embers in their chasubles without being burned.* Irish myth: *Cross.

D1841.3.3. *Sacred book or manuscript does not burn in fire.* *Loomis White Magic 31f.

D1841.4. *Man proof against wet.* (Cf. D1524.1, D1540, D1551, D2125, D2151.) India: Thompson-Balys.

F930.1. Book dropped in water by saint not wet.

D1841.4.1. *Man proof against wet from rain.* *Loomis White Magic 39; Irish: Plummer cxxxvii, *Cross; Welsh: MacCulloch Celtic 198. — Africa (Kaffir): Theal 76.

D1841.4.2. *Person proof against wet from snow.* Irish myth: Cross.

D1841.4.3. *Walking upon water without wetting the soles or garments.* *Loomis White Magic 40.

D1841.4.3.1. *The waters of seas, lakes, and streams turn aside and let the holy man walk through untouched by moisture.* (Cf. D1551.) *Loomis White Magic 40.

D1841.4.3.2. *Stones cast in the ocean keep dry.* India: Thompson-Balys.

D1841.4.4. *Rain or snow avoids certain places according to the desire of a saint or monk.* *Loomis White Magic 39, 43.

D1841.4.5. *Whale husband makes wife's eyes impervious to sea water.* Eskimo (Greenland): Rink 127.

D1841.5. *Invulnerability from weapons.* Irish myth: Cross.

D1841.5.1. *Man proof against weapons.* Irish myth: *Cross; Jewish: Neuman; Eskimo (Greenland): Holm 26, Rink 335.

D1841.5.1.1. *Invulnerability from hurled stones.* Jewish: Neuman.

D1841.5.2. *Magic animal proof against weapons.* Irish myth: *Cross; Eskimo (Cumberland Sound): Boas BAM XV 262.

D1841.5.3. *Axe will not cut man, however much he strikes himself.* India: Thompson-Balys.

D1841.6. *Immunity from drowning.* (Cf. F222.1.1.) Irish myth: *Cross.

D1841.6.1. *Magic animal proof against drowning.* Irish myth: *Cross.

D1841.7. *Magic animal proof against hound.* Irish myth: Cross.

D1841.8. *Man proof against poison.* (Cf. D1840.1.2.) Icelandic: Boberg.

D1841.9. *Invulnerability from demons.* Jewish: Neuman.

D1845. *Invulnerability for limited time.*

D1845.1. *Invulnerability for single day.* Greek: Frazer Apollodorus I 109 n. 4, 110 n. 1.

D1845.2. *Invulnerability only when dressed in certain clothes.* (Cf. D1344.) Jewish: Neuman.

D1846. *Attainment of invulnerability.* (Cf. D1840.) *Fb "hård" I 772b; Icelandic: *Boberg; Eskimo (Greenland): Rink 125, 138.

D1846.1. *Invulnerability by being burned and anointed with magic ointments.* (Cf. D1244.) Roscher Lexikon s.v. "Achilleus" I 24, *Grote I 218.

D1787. Magic results from burning.

D1846.2. *Invulnerability bestowed by many-headed monster.* (Cf. B15.1.2.) Zulu: Callaway.

D1846.3. *Magic horse renders rider invulnerable.* (Cf. B184.1.11.) Irish myth: *Cross.

D1846.4. *Invulnerability through bathing in dragon's blood.* *Von Sydow Sigurds Strid med Fåvne 27ff.; Lithuanian: Balys Index No. *650A.

B11. Dragon. D1500.1.9.3. Dragon's heart-blood as remedy. D1016. Magic blood of animal. D1788. Magic results from bathing.

D1846.4.1. *Attainment of invulnerability through magic bath.* Icelandic: Boberg.

D1846.5. *Invulnerability bestowed by saint.* (Cf. V220.) Irish myth: *Cross.

H1573.1.4. Man commanded by saint to leap into fiery furnace. Unharmed.

D1846.5.1. *Invulnerability by invoking saint.* Irish myth: Cross.

D1766.10. Magic results produced in name of saint.

D1846.5.2. *Pious man in city renders it invulnerable.* Jewish: Neuman.

D1846.6. *Man killed and restored as invulnerable.* Eskimo (Bering Strait): Nelson RBAE XVIII 503.

E0: Resuscitation.

D1847. *Loss of invulnerability.* Irish myth: Cross.

D1847.1. *Invulnerability lost if man forgets sweetheart.* English: Child I 189f.; India: Thompson-Balys.

D1850. Immortality. (Cf. D1346.) Irish myth: *Cross; Jewish: Neuman; India: Thompson-Balys.

A122. God half mortal; half immortal. A153.2. Magic food gives immortality to gods. E0. Resuscitation. F167.9. Otherworld people ever young, ever beautiful. F243.5. Fairies' food gives immortality. F251.5. Fairies as sprites who have been given immortality. V311. Belief in the life to come (immortality taught by druids).

D1850.1. *Immortality useless without eternal youth.* India: Thompson-Balys.

D1880. Magic rejuvenation. M416.2. Curse: eternal life without eternal youth.

D1850.2. *Woman changes into an immortal.* Chinese: Graham.

D1851. *Immortality bestowed.* Greek: Frazer Apollodorus I 44 n. 1 (Hercules).

D1851.1. *Immortality by burning.* Greek: Roscher Lexikon s.v. "Achilleus" I 24, Frazer Apollodorus II 69 n. 4, I 37 n. (burning and stripping off mortal flesh [Demophon]) *Carl-Martin Edsman Ignis Divinus: Le feu comme moyen de rajeunissement et d'immortalité (Publications of the New Society of Letters No. 34, Lund, 1949).

D1346.8. Magic ointment gives immortality. Burning at night and anointment by magic ointment by day. D1787. Magic results from burning.

D1851.2. *Immortality gained from bargain with Death.* Italian Novella: Rotunda.

D1413.1.3. Fig tree from which one cannot descend. D1724. Magic power from Death. D1825.3.1. Magic power of seeing Death. K100. Deceptive bargains. Z111. Death personified.

D1851.3. *Immortality bestowed by saint.* (Cf. V220.) Irish myth: Cross.

D1851.4. *Immortality bestowed by Christ.* (Cf. V211.) Irish myth: *Cross.

D1851.5. *Immortality bestowed by deity.* Greek: Grote I 174, 284, 287.

D1853. *Immortality exchanged.* Wounded Centaur immortal but cannot be cured. He gives away his immortality to Prometheus and is thus allowed to die. Greek: *Frazer Apollodorus I 191 n. 3.

D1853.1. *Immortality exchanged for death on alternate days.* Greek: Grote I 158.

D1854. *Giant immortal so long as he touches land of his birth.* Greek: Frazer Apollodorus I 44 n. 1.

D1778. Magic results from contact with earth.

D1855. *Time of death postponed.* (Cf. D1345, D1857.) Irish myth: Cross; Jewish: Neuman; Icelandic: Boberg.

D1855.1. *Witch delays person's death.* Africa (Ekoi): Talbot 234.

D1855.2. *Death postponed if substitute can be found.* Greek: Euripides Alcestis, *Grote I 108; India: Thompson-Balys.

E165. Resuscitation of wife by husband giving up half his remaining life. M292. Wife undertakes man's penances: also to go to heaven for him? T211.1. Wife dies so that husband's death may be postponed.

D1855.3. *Saint delays person's death.* (Cf. V220.) Irish myth: Cross.

D1855.4. *Death can be postponed if man does not break tabu for forty days.* India: Thompson-Balys.

C300. Looking tabu. C400. Speaking tabu.

D1855.5. *Life prolonged a thousand years by traveling six months each year.* India: Thompson-Balys.

D1855.6. *Death postponed for three generations.* Greek: *Grote I 202.

D1856. *Death evaded.* Person enters on the next life without dying. Greek: Fox 53 (Amphiaraos); Hebrew: Genesis 5:24, 2 Kings 2:11; U.S.: Baughman.

F11.2. Man goes to heaven without dying. V229.2.12.1. Seven Irish saints who never died.

D1856.1. *Hero (saint) taken to Paradise (Heaven) alive.*

D1856.1.1. *"The Two Sorrows of the Kingdom of Heaven": Elijah and Enoch pass to otherworld without dying.* Irish myth: *Cross.

D1856.2. *Three Nephites are granted quasi-immortal state by Jesus Christ at time of resurrection.* (Cf. V294.) U.S.: Baughman.

D1857. *Magic longevity.* Irish myth: *Cross.

A191.1. Great age of the gods. B81.13.12. Mermaid lives for 300 years under lake. B841. Long-lived animals.

D1857.1. *Old woman has lived for ages.* Irish myth: *Cross.

D1857.2. *Two hundred years of unfailing life and happiness offered to warrior by fairy woman in exchange for one day's delay of battle.* Irish myth: Cross.

D1860. Magic beautification. BP I 86ff., 99ff., 165ff., 207ff. (Gr. Nos. 11, 13, 21, 24); *Loomis White Magic 80, 82; Cox Cinderella 481 n. 12 (most of references there given). — Irish: *Cross, Beal XXI 335; Breton: Sébillot Incidents s.v. "beauté"; French Canadian: Barbeau JAFL XXIX 17; Jewish: Neuman; Buddhist myth: Malalasekera II 527. — N. A. Indian: *Thompson Tales 349 n. 259, (Zuni): Parsons JAFL XXXI 244 No. 16; Africa (Fjort): Dennett 43 No. 6, (Hottentot): Bleek 76 No. 35. — See also all references to D732 and D733.

A120.1. God as shape-shifter. D52. Changes to different appearance. D412.4.1. Transformation: packhorse to palfrey. D621.3. Ugly by day; fair by night. D682.4.2. "Spirit of poetry" as hideous youth becomes beautiful. D732. Loathly lady. D733. Loathly bridegroom. D733.1. Hairy anchorite. D1337. Magic object makes beautiful or hideous. D1338. Magic object rejuvenates. F129.4.3. Voyage to Isle of Shape. F234 Transformed fairy. F343.11. Fairy offers man change of form and feature for aid in battle. V331.3. Miraculous beautification upon conversion to Christianity.

D1860.0.1. *Magic beautification of fairy.* (Cf. D732, F234.) Irish myth: Cross.

D1862. *Magic beauty bestowed.* Jewish: Neuman.

D1862.1. *Magic beauty bestowed by supernatural wife.* S. A. Indian (Toba): Métraux MAFLS XL 44.

D1862.2. *Magic beauty bestowed by saint.* Jewish: Neuman.

D1863. *Beautification by stroking (tapping).* Africa (Ekoi): Talbot 207.

D1864. *Magic beautification through prayer by saint.* (Cf. D1766.1.) Irish myth: Cross.

D1865. *Beautification by death and resuscitation.*

E0. Resuscitation.

D1865.1. *Beautification by decapitation and replacement of head.* *Type 531. — Italian Novella: Rotunda; Eskimo (Bering Strait): Nelson RBAE XVIII 503.

D711. Disenchantment by decapitation. E12. Resuscitation by decapitation. E30. Resuscitation by arrangement of members. J2411.1. Imitation of magic rejuvenation unsuccessful.

D1865.2. *Beautification by boiling and resuscitation.* Greek: Frazer Apollodorus II 156 n. 2 (Pelops); N. A. Indian: *Thompson Tales 349 n. 258.

D1787. Magic results from burning. D1885. Rejuvenation by boiling. E15.1. Resuscitation by boiling. E728.1. Evil spirit cast out of person by killing and resuscitating. S112.1. Boiling to death. Often in pitch or oil.

D1865.2.1. *Girl becomes more beautiful as she is burned but her brother, who loves her incestuously, turns to charcoal.* India: Thompson-Balys.

J2411.1. Imitation of magic rejuvenation unsuccessful. Q414.0.3. Burning as punishment for incest (incontinence).

D1865.3. *Face of pious girl becomes angelic at death.* Irish: O'Suilleabhain 115.

D1866. *Other means of beautification.*

D1866.1. *Beautification by bathing.* Irish myth: Cross; Spanish: Boggs FFC XC 70 No. 531; India: Thompson-Balys; Indonesian: Dixon 216; Philippine (Tinguian): Cole 159, 161; Tonga: Gifford 186; Easter Island: Métraux Ethnology 388.

D562. Transformation by bathing. D1337.4. Bathing in magic cauldron gives beauty. D1788. Magic results from bathing. D1887. Rejuvenation by bathing. D1895. Magic aging by bathing. G264.0.1. Ogress bathes in pool; becomes beautiful maiden; becomes king's favorite wife.

D1866.2. *Beautification by removal of skin.* (Cf. D1889.6.) German: Grimm No. 179.

D1866.3. *Beautification by fasting.* Jewish: Neuman.

D1867. *Magic beautification of house.* Irish myth: *Cross; Africa (Fjort): Dennett 40 No. 5.

D1130. Magic buildings and parts. D1337.9. Magic needle transforms a room from plainness to beauty.

D1867.1. *Hut becomes mansion.* India: Thompson-Balys.

D1868. *Magic beautification of animal.*

D1868.1. *Broken-down nag becomes magnificent riding horse.* Type 314. — India: Thompson-Balys.

D1870. Magic hideousness. (Cf. D1337, D1860, M400.) See references to following motifs: D732, D733, D621.3. — BP I 86ff., 99ff., 165ff., 207ff. (Gr. Nos. 11, 13, 21, 24); *Loomis White Magic 82; Cox Cinderella 481 n. 12. References to BP and to Cox concern motif Q2 (Kind and Unkind) which usually involves magic hideousness. — Irish myth: *Cross; India: Thompson-Balys; Jewish: Neuman. — S. A. Indian (Carajá): Métraux MAFLS XL 48, (Toba): ibid. 87; Africa (Ekoi): Talbot 273.

D621.3. Ugly by day; fair by night. D732. Loathly lady. D733. Loathly bridegroom. H425.2. Horns grow on cuckold's head. M400. Curses.

D1871. *Girl magically made hideous.* Irish myth: Cross.

D1872. *Man made hideous.*

D1872.1. *Handsome man magically made ugly.* Irish myth: Cross.

D1873. *Object magically made hideous.*

D1873.1. *Picture magically made hideous.* India: Thompson-Balys.

D1880. Magic rejuvenation. Irish: Plummer clxxxiv, *Cross; Icelandic:

MacCulloch Eddic 180; Breton: Sébillot Incidents s.v. "vieille", "rajeunissement"; Jewish: Neuman; India: Thompson-Balys; Hindu: Keith 31; Buddhist myth: Malalasekera II 960. — N. A. Indian: *Thompson Tales 284 n. 50; Africa (Ekoi): Talbot 208, 238.

A154.1. Magic drink gives immortality to gods. D1338. Magic object rejuvenates.

D1881. *Magic self-rejuvenation.* Persian: Carnoy 277.

A191. Goddess rejuvenates self when old. B32.1. Phoenix renews youth. B758. Eagle renews youth. D56.1. Transformation: man to baby at will.

D1882. *Rejuvenation by supernatural person.* Irish myth: Cross.

D1882.1. *Rejuvenation by saint.* Irish myth: *Cross.

D1713. Magic power of hermit (saint). V220. Saints.

D1882.2. *Rejuvenation by fairy.* Irish myth: *Cross.

F302. Fairy mistress. Mortal man marries or lives with fairy woman.

D1883. *Eternal youth.* (Cf. F167.9, F172.) Irish myth: Cross; Eskimo (Greenland): Rink 424, 447.

D1349.2. Magic object produces immunity from old age. D1338.1.1. Fountain of youth. M416.2. Tithonus given eternal life without eternal youth.

D1884. *Rejuvenation by dismemberment.* (Cf. D1885.1.) *Dh II 154; BP III 198 n. 3; Gaster Thespis 266, 300.

S139.2. Slain person dismembered.

D1885. *Rejuvenation by boiling.* (Cf. D1865.) *Fb "ungdom" III 979ab. — Breton: Sébillot Incidents s.v. "rajeunissement"; Greek: Fox 114, Frazer Apollodorus I 121 n. 4.

D1787. Magic results from burning. E15.1. Resuscitation by boiling. S112.1. Boiling to death.

D1885.1. *Rejuvenation by dismemberment and boiling.* (Cf. D1884.) Girard de Rialle RTP I 74; *Fb "ungdom" III 979ab; Greek: Grote I 110.

D1886. *Rejuvenation by burning.* *Type 753; *BP III 198 (Gr. No. 147); *FB "ungdom" III 979; *Dh II 154, 162ff., 288; *Bolte Herrigs Archiv CII 241—266, CIV 355; Köhler-Bolte I 298; *Carl-Martin Edsman Ignis Divinus: Le feu comme moyen de rajeunissement et d'immortalité (Publications of the New Society of Letters No. 34, Lund 1949). — Icelandic: Ritterhaus 338; Breton: Sébillot Incidents s.v. "four"; German: Hartung Zs. f. Vksk. VII 89, Piger ibid. X 84; Greek: *Frazer Apollodorus I 121 n. 4; India: Thompson-Balys.

D1787. Magic results from burning. J2411.1. Imitation of magic rejuvenation unsuccessful.

D1886.1. *Rejuvenation by burning and throwing bones into tub of milk.* (Cf. D1338.4.) England: Child I 507b.

A1861.2. Creation of monkeys: old woman thrown into fire.

D1887. *Rejuvenation by bathing.* Irish myth: *Cross; Hindu: Keith 87, 141.

D562. Transformation by bathing. D1338.4. Bath in magic milk rejuvenates. D1788. Magic results from bathing. D1866. Beautification by bathing. D1895. Magic aging by bathing.

D1889. *Miscellaneous means of rejuvenation.*

D1889.1. *Rejuvenation by reading in book.* (Cf. D1266.) Fb "ungdom" III 979b.

D1889.2. *Rejuvenation by looking into mirror.* (Cf. D1163.) Fb "ungdom" III 979b.

D1889.3. *Rejuvenation by song of pelican.* (Cf. D1275.) Fb "ungdom" III 979b.

B751.2. Pelican kills young and revives them with own blood.

D1889.4. *Rejuvenation by smelling apple.* (Cf. D981.1, D1338.3.1.) Fb "ungdom" III 979b.

D1889.5. *Rejuvenation by going to other world and having digestive tract removed.* Chinese: Hartland Science 178.

D1889.6. *Rejuvenation by changing skin.* Penzer IX 48 n.; Icelandic: *Boberg; Eskimo (Cumberland Sound): Boas BAM XV 227; Africa (Congo): Grenfell (Baluba) 814f., (Wachaga): Gutman 120.

K1941.1. Disguised flayer tightens skin to look beautiful.

D1889.7. *Rejuvenation by being reborn.* Man in fish form eaten and reborn. (Cf. T511.) Irish myth: *Cross.

E600. Reincarnation. T500. Conception and birth.

D1889.8. *Rejuvenation by riding surf.* Marquesas: Beckwith Myth 502, Handy 60.

D1889.9. *Rejuvenation by drinking from magic horn.* Irish myth: Cross.

D1889.10. *Rejuvenation by conjuring.* Eskimo (Greenland): Rasmussen I 272, 322, III 248, Rink 238.

D1889.11. *Rejuvenation by jumping over cliff.* Eskimo (Greenland): Rink 403.

D1890. Magic aging. (Cf. D1857.) Fb "ungdom" III 979b; *Loomis White Magic 80; Penzer I 137. — Irish: Plummer clxxiv, *Cross; Breton: Sébillot Incidents s.v. "vieux"; Estonian: Hartland Science 201; Jewish: Neuman; India: Thompson-Balys; Chinese: Graham; N. A. Indian: *Thompson Tales 284 n. 50b.

D1341. Magic object makes person old.

D1891. *Transformation to old man to escape recognition.* Icelandic: FSS 27, Boberg; Maori: Dixon 60; Calif. Indian: Gayton and Newman 80.

D640. Reasons for voluntary transformation. K1810. Deception by disguise.

D1895. *Magic aging by bathing.* Irish myth: *Cross.

D562. Transformation by bathing. D1338.4. Bath in magic milk rejuvenates. D1788. Magic results from bathing. D1866. Beautification by bathing. D1887. Rejuvenation by bathing.

D1896. *Magic aging by contact with earth after otherworld journey.* Fb "jord" II 46a; Hartland Science 197ff. — Irish myth: *Cross; England, Wales: Baughman.

D1778. Magic results from contact with earth. F378.1. Tabu: touching ground on return from fairyland.

D1897. *Youngest of the three Magi becomes the senior through power of the Savior.* Irish myth: Cross.

D1900. Love induced by magic. (Cf. D1355, D1825.1.2.) *Type 580; Kittredge Witchcraft 104ff nn. 1—22 passim; Malory Morte Darthur VIII 1; K. Reuschel "Die Sage vom Liebeszauber Karls des Grossen in dichterischen Behandlungen der Neuzeit" (Philolog. u. volkskundliche Arbeiten K. Vollmöller dargeboten, 1908, pp. 371ff.); Zs. f. Vksk. XIX 243; Crane Miraculis 389ff. No. 34. — India: Thompson-

Balys; Penzer II 43; Philippine (Tinguian): Cole 77; Cherokee: Mooney RBAE XIX 259 No. 12; Irish myth: *Cross.

D1355. Love-producing magic object. G264. La Belle Dame Sans Merci. Witch entices men with offers of love and then deserts or destroys them. K1672. Dwarf himself falls in love with girl he has induced by magic love, and loses her as he is forced to remove his magic. T10. Falling in love. T21. Mutual love through accidental drinking of love philtre.

D1900.0.1. *Love purified by magic.* Irish myth: Cross.

D1900.1. *Favor with royalty induced by magic.* *Kittredge Witchcraft 108 nn. 32—48 passim; Heptameron No. 1; England: Baughman.

P0. Royalty and nobility.

D1901. *Witches induce love.* *Kittredge Witchcraft 30, 382 nn. 52—54. — England: Baughman; Icelandic: Boberg; Italian Novella: Rotunda.

D1903. *Power of inducing love given by animals.* (Cf. B500.) India: Thompson-Balys; Pawnee: Dorsey CI LIX 301 No. 83.

D1904. *Love-compelling man sickens of bargain.* A man given the power of making all women love him is smothered to death by them. N. A. Indian: *Thompson Tales 277 n. 19a.

C922. Death by smothering for breaking tabu. Q338. Immoderate request punished.

D1905. *Means of inducing love.* (Cf. D1355ff.)

K1300. Seduction.

D1905.1. *Girl's heart magically removed and fed to man draws her to him.* Cherokee: Mooney RBAE XIX 278 No. 30.

D1782. Sympathetic magic.

D1905.2. *Apple divided and eaten as love charm.* (Cf. D1355.7.) *Hdwb. d. Märchens s.v. "Baum".

D1905.3. *Love by curse.* Icelandic: *Boberg.

D2064.5. Magic sickness from curse. M436. Curse: prince to fall in love with prince's daughter.

D1908. *Love lost by magic.*

D1908.1. *Husband's love magically turns to hatred.* India: Thompson-Balys.

D1910. Magic memory. Penzer I 12 n. 1; Irish myth: *Cross; Jewish: Neuman.

D1366. Magic object causes memory. D2006. Magic reawakening of memory. F692. Person with remarkable memory. V223.4.1. Long lesson learned while asleep.

D1910.0.1. *Book written by man with marvelous memory.* Irish myth: *Cross.

D1911. *Person remembers all he has ever learned.* Irish myth: *Cross.

D1920. Other permanent magic characteristics.

F500. Remarkable persons. F600. Person with extraordinary powers. F622. Mighty blower. F660. Remarkable skill.

D1921. *Magic carrying power of voice.* Irish: Plummer clxxii, *Cross; England, U.S.: Baughman; Jewish: Neuman.

B741.4. Bellow of bull heard over entire land. F556. Remarkable voice. F688. Man with marvelous voice.

D1922. *Magic power of hearing.* Irish: Plummer clxxi, *Cross.

F641. Person of remarkable hearing.

D1923. *Power to hit whatever one aims at.* Fb "friskytte" I 373; *Hdwb. d. Abergl. III 2; India: Thompson-Balys.

D1653.1. Infallible weapon. F661. Skillful marksman.

D1924. *Magic immunity from fatigue.* Irish myth: *Cross.

D1925. *Fecundity magically induced.* India: Thompson-Balys.

D1347. Magic object produces fecundity. H1572. Test of fertility. T591.1. Magic remedies for barrenness or impotence.

D1925.1. *Barrenness removed by eating or drinking.* *Hartland Paternity I 30ff.; Irish myth: *Cross.

D1793. Magic results from eating or drinking.

D1925.2. *Barrenness removed by bathing.* *Hartland Paternity I 77ff.; Irish myth: *Cross.

D1788. Magic results from bathing.

D1925.3. *Barrenness removed by prayer.* Irish myth: *Cross.

D1766.1. Magic results produced by prayer.

D1925.4. *Barrenness removed by saint's blessing.* Irish myth: *Cross.

D1713. Magic power of hermit (saint).

D1926. *Craftsmanship magically bestowed by saint.* (Cf. D1713, D1722.) Irish myth: *Cross.

D1927. *Appetite magically diminished.* (Cf. V221.10.) Irish myth: *Cross.

D1931. *Hate induced by magic.* Irish myth: Cross; Icelandic: Boberg.

D1932. *Druids can pass through trees.* (Cf. F694.) Irish myth: Cross.

D1933. *Magic power of lighting empty lamp by breathing on it used for divination.* (Cf. D1311.) Irish myth: *Cross.

D1935. *Any work touched automatically done.* New Hebrides: Codrington 379, 397.

D1601. Object labors automatically.

D1936. *Magic fleetness of foot.*

D1936.1. *Donning skin makes woman fleet.* Eskimo (Greenland): Rink 156.

F681. Marvelous runner.

D1950—D2049. TEMPORARY MAGIC CHARACTERISTICS

D1960. **Magic sleep.** *Type 410; *BP I 440, III 261; *Fb "sove" III 472b. Irish: *Cross, O'Suilleabhain 35(a), Beal XXI 312; Icelandic: Panzer Sigfrid 113ff., Krappe Scandinavian Studies X (1928) 14—25, *Boberg; French Canadian: Barbeau JAFL XXIX 11; Jewish: Neuman; India: Thompson-Balys; Chinese: Eberhard FFC CXX 236; Philippine (Tinguian): Cole 144; Eskimo (Greenland): Rink 428, Rasmussen I 310, 367, II 168, 197.

D1364. Object causes magic sleep. E322.2. Dead wife returns to wake husband. H1484. Continual pricking with pin in order to remain awake. K51. Waking contest won by deception. K331.2. Owner put to sleep and goods stolen. Magic or drugs. M353. Prediction of bird that girl will have dead husband. (She disenchants him from magic sleep.)

D1960.1. *Seven sleepers.* (Rip Van Winkle.) Magic sleep extending over many years. **Huber Die Wanderlegende von den Siebenschläfern;

Type 763*; *Chauvin VII 102 No. 376; *Hartland Science 173ff.; *Frazer Pausanias II 121; Alphabet No. 283; *Loomis White Magic 115. — Irish myth: *Cross; Finnish-Swedish: Wessman 18 No. 163; Jewish: Neuman; N. A. Indian: cf. Thompson Tales 314 No. 143.

D2011. Years thought days. F377. Supernatural lapse of time in fairyland. Years seem days. F1099.3. Unnaturally long sleep.

D1960.1.1. *Mighty sleeper.* Irish myth: *Cross.

D1960.2. *Kyffhäuser.* King asleep in mountain (Barbarossa, King Marko, Holger Danske, etc.) will awake one day to succor his people. *BP III 460; *Feilberg Danske Studier (1920) 97ff.; **Weltig Der Sagenkreis des Kyffhäusers (Bremen, 1891); *Wehrhan Die Sage 47ff.; *Hartland Science 170ff.; *Krappe "Die Sage vom König im Berge" (Mitt. d. schles. Gesell. f. Volkskunde XXX (1935) 76—102). — Celtic: MacCulloch Celtic 15, 180; England, Scotland, U.S.: *Baughman; Lithuanian: Balys Index No. 3595; Armenian: Ananikian 34; Jewish: Neuman; Persian: Carnoy 327; India: Thompson-Balys, Keith 173.

A571. Culture hero asleep in mountain. A580. Culture hero's expected return. E502. The Sleeping Army. F545.1.3. Beard grows through table. (Usually told of king asleep in mountain.) F721.2. Habitable hill. N111.3.1. Fortune's wheel turned by dead king in mountain. N573. Sleeping king in mountain as guardian of treasure.

D1960.2.1. *King asleep in mountain will awake when his horse's shoes are worn down.* Every seven years the horse goes around the castle. He must wear his half-inch silver shoes to thinness of cat's ear before the king awakes. Howey 9.

D791.1. Disenchantment at end of specified time.

D1960.3. *Sleeping Beauty.* Magic sleep for definite period (e.g., a hundred years). *Type 410; India: Thompson-Balys.

B582.1.1.1. Goose brings master sleeping princess.

D1960.4. *Deathlike sleep.* Jewish: Neuman.

D1961. *Sleepless watcher magically put to sleep.* Usually has a magic watchful eye, which remains awake while his many other eyes sleep. (Argus). *Frazer Apollodorus I 109 n. 4; Köhler-Bolte I 101; *Fb "øje" III 1166.

F512.2.2. Argos. Has eyes all over body.

D1962. *Means of inducing magic sleep.* (Cf. D1364.)

B172.9. Magic birds cause hosts to sleep by shaking wings.

D1962.1. *Magic sleep through curse.* *Type 410.

D1792. Magic results from curse. M433. Endless sleep given Endymion.

D1962.2. *Magic sleep by lousing.* Picking the lice from the head of an old person or an ogre is used to put him to sleep. *Type 300; Hartland Perseus III 211; *Köhler-Bolte Zs. f. Vksk. VI 62 (to Gonzenbach No. 9). — English: Child V 487 s.v. "lousing"; India: Thompson-Balys; Jamaica: Beckwith MAFLS XVII 2 No. 1a; N. A. Indian: *Thompson Tales 326 n. 174; Eskimo (Greenland): Rasmussen I 364; Africa (Thonga): Junod 226.

D583. Transformation by lousing. G253. Witch's horns discovered by lousing her. K874. Deception by pretended lousing. K611.1. Escape by pretended lousing. Captive pretends to louse the captor but deceives him by cracking berries in the teeth (or the like).

D1962.3. *Magic sleep by hairdressing.* Head laid on anothers's lap. *Cox Cinderella 498 n. 34; MacCulloch Childhood 31; India: Thompson-Balys; N. A. Indian (Dakota): Schoolcraft Hiawatha 184.

D1962.3.1. *Magic sleep brought on by combing hero's hair lasts six months.* India: Thompson-Balys.

D1962.4. *Magic sleep by hypnotic suggestion.* MacCulloch Childhood 33.

D1962.4.1. *Lulling to sleep by "sleepy" stories (songs).* N. A. Indian: *Thompson Tales 322 n. 162, (Bella Coola): Boas JE I 98.

D1962.4.2. *Song (crónán) used to lull children to sleep.* Irish myth: *Cross.

B81.11. Mermaid's singing causes sleep.

D1962.5. *Snakes put to sleep by music on harp.* (Cf. B765, D1275.1.) Icelandic: Völsunga saga ch. 39 (37), Boberg.

D1962.6. *Magic sleep from breaking tabu.*

D1962.6.1. *Magic sleep when hero breaks fruit open too soon.* India: Thompson-Balys.

C963.3. Person returns to original vegetable form when tabu is broken.

D1964. *Magic sleep induced by certain person.*

D1964.1. *Savage elephant lulled to sleep by virgin.* Penzer III 172. (Cf. B13.1.)

T300. Chastity and celibacy.

D1964.2. *Magic sleep induced by disappointed suitor.* BP III 261.

K1210. Humiliated or baffled lovers. K2230. Treacherous lovers.

D1964.3. *Magic sleep induced by abductor.* (Cf. K1349.4.) Irish myth: *Cross.

D1964.4. *Magic sleep induced by druid.* (Cf. D1711.4.) Irish myth: *Cross.

D1964.5. *Magic sleep induced by saint.* (Cf. V220.) *Loomis White Magic 129.

D1964.6. *Magic sleep induced by deity.* Greek: Homer Iliad II 395, Odyssey XVIII 191.

D1965. *Guardian magically made to sleep while girl goes to lover.* (Cf. K1349.4, T30.) Irish myth: *Cross.

D1965.1. *Guardian magically made to sleep while lover visits maiden.* Irish myth: Cross.

D1967. *Person in magic sleep surrounded by protecting fire.* BP I 440; *Panzer Sigfrid 281 s.v. "Waberlohe".

D1380.1. Waberlohe. Magic fire surrounds and protects.

D1967.1. *Person in magic sleep surrounded by protecting hedge.* Type 410; German: Grimm Nos. 3, 50.

D1971. *Three-fold magic sleep.* Husband (lover) put to sleep by false bride. Only on the third night (the last chance) he wakes. *Types 303, 313; BP II 51, 273; Cox Cinderella 481. — Spanish: Boggs FFC XC 61 No 445A.

D762. Disenchantment by proper person waking from magic sleep. D1978.4. Hero wakened from magic sleep by wife who has purchased place in his bed from false bride. K1911.3. Reinstatement of true bride.

D1972. *Lover's magic sleep at rendezvous.* A lover (husband) is to meet his mistress but magically oversleeps. *Type 400; Chauvin V 145 No.

71 n. 1; *Fb "sove" III 472b; *Dickson 94 n. 78; Wesselski Mönchslatein 172 No. 138; Irish myth: *Cross; India: Thompson-Balys.

H1450. Vigilance tests. Q473.4. Importunate lover put asleep in street. T35.0.1. Lover late at rendezvous: detained by incessant talker. T92.4. Girl mistakenly elopes with the wrong lover. The preferred suitor overtakes them, finds them asleep and waits for them to awaken. He himself falls asleep and when he wakes they have gone.

D1973. *Magic sleep: in order to sleep off period of enchantment.* India: Thompson-Balys.

D1975. *Dragon-fighter's magic sleep.* While waiting for fight with dragon, hero falls into magic sleep. (Cf. D1962.2.) *Type 300; *Hartland Perseus III 211. — French Canadian: Barbeau JAFL XXIX 20; India: Thompson-Balys.

B11.11. Fight with dragon.

D1976. *Experiences during magic sleep.*

D1976.1. *Transportation during magic sleep.* Dickson 223; Irish myth: *Cross; Greek: Homer Odyssey XVIII 121; India: Thompson-Balys.

D2120. Magic transportation.

D1976.2. *Future spouse met during magic sleep.* Irish myth: *Cross.

D1731.2. Marvels seen in dreams. D1812.3.3. Future revealed in dream. H1301.2. Quest for far-off princess. T11.3.1. Lovers meet in their dreams.

D1978. *Waking from sleep.*

D1364.0.1. Ring wakes from magic sleep. H1481. Thumb cut and salt put on it in order to remain awake.

D1978.1. *Waking from magic sleep by cutting off finger.* Type 300; *Hartland Perseus III 211f.; India: Thompson-Balys.

D1978.2. *Waking from magic sleep by letting tear fall on sleeper.* Type 300; *Hartland Perseus III 211.

D1978.3. *Waking from magic sleep by removal of enchanting instrument.* BP I 436; *Bolte Zs. f. Vksk. XX 354; India: Thompson-Balys.

B511.3. Faithful horse pushes sleep-thorn out of its master's head, so that he awakes. D765.1.2. Disenchantment by removal of enchanting pin (thorn). E21. Resuscitation by withdrawal of wounding instrument.

D1978.4. *Hero wakened from magic sleep by wife who has purchased place in his bed from false bride.* (Cf. D1971.) Cox Cinderella 481; Type 313; BP II 51, 273; Indonesia: DeVries' list No. 176.

D762. Disenchantment by proper person waking from magic sleep. D1971. Three-fold magic sleep. K1911.3. Reinstatement of true bride.

D1978.5. *Waking from magic sleep by kiss.* *Type 410.

D735. Disenchantment by kiss.

D1980. Magic invisibility. *Type 306; *Bolte Reise der Söhne Giaffers 214; *Chauvin VII 39 No. 212B, 103 No. 377; *Loomis White Magic 51; *Fb "usynlig"; Penzer VIII 36f. — Irish: MacCulloch Celtic 65, 208, *Cross; Welsh: MacCulloch Celtic 189; Icelandic: *Boberg; Breton: Sébillot Incidents s.v. "invisibilité"; Jewish: *Neuman; India: Thompson-Balys, Keith 152; Chinese: Eberhard FFC CXX 49, 109f., 134 No. 92. — Africa (Zulu): Callavay 223, (Fang): Trilles 269.

B11.5.2. Dragon's power of magic invisibility. B184.1.6.1. Flight on invisible horse. B184.3.2.1. Magic invisible pig. D1361. Magic object renders invisible. D1361.19. Magic jewel renders invisible. F831.1. Invisible arrow.

D1981. *Certain persons invisible.* Jewish: Neuman; India: Thompson-Balys.

B11.5.2. Dragon's power of magic invisibility. E421.1. Invisible ghosts. E481. Land of the dead. F235.1. Fairies invisible. F412.1. Invisible spirit speaks. F531.6.5.1. Giants can make selves invisible. K531. Escape from battle by magic invisibility. T118.1. Monster husband invisible.

D1981.1. *Magic invisibility of gods.* Irish: MacCulloch Celtic 55, *Cross; Jewish: Neuman.

A120. Nature and appearance of the gods.

D1981.2. *Magic invisibility of saints.* (Cf. V229.8.) *Toldo IV 80; Irish myth: *Cross; Jewish: Neuman; Icelandic: Boberg.

D1981.3. *Magic invisibility of druids.* (Cf. D1711.4.) Irish myth: *Cross.

D1981.4. *Magic invisibility of ogre.* (Cf. G301.) India: Thompson-Balys.

D1981.5. *Magic invisibility of priests.* Jewish: Neuman.

D1981.6. *Magic invisibility of angels.* Jewish: Neuman.

D1982. *Certain objects invisible.*

F241.2.2. Fairies' cattle become invisible. Q552.18. Punishment: disappearance of ill-got gains.

D1982.1. *Magic door invisible to women.* *Chauvin VI 134 No. 286 n. 2.

C181. Tabu confined to women. D1146. Magic door.

D1982.2. *Ship made invisible.* Kittredge Witchcraft 46, 399 n. 176.

D1123. Magic ship. D1361.21. Ship becomes invisible.

D1982.3. *Chariot made invisible.* Irish myth: Cross.

F242.1.1. Fairy car becomes invisible.

D1982.4. *Food and drink appear and disappear in otherworld.* (Cf. D1030, D1040.) Irish myth: *Cross.

F166.4. Magic objects in otherworld. F171.7. Unseen hands lave feet in otherworld. F243. Fairies' food. F771.4.3. Abandoned castle.

D1982.5. *Boat made invisible.* Eskimo (Greenland): Rasmussen III 293.

D1983. *Invisibility conferred on person.*

D1983.1. *Invisibility conferred by a god.* (Cf. A180.) Irish myth: Cross; Greek: Fox 127 (Paris).

K531. Escape from battle by magic invisibility.

D1983.2. *Invisibility conferred by fairy.* (Cf. D1723.) Irish myth: Cross.

D1985. *Means of acquiring invisibility.* Penzer I 136, VI 149 n. 1.

D1361.8. Heart of unborn child renders person invisible.

D1985.1. *Invisibility by scarification.* Africa (Basuto): Jacottet 212 No. 31.

T537. Conception from scarification.

D1985.2. *Invisibility by reciting formula backwards.* *Penzer VI 149 n. 1.

D1361.26. Magic formula renders invisible. D1783. Reverse magic.

D2000. Magic forgetfulness. *Cox Cinderella 511; *Kittredge Witchcraft 55, 406 nn. 241, 242. — Irish myth: Cross; Icelandic: *Boberg; Breton: Sébillot Incidents s.v. "oubli"; Jewish: Neuman; India: Thompson-Balys; Eskimo (Greenland): Rink 457, Rasmussen III 145.

D1365. Object causes magic forgetfulness. D1896. Magic aging by contact with earth after otherworld journey. D1910. Magic memory.

D2003. *Forgotten fiancée.* Young husband visiting his home breaks tabu and forgets his wife. Later she succeeds in reawakening his memory. (For details of the ways in which the memory is lost and regained see D2004 and D2006. — *Type 313C, 425; Tegethoff 50ff.; *BP I 442, II 56, 527, III 338, 406, 443 (Gr. Nos. 56, 67, 113, 186, 193, 198); Cox Cinderella 511; *Fb "brud" IV 65a; Jiriczek Der Vergessenheitstrank in der Niebelungensage (Zs. f. vgl. Littgsch. N. F. VII 49): Köhler-Bolte I 169. — English: Child I 461 and note; Icelandic: *Boberg; Korean: Zong in-Sob 25; American Indian (European borrowings): Thompson CColl II 343, 367—371 (Micmac, New Mexican Spanish, Thompson River, Chilcotin), (cf. Seneca): Curtin-Hewitt RBAE XXXII 91 No. 5.

D1847.1. Invulnerability lost if man forgets sweetheart.

D2003.1. *Husband magically forgets wife.* India: Thompson-Balys.

F302.1.1. Mortals supplied with fairy mistresses during visit to fairyland. F377.1. Supernatural lapse of time in fairyland.

D2004. *Means of bringing about magic forgetfulness.*

C945. Magic forgetfulness for breaking tabu.

D2004.1. *Curse of forgetfulness.* *Cox Cinderella 512; Köhler-Bolte I 170. — Icelandic: *Boberg; Italian Novella: Rotunda.

D1792. Magic results from curse. M430. Curses on persons.

D2004.2. *Kiss of forgetfulness.* *Type 313; *Cox Cinderella 511 and practically all references given under D2003 (Forgotten Fiancée); *Fb "kys" II 349. — Italian Novella: Rotunda.

C120. Tabu: kissing. Usually causes disenchantment or magic forgetfulness. D565.5. Transformation by kiss. D735. Disenchantment by kiss. D1794. Magic results from kissing.

D2004.2.1. *Dog's licking of man produces forgetfulness.* Fb "glemme".

D1775. Magic results from licking.

D2004.3. *Forgetfulness by eating.* Fb "glemme" I 462, "spise" III 495. — Icelandic: *Boberg.

D1365.1.1. Lotus causes forgetfulness. D1793. Magic results from eating or drinking.

D2004.3.1. *Forgetfulness by drinking.* Herrmann Saxo II 590. — Africa (Fjort): Dennett 36 No. 4.

D1365.2. Drink causes forgetfulness. D1793. Magic results from eating or drinking.

D2004.4. *Forgetfulness by spitting.* Greek: Fox 63 (Polydos).

D1776. Magic results from spitting.

D2004.5. *Forgetting by stumbling.* A name or formula is magically forgotten when one stumbles (or jumps). Type 1687*. — Breton: Sébillot Incidents s.v. "nom"; Lithuanian: Balys Index No. *1687; Russian: Andrejev No. 1687*; India: Thompson--Balys; Japanese: Ikeda; N. A. Indian: *Thompson Tales 303 n. 109g; Africa (Kaffir): Theal 114, (Ila, Rhodesia): Smith and Dale II 394 No. 18.

J2671.2. Fool keeps repeating his instructions so as to remember them. (He usually forgets them.)

D2004.5.1. *Forgetting by stepping over log.* Papua: Ker 36.

D2004.6. *Magic forgetting of wife when husband removes shirt she has given him.* Fb "glemme" I 462.

D2004.7. *Forgetfulness from fright.* India: Thompson-Balys.

D2004.8. *Forgetfulness by mourning.* Jewish: Neuman.

D2004.9. *Forgetfulness caused by specific place.* Jewish: Neuman.

D2004.9.1. *Forgetfulness caused by Tower of Babel.* (Cf. F772.1.) Jewish: Neuman.

D2004.10. *Barking of brazen dogs causes forgetfulness.* (Cf. D1620.) Jewish: Neuman.

D2006. *Magic reawakening of memory.* (Cf. D1360, D1910.) Irish: Plummer lxxx, Cross.

D2006.1. *Forgotten fiancée reawakens husband's memory.*

K1911.3. Reinstatement of true bride. T56.3. Forgotten fiancée sends lover false diamond inscribed with Christ's last words: "Oh Lord, why hast Thou forsaken me?"

D2006.1.1. *Forgotten fiancée reawakens husband's memory by detaining lovers through magic.* Heroine takes up residence near home of her forgetful husband. She is apparently going to permit a lover to sleep with her when she detains him by having him try to place some magic birds on their roost. They continue to fall down throughout the night. (Or the lover is left magically sticking to a calf's tail or other object.) The thwarted lover tells of his experience, and in this way the attention of the husband is gained. *Type 313; Tegethoff 50; *BP II 231 n. 1; *Cosquin Lorraine II 28; Italian Novella: Rotunda; India: Thompson-Balys; Thompson River: Thompson CColl II 372 (European borrowing).

D1413.15. Magic window holds person fast. D1413.16. Magic door holds person fast. D1649.1.2. Magic birds keep falling off perch. H151.1. Attention drawn by magic objects: recognition follows. K555.3. Respite from wooer while he brings clothes all night. The girl wastes time trying them on. K1210. Humiliated or baffled lovers. K1217. Tale of the basin. Lover caught on magic basin and left in embarrassing position.

D2006.1.2. *Forgotten fiancée reawakens husband's memory by serving as milkmaid and talking to calf.* *Type 313; BP III 339 (Gr. 186).

H13.1. Recognition by overheard conversation with animal.

D2006.1.3. *Forgotten fiancée reawakens husband's memory by having magic doves converse.* *Type 313; Köhler-Bolte Zs. f. Vksk. VI 65; India: Thompson-Balys.

B211.3. Speaking bird. H11.1. Recognition by telling life history. H151.1. Attention drawn by magic objects: recognition follows.

D2006.1.4. *Forgotten fiancée buys place in husband's bed and reawakens his memory.* *Types 313, 425; *BP II 234ff., 527 n. 2; Tegethoff 52f. — Philippine: Fansler MAFLS XII 165.

T160. Consummation of marriage.

D2006.1.5. *Forgotten fiancée attracts attention by magically stopping wedding carriage of new bride.* *Type 313; BP II 517 (incident G).

D2070. Bewitching. T150. Happenings at weddings.

D2006.1.6. *Forgotten fiancée remembered by means of doll.* *Bolte Reise der Söhne Giaffers 221.

D2006.1.7. *Forgotten fiancée remembered by means of bird.* India: Thompson-Balys.

D2006.1.8. *Piece of wood revives memory.* (Cf. D956.) India: Thompson-Balys.

H10. Recognition through common knowledge.

D2006.1.9. *Forgotten wife remembered by seeing her initials.* India: Thompson-Balys.

D2006.1.10. *Forgotten wife gives food to beggar: husband's memory reawakened.* Buddhist myth: Malalasekera II 527.

D2006.2. *Sight of old home reawakens memory and brings about return from other world.* Hartland Science 200. — N. A. Indian: *Thompson Tales 330 n. 193; *Thompson Star Husband; Melanesia: Codrington 365.

C300. Looking tabu. C713.3. Tabu: wife of merman staying too long at home (on visits).

D2006.2.1. *Longing of human child of sky-mother to visit father on earth.* India: Thompson-Balys.

D2011. *Years thought days.* (Cf. F379.5.) Years spent in the other world or asleep seem as days because of magic forgetfulness. *Type 470; *Fb "tid" III 790a; Pauli (ed. Bolte) No. 561, 562; *Köhler-Bolte II 224ff., 406ff.; *Hartland Science 162ff. — Irish: MacCulloch Celtic 116, 119, 181f., *Cross; Breton: Sébillot Incidents s.v. "temps"; Welsh: MacCulloch Celtic 101; Scottish: McKay Bealoideas III 138; English: Child V 290a; Spanish Exempla: Keller; Lithuanian: Balys Index No. *472; India: Thompson-Balys; Chinese: Graham; Japanese: Ikeda; Eskimo (Greenland): Rasmussen III 299, (Bering Strait): Nelson RBAE XVIII 459; N. A. Indian: *Thompson Tales 314 n. 143.

A697.2.1. Years are days in Tusita world. D1365. Object causes magic forgetfulness. D1960.1. Seven sleepers (Rip van Winkle). E175. Death thought sleep. F172. No time, no birth, no death in otherworld. F377. Supernatural lapse of time in fairyland. Years seem days. K1870. Illusions.

D2011.1. *Years seem moments while man listens to song of bird.* **Hammerich Munken og Fuglen (København, 1933); *Pauli (ed. Bolte) No. 562; *Herbert III 67; Longfellow "The Golden Legend"; Hartland Science 188f. — Irish: Plummer clxxxvi, *Cross; Welsh: MacCulloch Celtic 104; Lithuanian: Balys Index No. 472A*; Estonian: Aarne FFC XXV No. 471*; Russian: Andrejev Ukazatel' Skazochnik No. 471.

B172.2. Magic bird's song. Brings joy and oblivion for many years. Wakes the dead. B292.5. Bird sings to console man. B251.2.1. Animals sing in honor of a saint. D1275. Magic song. D1365. Object causes magic forgetfulness.

D2011.1.1. *Day seems moment while saint listens to music made by bird's wing.* Irish myth: *Cross.

D2011.1.2. *Three days and three nights seem one hour as saint preaches.* (Cf. Z71.1.1.) Irish myth: Cross.

D2011.2. *Two friars perceive no passing of time from Shrovetide till following Easter while they talk of Christ.* Irish myth: Cross.

D2011.3. *Years are as moments to creator.* India: Thompson-Balys.

D2012. *Moments thought years.* In a moment a person seems to experience events of many years. Hartland Science 226f.; Wesselski Märchen 255 No. 65; *Krappe Bulletin Hispanique XXXV (1933) 114f., Scandinavian Studies 19 (1947) 217—224; Irish myth: *Cross.

F377. Supernatural lapse of time in fairyland. K1870. Illusions.

D2012.1. *King in the bath; years of experience in a moment.* This illusion takes place when the king puts his head under water. *Chauvin VII 106 No. 94; Penzer VII 244ff.; Hartland Science 225ff.

L411. Proud king displaced by angel. (King in the bath.)

D2012.2. *Wizard gives man the illusion that he has been away twenty (forty) years.* Italian Novella: Rotunda.

D2020. Magic dumbness. Breton: Sébillot Incidents s.v. "muet"; Spanish Exempla: Keller; Eskimo (Greenland): Rink 154.

C401. Tabu: speaking during certain time. D758. Disenchantment by maintaining silence. D1507. Magic object restores speech. D2161.3.6. Dumbness magically cured. F954. Dumb person brought to speak. G91.1.1. Man forced to eat dead father's (grandfather's) heart struck dumb. L124. Dumb hero.

D2021. *Causes of magic dumbness.*

D2021.1. *Dumbness as curse.* *Type 710; *BP I 21; Tawney I 5.

C944. Dumbness as punishment for breaking tabu. D1792. Magic results from curse. M430. Curses on persons. Q451.3. Dumbness as punishment.

D2025. *Magic recovery of speech.*

D1507. Magic object restores speech.

D2025.0.1. *Magic (loss and) recovery of speech.* Irish myth: Cross.

D2025.1. *Speech magically recovered on execution stake.* Type 710.

F954. Dumb person brought to speak.

D2025.2. *Speech magically recovered when certain bird is caught.* Africa (Kaffir): Theal 80.

D2025.3. *Speech magically recovered when third person guesses secret transaction.* Tawney I 5.

D2025.4. *Dumbness magically cured by astonishment.* Africa (Basuto): Jacottet 224 No. 33.

D2025.5. *Speech magically recovered on Hallowe'en* (Cf. V70.5.) Irish myth: *Cross.

D2030. Other temporary magic characteristics.

D2031. *Magic illusion.* *BP III 203; *Loomis White Magic 51; Irish myth: *Cross; Danish: Kristensen Danske Sagn VI (1900) 426ff., (1936) 193ff., Icelandic: MacCulloch Eddic 93, *Boberg.

D612.1. Illusory transformation of animals in order to sell and cheat. D1368. Magic object causes illusions. K1870. Illusions.

D2031.0.1. *Saints cause illusions.* Irish: Plummer clix, clxix, *Cross.

D1713. Magic power of hermit (saint). V220. Saints.

D2031.0.2. *Fairies cause illusions.* Irish myth: *Cross.

F221.1. Fairy house disappears at dawn. F260. Behavior of fairies.

D2031.0.3. *Magic illusion dissipated by sign of the cross.* Irish myth: Cross.

D1766.6. Magic results from sign of the cross.

D2031.0.4. *Druids cause illusions.* (Cf. D2031.4.1.) Irish myth: *Cross.

D2031.0.5. *Giantess' punishment is pure illusion.* Icelandic: Egils saga og Ásm. 58, Boberg.

D2031.1. *Magician makes people lift garments to avoid wetting in imaginary river.* *BP III 203; Dickson 222 n. 18; Danish: Kristensen Danske Sagn VI (1900) 426ff; FSS 22—23, Boberg; Estonian: Aarne FFC XXV 137 No. 103; Lappish: Qvigstad FFC LX 51 No. 99.

K1200. Deception into humiliating position. D1963.1. False magician exposed by clever girl.

D2031.1.2. *People swim in imaginary rising river.* Icelandic: *Boberg.

D2031.2. *Thread made to appear as a large log carried by a cock.* *BP III 203.

D2031.3. *Pursued animal runs through imaginary river.* Dickson 222 n. 17.

D2031.4. *Hideous person magically makes self seem beautiful.* Malone PMLA XLIII 417.

D2031.4.1. *Druid makes self appear ugly on one side, beautiful on other.* (Cf. D2031.0.4.) Irish myth: Cross.

F162.1.2.3. Objects on one side of palisade in otherworld black, on other side white. T551.4. Boy born with one side flesh and one iron.

D2031.4.2. *Magician appears as swineherd, dwarf, and giant in order to seduce queen and scorns her later in the same shapes.* Icelandic: *Boberg.

D658. Transformation to seduce woman.

D2031.4.3. *Magician appears as beggar or old man in order to free prisoners.* Icelandic: FSS 22—23, Boberg.

D2031.5. *Man magically made to believe himself bishop, archbishop, and pope.* When he continues to refuse payment to the magician, the latter shows him the reality. *Chauvin II 151 No. 11.

H1565.1. Test of gratitude: magician makes pupil believe himself superior. J2010. Uncertainty about own identity. J2300. Gullible fools. K231. Debtor refuses to pay his debt.

D2031.6. *Magic illusion as protection.*

D2031.6.1. *Man made to appear to pursuers as woman carrying babe.* Irish myth: Cross.

D2031.6.2. *Son made to appear to pursuers as spinning wheel, buck, and hog.* Icelandic: Boberg.

D2031.6.3. *Lonesome wife scares robbers by making it appear that her husband is at home.* Icelandic: Boberg.

D2031.6.4. *Pursuers confused in other ways by magic illusion.* Icelandic: *Boberg.

D2031.7. *Horse made to appear as tree-trunk.* Irish myth: Cross.

D2031.8. *Armies separated with illusion that each has won object of contention.* Irish myth: Cross.

F1097. Armies miraculously separated. K1872.1. Army appears like forest. K2350. Military strategy.

D2031.9. *Enemy's last arrow made to appear crooked so that he does not use it, and adversary gets time to kill him.* Icelandic: *Boberg.

D2031.10. *Spear made to appear as a reed in order to kill treacherously.* Icelandic: Boberg.

D2031.11. *Illusive fire stops men.* Danish: Kristensen Danske Sagn III (1895) 452—53, (1931) 310—11; Icelandic: Boberg.

D2031.12. *Sea water made to behave like solid earth.* Irish myth: Cross.

D2031.13. *Magic rath always seems distant, never near.* Irish myth: Cross.

D2031.14. *Illusion: mountains seem to be fighting.* India: Thompson-Balys.

D2031.15. *Goat appears to be two every time man aims.* India: Thompson-Balys.

D2031.16. *Vision of food arises to tempt fasting women.* India: Thompson-Balys.

D2031.17. *Storm appears to be island.* Eskimo (Central): Boas RBAE VI 622.

D2031.18. *Person appears to be in several places at once.* Buddhist myth: Malalasekera I 141.

D2032. *Magic avoidance of fatigue.* (Cf. D1924.) *Fb "hest" I 600.

D2033. *Thirst magically caused to disappear.* (Cf. D1349.1.) Irish myth: Cross.

D2034. *Crying induced by magic as trick to force child's mother.* Icelandic: Egils saga Einhenda 66, *Boberg.

C681. Compulsion to answer cry.

D2035. *Magic heaviness.* Loomis White Magic 49.

E411.0.3. Horse unable to draw evil dead man. F610.7. Strong man is so heavy that no horse can carry him all day. F833.1.2. Sword so heavy that only its owner can lift it.

D2036. *Magic homesickness.* Greek: Homer Odyssey XV 66, Iliad III 139.

C713.2. Tabu: wife of supernatural husband seeing old home. D2006.2. Sight of old home reawakens memory. T294. Husband (wife) of supernatural being longs for old home.

D2038. *Animal becomes magically larger.*

D55.1. Person becomes magically larger.

D2038.1. *Centipede becomes large enough to kill demon.* Chinese: Graham.

D2050—D2099. DESTRUCTIVE MAGIC POWERS

D2050. Destructive magic power.

D2060. Death or bodily injury by magic. (Cf. C920f., D1207.1, D1400, D2089.3.) Irish myth: Cross.

C901.3. Tabu imposed by magic. C943. Loss of sight for breaking tabu. F360. Malevolent or destructive fairies. F362.1. Fairies cause blindness. F1041.4. Person melts away from heat. M400. Curses. M400.1. Satire. M442. Curse: deformity. Q582. Fitting death as punishment. Q583. Fitting bodily injury as punishment. T591. Barrenness or impotence induced by magic. T611.4. Children magically prevented from suckling. V52.8. Saint's prayer brings death to enemy. V229.7. Invaders miraculously defeated by saints.

D2061. *Magic murder.* (Cf. D1402.) Icelandic: *Boberg; India: Thompson-Balys; Hawaii: Beckwith Myth 115, 120.

K910. Murder by strategy. Q411. Death as punishment.

D2061.1. *Kinds of death produced by magic.* (Cf. D1896.)

D2061.1.1. *Person magically reduced to ashes.* (Cf. D1896.) Irish myth: *Cross; India: Thompson-Balys, Penzer IV 232, 244; Chauvin V 16 n. 2, 293.

C927.2. Falling to ashes as punishment for breaking tabu. D1402.16. Magic mustard seed causes man to turn to ashes. D2082.1. Magic glance reduces tree to ashes.

D2061.1.1.1. *Person magically reduced to pile of bones.* Jewish: Neuman.

D2061.1.2. *Persons magically caused to dance selves to death.* Aztec: Alexander Lat. Am. 66.

C94.1.1. The cursed dancers. D2174. Magic dancing. D1415. Magic object compels person to dance. Q500. Tedious punishments.

D2061.1.3. *Poisoning by magic.* *Kittredge Witchcraft 136ff., 457f. nn. 1—29 passim; Irish myth: *Cross; England, U.S.: Baughman.

B33.1.4. Devastating birds with poisonous spells on their wings.

D2061.1.4. *Persons magically made to decay and die.* Irish myth: *Cross.

D926. Magic well. Q551.8.3. Deformity (putridity) as punishment for murder.

D2061.1.5. *Plague magically invoked.* Irish myth: Cross.

D2061.2. *Means employed in magic murder.*

D2061.2.1. *Death-giving glance.* (Cf. F555.7.) Hartland Perseus III 59f.; *Krappe Balor 1ff.; Penzer II 298, IV 232, VIII 75 n. 1; Chauvin V 16 n. 2, 293; Gaster Rabbis 225 No. 203. — Greek: Fox 35 (Gorgon); Irish myth: *Cross; England, Wales, U.S.: *Baughman; Jewish: Neuman; India: Thompson-Balys; Persian: Carnoy 336; N. A. Indian: Thompson Tales 344 n. 242, (Calif): Gayton and Newman 92; Eskimo (Mackenzie Area): Jenness 65.

A128.2. One-eyed god. B12.2. Basilisk's fatal glance. D581. Petrification by glance. F526.3. Gorgon. F555.7. Poisonous white hair in eyebrow that causes death to first person that sees it each day. G264.1. Woman is death of all who behold her.

D2061.2.1.1. *Evil eye sets bird on fire.* India: Thompson-Balys.

D2061.2.2. *Murder by sympathetic magic.* An object or an animal is abused or destroyed to bring about the death of a person. *Cox Cinderella 491; Herbert III 200; Oesterley No. 102; *Kittredge Witchcraft 73ff., 411ff. nn. 1—171; Irish myth: Cross; Heptameron No. 1.

E765. Life dependent on external object or event. G271.4. Exorcism of witches by sympathetic magic.

D2061.2.2.1. *Person whose shadow is pierced by spear falls dead.* Irish myth: Cross.

D2061.2.2.2. *Spell chanted over person's shadow brings death.* Irish myth: Cross.

D1273. Magic formula (charm). D1402. Magic object kills.

D2061.2.2.3. *Murder by abuse or destruction of image.* England, Scotland, U.S.: *Baughman.

D2061.2.2.4. *Body of victim abused.*

D2061.2.2.4.1. *Hair of victim burned, causing his death.* England: Baughman.

D2061.2.2.5. *Murder by abuse of clothing of victim.*

D2061.2.2.5.1. *Murder by boiling gloves of victim.* England: Baughman.

D2061.2.2.6. *Candle burned causes victim to waste away.* England, U.S.: *Baughman.

D2061.2.2.7. *Animals abused or destroyed to cause death of person.* England: *Baughman.

D2061.2.2.8. *Miscellaneous objects abused to cause death.*

D2061.2.2.8.1. *Needle, placed under hearth, burns and causes death of victim.* U.S.: Baughman.

D2061.2.3. *Murder by pointing.* (Cf. D2069.1.1.) N. A. Indian: *Thompson Tales 345 n. 242a, (Calif.): Gayton and Newman 56, Eskimo (Greenland): Rasmussen III 114, 240, 246.

D2061.2.4. *Death by cursing.* Irish myth: *Cross; Hebrew: 2 Kings 2:24, Neuman; Icelandic: Boberg; Eskimo: Kroeber JAFL XII 173, Turner RBAE XI 262.

D1792. Magic results from curse. D2175. Cursing by magic. D2176. Exorcising by magic. G269.4. Curse by disappointed witch. M400. Curses. M400.1. Satire. M430. Curses on persons. Q556. Curse as punishment. V52.8. Saint's prayer brings death to enemy.

D2061.2.4.1. *Death in sin (damnation) by cursing.* (Cf. E752.) Irish myth: *Cross.

D2061.2.4.2. *Curse of clergy causes man to die of wound.* Irish myth: Cross.

D2061.2.5. *Hunter reduced to ashes by power of heroine's chastity.* (Cf. D2061.1.1.) Penzer IV 244.

D1714. Magic power of chaste woman. T300. Chastity and celibacy.

D2061.2.6. *Person killed by spike magically made to appear on chair.* Irish myth: Cross.

D2061.2.7. *Murder by showing man caul with which he was born.* Irish myth: Cross.

D2061.2.8. *Horse made to hang himself on gate by magic.* Cheremis: Sebeok-Nyerges.

D2061.2.9. *Breathing on enemy drives him onto knife.* Eskimo (Mackenzie Area): Jenness 36.

D2062. *Maiming by magic.* Irish myth: *Cross.

C948. Mutilation as punishment for breaking tabu. D1403. Magic object maims. Q451.3. Loss of speech as punishment. Q551.8. Deformity as punishment. S160. Mutilations.

D2062.1. *Heart removed by magic.* Penzer I 129.

D2062.2. *Blinding by magic.* Irish myth: *Cross; German: Grimm No. 135; India: Thompson-Balys.

C943. Loss of sight for breaking tabu. D1331.2. Magic object blinds.

D2062.2.1. *Blinding by curse.* (Cf. M431.1.) Irish myth: *Cross.

D1792. Magic results from curse. D1981. Magic invisibility. Q451.7.0.2. Miraculous blindness as punishment.

D2062.2.1.1. *Person suffers from "crookedness in his eye" as result of curse.* Irish myth: Cross.

D2062.2.2. *Sight of holy person causes blindness.* Jewish: Neuman.

C311. Tabu: seeing the supernatural.

D2062.2.3. *Person caused to squint as punishment.* Irish myth: Cross.

D2062.2.4. *Enemies magically caused to lose sight of each other while hunting.* Irish myth: Cross (D1981.4).

D2062.2.5. *Magic blindness by snake bite.* India: Thompson-Balys.

D2161.4.10.6. Blindness cured by killing snake that caused it.

D2062.2.6. *When certain thief coughs, watchmen become blind.* India: Thompson-Balys.

K621. Escape by blinding the guard.

D2062.3. *Flesh magically does not regrow.* Irish myth: Cross; Icelandic: Boberg.

D2062.4. *Magic mutilation: sexual organs.*

D2062.4.1. *Bride enchanted by witch loses her sexual organs.* Cheremis: Sebeok-Nyerges.

D2062.4.2. *Castration by magic.* Eskimo (Greenland): Rasmussen III 294.

D2062.5. *Magic mutilation: temporary growths on person.* (Cf. D1375.) Philippine (Tinguian): Cole 39, 62, 701.

D2063. *Magic discomfort.* Icelandic: *Boberg.

D1372. Magic object causes continued sneezing. D1373. Magic object causes constant hunger. M438. Curse: humiliation. Q470. Humiliating punishment. T321.5. Magic sickness (discomfort) prevents lover raping woman.

D2063.1. *Tormenting by magic.* England: *Baughman.

D2063.1.1. *Tormenting by sympathetic magic.* Person (usually witch) tormented by abusing an animal or object. The usual methods of abuse are burning or sticking with pins. *Kittredge Witchcraft 97ff., 429ff. nn. 173—239 passim; England, U.S.: *Baughman; Feilberg DF X 165ff.; Icelandic: *Boberg.

D1355.3.2. Image (animal) pierced with pins as love charm. D1355.3.3. Fruit pierced with pins as love charm. D1782. Sympathetic magic. Q469.9.2. Punishment: piercing with needles.

D2063.2. *Magic restlessness in bed.* Fb "seng" III 187b.

D2063.3. *Magic insatiable thirst.* (Cf. D1373.0.1.) Irish myth: Cross; Chinese: Eberhard FFC CXX 105.

D2091.6. Enemies magically made to feel thirst.

D2063.3.1. *Druids cause magic thirst.* (Cf. P427.) Irish myth: Cross.

D2063.3.1.1. *Saints cause magic thirst.* Irish myth: Cross.

D2063.4. *Magic scratching (itching).* Icelandic: *Boberg.

D2063.5. *Magic discomfort: continued breaking of wind.* (Cf. D2079.1, G303.6.2.15.1.) Cheremis: Sebeok-Nyerges.

D2063.6. *Man magically made to bark like dog.* Buddhist myth: Malalasekera II 32.

D2064. *Magic sickness.* (Cf. D1837.) Icelandic: *Boberg; Spanish Exempla: Keller; Chinese: Graham; Eskimo (Greenland): Rink 458, 467, Rasmussen III 67, 292.

B177.1.1. Magic toad under king's bed causes magic sickness. B183.1.2. Magic mouse causes disease. C940. Sickness or weakness for breaking tabu. D53.1. Magic change to sick man. D1500.4. Magic object causes disease. E265. Meeting ghost causes misfortune. E501.18.9. Sight of wild hunt causes swelling of head. M431. Curse: bodily injury. Q551.6. Magic sickness as punishment.

D2064.0.1. *Magic love-sickness.* (Cf. D1355.) Irish myth: *Cross.

T24.1. Love-sickness.

D2064.0.2. *Magic heart-sickness.* Jewish: Neuman.

D2064.0.3. *Magic pestilence.* Jewish: Neuman.

D2064.1. *Magic sickness because girl has thrown away her consecrated wafer.* (Cf. C55, C940.1.) *Type 613; *BP I 322 n. 1; Irish: O'Suilleabhain 27, Beal XXI 308.

H1292.4.1. Question (propounded on quest): How can the princess be cured? Answer: She must recover consecrated wafer which rat has stolen from her first communion. V34.2. Princess sick because toad has swallowed her consecrated wafer.

D2064.2. *Sickness of princess dependent on witch's fire.* When fire is high, princess is very sick. Princess recovers when fire is put out. (Cf. D2065.4.) Köhler-Bolte I 335.

D1271. Magic fire. D1836.1. Ghost's strength waxes and wanes with height of fire. F1061. Flame as miraculous index.

D2064.3. *Sickness transferred to animal.* Fb "sygdom" III 609b; England: Baughman.

D1500.3. Magic object transfers disease to another person or thing. D2161.4.1. Cure by transferring disease to animal.

D2064.4. *Magic sickness because of Evil Eye.* (Cf. D2071.) Fb "sygdom" III 700a, "overse" II 771a; England, Scotland, Ireland, Wales, U.S.: *Baughman.

D2064.5. *Magic sickness from curse.* Irish myth: Cross; Icelandic: Boberg; India: Thompson-Balys; Eskimo (Greenland): Rink 372.

D1792. Magic results from curse. D1905.3. Love by curse.

D2064.6. *Magic sickness from wounding sick person.* Irish myth: Cross.

D2064.7. *Magic sickness from bit of weapon left in head.* Icelandic: Boberg.

D2064.8. *Magic sickness by making fruit plant dry and shrivel.* India: Thompson-Balys.

D2065. *Magic insanity.* (Cf. D2161.3.8.) *Kittredge Witchcraft 30, *382 n. 51, 124ff., 449f. nn. 1—23 passim; Irish myth: *Cross; Lithuanian: Balys Index 3512; Eskimo (Greenland): Rink 167, 259, 368, 445.

D1367. Magic object causes insanity. E265. Meeting ghost causes sickness (madness). F362.2. Fairies cause insanity. Q555. Madness as punishment.

D2065.1. *Madness from demonic possession.* Kittredge Witchcraft 124ff., 449f. nn. 1—23 passim; Italian Novella: Rotunda; India: Thompson-Balys.

F402.1. Deeds of evil spirits.

D2065.2. *Insanity from seeing strange sight.* Fb "vild" III 1052a.

E501.18.6. Sight of wild hunt renders person insane. E561.1. Sight of dead woman spinning drives people insane. F1041.8. Madness from strange sight.

D2065.2.1. *Magic insanity caused by hearing strange sound.* India: Thompson-Balys.

D2065.3. *Druids bereave men of senses.* (Cf. P427.) Irish: Plummer clix, *Cross.

D2065.4. *Insanity of princess dependent on height of fire.* (Cf. D2064.2.) Spanish: Boggs FFC XC 60 No. 435*.

D1271. Magic fire. D1836.1. Ghost's strength waxes and wanes with height of fire. F1061. Flame as miraculous index.

D2065.5. *Insanity because of Evil Eye.* (Cf. D2071.) Fb "øje" III 1167b.

D2065.6. *Person abducted by Echo crazed and dumb.* India: Thompson-Balys.

A497. Echo. R11.2.2.2. Abduction by Echo.

D2065.7. *Insanity from curse.* Irish myth: Cross.

D1792. Magic results from curse.

D2066. *Elfshot.* (F360.) Magic shooting of small objects into a person's (or animal's) body. Kittredge Witchcraft 133, 453ff. nn. 62—82 passim; *Fb "skud" III 333b, "ellefolk" I 241b. — Irish myth: Cross; England, Ireland: *Baughman.

D1516. Charms against elfshot.

D2066.1. *Elves get stones from fairies who get them from mermaids.* The devil does the finishing work on the stones. England: Baughman.

D2069. *Death or bodily injury by magic—miscellaneous.*

D2069.1. *Person magically caused to fall.*

D2069.1.1. *Person made to fall down by pointing at door.* (Cf. D2061.2.3.) Chinese: Graham.

D2069.2. *People magically compelled to bend arm.* Eskimo (Bering Strait): Nelson RBAE XVIII 501.

D2070. **Bewitching.** (Cf. D5, G200.) **Kittredge Witchcraft. — Irish myth: *Cross; Icelandic: Ynglinga saga 29, Boberg; Jewish: Neuman; Eskimo (Greenland): Rink 200.

D766.2.1. Disenchantment of bewitched person by placing cake in his mouth. D1385.2. Moly (plant) as antidote to spells and enchantments. D1385.5.1. Copper as defense against magic. D1385.6. Magic salve protects from enchantment. D1837. Magic weakness. G263. Witch enchants or transforms. G265.4.1. Witch causes animals to die.

D2070.1. *Magic hair-ball used for bewitching.* (Cf. D991.3, D1274.1.) North Carolina: Brown Collection I 668.

D991.3. Magic ball of hair.

D2071. *Evil Eye.* Bewitching by means of a glance. *Krappe Balor 9ff.; *Chauvin V 161 No. 84, VIII 143 No. 144 n. 1; *Fb "öje" III 1167ab, 1168a; *Hdwb. d. Abergl. I 686; Elworthy The Evil Eye (London, 1895); Jahn Über den Aberglauben des bösen Blicks bei den Alten; Pitre Le jettatura ed il mal occhio in Sicilia (Kolozsvár, 1884); Seligman Der böse Blick und Verwandtes (Berlin, 1910); Maclagen, R. C. The Evil Eye in the Western Highlands (London, 1902); Penzer II 298; *Hertz Abhandlungen 181ff. — Irish myth: *Cross; Icelandic: *Boberg; Jewish: Neuman; India: Thompson-Balys.

A128.2.1. God with Evil Eye. B12.2. Basilisk's fatal glance. D581. Petrification by glance. D993. Magic eye. D2061.2.1. Death-giving glance. D2064.4. Magic sickness because of Evil Eye. D2065.5. Insanity because of Evil Eye. D2082.1. Magic glance reduces tree to ashes. F592. Man's ferocious glance kills (causes swooning).

D2071.0.1. *Evil eye covered with seven veils.* *Krappe Balor 25; Gaster Oldest Stories 45.

D2071.0.1.1. *Evil eye covered with bag or hide while owner is stoned.* Icelandic: *Boberg.

D2071.0.2. *Evil eye from exposure to magic concoction.* Irish myth: Cross.

D2071.0.3. *Man with power of evil eye cannot look at any living thing before breaking fast in the morning without causing it to wither and die.* England: Baughman.

D2071.1. *Averting Evil Eye.* See references for D1070, Magic ornaments, a large number of which are used to keep off the Evil Eye. India: Thompson-Balys.

D2071.1.1. *Evil Eye averted by spitting.* (Cf. D1001, D1776.) *Fb "spytte" III 514b; Irish myth: Cross.

D2071.1.2. *Evil Eye averted by swinging cat over child's cradle.* Fb "overse" II 771a.

F321.1.4. Disposing of changeling. T582.2. Avoidance of evil spirits at childbirth.

D2071.1.3. *Simulated change of sex to baffle Evil Eye.* Penzer IX 163.

K521.4.1. Disguise in clothes of other sex so as to escape.

D2071.1.4. *Black as guard against Evil Eye.* Penzer I 212, 217.

D2071.1.5. *Countermagic against Evil Eye: returning glance of Evil Eye blights the original glancer.* India: Thompson-Balys.

D765. Disenchantment by reversing enchantment.

D2071.2. *Person kills with Evil Eye.*

D2071.2.1. *Person kills animals with glance of Evil Eye.* England, Ireland, U.S.: *Baughman.

D2072. *Magic paralysis.* Person or thing rendered helpless. (Cf. D1410.) *Type 952; *BP III 453; Chauvin V 16 n. 2; Tawney I 408, 417, 458; *Fb "stjæle" III 575a; Kittredge Witchcraft 201f. nn. 104—110; Alphabet 624; *Loomis White Magic 56f. — Irish myth: Cross; Icelandic: Göngu-Hrólfs saga 242, Boberg; Swiss: Jegerlehner Oberwallis 300 No. 10; Missouri French: Carrière; India: Thompson-Balys.

B15.7.12. Three-legged ass renders powerless by sharpness of eyes. D5.1. Enchanted person cannot move. D1336. Magic object gives weakness. D1411. Magic object binds person. D1412. Magic object pulls person into it. D1413. Magic object holds person fast. D1414.3. Magic wind causes arms to fall from warriors' hands. D1419.2. Magic object paralyzes. D1837. Magic weakness. D2006.1.5. Forgotten fiancée attracts attention by magically stopping wedding carriage of new bride. D2091.9. Magic paralysis drawn down on foe. D2171. Magic adhesion. K422. Thief rendered helpless by magic. Q551.7. Magic paralysis as punishment.

D2072.0.1. *Sword made magically helpless.* Fb "sværd" III 690a; Spanish Exempla: Keller; Jewish: Neuman.

D1414. Magic object renders weapon useless. D2086.1. Sword magically dulled.

D2072.0.2. *Animal rendered immovable.*

D2072.0.2.1. *Horse enchanted so that he stands still.* (Cf. D1654.12.) Fb "hest" IV 212a; Irish myth: Cross; England, Scotland, Ireland, Wales, U.S.: *Baughman.

D2072.0.2.1.1. *Horse (ox) unable to move wagon paralyzed by witch.* England, U.S.: *Baughman.

D2072.0.2.2. *Bird paralyzed.*

D2072.0.2.2.1. *Person charged with keeping birds from the crops confines them in barn (usually roofless) by magic while he goes to town.* England, Wales: *Baughman.

D2072.0.2.3. *Oxen paralyzed. England,* U.S.: *Baughman.

D2072.0.2.4. *Mule paralyzed by witch.* England: Baughman.

D2072.0.2.5. *Pigs paralyzed by witch.* England: Baughman.

D2072.0.2.6. *Dog paralyzed.* U.S.: Baughman; Eskimo (Greenland): Rink 452.

D2072.0.3. *Ship held back by magic.* (Cf. D1419.3, F302.3.1.2, F402.1.13.) *BP II 265 n. 1, IV 196 n. 1. — Irish myth: *Cross; Italian: Basile I No. 6; U.S.: Baughman; India: Thompson-Balys.

D1419.3. Magic object prevents ship from moving. D1654. Immovable object. D1654.6. Ship refuses to move. D2136.8. Ship moved by sacrifice. F420.5.2. Malevolent water-spirits. F420.5.2.7.4. Water-spirit holds ship. F494.1. Guardian spirit of land. F637. Strong man holds back ship. S263.4.1. Sacrifice to offended guardian gods who hold ship back.

D2072.0.4. *Bird overpowered by stepping on his shadow.* Drops the stolen meat. Zachariae 57.

E743. Soul as shadow. K1227.7. Girl asks undesired lover to follow her but not to step on her shadow.

D2072.0.5. *Person paralyzed.* (Cf. D5.1, G256.3, G257.) England, Scotland, U.S.: *Baughman.

A185.2.2. God makes man's hand rigid so he can no longer torment captive.

D2072.0.5.1. *Witch prevents person from drinking.* England: Baughman.

D2072.0.5.2. *Person who yawns cannot close mouth.* Eskimo (Greenland): Rasmussen I 255.

D2072.0.5.3. *Magic paralysis of tongue of a talkative wife.* *Loomis White Magic 126.

D2072.1. *Magic paralysis by Evil Eye.* (Cf. D2071.) Fb "øje" III 1167b. — Icelandic: *Boberg.

D2072.2. *Magic paralysis by curse.* Tawney II 467.

D1792. Magic results from curse. M430. Curses on persons.

D2072.2.1. *Charm used by witch to cause paralysis.* U.S.: Baughman.

D2072.3. *Magic paralysis caused by saint.* Irish myth: *Cross.

D2072.4. *Magic prevention of performance of task.* (Cf. H970.) Irish myth: *Cross.

D2072.5. *Robber-proof house: thieves are petrified when they enter house for unlawful purposes; are fed and welcomed, otherwise.* India: Thompson-Balys.

D1410. Magic object renders (person) helpless.

D2072.6. *Paralysis by singing magic song.* Eskimo (Greenland): Rink 351, Rasmussen III 111.

D2074. *Attracting by magic.* Icelandic: *Boberg.

D1412. Magic object pulls person into it. D1420. Magic object draws person (thing) to it. D1427.1. Magic pipe compels one to follow. D1441.1. Magic musical instrument calls animals together. D1649.2. Magic object comes at owner's call.

D2074.1. *Animals magically called.* (Cf. D1440, D2156.) *Toldo VIII 21; Irish myth: Cross; Icelandic: Þidriks saga II 271—75, Boberg; Jewish: Neuman; Eskimo (West Hudson Bay): Boas BAM XV 324.

B501. Animal gives part of body as talisman for summoning its aid. D2197. Magic dominance over animals.

D2074.1.1. *Mammals magically called.*

D2074.1.1.1. *Buffalo magically called.* Southern Ute: Lowie JAFL XXXVII 45.

B501.1. Buffalo give hero horns to blow for summoning them.

D2074.1.1.2. *Deer summoned by singing.* India: Thompson-Balys.

D1781. Magic results from singing.

D2074.1.1.3. *Bear summoned by magic.* Greek: Grote I 32.

D2074.1.2. *Fish or sea animals magically called.* Eskimo (West Hudson Bay): Boas BAM XV 324, (Greenland): Rink 116, 153; Marquesas, Tuamotu: Beckwith Myth 269, 289; Philippine (Tinguian): Cole 94.

D2074.1.2.1. *Coyote calls the largest fish.* N. A. Indian (Calif.): Gayton and Newman 83.

D2074.1.3. *Birds magically called.* Irish: O'Suilleabhain 86.

D2074.2. *Magic means of attracting.* Eskimo (Greenland): Rink 156, 286, Holm 30.

D1905.1. Girl's heart magically removed and fed to man draws her to him.

D2074.2.1. *Person summoned by thinking of him.* Chauvin V 5 n. 3; Penzer II 58.

D1777. Magic results from power of thought.

D2074.2.2. *Summoning by burning hair.* *Chauvin V 5 n. 3, 293.

D1787. Magic results from burning.

D2074.2.2.1. *Long-plaited hair struck on ground summons female goddess to aid of owner.* India: Thompson-Balys.

D2074.2.3. *Summoning by wish.* Eskimo (Mackenzie Area): Jenness 49.

D2074.2.3.1. *Mistress summoned by wish.* *Fb "ønske" III 1179a.

C31.6. Tabu: calling on supernatural wife.

D2074.2.3.2. *Ship summoned by wish.* Breton: Sébillot Incidents s.v. "navire".

D2074.2.4. *Genie called by writing his name on papers and burning them.* (Cf. D1421.) Chauvin V 244 No. 143.

C20. Tabu: calling on ogre or destructive animal. C432. Tabu: uttering name of supernatural creature. E384. Ghosts summoned by calling them by name. F403.2. Spirits help mortal. F404. Means of summoning spirits. P272. Foster-mother.

D2074.2.4.1. *Foster-mother summoned by saying her name.* Icelandic: *Boberg.

D2074.2.4.2. *Animals summoned by pronouncing their names.* India: Thompson-Balys.

D2074.2.4.3. *Helper summoned by calling his name.* India: Thompson-Balys (D1420.4).

D2074.2.4.4. *Order for spirit's help left on card.* *Krappe Archiv. f. d. Studium d. neueren Sprachen CLVIII 16ff.

D2074.2.5. *Summoning by prayer.* (Cf. V52.) Irish myth: Cross.

D1766.1. Magic results produced by prayer.

D2074.2.5.1. *Imprisoned cleric comes to answer saint's prayers in ritual.* Irish myth: Cross.

D2120. Magic transportation R165. Rescue by saint. R211. Escape from prison.

D2076. *Saint magically causes druids to bless instead of curse.* Irish myth: Cross.

D1719.1.1. Contest in magic between druid and saint.

D2078. *Imprisoning by magic.*

R0. Captives and fugitives.

D2078.1. *Witch made to enter boulder magically and imprisoned therein.* India: Thompson-Balys.

D2079. *Other forms of bewitching.*

D2079.1. *Magic compulsion to break wind under certain conditions.* (Cf. D2063.5.) N. A. Indian (Calif.): Gayton and Newman 83.

D2080. Magic used against property.

D2081. *Land made magically sterile.* (Cf. D1563.) *Kittredge Witchcraft 171, 488f. nn. 59, 63, 64; Greek: Frazer Apollodorus I 383 n. 5; Irish myth: *Cross; England, U.S.: *Baughman; Spanish: Boggs FFC XC 85 No. 750B.

B11.12.2. Dragon's shriek makes land barren. B16.4.4. Magic swine make land sterile. C934.2. Land made sterile because of broken tabu. D2143.2. Drought produced by magic. D2157. Magic control of soil and crops. F960.2.1. Nature fruitless after death of hero. F975. Garden becomes wilderness because of owner's wickedness. G112. Giant's fields fertile; others arid. H243. Nature fruitless if false judgment is passed. M400. Curses. M411.6.1. Druid's curse makes land sterile.

D2081.1. *Earth dried up in three years while hero is under earth.* Chinese: Graham.

D2082. *Trees killed by magic.* Breton: Sébillot Incidents s.v. "arbres".

D1563.4. Monster's blood makes tree (and surroundings) poisonous.

D2082.0.1. *Trees magically made fruitless.* Irish myth: *Cross.

D2082.0.2. *Tree magically withers.* India: Thompson-Balys.

D2082.1. *Magic glance reduces tree to ashes.* Another restores it. Penzer V 123.

D2061.1.1. Person magically reduced to ashes. D2071. Evil Eye.

D2082.2. *Anchorite consumes tree by one blast of his fiery breath.* India: Thompson-Balys.

D2083. *Evil magic in the dairy.* *Kittredge Witchcraft 163ff., 480ff.; Fb "smør" III 412—13.

D1018. Magic milk of animal. D1036. Magic dairy products. D1043. Milk as magic drink. D1335.2.3. Milk as magic strengthening drink. G265. Witch abuses property.

D2083.1. *Cows magically made dry.* Kittredge Witchcraft 480 n. 1; Irish myth: Cross; England, Scotland, U.S.: *Baughman; India: Thompson-Balys.

E251.3.2. Vampire milks cow dry. F366.1. Fairies milk mortal's cows dry.

D2083.2. *Cows made to give bad milk.* England, Canada: Baughman.

D2083.2.1. *Witches make cows give bloody milk.* *Kittredge Witchcraft 166, 484 n. 28; U.S.: Baughman.

D2083.2.2. *Witch causes cow to give curdled milk.* U.S.: Baughman.

D2083.3. *Milk transferred from another's cow by magic.* (Cf. D1605.2, C2087.) *Kittredge Witchcraft 163, 482 n. 4; England, Scotland, Ireland, U.S.: *Baughman; Lithuanian: Balys Index No. 5653.

D2083.3.1. *Milk transferred from another's cow by squeezing an axe-handle (or the like).* *Kittredge Witchcraft 163f., 482f. nn. 5—11; England, Scotland, U.S.: *Baughman.

D1782. Sympathetic magic.

D2083.3.2. *Witch transfers milk from another's cows by use of hair rope.* England, Scotland: *Baughman.

D2083.3.3. *Witch transfers milk from another's cows to a vessel.* England: *Baughman.

D2083.4. *Butter transferred from another by magic.* (Cf. D2087.) *Kittredge Witchcraft 168, 487f. nn. 38—43.

D2084.2. Butter magically kept from coming.

D2084. *Industrial processes magically interrupted.*

D2084.1. *Beer magically kept from brewing.* *Kittredge Witchcraft 170, 488 nn. 48—57; England: Baughman.

C671. The one compulsory song. Beer cannot be brewed until an old man sings the song of the origin of beer.

D2084.2. *Butter magically kept from coming.* (Cf. D1573, D2083.) *Kittredge Witchcraft 167, 485f. nn. 30—35; England, Ireland, U.S.: Baughman.

D2084.3. *Saint causes dyes to work incorrectly.* Irish myth: Cross.

D1713. Magic power of hermit (saint).

D2085. *Game animals magically made overwary.* Scotch: Campbell II 56.

D2085.1. *Curse (by saint) makes river (lake) barren of fish.* Irish myth: *Cross.

D1449.4. Charm prevents fish being caught. D1792. Magic results from curse. M411.8. Saint's curse.

D2086. *Weapons magically dulled.*

D2086.1. *Sword magically dulled.* **U. Priebe Stumpfmachen der Schwerten durch Zauber (Kiel Diss., Stettin, 1906); Zs. f. Vksk. XIII 213, XV 349, XVII 329; Icelandic: MacCulloch Eddic 46, 302, 260, *Boberg; Spanish Exempla: Keller; Jewish: Neuman.

D1414. Magic object renders weapon useless. D2072.0.1. Sword made magically helpless.

D2086.1.1. *Execution sword turned to wood.* India: Thompson-Balys.

D1391. Magic object saves person from execution. K500. Escape from death or danger by deception.

D2086.2. *Guns rendered ineffective by witch.* North Carolina: Brown Collection I 644.

D2086.3. *Weapons magically blown out of enemies' hands.* Icelandic: *Boberg.

D2087. *Theft by magic.*

K300. Thefts and cheats.

D2087.1. *Crops stolen by magic.* *Kittredge Witchcraft 172, 489 nn. 66—70.

D2083.3. Milk transferred from another's cow by magic. D2083.4. Butter transferred from another by magic.

D2087.2. *Hunter's prey stolen during night by magic.* Icelandic: Grímssaga L. 144, Boberg.

D2087.3. *Sheep or cattle disappear every night.* Icelandic: *Boberg.

D2087.3.1. *Cow and cowherd disappear every New Year's night.* Icelandic: Boberg.

D2087.4. *Men disappear every night.* Icelandic: Flateyjarbók I 282—83, *Boberg.

D2087.5. *Gold stolen by magic.* Icelandic: *Boberg.

D2087.6. *Food stolen by magic.* Icelandic: *Boberg.

D2087.7. *Witches rifle drawers of chests in house.* U.S.: Baughman.

D2087.8. *Witch steals potatoes, leaving no traces.* England: Baughman.

D2088. *Locks opened by magic.* Krappe Balor 2 n. 9; Irish myth: Cross; Icelandic: *Boberg.

D2088.0.1. *All locks opened on the night of Christ's Nativity.* (Cf. D1557.1.) Irish myth: Cross.

D2088.1. *Fairy gains entrance to locked city.* Irish myth: *Cross.

D2089. *Magic used against property—miscellaneous.*

D2089.1. *Man makes all of iron in enemy's storehouse disappear so weapons cannot be made.* India: Thompson-Balys.

K632. Mice gnaw enemies' bow-strings. K2350. Military strategy.

D2089.2. *Curse makes stones useless.* Irish myth: Cross.

D1792. Magic results from curse.

D2089.3. *Animals magically stricken dead.* (Cf. D2060.) Irish myth: Cross.

B275.3. Animals eating corpse of holy man die. Q558.14.1. Animals stricken dead for desecration of holy places. Q574.2. Mysterious death of animals as punishment for uncharitableness remitted.

D2089.3.1. *Swine magically kept from fattening.* Irish myth: Cross.

D2089.4. *Saint causes mill to turn backwards.* Irish myth: Cross.

D1713. Magic power of hermit (saint).

D2089.5. *Books illegible as result of curse.* (Cf. D1266.) Irish myth: Cross.

D1792. Magic results from curse.

D2089.6. *House destroyed by magic.* Chinese: Graham.

D2089.7. *Goods magically diminish.*

D2089.7.1. *Food dwindles as soon as it is cooked.* India: Thompson-Balys.

D2089.8. *Clothes burned by magic.* Eskimo (Greenland): Rink 393.

D2089.9. *Trail magically closed.*

D2089.9.1. *Trail magically covered with thorns.* Philippine (Tinguian): Cole 98.

D2089.10. *Fire drills magically made not to function.* Eskimo (Cumberland Sound): Boas BAM XV 243.

D2090. Other destructive magic powers.

D2091. *Magic attack against enemy.* Icelandic: *Boberg; Eskimo (Bering Strait): Nelson RBAE XVIII 516.

D2163. Magic defense in battle. K2350. Military strategy.

D2091.1. *Magic fire drawn down on foe.* (Cf. D1271.) Irish myth: *Cross.

F962.2. Fire from heaven.

D2091.2. *Magic plague of frogs drawn down on foe.* Irish myth: *Cross.

D2091.2.1. *Magic army of snakes and frogs drawn down on foe.* Jewish: Neuman.

D2091.3. *Streams of blood magically drawn down on foe.* Irish myth: *Cross.

F1084.1. Deep streams of blood flow during battle.

D2091.4. *Magic causes enemies to fight among selves.* Irish myth: *Cross; Icelandic: *Boberg; Jewish: Neuman; Eskimo (Greenland): Rink 189; Africa (Duala): Lederbogen Fables 62, (Ekoi): Talbot 127.

K1080. Persons duped into injuring each other.

D2091.5. *Storms magically drawn down on foe.* Irish myth: *Cross.

D2141. Storm produced by magic.

D2091.6. *Enemies magically made to feel thirst.* Irish myth: Cross.

D2063.3. Magic insatiable thirst.

D2091.7. *Magic lake (river) sent against enemy.* (Cf. D921.1.) Irish myth: *Cross.

D2091.7.1. *River magically caused to rise against enemy.* Irish myth: *Cross.

D2151.2. Magic control of rivers.

D2091.8. *Magic drought to destroy enemy.* Buddhist myth: Malalasekera II 37.

D2091.8.1. *Druids dry up water in enemy's camp.* (Cf. D1711.4.) Irish myth: *Cross.

D2151.2.3. Rivers magically made dry.

D2091.9. *Magic paralysis drawn down on foe.* (Cf. D2072.) Irish myth: *Cross.

D2091.10. *Magic heat causes enemies to melt away.* (Cf. D2144.3.) Irish myth: Cross.

D2091.10.1. *Stones, etc., magically made to burn feet of enemies.* Irish myth: Cross.

D2091.11. *Black cloud magically blown upon enemy.* Irish myth: Cross.

D1005. Magic breath.

D2091.12. *Plants and animals magically caused to shriek, frightening enemy.* Irish myth: Cross.

F990. Inanimate objects act as if living. K1883. Illusory enemies.

D2091.13. *Army stopped by saint's curse.* Irish myth: *Cross.

D1792. Magic results from curse.

D2091.14. *Magician shoots an arrow of each finger against enemy.* Icelandic: *Boberg.

D2091.15. *Magic earth-slip overcomes enemies.* Icelandic: Boberg.

D2091.16. *Enemy magically enclosed within walls.* Jewish: Neuman.

D2092. *Man caused to sink into mud.* Finnish: Kalevala rune 3.
F943. Sinking into mud in duel.

D2093. *Walls overthrown by magic (Jericho).* *Saintyves Essais 180ff.; Spanish Exempla: Keller; Jewish: Neuman.

D2094. *Pestilence magically sent upon (domestic) animals.* (Cf. D2064.) Irish myth: *Cross.

D2095. *Magic disappearance.*
D1405. Magic object causes person to disappear.

D2095.1. *Magic village and people disappear by magic.* India: Thompson-Balys.

D2096. *Magic putrefaction.* Irish myth: *Cross.
F1041.1.23. Putrescence flows from head when person presses forehead. Q552.16. Food and drink refused saint miraculously become putrid. Q575. Magic putrefaction of food as punishment for opposition to holy person remitted.

D2097. *Magic trouble-making.* (Cf. K2130.) Irish myth: *Cross.

D2098. *Ship magically sunk.* England: Baughman.

D2099. *Miscellaneous destructive magic powers.*

D2099.1. *Loss of skill through magic.* Eskimo (Greenland): Holm 84.

D2099.2. *Magic banishment.* Icelandic: *Boberg.

D2099.3. *House crushed by magic.* Eskimo (Greenland): Rink 272.

D2099.4. *Calabashes broken by magic.* Easter Island: Métraux Ethnology 367.

D2100—D2199 OTHER MANIFESTATIONS OF MAGIC POWER

D2100. Magic wealth. (Cf. D1450.) India: Thompson-Balys; Chinese: Graham.
B100. Treasure animal. B110. Treasure-producing parts of animals. B581. Animal brings wealth to man. C911. Golden finger as sign of opening forbidden chamber. C912. Hair turns to gold as punishment in forbidden chamber. D475. Transformation: object to treasure. D565.1. Midas' golden touch. Everything touched turns to gold. D852. Magic object acquired by wishing. D1450. Magic object furnishes treasure. D1470. Magic object acts as provider. D1761. Magic results produced by wishing. Q141. Reward: man's cows magically multiply. Q142. Magic treasure as reward for humility.

D2100.1. *Inexhaustible treasure.* (Cf. D1652.) Jewish: Neuman; India: Thompson-Balys, Tawney I 350f., 471.

D2100.2. *Coin multiplies itself.* (Cf. D1288, D2106.) *Loomis White Magic 87; India: Thompson-Balys.
C773.1.1. Tabu: asking for too great multiplication of coins.

D2101. *Treasure magically discovered.* *Type 613. See also N530—N549, Discovery of treasure.

D2101.1. *Treasure found by sprinkling ground with blood of white cock.* (Cf. D1314.) *Chauvin V 13f. No. 9; India: Thompson-Balys.

D2101.2. *Shower of jewels magically drawn from sky.* Buddhist myth: Malalasekera II 445.

D2102. *Gold magically produced.*
D475.1. Transformation: objects to gold. D1469.7. Wealth from drawing cow's feet over money box.

D2102.1. *Gold vomited.* Irish: Plummer xliv, *Cross.

D2102.2. *Valley fills with gold at command.* Gaster Rabbis 225 No. 205, Jewish: Neuman.

D2102.2.1. *Field turns to gold after ascetic plows it.* Buddhist myth: Malalasekera II 221.

D2102.3. *Saint magically produces treasure.* Irish myth: Cross.
D1713. Magic power of hermit (saint).

D2102.4. *"Golden" son of supernatural bride of king has the power of producing gold and gold buildings, ornaments etc.* India: Thompson-Balys.

D2102.5. *Magic corn eaten by animal becomes gold.* Chinese: Eberhard FFC CXX 221.
B103.1. Treasure-dropping animals.

D2103. *Silver magically produced.* India: Thompson-Balys.

D2105. *Provisions magically furnished.* (Cf. D1470.) Irish myth: *Cross; Icelandic: *Boberg; German: Grimm Nos. 90, 121, 179; India: Thompson-Balys; Chinese: Graham; Eskimo (Greenland): Rink 229, 325, 422, 454, Holm 40, Rasmussen I 239, 374, III 51, (Mackenzie Area): Jenness 63, (Cumberland Sound): Boas BAM 245; S. A. Indian (Chiriguano): Métraux BBAE CXLIII (3) 484, (Toba) ibid. (1) 368; Africa (Angola): Chatelain 115 No. 9, (Ibo): Thomas 119.
V224.2 Food (animals) eaten by saint miraculously replaced.

D2105.1. *Provisions provided in answer to prayer.* Irish myth: *Cross.
D1766.1. Magic results produced by prayer. V52. Miraculous power of prayer.

D2105.1.1. *Starvation prevented by composition of hymn.* (Cf. D1275.3.) Irish myth: Cross.

D2105.2. *Provisions provided by messenger from heaven.* Irish myth: Cross.

D2105.3. *Rubbish magically becomes food and clothing.* Irish myth: Cross.

D2105.3.1. *Trash magically becomes food.* Africa (Duala): Lederbogen Fables 66.

D2105.4. *Drink magically furnished.* Irish myth: *Cross.

D2105.5. *Saint causes fish to come out of lake to satisfy guests for whom he has no food.* (Cf. D1444.1, F986.2.) Irish myth: Cross.

D2105.6. *Showers of grain called down.* Buddhist myth: Malalasekera II 654.

D2105.7. *Fruit obtained from tree by magic.* Buddhist myth: Malalasekera II 409.

D2106. *Magic multiplication of objects.*

D2106.1. *Magic multiplication of objects by saints.* (Cf. D2100.2, V220.) *Toldo VI 289; Irish myth: *Cross; Spanish Exempla: Keller; India: Thompson-Balys.

D1573.1. Much butter made from little milk by power of Saint. D1599.3. Magic object multiplies objects. D1652.1.12.1. Loaves and fish, eaten at night, restored next morning through power of saint. D2182.1. Flow of cow's milk increased by saint. E155.5.1. Calf, slain at night, alive next day through power of saint. F166.11. Abundant food in otherworld. F815.2.1. Extraordinary amount of liquor pressed from single grain. F986.1. Clerics catch fish with regularity. H1022.4. Task: making shirt from piece of linen three inches square. V224.2. Food eaten by saint miraculously replaced.

D2106.1.1. *Saint causes waters to be filled with fish.* *Loomis White Magic 69f.; Irish myth: *Cross.

D2106.1.1.1. *Fish caught in waterless field.* *Loomis White Magic 70.

D2106.1.2. *Animals miraculously multiplied.* *Loomis White Magic 87.

D2106.1.3. *Multiplication of metal by saint.* *Loomis White Magic 87.

D2106.1.4. *Multiplication of the corpse of saint when different communities claim the body.* *Loomis White Magic 87.

D2106.1.5. *Multiplication of food by saint.* (Cf. D1652.1.) India: Thompson-Balys; Icelandic: Boberg.

D2106.2. *One sack of charcoal makes a hundred.* India: Thompson-Balys.

D2106.3. *Tree with all sorts of cakes hanging from its branches springs from one cake.* India: Thompson-Balys.

D2107. *Warrior's equipment magically furnished.*

D2107.1. *Horse and weapons needed by hero are provided after incense is offered to Nandia, the Bull.* India. Thompson-Balys.

D2120. Magic transportation. *Type 400, 566; Chauvin V 231 No. 130 n. 1. — Irish myth: Cross; Spanish: Boggs FFC XC 84 No. 750A*; India: Thompson-Balys; Buddhist myth: Malalasekera II 676; Chinese: Eberhard FFC CXX 102; Philippine (Tinguian): Cole 53.

B184.1.6.1. Flight on magic horse. B551.1. Fish carries man. D1520. Magic object affords miraculous transportation. D1523. Magic self-moving vehicle. D1976.1. Transportation during magic sleep. D2074.2.5.1. Imprisoned cleric comes to answer saint's prayers in ritual. F101.4. Escape from lower world by magic. R122. Prisoner whirled away in blaze of fire. V229.6.3. Druid raised in air, cast down, and brains scattered on stone by power of saint. V232.2. Angel carries mortal.

D2121. *Magic journey.* *Type 400; *Huet RTP XXXII 97, 145; Wesselski Theorie 23. — Irish myth: Cross; Italian Novella: Rotunda; Jewish: Neuman; India: Thompson-Balys; Chinese: Ferguson 128; Eskimo (Greenland): Rasmussen I 219; Africa (Benga): Nassau 214 No. 33.

F0. Journey to otherworld. F370. Visit to fairyland.

D2121.1. *Magic journey by wishing.* (Cf. D1761.) *Fb "ønske" III 1178b; India: Thompson-Balys.

D2121.2. *Magic journey with closed eyes.* Person must not open eyes while on the journey. (Cf. C300.) *Chauvin VII 59 No. 77, 102 No. 376, VIII 148 No. 146; Hartland Science 174 (Japanese). — Irish myth: Cross; India: Thompson-Balys; Chinese: Graham, Eberhard FFC CXX 234f.; Japanese: Ikeda; N. A. Indian: *Thompson Tales 338 n. 217; Eskimo (Greenland): Rasmussen II 14, III 103, 124, 257, Rink

147, 196, 219, (Bering Strait): Nelson RBAE XVIII 511, (Mackenzie Area): Jenness 52, (Smith Sound): Kroeber JAFL XII 171, (Central Eskimo): Boas RBAE VI 629.

D2121.3. *Magic journey through power of imagination.* Chauvin V 230f. No. 130.

D1777. Magic results from power of thought.

D2121.4. *Magic journey by making distance vanish.* The road is contracted or the earth folded up. *Chauvin V 231 No. 130. — Jewish: Neuman; Africa (Upoto): Einstein 134; N. A. Indian: *Thompson Tales 315 n. 145c; Eskimo (Greenland): Rasmussen III 247.

D2121.5. *Magic journey: man carried by spirit or devil.* Herbert III 362f. Nos. 135, 152. — Irish myth: Cross; England: Baughman; Icelandic: Boberg; Jewish: *Neuman; India: Thompson-Balys; Eskimo (Greenland): Rink 255, Rasmussen III 114.

E752.2. Soul carried off by demon (devil). N810. Supernatural helpers. V232.2. Angel carries mortal.

D2121.6. *Magic journey during which one must not think good or evil.* Swiss: Jegerlehner Oberwallis 322 No. 88.

F64. Journey to upper world by keeping thoughts continually on heaven.

D2121.7. *Magic journey in cloud.* (Cf. D2135.) Irish myth: Cross; Spanish: Boggs FFC XC 57 No. 425; Jewish: Neuman; Chinese: Graham; Korean: Zong in-Sob 224.

D1520.2. Magic transportation by cloud. F61.1. Ascent to sky on cloud. R122.2. Prisoner carried off in cloud.

D2121.7.1. *Magic journey in cloud of fire.* Irish myth: Cross.

D2121.7.2. *Magic journey in whirl of snow.* Icelandic: Ketilssaga H. 118, Boberg.

D2143.6. Magic control of snow.

D2121.7.3. *Magic transportation on smoke.* Easter Island: Métraux Ethnology 368.

D2121.8. *Magic journey by throwing knife into whirlwind.* *Taylor FFC LXX 24 n. 1; Lithuanian: Balys Index No. 3903; Livonian: Loorits FFC LXVI 60 No. 149.

D1520.28. Magic transportation in whirlwind.

D2121.9. *Magic transportation from kick of a horse.* Penzer VIII 57 n. 2.

D2121.10. *Magic journey on sunbeam.* Africa (Ganda): Baskerville The Flame Tree (London, 1925) 1ff. No. 1.

F1011. Sunbeam as support.

D2121.11. *Magic journey: man left on land appears in ship.* Irish myth: Cross.

D2121.12. *Power to go through closed doors.* Icelandic: Boberg.

F1088.4. Locks marvelously open. G304.2.3.1. Locks spring open for troll.

D2121.13. *Sailing in a leaky boat without sinking.* *Loomis White Magic 90.

D2121.14. *Saint rides on thorn tree and drags its roots through earth to dig out canal.* India: Thompson-Balys.

D2121.15. *Magic compulsion to make journey.* Eskimo (Greenland): Rink 123.

C650. The one compulsory thing.

D2122. *Journey with magic speed.* *Loomis White Magic 93; Penzer II 223 n. 1, VI 213, 279, VII 24, 225 n. 1, VIII 57 n. 2. — Irish: Plummer clxxxvi, *Cross; Icelandic: *Boberg; Breton: Sébillot Incidents s.v. "transport"; Jewish: *Neuman; India: Thompson-Balys; Chinese: Eberhard FFC CXX 195; Korean: Zong in-Sob 65, 73; Eskimo (Greenland): Holm 24; Africa (Vai): Ellis 207 No. 24, (Benga): Nassau No. 24 (version 2).

B11.5.4. Dragon's miraculous speed. B184.1.1. Horse (mule) with magic speed. D1521. Miraculous speed from magic object. D1924. Magic immunity from fatigue. F370. Visit to fairyland. F403.2.3.4. Familiar spirit brings news with magic speed. F411.0.1. Spirit travels with extraordinary speed. F681. Marvelous runner.

D2122.0.1. *Journey to otherworld with magic speed.* (Cf. F0.) Irish myth: Cross.

D2122.1. *Magic speed by eating magic grains (medicine).* N. A. Indian (Maliseet, European borrowing): Mechling JAFL XXVI 250; Africa (Basuto): Jacottet 214 No. 31.

D2122.2. *Hundred-league stride.* England: Baughman; Breton: Sébillot Incidents s.v. "pas"; Jewish: Neuman; N. A. Indian: Thompson Tales 315 n. 145, (Calif.): Gayton and Newman 59.

D1521.1. Seven-league boots.

D2122.3. *Magic journey as swift as thought.* (Cf. G242.) *Taylor FFC LXX 49ff.; *Fb "tanke"; England: Baughman; Swiss: *Jegerlehner Oberwallis 293 No. 1.

D1521.3. Sleigh as swift as thought. D1521.4. Carriage as swift as thought. F681.3. Marvelous runner swift as thought.

D2122.4. *Journey with speed of angels.* Irish myth: Cross.

D2122.5. *Journey with magic speed by saint.* Irish myth: Cross.

D2125. *Magic journey over water.* Jewish: Neuman; Irish myth: *Cross.

D2125.0.1. *Saint causes earth to rise underfoot, enabling him to cross water.* Irish myth: *Cross.

D2125.0.2. *Saint drives over bog as over land.* Irish myth: Cross.

D2125.1. *Magic power to walk on water.* *Pauli (ed. Bolte) No. 332; *Saintyves Essais 307ff.; *Toldo VI 310ff.; Cowell Jātaka II 77. — Irish: Plummer xxxi, cxlvii, Cross; Icelandic: Boberg; U.S.: Baughman; India: Thompson-Balys; Buddhist myth: Malalasekera II 112; Eskimo (Greenland): Rink 123, 407, Rasmussen III 192.

B184.1.4. Magic horse travels on sea or land. D1524.1. Magic object permits man to walk on water. D1524.2. Boots carry owner on sea. F931. Extraordinary occurrence connected with sea. P192.3 Fool can walk on water.

D2125.1.1. *Magic transportation by waves.* Icelandic: Völsunga saga ch. 41 (39), cf. 43 (41), Boberg; Tuamotu: Stimson MS (z-G. 13/249).

F931.4. Extraordinary behavior of waves.

D2125.1.1.1. *Saint rides blessed wave.* *Loomis White Magic 91.

D2125.2. *Magic transportation on a sheet of ice.* Icelandic: Boberg.

D2125.3. *Person crosses water in chariot.* Buddhist myth: Malalasekera I 96.

D2126. *Magic underwater journey.* Irish myth: *Cross; Chinese: Graham; Eskimo (Greenland): Rink 185, 417, 451.

D1525.1. Magic hood enables person to pass under water. F133. Submarine otherworld. F141. Water barrier to otherworld. F153. Otherworld reached by diving under water. F212. Fairyland under water. F345.1. Fairies teach mortal to walk under water. F691.0.1. Hero battles under lake for a day and night. F842.2.3.1. Underwater bridge. P192.4. Fool can live under water.

D2131. *Magic underground journey.* *Type 306; *Fb "løngang" II 515b; India: *Thompson-Balys; N. A. Indian: *Thompson Tales 316 n. 145c; Eskimo (Greenland): Rink 451, Rasmussen III 268, Holm 68, (Mackenzie Area): Jenness 42.

B184.1.2. Magic horse goes underground. D1533.2. Vehicle travels above or below ground. F721.1. Underground passages. Journey made through natural subways. F940. Extraordinary underground disappearance.

D2135. *Magic air journey.* *Penzer X 64 s.v. "air"; *Fb "ride" III 53a; *Toldo IV 77; *Loomis White Magic 91f.; Jones PMLA XXIII 563; Malone PMLA XLIII 412. — Irish myth: *Cross; Breton: Sébillot Incidents s.v. "voyages"; Jewish: *Neuman; India: Thompson-Balys; Buddhist myth: Malalasekera II 12, 43, 319; Chinese: Chavannes 500 Contes I 359 No. 94, Graham; Japanese: Coyajee JPASB XXIV 185; N. A. Indian: *Thompson Tales 316 n. 145d; Eskimo (Greenland): Rasmussen I 87, (Mackenzie Area): Jenness 40.

B41.2. Flying horse. B45. Air-going elephant. B542.2. Escape on flying horse. B552. Man carried by birds. D1118. Magic airships. D1118.1. Magic air-riding basket. D1520.2. Magic transportation by cloud. D1520.19. Magic transportation by carpet. D1531. Magic object gives power of flying. D1532. Magic object bears person aloft. D1626. Image flies through air. D1626.1. Artificial flying horse. D2121.7. Magic journey in cloud. D2122. Journey with magic speed. F61.3. Transportation from Heaven in mist. F68. Ascent to upper world by magic. F460.2.2. Mountain-folk ride through air on horses. K1334. Seduction (or wooing) on an aerial journey. R111.3.1. Girl rescued by traveling through air.

D2135.0.1. *Levitation.* Person able to raise self in the air. *Cowell Jātaka index s.v. "air"; *Toldo IV 77; Alphabet No. 459; *Loomis White Magic 47. — Irish myth: *Cross; England, Scotland, Wales, U. S.: *Baughman; Jewish: *Neuman; India: Thompson-Balys; Buddhist myth: Malalasekera II 490.

D1711. Magician. D2165.1. Escape by flying through the air. F411.2. Spirit floats in air. F1041.8.7. Mad warriors fly up into clouds. F1083.0.1. Object rises in air. R324.1. Escape from battle by flying in air.

D2135.0.2. *Object magically raised in air.* Irish myth: Cross; U.S.: Baughman.

D2135.0.2.1. *Stone cross magically raised in air.* Irish myth: Cross.

D2135.0.3. *Magic ability to fly.* Chinese: Eberhard FFC CXX 189.

D2135.1. *Power of flying from eating children's hearts.* Child V 482 s.v "hearts".

D1793. Magic results from eating or drinking.

D2135.2. *Magic air journey from biting an ear.* Tehauno: Boas JAFI XXV 244.

D2135.3. *Stones fly through the air at saint's bidding.* *Loomis White Magic 92.

D2135.4. *Magic transportation to highest summit by divine power.* India Thompson-Balys.

D2135.5. *Objects sent through air.* Buddhist myth: Malalasekera II 121]

D2136. *Objects magically moved.* Irish myth: *Cross.

D2136.1. *Rocks moved by magic.* Irish myth: *Cross; Welsh: MacCulloch Celtic 201 (rocks of Stonehenge), cf. Chaucer's Franklin's Tale; Greek: *Frazer Apollodorus I 17 (Orpheus); Jewish: *Neuman; N. A. Indian (Seneca): Curtin-Hewitt RBAE XXXII 192 No. 37, 310 No. 58; Eskimo (Greenland): Rink 258.

D1602.1. Stones, being removed, return to their places. D1641.2. Stones remove themselves. M261. Chaste woman promises herself to her lover when the rocks leave the coast. (They are moved by magic).

D2136.2. *Castle magically transported.* Breton: Sébillot Incidents s.v. "château"; India: Thompson-Balys.

D2136.2.1. *Mosque turns around in order to face in the true direction of Mecca after prayers of two saints.* India: Thompson-Balys.

F771.2.6. Revolving castle.

D2136.2.2. *Sunken palace magically raised.* Buddhist myth: Malalasekera II 30.

D2136.3. *Mountains (hills) magically transported.* Irish myth: Cross.

D2136.3.1. *Mountain moved by prayer.* *Herbert III 390 No. 290; *Wesselski Märchen 255ff. No. 66; *Pauli (ed. Bolte) Nos. 683, 684; Spanish Exempla: Keller.

F755. Living mountain.

D2136.4. *Lake magically transported.* (Cf. D1641.12.) Irish myth: Cross.

D2136.4.1. *Saint drives lake into sea.* Irish myth: Cross.

D2136.5. *Saint's possessions magically transported.* (Cf. V220.) Loomis White Magic 91f.; Irish myth: *Cross.

D2136.6. *Island magically transported.* (Cf. D936.) Irish myth: Cross; Tuamotu: Stimson MS (z-G. 3/1122, 1146, T-G. 3/912, z-G 13/499).

F737. Wandering island. J2287. Belief that island may be towed by ship.

D2136.7. *Well magically transported.* (Cf. D926, D1641.1, D1641.13.) Irish myth: Cross.

D2136.8. *Ship moved by sacrifice.* Greek: Fox 125; India: Thompson-Balys.

D1654.6. Ship refuses to move. D2072.0.3. Ship held back by magic. D2142. Wind produced by magic.

D2136.9. *Magic house removed.* Chinese: Graham, Eberhard FFC CXX 241; Philippine (Tinguian): Cole 64, 129, 130, 151; Eskimo (Cumberland Sound): Boas BAM XV 257.

D2136.10. *Objects magically sent to certain place.* Philippine (Tinguian): Cole 68, 69, 75, 140; Eskimo (Cumberland Sound): Boas BAM XV 245.

D2137. *Natural law suspended.*

D2137.1. *Witch keeps water from boiling.* England: Baughman.

D2140. Magic control of the elements. (Cf. D1540.) *Kittredge Witchcraft 152ff., 472ff. nn. 1ff., especially n. 4; French Canadian: Sister Marie Ursule; Jewish: *Neuman; India: Thompson-Balys; Icelandic: *Boberg.

A197. Deity controls elements. A280. Weather-god. A1130. Establishment of present order: weather phenomena. B172.8. Magic osprey produces lightning. D900. Magic weather phenomena. D1541. Magic object controls storms. F790. Extraordinary sky and weather phenomena. F961. Extraordinary behavior of heavenly bodies. G283. Witches have control over weather.

D2140.1. *Control of weather by saint's prayers.* (Cf. V220.) *Toldo VI 330; *Loomis White Magic 39; Irish myth: *Cross; Icelandic: *Boberg; Spanish Exempla: Keller.

D2140.1.1. *Saint has power to control winds and storms at will.* (Cf. A287.2.) *Loomis White Magic 45f.

D2140.2. *Shaman's wife controls weather.* Eskimo (Mackenzie Area): Jenness 84.

D2140.3. *Weather changed on confession of deed.* Eskimo (Cumberland Sound): Boas BAM XV 301.

D2141. *Storm produced by magic.* (Cf. D905, D1541.) *Krappe Bulletin Hispanique XXXV 109ff.; Irish myth: *Cross; Icelandic: *Boberg; Italian Novella: Rotunda; Jewish: *Neuman; Hawaii: Beckwith Myth 507; Eskimo (Greenland): Rink 223, 375, 450, 469, Rasmussen I 367, II 170, III 158, 270, (Central Eskimo): Boas RBAE VI 584, 622, (Cumberland Sound): Boas BAM XV 164, (West Hudson Bay): Boas BAM XV 321; N. A. Indian: *Thompson Tales 289 n. 61b, (Calif.): Gayton and Newman 61; S. A. Indian (Toba): Métraux MAFLS XL 162.

D905. Magic storm. D1541. Magic object controls storms. D1766.4.2. Storm raised because of cat christened by witches. D2091.5. Storms magically drawn down on foe. D2143.1.1. Rain produced by pouring water. E501.13.6. Wild hunt heralded by storm. K356. Thief makes magic storm in order to escape. Q222.1. Magic storm conceived as punishment for desecrating temple.

D2141.0.1. *Storm from calling on evil spirit.* *Kittredge Witchcraft 158, 477 nn. 57, 58. — Icelandic: Boberg.

D1721.1. Magic power from devil.

D2141.0.2. *Storm from calling up spirits to help find buried treasure.* (Cf. C401.3.) *Kittredge Witchcraft 158, 477 nn. 54—56.

C12. Devil invoked: appears unexpectedly. N530. Discovery of treasure.

D2141.0.3. *Storms produced by devil.* *Kittredge Witchcraft 152ff., 472ff. nn. 1—53 passim; North Carolina: Brown Collection I 660.

D1721.1. Magic power from devil.

D2141.0.4. *Storm at death of wizard.* Devil comes for him. (Cf. D2141.0.3.) Kittredge Witchcraft 159, 477 n. 59.

G278.1. Marvelous manifestation at death of witch.

D2141.0.5. *Storm at death of wicked person.* Devil comes for him. (Cf. D2141.0.3.) Kittredge Witchcraft 159, 477 nn. 60—64.

Q550.1. Supernatural manifestations at death of wicked person.

D2141.0.6. *Storm because of bird's singing.* Africa (Basuto): Jacottet 104 No. 15.

D1781. Magic results from singing.

D2141.0.7. *Storm raised by incantation.* (Cf. D1391.1.) Greek: Grote I 184, Philippine (Tinguian): Cole 121; Africa (Zulu): Callaway 203.

D2141.0.7.1. *Storm produced by prayer.* (Cf. D2143.3.) Jewish: Neuman.

D2141.0.8. *Storms raised by druids.* (Cf. D2142.0.3.) Irish: Plummer clix, *Cross.

D1711.4. Druid as magician.

D2141.0.8.1. *Storm calmed by wizard* (druid). (Cf. D2141.1.) Irish myth: *Cross.

D2141.0.9. *Storm raised by saint.* Irish myth: Cross.

D2141.0.10. *Woman hoists skirt to raise thunderstorm.* Hawaii: Beckwith Myth 113.

D1796. Magic from maiden walking naked in public. Z181. Nudity as sign of anger.

D2141.0.11. *Magic storm produced by animal.*

D2141.0.11.1. *Magic storm produced by serpent.* S. A. Indian (Toba): Métraux MAFLS XL 71.

D2141.0.12. *Magic storm by pointing root of tree at sky.* Africa (Cameroon): Ittman 71.

D2141.1. *Storm magically stilled.* (Cf. D2141.0.8.1.) *Fb "storm" III 596a; Irish myth: Cross; Spanish Exempla: Keller; Jewish: bin Gorion Born Judas[2] II 95, 342, 368; India: Thompson-Balys; Tonga: Gifford 117; Eskimo (Greenland): Rasmussen I 331.

V254.2. Ship in storm saved because of sailors' "Ave Maria".

D2141.1.1. *Church bell rung as protection against storm.* To thwart devil. (Cf. D1213.) *P. Sartori Das Buch von deutschen Glocken (Berlin, 1932); *Kittredge Witchcraft 158, 476 nn. 51—53; *Loomis White Magic 53.

V115. Church bells.

D2141.2. *Storm raised to defeat enemy.* India: Thompson-Balys.

K2350. Military strategy.

D2142. *Winds controlled by magic.*

D2142.0.1. *Magician (witch) controls winds.* *Kittredge Witchcraft 159, 478 nn. 67—8. — Icelandic: *Boberg.

D1711. Magician. G260. Evil deeds of witches.

D2142.0.1.1. *Witch sells power to control winds.* *Kittredge Witchcraft 159, 477f. nn. 65—74 passim.

D1721. Magic power from magician.

D2142.0.1.2. *Witch sits atop mast, causes winds to blow.* England: Baughman.

D2142.0.2. *Saint controls winds.* Irish myth: *Cross.

D1543.6. Wind carried in mantle. D1713. Magic power of Hermit (saint). V220. Saints.

D2142.0.3. *Druid controls winds.* (Cf. D2141.0.8.) Irish myth: *Cross.

D1711.4. Druid as magician.

D2142.0.4. *Leper controls winds.* Tuamotu: Stimson MS (T-G. 3/45).

D2142.0.5. *Wind controlled by girl's spirit.* Marquesas: Handy 29.

D2142.1. *Wind produced by magic.* Irish myth: *Cross; Finnish: Kalevala rune 10; Icelandic: *Boberg; Jewish: Neuman; Chinese: Werner 353; Marquesas: Handy 119; Tuamotu: Stimson MS (T—G. 3/109, z-G. 3/1323).

A532. Culture hero tames winds in caves. A1120. Establishment of present order: winds. C984.1. Great wind because of broken tabu. D906. Magic wind. D1543. Magic object controls wind.

D2142.1.1. *Wind raised by dog's wagging tail.* Irish myth: Cross.

D2142.1.2. *Wind raised by loosing certain knots.* (Cf. D906, D1282.1.) *Fb "vindknude"; Taylor FFC LXX; Danish: Kristensen Danske Sagn VI (1901) 414—16; Scotland: Baughman.

D1782. Sympathetic magic.

D2142.1.3. *Wind raised by calling on devil.* (Cf. D2141.0.3.) *Kittredge Witchcraft 161, 479 n. 81.

D1721.1. Magic power from devil.

D2142.1.4. *Wind raised by troubling vessel of water.* *Kittredge Witchcraft 160f., 479 nn. 79—80; England, Scotland, U.S.: *Baughman.

D1541.4. Magic fountain causes storm.

D2142.1.4.1. *Wind raised by throwing traitor's ashes into lake.* *Krappe Bulletin Hispanique XXXV (1933) 109.

D2142.1.5. *Wind raised by putting cat under bushel (barrel) (drowning cat).* (Cf. G283.2.1.) *Kittredge Witchcraft 161, 479 nn. 84—87; Ireland: Baughman.

D2142.1.6. *Wind raised by whistling.* Kittredge Witchcraft 160, 478f., nn. 77—8; *Fb "fløjte" I 326 a.

D2142.1.6.1. *Wind raised by blowing into tobacco pipe.* Kittredge Witchcraft 160, 478 n. 76.

D2142.2. *Wind stilled by magic.* Tuamotu: Stimson MS (z-G. 13/555), Beckwith Myth 289; Ibo (Nigeria): Thomas 118; Icelandic: Boberg.

A532. Culture hero tames winds in caves. A1122. Cave of winds.

D2142.2.1. *Wind stopped by revenant.* Irish myth: Cross.

D2143. *Precipitation controlled by magic.* Irish myth: Cross.

F962. Extraordinary precipitation.

D2143.1. *Rain produced by magic.* *Gaster Beiträge zur vgl. Sagen- und Märchenkunde 33ff.; Irish myth: *Cross; Icelandic: Boberg; Jewish: *Neuman; India: Thompson-Balys; Chinese: Werner 353, Eberhard FFC CXX 237; Korean: Zong in Sob 64; Philippine (Tinguian): Cole 97; Eskimo (Greenland): Holm 66; Africa (Upoto): Einstein 123, (Hottentot): Bleek 29 No. 14, (Ekoi): Talbot 247, (Basuto): Jacottet 126 No. 18.

A287. Rain-God. A1131. Origin of rain. D902. Magic rain. D1542. Magic object controls rain.

D2143.1.0.1. *Rain caused to fall in certain place (by rain-god).* India: Thompson-Balys.

D2143.1.0.2. *No rain falls on religious man.* Irish: O'Suilleabhain 110.

D2143.1.1. *Rain produced by pouring water.* (Cf. D1242.1.) *Fb "vand" III 1001b; Chrétien de Troyes "Yvain" lines 565ff.; Kölbing Zs. f. vgl. Littgsch. XI 442ff.; Lang Myth II 190f.; Holmberg Die Wassergottheiten 181ff.; *Hdwb. d. Abergl. III 1307; Andrews Les Fontaines des Génies (Alger, 1903); Wells 66 (Ywain and Gawain); Gaster Thespis 181; Irish myth: *Cross; Chinese: Werner 205.

D1541.4. Magic fountain causes storm (rain). D1782. Sympathetic magic.

D2143.1.2. *Rain produced by singing.* (Cf. D1275, D1781.) Africa (Gold Coast): Barker and Sinclair 64 No. 9.

D2143.1.3. *Rain produced by prayer.* (Cf. D1391.1, D2141.0.7.1.) Irish myth:

Cross; Greek: Frazer Apollodorus II 55 n. 2; Buddhist myth: Malalasekera II 412.

D1766.1. Magic results produced by prayer. V52. Miraculous power of prayer.

D2143.1.4. *Rain produced by spitting blood toward sky.* Chinese: Werner 264.

D1776. Magic results from spitting.

D2143.1.5. *Rain produced by plowing.* Penzer II 117f.

D2143.1.6. *Shower from magic anvil.* (Cf. D1469.3.) Irish myth: *Cross.

D1202. Magic anvil.

D2143.1.7. *Rain produced by striking rock.* Irish myth: Cross.

D2143.1.8. *Rainstorm produced by emptying contents of bag in road.* U.S.: Baughman.

D2143.1.9. *Witch draws rain or snow from clouds with wave of his hand.* Scotland: Baughman.

D2143.1.10. *Wizard sells charm to raise rainstorm to enable eloping couple to escape pursuers.* U.S.: Baughman.

R225. Elopement.

D2143.1.11. *Certain man must laugh in order for it to rain.* (Cf. D1773.) India: Thompson-Balys.

D2143.1.12. *Arrival of saint brings rain to rainless land.* India: Thompson-Balys.

D2143.1.13. *White elephant can make rain fall.* Buddhist myth: Malalasekera II 945.

D2143.2. *Drought produced by magic.* (Cf. D2081, D2157.) Irish myth: Cross; India: Thompson-Balys; Africa (Basuto): Jacottet 15 No. 22.

D1841.4. Man proof against wet from rain.

D2143.2.1. *Church spared in flood because of prayers.* Alphabet No. 77; Spanish Exempla: Keller.

D2143.2.2. *Magic spear stuck in earth dries up spring.* India: Thompson-Balys.

D2143.3. *Fog produced by magic.* Finnish: Kalevala rune 42; Icelandic: *Boberg; Eskimo (Greenland): Rink 451, Rasmussen I 109.

D1361.1. Magic mist of invisibility. F278.2. Fairies create concealing mist. K1886.2. Mists which lead astray. V229.8. Saints create magic concealing mist.

D2143.3.1. *Heavy fog is at once dispelled by a saint.* *Loomis White Magic 106.

D2143.4. *Hail produced by magic.* U.S.: Baughman; Africa (Basuto): Jacottet 20 No. 2, (Cameroon): Ittman 71.

D2143.4.1. *Hail produced by whistling tune.* (Cf. D1275.1, D1782.) Africa (Kaffir): Theal 185.

D2143.5. *Frost produced by magic.* U.S.: Baughman.

D2143.5.1. *Old woman has control over frost.* Fb "frost".

D2143.6. *Magic control of snow.* (Cf. F686.) Irish myth: *Cross.

D2143.6.1. *Snow taken away by planting certain root.* Swiss: Jegerlehner Oberwallis 308 No. 4.

D2143.6.2. *Wall of snow around hut in answer to prayer.* (Cf. D1766.1.) Estonian: Aarne FFC XXV 136 No. 97.

D2121.7.2. Magic journey in whirl of snow.

D2143.6.3. *Snow produced by magic.* Irish myth: Cross.

D2143.6.4. *Snow magically caused to melt (burn).* Irish myth: *Cross.

V238.2 Angels melt snow around saintly babe.

D2143.6.5. *Snow magically caused to last.* Irish myth: *Cross.

D2144. *Magic control of cold and heat.* (Cf. D1592.) Irish myth: Cross; Eskimo (Greenland): Rasmussen I 235.

D2151.0.1. Saint regulates temperature of waters.

D2144.1. *Cold produced by magic.* Icelandic: Boberg; Finnish: Kalevala rune 30.

D2144.1.1. *Porcupine as controller of cold.* (Cf. K896.1.) N. A. Indian: *Thompson Tales 302 nn. 106—7.

D2144.1.2. *Man with power to make everything freeze.* Wears cap over ear. Should he wear it straight everything would freeze. *Type 513; BP II 79ff.

D2144.2. *Contest of heat and cold.* Magicians contest with each other in producing heat or cold that will overcome the other. Bolte Zs. f. Vksk. IX 85; cf. Type 71. — Livonian: Loorits FFC LXVI 81 No. 14; N. A. Indian: *Thompson Tales 288 n. 61a.

A255. Star deity and drought demon fight. F685. Marvelous withstander of cold. H1512. Cold test. Attempt to freeze hero to death. H1541. Contest in enduring cold.

D2144.3. *Heat produced by magic.* (Cf. D2091.10, D2143.6.4.) Irish myth: *Cross.

F686. Body with marvelous heat.

D2144.3.1. *Cold water in winter made warm by a saint.* *Loomis White Magic 78.

D2144.4. *Burning by magic.* (Cf. D2158.)

D1382. Magic object protects against cold or burning. D1408.1. Magic sphere burns up country. D1787. Magic results from burning.

D2144.4.1. *Person burned through magic wishing (curse).* India: Thompson-Balys.

D2144.5. *Ice controlled by magic.*

D2144.5.1. *Ice produced by magic.* Eskimo (Greenland): Rink 164.

D2144.5.2. *Ice melted by magic.* Koryak: Jochelson JE VI 170: Eskimo (Greenland): Rink 164, Rasmussen II 223, (Cumberland Sound): Boas BAM XV 191f., (West Hudson Bay): Boas BAM XV 324, (Central Eskimo): Boas RBAE VI 619.

D2145. *Magic control of seasons.*

A1150. Determination of seasons. A1151. Theft of the seasons. A1153. Seasons produced by marriage of North and South.

D2145.1. *Winter magically produced.*

A1040. Continuous winter destroys the race.

D2145.1.1. *Local winter.* Winter produced in one place while it is summer everywhere else. N. A. Indian: *Thompson Tales 289 n. 61c.

D2145.2. *Summer produced by magic.*

D2145.2.1. *Summer magically lengthened.* (Cf. F162.1.1, F971.5.) Irish: Plummer lxxx, Cross.

D2145.2.2. *Fruit magically grows in winter.* Wells 161 (Sir Cleges); Irish myth: Cross.

D1664. Summer and winter garden. F971.5.1. Fruit produced out of season at saint's request. H1023.3. Task: bringing berries (fruit, roses) in winter.

D2145.2.2.1. *Vineyard in full fruit and blooming palm found in winter on the night of Christ's Nativity.* (Cf. V211.1.) Irish myth: Cross.

D2145.2.2.2. *Tree blooms out of season.* India: Thompson-Balys.

D2146. *Magic control of day and night.* (Cf. A725, D1546.)

A1170. Origin of day and night. D1546.2. Magic spell controls sun. J2272.1. Chanticleer believes that his crowing makes the sun rise.

D2146.1. *Day controlled by magic.*

D2146.1.1. *Day magically lengthened.* *Loomis White Magic 29; Saintyves Saints Successeurs 237; Irish: Plummer cxxxviii, *Cross; Hebrew: Joshua 10: 13, *Neuman; Chinese: Eberhard FFC CXX 237; N. A. Indian (Lillooet): Teit JAFL XXV 351.

D1546. Magic object controls heavenly bodies. D1546.2. Magic spell controls sun. D2146.2.5. Saint banishes night for a year. V222.0.1.3. Dazzling heavenly light by day and night marks place of saint's birth. F961.1.5. Sun shines at night.

D2146.1.1.1. *Druid causes sun to stand still for two days.* (Cf. D1719.1.1.) Irish myth: Cross.

D2146.1.1.2. *Supernatural person (adulterer) causes sun to stand still for nine months.* (Cf. T481.) Irish myth: *Cross.

D2146.1.2. *Day magically shortened.* Greek: Fox 164.

D2146.1.3. *Day produced by magic.* Irish myth: *Cross.

F961.1.5. Sun shines at night. H1023.16. Task: making sun and moon shine in the north. K1889.5. Illusory night.

D2146.2. *Night controlled by magic.*

D2146.2.1. *Night produced by magic.* (Cf. F965.2.) Irish myth: *Cross; Breton: Sébillot Incidents s.v. "nuit"; Philippine (Tinguian): Cole 59; Eskimo (Greenland): Rasmussen III 158.

F965.1. Darkness comes in daytime in order to save life of maiden about to be executed.

D2146.2.2. *Night magically lengthened.* Greek: *Frazer Apollodorus I 174 n. 1; Irish myth: Cross; Breton: Sébillot Incidents s.v. "nuit"; N. A. Indian (Crow): Simms FM II 299 No. 16.

D2146.2.3. *Night magically shortened.* Irish myth: Cross; Philippine (Tinguian): Cole 150; Marquesas: Handy 109; N. A. Indian (Yana): Curtin Creation Myths 436.

D2146.2.4. *Earth darkened because of Sun's defeat in race against Coyote.* N. A. Indian (Calif.): Gayton and Newman 83.

D2146.2.5. *Saint banishes night for a year.* Irish myth: *Cross.

A725.1. Sun does not set for a year through power of saint. D1713. Magic power of hermit (saint). D2146.1.1. Day magically lengthened. F961.1.5.1. Sun shines for twelve days and nights after death of holy person.

D2147. *Magic control of clouds.* Jewish: Neuman.

D2147.1. *Cloud magically made to cover sun.* Alphabet No. 627.

D2147.2. *Cloud magically appears.* India: Thompson-Balys; Tuamotu: Stimson MS (z-G. 13/499).

D2147.3. *A cloud evoked by a saint.* *Loomis White Magic 41.

D2148. *Earth magically caused to quake.* Irish myth: *Cross.
Q552.2.0.1. Quaking of earth as punishment. V211.2.3.1. Earth trembles at Crucifixion.

D2148.1. *Angel causes earth to quake, releasing prisoners for saint.* Irish myth: Cross.
D1557.1. Door (lock) magically opens for saint. V230. Angels.

D2148.2. *Saint is able to produce earthquakes at will.* *Loomis White Magic 45.

D2148.3. *Stopping the eruption of a volcano by a saint.* *Loomis White Magic 45.

D2149. *Magic control of the elements—miscellaneous.* Irish myth: Cross.

D2149.1. *Thunderbolt magically produced.* (Cf. D1713.) Irish myth: Cross; Marquesas: Handy 65.

D2149.1.1. *Witch produces lightning.* U.S.: Baughman.

D2149.2. *Saint magically causes mountain to melt away.* (Cf. D1713.) Irish myth: Cross.

D2149.3. *Saint causes sun to come down and cook for him.* India: Thompson-Balys.

D2149.4. *Magic control of gravitation.*

D2149.4.1. *Saint prevents rocks from falling.* India: Thompson-Balys.

D2149.4.2. *Ring that has dropped into water rises to surface.* India: Thompson-Balys.

D2149.5. *Rice paddies flooded or dried by toad's tears or laughter.* Chinese: Graham.

D2149.6. *Magic control of heavenly bodies.* (Cf. D2146.1.) Jewish: *Neuman.

D2149.7. *Magic control of rainbow.* Jewish: *Neuman.

D2150. Miscellaneous magic manifestations.

D2151. *Magic control of waters.* (Cf. D1242.1.) Irish myth: *Cross; Jewish: Neuman.
A167.2. Cupbearer of the gods controls waters. A1111. Impounded water. D1524. Magic object enables person to cross water. D1551. Waters magically divide and close. D1841.4. Man proof against wet. D2125. Magic power to walk on water. D2165.2. Escape from drowning by drying up all waters. F930. Extraordinary occurrences concerning seas or waters. F933.1. Miraculous spring bursts forth for holy person.

D2151.0.1. *Saint regulates temperature of waters.* Irish myth: *Cross.
D1713. Magic power of hermit (saint). F716.3. Fountain hot or cold as desired. V220. Saints.

D2151.0.2. *Waters made to dry up.* Jewish: Neuman; India: Thompson-Balys.

D2151.0.3. *Wall of water magically warded off.* (Cf. D1549.3.1.) Hawaii: Beckwith Myth 466.

D2151.1. *Magic control of seas.* (Cf. D911.) Irish: Plummer cxlvii, *Cross; Jewish: Neuman; India: Thompson-Balys; Eskimo (Greenland): Rink 230, 453.

F931. Extraordinary occurrence connected with sea.

D2151.1.1. *Sea produced by magic.* Greek: Frazer Apollodorus II 78 n. 1.

A920. Origin of the seas.

D2151.1.2. *Tide held back.* (Cf. D1545.) Tuamotu: Stimson MS (T-G. 3/730).

D2151.1.2.1. *Tide held back by Virgin Mary.* (Cf. V250.) *Ward Catalogue of Romances II 602; Crane Miraculis 91 No. 22.

D2151.1.2.2. *Tide held back by saint.* (Cf. D1713, V220.) *Loomis White Magic 40; Irish myth: *Cross.

D2151.1.2.3. *Grave on shore rises with the tide.* (Cf. D1641.8.) Irish myth: Cross.

D2151.1.3. *Sea calmed by prayer.* (Cf. D1766.1, D2151.3.) Irish myth: Cross; Tuamotu: Stimson MS (T-G 3/109).

D2151.1.4. *Sea appears like flowery plain.* (Cf. F931.3.1.) Irish myth: *Cross.

D2151.2. *Magic control of rivers.* *Loomis White Magic 40f.; Irish: Plummer cxlvii—cxlviii, *Cross; Icelandic: *Boberg; Jewish: Neuman; Persian: Carnoy 339.

A930. Origin of streams. D915. Magic river. D1549.3. Magic object controls river. D2091.7.1. River magically caused to rise against enemy. F932. Extraordinary occurrences connected with rivers.

D2151.2.1. *Direction of river's flow magically reversed.* *Loomis White Magic 40; Irish myth: Cross; Korean: Zong in-Sob 70.

D2151.2.1.1. *River with flow magically divided.* (Part stands still, rest flows.) Africa (Wakweli): Bender 87.

D2151.2.2. *Saint causes river to rise and overflow.* *Loomis White Magic 95; Irish myth: *Cross.

F932.8. River rises and overflows. V220. Saints.

D2151.2.3. *Rivers magically made dry.* (Cf. D2165.2.) Irish myth: *Cross.

D2091.8.1. Druids dry up water in enemy camp.

D2151.2.3.1. *Evil spirit holds back water.* India: Thompson-Balys.

A1111. Impounded water.

D2151.2.4. *Saint causes a river to freeze over in summer.* *Loomis White Magic 41.

D2151.2.5. *Stream magically appears.* N. A. Indian (Klikitat): Jacobs U Wash II 31.

D2151.2.5.1. *River appears at prayer of desert travelers.* U.S.: Baughman.

D2151.2.6. *River magically widened.* S. A. Indian (Chiriguano): Métraux BBAE CXLIII (3) 484.

D2151.3. *Magic control of waves.* (Cf. D911.1, D2151.1.3.) Irish myth: Cross.

D2151.3.1. *Magic tidal wave.* Marquesas: Handy 65; Tuamotu: Stimson MS (T-G 3/109); Eskimo (Greenland): Rasmussen III 300, (Bering Strait): Nelson RBAE XVIII 516; Africa (Ekoi): Talbot 386.

D2151.3.2. *Dashing waves do not touch saint.* (Cf. D1388.) Irish myth: *Cross; India: Thompson-Balys; Buddhist myth: Malalasekera I 875.

F930.1.0.1. Dashing sea does not touch saint's cowl.

D2151.4. *Magic calming of whirlpool.* Irish: Plummer xxxi, *Cross; Buddhist myth: Malalasekera II 841.

D2151.5. *Magic control of pond (tank).*

D2151.5.1. *Water raised from tank by singing.* (Cf. D1781.) India: Thompson-Balys.

D2151.5.1.1. *Water raised from tank by burying ring in it.* India: Thompson-Balys.

D2151.5.2. *Pond magically dried up.* Tuamotu: Stimson MS (z-G. 13/499).

D2151.6. *Magic control of wells (springs).* (Cf. A941.5, D927, D1567, F933.) Irish myth: Cross.

D2151.6.1. *Saint causes wells to fail.* Irish myth: Cross; Tuamotu: Stimson MS (T-G 3/403); N. A. Indian (Klikitat): Jacobs U Wash II 31.

D2151.6.2. *Man makes all waters of spring flow into a small brass pot.* India: Thompson-Balys.

D2151.7. *Magic control of lakes.* (Cf. D921.) Irish myth: *Cross.

D2151.7.1. *Saint causes lake to dry up.* Irish myth: *Cross.

D2151.8. *Magic flood.* (Cf. D1542.3, D1549.3.1.) Mangaia (Cook Islands): Beckwith Myth 103; Samoa: Clark 74; Marquesas: Handy 109.

A1010. Deluge.

D2152. *Magic control of mountains.* (Cf. D932.) Irish myth: Cross.

D2152.1. *Magic leveling of mountain.* Welsh: MacCulloch Celtic 190; Irish myth: *Cross; Chinese: Eberhard FFC CXX 236; Africa (Bakuba): Einstein 160.

A960. Creation of mountains. D932. Magic mountain. D1549.4. Saint's bachall brings down mountain on heads of enemies. F626.1. Strong man pulls down mountain.

D2152.2. *Magician able to cast mountains upon enemies.* (Cf. D1711.) Irish myth: Cross.

D2152.3. *Mountain magically blown away.* Irish myth: Cross.

D2152.4. *Magic heightening of mountain.* Irish myth: Cross; N. A. Indian (Klikitat): Jacobs U Wash II 31.

D2152.5. *Mountain moved by saint.* *Loomis White Magic 92.

D2153. *Magic control of rocks.*

D2153.1. *Rock in sea created by magic.* Finnish: Kalevala rune 43; India: Thompson-Balys.

A970. Origin of rocks and stones.

D2153.1.1. *Island created by magic.* Eskimo (Ungava): Turner RBAE XI 264.

D2156. *Magic control over animals.* (Cf. D2070.) Irish myth: *Cross.

B771.2. Animal tamed by holiness of saint. D1440. Magic object gives power over animals. D2182. Flow of cow's milk increased by licking saint's garments.

D2156.1. *Magic power to make does give milk.* (Cf. B188.) Irish myth: Cross.

D2156.2. *Miraculous increasing of milk from one cow.* (Cf. D1440.1, D2106.) *Loomis White Magic 86.

D1652.3. Cow with inexhaustible milk.

D2156.2.1. *Cow supplies sufficient milk for the saint and all his disciples.* *Loomis White Magic 62.

D2156.3. *Saint forces a beast (leopard, wolf) to bring back stolen child (domestic animal) to his mother (owner).* *Loomis White Magic 50f.

D2156.4. *Wild boar reprimanded about its maraudings by saint.* The command is obeyed. *Loomis White Magic 62.

D2156.5. *Vicious snakes easily controlled by saint.* *Loomis White Magic 63f.; *Krappe Traditio V (1947) 323—330.

D2156.5.1. *Saint orders a serpent which had bitten a man to withdraw its venom.* *Loomis White Magic 63.

D2156.5.2. *Snakes expelled from human body by saint's intervention.* *Loomis White Magic 64.

D2156.6. *Saint destroys disastrous insects.* *Loomis White Magic 66.

D2156.7. *Saint orders the cicadas to sing the praises of God or be silent, because they disturb his preaching.* *Loomis White Magic 66.

D2156.8. *Wolf is forced by saint to be substitute for eaten calf.* *Loomis White Magic 59.

D2156.9. *Saint causes cuckoo to call in winter.* *Loomis White Magic 43; Irish myth: Cross.

D2156.10. *Horses (oxen) from sea put temporarily into man's service.* *Loomis White Magic 64.

D2156.11. *Saint kills lion with his slipper.* India: Thompson-Balys.

D2157. *Magic control of soil and crops.*

D965. Magic plants (grain). D1487.3. Magic spell makes tree grow. D1563. Magic object controls condition of soil. D1652.1.10. Inexhaustible wheat. F815. Extraordinary plants. F970. Extraordinary behavior of trees and plants. S274. Sacrifice as an agricultural rite. V211.1.8.3. Christ as infant in mother's arms causes bare hillside to become field of wheat as protection.

D2157.1. *Land made magically fertile.* (Cf. D1563, D2081, F349.4, F733.) Dickson 122 nn. 69, 70; *Hdwb. d. Abergl. III 145; Loomis White Magic 82; Irish myth: *Cross; Spanish: Boggs FFC XC 85 No. 750B; India: Thompson-Balys.

D2157.1.1. *Saint scratches surface of earth with his spear and treasures of gold and silver are revealed.* India: Thompson-Balys.

D2157.2. *Magic quick growth of crops.* Dh II 61ff.; Irish: Cross, O'Suilleabhain 15, 18, Beal XXI 305f.; Icelandic: *Boberg; England, Scotland: Baughman; Lithuanian: Balys Legends Nos. 200ff.; India: Thompson-Balys; Hawaii: Beckwith Myth 120.

F815.1. Vegetables (plants) which mature in miraculously short time.

D2157.2.0.1. *Rice grows in single day.* India: Thompson-Balys.

D2157.2.1. *Magic quick growth of saint's crops.* Irish myth: *Cross.

D2157.2.2. *Saint causes wheat to ripen prematurely in the time of a famine.* *Loomis White Magic 95.

D2157.3. *Withered and dead trees suddenly blossom at saint's command.* *Loomis White Magic 94.

D2157.3.1. *Apple trees bear as result of saint's blessing.* (Cf. D950, D981.1, F971.4.) Irish myth: *Cross.

D2157.3.2. *Tree regains life and verdure after treasure it hides in its roots is given away.* India: Thompson-Balys.

D2157.4. *Miraculous speedy growth of a tree.* *Loomis White Magic 95.

D2157.5. *Poor soil transformed into lovely garden overnight.* India: Thompson-Balys.

D2157.6. *Field cultivated and sowed by magic.* India: Thompson-Balys.

D2158. *Magic control of fires.* (Cf. D1271.) Irish myth: *Cross; Icelandic: *Boberg; Jewish: Neuman.

D1566. Magic object controls fire. D1656. Incombustible objects. D1841.3. Burning magically evaded. F171.6.5. Man in otherworld kindles fire. It burns out repeatedly while he is gathering more wood. F222.1.1. Fairies' underground palace cannot be burned by fire. Q552.18.1.1. Cowl demanded as ransom from saint bursts into flame.

D2158.1. *Magic kindling of fire.* (Cf. D1566.1.) Spanish Exempla: Keller.

Q492. Woman must relight magic fires as punishment.

D2158.1.1. *Fox produces fire by striking tail to ground.* Chinese: Werner 370.

D2158.1.2. *Saint sets fire to stone.* Irish myth: Cross.

D2158.1.3. *Fire obeys the saints.* *Loomis White Magic 30f.

D2158.1.3.1. *Control of conflagrations by a saint personally or by his relics.* *Loomis White Magic 30.

D2158.1.3.2. *Fire turns aside and refuses to catch hold of holy garments, wooden altars and similar sacred things.* *Loomis White Magic 31.

D2158.1.4. *Magician opens his eyes and forest burns for twenty-four miles in front of him.* India: Thompson-Balys.

D1408.1. Magic sphere burns up country.

D2158.1.5. *Saint creates fire unnaturally when needed.* *Loomis White Magic 35.

D2158.1.5.1. *Saint kindles her lamp or candle without using fire.* *Loomis White Magic 32.

D2158.1.5.2. *Cooking and baking done without fire.* *Loomis White Magic 35.

D2158.2. *Magic extinguishing of fires.* (Cf. D1656, Q492.) Köhler-Bolte I 417; *Oertel Studien zur vgl. Littgsch. VIII 113; Irish: Plummer cxxxviii, *Cross; Icelandic: *Boberg; Buddhist myth: Malalasekera II 816; Hawaii: Beckwith Myth 176.

D1391.1. Miraculous rain extinguishes fire used at stake.

D2161. *Magic healing power.* *Type 712; *Kittredge Witchcraft 30, 385 n. 64; *Fb "sygdom" III 699b; *Weinrich Antike Heilungswunder (Giessen, 1909); Wesselski Mönchslatein 136 No. 116; Irish myth: Cross; Jewish: Neuman; India: Thompson-Balys; Hawaii: Beckwith Myth 118; Eskimo (Cumberland Sound): Boas BAM XV 170, 193, 240, 248, (Mackenzie Area): Jenness 43, 82, (Greenland): Rink 279, 327, 370, 431, 440, 459, 467, Rasmussen III 172, 190, 209.

A454. God of healing. A1438. Origin of medicine (healing). B510. Healing by animal. D1342. Magic object gives health. D1500. Magic object controls disease. D1766.1.4. Pain stopped by prayer. E780. Vital bodily members. F344. Fairies heal mortals. F950. Marvelous cures. J1115.2. Clever physician. P424. Physician. V221. Miraculous healing by saints.

D2161.1. *Magic cure for specific diseases.* (Cf. D2161.5.2.5, D2161.5.2.6.)

D2161.1.1. *Magic cure of leprosy.* (Cf. D1502.4.) Irish: Plummer lxxx, *Cross.

A941.5.3. Spring breaks forth through power of saint at place where leper pulls out clump of rushes. F955. Miraculous cure. V221.3. Saint cures leprosy.

D2161.1.2. *Magic cure for fever.* (Cf. D1502.3.) *Kittredge Witchcraft 31, 385 n. 65; Irish myth: *Cross.

D2161.1.3. *Woman's labor pains magically eased.* Buddhist myth: Malalasekera I 23.

D2161.2. *Magic cure of wound.* (Cf. D1503.) Finnish: Kalevala rune 9; English: Wells 80 (Sir Tristrem); Irish myth: *Cross; Jewish: Neuman; India: Thompson-Balys; Buddhist myth: Malalasekera II 1224; Eskimo (Greenland): Rink 113, 440.

F959.3. Miraculous cure of wound.

D2161.2.1. *Steaks cut from live cow who heals herself by magic.* Swiss: Jegerlehner Oberwallis 294 No. 7.

E32. Resuscitated eaten animal.

D2161.2.2. *Flow of blood magically stopped.* (Cf. D1504.) Finnish: Kalevala rune 8.

D2161.2.3. *Magic cure of burns.* Irish myth: *Cross.

D2161.3. *Magic cure of physical defect.*

D1507. Magic object restores speech. D2025. Magic recovery of speech.

D2161.3.1. *Blindness magically cured.* (Cf. D1505.) Fb "blind" IV 45b; Irish myth: *Cross; Spanish Exempla: Keller; Italian Novella: Rotunda; Jewish: Neuman; India: Thompson-Balys; Buddhist myth: Malalasekera II 1153, 1234.

E781. Eyes successfully replaced. F952. Blindness miraculously cured. V221.12. Saint cures blindness.

D2161.3.1.1. *Eyes torn out magically replaced.* Irish: Thompson-Balys.

D2161.3.2. *Magic restoration of severed hand.* Krappe Zeitschrift für Englische Philologie XLIX 361—369; Irish myth: *Cross; Icelandic:

Lagerholm 66—68, Boberg; Spanish Exempla: Keller; French Canadian: Sister Marie Ursule, Nouvelles de Sens No. 12; India: Thompson-Balys.

A128.4. God with one hand. E782.1. Hands restored.

D2161.3.3. *Magic cure of broken limbs.* Irish myth: *Cross; India: Thompson-Balys; Eskimo (Mackenzie Area): Jenness 43.

D2161.3.3.1. *Witch burns her child's legs for wood, then covers child with sheet and child is whole.* India: Thompson-Balys.

D2161.3.4. *Baldness magically cured.*

D2161.3.4.1. *Feathered skin magically grafted to bald head.* Irish myth: Cross.

E785.1.1. Ewe's hide grafted to skinless head of wounded man.

D2161.3.5. *Deafness magically cured.* Irish myth: *Cross.

D2161.3.6. *Dumbness magically cured.* (Cf. D2020.) Irish myth: *Cross; Jewish: Neuman.

D1507. Magic object restores speech. F954. Dumb person brought to speak. V221.11. Saint cures dumb person.

D2161.3.6.1. *Magic restoration of cut-out tongue.* Irish myth: Cross.

S163. Mutilation: cutting out tongue.

D2161.3.7. *Lameness magically cured.* Irish myth: Cross.

D2161.3.7.1. *Lame animal magically cured.* Irish myth: *Cross.

D2161.3.8. *Insanity magically cured.* (Cf. D2065.) Irish myth: *Cross; Jewish: Neuman.

D1367. Magic object causes insanity. F362.2. Fairies cause insanity. F959.1. Madness miraculously cured. P192. Madmen. V221.4. Saint subdues (cures) madman.

D2161.3.8.1. *Remedy for epilepsy.* Irish myth: *Cross.

D2161.3.9. *Bad breath magically cured.* Irish myth: Cross.

D2161.3.10. *Sterility magically cured.* Jewish: Neuman.

D2161.3.11. *Barrenness magically cured.* (Cf. D1347.2, D1501.1, D1925.1.) Jewish: Neuman.

S271. Barrenness removed by sacrifice of child. T591. Barrenness induced by magic.

D2161.4. *Methods of magic cure.*

D2161.4.0.1. *Cure after following instructions received from saint in dream.* India: Thompson-Balys.

D2161.4.1. *Cure by transferring disease to animal.* (Cf. D1500.3.) *Kittredge Witchcraft 94, 424f. nn. 137—145; England, U.S.: *Baughman; Irish myth: *Cross.

D1782. Sympathetic magic. D2064.3. Sickness transferred to animal. E595. Cures by transferring disease to dead.

D2161.4.2. *Disease transferred to object.*

D2161.4.2.1. *Ghost transfers boil to a post.* Africa (Ekoi): Talbot 7.

D2161.4.2.2. *Saint transfers disease to his bell (bachall).* (Cf. D1500.3.2, D2161.5.1.) Irish myth: *Cross.

D2161.4.2.3. *Saint transfers thorn in foot to rock.* Irish myth: Cross.

D2161.4.2.4. *Disease transferred to tree.* India: Thompson-Balys.

D2161.4.3. *Cure by passing through earth at crossroads.* Kittredge Witchcraft 31, 386 n. 66.

D1786. Magic power at crossroads. D1795. Magic by creeping (running, pulling) through a hole.

D2161.4.4. *Person cured by repairing image that has same deformity.* *Kittredge Witchcraft 74, 414 n. 13.

D1782. Sympathetic magic.

D2161.4.5. *Cure by passing patient through cleft of tree (other loop).* (Cf. F950.3.) *Kittredge Witchcraft 148, 467 n. 92; *Oertel Studien zur vgl. Littgsch. VIII 115; Hdwb. d. Abergl. II 477 s.v. "durchkriechen"; A. F. Schmidt Hultræer i Danmark (Danske Studier 1932, 33ff.); Kr. Nyrop Kludetræet (Dania I (1890), 1ff. and 309); Irish myth: Cross; England, U.S.: *Baughman.

D1795. Magic by creeping (running, pulling) through a hole.

D2161.4.6. *Animal buried alive to cure disease.* Kittredge Witchcraft 95ff., 424f. nn. 146—154; *Fb "levende" II 403b—404; Feilberg Levende begravet (Aarbog for dansk kulturhistorie 1892).

D2161.4.7. *Animal burned to cure disease.* Especially for disease among animals. Kittredge Witchcraft 95ff., 426f. nn. 155—169.

D2161.4.8. *Cure by burning grain where man has died.* (Cf. D1787.) Or where he is buried. Kittredge Witchcraft 31, 386 n. 68.

D2161.4.9. *Baptism as magic cure.* (Cf. V81.) Kittredge Witchcraft 145, 464 n. 61; England: Baughman.

D2161.4.9.1. *Other religious ceremony as magic cure.* Sign of cross, prayer, etc. Irish myth: *Cross; Jewish: Neuman.

D1766.1. Magic results produced by prayer. V52. Miraculous power of prayer. V86. Sign of the cross.

D2161.4.10. *Disease cured by same thing (person) that caused it.* **Wesselski Erlesenes 13ff.

D791.2. Disenchantment by only one person. D827. Magic object received through particular intermediaries. Only one person can help secure it. M431.5. Curse: wound not to heal. Z300. Unique exceptions.

D2161.4.10.0.1. *Only one person possesses power to heal certain wound.* Irish myth: *Cross.

D2161.4.10.1. *Wound healed by same spear that caused it.* Greek: Fox 125.

D2161.4.10.2. *Wound healed only by person who gave it.* (Or by member of his family.) (Cf. D2161.2.) *Schoepperle Tristan and Isolt 375ff.; Irish myth: *Cross; Icelandic: *Boberg.

D2161.4.10.2.1. *Fairy wounded by mortal is healed only by obtaining mortal's blessing.* (Cf. D659.5.) Irish myth: *Cross.

F254. Mortal characteristics of fairies.

D2161.4.10.2.2. *Snake sucks poison from snake bite.* India: Thompson-Balys.

A2145.3. Snake created to suck poison from earth.

D2161.4.10.3. *Healing with hair of dog that bit one.* **Wesselski Erlesenes 13ff.

D2161.4.10.4. *Sorrowing father magically restored as lost son approaches.* He had lost strength, sight and hearing when son left home. Scotland: Campbell-McKay No. 25.

D2161.4.10.5. *Blindness cured by killing snake that caused it.* India: Thompson-Balys.

D2062.2.5. Magic blindness by snakebite.

D2161.4.11. *Cure by putting children on roof (in oven).* *Kittredge Witchcraft 31, 385 n. 65.

D2161.4.12. *Magic cure during sleep.* *Kittredge Witchcraft 221f., 529 n. 83—88.

D2161.4.13. *Eating of human hearts as cure for insomnia.* Chauvin VI 61 No. 229.

D2161.4.14. *Magic cure by bathing.* (Cf. D1788.) Irish myth: *Cross; India: Thompson-Balys.

D2161.4.14.1. *Magic cure by bathing in milk.* Irish myth: *Cross.

D1018. Magic milk of animal. D1788. Magic results from bathing. F872.1. Bath of milk. P427.5.1. Wounded soldiers healed by being bathed in pool of milk through power of druid.

D2161.4.14.1.1. *Wounds from poisoned arrows healed by bath of milk.* Irish myth: Cross.

D2161.4.14.2. *Magic cure by bathing in consecrated water* (lake, etc.). (Cf. D1500.1.18.5, V132.) Irish myth: *Cross.

D2161.4.14.3. *Cure by washing in dew.* U.S.: Baughman.

D2161.4.15. *Magic cure by lying on saint's shadow.* Irish myth: *Cross.

D2161.4.16. *Magic cure by touching.* India: Thompson-Balys.

D565. Transformation by touching.

D2161.4.16.1. *Magic healing by passing hand over affected parts.* India: Thompson-Balys.

D2161.4.17. *Magic cure by licking.* (Cf. D1775.) India: Thompson-Balys.

D2161.4.18. *Cure by putting lock of patient's hair in hole of post or tree, then plugging hole with wood.* U.S.: *Baughman.

D2161.4.19. *Methods of magic cure—miscellaneous.*

D2161.4.19.1. *Barber begins to recover after he reveals raja's secret.* India: Thompson-Balys.

N465. Secret physical peculiarity discovered by barber.

D2161.5. *Magic cure by certain person.*

D2161.5.1. *Cure by holy man.* *Kittredge Witchcraft 124ff., 449f. nn. 1—33 passim; *Toldo I 331; Irish myth: *Cross; Spanish Exempla: Keller; Jewish: Neuman.

D1713. Magic power of hermit (saint). F950.7. Marvelous cure: Jesus cures centurion's wife without seeing her. F954.2.2. Dumbness cured by saint's question. F959.3.4.1. Saint's palm over wound causes spearhead to come forth. V221. Miraculous healing by saints.

D2161.5.2. *Cure by Virgin Mary.* (Cf. V256.) *Ward Catalogue of Romances II 609 No. 23, 617 No. 38, 619 No. 22, 630 No. 23, 649 No. 47.

D2161.5.2.1. *Cure at shrine of Virgin Mary.* Ward II 648 No. 40 and passim; *Crane Miraculis 89 No. 17.

D2161.5.2.2. *Cure by relic of Virgin Mary.* Type 754*; Ward II 644 No. 3, 645 Nos. 6, 8.

D2161.5.2.3. *Cure by milk of Virgin Mary.* Ward II 613 No. 32; *Crane Miraculis 95 No. 30; English: Wells 167 (Vernon Miracles).

D2161.5.2.4. *Severed limbs replaced by Virgin Mary.* (Cf. D2161.3.) *Crane Miraculis 89 No. 18; Wells 167 (Vernon Miracles), 169 (The Clerk who would see the Virgin); Spanish Exempla: Keller.

D2161.5.2.5. *Cure of spider bite by the Virgin Mary.* Spanish Exempla: Keller.

D2161.5.2.6. *Terrible headaches cured by Virgin Mary.* Spanish Exempla: Keller.

D2161.5.3. *Cure by deity.* India: Thompson-Balys.

A180. Gods in relation to mortals.

D2161.5.4. *Cure by Moses.* Irish myth: Cross.

D2161.5.5. *Cure by angel.* (Cf. V232.) Irish myth: Cross; Jewish: Neuman.

D2161.5.6. *Cure by surviving twin.* England: Baughman.

D2161.5.7. *Cure by seventh son of seventh daughter.* England: Baughman.

Z71.5. Seven as formalistic number.

D2161.6. *Diseases cured at particular time.*

D2161.6.1. *All diseases healed at birth of Christ.* (Cf. V211.1.) Irish myth: Cross.

D2161.6.2. *Diseases cured in Messeanic era.* (Cf. A1095.) Jewish: Neuman.

D2161.6.3. *Diseases cured at holy man's birth.* Jewish: Neuman.

D2162. *Magic control of disease.* (Cf. D1500.) Irish myth: *Cross.

D2162.1. *Saint ends epidemic by fasting.* Irish myth: *Cross.

D1766.8. Magic results from fasting. P623. Fasting (as a means of distraint). S263.5.1. Saints sacrifice themselves (to avert plague). V73.1. Fast to prevent pestilence.

D2162.2. *Epidemic stops at river (sea) at saint's command.* (Cf. D1735.1.) Irish myth: *Cross.

D1586. Magic object relieves from plague. D1765. Magic results produced by command.

D2162.3. *Locality sanctified against pestilence (by angel) as result of prayer and fasting.* (Cf. D1586.) Irish myth: *Cross.

D1586. Magic object relieves from plague. D1766.1. Magic results produced by prayer. D1766.8. Magic results from fasting. V232. Angel as helper.

D2162.4. *People living on mountain dedicated to angel free from plague.* *Loomis White Magic 106.

D2163. *Magic defense in battle.* (Cf. K2350.) Tawney I 362, 367n., Jewish: Neuman.

D1380. Magic object protects. D2091. Magic attack against enemy. K2350. Military strategy.

D2163.1. *Broken weapons magically restored.* (Cf. D1080, F1098, H1023.8.) Irish myth: *Cross.

D2163.2. *Magic reinforcements.* Hero's followers magically multiplied or whole new army conjured up. Icelandic: Boberg; Finnish: Kalevala rune 27; Maori: Dixon 61.

A172. Gods intervene in battle. A185.1. God aids half mortal son in battle. A536. Demigods act as allies of mortals. E155.1. Slain warriors revive nightly. F349.2. Fairy aids mortal in battle. F585.2. Magic phantom army. Created out of puffballs and withered leaves.

D2163.2.1. *Heavenly help in battle.* *Loomis White Magic 122.

N848. Saint as helper. V229.7. Invaders miraculously defeated by saints.

D2163.3. *Virgin Mary intercepts an arrow in battle.* (Cf. V250.) *Ward II 625 No. 3.

D2163.4. *Magic mist as defense in battle.* (Cf. D902.1.) Irish myth: *Cross.

V229.7.1. Saint drives away an army by bringing cloud upon it.

D2163.5. *Saint's prayer wins battle.* Irish myth: *Cross.

D1766.1. Magic results produced by prayer.

D2163.5.1. *Saint's prayer brings large flight of birds carrying stones in talons.* These missiles dropped upon enemies cause terror. *Loomis White Magic 123.

D2163.5.2. *Saint changes vicious king's heart to peaceful thoughts.* *Loomis White Magic 123.

D2163.5.2.1. *Letter read by holy man stops emperor from devastating country.* India: Thompson-Balys.

D2163.6. *Obstructions magically produced before enemy.* Irish myth: *Cross.

D672. Obstacle flight.

D2163.6.1. *Saint causes great forest to spring up between opposing forces.* *Loomis White Magic 123.

D2163.6.2. *Saint causes wall of cakes to spring up between opposing armies.* India: Thompson-Balys.

D2163.7. *Enemy's army deceived by illusion produced by saint.* *Loomis White Magic 122.

D2163.8. *Saint's blessing brings victory.* *Loomis White Magic 123.

D2163.9. *Saint protects followers against bullets by stretching sheet over their heads.* India: Thompson-Balys.

D2165. *Escapes by magic.* (Cf. D1395.) English: Wells 43 (Arthour and Merlin); Irish: Plummer cxxxix, *Cross; Icelandic: Þorsteins saga Vikingssona 400, Boberg; India: Thompson-Balys.

D1391. Magic object saves person from execution. K500. Escape from death or danger by deception. R100. Rescues. R210. Escapes.

D2165.1. *Escape by flying through the air.* (Cf. D2135.0.1, R324.1.) Irish myth: Cross.

D2165.2. *Escape from drowning by drying up all waters.* (Cf. D2151.2.3.) Irish myth: Cross.

D2165.3. *Magic used to prevent pursuit.* Eskimo (Mackenzie Area): Jenness 82.

D2165.4. *Opening in house made by magic so as to escape.* Buddhist myth: Malalasekera II 101.

D2166. *Magic help from falling.* Hottentot: Bleek 78.

D2167. *Corpse magically saved from corruption.* (Cf. V52.14.) Tawney II 540; Saintyves De l'incorruption des corps saints (Bull. et. Mem. de la Soc. d'Anthrop. des Paris, 7th ser. IV [1923] 84—100). — Irish myth: *Cross; Icelandic: Boberg; Breton: Sébillot Incidents s.v. "cadavre"; Spanish Exempla: Keller; Jewish: *Neuman; Easter Island: Métraux Ethnology 311.

D1585. Magic object saves corpse from corruption. E182. Dead body incorruptible. F746. No putrefaction on extraordinary island. Hair, and nails of dead grow. F986.4. Stranded fish do not decay for a year. T84.5. Lover's body kept embalmed for years by grieving mistress.

D2167.1. *Food magically saved from corruption.* Irish myth: *Cross.

D2167.2. *Book magically saved from decay.* Irish myth: Cross.

D2167.3. *Flowers magically kept from withering.* Buddhist myth: Malalasekera II 501.

D2168. *Magic used against poison.* (Cf. D1515.) Irish myth: Cross.

D2168.1. *Poison magically separated from drink.* Irish myth: Cross.

B781. Animal "drinks apart" mixed liquids. F1092. Vessel of poisoned ale inverted: only poison flows out.

D2171. *Magic adhesion.* (Cf. D1413.) *Type 593; Fb "holde" IV 219b; Welsh: MacCulloch Celtic 102; Irish myth: *Cross; Icelandic: *Boberg; Jewish: Neuman; India: Thompson-Balys.

C994. Punishment by adhesion for breaking tabu. D2006.1. Forgotten fiancée reawakens husband's memory by detaining lovers through magic: magic adhesion to objects. F61.2.1. Ascent to sky by sticking to magic feather. H341.1. Princess brought to laughter by people sticking together. K1217. Tale of the basin. Lover caught on magic basin and left in embarrassing position.

D2171.1. *Object magically attaches itself to a person.* Irish myth: *Cross; India: Thompson-Balys; Japanese: Ikeda; Africa (Ekoi): Talbot 394, (Gold Coast): Barker and Sinclair 66 No. 9.

A1312.1. Origin of knee-caps. A stone that magically joins self to woman's body. F155. Journey to otherworld by clinging magically to an object. H251.3.8. Magic object clings to hand of guilty person. H411.4.2. Magic cup as chastity test: sticks to hand of adulterer. Q551.2.1. Magic adhesion to object as punishment for opposition to holy person.

D2171.1.1. *Seat (chair) caused to stick to person.* (Cf. D1413.6.) Icelandic: Boberg; England, U.S.: *Baughman.

D2171.1.2. *Tankard caused to stick to person's lips.* Wales: Baughman.

D2171.1.3. *Person magically sticks to floor (ground).* Irish myth: Cross (D2171.7); Jewish: *Neuman; Eskimo (Greenland): Rink 325, (Cumberland Sound): Boas BAM XV 237.

D2171.2. *Magic adhesion to monster (witch, ogre, etc.)* (Old Man of the Sea, Burr-Woman). *Basset 1001 Contes I 190f; Estonian: Aarne FFC XXV 126 No. 58; Livonian: Loorits FFC LXVI 42 No. 30; N. A. Indian: *Thompson Tales 330 n. 191e.

E262. Ghost rides on man's back. E501.15.3. Wild huntsman makes people carry him on their backs. G311. Old man of the sea. Burr-woman. Ogre who jumps on one's back and sticks there magically.

D2171.3. *Magic adhesion to animal.* (Cf. F155.) *Fb "holde" IV 219b; Irish myth: Cross.

Q551.2. Punishment: animal skin grows on man's back.

D2171.3.1. *Magic adhesion to goose.* *Type 571.

D2171.3.2. *Magic adhesion to swan.* Fb "holde ved" I 639.

D2171.3.3. *Magic adhesion to turtle.* N. A. Indian: *Thompson Tales 330 n. 191e.

D2171.3.4. *Magic adhesion to hose.* Cheremis: Sebeok-Nyerges; India: Thompson-Balys.

D2171.4. *Objects magically stick together.* (Cf. D1413.)

D2171.4.1. *Pitcher magically sticks to ground.* Africa (Basuto): Jacottet 168 No. 24.

D2171.4.2. *Cauldron magically sticks to wall.* Irish myth: Cross.

D2171.4.3. *Witch causes towel to adhere to wall.* U.S.: Baughman.

D2171.5. *Persons magically stick together.* (Cf. D1171.2, D1413.14.) India: Thompson-Balys.

H341.1. Princess brought to laughter by people sticking together.

D2171.6. *Clothes cling supernaturally to body.* *Loomis White Magic 56.

D2171.7. *Man's feet fixed to pavement so that he cannot move until he makes vow.* *Loomis White Magic 56, Irish myth: Cross.

D2171.8. *Witch causes milk to stay in overturned pail.* U.S.: Baughman.

D2172. *Continuing magic acts.*

C916. Continuous action started by breaking tabu.

D2172.1. *Magic repetition.* Person must keep on doing or saying thing until released. Type 593; Lang Eng. Fairy Tales 74; Lithuanian: Balys Historical.

D2172.2. *Magic gift: power to continue all day what one starts.* One woman measures linen; another throws water on pig. BP II 215, 438; *Hdwb. d. März. s.v. "Erste" nn. 112—149; Irish: Beal XXI 306; Lithuanian: Balys Index No. 750A[1]*.

D1470.1. Magic wishing object. D1720.1. Man given power of wishing. D1761. Magic results produced by wishing. J2073.1. Wise and foolish wish: keep doing all day what you begin. Q3. Moderate request rewarded; immoderate punished.

D2173. *Magic singing.* India: Thompson-Balys.

D1615. Magic singing object.

D2174. *Magic dancing.* Enchanted persons dance till released. Type 306; BP III 78; *Bolte Zs. f. Vksk. XIX 309 n. 1; England, Wales, U.S.: *Baughman; India: Thompson-Balys.

C94.1.1. The cursed dancers. Dancers rude to holy man cursed and must keep dancing till Judgment Day. D1415. Magic object compels person to dance. D2061.1.2. Persons magically caused to dance selves to death. F1015.1.1. The danced-out shoes.

D2175. *Cursing by magic.* Icelandic: MacCulloch Eddic 299, 268, 111; Jewish: Neuman; Irish myth: Cross.

D525. Transformation through curse. D2061.2.4. Death by cursing. M400. Curses.

D2175.1. *Cursing by means of a well.* (Cf. D926, D1766.2.1, D1792.2, V134.) Kittredge Witchcraft 34, 394 n. 113.

D2175.2. *Saint's bachall used in cursing.* Irish myth: *Cross.

D2175.3. *Magic satire (magic song) as curse.* Irish myth: Cross.

D2175.4. *Saint's bell used in cursing.* Irish myth: *Cross.

D2175.5. *Curse magically changed to blessing.* Jewish: Neuman.

D2176. *Exorcising by magic.* Irish myth: *Cross; Jewish: Neuman; India: Thompson-Balys.

D1273. Magic formula (charm). D1385. Magic object protects from evil spirits. D1746. Spirit gives man the power of exorcising him out of anyone he possesses. E440. Walking ghost "laid". E443. Ghost exorcised and laid. F321.1.3. Exorcising changeling. F382. Exorcising fairies. F405. Means of combating spirits. F471.1.2.1. Exorcising the Nightmare. G271. Witch exorcised. G271.2. Witch exorcised by holy water. G303.16.14. The devil exorcised. M400. Curses. M400.1. Satire. V10. Religious sacrifices. V70. Religious feasts and fasts.

D2176.0.1. *Saint sanctifies locality against death.* Irish myth: Cross.

D1713. Magic power of hermit (saint).

D2176.1. *Snakes banned by magic.* Irish: Plummer clxx, *Cross, O'Suilleabhain 66; Swiss: Jegerlehner Oberwallis 310 No. 33.

A531.2. Culture hero banishes snakes. A2434.2.3. Why there are no snakes in Ireland. M318. Prophecy: no snakes in Ireland. V229.3. Saint banishes snakes.

D2176.2. *Lice banned by magic.* Irish: Plummer clxx, Cross.

D2176.3. *Evil spirit exorcised.* Jewish: *Neuman.

D1385. Magic object protects from evil spirits. E728. Evil spirit possesses person. F382. Exorcising fairies. Fairies disappear when some name or ceremony of the Christian Church is used. F405.1. Priest bans spirit with sword. G303.16.14. The devil exorcised.

D2176.3.1. *Evil spirit exorcised by burning fish.* *S. Prato La Tradition III No. 2 (1889) (Tobit); Jewish: *bin Gorion Born Judas[2] II 360f.

D1787. Magic results from burning.

D2176.3.1.1. *Evil spirit exorcised by burning medicine.* India: Thompson-Balys.

D2176.3.2. *Evil spirit exorcised by religious ceremony.* (Cf. V10ff.) Holy name, sign of cross, prayer, etc. Fb "Jesus" II 41; Irish: Beal XXI 325; Italian Novella: Rotunda; *Chauvin VIII 41 No. 8AB; India: Thompson-Balys, Penzer III 37; Korean: Zong in-Sob 60, 128.

D2176.3.3. *Evil spirit exorcised by saint.* Irish myth: *Cross; India: Thompson-Balys.

D1713. Magic power of hermit (saint). G303.16. How the devil's power may be escaped. V229.5. Saint banishes demons.

D2176.3.3.0.1. *Evil spirits exorcised by death of saint.* Irish myth: Cross.

D2176.3.3.1. *Demons in stone images driven out by holy man (saint).* Irish myth: *Cross.

V356.2. Heathen idols and temples topple before the saint's presence.

D2176.3.3.2. *Saint purifies spring by driving out demon.* *Loomis White Magic 76.

D2176.3.3.3. *Saint throws ink bottle at devil who annoys him.* *Loomis White Magic 76.

D2176.3.3.4. *Saint's breath drives away the devil.* *Loomis White Magic 46.

D2176.3.4. *Devil cast out of man possessed.* Lithuanian: Balys Index No. 3368; Legends Nos. 702—710.

E728. Evil spirit cast out of person. G303.16.14. The devil exorcised.

D2176.4. *Magic book conjured away by throwing it on stream.* *Fb "Cyprianus" I 166b.

D2176.5. *Burning cut hair to prevent witchcraft.* *Fb "hår" I 771a; Spanish Exempla: Keller.

D2176.6. *Exorcising invisible man by flailing air with peach branch.* Chinese: Graham.

D2177. *Imprisoning by magic.* (Cf. R40.) Irish myth: Cross.

D2177.1. *Demon enclosed in bottle.* *Type 331; *Goebel Jüdische Motive im märchenhaften Erzählungsgut (Gleiwitz, 1932) 52ff.; Swiss: Jegerlehner Oberwallis 311 No. 39, 314 No. 105, 320 No. 34; Jewish: Neuman; Chinese: Graham; Philippine: Fansler MAFLS XII 439.

D55.2.4. Ten serving-women carried in bottle. G302. Demons. Malevolent creatures (not usually further defined). K717. Deception into bottle. R181. Demon enclosed in bottle released.

D2177.1.1. *Demons imprisoned by magic.* Nouvelles Recreations 13.

D2177.2. *Demon imprisoned in pomegranate.* Africa (Swahili): Stigand 122ff. No. 19.

D2177.3. *Evil spirits imprisoned in stone.* Irish myth: Cross.

D2177.4. *Evil spirits kept out by stone wall.* India: Thompson-Balys.

D2178. *Objects produced by magic.* Irish myth: *Cross: Missouri French: Carrière.

A900. Topography. D852. Magic object acquired by wishing. D915.1. River produced by magic. D921.1. Lake (pond) produced by magic. D925.1. Fountain magically made. D926.1. Island made by magic. D927.1. Spring made by magic. D941.1. Forest produced by magic. D961.1. Garden produced by magic. D1022.0.1. Wings grown by magic. D1030.1. Food supplied by magic. D1050.1. Clothes produced by magic. D1005.1.1. Boots produced by magic. D1071.0.1. Jewels produced by magic. D1081.1. Sword of magic origin. D1111.1. Carriage produced by magic. D1122.1. Canoe made by magic. D1130.1. Fort produced by magic. D1131.1. Castle produced by magic. D1132.1. Palace produced by magic. D1133.1. House produced by magic. D1151.1. Magic bench. D1258.1. Bridge made by magic. D1620. Magic automata. V224. Miraculous replacement of objects (animals) for saint.

D2178.1. *City built by magic.* Penzer VII 73f.; India: Thompson-Balys.

D2178.2. *Cattle produced by magic.* Africa (Kaffir): Theal 77.

D2178.3. *Pavilions produced by magic.* Penzer VIII 92.

D2178.4. *Animals created by magic.* India: Thompson-Balys; Eskimo (Mackenzie Area): Jenness 42.

A1700. Creation of animals.

D2178.4.1. *Magic production of rabbits.* N. A. Indian (Calif.): Gayton and Newman 82.

C916.2. Animals produced when forbidden drum is beaten.

D2178.4.2. *Noxious animals produced by magic.* Jewish: Neuman.

D2178.5. *People created by magic.* India: Thompson-Balys.

A1200. Creation of man.

D2178.6. *Ceremonial presents produced by magic.* Chinese: Graham.

D2178.7. *Whatever goldsmith proposes to make comes into existence by itself in the forge.* India: Thompson-Balys.

D2178.8. *Tree produced by magic.* Buddhist myth: Malalasekera II 347.

D2178.9. *Flower produced by magic.* Buddhist myth: Malalasekera II 135f.

D2182. *Flow of cow's milk increased by licking saint's garment.* (Cf. D1052, D1652.3.) Irish: Plummer clxxxi, Cross.

D1775. Magic results from licking. V220. Saints.

D2182.1. *Flow of cow's milk increased by saint.* Irish myth: *Cross.

D2182.2. *Flow of cow's milk increased by song (music).* (Cf. D1275.) Irish myth: *Cross.

D2183. *Magic spinning.* Usually performed by a supernatural helper. *Types 500, 501; *von Sydow Två spinnsagor.

F346. Fairy helps mortal with labor.

D2184. *People magically continue hurting themselves.* Try to drive ox but drive themselves; to stab it but stab themselves; etc. Africa (Basuto): Jacottet 76 No. 12.

D2184.1. *People magically made to strike selves blows aimed at another.* Irish myth: Cross.

D2185. *Magician carries woman in glass coffin.* She comes out at his will. Icelandic: *Boberg; *Chauvin V 190 No. 11.

D55.2.4. Ten serving-women carried in bottle. They change size at will. D491. Compressible objects. F852.1. Glass coffin. F1034. Magician carries mistress with him in his body. J882.2. Man with unfaithful wife comforted when he sees jealous husband who carefully guards wife cuckolded.

D2185.1. *Fairy personage (god?) houses mistress in crystal bower.* (Cf. F165.3.5.1.) Irish myth: Cross.

D2186. *Cat in wood-pile prevents axe from cutting.* *Type 1001.

D2188. *Magic disappearance.* (Cf. D1641.) Buddhist myth: Malalasekera II 484; Eskimo (Greenland): Rink 457, Rasmussen III 264, (Kodiak): Golder JAFL XVI 25, (Cumberland Sound): Boas BAM XV 257.

D2188.1. *Ability to disappear or appear at will.* India: Thompson-Balys.

D2188.1.1. *Garment appears and disappears in reply to command.* Spence 76.

D1765. Magic results produced by command.

D2188.2. *Person vanishes.* Jewish: Neuman; Philippine (Tinguian): Cole 48, 54, Tuamotu: Stimson MS (z-G. 3/1241).

D2188.2.1. *Man disappears, leaving only his ring.* India: Thompson-Balys.

D2188.3. *Village vanishes.* Chinese: Eberhard FFC CXX 157.

D2191. *Roast ducks fly (by magic).* Fb "and" IV 12b.

D2192. *Work of day magically overthrown at night.* *Fb "kirke" II 125 a; Wells 42 (Arthour and Merlin); Irish myth: *Cross; Icelandic: Boberg; Lithuanian: Balys Index No. 3602; India: Thompson-Balys; Chinese: Graham; Hawaii: Beckwith Myth 465; Ellice Island: ibid.

270; Marquesas: ibid. 269; Tuamotu: ibid. 267; Tahiti: ibid. 266; Maori: ibid. 265; Africa (Duala): Lederbogen Fables 59.

C931. Building falls because of breaking of tabu. G303.14.1.2. Devil destroys by night what is built by day. H1129.5. Task: building a fire; whole tree burns up while man is bringing another. H1104.1.2. Task: thatching roof with bird feathers; half blow away while other half are sought. Q556.5. Saint decrees offenders will not be able to fortify their dwellings. Fences fall, earth gapes when dug. S261. Foundation sacrifice. A human being buried alive at base of the foundation of a building or bridge.

D2192.1. *Supernatural agency moves new church foundation (or building materials) to another site, at night.* England, Scotland: *Baughman.

D2193. *Flowers drop on washing hands.* Italian Novella: Rotunda.

D2194. *Dung drops on washing hands.* Italian Novella: Rotunda.

D2195. *Blighted garden magically restored to beauty.* India: Thompson-Balys.

D2195.1. *Flower blooms when touched.* India: Thompson-Balys.

D1799.4. Magic powers from touching.

D2196. *Saint causes fiery sword to come between hostile king and queen.* Irish myth: Cross.

F833.4. Fiery sword.

D2197. *Magic dominance over animals.* (Cf. D1440, D2074.1.) Jewish: Neuman.

D2198. *Magic control of spirits (angels).* Jewish: *Neuman.

D2199. *Additional magic manifestations.*

D2199.1. *Bottomless tub (vat) holds water through power of saint.* (Cf. H1023.2.1.) Irish myth: *Cross.

D2199.2. *Tools sharpened through power of saint.* Slaves forced to hew down yew tree with dull tools: hands bleed. (Cf. H1110, P170.) Irish myth: Cross.

E. THE DEAD

DETAILED SYNOPSIS

E0 —E199. Resuscitation
- E0. Resuscitation
- E10. Resuscitation by rough treatment
- E30. Resuscitation by arrangement of members
- E50. Resuscitation by magic
- E80. Water of life
- E90. Tree of life
- E100. Resuscitation by medicines
- E120. Other means of resuscitation
- E150. Circumstances of resuscitation

E200—E599. GHOSTS AND OTHER REVENANTS

E200—E299. Malevolent return from the dead
- E200. Malevolent return from the dead
- E210. Dead lover's malevolent return
- E220. Dead relative's malevolent return
- E230. Return from dead to inflict punishment
- E250. Bloodthirsty revenants
- E260. Other malevolent revenants
- E280. Ghosts haunt buildings

E300—E399. Friendly return from the dead
- E300. Friendly return from the dead
- E310. Dead lover's friendly return
- E320. Dead relative's friendly return
- E340. Return from dead to repay obligations
- E360. Other reasons for friendly return from the dead
- E380. Ghost summoned
- E390. Friendly return from the dead—miscellaneous

E400—E599. Ghosts and revenants—miscellaneous
- E400. Ghosts and revenants—miscellaneous
- E410. The unquiet grave
- E420. Appearance of revenant
- E430. Defense against ghosts and the dead
- E440. Walking ghosts "laid"
- E460. Revenants in conflict
- E470. Intimate relations of dead and living
- E480. Abode of the dead
- E490. Meetings of the dead
- E500. Phantom hosts
- E510. Phantom sailors
- E520. Animal ghosts
- E530. Ghosts of objects
- E540. Miscellaneous actions of revenants

E600—E699. Reincarnation
- E600. Reincarnation
- E610. Reincarnation as animal

E630. Reincarnation in object
E650. Reincarnation: other forms
E670. Repeated reincarnation
E690. Reincarnation: miscellaneous

E700—E799. The soul
E700. The soul
E710. External soul
E720. Soul leaves or enters the body
E730. Soul in animal form
E740. Other forms of the soul
E750. Perils of the soul
E760. Life index
E770. Vital objects
E780. Vital bodily members

E. THE DEAD

E0—E199. Resuscitation.

E0. **Resuscitation.** Zwierzina Die Legenden der Märtyrer vom unzerstörbaren Leben (Innsbrucker Festgruss dargebracht der 50. Versammlung deutscher Philologen in Graz (1909) 130—158; Type 516; Clouston Tales II 407ff.; *Penzer X Index s.v. "Resuscitation"; *Jacobs' list s.v. "Resuscitation"; Greek: Grote I 206; Italian: Basile Pentamerone IV No. 9, Rotunda; Breton: Sébillot Incidents s.v. "resurrection"; Irish: Plummer xxxv, *Cross; Icelandic: *Boberg; Jewish: *Neuman; India: *Thompson-Balys; Chinese: Eberhard FFC CXX 169; Korean: Zong in-Sob 139; Polynesia: *Beckwith Myth Chapter X passim; Marquesas: Handy 83; Tuamotu: Stimson MS (z-G. 13/127); Eskimo (Greenland): Rink 291, 359, 373, 417, 444, 452, Holm 26, 89, (Cumberland Sound): Boas BAM XV 241; N. A. Indian (California): Gayton and Newman 73; S. A. Indian (Toba): Métraux MAFLS XL 102, (Tupinamba): Métraux BBAE CXLIII (3) 132, (Apapocuva-Guaraní): *Métraux RMLP XXXIII 133; Africa (Benga): Nassau 213 No. 33, (Upoto): Einstein 142, (Wuchaga): Gutman 35.

A165.12.1. God resuscitates man. A571. Culture hero asleep in mountain. A580. Culture hero's expected return. B125. Lion, bear, and wolf resuscitate master. B192.1. Magic pig burned to prevent resuscitation. B301.5. Faithful animals resuscitate master. B512. Medicine shown by animal. B515. Resuscitation by animals. D610. Repeated transformation. D719.1. Disenchantment by burying victim and sowing grain over him. D772.1. Disenchantment by recognition. D1585. Magic object saves corpse from corruption. D1850. Immortality. D1865. Beautification by death and resuscitation. D1960.1. Seven Sleepers (Rip van Winkle). Magic sleep extending over many years. D1960.2. King asleep in mountain (Barbarossa, King Marko, Holger Danske). Will awake one day to succor his people. D2167. Corpse magically saved from corruption. E463. Living man in dead man's shroud. Refuses to let corpse return to grave before he tells how to resuscitate woman living man has killed. E728.1. Evil spirit cast out of person by killing and resuscitating. E755.0.1. Resurrected boys choose to return to heaven. G513. Ogre killed and resuscitated so as to be of help to hero. J2311.3. Sham revenant. K1926. The false daughter: accepted as one's resurrected child. M364.4. Place of saint's resurrection prophesied. N694. Apparently dead woman revives as she is being prepared for burial. Q151.11. Resuscitation as revenant. V257. Virgin Mary resurrects priest in order to have him forgive his murderer. V268.1. Boy under protection of Virgin Mary pulled from well alive after a week. V311. Belief in the life to come. V363. Jewish child resurrected after being burned to ashes for eating consecrated bread in Christian church.

E1. *Person comes to life.* Alphabet No. 683; Köhler-Bolte II 164; Lithuanian: Balys Index No. 3506; Italian Novella: Rotunda; Jewish: *Neuman; India: *Thompson-Balys; Tonga: Gifford 130; Africa (Basuto): Jacottet 180 No. 25, (Zulu): Callaway 51.

E1.1. *Saint cut into pieces or decapitated comes back to life.* *Loomis White Magic 83f.

E1.2. *Dead man re-enters body and speaks of experience in heaven.* India: Thompson-Balys.

E2. *Dead tree comes to life.* Irish myth: Cross; India: *Thompson-Balys; Africa (Zulu): Callaway 47.

D1571. Magic object revivifies trees. E30.1. Felled tree restored by reassembling all cut parts. F971.1. Dry rod blossoms.

E3. *Dead animal comes to life.* (Cf. B192.1.) Irish myth: *Cross; Jewish: *Neuman; India: Thompson-Balys.

E32. Resuscitated eaten animal. E121.4. Resuscitation by saint. E168. Cooked animal comes to life. E171 Flayed animal resuscitated.

E4. *Sun revived by own power after being killed by moon.* S. A. Indian (Eastern Brazil): Lowie BBAE CXLIII (1) 434.

E10. Resuscitation by rough treatment.

D710. Disenchantment by rough treatment. D1884. Rejuvenation by dismemberment. S180. Wounding or torturing.

E11. *Resuscitation by beating.* *Penzer VI 265f.; Köhler-Bolte I 140; India: *Thompson-Balys; Indonesia (Soemba): Dixon 331 n. 108; N. A. Indian: *Thompson Tales 353 n. 273; Africa (Basuto): Jacottet 124 No. 17.

D566. Transformation by striking. D712.5. Disenchantment by beating.

E11.1. *Second blow resuscitates.* First kills. Welsh: MacCulloch Celtic 93.

C742. Tabu: striking monster twice. Though the monster begs that hero strike him again, hero refuses. Monster would otherwise revive. D1663.1. Wands of life and death. Pointed with one end, kill; with the other, resuscitate. E82. Water of life and death. One water kills, the other restores to life.

E11.2. *Resuscitation by striking with arrow.* N. A. Indian (California): Gayton and Newman 73.

E11.3. *Resuscitation by touching body during conjuration.* Eskimo (Greenland): Rink 452, Rasmussen II 349.

E12. *Resuscitation by decapitation.* *Type 531; *BP III 18ff.

D711. Disenchantment by decapitation. D1865.1. Beautification by decapitation and replacement of head. E446.3. Ghost laid by decapitating body.

E12.1. *Red thread on neck of person who has been decapitated and resuscitated.* *BP III 19; Hdwb. d. Abergl. I 866.

F662.1.1. Birds hatched from broken eggs repaired by skillful tailor have red line around necks. This indicates where eggs were broken.

E12.2. *Head of decapitated person is replaced backwards.* Later is readjusted. Italian Novella: Rotunda.

E13. *Resuscitation by jumping (stepping) over.* N. A. Indian: *Thompson Tales 350 n. 261; S. A. Indian (Chiriguano): Métraux RMLP XXXIII 177.

E13.1. *Resuscitation by stepping on corpse.* S. A. Indian (Chiriguano): Métraux RMLP XXXIII 177.

E14. *Resuscitation by dismemberment.* (Cf. E30, E32.) (Usually combined with burning; cf. E15.) *Type 753; *BP II 162; Irish: O'Suilleabhain 33, Beal XXI 311f.; Africa (Mpongwe): Nassau 76 No. 15.

S139.2. Slain person dismembered.

E15. *Resuscitation by burning.* *Type 753; *BP III 193ff.; DeCock Studien 14; Breton: Sébillot Incidents s.v. "cadavre"; Easter Island: Métraux Ethnology 68; N. A. Indian: *Thompson Tales 350 n. 260; Africa (Basuto): Jacottet 132 No. 18, 136 No. 19.

A1861.2. Creation of monkeys: old women thrown into fire. In unsuccessful imitation of Christ, the smith throwns an old woman into the fire. She becomes a monkey. D1787. Magic results from burning. E446.2. Ghost laid by burning body. S112. Burning to death.

E15.0.1. *Bone of man being burned jumps out of fire.* Africa (Pahouin): Largeau 197.

E15.1. *Resuscitation by boiling.* Greek: Frazer Apollodorus II 156 n. 2, Cook Zeus I 677ff.; Breton: Sébillot Incidents s.v. "cadavre"; N. A. Indian: *Thompson Tales 350 n. 260.

D1865.2. Beautification by boiling and resuscitation. D1885. Rejuvenation by boiling. S112.1. Boiling to death. Often in pitch or oil.

E15.2. *Resuscitation by sweating.* N. A. Indian: *Thompson Tales 340 n. 225, 350 n. 260, (Modoc): Curtin Myths of the Modocs (Boston, 1912) 31.

E15.3. *Resuscitation by stewing.* Chinese: Graham.

E16. *Resuscitation by stinging.* Corpse is laid on an ant-heap. MacCulloch Childhood 81 n. 3; Australian: Parker 13.

E17. *Resuscitation by licking corpse.* Africa (Kaffir): Theal 153.

D565.3. Transformation by licking. D1775. Magic results from licking.

E17.1. *Resuscitation when snake licks bite he has inflicted upon his victim.* India: Thompson-Balys.

E18. *Resuscitation by tickling.* N. A. Indian (Tlingit): Golder JAFL XX 292.

E21. *Resuscitation by withdrawal of wounding instrument.* Italian: Basile Pentamerone II No. 8; India: Thompson-Balys; N. A. Indian (Twana): Curtis N. A. Indian IX 164 ff., (Southern Paiute): Lowie JAFL XXXVII 185 No. 19; Eskimo (Kodiak): Golder JAFL XXI 18.

D765.1.2. Disenchantment by removal of enchanting pin (thorn). D1978.3. Waking from magic sleep by removal of enchanting instrument. N694.1. Apparently dead woman revives when dropped.

E21.1. *Resuscitation by removal of poisoned apple.* By shaking loose the apple from the throat of the poisoned girl the prince brings her to life. *Type 709; *BP I 450ff.; Hdwb. d. Märchens s.v. "Apfel" n. 8; India: Thompson-Balys.

E21.1.1. *Resuscitation by removal of poisoning cobra flesh from dead man's mouth.* India: Thompson-Balys.

E21.2. *Resuscitation when strangling corset-lace breaks.* Girl laced so tightly in corset that she faints. Brothers carry her to her grave. They stumble. Corset-lace breaks and girl revives. Spanish: Boggs FFC XC 63 No. 453; Italian Novella: Rotunda.

Q331.2.2. Vain woman wears corset so tightly that it stifles her to death.

E21.3. *Resuscitation by removal of poisoned comb.* *Type 709; Africa (Swahili): Baker FL XXXVIII 299ff.

E21.4. *Resuscitation by removal of poisoned slippers.* Africa (Tonga): Junod 266ff., (Swahili): Baker FL XXXVIII 299ff. No. 16.

S111.7. Murder with poisoned slippers.

E21.5. *Resuscitation by sucking poison from wound.* India: *Thompson-Balys.

E23. *Resuscitation by catching in snare.* Jamaica: *Beckwith MAFLS XVII 267 No. 74.

E25. *Resuscitation my frightening dead.* Frequently combined with E61. N. A. Indian: *Thompson Tales 319 n. 153. See also references to E61.

E26. *Resuscitation by shouting at dead.* Scottish: Campbell-McKay No. 1; N. A. Indian (California): Gayton and Newman 88.

E26.1. *Resuscitation by command to arise.* (Cf. E67.) Type 785; India: *Thompson-Balys.

E27. *Resuscitation by slinging against something.* Eskimo (Bering Strait): Nelson RBAE XVIII 510.

D712.2. Disenchantment by slinging against something.

E29. *Resuscitation by rough treatment—miscellaneous.*

E757. Disenchantment by holding enchanted person during successive transformations.

E29.1. *Resuscitation by biting victim's bone.* N. A. Indian (Joshua): Farrand-Frachtenberg JAFL XXVIII 240 No. 19.

E29.2. *Resuscitation by rubbing victim's bones on ground.* Madagascar (Antankarana): Renel Contes de Madagascar (Paris, 1910, 1930) I 94ff. No. 14.

E29.3. *Resuscitation by pricking anus.* N. A. Indian (California): Gayton and Newman 57, 81.

E29.4. *Resuscitation by plucking the flower into which one is incarnated.* India: Thompson-Balys.

E29.4.1. *Resuscitation by felling the tree into which one is incarnated and splitting trunk into two parts.* India: Thompson-Balys.

E29.5. *Resuscitation by cutting off heads of birds which contained the soul of dead person.* India: Thompson-Balys.

E715.1. Separable soul in bird.

E29.6. *Resuscitation by urinating on dead man's bone.* Korean: Zong in-Sob 38.

E29.7. *Resuscitation by striking with lightning.* Hawaii: Beckwith Myth 410.

E30. Resuscitation by arrangement of members. Parts of a dismembered corpse are brought together and resuscitation follows. (Sometimes combined with other methods.) *Type 720; *BP I 422f.; Köhler-Bolte I 140, 555; Gaster Thespis 300. — Finnish: Kalevala rune 15; Breton: Sébillot Incidents s.v. "os"; Italian: Basile Pentamerone I No. 2; Swiss: Jegerlehner Oberwallis 315 No. 119, 329 No. 38; Egyptian: Müller 114 (Osiris); Greek: Fox 22 (Arkas); Siberian: Holmberg Siberian 494; India: *Thompson-Balys; Marquesas: Handy 104; Tuamotu: Stimson MS (z-G. 3/1117); Eskimo (Greenland): Rink 276; N. A. Indian: *Thompson Tales 308 n. 114, (California): Gayton and Newman 71, Hatt Asiatic Influences 69f.; S. A. Indian (Yuracare): Alexander Lat. Am. 315, Métraux BBAE CXLIII (3) 503. — Africa (Fjort): Dennett 64 No. 12, (Angola): Chatelain 95 No. 5, (Bushman): Bleek and Lloyd 33, 137, (Ibo of Nigeria): Thomas 160, (Basuto): Jacottet 132 No. 18, 168 No. 24, (Thonga): Junod 242, (Zulu): Callaway 51, 230; Cape Verde Islands: Parsons MAFLS XV (1) 141.

D717. Disenchantment by laying collected bones in a seven-fold cloth and spreading another above it. D1865.1. Beautification by decapitation and replacement of head. D1884. Rejuvenation by dismemberment. E14. Resuscitation by dismemberment. E80. Water of life. E101. Resuscitation by salve (oil). E607.1. Bones of dead collected and buried. Return in another form directly from grave. V63. Bones of dismembered person assembled and buried.

E30.1. *Felled tree restored by reassembling all cut parts.* (Cf. E2.) Polynesian: Dixon *68 n. 38.

E31. *Limbs of dead voluntarily reassemble and revive.* *Köhler-Bolte I 130; Gaster Thespis 300; Jewish: Neuman; N. A. Indian (California): Gayton and Newman 92.

D1619.2. Eaten object speaks from inside person's body. G635.2. Ogre's limbs reassemble after they are cut off. H1411.1. Fear test: staying in haunted house where corpse drops piecemeal down chimney.

E32. *Resuscitated eaten animal.* (Cf. E171.) An animal is eaten. When his bones are reassembled he revives. *Von Sydow Tors Färd til Utgård (Danske Studier [1910] 65); Type 870B (FFC LXXXIII); Krohn Skandinavisk Mythologi 207ff.; BP I 422f.; Karjalainen FFC LXIII 14; Alphabet No. 370; MacCulloch Childhood 101; Clouston Tales II 395; Günter 83 nn. 94—96; *Loomis White Magic 68, 84f.; Archiv. f. slavische Philologie XIX 255. — Irish: Plummer cxliii, *Cross, O'Suilleabhain 66, Beal XXI 325; English: Child I 505b; Swiss: Jegerlehner Oberwallis 306 No. 8, 313 No. 93; Jewish: bin Gorion III 19, *Neuman; India: *Thompson-Balys; Buin: Wheeler No. 15; N. A. Indian: *Thompson Tales 308 n. 114a; Africa (Zulu): Callaway 272, (Thonga): Junod 229, (Basuto): Jacottet 124 No. 17.

D2161.2.1. Steaks cut from live cow who heals herself by magic. E3. Animal comes to life. E121.4. Resuscitation by saint. E155. Periodic resuscitation. E155.5. Eaten pigs (calf) revive nightly. E168. Cooked animal comes to life. F243.3.1. Animals eaten by fairies become whole again. H1331.2.3. Quest for pigs killed by night and revived by day. V224.2. Food (animals) eaten by saint miraculously replaced.

E32.0.1. *Eaten person resuscitated.* Irish myth: Cross; India: Thompson-Balys; Tonga: Beckwith Myth 483.

E32.1. *Insect swallowed by man comes out alive.* *Loomis White Magic 66.

E32.2. *Animals which devour each other are restored to their original forms by command of a saint.* *Loomis White Magic 63.

E32.3. *Dismembered pigs come alive again if only bones are preserved.* Irish myth: *Cross.

B192.1. Magic pig burned to prevent resuscitation.

E33. *Resuscitation with missing member.* In reassembling the members, one has been inadvertantly omitted. The resuscitated person or animal lacks this member. *Type 313; MacCulloch Childhood 97ff.; Von Sydow Danske Studier (1910) 65ff., 145ff.; Köhler-Bolte I 259, 273 n. 1, *586. — Greek: Fox 119 (Pelops); India: Thompson-Balys; Eskimo (Greenland): Rink 99, Rasmussen I 218, III 79, (Bering Strait): Nelson RBAE XVIII 501, (N. W. Canada): Petitot 84, 226, (Smith Sound): Kroeber JAFL XII 170; N. A. Indian: *Thompson Tales 308 n. 114b; S. A. Indian (Yuracare): Alexander Lat. Am. 314.

A128. Mutilated god. D702.1. Disenchantment with missing member. H57. Recognition by missing member.

E33.1. *Cooked part of white cow is brown after resuscitation.* Irish myth: Cross; England: Baughman.

B184.2.0.1. Magic white cow.

E34. *Resuscitation with misplaced head.* (Cf. M221.) In restoration of several persons simultaneously through reassembling of members, the heads are placed on the wrong bodies. Sometimes the damage is repaired, sometimes not. *Kittredge Gawain 155 n. 1; *Wesselski Märchen 239, 241 n. 2; Irish myth: *Cross; Italian Novella: Rotunda; India: *Thompson-Balys; N. A. Indian: *Thompson Tales 309 n. 114c.

E783.1. Head cut off and successfully replaced.

E34.1. *Resuscitation with head on backwards.* (Cf. F511.0.6.) *Type 303; Irish myth: *Cross; Italian Novella: Rotunda (E12.2).

E501.7.3. Wild huntsmen with heads on backward.

E35. *Resuscitation from fragments of body.* Cook Islands: Beckwith 253; S. A. Indian (Eastern Brazil): Lowie BBAE CXLIII (1) 434.

E35.1. *Resuscitation by sewing parts of body together.* India: Thompson-Balys.

E37. *Resuscitation by assembling members and leaving in cask for certain time.*

E37.1. *Failure to resuscitate because of premature disturbance of members to be left in cask for certain time.* Köhler-Bolte I 140, 585; Lithuanian: Balys Index No. 3670; India: Thompson-Balys.

E38. *Resuscitation by replacement of soul.* Crane Miraculis 84 No. 7; Irish myth: *Cross; Chinese: Werner 93, 268; Hawaii: Dixon 76, Beckwith Myth 145, 152; Maori: Dixon 78; Marquesas: Handy 113; Eskimo (Greenland): Rasmussen II 101.

E726. Soul enters body and animates it.

E38.1. *Resuscitation by returning dead person's soul (breath) to body.* India: Thompson-Balys.

E41. *Resuscitation from excrement of one who has eaten person (animal).* India: Thompson-Balys; Tonga: Gifford 140, Beckwith Myth 483, 504; S. A. Indian (Kaiguá): Métraux RMLP XXXIII 139.

E42. *Resuscitation from ashes of dead man.* India: Thompson-Balys.

E66.1. Resuscitation of cremated man by blowing on the ashes.

E42.1. *Resuscitation from dust.* India: *Thompson-Balys.

E50. Resuscitation by magic. Irish myth: Cross; Icelandic: *Boberg; India: Thompson-Balys; Hawaii: Beckwith Myth 154 and Chapter X passim; Tuamotu: Stimson MS (T-G 3/49, z-G 3/1353, z-G 13/1241); Eskimo (Bering Strait): Nelson RBAE XVIII 504, (Greenland): Rink 260, Rasmussen III 296, (Cumberland Sound): Boas BAM XV 193; Africa (Cameroon): Rosenhuber 43.

E121. Resuscitation by supernatural person. E251.2.1. Vampire brought to life through endurance of punishment by her victim.

E52. *Resuscitation by magic charm.* (Cf. D1273.) Irish myth: *Cross; India: Thompson-Balys, *Penzer VI 261ff.; Eskimo (Greenland): Rasmussen II 348, III 102.

E53. *Resuscitation by fetish.* Africa (Fjort): Dennett 64 No. 12.

D1274. Magic fetish.

E53.1. *Resuscitation by mummified dog.* Dog is kept in box. Revives and resuscitates dead hero. N. A. Indian (Central Algonquin): Skinner JAFL XXVII 98.

E53.2. *Resuscitation of dead by making image of deceased of breadfruit wood.* When spirit enters this, image disappears and person is found alive. Marquesas: Handy 113.

E55. *Resuscitation by music.* MacCulloch Childhood 84; Fb "spille" III 488a; N. A. Indian: *Thompson Tales 319 n. 153b.

D1275.1. Magic music.

E55.1. *Resuscitation by song.* Icelandic: Göngu-Hrólfs saga 337—38, Boberg; India: Thompson-Balys; Tsimshian: Boas BBAE XXVII 215; Eskimo (Greenland): Rink 452.

B172.2. Magic bird's song. Wakes the dead. D1275. Magic song. D1781. Magic results from singing.

E55.2. *Resuscitation by playing flute.* Breton: Sébillot Incidents s.v. "flute".

D1223.1. Magic flute.

E55.3. *Resuscitation by blowing trumpet.* Africa (Ekoi): Talbot 62f.

D1221. Magic trumpet.

E55.4. *Resuscitation by playing violin.* *Cosquin Lorraine II 7, 286.

D1233. Magic violin (fiddle).

E55.5. *Resuscitation by playing guitar.* Sicilian: Gonzenbach I 306 No. 45.

D1234. Magic guitar. K113.8. Alleged resuscitating guitar sold.

E58. *Resuscitation by weeping (tears).* Herbert III 62 (Odo of Cheriton); Fb "opskrig" II 754; Africa (Angola): Chatelain 43 No. 1 (Version B).

E381. Ghost summoned by weeping.

E58.1. *Resuscitation by universal weeping.* Return of deity from dead granted if all men will weep. One person refuses. *Dh II 211; Hdwb. d. Märch. I 439a s.v. "Eddamärchen" nn. 270, 271; MacCulloch Eddic 130.

E61. *Resuscitation by shooting arrow.* (Usually combined with E25.) Chinese: Graham; N. A. Indian (Ojibwa): Schoolcraft Hiawatha 58, (Missisagua): Chamberlain JAFL III 150, (Blackfoot): Wissler and Duvall PaAM II 146, (Gros Ventre): Kroeber PaAM I 99 No. 23, (Arapano): Dorsey and Kroeber FM V 269 No. 119, 344ff. Nos. 139—145.

E62. *Resuscitation by vigil at tomb.* Vigil is for stated time, three weeks and three days, or the like. Köhler in Gonzenbach II 209 No. 11; Köhler-Bolte Zs. f. Vksk. VI 62.

H1460. Task: vigil at tomb.

E62.1. *Resuscitation by fasting.* Irish myth: *Cross.

D1733.3.1. Magic power by fasting. P623. Fasting as a means of distraint.

E63. *Resuscitation by prayer.* Types 516, 612; Rösch FFC LXXVII 143. — Irish myth: *Cross, Scala Celi No. 949; Jewish: bin Gorion Born Judas VI 218, Neuman; India: *Thompson-Balys; Maori: Dixon 82.

D1766.1. Magic results produced by prayer. E121.1. Resuscitation by a god. E121.4. Resuscitation by saint. E121.5.2. Resuscitation through prayers of holy man.

E63.1. *Body placed in building and worshipped until it comes to life.* (Cf. E62.) Hawaii: Beckwith Myth 420.

E63.2. *Resuscitation by nine-day dance and prayers.* Hawaii: Beckwith Myth 184.

E64. *Resuscitation by magic object.*

E11. Resuscitation by beating with magic whip. K113. Pseudo-magic resuscitating object sold.

E64.1. *Resuscitation by staff.* (Cf. D1254.) India: *Thompson-Balys; Chinese: Graham; N. A. Indian (Southern Paiute): Lowie JAFL XXXVII 108 No. 5, 117 No. 7, 169f. Nos. 5a, 6; Eskimo (Greenland): Rasmussen I 115; Africa: Werner African 171, (Zulu): Callaway 233.

E64.1.1. *Staff of life and death.* Black staff kills; brown one restores to life. India: Thompson-Balys; Africa (Basuto): Jacottet 266 No. 40.
D1663.1. Wands of life and death. E82. Water of life and death. One water kills, the other restores to life.

E64.1.1.1. *Silver stick kills; gold one restores to life.* India: Thompson-Balys.

E64.1.1.2. *Leaves of life and death.* India: Thompson-Balys.

E64.1.1.3. *Fly-whisk of life and death.* India: Thompson-Balys.

E64.2. *Resuscitation by magic cauldron.* (Cf. D1171.2.) Irish myth: Cross.

E64.3. *Resuscitation by magic bell.* (Cf. D1213.) Jewish: Neuman.

E64.3.1. *Resuscitation by saint's bell.* Irish: Plummer clxxvi, Cross.

E64.4. *Resuscitation by magic bachall.* (Cf. D1277.)

E64.4.1. *Resuscitation by saint's bachall.* *Loomis White Magic 105; Irish: Plummer clxxv, *Cross.

E64.5. *Resuscitation by magic cup.* (Cf. D1171.6.)

E64.5.1. *Resuscitation by Holy Grail.* Welsh, Irish: MacCulloch Celtic 203; Irish myth: *Cross.

E64.6. *Resuscitation by candle.* (Cf. D1162.2.) Cape Verde Islands: Parsons MAFLS XV (1) 111 No. 39.

E64.7. *Resuscitation by book.* (Cf. D1266.) Fansler MAFLS XII 137.

E64.7.1. *Resuscitation by manuscript.* Cheremis: Sebeok-Nyerges.

E64.8. *Resuscitation by perfume.* (Cf. D1245.) Philippine: Dixon 235 n. 47, (Tinguian): *Cole 18 n. 1, 44, 51, 90, 98, 131.

E64.8.1. *Resuscitation by heavenly fragrance.* Jewish: Neuman.

E64.9. *Resuscitation by magic feather.* (Cf. D1021.) N. A. Indian (Kato): Goddard UCal V 208 No. 9, (Tsimshian): Boas RBAE XXXI 127.

E64.10. *Resuscitation by piece of felt.* (Cf. D1051.) Georgian: Wardrop Georgian Folk-Tales (London, 1894) 15 No. 3.

E64.11. *Resuscitation by magic robe (blanket).* (Cf. D1052.) N. A. Indian (Pawnee): Dorsey CI LIX 329 No. 88, (Tlingit): Swanton BBAE XXXIX 36 No. 8.

E64.12. *Resuscitation by sacred relics.* Irish myth: Cross.
V140. Sacred relics.

E64.13. *Resuscitation by ring.* BP III 537; India: Thompson-Balys.

E64.14. *Resuscitation by magic bag.* (Cf. D1193.) Zs. f. d. Phil. XXVI 23.

E64.15. *Resuscitation by magic gold.* Zs f. d. Phil. XXVI 23.
D1252.3. Magic gold. D1507.8. Magic gold taken from hill restores speech when it is laid under the tongue of dumb person.

E64.16. *Resuscitation by animal's tail.*

E64.16.1. *Resuscitation by yak's tail.* India: Thompson-Balys.

E64.17. *Resuscitation by magic stone.* (Cf. D931.) India: Thompson-Balys.

E64.18. *Resuscitation by leaf.* India: Thompson-Balys.

E64.19. *Resuscitation from bird dung.* (Cf. D1026.1.) India: Thompson-Balys.

E64.20. *Resuscitation by magic baskets.* Africa (Fang): Einstein 155.

E64.21. *Resuscitation by handkerchief.* S. A. Indian (Chiriguano): Métraux RMLP XXXIII 182.

E65. *Resuscitation by kiss.* Type 885*. — India: Thompson-Balys.
D1794. Magic results from kissing.

E66. *Resuscitation by breathing on corpse.* Greek: Fox 22; Irish myth: *Cross; India: *Thompson-Balys; Melanesia: Codrington JAI X 272; N. A. Indian: *Thompson Tales 319 n. 153a; Eskimo (Greenland): Rink 280, Rasmussen III 124, Holm 68, (Cumberland Sound): Boas BAM XV 247; Africa (Benga): Nassau 213 No. 33.
D1782. Sympathetic magic. D1784. Magic results from breathing.

E66.1. *Resuscitation of cremated man by blowing on the ashes.* India: Thompson-Balys; S. A. Indian (Bakairi, Amazon): Alexander Lat. Am. 312.
E42. Resuscitation from ashes of dead man.

E67. *Resuscitation by talking to corpse.* Type 450; Scottish: Campbell-McKay No. 17.
E26. Resuscitation by shouting at dead.

E68. *Apparently dead persons revived when certain thing happens.* Proper prince appears, or the like. Chauvin V 263 No. 154.

E71. *Resuscitation by wishing.* N. A. Indian (Seneca): Curtin-Hewitt RBAE XXXII 123 No. 19.

E72. *Resuscitation by smelling of moss.* N. A. Indian (Menomini): Hoffman RBAE XIV 181.

E73. *Resuscitation by incantation.* Chinese: Graham.

E74. *Resuscitation by waving magic object.* India: Thompson-Balys.

E75. *Resuscitation by writing deity's name.* Jewish: *Neuman.
C431. Tabu: uttering name of God.

E79. *Resuscitation by magic—miscellaneous.*

E79.1. *Resuscitation by passing helpful animal over corpse.* Chinese: Graham.

E79.1.1. *Resuscitation by bird flying over dead.* Jewish: Neuman.

E79.2. *Resuscitation by reversing positions of two blocks of wood.* India: Thompson-Balys.

E79.3. *Resuscitation by touch of eagle.* Jewish: Neuman.

E80. Water of Life. Resuscitation by water. Types 550, 551; *BP I 513, II 400; **Wünsche Lebensbaum; Chauvin VI 73f.; Hertz Abhandlungen 47ff.; *Fb "vand" III 1001b, "livets vand" II 439b, "flaske" I 309a; Dawkins Alexander and the Water of Life (Medium Aevum IX 173—192); Jacobs' list s.v. "Water of Life"; Köhler-Bolte I 186, 562. — Icelandic: Hrólfssaga Gautrekssonar (ed. Detter) 46, 64; Russian: Ralston Russian Folk-Tales (London 1873) 231ff.; Italian Novella:

Rotunda; Babylonian: Spence 130 (Ishtar); India: *Thompson-Balys, Penzer X 210 s.v. "Life, water of"; Buddhist myth: Malalasekera II 347; Arabian: Burton Nights S VI 213ff., 221; Siberian: Holmberg Siberian 494; Indonesian: DeVries Volksverhalen II 359 No. 104; Pelew Islands: Dixon 252; Hawaii: Beckwith Myth 74, 121, 153, 264; Fiji: ibid. 76; N. A. Indian: *Thompson Tales 355 n. 279a; (Calif. Indian): Gayton and Newman 64; Africa (Bushman): Bleek and Lloyd 27, 67, 137.

B172.5. Magic falcon gets water of life for hero. B512. Medicine shown by animal. D926.1. Drinking from well prevents death. D1242.1. Magic water. D1338.1.1. Fountain (water) of youth. D1338.1.2. Water of youth. D1346.1.1. Water of life destroyed to prevent immortality: too long life would become tiresome. D1500.1.18. Magic healing water. D1505.5. Magic water restores sight. F162.6.2. Lake with Water of Life in otherworld. H1321.1. Quest for Water of Life. T323.2. Maiden kills undesired suitor but does not use the resuscitating water.

E80.1. *Resuscitation by bathing.* Herbert III 197; Irish myth: *Cross; India: Thompson-Balys, Penzer IV 145; West Indies: Flowers 427.

D925. Magic fountain. D926. Magic well. D1788. Magic results from bathing.

E80.1.1. *Resuscitation by bathing in milk.* (Cf. D1018, D1503.7.1, E102.1.) Irish myth: *Cross; India: Thompson-Balys.

E80.2. *Resuscitation by wet cloth over corpse.* India: Thompson-Balys.

E134. Resuscitation by laying flesh on pyre and covering with cloth.

E80.3. *Resuscitation by water (in basket, overnight).* N. A. Indian (California): Gayton and Newman 68.

E80.4. *Resuscitation by holy water.* Irish myth: *Cross; Icelandic: *Boberg.

D1242.1.2. Holy water as magic object.

E80.4.1. *Resuscitation by dew from heaven.* Jewish: *Neuman.

E82. *Water of life and death.* One water kills, the other restores to life. *BP III 31 n. 1; Greek: Fox 281 (blood of life and death); India: Thompson-Balys; N. A. Indian: *Thompson Tales 355 n. 279b.

D1663.1. Wands of life and death. E11.1. Second blow resuscitates. First kills. E64.1.1. Staff of life and death.

E84. *Water of death.* India: Thompson-Balys.

E90. Tree of Life. (Cf. D950.) Resuscitation by touching its branches. *MacCulloch Childhood 83; *Wünsche Lebensbaum. — Irish myth: *Cross; Siberian: Holmberg Siberian 354; India: *Thompson-Balys; S. A. Indian (Guianas, Chaco, Arawakan Chaná): Métraux BBAE CXLIII (1) 369.

A151.7.1.1. God's home under tree of life. A652. World-tree. A878. Earth-tree. D1346.4. Tree of immortality. F162.3.1. Tree of Life in otherworld

E90.1. *Sun and moon steal wonderful tree which revives dead man or animal.* India: Thompson-Balys.

E100. Resuscitation by medicines. Greek: Aeschylus Agamemnon line 1020; India: *Thompson-Balys; Africa (Ekoi): Talbot 7, 34; (Benga): Nassau 98, 213 Nos. 5, 33, (Gold Coast): Barker and Sinclair 117 No. 20, (Kaffir): Theal 66, (Vai): Ellis 196 No. 14, 200 No. 18, 243 No. 49, (Cameroon): Ittman 72f., (Wakweli): Bender 96.

D1240. Magic waters and medicines.

E101. *Resuscitation by salve (oil).* (Cf. D1244.) BP I 127; Fb "salve" III 150b. — Irish myth: *Cross; Italian: Gonzenbach I 318 No. 48; India: *Thompson-Balys; Philippine (Tinguian): *Cole 18 n. 1, 44, 51.

E102. *Resuscitation by magic liquid.* (Cf. D1242.) *Krappe Balor 132ff. — Irish myth: Cross; Icelandic: Boberg; Spanish: Boggs FFC XC 61 No. 445A; India: *Thompson-Balys; Korean: Zong in-Sob 47.

E102.1. *Resuscitation by magic milk.* Irish myth: *Cross.

E80.1.1. Resuscitation by bathing in milk.

E102.2. *Resuscitation by sprinkling ambrosia.* (Cf. E80.) India: Thompson-Balys.

E105. *Resuscitation by herbs (leaves).* Type 612; BP I 126ff., *128; *Bolte Zs. f. Vksk. XX 354 n. 2; *Kittredge Gawain 153 n. 4; *Wesselski Märchen 239f. No. 50; Jacobs' list s.v. "Life-restoring herb"; Penzer VI 18 n. 1. — Irish myth: *Cross; Greek: Frazer Apollodorus I 312 n. 2; Jewish: Neuman; Italian: Basile Pentamerone I No. 7, V No. 7, Rotunda; India: *Thompson-Balys; Philippine: Fansler MAFLS XII 135; Africa (Ekoi): Talbot 7, (Thonga): Junod 56.

B512. Medicine shown by animal. D955. Magic leaf. D965. Magic plant.

E106. *Resuscitation by magic apple.* *Type 590; BP III 1; Fb "æble" IV 1135b; Hdwb. d. Märchens I 90b s.v. "Apfel" n. 2.

D981.1. Magic apple. H1323.3. Quest for apple of life.

E107. *Resuscitation by magic pill.* (Cf. D1243.) Chinese: Werner 159.

E108. *Resuscitation by magic powder.*

E108.1. *Resuscitation by magic powder blown into nose.* Africa (Kordofan): Frobenius Atlantis IV 101ff. No. 11.

E113. *Resuscitation by blood.* Type 516; Rösch FFC LXXVII 143; *BP I 46ff.; *Fb "blod" IV 46b, 47a; Jacobs' list s.v. "Blood resuscitates". — Greek: Frazer Apollodorus II 16 n. 1; Italian: Basile Pentamerone IV No. 9; India: *Thompson-Balys. — Tonga: Gifford 185; Tuamotu: Stimson MS (T-G 3/912); N. A. Indian (Seneca): Curtin-Hewitt RBAE XXXII 96 No. 7; S. A. Indian (Chiriguano): Métraux RMLP XXXIII 165.

B751.2. Pelican kills young and revives them with own blood. D766.2. Disenchantment by application of blood. D766.2.1. Disenchantment of bewitched person by placing cake in his mouth. D1003. Magic blood — human.

E113.1. *Resuscitation by animal's blood.* Cheremis: Sebeok-Nyerges.

E113.1.1. *Resuscitation by raven's blood.* Cheremis: Sebeok-Nyerges.

E114. *Resuscitation by spittle.* (Cf. D1001.) Type 516; Rösch FFC LXXVII 143. — Sicilian: Gonzenbach I 156 No. 25; Philippine (Tinguian): Cole 99, 157; Tonga: Gifford 185; N. A. Indian (Thompson River): Teit JAFL XXIX 305 (European borrowing).

D1001. Magic spittle.

E115. *Resuscitation by wax from deer's ear.* Scotch: Campbell Tales II 309 No. 44.

E116. *Resuscitation by use of animal fat.* Italian Novella: Rotunda.

E117. *Resuscitation by gall of slain giant.* Cheremis: Sebeok-Nyerges.

E120. Other means of resuscitation.

B515. Resuscitation by animals.

E121. *Resuscitation by supernatural person.* MacCulloch Childhood 84 n. 2; Melanesia: *Wheeler No. 66f.

E50. Resuscitation by magic.

E121.1. *Resuscitation by a god.* (Cf. A454.) Irish: Beal XXI 329; Greek: *Frazer Apollodorus I 234 n. 3 (Theseus), Fox 119 (Pelops), 126 (Protesilaos), 144 (Alkestis, Glaukos), 220 (Adriadne, Semele), 280 (Asklepios); Icelandic: Boberg (Odin); Jewish: *Neuman; India: *Thompson-Balys; Chinese: Werner 339.

A180. Gods in relation to mortals. E63. Resuscitation by prayer.

E121.1.1. *Resuscitation by concerted effort of the gods.* Greek: Fox 119 (Pelops).

E121.1.2. *Resuscitation by power of goddess.* *India: Thompson-Balys.

E121.1.3. *Man sent back to earth by Death, for it is not yet his time to die.* India: Thompson-Balys.

E121.1.3.1. *Hero resuscitated by his bride, daughter of king of death.* India: Thompson-Balys.

E121.2. *Resuscitation by Christ.* Types 750***, 753; Irish myth: Cross.

E121.3. *Resuscitation by Virgin Mary.* (Cf. V268.) *Type 710; *Crane Miraculis 85 No. 8; *Ward Catalogue of Romances II 633 No. 31; Wells Manual of Writings 170; Irish myth: *Cross.

E121.4. *Resuscitation by saint.* Köhler-Bolte II 163ff.; Alphabet Nos. 130, 374, 375, 376, 559, 628; *Loomis White Magic 83f.; Irish: Plummer xxxv, *Cross; Icelandic: Boberg; Sicilian: Gonzenbach I 156 No. 25; Jewish: bin Gorion III 20; India: *Thompson-Balys. See also Acta Sanctorum passim.

D1713. Magic power of hermit (saint). E3. Animal comes to life. E32. Resuscitated eaten animal. E63. Resuscitation by prayer. E755.0.1. Resurrected boys choose to return to heaven. P19.5. King raised from dead (by saint). Q574. Mysterious death as punishment remitted. V220. Saints.

E121.4.1. *The cooked and revived child.* Saint to a woman: "Cook me what you like most." Gullible woman cooks son. Saint revives child. Lithuanian: Balys Legends Nos. 80f.

F168. Cooked animal comes to life. V221. Miraculous healing by saints.

E121.5. *Resuscitation by holy man (priest, etc.)* Irish: O'Suilleabhain 31, 90, Beal XXI 310; Spanish Exempla: Keller; Jewish: *Neuman; Icelandic: *Boberg; India: Thompson-Balys.

E121.5.1. *Resuscitation by rabbi.* Gaster Exempla 218 No. 149.

E121.5.2. *Resuscitation through prayers of holy man.* (Cf. E63.) Nouvelles de Sens No. 24.

E121.5.3. *Resuscitation by prophet.* Jewish: Neuman.

E121.6. *Resuscitation by demon.* Hindu: Tawney I 132.

E121.6.1. *Resuscitation by demon's entering corpse.* Irish myth: *Cross.

F408. Habitation of spirit. G303.18. Devil enters body of another.

E121.7. *Resuscitation by magician.* (Cf. D1711.) Irish myth: Cross; Icelandic: Boberg; India: *Thompson-Balys; N. A. Indian (Lilooet): Teit JAFL XXV 332, (Mewan): Merriam Dawn of the World (Cleveland, 1910) 188; Eskimo (Cumberland Sound): Boas BAM XV 247.

E121.7.1. *Resuscitation by druid.* (Cf. P427.5.) Irish myth: Cross.

E121.8. *Resuscitation by fairy.* Irish myth: *Cross; India: Thompson-Balys.

F243.3.1. Animals eaten by fairies become whole again.

E122. *Resuscitation by animals.* Jewish: Neuman.

E122.1. *Resuscitation by cuckoo.* Lithuanian: Balys Index No. *455.
B459.1. Helpful cuckoo.

E122.2. *Resuscitation by snake.* India: *Thompson-Balys.

E125. *Resuscitation by relative*

E125.1. *Resuscitation by son.* India: Thompson-Balys.

E125.2. *Resuscitation by sister(s).* Hawaii: Beckwith Myth 152.

E125.3. *Resuscitation by brother.* Jewish: Neuman.

E127. *Resuscitation by friends.* India: Thompson-Balys.

E132. *Resuscitation through ashes thrown on funeral pyre.* *Penzer IX 68 n. 2.

E133. *Resuscitation by warming dead man.* German: Grimm No. 4.

E134. *Resuscitation by laying flesh on pyre and covering with cloth.* India: Thompson-Balys.
E80.2. Resuscitation by wet cloth over corpse.

E134.1. *Resuscitation by covering body for certain time.* Chinese: Eberhard FFC CXX 72, 80, 102.

E136. *Resuscitation by heavenly voice.* Jewish: Neuman.

E138. *Resuscitation by carrying corpse to its home.*

E138.1. *Deer foster parent of hero comes alive from its burial hill when youth returns to spot and carries him off to jungle again.* India: Thompson-Balys.

E141. *Resuscitation: ghosts deceived so that they cannot find way back to grave.* India: Thompson-Balys.
E432.1. Haunting ghost deceived so that he cannot find road to return.

E142. *Resuscitation by polishing sword that contains dead man's life.* India: *Thompson-Balys.
E711.10. Soul in sword.

E149. *Means of resuscitation—miscellaneous.*

E149.1. *Human bone, found in demon's stomach wrapped in silk with bow and arrow, becomes a boy.* India: Thompson-Balys.

E149.2. *Resuscitation of decapitated princess by hero by imitating ogre's actions of night before: passing sword three times up and down her throat.* India: Thompson-Balys.

E149.3. *Resuscitation from touch of a child at his first walking.* India: Thompson-Balys.

E150. Circumstances of resuscitation.

E151. *Repeated resuscitation.* A person dies and is resuscitated repeatedly. *Zwierzina Legenden der Märtyrer vom unzerstörbaren Leben (Innsbrucker Festgruss dargebracht der 50. Versammlung deutscher Philologen in Graz). — Irish myth: *Cross; Icelandic: Boberg; Georgian: Wardrop Georgian Folk-Tales (London, 1894) 59 No. 10; India: Thompson-Balys. — N. A. Indian (Micmac): Rand 296 No.

51, (Chilcotin): Farrand JE II 22 No. 8, (Yuki): Kroeber UCal IV 185, (Osage): Dorsey FM VII 43 No. 36, (Navaho): Matthews MAFLS V 93; Eskimo (Greenland): Rink 298f., 463; S. A. Indian (Ackawoi): Alexander Lat. Am. 270; Africa (Hottentot): Bleek 75 No. 36.

E610. Repeated transformation. G335. Ogre decapitates captive princess before he leaves palace, resuscitates her on return. K856. Fatal game: dying and reviving. Hero has power of resuscitation but fails to revive his enemy.

E152. *Body still warm restored to life.* Hawaii: Beckwith Myth 152.

E155. *Periodic resuscitation.* (Cf. D620.) Return to life at regular intervals. *Cosquin Contes indiens 18ff.; Irish myth: *Cross; India: Thompson-Balys.

E322.3. Wife in heaven by day, with husband by night. T113. Marriage to man alive by night but dead by day.

E155.1. *Slain warriors revive nightly.* Continue fighting the next day. *Krappe Balor 132ff.; Hdwb. d. Abergl. III 546; Irish myth: *Cross, Beal IV 342, 454, V 210; Icelandic: De la Saussaye 176, Fb "kamp", Panzer Hilde-Gudrun 327ff., Herrmann Saxo II 364, *Boberg; Hindu: Tawney I 476.

A162.1.0.1. Recurrent battle. A661.1. Valhalla: warriors die and are resurrected daily. D2163. Magic defense in battle. E497. Fighting warriors show the way of their past life and of their death. F585.2. Magic phantom army. K1089. Goddess arouses heroes' jealousy and eternal fighting. K1863. Death feigned to learn how soldiers are resuscitated.

E155.1.1. *Constant replacement of fighters.* In contest between gods and demons, latter are constantly slain and replaced. Hindu: Keith 150.

A162.2. Combat between god of light and dragon of ocean.

E155.1.2. *Soldiers of magic army constantly revived.* Irish myth: *Cross; India: Thompson-Balys.

E155.2. *Annual resuscitation of a god.* (Cf. A192.1.) Greek: Fox 156 (Zeus), 218 (Dionysus), 230 (Persephone); Babylonian: Spence 132 (Adonis, Tammuz).

E155.3. *Nightly resuscitation of man with external soul.* When enemy takes off necklace containing the soul he revives, but dies again when it is put on. India: Thompson-Balys.

E711.4. Soul in necklace.

E155.4. *Person dead during day, revived at night.* India: *Thompson-Balys.

T113. Marriage to man alive by night but dead by day.

E155.4.1. *Woman alive by day, dead by night.* Irish myth: Cross.

E155.5. *Slain pigs revive nightly.* Irish myth: *Cross.

B184.3.1. Magic boar. D1652.1.9.1. Inexhaustible pig. E32. Resuscitated eaten animal. E32.3. Dismembered pigs come alive again if only bones are preserved. F241.3.1. Fairy swine. H1331.2.3. Quest for pigs killed by night and revived by day.

E155.5.1. *Calf, slain at night, alive next day through power of saint.* Irish myth: *Cross.

D1652.1.10.1. Loaves and fish, eaten at night, restored next morning through power of saint. D2106.1. Magic multiplication of objects by saints. E32. Resuscitated eaten animal. V224.2 Food (animals) eaten by saint miraculously replaced.

E155.6. *King eaten every morning: revived daily.* India: Thompson-Balys.

E156. *Gradual resuscitation — one organ at a time.* Korean: Zong in-Sob 47.

E161. *Killed game revives and flies away.* N. A. Indian: Thompson Tales 303 n. 109e; Africa (Angola): Chatelain 159 No. 20.

E162. *Resuscitation impossible after certain length of time.* N. A. Indian (Seneca): Curtin-Hewitt RBAE XXXII 97 No. 7 (ten days); Africa (Vai): Ellis 200 No. 18 (three days).

E162.0.1. *Resuscitation after great length of time.* (Cf. D1857.) Irish myth: *Cross.

E162.1. *Resuscitation even possible after three days.* Icelandic: Göngu-Hrólfs saga 308.

E162.2. *Dead man tries in vain to come back to life.* (Cf. E1.) Eskimo (Greenland): Rasmussen II 347.

E163. *Man kept alive by consecrated sword.* (Cf. D1081, E765.3.0.1.) Irish: Plummer clxxxv, *Cross.

E165. *Resuscitation of wife by husband giving up half his remaining life.* (Sometimes vice versa). *Type 612; *BP I 126, 129; *Wesselski Märchen 188; *Chauvin VIII 120 No. 104; Greek: Frazer Apollodorus I 93, 193; Jewish: bin Gorion I 372; India: *Thompson-Balys, Penzer VIII 117; Indonesia: De Vries's list No. 226; Africa: Frobenius Atlantis IX No. 108.

D1855.2. Death postponed if substitute can be found. K2213.5. The faithless resuscitated wife. T211.1. Wife dies so that husband's death may be postponed.

E165.1. *One man prays either to keep friend from death or for both to die.* Both allowed to live. Jewish: bin Gorion II 171f., 349.

P310. Friendship.

E165.2. *Husband resuscitated after wife's nose is cut off and thrown over grave.* India: Thompson-Balys.

E166. *Return from dead granted for definite time.* Irish myth: Cross; Greek: Fox 126 (three hours); Hindu: Keith 114 (100 years).

E167. *Man given ability to return to life if killed.* Eskimo (Greenland): Rasmussen II 301.

E168. *Cooked animal comes to life.* (Cf. E155.5.) Irish myth: *Cross; India: Thompson-Balys.

E32. Resuscitated eaten animal.

E168.1. *Roasted cock comes to life and crows.* English: Child I 233—242, 505, II 8, 501b, III 502f., IV 451f., V 212a, 288a.

E171. *Flayed animal resuscitated.* Irish myth: Cross.

E174. *Bones wrapped in sheepskin inscribed with holy name revive.* Jewish: *Neuman.

E174.1. *Ashes of burnt hero revive.* Jewish: *Neuman.

E175. *Death thought sleep.* Resuscitated person thinks he has been sleeping. He exclaims, "How long I have been asleep!" *Köhler-Bolte 555; Wesselski Märchen 192. — India: *Thompson-Balys; Philippine: Dixon 235; N. A. Indian: *Thompson Tales 319 n. 154, (Calif.):

Gayton and Newman 57; S. A. Indian (Yuracare): Métraux BBAE CXLIII (3) 502.

D2011. Years thought days. F377. Supernatural lapse of time in fairyland. Years seem days.

E176. *Resuscitation in order to baptize.* Irish myth: Cross.

E177. *Resuscitated man relates visions of beyond.* (Cf. E480, V511.) Irish myth: Cross.

E178. *Resurrection at Judgment Day.* Jewish: *Neuman.

E751. Souls at Judgment Day.

E181. *Means of resuscitation learned.* India: Thompson-Balys.

B512. Medicine shown by animal.

E181.1. *Husband advised how to resuscitate his wife: lift her up and turn her around so her head rests upon the brick which had been under her feet.* India: Thompson-Balys.

E181.1.1. *Man advised how to resuscitate his mother: break waternuts on her head: she would revive and live one year for each nut broken.* India: Thompson-Balys.

E181.2. *Student revives whole family following instructions given by demon.* Chinese: Graham.

E182. *Dead body incorruptible.* Beard and fingernails continue to grow. Irish myth: *Cross; Icelandic: *Boberg.

D2167. Corpse magically saved from corruption.

E185. *Resuscitation when murder is discovered.* India: Thompson-Balys.

E185.1. *Resuscitation after murderer is buried in the earth, wood laid over him, and a lighted lamp on its top.* India: Thompson-Balys.

E186. *Failure at resuscitation.*

J2411.1. Imitation of magic rejuvenation unsuccessful.

E186.1. *Attempted resuscitation fails because of overanxiety.* S. A. Indian (Kaiguá): Métraux RMLP XXXIII 139.

E200—E599. GHOSTS AND OTHER REVENANTS

E200—E299. Malevolent return from the dead.

E200. Malevolent return from the dead. *Fb "spøgelse" III 520b; *Carrington and Nandor Haunted People (New York, 1951); English: Child IV 416, V 303b; U.S. (New York State): *L. C. Jones JAFL LVII 237ff., New York History XXIV 177ff., Spooks of the Valley (Boston, 1948); (Pennsylvania): Balys MWF II 47—52; Icelandic: *Boberg; Norwegian: *Solheim Register 17; India: Thompson-Balys; Easter Island: Métraux Ethnology 316; Eskimo (Greenland): Rasmussen III 64.

E210. Dead lover's malevolent return. *R. Arbesmann The Dead Bridegroom in South American Folklore (Thought XIX [March 1944] 95—111); North Carolina: Brown Collection I 681; Estonian: Aarne FFC XXV 114 No. 8.

E310. Dead lover's friendly return.

E211. *Dead sweetheart haunts faithless lover.* English: Child I 426; U.S.: Baughman, (North Carolina): Brown Collection I 676, (New York): Jones JAFL LVII 245; Corsican: Ortoli Contes Pop. de la Corse (Paris, 1883) 322, 330.

E211.1. *Dead sweetheart in the form of a white rabbit follows seducer.* England: *Baughman.

E211.2. *Dead sweetheart appears to seducer every evening, even after he has married another woman.* England: Baughman.

E212. *Dead lover sets tasks.* If girl does not perform them (or answer his questions) he will carry her off. Child IV 439ff.

E214. *Dead lover haunts faithless sweetheart.*

E214.1. *Dead lover returns to dance with fickle sweetheart at her wedding.* U.S.: Baughman.

E215. *The Dead Rider (Lenore).* Dead lover returns and takes sweetheart with him on horseback. She is sometimes saved at the grave by the crowing of the cock, though the experience is usually fatal. *Type 365; *Fb "død" I 228a, "ride" III 53a, "spøgelse" III 520ab; Krumbacher Zs. f. vgl. Litt. N. F. I (1887) 214—220; Wlislocki ibid. N.F. XI (1897) 467; Borker Germania XXXI 117; Dieterich Zs. f. Vksk. XII 147; — England: Child V 60ff., 303; England, U.S.: *Baughman; Finnish-Swedish: Wessman 4 No. 28.

B131.4. Bird reveals dead rider. E266. Dead carry off living. E581. Dead person rides.

E217. *Fatal kiss from dead.* English: Child I 439, II 229ff., 236f., III 512f., IV 474f.

E218. *Spells to recall dead lover.* Boiling dead man's head, bones, or carcass in a pot, or burning a piece of lover's clothing or cat in a hot oven. English: Child V 61.

D1787. Magic results from burning.

E220. Dead relative's malevolent return. *Fb "spøgelse" III 520b; Lithuanian: Balys Index No. 3531; West Indies: Flowers 428.

E320. Dead relative's friendly return.

E221. *Dead spouse's malevolent return.* Usually to protest with survivor because of evil ways. English: Child II 281 No. 86; Danish: Grundtvig Danmarks Gamle Folkeviser No. 89b; Lithuanian: Balys Index No. 3526; Estonian: Aarne FFC XXV 114 No. 6; Finnish-Swedish: Wessman 6 No. 47; New York: Jones JAFL LVII 245; West Indies: Flowers 428.

E321. Dead husband's friendly return. P210. Husband and wife. T200. Married life.

E221.1. *Dead wife haunts husband on second marriage.* *Pauli (ed. Bolte) No. 146; Scotch: Macdougall and Calder 185; England, U.S.: *Baughman.

E322. Dead wife's friendly return.

E221.2. *Dead wife returns to reprove husband's second wife.* Scotland, U.S.: *Baughman; N. A. Indian (Pawnee): Grinnell Pawnee Hero Stories 129.

E221.2.1. *Dead wife returns to reprove husband's second wife for abusing her step-children.* N. A. Indian (Fox): Jones PAES I 153.

E323.2. Dead mother returns to aid persecuted children. S31. Cruel stepmother.

E221.3. *Dead husband returns to reprove wife's second husband (lover).* Lithuanian: Balys Ghosts.

E221.4. *Dead husband returns to protest wife's spending his money.* U.S.: Baughman.

E221.5. *Dead wife torments husband who has let her die of neglect.* England, U.S.: *Baughman.

E222. *Dead mother's malevolent return.* Irish: O'Suilleabhain 94, 104, Beal XXI 330, 333.

E222.0.1. *Mother haunts daughter.* England: Baughman.

E222.1. *Mother's ghost tries to tear daughter to pieces.* English: Child V 303b.

E222.2. *Dead mother haunts daughter who marries against mother's will.* England: Baughman.

E222.3. *Dead mother returns to invoke curse on murderer-son.* Greek: Aeschylus Eumenides line 115.

E225. *Ghost of murdered child.* English: *Child I 218 No. 20; Tobler 30; Estonian: Aarne FFC XXV 114 No. 9; Finnish: Aarne FFC XXXIII 39 No. 9; Lappish: Qvigstad FFC LX 40 No. 3; New York: Jones JAFL LVII 241, 244; Eskimo (Greenland): Rink 392, 410, (Smith Sound): Kroeber JAFL XII 181.

A737.4. Ghosts of sun's children return to cause eclipse. S12. Cruel mother. S300. Abandoned or murdered children.

E225.1. *Ghost of abortion.* Eskimo (Greenland): Rink 274, 392, 410, 439, Holm 88, Rasmussen III 181f.

E226. *Dead brother's return.*

E226.1. *Dead brother reproves sister's pride.* English: Child I 428ff.

E228. *The dead daughter reproaches her mother for putting her dowery into coffin.* Lithuanian: Balys Ghosts.

E229. *Dead relative's malevolent return—miscellaneous.*

E229.1. *"If I were not your next of kin."* Ghost tells man that otherwise he would tear him into pieces. Swiss: Jegerlehner Oberwallis 320 No. 29.

E230. Return from dead to inflict punishment.

E373. Ghosts bestow gifts on living.

E231. *Return from dead to reveal murder.* Fb "gjenganger" I 443b, "lig" II 411b; Wimberly 261; England, U.S.: *Baughman; New York: Jones JAFL LVII 245; North Carolina: Brown Collection I 677; West Indies: Flowers 429; Jewish: bin Gorion V 213, 306, *Neuman; India: *Thompson-Balys; Japanese: Ikeda. — N. A. Indian (Fox): Jones PAES I 93ff., (Seneca): Curtin-Hewitt RBAE XXXII 173 No. 33, 670 No. 129; Eskimo (Greenland): Holm 39, Rasmussen III 145, Kroeber JAFL XII 181, (Cumberland Sound): Boas BAM XV 236; Africa (Fang): Tessman 118.

E613.0.1. Reincarnation of murdered child as bird. E632. The Singing Bone. E633. Reincarnation as dish. Bones made into dish. These speak. N270. Crime inevitably comes to light. Q211. Murder punished.

E231.1. *Ghost tells name of murderer.* Wales: Baughman.

E231.2. *Ghost skeleton points lance at murderer.* U.S.: Baughman.

E231.3. *Ghost light hovers over hiding place of body of murdered person.* England, U.S., Wales: *Baughman.

E231.4. *Noise of chains leads to buried ghost.* (Cf. E402.1.4.) England: Baughman.

E231.5. *Ghost returns to murderer, causes him to confess.* England, U.S.: *Baughman.

E232. *Return from the dead to slay wicked person.* Alphabet No. 772; Irish myth: Cross; Icelandic: Boberg; S. A. Indian (Brazil): Oberg 111.

E232.1. *Return from dead to slay own murderer.* U.S.: *Baughman.

E232.2. *Ghost returns to slay man who has injured it while living.* England, U.S.: *Baughman.

E232.3. *Ghost kills man who interferes with ghostly activity.* U.S.: Baughman.

E232.4. *Ghost returns to slay enemies.* U.S.: Baughman; S. A. Indian (Guaporé River): Lévi-Strauss BBAE CXLIII (3) 378.

E234. *Ghost punishes injury received in life.*

E234.0.1. *Ghost returns to demand vengeance.* (Cf. E232.2.) U.S.: *Baughman.

E234.1. *Ghost slaps face of son who cheated him out of property.* A cancer grows on son's face. Canada: Baughman.

E234.2. *Ghost stampedes stolen cattle being driven past his ranch.* U.S.: Baughman.

E234.3. *Return from dead to avenge death (murder).* Irish myth: Cross; England, U.S.: *Baughman (E233).

E234.4. *Ghost an unjustly executed man.* Real murderer found. Chinese: Eberhard FFC CXX 194.

E235. *Return from dead to punish indignities to corpse, or ghost.* Ireland: Baughman; New York: Jones JAFL LVII 245; Lithuanian: Balys Index No. 3532; India: Thompson-Balys.

E235.1. *Ghost punishes person who mocks him.* Fb "sjæl" III 214b, "gjenganger" I 443b; Spanish Exempla: Keller; U.S.: Baughman.

E235.2. *Ghost returns to demand proper burial.* Fb "lig" II 411b; Irish: *Cross, Baughman; Jewish: Neuman; Hawaii: Beckwith Myth 199.

E235.2.1. *Dead man speaks demanding proper funeral rites.* India: Thompson-Balys.

E235.2.2. *Ghost returns because corpse was not properly burned.* India: Thompson-Balys.

E235.3. *Return from dead as punishment for trying to raise ghost.* (Cf. E384ff., F491.7.) Ghost accuses man of stealing a trifle and thus has revenge. Fb "stjæle" III 575b; England: *Baughman.

E235.4. *Return from dead to punish theft of part of corpse.* (Cf. E419.7.) Finnish-Swedish: Wessman 6 No. 49.

E235.4.1. *Return from dead to punish theft of golden arm from grave.* *Type 366; Köhler-Bolte I 47, 133. — Gascon: Bladé II 324 No. 4; English: Baughman.

E235.4.2. *Return from dead to punish theft of leg from grave.* *Type 366; BP III 480; Köhler-Bolte I 133; Fb "rædehistorie". — English: Baughman; French: Cosquin Lorraine II 76 No. 41; Gascon Bladé II 328 No. 5.

E235.4.3. *Return from dead to punish theft of bone from grave.* *Type 366; Fb "menneskeben" II 579a; Köhler-Bolte I 133; England, U.S.: Baughman; Breton: Sébillot Incidents s.v. "os".

E235.4.4. *Return from dead to punish theft of liver from man on gallows* *Type 366; *BP III 478; Fb "lever" II 404b.

E235.4.5. *Return from dead to punish theft of skull.* England, Wales, U.S.: *Baughman; Estonian: Aarne FFC XXV 115 Nos. 14, 15; Swiss: Jegerlehner Oberwallis 328 No. 29.

E235.4.6. *Return from dead to punish theft of teeth.* U.S. (S. Carolina): Baughman.

E235.5. *Return from dead to punish kicking of skull.* (Cf. C13.) N. A. Indian (Tlingit): Swanton BBAE XXXIX 247 No. 86.

E235.6. *Return from dead to punish disturber of grave.* England, U.S.: Baughman; Jewish: bin Gorion II 160, 348, 360, Neuman.

E235.7. *Return from the dead to capture thief.* Spanish Exempla: Keller.

E235.8. *Corpse of saint sits up and looks at people who open grave and come to claim his body.* India: Thompson-Balys.

E236. *Return from dead to demand stolen property.* *Fb "spøgelse" III 520a; Icelandic: Boberg; Lithuanian: Balys Index No. 3565; N. Carolina: Brown Collection I 676.

E236.1. *Return from dead to demand clothing stolen from grave.* Type 366; Fb "død" I 228, "ligskjorte" II 425; *BP III 482 n. 1; Estonian: Aarne FFC XXV 116 No. 16; Lithuanian: Balys Index No. 3534.

H1431. Fear test: stealing clothes from ghosts. K426. Apparently dead woman revives when thief tries to steal from her grave.

E236.1.1. *Return from dead to demand ring stolen from corpse.* Lithuanian: Balys Index No. 3533, Balys Ghosts; England, U.S.: Baughman; U.S. (N. Carolina): Brown Collection I 676.

E236.2. *Return from dead to demand stolen children.* Tobler 84.

E236.3. *Return from the dead to warn thief that he will be punished.* Italian Novella: Rotunda.

E236.4. *Return from the dead because last will was not fulfilled.* Lithuanian: Balys Ghosts.

E236.4.1. *Ghost appears at time of death, foils lawyer who is counterfeiting a will for the newly-deceased.* England, Holland: *Baughman.

E236.4.2. *Ghost appears to remind his brother of the terms of his will.* U.S.: Baughman.

E236.5. *Return from dead to demand money stolen from corpse.* Am. Negro (Georgia): Harris Nights 161 No. 29.

E431.11. Coin placed in mouth of dead. K374. Grave robbing to secure obols in mouth of dead.

E236.6. *Ghost drives away his relatives who are trying to get estate from his wife.* England, U.S.: Baughman.

E236.7. *Ghostly noises disturb village until stolen church plate is returned.* (Cf. E402.) England: Baughman.

E236.8. *Ghost seeks repayment of stolen money.* England, Wales: *Baughman.

E238. *Dinner with the dead. Dead man is invited to dinner.* Takes his host to other world. *Type 470; **MacKay; Hartland Science 192f.; U.S.: Baughman; Breton: Sébillot Incidents s.v. "repas"; Lithuanian: Balys Index No. 470A*; Estonian: Aarne in FFC XX No. 472*; Spanish: Boggs FFC XC No. 835*. Cf. Eskimo (Greenland): Holm 79.

C13. The offended skull (statue). C210. Tabu: eating in other world. E481. Land of dead.

E238.1. *Dance with the dead.* Girl invites dead to come from grave and dance with her. Difficult escape. Lithuanian: Balys Index No. 365B*; Balys Ghosts (E225.8); Prussian: Plenzat 20.

G303.10.4.1. Devil dances with maid until she dies. Q386.1. Devil punishes girl who loves to dance.

E241. *Ghosts punish intruders into ghost town.* Africa (Ekoi): Talbot 238, 240.

E242. *Ghosts punish intruders into mass (procession) of ghosts.* Köhler-Bolte I 133; Gascon: Bladé II 266 No. 3; Estonian: Aarne FFC XXV 112f. Nos. 1, 2; Lithuanian: Balys Index No. 3558; Finnish: Aarne FFC XXXIII 39 No. 1; Lappish: Qvigstad FFC LX 39 No. 1; Livonian: Loorits FFC LXVI 48 Nos 64, 65.

E491. Procession of the dead. E492. Mass (church service) of the dead.

E243. *Ghosts attack bishop who has suspended priest for singing for all Christian souls.* Alphabet No. 686; Spanish Exempla: Keller.

E245. *Ghosts punish failure to provide for their wants.* Haunt man because he does not leave food and drink for them. Corsican: Ortoli Contes de la Corse (Paris, 1883) 337; Africa (Kweli): Sieber 90.

E246. *Ghosts punish failure to sacrifice to them.* Greek: Grote I 278; S. A. Indian (Brazil): Oberg 109; Africa: Werner African 198.

E247. *Ghost kills man who had had ghost exorcised for too short a time.* England: Baughman.

E250. Bloodthirsty revenants.

E251. *Vampire.* Corpse which comes from grave at night and sucks blood. (Cf. B16.7.1, E268.) *Types 307, 363; *Jellinek Zs. f. Vksk. XIV 322 (327 bibliography of literary treatments); *v. Negelein ibid. XIV 19; *Jaworskij ibid. VIII 331; *Hock Die Vampyrsagen und ihre Verwertung in der deutschen Literatur (Berlin, 1900); *Penzer VI 136, X 346 s.v. "vampires", 350 s.v. "Vetala"; *Fb "blod" IV 47a, "vampyr" IV 361b; *Kittredge Witchcraft 43, 397 n. 160; *Havecost Die Vampirsage in England (1914); Stetson The Animistic Vampire in New England (AA o.s. IX [1896] 1ff.); *Encyc. Rel. Ethics s.v. "Vampire"; Summers **The Vampire in Europe (London, 1929), **The Vampire, its Kith and Kin (London, 1928); *Feilberg Am Urquell III 331ff., VI 84; Wehrhan Die Sage 62; *E. Jobbé-Duval Les morts malfaisants (Paris, 1924) — England: Tupper and Ogle, Map 125f.; Breton: Sébillot Incidents s.v. "vampirisme"; Lithuanian: Balys Index No. 3543; Greek: Fox 278 (Stringes); Slavic: Máchal 231f.; Assyrian: Spence 265; India: *Thompson-Balys; Indonesian: Dixon 231f.; Kai (German New Guinea): ibid. 143; West Indies: Flowers 429; N. A. Indian: *Thompson Tales 357 n. 287e; S. A. Indian (Araucanian): Alexander Lat. Am. 329.

E440. Walking ghost "laid". G352. Cat as ogre. Sucks blood.

E251.1. *Vampire's power overcome.* Penzer VI 138.

E251.1.1. *Vampire's power overcome by endurance and prayer.* Hero continues to pray without looking or speaking while vampire punishes him. *Type 307; Japanese: Ikeda.

C300. Looking tabu. C400. Speaking tabu. H1460. Test: vigil at tomb. V52.3. Continuous prayer sustains man through frightful vigil.

E251.1.2. *Hand of vampire severed by cutting off hand of drawn figure.* Penzer IX 27 n. 1.

E251.2. *Vampire brought to life.*

E251.2.1. *Vampire brought to life through endurance of punishment by her victim.* *Type 307.

E251.2.2. *Prince plucks from grave of vampire a flower which later becomes a girl.* *BP II 126f.

E251.2.3. *Vampire brought to life by being fed human food and drink.* Africa (Ronga): Junod Les Chants et les Contes des Ba-Ronga de la baie de Delagoa (Lausanne, 1897) 317ff. No. 30.

E251.3. *Deeds of vampires.*

E251.3.1. *Vampires eat corpses.* *Type 363. — Cf. Fb "hud" I 661; India: Thompson-Balys.

E251.3.1.1. *Ghosts roast girl daily in oven and devour her flesh.* India: Thompson-Balys.

D1652.1. Inexhaustible food.

E251.3.2. *Vampire milks cows dry.* *Kittredge Witchcraft 166, 485 n. 27.

D2083.1. Cows magically made dry.

E251.3.3. *Vampire sucks blood.* U.S.: *Baughman.

E251.3.4. *Ghost sucks people's breath.* Chinese: Eberhard FFC CXX 173.

E251.4. *Form of Vampire.*

E251.4.1. *Vampire with elephant face.* Penzer VII 163.

E251.4.2. *Vampire with ass's ears.* Penzer VII 163.

E251.4.3. *Vampire with eyes of owls.* Penzer VII 163.

E251.4.4. *God with form and characteristics of vampire.* India: Thompson-Balys.

A139.4. Vampire goddess.

E251.5. *Vampire plant.* U.S.: Baughman.

E253. *Ghost tries to kill person for food.* Africa (Nyang): Ittman 58.

E255. *Ghosts flay corpse.* Fb "hud" I 661.

E256. *Ghosts eat corpse.* Africa (Ekoi): Talbot 238.

G20. Ghouls. Persons eat corpses.

E257. *Ghosts seek firewood to roast man.* Africa (Ekoi): Talbot 99.

E259. *Bloodthirsty revenants—miscellaneous.*

E259.1. *Corpse bites off woman's nose.* India: Thompson-Balys.

E259.2. *Ghosts may eat only female animals.* Africa (Bulu): Krug 108f.

E260. Other malevolent revenants.

E261. *Wandering ghost makes attack.* Unprovoked and usually unmotivated. Irish: Jacobs Celtic 200, Kennedy 180, O'Suilleabhain 30, 99, Beal XXI 309, 331; New York: Jones JAFL LVII 246; Icelandic: *Boberg; Lithuanian: Balys Index No. 3542, Legends No. 712; Russian: Ralston 271, 274, 313; Finnish-Swedish: Wessman 27 Nos. 229—240; cf. 2 Nos. 15—17; Lappish: Qvigstad FFC LX 40 No. 11; N. A. Indian (Kathlamet): Boas BBAE XXVI 182, 184, (Tahltan): Teit JAFL XXXII 225.

E261.1. *Wandering skull pursues man.* *Brown The Wandering Skull (Am. Journ. Philology XI 423ff.); Indonesian: DeVries Volksverhalen I 299; N. A. Indian (Zuñi): Benedict 342.

R261.1. Pursuit by rolling head.

E261.1.1. *Ghost's flying head attacks slayer.* Japanese: Anesaki 307.

G361.2. Great head as ogre.

E261.1.2. *Speaking skull tells about previous life, reveals future events, etc.* Krappe Moyen Âge XXVII (1926); India: *Thompson-Balys.

E261.1.3. *Hero attacked by revenant with half a head, carrying man with half a body.* (Cf. E461, E422.1.1, F511.0.5.) Irish myth: Cross.

E261.2. *Dead arises when shroud bursts and pursues attendant.* Estonian: Aarne FFC XXV 113 No. 3; Lithuanian: Balys Index No. *369; Finnish: Aarne FFC XXXIII 39 No. 3; Lappish: Qvigstad FFC LX 40 No. 4.

E261.2.1. *Coffin bursts; dead arises and pursues attendant.* Lithuanian: Balys Ghosts.

E261.3. *Man attacked on Christmas night by dancing ghosts.* Finnish: Swedish Wessman 6 No. 46.

E493. Dead men dance.

E261.4. *Ghost pursues man.* North Carolina: Brown Collection I 677, 681; Eskimo (Greenland): Rink 409, 463, Rasmussen III 182, (Mackenzie Area): Jenness 62.

E261.4.1. *Ghost of witch in her coffin chases man.* U.S.: Baughman.

E261.5. *Ghost beats living man with whip.* U.S.: Baughman.

E262. *Ghost rides on man's back.* *Fb "ryg" III 103a, "spøgelse" III 520a; E. H. Meyer Germanische 76; Schönbach Sitzungsberichte d. Phil. Hist. Classe der Kaiserl. Akad. d. Wiss. zu. Wien CXXXIX (1890) 135; Icelandic: Boberg; Lithuanian: Balys Index No. 3511.

D2171.2. Magic adhesion to monster (witch, ogre etc.). F420.5.2.10. Waterman sits on back of persons as heavy burden. F471.1. The Nightmare (Alp). F472. Huckauf. G241.2. Witch rides on person. G311. Old man of the sea. Burr-woman. Ogre who jumps on one's back and sticks there magically.

E263. *Adulteress returns from dead as devastating dragon.* *Herbert III 18, 279.

B11. Dragon. B16. Devastating animals. E410. The unquiet grave. G346. Devastating monsters. Q241. Adultery punished.

E264. *Ghost drives priest into oven.* Fb "ovn" II 774a.

E265. *Meeting ghost causes misfortune.* Fb "spøgelse" III 519b.

E265.1. *Meeting ghost causes sickness.* (Cf. D2064.)

E265.1.1. *Blow received from a spirit at night; that side paralyzed.* Lithuanian: Balys Ghosts; England: *Baughman.

E265.1.2. *Ghost of father slaps son's face; a cancer grows there.* Canada: Baughman.

E265.1.3. *Ghost strikes man in face, making his mouth crooked.* Ireland: Baughman.

E265.2. *Meeting ghost causes person to go mad.* (Cf. D2065.) Ireland, U.S.: Baughman.

E265.3. *Meeting ghost causes death.* (Cf. E574.) England, U.S.: *Baughman.

E266. *Dead carry off living.* Wimberly 257; Eskimo (Greenland): Rink 468; Africa (Bulu): Krug 109.

E215. The dead rider (Lenore).

E266.1. *Ghost of suicide drags people into stream.* England: *Baughman.

E266.1.1. *Ghost claims a life every seven years by drowning person in river.* England: *Baughman.

E266.2. *Ghost leads people to commit suicide.* U.S.: Baughman.

E267. *Dead tears living to pieces.* Wimberly 264.

E268. *Ghost (revenant) kills by spewing water from his mouth on Hallowe'en.* (Cf. F211.1.1.1.) Irish myth: *Cross.

E271. *Sea-ghosts.* Ghosts which haunt the sea. Lappish: Qvigstad FFC LX 40ff. Nos. 6, 17—22.

E271.1. *Ghost brings disaster on sailors.* U.S., England: *Baughman.

E271.2. *Sea-ghost predicting death.* Norwegian: Solheim Register 17.

E272. *Road-ghosts.* (Cf. E332ff., E582.) Ghosts which haunt roads. Lappish: Qvigstad FFC LX 40 No. 10; England, U.S.: *Baughman; New York: Jones JAFL LVII 248; North Carolina: Brown Collection I 674.

F402.1.1. Spirit leads person astray. F402.1.2. Spirit blocks person's road.

E272.1. *Ghost rides in cart.* Horse can scarcely pull cart, later dies or goes mad. (Cf. D1654.9, E332, E411.0.3.) Ireland, England: Baughman.

E272.2. *Ghost rides behind rider on horse.* (Cf. E215.) England, U.S.: *Baughman.

E272.3. *Ghost frightens people off bridge into stream.* England, Wales: *Baughman.

E272.4. *Ghost chases pedestrian on road.* England: Baughman.

E272.5. *Ghost misleads traveler on road.* See similar actions of fairies, witches, Will-o-the-wisp. (Cf. F402.1.1.) Wales: Baughman.

E273. *Churchyard ghosts.* Fb "spøgelse" III 519b; Lappish: Qvigstad FFC LX 40 No. 8; North Carolina: Brown Collection I 675.

E334.2. Ghost haunts burial spot. H1416. Fear test: spending night by grave.

E273.1. *Ghosts prevent burial of corpse.* Finnish-Swedish: Wessman 6 No. 44.

E274. *Gallows ghost. Ghost haunts gallows.* Lappish: Qvigstad FFC LX 40 No. 9; U.S.: Baughman.

H1415. Fear test: staying under gallows at night.

E275. *Ghost haunts place of great accident or misfortune.* Finnish-Swedish: Wessman 25 No. 225.

E275.1. *Ghost haunts mine after tragedy.* (Cf. E336.) England, U.S.: *Baughman.

E276. *Ghosts haunt tree.* North Carolina: Brown Collection I 679.

E278. *Ghosts haunt spring.* North Carolina: Brown Collection I 678.

E279. *Malevolent revenants—miscellaneous.*

E279.1. *The ghost haunts outside at night in human shape.* Lithuanian: Balys Ghosts.

E279.2. *Ghost disturbs sleeping person.* (Cf. E281.2.) England, U.S.: *Baughman.

E279.3. *Ghost pulls bedclothing from sleeper.* England, Ireland, Scotland, U.S., Wales: *Baughman.

E279.4. *Ghost haunts park, terrifies watchers.* England: Baughman.

E279.5. *Ghost violently brands drunkard with "D".* U.S.: Baughman.

E279.6. *Ghost punishes person who molests him.* England, Ireland, Wales: *Baughman.

E279.7. *Ghosts blow smithy into air.* India: Thompson-Balys.

E280. Ghosts haunt buildings. (Cf. H1411.)

E281. *Ghosts haunt house.* (It is sometimes hard to tell whether haunters are supposed to be ghosts or familiar spirits of some kind.) *Type 326; BP I 22ff.; Scotch: Campbell Tales II 290, 299; Irish: O'Suilleabhain 33, Beal XXI 310; England, Scotland, U.S.: Baughman (F470); North Carolina: Brown Collection I 669, 671; New York: Jones JAFL LVII 248; Swiss: Jegerlehner Oberwallis 311 No. 46, 323 No. 101; Lithuanian: Balys Index No. 3505; Finnish-Swedish: Wessman 25 Nos. 220—222.

E279.2. Ghost disturbs sleeping person. E338.1. Non-malevolent ghost haunts house or castle. F480. House spirits. H1411. Fear test: staying in haunted house.

E281.0.1. *Ghost kills man who stays in haunted house.* U.S.: Baughman.

E281.1. *Hungry ghosts haunt house seeking food.* Africa (Ekoi): Talbot 241.

E281.2. *Ghostly horse enters house and puts hoofs on breast of sleeper.* Tobler 50.

E521. Ghost of horse. F471.1. The Nightmare (Alp). Presses person in dream.

E281.3. *Ghost haunts particular room in house.* England, Scotland, U.S.: *Baughman.

E282. *Ghosts haunt castle.* (Cf. F771.4.5.) Type 1160. — Breton: Sébillot Incidents s.v. "château".

E338.1. Non-malevolent ghost haunts house or castle.

E283. *Ghosts haunt church.* *Type 326. — Breton: Sébillot Incidents s.v. "église", "chapelle"; Lappish: Qvigstad FFC LX 40 No. 7.

E338.2. Non-malevolent ghost haunts church.

E284. *Ghost haunts cloister.* Herbert III 83 (Étienne de Bourbon).

H1412. Fear test: spending night in church.

E285. *Ghost haunts well, prevents drawing water after dark.* England: Baughman.

E290. Malevolent return from the dead—miscellaneous.

E291. *Ghosts protect hidden treasure.*

D2141.0.2. Storm from calling up spirits to help find buried treasure. E371. Return from dead to reveal hidden treasure.

E291.1. *Person burying treasure kills person to supply guardian ghost.* U.S.: Baughman.

E291.2. *Form of treasure-guarding ghost.*

E291.2.1. *Ghost in human form guards treasure.* Canada, England, U.S., Wales: *Baughman.

N576. Ghosts prevent men from raising treasure.

E291.2.2. *Ghost animal guards treasure.* U.S.: *Baughman.

B576.2. Animals guard treasure.

E292. *Ghost causes storms.* England: *Baughman.

E293. *Ghosts frighten people (deliberately).* England, U.S.: *Baughman.

E293.1. *Ghost scares thief, prevents theft.* England: *Baughman.

E293.2. *Ghost scares card players.* U.S., Wales: *Baughman.

E299. *Miscellaneous acts of malevolent ghosts.*

E299.1. *Ghost causes machinery to run unattended.* Canada, England, U.S.: *Baughman.

E299.2. *Ghost prevents removal of box from abbey.* The box takes on miraculous weight. England: Baughman.

D1654. Immovable object.

E299.3. *Ghost upsets farmers' wagons.* England: Baughman.

E299.4. *Ghost breaks windows.* U.S.: Baughman.

E299.5. *Ghost unties boats, setting them adrift.* Canada: Baughman.

E300—E399. Friendly return from the dead.

E300. Friendly return from the dead. Irish: *Cross, Beal XXI 331; Jewish: Neuman.

A581. Culture hero (divinity) returns. B134.5. Dog returns from dead. E366. Return from dead to give counsel. F80. Journey to lower world. V229.1. Saint commands return from dead with supernatural information.

E310. Dead lover's friendly return. (Cf. E210.) Irish myth: *Cross; Icelandic: Boberg; German: Erk-Böhme Deutscher Liederhort No. 201a; N. A. Indian (Pawnee): Grinnell Pawnee Hero Stories (New York, 1889) 191, Dorsey CI LIX 126 No. 34, (Sioux): Dorsey RBAE XI 490, (Zuñi): Cushing 19.

E311. *Return from dead to return and ask back love tokens.* English: Child II 228.

E320. Dead relative's friendly return.

E220. Dead relative's malevolent return.

E321. *Dead husband's friendly return.*

E221. Dead spouse's malevolent return. P210. Husband and wife. T230. Faithlessness in marriage.

E321.1. *Dead husband sends his ring to his wife.* Fb "ring".

E321.2. *Dead husband returns and lives with his wife.* He is invisible to others. (Cf. F378.) N. A. Indian (Teton): Dorsey AA o.s. II (1889) 148.

E321.2.1. *Dead husband returns, helps wife knit socks, piece quilts.* She shows his work as proof. U.S.: Baughman.

E321.2.2. *Dead man visits his wife every night.* India: Thompson-Balys.

E321.3. *Dead husband returns, asks wife to make him coffee.* U.S.: Baughman.

E321.4. *Ghost often visits his widow and her new husband.* England: Baughman.

E321.5. *Ghost appears often to wife and daughter.* U.S.: Baughman.

E322. *Dead wife's friendly return.* (Cf. E221.2.) Irish: O'Suilleabhain 104, Beal XXI 333; India: Thompson-Balys; N. A. Indian (Iroquois): Smith RBAE II 103, (Pawnee): Grinnell Pawnee Hero Stories (New York, 1889) 129, (Osage): Dorsey FM VII 43 No. 36.

E322.1. *Dead wife returns and bears children for husband.* *Jellinek Zs. f. Vksk. XIV 323.

T211. Faithfulness to marriage in death.

E322.2. *Dead wife returns to wake husband.* *Types 403, 450. — New York: Jones JAFL LVII 245.

E322.2.1. *Dead wife returns and asks husband to go with her to spirit world.* India: Thompson-Balys.

E322.3. *Wife in heaven by day, with husband by night.* Hindu: Tawney II 577.

E155. Periodic resuscitation.

E322.4. *Dead wife returns in form of bird.* Scotch: Macdougall and Calder 183; India: Thompson-Balys.

E322.5. *Man carries his dead wife with him.* *Jellinek Zs. f. Vksk. XIV 323f.

E322.6. *Dead wife returns to live with her husband until his death.* U.S.: *Baughman; S. A. Indian (Cashinawa): Métraux BBAE CXLIII (3) 685.

E322.7. *Dead wife returns to another person to have him write a letter to her husband.* England: Baughman.

E322.8. *Return from dead and remarriage to husband.* Chinese: Graham.

E322.9. *Man talks to dead wife in grave.* Eskimo (Greenland): Rink 453.

E323. *Dead mother's friendly return.* *Jellinek Zs f. Vksk. XIV 323f.; *Fb "moder" II 600b, "spøgelse" III 520a; Breton: Sébillot Incidents s.v. "mère"; Lithuanian: Balys Index No. 3527; Jewish: *Neuman.

B313.1. Helpful animal reincarnation of parent. The dead mother appears to the heroine in the form of an animal. D842. Magic object found on mother's grave.

E323.1. *Dead mother returns to see baby.* U.S.: Baughman.

E323.1.1. *Dead mother returns to suckle child.* *Types 403, 450; *BP I 96; *Jellinek Zs. f. Vksk. XIV 323; Finnish-Swedish: Wessman 4 No. 27; India: *Thompson-Balys; Chinese: Eberhard FFC CXX 260; N. A. Indian: *Thompson Tales 350 n. 263, (Luiseño): DuBois UCal VIII 153; Africa (Kweli): Sieber 89; Jamaica: Beckwith MAFLS XVII 266 No. 74, 275 No. 88.

D688. Transformed mother suckles child. S410. Persecuted wife. T611. Suckling of children.

E323.1.2. *Dead mother returns to care for neglected baby.* Tobler 92f.; India: Thompson-Balys; Papua: Ker 131; Eskimo (Greenland): Rasmussen III 67.

E323.2. *Dead mother returns to aid persecuted children.* *Types 510A, 511, 923; Cox 475 n. 4; *BP I 165ff.; *MacCulloch Childhood 108; *Cosquin Contes indiens 504ff.; Italian: Basile Pentamerone I No. 6; Jewish: Neuman; Oceanic (Hawaii, Indonesia, Micronesia, Melanesia): Dixon 89 nn. 97—100; West Indies: Flowers 429; Africa (Cameroons): Mansfield 228.

E221.2.1. Dead wife returns to reprove husband's second wife for abusing her step-children.

E323.2.1. *Dead mother (in animal form) returns to aid persecuted children.* Chinese: Graham.

E323.3. *Dead mother called up from grave to give her son charms.* Icelandic: MacCulloch Eddic 124.

E323.4. *Advice from dead mother.* India: Thompson-Balys; Africa (Hausa): Equilbecq III 291ff.

E323.5. *Mother returns to search for dead child.* England, Ireland: *Baughman.

E323.6. *Mother returns to encourage daughter in great difficulties.* England: Baughman.

E323.7. *Dead mother makes son strong.* Eskimo (Greenland): Rink 158.

E324. *Dead child's friendly return to parents.* Frequently to stop weeping. (Cf. P230.) *BP II 485; *Fb "hånd" I 765a; Dieterich Zs. f. Vksk. XII 147; Irish: O'Suilleabhain 41, Beal XXI 315; English: Child II 238f., III 244f., 247, V 241, Baughman; U.S.: Baughman; Lithuanian: Balys Index No. 3525; Spanish Exempla: Keller; Chinese: Werner 314; N. A. Indian (Pawnee): Grinnell Pawnee Hero Stories (New York, 1889) 145; Eskimo (Greenland): Rink 161.

C762.2. Tabu: too much weeping for the dead. E361. Return from the dead to stop weeping.

E324.1. *Voice of son answers his mother from the grave only when called by his pet name.* India: Thompson-Balys.

E324.2. *Ghost family visits grave of father.* England: Baughman.

E325. *Dead sister's friendly return.* Irish: O'Suilleabhain 98; Eskimo (Greenland): Rasmussen III 178.

E326. *Dead brother's friendly return.* Dieterich Zs. f. Vksk. XII 147; Irish: O'Suilleabhain 102, Beal XXI 332; Eskimo (Greenland): Rink 446.

E361.1. Tear from upper world of mortals falls on departed in lower world. Dead brother sends message of comfort to living.

E327. *Dead father's friendly return.* Cheremis: Sebeok-Nyerges; U.S.: Baughman; Greek: Aeschylus Prometheus Bound 195; Latin: Virgil Aeneid V 724; Chinese: Graham.

E327.1. *Dead father returns to daughter to stop her weeping.* (Cf. E324.) Scotland: Baughman.

E327.2. *Dead father returns to encourage daughter in childbirth.* U.S.: Baughman.

E327.3. *Dead father returns to clear son's name of crime.* England: *Baughman.

E327.4. *Ghost of father returns to rebuke child.* U.S.: Baughman.

E327.5. *Dead father returns in form of bird.* (Cf. E322.4.) India: Thompson-Balys.

E330. **Locations haunted by non-malevolent dead.** (Cf. E270—E284 for locations haunted by malevolent ghosts.).

E332. *Non-malevolent road ghosts.* (Cf. E272, E581, E582.)

E332.1. *Ghost appears at road and stream.* England, U.S., Wales: *Baughman.

E332.2. *Person meets ghost on road.* Canada, England, U.S.: *Baughman.

E332.3. *Ghost on road asks traveler for ride.* (Cf. E581, E582.)

E332.3.1. *Ghost rides on horseback with rider.* (Cf. E215.) U.S.: Baughman.

E332.3.2. *Ghost rides in carriage, disappears suddenly at certain spot.* England, U.S.: *Baughman.

E332.3.3. *Ghost asks for ride in automobile.*

E332.3.3.1. *The Vanishing Hitchhiker.* Ghost of young woman asks for ride in automobile, disappears from closed car without the driver's knowledge, after giving him address to which she wishes to be taken. Driver asks person at address about the rider, finds she has been dead for some time. (Often driver finds that ghost has made similar attempts to return, usually on anniversary of death in automobile accident. Often ghost leaves some item such as a scarf or a traveling bag in car.) **Beardsley and Hankey California Folklore Quarterly I 303ff.; Hawaii, U.S.: *Baughman.

E332.3.3.2. *Deity as ghostly rider.* Hawaii: *Baughman.

E333. *Non-malevolent churchyard ghost.* (Cf. E273.) England, U.S.: *Baughman.

E334. *Non-malevolent ghost haunts scene of former misfortune, crime, or tragedy.* (See E336, E337, E338, E339.) England, U.S.: *Baughman.

E334.1. *Ghost haunts scene of former crime or sin.* England, U.S.: *Baughman.

E334.2. *Ghost haunts burial spot.* (Cf. E411.1.) England, U.S.: *Baughman.

E334.2.1. *Ghost of murdered person haunts burial spot.* (Cf. E413.) Canada, England, Ireland, Scotland, U.S., Wales: *Baughman.

E334.2.2. *Ghost of person killed in accident seen at death or burial spot.* England, U.S., Wales: *Baughman.

E334.2.3. *Ghost of tragic lover haunts scene of tragedy.* (Cf. E337.3.) England, U.S.: *Baughman.

E334.3. *Ghost of person abandoned by faithless lover.* (Cf. E211ff.) England, Wales, U.S.: *Baughman.

E334.4. *Ghost of suicide seen at death spot or near by.* (Cf. E411.1.1, E431.16.) England, Scotland, U.S., Wales: *Baughman.

E334.5. *Ghost of soldier haunts battlefield.* England: *Baughman.
E502. The sleeping army.

E336. *Non-malevolent mine ghosts.* (Cf. E275.1, E334.5.1, F456.)

E336.1. *Helpful mine ghosts.* England, U.S.: *Baughman.

E336.2. *Mine ghosts annoy miners.* England, U.S.: *Baughman.

E337. *Ghost reenacts scene from own lifetime.* U.S.: Baughman.

E337.1. *Sounds of re-enacted actions.* (Cf. E402.)

E337.1.1. *Murder sounds heard just as they must have happened at time of death.* England, U.S., Wales: *Baughman.

E337.1.2. *Sounds of accident re-enact tragedy.* U.S.: *Baughman.

E337.1.3. *Sounds of revelry heard.* England, U.S.: *Baughman.

E337.1.4. *Sounds of driving cattle: horse's hoofs, whip-popping, calling to cattle, rattle of spurs: ghost of slain cowboy.* U.S.: Baughman.

E337.2. *Re-enactment of tragedy seen.* England, U.S.: *Baughman.

E337.3. *Lovers' tragedy re-enacted.* (Cf. E334.5.) England, U.S.: *Baughman.

E338. *Non-malevolent ghost haunts building.* See E281, E402. England, Ireland, Scotland, U.S., Wales: *Baughman.

E338.1. *Non-malevolent ghost haunts house or castle.* England, Scotland, U.S., Wales: *Baughman.

E338.2. *Non-malevolent ghost haunts church.* (Cf. E283.) England: *Baughman.

E338.3. *Non-malevolent ghost haunts cloister.* England: Baughman.

E340. Return from dead to repay obligation.

E341. *The grateful dead.* Irish: *Cross, Beal XXI 313; Icelandic: Boberg.
B350. Grateful animals. B541.2. Fox rescues man from sea. D812.4.1. Magic object received from the dead in lower world. D1658. Grateful objects. H972. Tasks accomplished with help of grateful dead. N800. Helpers. Q47. Kindness to orphans repaid by dead parents. R163. Rescue by grateful dead man. T66.1. Grateful dead man helps hero win princess. T172.2.1. Grateful dead man kills princess' monster husband. V45. Mass said for dead. They arise and say "Amen!" W27. Gratitude.

E341.1. *Dead grateful for having corpse ransomed.* Corpse is being held unburied because of nonpayment of debts. Hero pays debt and secures burial of corpse. — *Types 505—508; **Liljeblad Die Tobiasgeschichte und andere Märchen mit toten Helfern; *BP III 490ff.; Köhler-Bolte I 5, 222ff., 424; **Gerould The Grateful Dead (London,

1908); *Goebel Jüdische Motive in märchenhaftem Erzählungsgut (Gleiwitz, 1932) 38ff.; *Fb "lig" II 412b, "død" I 228a. — Breton: Sébillot Incidents s.v. "mort"; Swiss: Jegerlehner Oberwallis 299 No. 13; Jewish: bin Gorion I 176, 374, V 76, 299, VI 224, 316; India: Thompson-Balys; N. A. Indian (Thompson River): Teit JE VIII 385 No. 93.

Q42.1. Spendthrift knight. Divides his last penny. He is later helped by the grateful person. Q271.1. Debtor deprived of burial. V62.1. Funeral rites forbidden.

E341.1.1. *Dead grateful for having been spared indignity to corpse.* Kind man has given it burial. U.S.: Baughman; Italian Novella: Rotunda; India: Thompson-Balys.

E341.2. *Dead grateful for food.* N. A. Indian (Canadian Dakota): Wallis JAFL XXXVI 48.

E541.1. Food placed out for returning souls of dead.

E341.3. *Dead grateful for prayers.* Tatlock MPh XXII 211f.; Alphabet Nos. 18, 519, 587; Nouvelles de Sens No. 15; Irish: O'Suilleabhain 102, Baughman.

E415.5. Priest cannot rest because he has failed to say certain masses. V50. Prayer.

E341.4. *Dead grateful for clothes (shirt).* Lithuanian: Balys Ghosts.

E341.5. *Grateful priest returns to save gambler from devil.* Irish: O'Suilleabhain 36.

E342. *Dead return to fulfill bargain.* Irish myth: *Cross.

M200. Bargains and promises.

E345. *Dead returns to repair injury.* Fb "spøgelse" III 521b.

E345.1. *Dead returns to replace boundary marks he has removed.* (Cf. E416.) *Fb "skjel" III 264a; Tobler 93; England, Wales, U.S.: *Baughman; New York: Miller NYFQ I 105f.; Irish: Beal XXI 310, O'Suilleabhain 33.

E351. *Dead returns to repay money debt.* Herbert III 96 No. 38; Swiss: Jegerlehner Oberwallis 327 No. 23; cf. French Canadian: Barbeau JAFL XXIX 13; Irish: O'Suilleabhain 53, 97, Beal XXI 319, 331; Scotland: Baughman; India: Thompson-Balys.

E352. *Dead returns to restore stolen goods.* *BP III 235; Tobler 65; Fb "gjenganger" I 443b. — Irish: O'Suilleabhain 98, Beal XXI 331; England: *Baughman; Swiss: Jegerlehner Oberwallis 313 No. 80, 327 No. 23.

E353. *Dead man asks that certain girl be married to him because in life he seduced her.* Lithuanian: Balys Ghosts.

E495. Wedding of the dead.

E360. Other reasons for friendly return from the dead.

E361. *Return from the dead to stop weeping.* *BP II 485; Wimberly 110, 230ff.; Hdwb. d. Märchens I 433a s.v. "Eddamärchen"; Hdwb. d. Abergl. II 831; Legenda Aurea (ed. Grässe) 132; *Fb "hånd" I 765a, "tåre" III 947a, "græde" IV 187b; Dieterich Zs. f. Vksk. XII 147. — Icelandic: *Boberg; English: Child II 234ff., 512., III 513, V 62, 294; Finnish-Swedish: Wessman 2 No. 18; Persian: Carnoy 345.

A189.2. God summoned by weeping. C762.2. Tabu: too much weeping for dead. D516. Transformation through excessive grief. E324. Dead child's friendly return to parents. Frequently to stop weeping. E381. Ghost summoned by weeping.

E361.1. *Tear from upper world of mortals falls on departed in lower world. Dead brother sends message of comfort to living.* N. A. Indian (Thompson River): Alexander N. Am. 137.

E326. Dead brother's friendly return. F81.1. Orpheus. Journey to land of dead to bring back person from the dead.

E361.2. *Return from dead to give consoling message.* Irish myth: *Cross.

E361.3. *Dead son tells mother that no mortal escapes death.* India: Thompson-Balys.

E363. *Ghost returns to aid living.*

H972. Tasks accomplished with aid of grateful dead.

E363.1. *Ghost aids living in emergency.* England, U.S.: *Baughman.

E363.1.1. *Ghost substitutes for bride on her wedding journey.* India: Thompson-Balys.

E363.2. *Ghost returns to protect the living.* England, U.S., Wales: *Baughman; India: Thompson-Balys.

E363.3. *Ghost warns the living.* England, Scotland, U.S.: *Baughman.

E363.4. *Dead reassures living.* England, U.S.: *Baughman.

E363.5. *Dead provide material aid to living.* England, U.S.: *Baughman.

E363.5.1. *Ghost of murdered girl appears and lends jewels needed for a ball in exchange for flowers.* India: Thompson-Balys.

E363.6. *Ghost aids living otherwise.* England, Scotland: *Baughman.

E364. *Dead returns to say farewell.* Lithuanian: Balys Index No. 3502, Balys Ghosts.

E365. *Return from dead to ask forgiveness.* *Fb "tilgive", Feilberg DF X 74f; Irish myth: *Cross; Wales, U.S.: *Baughman; Estonian: Aarne FFC XXV 115 No. 13.

H1244. Forgiveness the reward of successful quest.

E365.1. *Return of the dead to grant forgiveness.* Italian Novella: Rotunda.

E366. *Return from dead to give counsel.* (Cf. V229.1.) *Type 510; Irish: *Cross, O'Suilleabhain 101, Beal XXI 332; Icelandic: *Boberg; Sicilian: Gonzenbach I 10 No. 3; Finnish-Swedish: Wessman 4 no. 29; Jewish: Neuman; India: *Thompson-Balys; Chinese: Eberhard FFC CXX 191; Korean: Zong in-Sob 133ff. — N. A. Indian (Iroquois): Smith RBAE II 104, (Onondaga): Jewitt RBAE XXI 148, 262, (Skidi Pawnee): Dorsey MAFLS VIII 49 No. 10, (Arapaho): Dorsey and Kroeber FM V 49, 259 Nos. 15, 110; Eskimo (Greenland): Rasmussen II 219; S. A. Indian (Brazil): Oberg 110; Africa (Jaunde): Heepe 260, (Fang): Tessman 99f., 173, 193.

E366.1. *Laughing skull advises hero.* (Cf. E545.) *Cosquin Études 351ff.

E366.2. *Hanged man warns youth against visiting sweetheart.* Takes youth's place and receives shot meant for him. Lithuanian: Balys Index No. 3566, Balys Ghosts.

E366.3. *Talking bones of eaten man advise hero.* India: Thompson-Balys.

E367. *Return from dead to preach repentance.* Wesselski Arlotto I 201 No. 29; Irish: Beal XXI 332, O'Suilleabhain 100; Spanish Exempla: Keller; Finnish-Swedish: Wessman 3 No. 23.

E367.1. *Person who has spent two years in hell speaks of importance of religious experience.* Irish myth: *Cross.

E367.2. *Saint returns from dead to give blessing.* Irish myth: *Cross.

E367.3. *Return from dead to prophesy coming of Christ.* (Cf. M363, M364.7.2.) Irish myth: *Cross.

E367.4. *Return from dead to convert to Christianity.* Irish myth: *Cross.
A581.3. Culture hero returns to prove power of saint.

E367.5. *Ghost of woman chides unbeliever.* Eskimo (Greenland): Rasmussen III 291.

E368. *Pupil returns from dead to warn master of futility of his studies.* *Crane Vitry 145f. No. 31; Alphabet Nos. 151, 700; Spanish Exempla: Keller.

E371. *Return from dead to reveal hidden treasure.* (Cf. E276, E291, E419.11.2.) *Fb "spøgelse" III 521b; Tobler 34f.; Loomis White Magic 53; England, Wales, Ireland, Canada, U.S.: *Baughman; Buddhist myth: Malalasekera I 827.
C401.3. Tabu: speaking while searching for treasure.

E371.1. *Return from dead to reveal whereabouts of stolen goods.* Irish myth: Cross.

E371.2. *Return from dead to repeat forgotten epic.* (Cf. A581, J1563.7.) Irish myth: *Cross.

E371.3. *Poet sings day after his death.* (Cf. E342, E546.) Irish myth: *Cross.

E372. *Return from the dead to seek hidden treasure.* U.S.: Baughman.

E373. *Ghosts bestow gifts on living.*
B217.3. Animal languages learned from ghosts (spirits). D812.4. Magic object received from ghost. D1815.0.1. Gift of tongues received from ghosts.

E373.1. *Money received from ghosts as reward for bravery.* A voice says: "I am letting it fall." The man: "Let it." Money falls to the ground. *Chauvin V 78 No. 22 n. 1; Estonian: Aarne FFC XXV 123 No. 46; cf. Finnish-Swedish: Wessman 24 No. 216; Lithuanian: Balys Index No. 3626; India: Thompson-Balys.
E389.2. Ghost summoned to get something from it. F403.1. Spirits give money to mortal. H1411.1. Fear test: staying in haunted house where corpse drops piecemeal down chimney. Dead man's members call out to hero, "Shall we fall, or shall we not?"

E373.2. *Sword received from summoned dead father.* Icelandic: Boberg.

E373.3. *Woman's hand rises from grave and gives man performing vigil letter of salvation.* India: Thompson-Balys.

E373.4. *Dead returns to supply tribe with money demanded by landlord.* Jewish: Neuman.

E374. *Dead returns to life and tells of journey to land of dead.* India: Thompson-Balys.

E374.1. *Return of the dead to keep promise and tell of land of the dead.* Two friends promise each other that the first to die will do so. Italian Novella: Rotunda; Lithuanian: Balys Index No. 3570.

F81. Descent to lower world of dead. M250. Promises connected with death. P310. Friendship.

E375. *Return from dead to prevent flight of thief.* Irish myth: Cross.

K420. Thief loses his goods or is detected.

E376. *Ghost returns to confess misdeed.* England: Baughman.

E376.1. *Saint returns from dead to exonerate cleric.* Irish myth: Cross.

E377. *Return from dead to teach living.* Jewish: Neuman.

E377.1. *Dead poet leaves grave mound to teach poem to herdsman: latter becomes great poet.* Icelandic: Boberg.

E379. *Friendly return from the dead—other motifs.*

E379.1. *Return from dead to rescue from drowning.* Irish myth: Cross.

E379.2. *Anchorite's body rises out of river in favor to disciple.* India: Thompson-Balys.

E379.3. *Return from dead to protect friends.* S. A. Indian (Guaporé River): Lévy-Strauss III 378.

E379.4. *Ghost as confederate of man.* India: Thompson-Balys.

E379.5. *Return from dead to make up enough men to perform ritual.* Jewish: Neuman.

E380. Ghost summoned. *Fb "mane" II 547a; Irish: Beal XXI 310; Scotland: Baughman; Lithuanian: Balys Index No. 3513; Jewish: *Neuman; Icelandic: *Boberg.

E380.1. *Summoning souls punished: in hour of man's death they overwhelm him.* India: Thompson-Balys.

C10. Tabu: profanely calling up spirit (devil, etc.).

E381. *Ghost summoned by weeping.* See all references to E361. *Jellinek Zs. f. Vksk. XIV 323f; India: Thompson-Balys; N. A. Indian: *Thompson Tales 281 n. 41.

A189.2. God summoned by weeping. E58. Resuscitation by weeping (tears).

E382. *Ghost summoned by pouring blood of sacrifices into trench.* Greek: Fox 145.

F404. Means of summoning spirits. V10. Religious sacrifices.

E383. *Ghosts summoned by sacred book.* Irish: O'Suilleabhain 32; Estonian: Aarne FFC XXV 138 No. 107; Finnish: Aarne FFC XXXIII 48 No. 107; Lithuanian: Balys Legends Nos. 597—601; Korean: Zong in-Sob 205.

D1266. Magic book. D1421.1.3. Magic book summons genie.

E384. *Ghost summoned by music.*

F491.5. Raising will-o-the-wisp.

E384.1. *Ghost summoned by beating drum.* England: Baughman.

E384.2. *Ghost raised inadvertently by whistling.* England: Baughman.

E384.3. *Ghost summoned by blast on horn (whistle).* Scottish: Campbell-McKay No. 29; S. A. Indian (Brazil): Oberg 110.

E385. *Vigil of husband at wife's grave calls her forth.* N. A. Indian (California): Gayton and Newman 99.

E410. The unquiet grave.

E385.1. *Husband ignored or discouraged by ghost wife.* N. A. Indian (California): Gayton and Newman 99.

E386. *Other means of summoning ghost.*

E386.1. *Ghost summoned by holy water.* Icelandic: MacCulloch Eddic 312.

E386.2. *Ghost summoned by charm.* Icelandic: Herrmann Saxo II 98; MacCulloch Eddic 298—300, 312.

E386.3. *Ghosts summoned by calling them by name.* Icelandic: *Boberg; England: Baughman.

D2074.2.4.1. Foster-mother summoned by saying her name.

E386.4. *Walking around a grave twelve times backward will raise the ghost.* England: Baughman.

E386.5. *Light remark about what person would do if ghost appeared causes ghost to appear.* (Cf. C10, C13.) England: Baughman.

E387. *Reasons for summoning of ghosts.*

E387.1. *Ghost summoned in order to talk to it.* Icelandic: *Boberg.

E545. The dead speak. M301.14. Summoned dead prophesies.

E387.1.1. *Dead called from their graves to make statement.* *Loomis White Magic 53.

E387.2. *Ghost summoned to get something from it.*

E373. Ghosts bestow gifts on living.

E387.2.1. *Father summoned to get his sword.* Icelandic: Hervararsaga 17—33, 102—13.

E387.3. *Ghost summoned for purposes of necromancy.* Jewish: Neuman.

E389. *Ghost summoned—miscellaneous.*

E389.1. *Ghost must be summoned by king else he appears head downward.* Jewish: Neuman.

E389.2. *Summoned ghost audible and visible only to person who has summoned him.* Jewish: Neuman. Cf. Shakespeare Hamlet ("ghost scene").

E390. Friendly return from the dead—miscellaneous.

E400—E599. Ghosts and revenants — miscellaneous.

E400. Ghosts and revenants — miscellaneous. *Wimberly 451f. s.v. "Ghost", "ghosts"; *Hdwb. d. Abergl. s.v. "Gespenst"; *Bolte Zs. f. Vksk. XX 353; *Feilberg Sjæletro (København, 1914). — Irish: O'Suilleabhain 62, Beal XXI 324; Breton: Sébillot Incidents s.v. "revenant"; Slavic: Máchal 230; Livonian: Loorits FFC LXVI 44f. Nos. 40—77 passim; Estonian: Loorits Grundzüge I 153—170, 506—519; Lappish: Qvigstad FFC LX 41 Nos. 12—16; Finnish-Swedish: Wessman

1ff., Landtman Finlands Svenska Folkdiktning VII pt. 1, 199f. — Melanesian: Dixon 142ff.

C16. Tabu: offending spirits of the dead. C334. Tabu: looking over cemetery walls, lest one see ghosts. C497. Tabu: speaking to the dead. C541.1. Tabu: dead body not to be on ship. C541.2. Head of slain man must not be moved. D1162.2.1. Hand-of-glory. Magic candle made of criminal's hand. D1317.10. Wagon refuses to move because ghost is sitting in it. D1318.5.2. Corpse bleeds when murderer touches it. D1361.7. "Hand of glory" renders light invisible. D1385.1. Earth from saint's grave expels demons. D1500.1.7.1. Powdered skull as remedy. D1500.1.6.1. Corpse's hand as remedy. D1500.1.15.2. Ring made of coffin-hinge as remedy. D1502.2.1. Dead man's tooth as cure for toothache. D1715. Magic power of dying man's words. D1816.2.1. Lost object found by throwing spade at ghost. Where spade sticks one will find the lost object. D1821.8. Possession by spirit of dead person gives second sight. D1836.1. Ghost's strength waxes and wanes with height of fire. D2161.4.2.1. Ghost transfers boil to a post. D2167. Corpse magically saved from corruption. F841.1.5. Ship Naglfar. Made of parings of fingernails of the dead. H1151.10. Task: bringing branch from tree guarded by ghost. J1782. Things thought to be ghosts.

E401. *Voices of dead heard from graveyard.* Irish: O'Suilleabhain 63, Beal XXI 324; Finnish-Swedish: Wessman 2 No. 20.

E401.0.1. *Ghostly voice heard on battlefield.* (Cf. E502, F418.) Irish myth: Cross.

E402. *Mysterious ghostlike noises heard.* (Song, animal cries, footsteps, etc.) (Cf. E337.1, E236.7.) Finnish-Swedish: Wessman 24 Nos. 211—214; New York: Jones JAFL LVII 250; England: *Baughman.

E402.1. *Noises caused by ghost of person.*

E402.1.1. *Vocal sounds of ghost of human being.* (Cf. E545.)

E402.1.1.1. *Ghost calls.* England, U.S.: *Baughman.

E402.1.1.2. *Ghost moans.* (Cf. E547.) Ireland, U.S.: *Baughman.

E402.1.1.3. *Ghost cries and screams.* England, Scotland, U.S.: *Baughman.

E402.1.1.4. *Ghost sings.* (Cf. E546.) England, U.S.: *Baughman.

E402.1.1.5. *Ghost snores.* U.S.: Baughman.

E402.1.1.6. *Ghost sobs.* (Cf. E551.) England: Baughman.

E402.1.2. *Footsteps of invisible ghost heard.* England, Scotland, U.S.: *Baughman.

E402.1.3. *Invisible ghost plays musical instrument.* (Cf. E548.) England, Scotland, U.S.: *Baughman.

E402.1.3.1. *Ghost sounds conch shell.* Hawaii: Beckwith Myth 349.

E402.1.4. *Invisible ghost jingles chains.* (Cf. E231.4.) England, Ireland, U.S.: *Baughman.

E402.1.5. *Invisible ghost makes rapping or knocking noise.* (Cf. F470.) England, U.S.: *Baughman.

E402.1.6. *Crash as of breaking glass, though no glass is found broken.* England, U.S.: *Baughman.

E402.1.7. *Ghost slams door.* Canada: Baughman.

E402.1.8. *Miscellaneous sounds made by ghost of human being.* Canada, England, U.S., Wales: *Baughman.

E402.2. *Sounds made by invisible ghosts of animals.* (Cf. E520.)

E402.2.1. *Crowing of ghost rooster.* England: Baughman.

E402.2.2. *Braying of ghost donkey.* England: Baughman.

E402.2.3. *Hoofbeats of ghost horse.* (Cf. E423.1.3, E521.1, E535.1ff.) U.S.: *Baughman.

E402.3. *Sound made by ghostly object.* (Cf. E530.) U.S.: Baughman.

E402.4. *Sound of ethereal music.* U.S.: *Baughman.

E410. The unquiet grave. (Cf. D2151.1.2.3.) Dead unable to rest in peace. Aside from the references given in the numbers immediately following, see E200—E399 passim. Jewish: *Neuman; Icelandic: *Boberg; India: Thompson-Balys; Eskimo (Greenland): Rasmussen III 48.

E263. Adulteress returns from dead as devastating dragon. E451.1. Ghost paid when crime has been confessed.

E410.1. *Ground trembles or rumbles when ghost rises from grave.* N. A. Indian (California): Gayton and Newman 99.

E410.2. *Ghost shakes off earth when he rises from grave.* N. A. Indian (California): Gayton and Newman 99.

E411. *Dead cannot rest because of sin.* *Herbert III 380 No. 127; Alphabet Nos. 198, 300, 386, 701, 703, 752; Irish: Beal XXI 330, O'Suilleabhain 96; Icelandic: *Boberg; Finnish-Swedish: Wessman 4 Nos. 31—34; Spanish Exempla: Keller; England, Wales: *Baughman; New York: Jones JAFL LVII 242; Africa (Fang): Trilles 134.

E501.3. Wild huntsmen wander because of sin. Q502.1. The Wandering Jew. Q503. Wandering after death as punishment.

E411.0.1. *Hand of sinner sticks out of grave.* *BP II 550.

E411.0.2. *Unquiet dead sinner taken to priest for absolution.* Type 760; Alphabet Nos. 17, 178, 303, 331, 337.

V20. Confession of sins.

E411.0.2.1. *Return from dead to do penance.* Alphabet Nos. 363, 616. — Lithuanian: *Balys Ghosts; U.S.: Baughman.

E451.2. Ghost laid when penance is done.

E411.0.2.2. *Unconfessed person cannot rest in grave.* Spanish Exempla: Keller; England: Baughman.

E411.0.3. *Horse unable to draw evil dead man.* McKay Bealoideas III 141; Icelandic: *Boberg; Estonian: Aarne FFC XXV 113 No. 4; Finnish: Aarne FFC XXXIII 39 No. 4; Finnish-Swedish: cf. Wessman 1 Nos. 7—9; U.S.: *Baughman.

D1317.10. Wagon refuses to move because ghost is sitting in it. D1654.9. Corpse in coffin refuses to be moved in wagon. D2035. Magic heaviness. E272.1. Ghost rides in cart. E499.3. Pot so heavy with ghosts that girl cannot lift it. F610.7. Strong man is so heavy that no horse can carry him all day. F833.1.2. Sword so heavy that only its owner can lift it.

E411.0.3.1. *Dead body cannot be moved from where it lies.* India: Thompson-Balys.

E411.0.4. *Sinner wanders between earth and heaven.* Fb "selvmord" III 183b.

Q503. Wandering after death as punishment.

E411.0.5. *Other dead drive sinner from graveyard.* Fb "lig" II 412b.

E411.0.5.1. *Rich man dragged from grave by demons in hallowed ground and flung into grave in unblessed ground.* Spanish Exempla: Keller.

E411.0.6. *Earth rejects buried body.* (Cf. V62.1.) Loomis White Magic 44; Irish myth: *Cross; Lithuanian: Balys Index No. 3748; Danish: Boberg; Jewish: Neuman.

E411.0.7. *Demons cast evil man from grave leaving only his shroud.* Spanish Exempla: Keller.

E411.0.8. *Saint's body miraculously moves so that it is laid properly north and south, not northeast and southwest.* India: Thompson-Balys.

E411.1. *Murderer cannot rest in grave.* *Type 760; Jellinek Zs. f. Vksk. XIV 323; Fb "gjenganger" I 443b, "lig" II 412b; Tobler 83, 90. — Finnish-Swedish: Wessman 4 No. 32; England, U.S.: *Baughman; North Carolina: Brown Collection I 678; Greek: Aeschylus Eumenides 100.

E501.3.3. Wild huntsman wanders because of parricide. K2320. Death by frightening. Q211. Murder punished.

E411.1.1. *Suicide cannot rest in grave.* (Cf. E334.7, E431.16.) Fb "lys" II 481b, "selvmord" III 183b; Hartland Science 238; Tobler 22. — Finnish-Swedish: Wessman 4 No. 35, 7 No. 53; Lithuanian: Balys Ghosts; England, U.S.: *Baughman.

E501.3.2. Wild huntsman wanders because of suicide. Q211.5. Suicide punished.

E411.1.1.1. *Suicides must walk the earth until time for their natural death.* England: *Baughman.

E411.2. *Adulterous person cannot rest in grave.* *Pauli (ed. Bolte) No. 228; English: Wells 61 (Awntyrs off Arthure at the Terne Wathelyne), Baughman; India: Thompson-Balys.

Q241. Adultery punished.

E411.2.1. *Priest's concubine cannot rest in grave.* Herbert III 380; Wesselski Mönchslatein 163 No. 125.

E501.2.4. Courtisans in wild hunt. Q243. Incontinence punished. V465.1.1. Incontinent monk (priest).

E411.2.2. *The devil's concubine haunts after her death.* Lithuanian: Balys Ghosts.

E411.3. *Perjurer cannot rest in grave.* *Fb "sværge" III 692b, 693a.

Q263. Lying (perjury) punished.

E411.4. *Usurer cannot rest in grave.* Herbert III 83; Alphabet Nos. 704, 784; Spanish Exempla: Keller.

Q273. Usury punished. Q273.2. Usurer refused burial. V441. Charity of usurers ineffective.

E411.5. *Swindler cannot rest in grave.* Fb "gjenganger" I 443b; Spanish: Boggs FFC XC 47 No. 326A*; England: *Baughman.

Q274. Swindler punished.

E411.6. *Person who never said "good morning" cannot rest in grave.* Tobler 64.

E411.7. *Monk who dies without his cowl cannot rest in grave.* Alphabet No. 501.

E411.8. *Pilate appears periodically at Mt. Pilatus and washes his hands.* *Hauffen Zs. f. Vksk. X 435.

E411.9. *Magician who has sold his soul to the devil hires his servant to bury him properly: the coffin bursts.* (Cf. E261.2.1.) Lithuanian: Balys Ghosts.

M211. Man sells soul to devil.

E411.10. *Persons who die violent or accidental deaths cannot rest in grave.* See all references to E334ff., especially E334.5, E411.1, E411.1.1, E413, E414. U.S.: Baughman.

E412. *Person under religious ban cannot rest in grave.*

E501.3.4. Wild huntsman wanders because of unshriven death.

E412.1. *Excommunicated person cannot rest in grave.* Jellinek Zs. f. Vksk. XIV 323.

V84. Excommunication.

E412.2. *Unbaptized person cannot rest in grave.* *Fb "udøbt" III 960a; Tobler 47; Irish: Beal XXI 315, O'Suilleabhain 41; England: Baughman; Lithuanian: Balys Index No. 3557.

E501.2.7. Unbaptized children in wild hunt. E501.5.4. Unbaptized children pursued in wild hunt. E613.0.2. Reincarnation of unbaptized children as bird. F251.3. Unbaptized children as fairies. F360.1. Fairies pursue unbaptized children.

E412.2.1. *Unchristened person cannot rest in grave nor enter heaven.* Scotland: Baughman.

E412.2.2. *Mother of unbaptized child cannot rest in grave.* U.S.: Baughman.

E412.3. *Dead without proper funeral rites cannot rest.* Hdwb. d. Abergl. IX Nachträge 228ff.; Fb "spøgelse" III 521b; Ireland, U.S.: *Baughman; Greek: Fox 145; Finnish-Swedish: Wessman 3 No. 25; Jewish: Neuman; India: Thompson-Balys; Hawaii: Beckwith Myth 123; Eskimo (Greenland): Rasmussen II 342.

V60. Funeral rites.

E412.3.1. *Dead man comes back because he was buried without a cap.* Lithuanian: Balys Ghosts.

E412.3.2. *Naked ghost asks for shirt and promises luck on market for man.* Lithuanian: Balys Ghosts.

E412.3.2.1. *Ghost asks to wash his shirt.* Lithuanian: Balys Ghosts.

E412.3.3. *Dead man asks for shoes (was buried without them).* Lithuanian: Balys Ghosts.

E412.4. *Child cursed by father cannot rest in grave.* Finnish-Swedish: Wessman 2 No. 19; Lithuanian: Balys Index No. 3591.

E412.5. *Ghost of church desecrator cannot rest.* U.S.: Baughman.

E413. *Murdered person cannot rest in grave.* (See all references to E231, E334, E337.1.1, E337.3.) *Fb "spøgelse" III 521a, "gjenganger" I 443b; Jellinek Zs. f. Vksk. XIV 323; Tobler 47; England, Wales, U.S.: *Baughman; North Carolina: Brown Collection I 682; Finnish-Swedish: Wessman 5 Nos. 37—38; Kristensen Danske Sagn V (1897) 102ff., 334ff., (1934) 78ff., 252ff.

E231. Return from dead to reveal murder. E613.0.1. Reincarnation of murdered child as bird.

E414. *Drowned person cannot rest in peace.* (Cf. E334.4.) Fb "spøgelse" III 521b; Kristensen Danske Sagn V (1897) 90ff., 359ff., (1934) 70ff., 265ff.; Icelandic: *Boberg; Finnish-Swedish: Wessman 5 No. 40.

E414.1. *Person otherwise killed by accident cannot rest in grave.* Icelandic: *Boberg; India: Thompson-Balys.

E415. *Dead cannot rest until certain work is finished.* U.S.: Baughman (E354); North Carolina: Brown Collection I 679; New York: Jones JAFL LVII 245; West Indies: Flowers 430.

E415.1. *Ghost returns to hunt lost article.* Finnish-Swedish: Wessman 3 No. 24; U.S.: *Baughman (E328).

E415.1.1. *Ghost unlaid until iron he hid in life is found.* India: Thompson-Balys.

C531. Tabu: touching with iron.

E415.1.2. *Return from dead to uncover secretly buried treasure.* India: Thompson-Balys.

N550. Unearthing hidden treasure.

E415.2. *Dead rich man returns to rebuke his children who have kept the money he promised to the church.* Spanish Exempla: Keller.

E415.3. *Ghost of priest cannot rest because he failed to say certain masses for the dead.* (Cf. E341.3, Q521.6.) Canada, Ireland, U.S.: *Baughman.

E415.4. *Dead cannot rest until money debts are paid.* (See E351.) U.S.: Baughman.

E416. *Man who removes landmarks cannot rest in grave.* (Cf. E345.1.) Kuhn Sagen aus Westfalen I 40f. No. 34, 118 No. 127, 177 No. 187; Sikes British Goblins (London, 1880) 149; Hoffman JAFL II 33; Frahm Am Urquell II 202; Kristensen Danske Sagn V (1897) 404ff.. (1934) 308ff.

Q275. Remover of landmarks punished.

E417. *Dead person speaks from grave.* Madagascar: Sibree FLJ I 202ff., Larrouy RTP IV 305.

E419. *Other restless dead.* England: Baughman.

E419.1. *Soul wanders and demands that a temple be built for him.* Chinese: Werner 314.

V112. Temples.

E419.2. *Dead find no rest since someone daily knocks at grave.* Fb "sjæl" III 214b.

E419.3. *Dead find no rest since grass is pulled on grave.* Fb "sjæl" III 214b.

E419.4. *Dead move when cemetery is moved.* Finnish-Swedish: Wessman 6 No. 42.

E419.5. *Dead arise when one plays organ for first time in church.* Finnish-Swedish: Wessman 8 No. 64.

E419.6. *Lovers buried apart found in one grave each morning.* (Cf. E631.0.1.) Irish myth: *Cross.

T80. Tragic love.

E419.7. *Person with missing bodily member cannot rest in grave.* (Cf. E235.) U.S.: *Baughman.

E419.8. *Ghost returns to enforce its burial wishes or to protest disregard of them.* England, U.S.: *Baughman.

E419.9. *Ghost flits between two graves reputed to contain body.* U.S.: Baughman.

E419.10. *Concern of ghost about belongings of its lifetime.* England, U.S.: *Baughman.

E419.11. *People who bury metal cannot rest in grave.* England, Wales: *Baughman.

E419.12. *Fate of ghosts of persons eaten by tigers.* India: Thompson-Balys.

E420. Appearance of revenant.

E421. *Spectral ghosts.* Irish myth: Cross; Icelandic: Boberg; Breton: Sébillot Incidents s.v. "fantôme"; North Carolina: Brown Collection I 684; New York: Jones JAFL LVII 239.

D1812.5.1.17. Spectre as evil omen.

E421.1. *Invisible ghosts.* *Tobler 92ff.; N. A. Indian (Tahltan): Teit JAFL XXXII 226; England, Wales: *Baughman; North Carolina: Brown Collection I 681; Jewish: Neuman.

D1361. Magic object renders invisible. D1980. Magic invisibility. E482. Land of shades. E501.9. Wild huntsmen invisible. F412.1. Invisible spirit speaks. F585. Phantoms.

E421.1.1. *Ghost visible to one person alone.* Spanish Exempla: Keller; New York: Jones JAFL LVII 243; Eskimo (Greenland): Rasmussen III 64; N. A. Indian (Teton): Dorsey AA o.s. II (1889) 148.

Z300. Unique exceptions.

E421.1.1.0.1. *First-born of a family cannot see ghosts.* England: Baughman.

E421.1.1.1. *Persons born at midnight can see ghosts.* England: *Baughman.

E421.1.1.2. *Only sorcerers can see ghosts.* Eskimo (Greenland): Rasmussen III 181.

E421.1.2. *Ghost visible to horses alone.* *Fb "hest" I 600a, IV 212a; Finnish-Swedish: Wessman 26 No. 227; England, Scotland, U.S.: *Baughman; North Carolina: Brown Collection I 678.

B733. Animals are spirit-sighted. Scent danger.

E421.1.3. *Ghost visible to dogs alone.* England: Baughman; North Carolina: Brown Collection I 681; India: Thompson-Balys.

B134. Truth-telling dog.

E421.1.4. *Ghosts visible only to sheep.* England: Baughman.

E421.1.5. *Ghosts visible only to seals.* Greenland: Baughman.

E421.1.6. *Ghost visible only to wild fowls.* Greenland: Baughman.

E421.2. *Ghosts cast no shadow.* *Fb "skygge" III 347a; *Handwb. d. Abergl. IX Nachträge 138ff; *Penzer IV 239 n. 2; U.S.: Baughman; North Carolina: Brown Collection I 682.

E421.2.1. *Ghost leaves no footprints.* Canada, England: *Baughman.

E421.3. *Luminous ghosts.* (Cf. E530.1, E742.) Tobler 83f.; Swiss: Jegerlehner Oberwallis 334b s.v. "Geister"; New York: Jones JAFL LVII 240.

D1645. Self-luminous objects. E487. Glowing beds of dead. E501.4.1.2. Dogs with fiery tongues in wild hunt. E501.4.1.3. Dogs with fiery eyes in wild hunt. E501.4.2.5. Horse with fiery eyes in wild hunt. E501.7.6. Wild huntsmen luminous. E594. Dead man wanders with torch. F401.2. Luminous spirits. F574. Luminous persons. F491. Will o' the Wisp.

E421.3.1. *Ghost as glowing wheel.* *Fb "hjul" I 626b, "spøgelse" III 521a, "gloende" IV 181b.

E421.3.2. *Ghost as firebrand.* Fb "spøgelse" III 520b.

E421.3.3. *Ghost with glowing face.* *Fb "gloende" I 465b; England: *Baughman.

E421.3.4. *Ghost as fiery bull.* Tobler 81; England, Ireland: *Baughman.

E421.3.5. *Ghosts in glowing wagon.* Fb "karet" II 91b.

E421.3.6. *Ghosts as dogs with glowing tongues and eyes.* (Cf. E423.1.1, E522.) *Fb "hund" I 676a; Swiss: Jegerlehner Oberwallis 334b s.v. "Geister"; England, Wales, U.S.: *Baughman.

E421.3.7. *Flames issue from corpse's mouth.* Penzer II 62; Icelandic: *Boberg.

E421.4. *Ghosts as shadow.* U.S.: *Baughman.

E421.2. Ghosts cast no shadow.

E421.5. *Ghost seen by two or more persons; they corroborate the appearance.* England: *Baughman.

E422. *The living corpse.* Revenant is not a specter but has the attributes of a living person. He wanders about till his "second death", complete disintegration in the grave. (Cf. E261.1.3, E268, E461.) *Naumann Primitive Gemeinschaftskultur (Jena, 1921) 18ff.; *Wimberly 229, 239, 256ff.; *Klare Acta Philologica Scandinavica VIII 1—56; *Gould Scandinavian Studies and Notes IX 167; *Fb "spøgelse" III 519b; Estonian: Loorits Grundzüge I 70—152; Lithuanian: Balys Index No. 3590, Ghosts; Finnish-Swedish: Wessman 21 No. 199; Finnish: Holmberg Finno-Ugric 3f.; Irish: *Cross, Baughman; North Carolina: Brown Collection I 682; New York: Jones JAFL LVII 239f., 243; West Indies: Flowers 430; Africa: Werner African 180f., (Ekoi): Talbot 7 (dies a second time and becomes more dead).

E722.3.2. Soul wanders till corpse decays.

E422.0.1. *Hanged man thirsty; demands water to drink.* Irish myth: *Cross.

E422.1. *Body of living corpse.*

E422.1.1. *Headless revenant.* *Fb "hoved" I 655b, "hovedløs" IV 223a; Irish myth: Cross; Icelandic: Boberg; Swiss: Jegerlehner Oberwallis 300 No. 6, 301 No. 18, 311 No. 46; India: *Thompson-Balys; England, U.S.: *Baughman; North Carolina: Brown Collection I 680, 683, 693.

B15.1.1. Headless animals. E261.1.3. Hero attacked by revenant with half a head. E501.4.2.7. Headless horse in wild hunt. E501.7.1. Wild huntsmen headless. E521.1. Headless ghost of horse. E526.0.1. Headless ghost of hog. F401.4.1. Spirit has half head. F511.0.1. Headless person.

E422.1.1.1. *Two-headed ghost.* Swiss: Jegerlehner Oberwallis 334b s.v. "Geister"; England, Scotland, U.S.: Baughman.

E422.1.1.2. *Revenant with ball of fire in place of head.* England: Baughman.

E422.1.1.3. *Actions of headless revenant.*

E422.1.1.3.1. *Headless ghost rides horse.* England, U.S.: *Baughman.

E422.1.1.4. *Headless ghost carries head under arm.* (Cf. F511.0.4.) England, U.S.: *Baughman.

E422.1.2. *Armless revenant.* Wimberly 235.

E422.1.3. *Revenant with ice-cold hands.* *Fb "hånd" I 765b; Kristensen Danske Sagn V (1897) 554ff., (1934) 400ff.; England, U.S.: *Baughman.

E578.1. Revenants want to warm themselves. E578.2. Man warms dead man: he revives.

E422.1.4. *Revenant with cold lips.* Wimberly 235.

E422.1.5. *Revenant with bad breath.* *Wimberly 233.

E422.1.6. *Revenant with chicken feet.* Gaster Germania XXV (1880) 290ff.

F231.2.1. Fairies with bird feet. F451.2.2.2. Dwarf with bird feet. G216.1. Witch with goose feet.

E422.1.6.1. *Ghost with feet twisted backward.* India: *Thompson-Balys.

F451.2.2.1. Dwarf's feet twisted backward.

E422.1.6.2. *Revenant with thin legs.* Irish: O'Suilleabhain 96.

E422.1.7. *Revenant with chip of resin between teeth.* Estonian: Aarne FFC XXV 116 No. 18; Finnish: Aarne FFC XXXIII 40 No. 18.

E422.1.8. *Revenant with peculiar nails.* Icelandic: Boberg.

F531.1.6.1. Giant with nails like claws.

E422.1.9. *Living corpse returns every night, shows gradual wasting away of body.* U.S.: Baughman.

E422.1.10. *Dismembered corpse.*

E422.1.10.1. *Dismembered corpse reassembles.* (Cf. E31.) U.S.: *Baughman.

E422.1.11. *Revenant as part of body.*

E422.1.11.1. *Revenant as an eye.* U.S.: Baughman.

E422.1.11.2. *Revenant as face or head.* England, U.S.: *Baughman.

E422.1.11.3. *Ghost as hand or hands.* England, U.S.: *Baughman.

E422.1.11.4. *Revenant as skeleton.* U.S.: Baughman.

E422.1.11.5. *Revenant as blood.* U.S.: *Baughman.

E422.1.11.5.1. *Ineradicable bloodstain after bloody tragedy.* England, Ireland, U.S.: *Baughman. Danish: Kristensen Danske Sagn IV 267ff.

E422.2. *Color of revenant.* (Cf. F527.)

E422.2.1. *Revenant red.* Fb. "rød" III 117a.

E422.2.2. *Revenant green.* Wimberly 240.

F233.1. Green fairy. F440.1. Green vegetation spirit.

E422.2.3. *Revenant gray.* Tobler 64, 89.

E422.2.4. *Revenant black.* Irish: Cross, O'Suilleabhain 63, Beal XXI 324.

E422.3. *Size of revenant.*

E422.3.1. *Revenant as small man.* Wimberly 244; Tobler 64, 89; England: *Baughman.

E422.3.2. *Revenant as a very large man (giant).* (Cf. F531.) Scotland, Canada, U.S.: *Baughman; Cheremis: Sebeok-Nyerges.

E422.4. *Dress of revenant.*
E501.8. Clothing of wild huntsmen.

E422.4.1. *Revenant with hat of birch.* Wimberly 243. Note: in the motifs immediately following, it is frequently impossible to tell whether the spectral ghost (E421) or the living corpse (E422) is thought of.

E422.4.2. *Ghost with bonnet pulled down over her face.* North Carolina: Brown Collection I 681.

E422.4.3. *Ghost in white.* North Carolina: Brown Collection I 681f.
E425.1.1. Revenant as lady in white.

E422.4.4. *Revenant in female dress.* England, Scotland, U.S., Wales: *Baughman.

E422.4.5. *Revenant in male dress.* England, U.S.: *Baughman.

E422.4.6. *Revenant in red cap.* North Carolina: Brown Collection I 670.

E423. *Revenant in animal form.* *Rosén Om Själavandringstro; *Fb "spøgelse" III 521a; Breton: Sébillot Incidents s.v. "mort"; Scotland, England, U.S.: *Baughman; New York: Jones JAFL LVII 243.
E501.4. Animals follow wild huntsman. E501.5.5. Animals pursued in wild hunt. E610. Reincarnation as animal. E730. Soul in animal form. F167.1. Animals in otherworld. F401.3. Spirit in animal form.

E423.1. *Revenant as domestic animal.*

E423.1.1. *Revenant as dog.* (Cf. E421.3.6.) *Rosén Om Själavandringstro 14; *Fb "spøgelse" III 521a, "hund" I 675b, 676a, "præst" II 886a; Tobler 49, 54, 68; Swiss: Jegerlehner Oberwallis 313 No. 92; German: Grimm No. 4; England, Scotland, Wales, U.S.: *Baughman; New York: Jones JAFL LVII 243; North Carolina: Brown Collection I 675, 684.
E521.2. Ghost of dog.

E423.1.1.1. *Color of ghostly dog.* Canada, England, U.S., Wales: *Baughman.

E423.1.1.2. *Features of ghostly dog.*

E423.1.1.2.1. *Headless ghostly dog.* (Cf. B15.1.1, E422.1.1.) England, U.S.: *Baughman.

E423.1.1.2.2. *Human-headed ghostly dog.* (Cf. B25.) England: *Baughman.

E423.1.2. *Revenant as cat.* Type 326; Rosén Om Själavandringstro 16; *Fb "kat" II 107b; Tobler 42, 47, 56; England, U.S.: *Baughman.
B292.6. Black cat as servant of giant. G225.3. Cat as servant of witch.

E423.1.3. *Revenant as horse.* (Cf. F401.3.1.) Rosén Om Själavandringstro 16; *Handwb. d. Abergl. VI 1614f., IX Nachträge 168; New York: Jones JAFL LVII 243; India: Thompson-Balys.
E521.1. Ghost of horse.

E423.1.3.1. *Revenant as three-legged horse.* Swiss: Jegerlehner Oberwallis 313 No. 81, 326 No. 18.
E521.1.2. Three-legged ghost of horse.

E423.1.3.2. *Revenant as mare.* Herbert III 380.

E423.1.3.3. *Revenant as headless horse.* (See E422.1.1, E535.1.) England, Wales: *Baughman.

E423.1.3.4. *Revenant as white horse.* England, U.S.: *Baughman.

E423.1.3.5. *Actions of ghostly horse.* England: *Baughman.

E423.1.4. *Revenant as ass.* Tobler 89; England, U.S.: *Baughman.

E423.1.5. *Revenant as swine.* Swiss: Jegerlehner Oberwallis 316 No. 134f.; England, Ireland, U.S.: *Baughman; Irish: Beal XXI 310, O'Suilleabhain 31.

E501.4.3. Boar (sow) in wild hunt. E521.5. Ghost of hog. F460.1.1.1. Mountain-man in shape of hog. F480.1. House-spirit in form of a sow.

E423.1.6. *Revenant as lamb.* Tobler 56; England: Baughman.

E423.1.7. *Revenant as ram.* Tobler 51.

E423.1.8. *Revenant as cow.* Tobler 50. — Swiss: Jegerlehner Oberwallis 334b s.v. "Geister"; England, U.S.: *Baughman.

E423.1.8.1. *Revenant as calf.* (Cf. E521.4.) Cheremis: Sebeok-Nyerges.

E423.1.9. *Revenant as goat. England.* U.S.: *Baughman; New York: Jones JAFL LVII 243.

E423.2. *Revenant as wild animal.*

E423.2.1. *Revenant as bear.* (Cf. E522.2.) Tobler 56.

E552. Ghost in form of bear sneezes.

E423.2.2. *Revenant as rabbit (hare).* *Fb "hare" I 556a; Rosén Om Själavandringstro 15; Tobler 52; England: *Baughman; Irish: O'Suilleabhain 56.

E423.2.3. *Revenant as fox.* Fb "ræv" III 113a; Swiss: Jegerlehner Oberwallis 310 No. 24.

E522.1. Ghost of fox.

E423.2.4. *Revenant as hedgehog.* Hartland Science 247.

E423.2.5. *Revenant as seal.* Icelandic: *Boberg.

E423.2.6. *Revenant as deer.* U.S.: *Baughman.

E423.2.7. *Revenant as wolf.* U.S.: *Baughman.

E423.2.8. *Revenant as rat.* England, Ireland: *Baughman.

E423.2.9. *Revenant as "man-monkey".* England: *Baughman.

E423.2.10. *Revenant in tiger form.* Chinese: Graham.

E423.2.11. *Revenant as mouse.* Africa (Wachaga): Gutman 35.

E423.2.12. *Revenant as squirrel.* Africa (Wachaga): Gutman 35.

E423.3. *Revenant as bird.* Tobler 34; Krappe Balor 96—97; Irish: Cross, Beal XXI 332, O'Suilleabhain 99; England, U.S.: *Baughman; New York: Jones JAFL LVII 243.

A132.6.2. Goddess in form of bird. E732. Soul in form of bird. F234.1.15. Fairy in form of bird. V231.1. Angel in bird shape.

E423.3.1. *Revenant as dove.* Tobler 30; Krappe Balor 96—97; Irish myth: Cross; U.S.: Baughman.

E423.3.2. *Revenant as swan.* Tobler 34; England: Baughman.

E423.3.3. *Revenant as partridge.* Tobler 32.

E423.3.4. *Revenant as raven.* Swiss: Jegerlehner Obervallis 329 No. 56; Danish: Kristensen Danske Sagn II (1893) 127ff., 132, (1928) 91ff.; Krappe Balor 96—97.

E423.3.5. *Revenant as owl.* Tobler 31f.; Krappe Balor 96—97; U.S.: *Baughman; India: Thompson-Balys.

E423.3.6. *Revenant as hen.* Sometimes with chickens. Tobler 33.

E423.3.7. *Revenant as goose.* Type 403; Tobler 34; England: *Baughman.

E423.3.8. *Revenant as crow.* Krappe Balor 97.

E423.3.9. *Revenant as sea-gull.* Krappe Balor 97.

E423.3.10. *Revenant as duck.* Type 403; England: Baughman.

E423.3.11. *Revenant as bean-goose.* Wales: *Baughman.

E423.4. *Revenant as frog.* Tobler 86.

E423.5. *Revenant as snake (serpent).* Tobler 22, 55f. — Swiss: Jegerlehner Oberwallis 334b s.v. "Geister"; New York: Jones JAFL LVII 243.

E423.6. *Revenant as centaur.* U.S.: Baughman.

E423.7. *Revenant as fly.* England: Baughman.

E423.8. *Revenant as spider.* England: Baughman.

E423.9. *Revenant as eel.* Irish: O'Suilleabhain 93.

E424. *Revenant as dwarf.* *Gould They who await the Second Death (Scandinavian Studies and Notes IX 167); Tobler 65.

E439.2. Dwarfs magically keep ghosts from rising. F451. Dwarf as underground spirit.

E425. *Revenant in human form.*

E425.1. *Revenant as woman.*

E425.1.1. *Revenant as lady in white.* *M. Waehler Die Weisse Frau (Erfurt, 1931); Fb "jomfru" II 43a; Tobler 68, 90; New York: Jones JAFL LVII 239; England, Scotland, Wales, U.S.: *Baughman.

E338. Female ghost haunts house. E422.4. Dress of revenant. E422.4.3. Ghost in white. N572.1. "White woman" as guardian of treasure.

E425.1.2. *Revenant as naked woman.* Pauli (ed. Bolte) No. 228; Tobler 67.

E425.1.3. *Revenant as seductive woman.* Swiss: Jegerlehner Oberwallis 303 No. 24.

E425.1.4. *Revenant as woman carrying baby.* Tobler 90; U.S.: Baughman.

E425.1.5. *Revenant as woman riding hog.* Walz MLN XVI 130ff.

E425.1.6. *Revenant as horrible female figure.* Covered with snakes and toads. English: Wells 61 (The Awntyrs off Arthure at the Terne Wathelyne).

E425.1.7. *Revenant as woman with seal's head.* Icelandic: *Boberg.

E425.2. *Revenant as man.* Irish: O'Suilleabhain 101, 103, Beal XXI 332f.

E425.2.1. *Revenant as old man.* German: Grimm No. 4; Swiss: Jegerlehner Oberwallis 334b s.v. "Geister".

E425.2.2. *Revenant as man with horse's head.* England: Baughman.

E425.2.3. *Revenant as priest or parson.* (Cf. E338.5, E417.) England, Ireland, U.S.: *Baughman.

E425.2.4. *Revenant as American Indian.* U.S.: *Baughman.

E425.2.5. *Revenant as piper.* Irish: O'Suilleabhain 62.

E425.3. *Revenant as child.* Tobler 66f.; England: *Baughman; Irish: O'Suilleabhain 100, Beal XXI 332.

E426. *Revenant as object.*

E426.1. *Ghost in shape of a bag.* Lithuanian: Balys Ghosts.

E426.2. *Revenant as a rolling cask.* Cheremis: Sebeok-Nyerges.

E430. Defense against ghosts and the dead. Frazer The Fear of the Dead (London, 1933—36); Swiss: Jegerlehner Oberwallis 335b s.v. "Geister"; Irish myth: *Cross; Icelandic: MacCulloch Eddic 309; New York: Jones JAFL LVII 251.

D2176. Exorcising by magic. F380. Defeating or ridding oneself of fairies. F405. Means of combatting spirits. S139.2.2. Other indignities to corpse.

E431. *Precautions at funeral against revenant.*

V60. Funeral rites.

E431.0.1. *Test for presence of demons in corpses.* Irish myth: Cross.

E431.1. *Burial service read into hat to prevent dead walking.* *Fb "hat" I 563b, "gjenganger" I 444a.

E431.2. *Water thrown on corpse to prevent return.* *Fb "død" I 228a, "gjenganger" I 444a.

E431.3. *Mould thrown on corpse to prevent return.* Fb "muld" II 619a.

D1278.1. Magic churchyard mould. E446.2. Ghost laid by burning body. E501.17.7.1. Wild huntsman released from wandering by mould from Christ's grave.

E431.4. *Coffin carried through hole in wall to prevent return of dead.* Fb "gjenganger" I 444a; Frazer JAI XV 70; England, Scotland: *Baughman; Indonesia: Kruyt Het Animisme 264ff., Elshout De Kenja-Dejaks uit het Apo-Kajanggebied (Den Haag, 1926) 62.

E431.5. *Limbs of dead fettered to prevent return.* Von Trauwitz-Hellweg Urmensch und Totenglaube. 134ff.; Meyer Germanen 102; Wimberly 254; England: *Baughman; Africa: Frobenius Atlantis I 15f.

E431.6. *Turf laid on breast of dead to prevent return.* Wimberly 256.

E431.7. *Beheaded man's head laid at feet to prevent return.* *Fb "hoved" I 655b; England: Baughman; New York: Jones JAFL LVII 252.

E446.3. Ghost laid by decapitating body.

E431.7.1. *Beheaded man's head laid at back to prevent return.* *Fb "hoved" I 655b; Icelandic: *Boberg.

E431.7.2. *Decapitating in order to prevent return.* Icelandic: *Boberg.

E431.7.2.1. *Head of beheaded man separated from body (by walking between them) to prevent return.* (Cf. E721.1.2.2.) Irish myth: *Cross.

E431.8. *Dog buried alive to prevent ghosts from walking.* *Fb "hund" I 677a.

E431.9. *Ashes of dead thrown on water to prevent return.* Levy-Bruhl L'âme primitive 332ff.; Icelandic: *Boberg; Finno-Ugric: Holmberg Finno-Ugric 386, Mansikka Religion der Ostslaven (Helsinki, 1922) 220, 231; Jamaica: *Beckwith MAFLS XVII 266 No. 72.

G655. Ogre's ashes cast on stream cause rapids to stop. Q414.3. Punishment: burning and scattering ashes.

E431.9.1. *Head of corpse thrown on water to prevent return.* Icelandic: Boberg.

E446.3. Ghost laid by decapitating body.

E431.9.2. *Corpses thrown in water to prevent return.* Icelandic: *Boberg.

E431.10. *Corpse buried under stone so that sun will not shine on him again.* Swiss: Jegerlehner Oberwallis 305 No. 1.

E431.10.1. *Corpse buried under stones.* Icelandic: *Boberg.

E431.11. *Coin placed in mouth of dead to prevent return.* *Fb "død" I 228a; Wesselski Archiv Orientální I 77; India: Thompson-Balys.

A672.1. Ferryman on river in lower world. A672.1.1. Charon exacts fee. E237. Return from dead to demand money stolen from corpse. E489.3. Forgetting Charon's fee. K274. Grave robbing to secure obols in mouth of dead. V64.1. Shipwrecked each get a piece of the chief's gold ring in order to have gold with them in death.

E431.12. *Pins stuck in soles of dead man's feet to prevent return.* Fb "død" I 228a.

E431.13. *Corpse burned to prevent return.* Icelandic: *Boberg.

E446.2. Ghost laid by burning body. V61.2. Dead burned on pyre.

E431.14. *Tall wall around grave to prevent return.* Icelandic: Eyrbyggja saga ch. XXXIV 14 in ASB VI, Boberg.

E431.15. *People touch corpse before burial to avoid seeing ghost of dead person after burial.* England: *Baughman.

E431.16. *Burial of suicide to prevent walking.* (Cf. E334.7, E411.1.1, E441.)

E431.16.1. *Suicide buried head (or face) downward.* (If corpse moves it only goes deeper into ground.) England: *Baughman.

E431.16.2. *Suicide buried with stake through heart (body).* (Cf. E442.) England, U.S.: *Baughman.

E431.16.3. *Suicide buried at crossroads.* (Cf. E434.4.) England: Baughman.

E431.17. *Criminals buried at crossroads to prevent walking.* (Cf. E434.4.) Wales: Baughman.

E431.18. *Body cut up and buried in vessels, buried in bag.* England: Baughman.

E431.19. *Burial of corpse at midnight to prevent walking.* England: Baughman.

E431.20. *Coffin with iron band made to keep corpse from returning as tiger.* Chinese: Graham.

E432. *Ghost deceived.*

E432.1. *Haunting ghost deceived so that he cannot find road to return.* Jellinek Zs. f. Vksk. XIV 323.

K500. Escape from death or danger by deception.

E432.2. *Dead man visiting wife deceived by wife's absurd actions — "no more absurd than ghost visiting wife".* (Cf. E321.2, E474.) Lithuanian: Balys Index No. 3547; Balys Ghosts.

J1530. One absurdity rebukes another.

E432.3. *Woman drying hair scares soul returning from the dead.* Eskimo (Greenland): Rink 452.

E433. *Ghosts placated by sacrifices.* India: Thompson-Balys; Africa (Ekoi): Talbot 7, 9.

E541.1. Food placed out for returning souls of dead. V10. Religious sacrifices.

E433.1. *Mould put on table for the dead.* Fb "muld" II 619a.

E433.2. *Possessions buried with dead.* India: Thompson-Balys.

E433.3. *Animals sacrificed so that dead have food on way to other world.* India: Thompson-Balys.

E433.4. *Ghosts pleased by human sacrifices.* India: Thompson-Balys.

E433.4.1. *Ghosts killed by sacrifice of buffaloes.* India: Thompson-Balys.

E434. *Magic protection against revenants.* Irish myth: Cross.

D1385. Magic object protects from evil spirits. D1385.4. Silver bullet as protection against ghosts. D1385.5.1. Copper as defense against ghosts. D1385.8. Saint's bachall keeps off ghosts. D1381.11.1. Magic circle protects from ghosts. E442. Ghost laid by piercing grave with stake.

E434.1. *Hiding from ghosts under church bell.* *Fb "kirkeklokke" II 131a, "gjenganger" I 443b.

D1213. Magic bell. G303.16.12. Ringing of church bell causes devil to lose his power. G304.2.4.1. Trolls cannot endure church-bells. V115. Church bells.

E434.2. *Hiding from ghosts in pulpit.* Fb "predikestol" II 882b.

V117. Pulpits.

E434.3. *Ghosts cannot cross rapid stream.* *Fb "gjenganger" I 443b; U.S.: Baughman.

E915. Magic river. G273.4. Witch powerless to cross stream.

E434.4. *Ghosts cannot pass crossroads.* (Cf. E431.16, E431.17.) Fb "korsvej" II 277a.

D1786. Magic power at crossroads. G273.5. Witches powerless at crossroads.

E434.5. *Steel as protection against revenants.* Fb "stål" III 647a.

D1252.1. Magic steel. G272.1. Steel powerful against witches.

E434.6. *Keys as protection against revenants.* (Cf. D1176.) Wimberly 255.

E434.7. *Knives as protection against revenants.* (Cf. D1173.) Wimberly 255.

E434.8. *Ghost cannot pass cross or prayerbook.* (Cf. D1266.) Swiss: Jegerlehner Oberwallis 335b s.v. "Geister"; Icelandic: Boberg.

E434.8.1. *Ghost cannot harm person wearing a cross.* England: Baughman.

E434.9. *Candle light protection against ghost.* Icelandic: Bárdar saga Snaefellsáss, ed. Vigfússon 1860, 42—43, Boberg.

E434.10. *Ghost cannot cross new door sill.* U.S.: Baughman.

E436. *Ghost detected.*

E436.1. *Ghost detected by strewing ashes.* Their footprints remain in the ashes. Fb "spor" III 500a; Gaster Germania XXV (1880) 290ff.; Dh III 153; Hdwb. d. Abergl. III 297; Güntert Kalypso 75; Kruyt Het Animisme 398; Mansikka Religion der Ostslaven (Helsinki, 1922) 181, 184.

F381.2. Fairy leaves when mortal strews peas in his path. F405.6. Grain scattered as a means of dispersing spirits. J1146. Detection by strewing ashes.

E436.2. *Cats crossing one's path sign of ghosts.* North Carolina: Brown Collection I 677.

E436.3. *Bats flying in house sign of ghosts.* North Carolina: Brown Collection I 677.

E437. *Revenants banished.* Icelandic: *Boberg.

E437.1. *Revenants banished to glaciers and uninhabited places.* Swiss: Jegerlehner Oberwallis 296 No. 27.

E437.2. *Ghost laid in body of water.* England, Ireland, Wales: *Baughman.

E437.3. *Ghost driven into body of dead crow, buried under path.* England: Baughman.

E437.4. *Ghost laid under stone.* England: *Baughman.

E437.5. *Ghost laid under tree.* England: Baughman.

E437.6. *Ghost laid and confined inside building.* England, U.S.: *Baughman.

E437.7. *Ghost laid and confined in sheepfold.* England: Baughman.

E439. *Other protection against revenants.*

E439.1. *Revenant forced away by shooting.* Swiss: Jegerlehner Oberwallis 335b s.v. "Geister"; Africa (Cameroons): Mansfield 227.

F405.2. Spirits driven off by knife-thrusts and pistol shots.

E439.2. *Dwarfs magically keep ghosts from rising.* Icelandic: Göngu Hrolfssaga 337.

E439.3. *Dog saves man from malevolent living corpse.* Dog killed, man safe. (Cf. B524.1.1.) Lithuanian: Balys Legends Nos. 698f.

E439.4. *Seeds of poppy poured into revenant's mouth.* Lithuanian: Balys Ghosts.

E439.5. *Revenant forced away by fire.* Icelandic: *Boberg.

E439.6. *Ghosts cannot come near spayed bitch.* England: Baughman.

E439.7. *Ghost will not approach a light left burning.* England, U.S.: *Baughman.

E439.8. *Ghost will vanish if seer walks around it nine times.* (Cf. D1791, D1273.1.5.) England: Baughman.

E439.9. *Ghost will not return if door is removed and hung backwards.* (Cf. D1783.) England: Baughman.

E439.10. *Ghost will not come near person who anoints self with new honey.* U.S.: Baughman.

E440. Walking ghost "laid". *Jellinek Zs. f. Vksk. XIV 324; *v. Negelein ibid. XIV 20ff.; Irish: Beal XXI 332; Icelandic: *Boberg; Spanish: Boggs FFC XC 53 No. 400A*; Estonian: Aarne FFC XXV 114 No. 6.

E251. Vampire. E501.17.7. Wild huntsman released from wandering.

E441. *Ghost laid by reburial.* Icelandic: Boberg; Estonian: Aarne FFC XXV 115 No. 12; Finnish: Aarne FFC XXXIII 39 No. 12; Lithuanian: Balys Index No. 3590; U.S.: Baughman. Cf. Gaster Exempla 222 No. 175.

E441.1. *Ghost laid when leg is buried.* Fb "løse" II 517a.

E441.2. *Ghost laid by placing stones in throat of the corpse.* Cheremis: Sebeok-Nyerges.

E441.3. *Corpse exhumed and heart cremated to lay ghost.* Africa (Bena Makuni): Torrend Specimens of Bantu Folklore 72.

E442. *Ghost laid by piercing grave (corpse) with stake.* (Cf. D712.10, E431.16.2.) *Fb "pæl" II 904ab, "jærn" II 61a; England, U.S.: *Baughman; Icelandic: *Boberg; Irish myth: Cross; Lithuanian: Balys Index No. 3546B, Legends No. 698, Ghosts; S. A. Indian (Cashinawa): Métraux BBAE CXLIII (3) 686.

F405.9. Spirit overcome by driving stake through body it inhabits. S139.2.2.10. Ash stakes thrust through bodies of slain warriors.

E442.1. *Hunting woman beaten with sticks of rowan-tree and ankles of corpse tied with branches of same tree.* Lithuanian: Balys Ghosts.

E442.2. *Ghost laid by burial outside village on far side of stream, with four iron nails driven into the corners of the grave.* India: Thompson-Balys.

E443. *Ghost exorcized and laid.* *Fb "bande" IV 24a, "Jesus" II 41a; Tobler 65; Estonian: Aarne FFC XXV 115 No. 11; Finnish: Aarne FFC XXXIII 39 No. 11; Finnish-Swedish: Wessman 7 No. 51, 27 No. 243; New York: Jones JAFL LVII 251; West Indies: Flowers 430.

D1379.2. Magic writings (runes) cause dead to speak. D2176. Exorcising by magic. E164. Dead body caused to speak by setting door ajar.

E443.0.1. *Laying ghost causes great storm.* (Cf. D2141.) England: *Baughman.

E443.0.2. *Protection during ghost-laying ceremony.* England: Baughman.

E443.1. *Ghost laid by blessing grave.* Estonian: Aarne FFC XXV 115 No. 10.

E443.2. *Ghost laid by prayer.* Fb "løse" II 517b; Icelandic: Boberg; Swiss: Jegerlehner Oberwallis 336 s.v. "Geister, Erlösung".

D1766.1. Magic results produced by prayer. F420.5.3.5. Nix flees from benediction in church.

E443.2.1. *Ghost laid by saying masses.* Irish: O'Suilleabhain 95, 99, Beal XXI 330, 332; Scotch: Macdougall and Calder 319; English: Wells 61 (Awntyrs off Arthure at the Terne Wathelyne); U.S.: Baughman (E341.3.2.).

E443.2.1.1. *The dead man: "Sell my golden teeth and pay for a mass for my soul."* Lithuanian: Balys Ghosts.

E443.2.2. *Ghost laid by formulistic prayer.* England: *Baughman.

E443.2.3. *Ghost laid by confessor to priest.* Irish: O'Suilleabhain 99.

E443.2.4. *Ghost laid by priest (minister).* England, Ireland, U.S.: *Baughman.

E443.2.4.1. *Ghost laid by group of ministers.* By prayer and services, usually with "bell, book, and candle" or some modification of the procedure. England, U.S.: *Baughman.

E443.3. *Ghosts exorcized by name.* Fb "navn" II 675b.

C432.1. Tabu: uttering name of supernatural creature.

E443.4. *Ghost laid by raising a cross.* Icelandic: Boberg; Swiss: Jegerlehner Oberwallis 336 s.v. "Geister, Erlösung".

V86. Sign of the Cross.

E443.5. *Ghost laid by adjuring it to leave "in the name of God."* Wales: Baughman.

E443.6. *Ghost laid by baptizing children in its presence.* England: *Baughman.

E443.7. *Ghost laid by fasting.* England: Baughman.

E443.8. *Ghost laid by Bible.* England, U.S.: *Baughman.

E443.9. *Ghost laid by consecrated water.* Icelandic: *Boberg.

E444. *Ghost laid by talisman.* Breton: Sébillot Incidents s.v. "fantôme"; Eskimo (Mackenzie Area): Jenness 62.

D1274. Amulet. D1385. Magic object protects from evil spirit.

E445. *Ghost laid by barring off.*

E445.1. *Ghost comes through certain crevice: when this is barred she never returns.* Tobler 92.

E446. *Ghost killed and thus finally laid.* N. A. Indian (Sioux): Dorsey RBAE XI 491f., (Fox): Jones PAES I 101 No. 7, (Osage): Dorsey FM VII 26 No. 21; Eskimo: Kroeber JAFL XII 181, (Greenland): Holm 55, Rasmussen III 182.

E422. The living corpse.

E446.1. *Corpse magically killed and laid.* N. A. Indian (Tlingit): Swanton BBAE XXXIX 248 No. 86.

E446.2. *Ghost laid by burning body.* *Fb "spøgelse" III 522a, "brænde" IV 69a. — Icelandic: *Boberg.

D1787. Magic results from burning. E15. Resuscitation by burning. E431.9. Ashes of dead thrown on water to prevent return. E431.13. Corpse burned to prevent return. S112. Burning to death. V61.2. Dead burned on pyre.

E446.2.1. *Ghost laid by burning lock of hair.* Spanish Exempla: Keller.

E446.3. *Ghost laid by decapitating body.* Icelandic: *Boberg; Lithuanian: Balys Index No. 3546A, Legends No. 621.

D711. Disenchantment by decapitation. E12. Resuscitation by decapitation. E431.7. Beheaded man's head laid at feet to prevent return. E431.9.1. Head of corpse thrown on water to prevent return.

E446.3.1. *Ghost laid by beating body to pieces.* Irish: O'Suilleabhain 99.

E446.4. *Slain ghost carried off by other ghosts.* India: Thompson-Balys.

E446.5. *Ghost laid by pushing it into water.* S. A. Indian (Cashinawa): Métraux RBAE CXLIII (3) 685.

E451. *Ghost finds rest when certain thing happens.*

E451.1. *Ghost laid when crime has been confessed.* (Cf. E412.5.) Fb "løse" II 517a.

E411. Dead cannot rest because of a sin.

E451.1.1. *Corpse cannot be laid until after he has confided the secret of magic charms.* India: Thompson-Balys.

E451.2. *Ghost laid when penance is done.* (Cf. E411.0.2.1.) Swiss: Jegerlehner Oberwallis 336 s.v. "Geister, Erlösung".

Q520. Penances.

E451.3. *Ghost laid when vow is fulfilled.* (Cf. E415.3.) Swiss: Jegerlehner Oberwallis 336 s.v. "Geister, Erlösung"; Danish: Kristensen Danske Sagn V (1897) 266ff., (1934) 196ff.; Icelandic: Boberg; India: Thompson-Balys.

E451.4. *Ghost laid when living man speaks to it.* Fb "løse" II 517a; Swiss: Jegerlehner Oberwallis 336 s.v. "Geister, Erlösung".

E451.4.1. *Ghost asked to identify self "in name of God."* U.S.: Baughman.

E451.5. *Ghost laid when treasure is unearthed.* Fb "løse" II 517b; India: Thompson-Balys; Japanese: Ikeda (Cf. E371ff.).

N550. Unearthing hidden treasure.

E451.5.1. *Money must be distributed to beggars so that ghost may be laid.* Lithuanian: Balys Ghosts.

E451.6. *Beggar's ghost laid when pig bought with money taken from him is brought to his grave.* Sinks in grave. Lithuanian: Balys Index No. *842.

E451.7. *Bearded woman ghost laid by shaving her.* Lithuanian: Balys Index No. 3560; Livonian: Loorits FFC LXVI 72 No. 216.

E451.8. *Ghost laid when house it haunts is destroyed or changed.* U.S.: *Baughman.

E451.9. *Ghost laid when revenge is accomplished.* Korean: Zong in-Sob 122f.

E451.10. *Ghost laid when rest of poem is recited.* Japanese: Ikeda.

E452. *Ghost laid at cockcrow (dawn).* Fb "spøgelse" III 519b, "kok" IV 272b; Köhler-Bolte III 581; Wimberly 248. — Breton: Sébillot Incidents s.v. "coq"; Scotch: Campbell Tales II 94—112 passim; English: Child II 228, V 294; Finnish, Swedish: Wessman 1 No. 6; India: *Thompson-Balys; Melanesian, Polynesian: *Dixon 141 n. 24; Kai

(German New Guinea): ibid. 144; N. A. Indian (Seneca): Curtin-Hewitt RBAE XXXII 96 No. 7, (Teton): Dorsey AA o.s. II (1889) 151.

C752.2.1. Tabu: supernatural creatures being abroad after sunrise. E501.11.1.2. Wild hunt abroad until cockcrow. E587.3. Ghosts walk from curfew to cockcrow. F383.4. Fairy must leave at cockcrow. F451.3.2. Dwarfs turn to stone at sunrise. G273.3. Witch powerless at cockcrow. G636. Ogress powerless after cockcrow. Z65.2. Series: white cock, red cock, black cock. Crow at dawn and scatter ghosts.

E452.1. *Dead quiescent during day.* N. A. Indian (California): Gayton and Newman 99.

E452.2. *Ghost invisible during day.* N. A. Indian (California): Gayton and Newman 99.

E453. *Ghost transformed into animal.* (Cf. D100, E423.) England: *Baughman.

E454. *Ghost is laid by giving it a never-ending or impossible task.* (Cf. H900, H1010.) England, U.S.: *Baughman.

E456. *Man raises corpses and gets their shrouds, then "lays" them again.* India: Thompson-Balys.

E459. *Other exorcism practices.*

E459.1. *Ghost demands a body and soul before it will agree to be laid.* Monk provides cock and sole of shoe. England: Baughman.

E459.2. *Ghost laid when bones are brought to home country from foreign soil.* England: Baughman.

E459.3. *Ghost laid when its wishes are acceded to.* England: Baughman.

E459.4. *Ghost bound and jailed.* England: Baughman.

E459.5. *Ghost laid at midnight.* U.S.: Baughman.

E459.6. *Ghost laid by burying bell from church in one pond, the clapper in another.* If the two ever come together again, the ghost can walk. England: Baughman.

E459.7. *Ghost laid when his skull is thrown into the Ganges.* India: Thompson-Balys.

E460. Revenants in conflict.

E461. *Fight of revenant with living person.* (Cf. E261.1.3.) Fb "spøgelse" III 520b; Irish myth: *Cross; Icelandic: *Boberg; Lithuanian: Balys Index No. 3542, Legends No. 882; N. A. Indian (Teton): Dorsey AA o.s. II (1889) 150, (Passamaquoddy): Leland Algonquin Legends 349, (Seneca): Curtin-Hewitt RBAE XXXII 96 No. 7.

E461.1. *Revenant challenged to combat.* Swiss: Jegerlehner Oberwallis 298 No. 12; Wales: Baughman.

E461.2. *Fight of living person with dead in the grave.* Andrews MPh X 601ff.; Icelandic: Herrmann Saxo II 367ff., MacCulloch Eddic 309—11, *Boberg.

P312.3. Blood-brethren promise that he who survives the other shall watch three nights in his grave mound.

E462. *Revenant overawed by living person.* *Fb "student"; Icelandic: Boberg; Welsh: Baughman.

K1700. Deception through bluffing.

E463. *Living man in dead man's shroud.* Refuses to let corpse return to grave before he tells how to resuscitate woman living man has killed. Estonian: Aarne FFC XXV 114 No. 7; Lithuanian: Balys Index No. 3543.

E464. *Revenant tricked or jeered into a bottle, corked up and put in safe place.* (Cf. D2177.1.) England: *Baughman.

E465. *Revenant rewards its conqueror.* Irish: Curtin Myths and Folklore of Ireland (Boston, 1889) 127; Egypt (ancient): Petrie II 87.

Q82. Reward for fearlessness. Reward given by devil or ghost.

E467. *Revenants fight each other.* *Krappe Balor 145ff.; Fb "spøgelse" III 520b; Icelandic: *Boberg.

E467.1. *Two dead men struggle over living man.* Lithuanian: Balys Index No. 3548, Balys Ghosts.

E470. Intimate relations of dead and living.

E471. *Ghost kisses living person.* *Fb "gjenganger" I 444a.

E472. *Revenant sleeps in same bed with living but without contact.* U.S.: Baughman.

E474. *Cohabitation of living person and ghost.* This usually involves sexual relations. (Cf. E321.2, E322.6, E339, E378.) Liebrecht 49; Aly Volksmärchen bei Herodot (Göttingen, 1921) 153; H. Schreuer Zs. d. vgl. Rechtswissenschaft XXXIII (1916) 350 n.; Corsican: Ortoli 332; India: Thompson-Balys; Icelandic: Boberg; New Hebrides: Codrington 379; N. A. Indian (Tlingit): Swanton BBAE XXXIX 249 No. 86, (Teton): Dorsey JAFL I 68, (Blackfoot): Wissler and Duvall PaAM II 154 No. 10 (head of murdered woman continues to live with husband), Grinnell Blackfoot Lodge Tales (New York, 1923) 70, (Hopi): Voth FM VIII 33, (Zuñi): Cushing 48 No. 2, (Thompson River): Teit JE VIII 281 No. 46, (Quileute): Farrand-Mayer JAFL XXXII 268 No. 12, (Klickitat): Alexander N. Am. 147; Eskimo (Greenland): Rink 454, Rasmussen III 84; Africa (Ekoi): Talbot 280.

T110. Unusual marriage. T113. Marriage to man alive by night but dead by day. T466. Necrophilism: sexual intercourse with dead human body.

E474.1. *Offspring of living and dead person.* (Cf. E322.1, T540.) *Fb "barn" IV 27a; Tupper and Ogle Walter Map 98; Irish myth: Cross.

E477. *Body in coffin moves so as to make room for his recently deceased friend.* *Loomis White Magic 92.

E480. Abode of the dead. Irish myth: *Cross; Jewish: *Neuman.

E177. Resuscitated man relates visions of beyond. F167. Inhabitants of other world. F323. Fairy women take body of dead hero to fairyland.

E480.1. *Abode of animal souls.* (Cf. E730.1.) Jewish: *Neuman.

E480.2. *Three worlds of dead.* Hawaii: Beckwith Myth 155, 160.

E480.3. *Men must enter spirit world armed.* S. A. Indian (Brazil): Oberg 110.

E481. *Land of the dead.* *Types 470, 471; *Köhler-Bolte II 224ff.; *Encyc. Rel. and Ethics II 680ff.; **Wiedeman Die Toten und ihre Reiche im Glauben der alten Ägypten (Leipzig, 1910); A. Jeremias Hölle und Paradies bei den Babyloniern (Leipzig, 1903); Dickson 94f. n. 78; Feilberg DF X 1; Herbert Catalogue of Romances III 585; Finnish: Kalevala rune 16; India: Thompson-Balys; N. A. Indian: *Alexander N.

Am. 274 n. 10; Africa: Werner African 180ff., (Ekoi): Talbot 7, 59, 226, 240, (Benga): Nassau 208 No. 33.

A310. God of the world of the dead. F160.0.2. Fairy otherworld confused with land of the dead. V52.16. Prayer for protection on journey to land of dead.

E481.0.1. *Spain as land of the dead.* (Cf. F130.2.) Irish myth: *Cross.

E481.0.2. *Quarrel of dead and living causes removal of dead to own land.* India: Thompson-Balys.

E481.1. *Land of dead in lower world.* *Krappe Etude 45ff.; **M. Landau Hölle und Fegefeuer in Volksglauben, Dichtung, und Kirchenlehre (Heidelberg, 1909); Krappe Revue Celtique XLIX (1932) 96—102; Icelandic: *Boberg; Greek: Fox 146, Grote I 62; Finnish: Holmberg Finno-Ugric 72; Jewish: *Neuman, Gaster Thespis 183, 187f.; Siberian: Holmberg Siberian 485; Buddhist myth: Malalasekera I 199f.; Chinese: Eberhard FFC CXX 200f.; Tonga: Gifford 183; Melanesia: Wheeler 33, 47; Papua: Ker 81; Hawaii: Beckwith Myth 146, 155; N. A. Indian: *Alexander N. Am. 274 n. 10; S. A. Indian (Metaco): Métraux MAFLS XL 24.

A671. Hell. Lower world of torment. E755.2. Souls in hell. F81. Descent to lower world of dead. Q560. Punishments in hell. Q565. Man admitted to neither heaven nor hell. He has tricked the devil.

E481.1.1. *Old woman ruler of dead in lower world.* (Cf. A481.9.) Finnish: Holmberg Finno-Ugric 75.

A310.1. Goddess of the world of the dead.

E481.1.2. *Houses in lower world of dead.* (Cf. F163, F220.) Finnish: Holmberg Finno-Ugric 74.

E481.2. *Land of dead across water.* Icelandic: Boberg; Siberian: Holmberg Siberian 486; N. A. Indian (Haida): Swanton JE V 34.

F93. Water entrance to lower world. F134. Otherworld on island.

E481.2.0.1. *Island of the dead.* *Meyer Der irische Totengott und die Toteninsel (Stzb. d. preussischen Akad. d. Wissenschaften XXXII [1919] 537); *Krappe Balor 102; Irish myth: *Cross; Hawaii: Beckwith Myth 72.

A692. Islands of the blest. E481.4.1. Avalon. F129.7. Voyage to the Isle of the Dead. F134. Otherworld on island. F730. Extraordinary islands.

E481.2.1. *Bridge to land of dead.* Type 471; *Fb "bro" IV 62b; Wimberly 110ff.; Ward Catalogue of Romances II 399, 420, 607, Herbert ibid. III 279; Moe Samlede Skrifter III 212, 226ff.; Frazer Immortality III 150; Icelandic: *Boberg; Finnish: Holmberg Finno-Ugric 74; India: *Thompson-Balys; Persian: Carnoy 344; Kachin: Scott Indo-Chinese 265; N. A. Indian: Brinton Myths of the New World (New York, 1868) 248, Skinner PaAM XIII 86.

A661.0.5. Bridge of heaven. A661.0.5.1. Soul bridge. A673. Hound of hell. Cerberus (monstrous dog) guards the bridge to the lower world. A778.2.1. Milky Way as path of souls (demons). E496. Ghosts gathered on a bridge. E750.2.1. Dead person of good life goes over bridge to other world without fear. F152. Bridge to otherworld. F842. Extraordinary bridge.

E481.2.1.1. *Frightening thing at bridge to land of dead.* N. A. Indian (California): Gayton and Newman 99.

E481.2.1.2. *Unstable bridge to land of dead.* N. A. Indian (California): Gayton and Newman 99.

F842.2.1. Perilous trap bridge.

E481.2.2. *Boat to land of dead.* Icelandic: De la Saussaye 292, *Boberg; Irish myth: Cross; Finnish: Holmberg Finno-Ugric 75.

F93.0.1. Boat to lower world. F213.1. Magic boat to fairyland.

E481.3. *Abode of dead in mountain.* Patch PMLA XXXIII 614 n. 48; Icelandic: *Boberg; Swiss: Jegerlehner Oberwallis 335b s.v. "Geister"; Gaster Oldest Stories 156.

A151. Home of the gods. A571. Culture hero asleep in mountain. F92.4. Entrance to lower world through mountain. F131. Otherworld in hollow mountain. F131.1. Mountain of Venus. F132. Otherworld on lofty mountain. F211.1. Entrance to fairyland through door in knoll. F721.2. Habitable hill. F750. Extraordinary mountains and other land features.

E481.3.1. *Abode of the dead in hills, barrows.* Icelandic: *Boberg.

F451.4.1.9. Burial places (barrows, howes) as homes of dwarfs. F456.1. Trolls live in howe (barrow, grave). V1.11. Hill worship.

E481.3.2. *Abode of the dead in stones.* Icelandic: MacCulloch Eddic 312.

F451.4.1.10. Dwarfs live in stones.

E481.4. *Beautiful land of dead.* (Rosengarten). Icelandic: *Boberg; Finnish: Holmberg Finno-Ugric 79f.

A151.2. Garden of the gods. A661. Heaven. A692. Islands of the blest. F111. Journey to earthly paradise. F162.1. Garden in otherworld. F210. Fairyland.

E481.4.1. *Avalon.* (Cf. F323.) Happy otherworld where dead are healed. Irish myth: *Cross; English: Wells 31 (Geoffrey of Monmouth), 33 (Layamon's Brut), 50 (Le Morte Arthure); Hartland Science 204 (Olger the Dane).

A571.2. Culture hero still alive on mysterious island. F0.1. Names for otherworld. F111. Journey to earthly paradise. Land of happiness. F125. Journey to otherworld where people are made whole. F344. Fairies heal mortals. F399.1. Fairies bear dead warrior to fairyland.

E481.5. *Ghost lives midway between heaven and earth.* Fb "spøgelse" III 519b.

E481.6. *Land of dead in one of the cardinal directions.*

F136. Direction of otherworld.

E481.6.1. *Land of dead in north.* Icelandic: Boberg; Finnish: Holmberg Finno-Ugric 77f.; N. A. Indian (California): Gayton and Newman 101.

A671.0.1. Hell located to the north. F531.6.2.4. Giants live in the utmost northwest. G633. North as abode of evil spirits.

E481.6.2. *Land of dead in west.* (Cf. A692.1.) Finnish: Holmberg Finno-Ugric 77f.; Irish myth: *Cross; N. A. Indian (California): Gayton and Newman 99.

A561. Divinity's departure for west.

E481.6.3. *Land of dead in east.* Icelandic: Boberg.

E481.7. *Icy inferno.* (Cf. E481.6.1.) Krappe Études 46 n. 2.

A671.3. Frigidity of hell. E756.2.5. Icy hell. Q567. Punishments by cold in hell.

E481.8. *Land of dead in sky.* India: *Thompson-Balys; Cook Islands: Beckwith Myth 76.

A661. Heaven.

E481.8.1. *Account book of men summoned to death kept in heaven.* India: Thompson-Balys.

E481.8.2. *Moon as land of dead.* Samoa: Clark 181.

E481.8.3. *Venus as land of dead.* Africa (Fang): Trilles 136.

E481.8.4. *Dead in house of cloud.* Eskimo (Greenland): Holm 79.

E481.9. *King of world of dead.* (Cf. E481.1.1.) Irish myth: Cross (E481.1.1.1); Icelandic: Boberg; India: Thompson-Balys; Africa (Baholoholo): Einstein 216.

A108.1. God of the dead. A310. God of the world of the dead.

E482. *Land of shades.* Everything is done by unseen people. Type 425; Tegethoff 14; *Siuts 218ff.; Ward Catalogue of Romances II 425 (Voyage of St. Brandon); N. A. Indian: *Thompson Tales 339 n. 221.

D1981. Certain persons invisible. E421.1. Invisible ghosts. E501.9. Wild huntsmen invisible. F412.1. Invisible spirit speaks. F585. Phantoms. H1239.2. Hero served by unseen hands. T118.1. Monster husband invisible.

E485. *Land of skulls.* Africa (Ekoi): Talbot 275.

A2223.2. Bird carries deity's daughter home from land of skulls: given brilliant plumage.

E485.1. *Land of skeletons.* Eskimo (Cumberland Sound): Boas BAM XV 230.

E487. *Glowing beds of dead.* Youth in land of dead puts staff into one of the beds. The iron glows and the wood burns. Irish: O'Suilleabhain 63, 102, Beal XXI 324, 333; Swiss: Jegerlehner Oberwallis 309 No. 7.

E421.3. Luminous ghosts.

E489. *Abode of the dead—miscellaneous.*

F93.1.1. Dead place net across river to prevent living man from returning to earth. F105. Dead opposes return of living from land of the dead.

E489.1. *Dead awaken after three days to new life and great wisdom.* Fb "død" I 228a.

E489.2. *Life in land of dead contrary to ours.* People grow younger and smaller till they become nothing and are reborn. Finnish: Holmberg Finno-Ugric 73.

E489.3. *Forgetting Charon's fee.* Philosopher forgets to put coin in mouth before death (Charon's fee). Charon: "Don't you know the custom?" Answer: "Yes, but I couldn't put off dying for a quarter!" — Italian Novella: Rotunda.

A672.1.1. Charon exacts fee to ferry souls across Styx. E431.11. Coin placed in mouth of dead to prevent return.

E489.4. *Man's spirit in land of dead prophesies his own future death.* India: Thompson-Balys.

M341. Death prophesied.

E489.5. *Dancing in afterworld.* N. A. Indian (California): Gayton and Newman 99.

E493. Dead men dance.

E489.6. *Culture hero gambles with ruler of the afterworld: result, death or increase in game.* N. A. Indian (California): Gayton and Newman 85.

A310. God of the world of the dead. A1335. Origin of death. E577.2. Dead persons play cards.

E489.7. *Judas Iscariot appears in midst of sea on rock washed alternately by fiery and icy waves.* (Cf. Q560.2.3.) Irish myth: *Cross.

E489.8. *Why living cannot go to land of the dead.* Chinese: Graham.

E489.9. *In land of dead the dead walk on grass without bending it and on mud without sinking.* (Cf. F973.2.) Chinese: Graham.

E489.10. *Land of dead "in Abraham's bosom".* Jewish: *Neuman.

E489.11. *Inhabitants of land of dead have great thirst.* Jewish: *Neuman.

E490. Meetings of the dead.

E491. *Procession of the dead.* *BP III 472 n. 1; Fb "gjenganger" I 443b, "Nytårsaften" II 707b; Finnish-Swedish: Wessman 23 No. 204; Swiss: Jegerlehner Oberwallis 323 Nos. 100, 105, 326 Nos. 15, 17; *Geiger Archives suisses des Traditions Populaires XLVII 71—76; West Indies: Flowers 431; Pochulata: Boas JAFL XXV 226; Spanish: Boas ibid. 251; India: *Thompson-Balys.

D1825.7.1. Person sees phantom funeral procession before funeral actually takes place.

E492. *Mass (church service) of the dead.* Held at midnight. *BP III 472, 545; Krappe Balor 116ff., 121 n. 11, JAFL LX 159ff.; *Fb "død" I 228a, "kirke" II 125b; *Grunwald Hessische Blätter f. Vksk. XXX—XXXI 316; Danish: Kristensen Danske Sagn II (1895) 280ff., (1928) 176ff.; Norwegian: Solheim Register 17; Icelandic: Boberg; Lithuanian: Balys Index No. 3558; Jewish: *Neuman; New York: Jones JAFL LVII 242.

E242. Ghosts punish intruders into mass (procession) of ghosts. E546. The dead sing. V49.1. Werwolves hold mass.

E493. *Dead men dance.* *Fb "spøgelse" III 520a, "danse" IV 93a, "sjæl" III 214b, "kirkegaard" II 128b; Swiss: Jegerlehner Oberwallis 335 s.v. "Geister"; England, U.S.: *Baughman; N. A. Indian (Pawnee): Grinnell 192, (Hupa): Goddard UCal I 239 No. 25, (Luiseño): DuBois UCal VIII 154, (Zuñi): Cushing 48 No. 2, (Cherokee): Mooney RBAE XIX 252 No. 5, 331 No. 78, (Kwakiutl): Boas and Hunt JE III 106; Africa: Werner African 188f.

C94.1.1. The cursed dancers. E261.3. Man attacked on Christmas night by dancing ghosts.

E494. *Ball game in lower world.* (Cf. E577.1.) N. A. Indian (Thompson River): Alexander N. A. Myth 137; *Icelandic: Boberg.

H1433. Fear test: playing game with reassembled dead man.

E495. *Wedding of the dead.* Finnish-Swedish: Wessman 23 No. 208.

E495.1. *Ghostly marriage party.* India: Thompson-Balys.

E495.2. *Marriage (ceremony) to a ghost.* India: *Thompson-Balys.

E496. *Ghosts gathered on a bridge.* *Fb "bro" IV 62b.

E481.2.1. Bridge to land of dead. F152. Bridge to other world.

E497. *Fighting warriors show the way of their past life and of their death.* Icelandic: Boberg.

A661.1. Valhalla. E155.1. Slain warriors revive nightly.

E499. *Meetings of the dead—miscellaneous.*

E499.1. *Gay banquet of the dead.* (Cf. E541.) England, U.S.: *Baughman; N. Y.: Jones JAFL LVII 241.

E499.2. *Orchestra of ghosts.* U.S.: Baughman.

E499.3. *Pot so heavy with ghosts that girl cannot lift it.* (Cf. D1317.10.) India: Thompson-Balys.

E499.4. *Dead in lower world complain about odor of human visitor.* N. A. Indian (California): Gayton and Newman 99.

G84. Fee-fi-fo-fum.

E500. Phantom hosts.

E501. *The Wild Hunt.* (Cf. F282.) (Die Wilde Jagd, Das Wütende Heer, Odinsjæger, Chasse Fantastique.) A ghostly hunter and his rout continue the chase. **Plischke (bibliography); **Schweda; *Wahner Der Wilde Jäger in Schlesien; Lorentzen; Brunk Der wilde Jäger im Glauben des pommerschen Volkes (Zs. f. Vksk. XIII 179); *Zingerle 589f. (bibliography): Jacobsen Harlekin og den vilde Jæger (Dania IX 1); Heilberg Theodorich som den vilde Jæger (Dania IX 239); Olrik Odinsjægeren i Jylland (Dania VIII 139); *Fb "Odinsjæger" III 730ff.; RTP II 156, VI 291, VII 175, 328, VIII 566, IX 91, 411, XIII 186, 695f.; XIV 83, XVI 453, 531, XVII 504f.; Hartland Science 234ff.; Wehrhan 84; Walhouse FL VIII (1897) 196; *O. Höfler Kultische Geheimbünde der Germanen Bd. I: Das germanische Totenheer (Frankfurt a. M., 1934); Tupper and Ogle Walter Map 234. Musical treatments: Raff Symphony No. 3 (1869); J. Triebensee "Die wilde Jagd" (opera, Budapest, 1824); H. Payer "Der wilde Jäger" (opera, Vienna, 1806); V. E. Nessler "Der wilde Jäger" (opera, Leipzig, 1881); M. J. Beer "Der wilde Jäger" (cantata, Olmütz, 1888); A. Schultz "Der wilde Jäger" (opera, Brunswick, 1887); Müller-Reuter "Hackelberends Begräbnis" (choral ballad, 1902); C. Franck "Le Chasseur Maudit" (symphonic poem, 1883). For classical parallels see H. Hepding Attis 124; Gruppe Griechische Religionsgeschichte (1907) 1290 n. 2; Samter Geburt, Hochzeit, Tod 206 n. 5. — Irish: *Cross; Beal XXI 322; Lithuanian: Balys Index No. 3518; Norwegian: *Solheim Register 17.

A778.1.1. Milky Way is the Wild Hunt. F280. Fairies travel in eddies of wind. F432. Wind-spirit.

E501.1. *Leader of the Wild Hunt.* *Rühlemann passim.

E501.1.1. *King as wild huntsman.* (Cf. E501.1.7.) Schweda 38; *Fb "Odins jæger" II 731b; Hartland Science 234, 236; RTP XVII 504f.

E501.1.2. *Nobleman as wild huntsman.* Schweda 38; Fb "Odins jæger" II 731b.

E501.1.3. *Rich man as wild huntsman.* Schweda 38.

E501.1.4. *Forester as wild huntsman.* Schweda 38.

E501.1.5. *Freemason as wild huntsman.* Schweda 38.

E501.1.6. *Saint as leader of wild hunt.* RTP XVII 504f.

E501.1.7. *Historic or romantic hero as leader of wild hunt.* Plischke 41; RTP XVII 504f.

E501.1.7.1. *King Herla as wild huntsman.* *Liebrecht 28; Tupper and Ogle Walter Map 18.

E501.1.7.2. *Theodoric as wild huntsman.* *Heilberg Dania IX 239, Nyrop ibid. X 177; BP IV 140; Oesterley No. 190.

E501.1.7.3. *Wild Edric as leader of Wild Hunt.* England: *Baughman.

E501.1.8. *Woman as leader of wild hunt.* Favorites are Herodias, Diana, Frau Holle. — Plischke 47; Schwartz Zs. f. Vksk. VII 231.

F475.1. Dame Berchta (Frau Holle).

E501.1.8.1. *Herodias as leader of wild hunt.* Zachariae Zs. f. Vksk. XXII (1912) 238 n. 7; Germania XVI (1871) 217; Dunlop-Liebrecht 474 n. 170; Grimm Deutsche Mythologie 599; La Tradition IV 69; *Kloss

MLN XXIII 82; *Grunwald Hessische Blätter f. Vksk. XXX—XXXI 317.

E501.1.8.2. *Artemis as leader of wild hunt.* Gruppe Griechische Religionsgeschichte 840 n. 5, 1292.

E501.1.8.3. *Hecate as leader of wild hunt.* Pauly-Wissowa s.v. "Hekate"; Rohde Psyche II 84.

E501.2. *Participants in wild hunt.*

E501.2.1. *Knights in wild hunt.* Plischke 29.

E501.2.2. *Ladies in wild hunt.* Plischke 29.

E501.2.3. *Witches in wild hunt.* (Cf. G200.) Plischke 29.

E501.2.4. *Courtisans in wild hunt.* (Cf. E501.5.1.2.) Plischke 29.
E411.2.1. Priest's concubine cannot rest in grave.

E501.2.5. *Churchmen in wild hunt.* Plischke 29.

E501.2.6. *Soldiers in wild hunt.* Plischke 29.

E501.2.7. *Unbaptized children in wild hunt.* Plischke 30; *Fb "udøbt" III 960a.
E412.2. Unbaptized person cannot rest in grave. E501.5.4. Unbaptized children pursued in wild hunt. F251.3. Unbaptized children as fairies. F360.1. Fairies pursue unbaptized children.

E501.3. *Wild huntsmen wander because of sin.* Schweda 38.
E411. Dead cannot rest because of a sin. E501.2.4. Courtisans in wild hunt. Q503. Wandering after death as punishment. V520. Salvation.

E501.3.1. *Wild huntsman wanders because of cruelty.* Schweda 38.
Q285. Cruelty punished.

E501.3.2. *Wild huntsman wanders because of suicide.* Schweda 38.
E411.1.1. Suicide cannot rest in grave. Q211.5. Suicide punished.

E501.3.3. *Wild huntsman wanders because of parricide.* Harow RTP XX 369.
E411.1. Murderer cannot rest in grave. Q211.1. Parricide punished.

E501.3.4. *Wild huntsman wanders because of unshriven death.* Schweda 38.
E411.1. Adulterous person cannot rest in grave. V20. Confession of sins.

E501.3.5. *Wild huntsman wanders for failure to keep fast day.* Plischke 29.
V70. Religious feasts and fasts.

E501.3.6. *Wild huntsman wanders for hunting on Sunday.* *Fb "Søndag" III 741a, "Odins jæger" II 731b.
A751.1.1. Man in moon burns brush as punishment for doing so on Sunday. C58. Tabu: profaning sacred day. Q223. Punishment for neglect of services to gods (God). V71. Sabbath.

E501.3.7. *Wild huntsman wanders because he wished to continue hunt after death.* Fb "jagt" II 36, "jagen" II 35; RTP XIII 695f.

E501.3.8. *Wild huntsman wanders for disturbing church service.* Plischke 34.
Q222. Punishment for desecration of holy places.

E501.3.9. *Wild huntsmen cannot die until evil in world has been made right and things return as they had been.* England: Baughman.

E501.3.10. *Wild huntswoman wanders because of murder of daughter.* England: Baughman.

E501.4. *Animals follow wild huntsman.*

B575. Animal as constant attendant of man. E423. Revenant in animal form. E520. Animal ghosts. F167.1. Animals in otherworld. F401.3. Spirit in animal form.

E501.4.0.1. *Animals in wild hunt reincarnation of murdered person.* Plischke 31.

E501.4.1. *Dogs in wild hunt.* Schweda 25; England: Baughman; Irish: O'Suilleabhain 50f., 56, Beal XXI 318f.

E522. Ghost of dog.

E501.4.1.1. *Enormous pack of dogs in wild hunt.* Overcome people by their mass. Plischke 32.

E501.4.1.2. *Dogs with fiery tongues in wild hunt.* Schweda 25; *Schwartz Zs. f. Vksk. VII 232; Fb "Odins jæger" II 732a; England: Baughman.

B19.4. Glowing animals. E421.3. Luminous ghosts.

E501.4.1.3. *Dogs with fiery eyes in wild hunt.* Schweda 25.

B15.4.2. Dog with fire in eyes. E421.3. Luminous ghosts.

E501.4.1.4. *Dogs with eyes hanging out over mouth in wild hunt.* Fb "øje" III 1165b.

E501.4.1.5. *Black dogs in wild hunt.* Schweda 25; England: Baughman.

E501.4.1.6. *Three-legged dogs in wild hunt.* *Zingerle Sagen aus Tirol 590; H. Usener Dreiheit (Rheinisches Museum f. Philologie N. F. LVIII (1903) 1ff., 161ff.).

B15.6.1. Three-legged quadruped.

E501.4.1.7. *Winged dogs in wild hunt.* RTP XVII 505.

E501.4.1.8. *Dogs in single file in wild hunt.* Schweda 25.

E501.4.1.9. *Dogs on leash in wild hunt.* Schweda 25.

E501.4.1.10. *Baying dogs in wild hunt.* Schweda 25; Fb "hund" I 676a.

E501.4.2. *Wild huntsman's horse.* *Howie 51.

E521. Ghost of horse.

E501.4.2.1. *White horse in wild hunt.* *Schwartz Zs. f. Vksk. VII 235; Schweda 25.

E501.4.2.2. *Black horse in wild hunt.* Schweda 25.

E501.4.2.3. *Brown horse in wild hunt.* Schweda 25.

E501.4.2.4. *Horse in wild hunt breathes fire.* Schweda 25; Schwartz Zs. f. Vksk. VII 235.

B15.5.1. Horse with fire-breathing nostrils. B742. Animal breathes fire.

E501.4.2.5. *Horse with fiery eyes in wild hunt.* Schweda 25.

B19.4. Glowing animals. E421.3. Luminous ghosts.

E501.4.2.6. *Two-legged horse in wild hunt.* Plischke 30.

B15.6. Animals with unusual legs or feet. E521.2. Three-legged ghost of horse.

E501.4.2.7. *Headless horse in wild hunt.* Plischke 30.

E422.1.1. Headless revenant. E521.1. Headless ghost of horse.

E501.4.3. *Boar (sow) in wild hunt.* Plischke 31

E423.1.5. Revenant as swine. E526. Ghost of hog.

E501.4.3.1. *One-eyed sow in wild hunt.* Plischke 31.

E501.4.3.2. *Blind wild boar in wild hunt.* Plischke 32.

E501.4.4. *Two ravens follow wild huntsman.* *Zingerle Sagen aus Tirol 588.

A165.1.1. Ravens as attendants of god. B575. Animal as constant attendant of man.

E501.4.5. *Owl (ghost of nun) in wild hunt.* Plischke 34.

E501.5. *Object of wild hunt's pursuit.*

E501.5.1. *Wild hunter pursues a woman.* Plischke 65; Fb "Odins jæger" II 732b; Schwartz Zs. f. Vksk. VII 233.

E501.5.1.1. *Naked woman pursued and cut in two by rider.* *Pauli (ed. Bolte) No. 228; *Herbert III 134.

E501.5.1.2. *Prostitutes pursued in wild hunt.* (Cf. E501.2.4.) Plischke 65.

Q243.1. Prostitution punished.

E501.5.1.3. *Witches pursued in wild hunt.* Plischke 65.

E501.5.2. *Fairies pursued in wild hunt.* Fb "Odins jæger" II 732ab.

E501.5.3. *Wood-spirits pursued in wild hunt.* Plischke 66.

E501.5.4. *Unbaptized children pursued in wild hunt.* Plischke 65.

E412.2. Unbaptized person cannot rest in grave. E501.2.7. Unbaptized children in wild hunt. F251.3. Unbaptized children as fairies. F360.1. Fairies pursue unbaptized children.

E501.5.5. *Animals pursued in wild hunt.*

E423. Revenant in animal form. F167.1. Animals in otherworld.

E501.5.5.1. *Hare pursued in wild hunt.* Plischke 66.

E501.5.5.2. *Deer pursued in wild hunt.* Schwartz Zs. f. Vksk. VII 232; RTP XXII 466.

E501.6. *Ghostly warner of wild hunt's approach.* Plischke 38.

E501.7. *Personal appearance of wild huntsmen.*

E501.7.1. *Wild huntsmen headless.* *Zingerle 589; Schweda 28.

E422.1.1. Headless revenant.

E501.7.2. *Wild huntsmen with deer-heads.* Plischke 29.

E501.7.3. *Wild huntsmen with heads on backward.* Plischke 29.

E34. Resuscitation with misplaced head.

E501.7.4. *Wild huntsmen carrying skull under arms.* Plischke 29.

E501.7.5. *Wild huntsmen with entrails stringing from open bodies.* Plischke 29.

E501.7.6. *Wild huntsmen luminous.* Zingerle 4 No. 6.

E421.3. Luminous ghosts. F401.2. Luminous spirits.

E501.7.6.1. *Wild huntsmen exhale fire.* Schweda 28.

E501.7.6.2. *Wild huntsmen have fiery eyes.* Schweda 29.

E501.7.6.3. *Wild huntsmen leave fiery tracks.* Schweda 28.

E501.7.6.4. *Wild huntsmen surrounded by fire.* Schweda 29.

E501.7.7. *Wild huntsmen with long hair.* Schweda 29.

E501.8. *Clothing of wild huntsmen.*

E501.8.1. *Wild huntsmen dressed in black.* Schweda 29.

E501.8.2. *Wild huntsmen dressed in red.* Schweda 29.

E501.8.3. *Wild huntsmen dressed in white.* Schweda 29.

E501.8.4. *Wild huntsmen dressed in ancient costume.* Schweda 29.
F401.1. Spirits dressed in antique clothes.

E501.8.5. *Wild huntsmen belted and tied up.* Plischke 35.

E501.8.6. *Wild huntsman with black fur cap and white staff.* Hartland Science 236.

E501.9. *Wild huntsmen invisible.* Tobler 92.
E421.1. Invisible ghosts. E482. Land of shades. F412.1. Invisible spirit speaks.

E501.10. *Objects as part of wild hunt.*

E501.10.1. *Empty shoe follows wild hunt.* Plischke 35.

E501.10.2. *Worn-out broom at head of wild hunt.* Plischke 35.

E501.10.3. *Wagon accompanies wild hunt.* Plischke 36.

E501.11. *Time of appearance of wild hunt.*
E587. Ghosts walk at certain times.

E501.11.1. *Wild hunt appears at night.* *Schwartz Zs. f. Vksk. VII 235.

E501.11.1.1. *Wild hunt appears at midnight.* Schweda 16; Plischke 52.

E501.11.1.2. *Wild hunt abroad until cockcrow.* Schweda 16.
C752.2.1. Tabu: Supernatural creatures to be abroad after sunrise. E452. Ghost laid at cockcrow (dawn). F451.3.2.1. Dwarfs turn to stone at sunrise.

E501.11.1.3. *Wild hunt appears on St. John's Night.* Schweda 16.
V70. Religious feasts and fasts.

E501.11.1.4. *Wild hunt appears on stormy nights.* Plischke 55.

E501.11.2. *Wild hunt appears at certain seasons.*

E501.11.2.1. *Wild hunt appears in winter.* Schweda 16; Plischke 54.

E501.11.2.2. *Wild hunt appears between Christmas and Twelfth Night.* Plischke 54.

E501.11.2.3. *Wild hunt appears on feast-days.* Schweda 16; Plischke 55; Fb "Odins jæger" II 732ab.

E501.11.3. *Wild hunt appears periodically.*

E501.11.3.1. *Wild hunt appears every seven years.* Plischke 64.
E585.1. Dead person visits earth every seven years.

E501.11.3.2. *Wild hunt appears yearly at same moment.* Plischke 74.

E501.12. *Place of appearance of wild hunt.*

E501.12.1. *Wild hunt appears in woods.* Schweda 13; Plischke 57.

E501.12.2. *Wild hunt appears in churchyard.* Schweda 13.

E501.12.3. *Wild hunt appears at crossroads.* Schweda 13; Plischke 61.
D1786. Magic power at crossroads.

E501.12.4. *Wild hunt appears by body of water.* Schweda 13; North Carolina: Brown Collection I 678.

E501.12.5. *Wild hunt appears by hill or mountain.* Schweda 14; Plischke 57.

E501.12.6. *Wild hunt appears in a field.* Schweda 14.

E501.12.6.1. *Wild hunt appears in old battlefield.* Plischke 29, 59.

E501.12.7. *Wild hunt appears at desert spot.* Schweda 14.

E501.12.8. *Wild hunt appears at castle.* Schweda 14.

E501.12.9. *Wild hunt appears over city.* Schweda 14.

E501.12.10. *Wild hunt appears at old mill.* Schweda 14.

E501.13. *Phenomena at appearance of wild hunt.*

E501.13.1. *Wild hunt heralded by noise.* Schweda 20, Plischke 36.

E501.13.1.1. *Wild hunt heralded by detonation.* Schweda 21.

E501.13.1.2. *Wild hunt heralded by rattle of chains.* Schweda 20; New York: Jones JAFL LVII 250.

E501.13.1.3. *Wild hunt heralded by clash of swords.* Plischke 29.

E501.13.1.4. *Wild hunt heralded by ringing of bells.* Schweda 21.

E501.13.2. *Wild hunt heralded by music.* Plischke 36.

E501.13.3. *Wild hunt heralded by noise of horses.*

E501.13.3.1. *Wild hunt heralded by stamping of horses.* Schweda 21.

E501.13.3.2. *Wild hunt heralded by neighing of horses.* Schweda 21.

E501.13.4. *Wild hunt heralded by baying of hounds.* Schweda 21.

E501.13.5. *Wild hunt heralded by shouts of huntsmen.* Schweda 21, Tobler 92.

E501.13.6. *Wild hunt heralded by storm.* Plischke 37.
D2141. Storm produced by magic.

E501.13.7. *Wild hunt heralded by fire.* Schweda 21.

E501.14. *Course of wild hunt.*

E501.14.1. *Wild hunt chases in air.* Plischke 62; Mazeret RTP XXV 313.

E501.14.1.1. *Wild hunt in air very close to ground.* Plischke 63.

E501.14.2. *Wild hunt courses in particular direction.* Plischke 63.

E501.14.3. *Wild hunt goes thrice around pond.* Schweda 29.

E501.14.4. *Wild hunt goes several times around a hill.* Schweda 29.

E501.14.5. *Wild hunt goes around the entire earth.* Plischke 64.

E501.14.6. *Wild hunt goes through houses when front and back doors are on a line.* (Cf. E501.17.5.4.) Plischke 64; Fb "port" II 862b, "Odins jæger" II 732b.

F406.1. Doors left open to let night creatures pass to and fro.

E501.15. *Behavior of wild huntsmen.*

E501.15.1. *Wild huntsman blows horn.* Schwartz Zs. f. Vksk. VII 232.

E501.15.2. *Wild huntsman has his horse beaten.* *Zingerle 589.

E501.15.3. *Wild huntsman makes people carry him on their backs.* Harou RTP XX 368.

D2171.2. Magic adhesion to monster (witch, ogre, etc.) G311. Old man of the sea.

E501.15.4. *Wild huntsman repays with leaves (shavings) that turn to gold.* Plischke 36; Zingerle 589.

D475.1. Transformation: objects to gold. F451.1.4. Dwarf's gold. Seemingly worthless gift given by dwarfs turns to gold.

E501.15.5. *Living smith must repair wagon belonging to wild hunt.* Plischke 36.

E501.15.6. *Behavior of wild huntsman's dogs.*

E501.15.6.1. *Wild huntsman asks people to hold his dogs.* Fb "Odins jæger" II 732a.

E501.15.6.2. *Wild huntsman turns his dogs loose on those he meets.* Harou RTP XX 368.

E501.15.6.3. *Bite of wild huntsman's dogs drives other dogs mad.* *Fb "hund" I 676a, "Odins jæger" II 732a.

E501.15.6.4. *Wild huntsman's dogs cannot pass over grave.* Must be lifted over. Plischke 33.

E501.15.6.5. *Wild huntsman's dog cannot be dislodged from house it has entered.* Plischke 33.

E501.15.6.6. *Wild huntsman's dogs eat dough, bread, meal, etc.* Plischke 33; *Zingerle 590.

E501.15.6.7. *Wild huntsman's dog when seized becomes stick (black coal).* Plischke 32.

E501.15.7. *Wild huntsman waters his horse.* Fb "Odins jæger" II 732a.

F241.1.2.1. Trolls' horses water at peasant's well.

E501.15.8. *Wild huntsman lives in room on farm.* Fb "Odins jæger" 732b.

E501.16. *Phenomena at disappearance of wild hunt.*

E501.16.1. *Wild hunt disappears with loud noise.* Schweda 21.

E501.16.2. *Wild hunt disappears with movement of tree tops.* Schweda 21.

E501.16.3. *Wild hunt disappears with blast of wind.* Schweda 21.

E501.16.4. *Wild hunt disappears in column of fire.* Schweda 21.

E501.16.5. *Wild hunt disappears during storm.* Schweda 21.

E501.17. *Evading or combating the wild hunt.*

E501.17.1. *Wild hunt powerless against certain persons.*

E501.17.1.1. *Wild hunt powerless against herdsmen.* Schweda 31.

E501.17.1.2. *Wild hunt powerless against churchmen.* Schweda 32.

E501.17.2. *Wild hunt powerless beyond certain range.* Schweda 32.

E501.17.3. *Wild hunt powerless at crossroads.* Schweda 32; Plischke 32, 37; RTP XX 163.

D1786. Magic power at crossroads.

E501.17.4. *Wild hunt's power evaded.*

E501.17.4.1. *Power of wild hunt evaded by prayer.* Schweda 31; Plischke 79.

D1766.1. Magic results produced by prayer.

E501.17.4.2. *Power of wild hunt evaded by formula.* (Cf. D1273.) Schweda 32.

E501.17.4.3. *Power of wild hunt evaded by sacrificing to huntsman's dogs.* Fb "kvie" II 338.

D1766.2. Magic results produced by sacrifices.

E501.17.4.4. *Power of wild hunt evaded by silence.* Schweda 31; England: Baughman.

E501.17.5. *Wild hunt avoided.*

E501.17.5.1. *Wild hunt avoided by keeping on one's road.* Sometimes in middle of road or on right side of road. Schweda 31; Plischke 77.

E501.17.5.2. *Wild hunt avoided by getting out of its course.* Plischke 76.

E501.17.5.3. *Wild hunt avoided by keeping in house with windows closed.* (Cf. E501.14.6.) Plischke 76.

E501.17.5.4. *Wild hunt avoided by throwing self to earth.* Plischke 76.

E501.17.5.5. *Wild hunt avoided by staying within circle.* (Cf. D1272.) Plischke 76.

E501.17.5.6. *Wild hunt avoided by holding bread.* (Cf. D1031.1.) Plischke 78.

E501.17.5.7. *Wild hunt avoided by holding certain plant.* (Cf. D965.) Plischke 78.

E501.17.5.8. *Sound of wild hunt avoided by sticking fingers in ears.* Fb "øre" III 1181a.

E501.17.6. *Wild huntsman pacified.*

E501.17.6.1. *Wild huntsman pacified by sacrifice.* *Fb "ofre" II 735a.

V10. Religious sacrifices.

E501.17.6.2. *Wild huntsman pacified with food.* Fb "Odins jæger" II 732b.

E501.17.7. *Wild huntsman released from wandering.*

E440. Walking ghost "laid".

E501.17.7.1. *Wild huntsman released from wandering by mould from Christ's grave.* Fb "Kristi grav".

D1278.1. Magic churchyard mould. E431.3. Mould thrown on corpse to prevent return.

E501.17.8. *Wild hunt forced to depart.*

E501.17.8.1. *Wild hunt frightened away by scolding.* Plischke 75.

E501.18. *Evil effects of meeting wild hunt.*

E501.18.1. *Wild hunt harmful to certain persons.*

E501.18.1.1. *Wild hunt harmful to mockers.* Schweda 31; Plischke 69, 72.

Q225. Punishment for scoffing at church teachings.

E501.18.1.2. *Wild hunt harmful to thieves.* Schweda 31.

Q212. Theft punished.

E501.18.1.3. *Wild hunt harmful to the curious.* Schweda 31.

Q341. Curiosity punished.

E501.18.1.3.1. *Wild hunt throws down man's dead child when asked for part of game.* England: Baughman.

E501.18.2. *Wild hunt throws human flesh on persons who see it.* This cannot be removed. Schweda 32; Plischke 72.

E501.18.3. *Wild hunt throws horses' feet on persons who see it.* This cannot be removed. Schweda 32; Plischke 72.

E501.18.4. *Wild hunt carries person off.* Plischke 69; England: Baughman.

E501.18.5. *Wild hunt throws person to ground.* Plischke 70.

E501.18.6. *Sight of wild hunt renders person insane.* Plischke 70.

D2065.2. Insanity from seeing strange sight.

E501.18.7. *Sight of wild hunt blinds person.* Plischke 70.

E501.18.8. *Sight of wild hunt causes swelling of head.* Plischke 71.

D2064. Magic sickness.

E501.18.9. *Sight of wild hunt causes one to stick axe or knife in foot.* Plischke 71.

E501.18.10. *Sight of wild hunt causes death.* Schweda 32; Ireland: Baughman.

E501.19. *Remedy for effects of seeing wild hunt.*

E501.19.1. *Effects of wild hunt remedied by seeing it a year later in same place.* Plischke 74.

E501.19.2. *Effects of wild hunt remedied by asking the huntsmen for salt.* Plischke 74.

E501.19.3. *Effects of wild hunt remedied by asking the huntsmen for parsley.* Plischke 74.

E501.19.4. *Effects of wild hunt remedied by asking to partake in booty of hunt.* This booty is the same kind as the hunt has already thrown down. (Cf. E501.18.2.) Plischke 74.

E501.19.5. *Effects of wild hunt remedied by eating part of flesh thrown down by it.* (Cf. E501.18.2.) Plischke 75.

E501.19.6. *Effects of wild hunt remedied by prayer.* Plischke 75.
D1766.1. Magic results produced by prayer.

E501.20. *Wild hunt as omen.*
D1812.5. Future learned through omens.

E501.20.1. *Wild hunt as omen of disaster.* RTP XII 186.

E501.20.1.1. *Wild hunt as omen of war.* Plischke 67; Fb "krig" II 296a; England: Baughman.

E501.20.1.2. *Wild hunt as omen of pestilence.* Plischke 67.

E501.20.2. *Wild hunt as omen of plentiful year.* Plischke 68.

E501.20.3. *Wild hunt as weather omen.* Plischke 68.

E502. *The Sleeping Army.* Soldiers killed in battle come forth on occasions from their resting place (hill, grave, grotto) and march about or send their leader to do so. — *Schweda 59ff.; *Hartland Science 216ff.; Howey 9; Irish myth: *Cross; England, Scotland, Ireland, U.S.: *Baughman; India: Thompson-Balys.
A151.1.1. Home of gods inside of hill. A162.1.0.1. Recurrent battle. A165.7. Army of the gods. C549.2. Tabu: touching soldiers of enchanted (sleeping) army and their horses. D1960.2. King asleep in mountain (Barbarossa, King Marko, Holger Danske, etc.) Will awake one day to succor his people. E155.1. Slain warriors revive nightly. E334.5. Ghost of soldier haunts battlefield. E401.0.1. Ghostly voice heard on battlefield. F721.2. Habitable hill.

E510. Phantom sailors and travelers.

E511. *The Flying Dutchman.* A sea captain because of his wickedness sails his phantom ship eternally without coming to harbor. **G. Kalff De Sage van den Vliegenden Hollander (Zupthen, 1923); **Engert Die Sage vom Fliegenden Holländer; **W. Söderhjelm Flygande holländeren (Helsingfors, 1890); *Andraea Anglia Beiblatt XIII (1902) 47; Golther Zur deutschen Sage und Dichtung 7; Fb "skib" III 243a; England, U.S.: *Baughman.
Q503. Wandering after death as punishment.

E511.1. *Reason for Flying Dutchman's punishment.*
Q200. Deeds punished.

E511.1.1. *Flying Dutchman sails because of cruelty.* See all references to E511.

E511.1.2. *Flying Dutchman sails because of pact with Devil.* Engert 21ff.

E511.1.3. *Flying Dutchman sails because he defied the storm.* Engert passim.
C41. Tabu: offending water-spirit.

E511.2. *Flying Dutchman's ship.*

E511.2.1. *Flying Dutchman has dead men as sailors.* Fb "skib" III 243a.

E512. *Phantom cart driver wanders because of blasphemy.* "Peter Rugg the Missing Man." Boasts that he will reach home despite storm or never see his home again. He always travels in hard shower of rain or just ahead of one. U.S.: *Baughman.

E520. Animal ghosts. Hdwb. d. Abergl. s.v. "Geist"; Finnish-Swedish: Wessman 22 No. 201; New York: Jones JAFL LVII 243.

E423. Revenant in animal form. E501.4. Animals follow wild huntsman. E730.1. Souls of animals. F234.1. Fairy in form of an animal. F401.3. Spirit in animal form.

E521. *Ghost of domestic beast.*

E521.1. *Ghost of horse.* *Howey 31; *Fb "stud" III 619b, "hest" I 599b, "helhest" I 584b; *Kittredge Witchcraft 177 n. 31; *Handwb. d. Abergl. IX Nachträge 164ff.; England: Baughman.

E281.2. Ghostly horse enters house and puts hoofs on breast of sleeper. E402.2.3. Hoofbeats of ghost horse. E423.1.3. Revenant as horse. E501.4.2. Wild huntsman's horse. E535.1. Phantom coach and horses.

E521.1.1. *Headless ghost of horse.* *Howey 62; *Fb "stud" III 619b, "hest" I 599b, "helhest" I 584b; Japanese: Ikeda.

E422.1.1. Headless revenant. E501.4.2.7. Headless horse in wild hunt.

E521.1.2. *Three-legged ghost of horse.* Fb "helhest" I 584b; Hdwb. d. Abergl. II 15, 420, 1011, III 1517.

B15. Animals with unusual limbs or members. B15.6. Animals with unusual legs or feet. E423.1.3.1. Revenant as three-legged horse. E501.4.2.6. Two-legged horse in wild hunt. F241.1.3. Fairies ride on three-legged horses.

E521.1.3. *Ghost of race horse wins race in competition with living horses.* U.S.: Baughman.

E521.2. *Ghost of dog.* Hdwb. d. Abergl. s.v. "Geist"; Finnish-Swedish: Wessman 22 No. 202; Jewish: *Neuman; Texas: Bishop Pub. Texas Folklore Soc. XV 119—21; Eskimo (Bering Strait): Nelson RBAE XVIII 488, (Cumberland Sound): Boas BAM XV 228.

E423.1.1. Revenant as dog. E501.4.1. Dogs in wild hunt.

E521.2.1. *Ashes of dead dog speak.* *Jamaica: Beckwith MAFLS XVII 265 No. 72.

E521.2.2. *Headless ghost of dog.* North Carolina: Brown Collection I 682.

E521.3. *Ghost of cat.* (Cf. E423.1.2.) Kittredge Witchcraft 497 n. 41.

E521.4. *Ghost of calf.* (Cf. E423.1.8.1.) *Fb "kalv" II 79a; U.S.: Baughman.

E521.5. *Ghost of hog.* Fb "svin" III 676b.

E423.1.5. Revenant as swine. E501.4.3. Boar (sow) in wild hunt.

E521.5.0.1. *Headless ghost of hog.* (Cf. E422.1.1.) Fb "svin" III 676b.

E521.5.1. *Ghost of sow.* Fb "so" III 450a.

E522. *Ghost of wild beast.*

E522.1. *Ghost of fox* (Cf. E423.2.3.) Swiss: Jegerlehner Oberwallis 310 No. 24.

E522.2. *Ghost of bear.* (Cf. E423.2.1.) Eskimo (Greenland): Rasmussen III 87.

E523. *Ghost of fish.* Eskimo (Mackenzie Area): Jenness 33.

E524. *Ghost of bird.* (Cf. E423.3.)

E524.1. *Ghost of goose.* Fb "gasse" I 425a.

E524.2. *Ghost of cock.*

E524.2.1. *Cooked cock crows.* Fb "kok" IV 272b.

E530. Ghosts of objects. Hdwb. d. Abergl. s.v. "Geist"; Finnish-Swedish: Wessman 23 No. 205.

E402.3. Sound made by ghostly object.

E530.1. *Ghost-like lights.* Finnish-Swedish: Wessman 23 No. 210; England, Scotland, U.S.: *Baughman.

E276.2.4. Ghostly lights frighten treasure seekers. E371.10. Ghost light leads to hidden treasure. E742. Soul as light. F491.1. Will-o-the-wisp.

E530.1.1. *Ghost light follows ghost.* U.S.: *Baughman.

E530.1.2. *Ball of fire haunts murderer.* U.S.: *Baughman.

E530.1.3. *Ghost light haunts burial spot.* England, Scotland, U.S., Wales: *Baughman.

E530.1.4. *Ghost light on farm indicates that occupants will move shortly.* Scotland: Baughman.

E530.1.5. *Ghost light indicates impending calamity.* Scotland: *Baughman.

E530.1.6. *Ghost light serves as death omen.* (Cf. D1812.5.) England, Scotland, U.S., Wales: *Baughman.

E530.1.7. *Ghost light indicates route funeral will take.* (Cf. D1825.7.1.) England, Scotland, U.S., Wales: *Baughman.

E531. *Ghost-like building.* Finnish-Swedish: Wessman 23 No. 207; England, U.S.: *Baughman.

E532. *Ghost-like picture.* U.S.: *Baughman.

E533. *Ghostly bell.*

E533.1. *Ghostly bell sounds from under water.* England: *Baughman.

F993. Sunken bell sounds.

E533.2. *Self-tolling bell.* England: Baughman.

E534. *Phantom spinning-wheel makes noise.* North Carolina: Brown Collection I 678.

E535. *Ghostlike conveyance (wagon, etc.).* Finnish-Swedish: Wessman 22 No. 203; New York: Jones JAFL LVII 241—243.

E535.1. *Phantom coach and horses.* England, Ireland, U.S., Wales: *Baughman.

E535.2. *Ghostly wagon.* England, U.S.: *Baughman.

E535.3. *Ghost ship.* (Cf. E510.) Canada, England, U.S.: *Baughman; Childs NYFQ V 146ff.; Jones JAFL LVII 244.

D1812.5.1.10. Sight of phantom ship a bad omen.

E535.3.1. *Phantom canoe.* New York: Jones JAFL LVII 244.

E535.3.2. *Phantom boat.* Tahiti: Henry 91.

E535.4. *Phantom railway train.* U.S.: *Baughman; Jones JAFL LVII 241, 244.

E538. *Ghoulish ghost objects.*

E538.1. *Spectral coffin.* U.S.: Baughman.

E538.2. *Ghostly rope of suicide appears.* U.S.: Baughman.

E539. *Other ghostly objects.*

E539.1. *Oven door jumps into room; money thought to be under spot where it lands.* England: Baughman.

E539.2. *Pot jumps in house to indicate money hidden underneath it.* England: Baughman.

E539.3. *Ghostly wool-packs roll over fields, down hill.* England: *Baughman.

E539.4. *Ghostly chair.*

E539.4.1. *Ghostly chair in cellar jumps up and down on three legs, points with fourth at spot on floor.* Witnesses dig up body from under floor. U.S.: Baughman.

E539.5. *Coal in bin jumps around and gurgles.* U.S.: Baughman.

E540. Miscellaneous actions of revenants.

D2142.2.1. Wind stopped by revenant. E281.2. Ghostly horse enters house and puts hoofs on breast of sleeper. E474.1. Child begotten on dead woman. N576. Ghosts prevent men from raising treasure. P319.5. Hands of friends extend through sides of tombs and clasp in death. V222.7. Dead holy man stretches hand from tomb to honor saint.

E541. *Revenants eat.* (Cf. E499.1.) *Fb "lig" II 412b, "spøgelse" III 518ab.; India: Thompson-Balys.

E541.1. *Food placed out for returning souls of dead.* Germanic: Celander Nordisk Jul I 203ff., Wuttke Volksaberglaube 471, Archiv f. Religionsgeschichte XIX (1918) 134; Lappish: Rheen Svenska Landsmålen XVII (1898) 27; Slavic: Máchal 230; India: Thompson-Balys.

E341.2. Dead grateful for food. E433. Ghosts placated by sacrifices. F406.2. Food left out for spirits at night.

E541.2. *Ghost eats living human beings.* Cheremis: Sebeok-Nyerges.

E541.3. *Dead come forth and eat grave-offerings.* India: Thompson-Balys; Eskimo (Bering Strait): Nelson RBAE XVIII 488, (Labrador): Hawkes GSCan XIV 154.

E541.4. *Revenants drink.* India: Thompson-Balys.

E541.4.1. *Amputated head asks for drink.* India: Thompson-Balys.

F556. Remarkable voice.

E541.5. *Dead beg food from living.* Africa (Bantu): Einstein 193.

E542. *Dead man touches living.*

V222.7. Dead holy man stretches hand from tomb to honer saint.

E542.1. *Ghostly fingers leave mark on person's body.* U.S.: Baughman.

E542.1.1. *Ghostly fingers leave mark on man's hand.* *Fb "hånd" I 765b.

E542.1.2. *Ghost touches man's neck, leaves impression of hand on neck.* U.S.: Baughman.

E542.1.3. *Ghost strikes man on mouth; leaves his mouth crooked.* Ireland: Baughman.

E542.1.4. *Ghost strikes man on face.*

E542.1.4.1. *Ghost strikes man on face: cancer grows there.* Canada: Baughman.

E542.1.4.2. *Ghost strikes man on face: marks remain permanently.* U.S.: Baughman.

E542.2. *Dead man's hand touches birthmark and thus removes it.* *Fb "død" I 228a.

E542.3. *Ghost throws man into ditch, leaving his side numb.* England: Baughman.

E542.4. *Ghost touches man's hat, scorching it and turning lock of his hair white.* U.S.: Baughman.

E543. *Dead drag boat to strand.* Finnish-Swedish: Wessman 5 No. 41.

E544. *Ghost leaves evidence of his appearance.* (Cf. E322.3.3.1, E542.1ff.) Scotland, U.S.: *Baughman.

E544.1. *Ghost leaves object after appearance.* U.S.: Baughman.

E544.1.1. *Ghost leaves behind a crucifix.* England: Baughman.

E544.1.2. *Ghost leaves a ring with the living.* England: Baughman.

E544.1.3. *Ghost of drowned man leaves puddle of salt water where he stands.* U.S.: *Baughman.

E544.2. *Ghost pulls off blanket from sleeper.* Lithuanian: Balys Ghosts, Index No. 3540.

E545. *The dead speak.* Irish myth: *Cross; Icelandic: *Boberg; Jewish: *Neuman ; West Indies: Flowers 431; India: Thompson-Balys.
D1610.5. Speaking head. D1615.7. Singing head. E389.1. Ghost summoned in order to talk to it. M301.14. Summoned dead prophesies.

E545.0.1. *Words uttered from the tomb.* *Loomis White Magic 53; Icelandic: Boberg; India: Thompson-Balys.

E545.0.2. *The dead are silent.* Irish myth: *Cross.
C400. Speaking tabu. C405. Silence preserved in fairyland.

E545.1. *Conversation between the dead.* Gaster Exempla 206 No. 110; Jewish: *Neuman.

E545.2. *Dead predict death.* (Cf. E363.3.) Wimberly 268; England, U.S.: *Baughman.

E545.3. *Dead announce own death.* (Cf. E723ff.) Wimberly 268.

E545.4. *Dead will not speak of their condition.* England: Child II 231—3.

E545.5. *Questions to dead are dangerous.* *Fb "død" I 228a; Boberg.
D1815.1. Knowledge of ghost language.

E545.6. *Dead speak on Hallowe'en.* (Cf. V70.5.) Irish myth: Cross.

E545.6.1. *Thirsty when hanged, corpse asks for water on Hallowe'en.* Irish myth: Cross.

E545.7. *Holy man converses with entombed dead.* Irish myth: *Cross.
D1713. Magic power of hermit (saint).

E545.8. *Fairy converses with dead.* Irish myth: Cross.
F260. Behavior of fairies.

E545.9. *Dead holy man begs grave-digger not to bury sinner on top of him.* Irish myth: Cross.

E545.10. *Corpse exclaims over miracle.* Irish myth: Cross.

E545.11. *Ghost chooses own requiem.* Irish myth: Cross.

E545.12. *Ghost directs man to hidden treasure.* India: Thompson-Balys.
N538. Treasure pointed out by supernatural creature.

E545.13. *Man converses with dead.* Jewish: Neuman.

E545.14. *The dead hear saint's bell.* (Cf. D1213.) Irish myth: Cross.

E545.15. *Saint after his death gives directions where he wants to be buried.* *Loomis White Magic 53.

E545.16. *Dead predict calamity or disaster.*

E545.16.1. *Dead predict war.* (See E575.) U.S.: Baughman.

E545.17. *The dead foretell the future.* (Cf. E363.3, E576.) U.S.: Baughman; Jewish: *Neuman.

E545.18. *Ghost asks to be taken to former home.* (See all references to E332.3.3.1.) U.S.: Baughman.

E545.19. *Addressing the dead.*

E545.19.1. *The dead cannot speak until spoken to.* England, U.S., Wales: *Baughman.

E545.19.2. *Proper means of addressing ghosts.* England, U.S., Wales: *Baughman.

E545.20. *Part of ghost speaks.*

E545.20.1. *Strand of hair from drowned woman speaks.* U.S.: Baughman.

E545.21. *Heads of slain people in magician's house advises hero.* India: Thompson-Balys.

E545.22. *Conversation between God and Adam's corpse.* Jewish: *Neuman.

E545.23. *Dead must be answered in whispers.* Eskimo (Labrador): Hawkes GSCan XIV 153, (Ungava): Turner RBAE XI 266, (Greenland): Rink 302, Rasmussen II 269.

E546. *The dead sing.* (Cf. E371.3.) *Type 403_1; *Fb "hvid" I 700b; Irish myth: *Cross; New York: Jones JAFL LVII 244.
E492. Mass (church service) of the dead.

E547. *The dead wail* (Cf. E402ff.) Fb "kirkeklokke" II 131a; Jewish: Neuman.

E547.1. *The dead groan.* North Carolina: Brown Collection I 681, 685.

E548. *Dead make music on their ribs.* Irish: Curtin Myths and Folklore of Ireland 25; India: Thompson-Balys; New York: Jones JAFL LVII 244.

E551. *Dead man sobs.* (Cf. E402.1.1.) Swiss: Jegerlehner Oberwallis 296 No. 21.

E552. *Ghost in form of bear sneezes.* (Cf. E423.2.1.) Tobler 56.

E553. *Ghost becomes log during day.* N. A. Indian (California): Gayton and Newman 101.

E554. *Ghost plays musical instrument.* U.S.: Baughman.

E554.1. *Ghost plays organ.* North Carolina: Brown Collection I 676.

E555. *Dead man smokes pipe.* Fb "tobak" III 814a, "spøgelse" III 520a; U.S.: Baughman; N. A. Indian (Seneca): Curtin-Hewitt RBAE XXXII 219 No. 41, (Teton): Dorsey AA o.s. II (1889) 150.

E556. *Ghost drinks.* U.S.: Baughman.

E556.1. *Ghost drinks liquor.* England, U.S.: Baughman.

E556.1.1. *The dead man asks for whiskey.* Lithuanian: Balys Ghosts.

E557. *Dead man writes.* Fb "spøgelse" III 520a.

E557.1 *Ghost writes on wall the answers to problems of person in trouble.* U.S.: Baughman.

E558. *Ghosts forced to labor.* India: Thompson-Balys.

E561. *Dead person spins.* Fb "spøgelse" III 520a, "spinde" III 492a; England, Scotland, U.S.: *Baughman.

E561.1. *Sight of dead woman spinning drives people insane.* *Fb "spinde" III 492a.

C311.1.1. Tabu: looking at ghosts. D2065.2. Insanity from seeing strange sight.

E562. *Dead person weaves.* Fb "spøgelse" III 520a; England: *Baughman.

E563. *Dead person knits.* Fb "spøgelse" III 520a.

E564. *Man who has died and returned to life becomes diviner.* India: Thompson-Balys.

E565. *Ghosts clank chains.* (Cf. E501.13.1.2., E755.2.2.) North Carolina: Brown Collection I 675.

E567. *Dead person threshes.* Fb "spøgelse" III 520a.

E568. *Revenant lies down and sleeps.* U.S.: Baughman.

E568.1. *Revenant leaves impression of body in bed.* England, U.S. *Baughman.

E571. *Ghostly barber.* *Type 326; *BP I 24; *Fb "balbere" IV 23a.

E572. *Ghost walks through solid substance.* U.S.: *Baughman.

E573. *Ghost tried in court.* **Jacoby Zs. f. Vksk. XXIII (1913) 184; Jewish: Neuman.

B272. Animals defendant in court.

E574. *Appearance of ghost serves as death omen.* (Cf. D1812.5.1.1, E265.3, E501.20.) England, Scotland, U.S., Wales: *Baughman.

E575. *Ghost as omen of calamity or ill fortune.* England, U.S.: *Baughman.

E576. *Dead man praises God.* Jewish: *Neuman.

E576.1. *Dead intercedes before God for mortal.* Jewish: *Neuman.

E577. *Dead persons play games.* U.S.: Baughman; Eskimo (Labrador): Hawkes GSCan XIV 153.

E577.1. *Dead persons play ball.* (Cf. E494.) Wimberly 233.

E577.2. *Dead persons play cards.* *Type 326; Fb "spøgelse" III 520a; U.S.: Baughman.

E577.2.1. *Playing cards with a dead man (ghost).* Lithuanian: Balys Legends Nos. 678ff.

H1421. Playing cards with devil in church. N4. Devil plays cards.

E577.3. *Dead persons bowl.* Type 326; cf. Washington Irving's "Rip Van Winkle".

E578. *Dead persons build fires.* Type 326; Russian: Ralston 314; India: Thompson-Balys.

E578.1. *Revenants want to warm themselves.* Type 326.

E422.1.3.Revenant with ice-cold hands or feet.

E578.2. *Ghosts warm themselves around fire.* India: Thompson-Balys.

E581. *Dead person rides.* Fb "spøgelse" III 520a; North Carolina: Brown Collection I 680—682.

E215. The Dead Rider (Lenore). E332.3. Ghost on road asks traveler for ride.

E581.1. *Whirlwind as ghost's vehicle.* N. A. Indian (California): Gayton and Newman 84.

D1520.28. Magic transportation in whirlwind. F411.1. Demon travels in whirlwind. F455.3.4. Troll rides in whirlwind.

E581.2. *Ghost rides horse.* England, U.S.: *Baughman.

E422.1.1.3.1. Headless ghost rides horse.

E581.2.1. *Ghost jumps on horse behind man.* (Cf. E262.) North Carolina: Brown Collection I 681.

E581.3. *Ghost rides cow.* U.S.: *Baughman.

E581.4. *Ghost rides bus.*

E581.4.1. *Ghost rides on bus, disappears before it crosses bridge.* U.S.: Baughman.

E581.5. *Ghost rides heavy iron chest.* U.S.: Baughman.

E581.6. *Ghost rides giant demijohn.* U.S.: Baughman.

E581.7. *Ghost sails over sound on bundle of straw.* Fb "halmknippe" I 539b.

E582. *Dead person drives horses.* Fb "spøgelse" III 520a; England: Baughman.

E583. *Dead persons draw chariot.* India: Thompson-Balys, Tawney I 457.

E585. *Dead person visits earth periodically.* (Cf. E332.3.3.1, E535.3.)

E585.1. *Dead person visits earth every seven years.* Fb "spøgelse" III 519b; Tobler 66.

E501.11.3.1. Wild hunt appears every seven years.

E585.2. *Spectre rides to castle every seven years.* Irish myth: Cross.

E585.3. *Revenant revisits earth every day.* U.S.: Baughman.

E585.3.1. *Revenant revisits earth nightly.* Africa (Fang): Trilles 269.

E585.4. *Revenant revisits earth yearly.* S. A. Indian (Brazil): Oberg 109.

E586. *Dead returns soon after burial.* India: Thompson-Balys.

E586.0.1. *Ghost returns before burial.* U.S.: Baughman.

E586.1. *Dead returns on burial day.* Fb "spøgelse" III 519ab; Spanish Exempla: Keller; England, U.S.: *Baughman.

E586.2. *Dead returns third day after burial.* Fb "sjæl" III 214b, "spøgelse" III 519b; N. A. Indian (California): Gayton and Newman 101; Eskimo (Labrador): Hawkes GSCan XIV 153.

E586.3. *Dead return second day after burial.* N. A. Indian (California): Gayton and Newman 99.

E586.4. *Dead sent back to life because his name is not in heavenly roll.* India: Thompson-Balys.

E587. *Ghosts walk at certain times.*

E501.11. Time of appearance of wild hunt.

E587.1. *Ghosts walk at midday.* Fb "middag" II 585b.

E587.2. *Ghosts walk on Hallowe'en.* (Cf. F211.1.1.1.) Irish myth: Cross; U.S.: Baughman.

F900.1. Wonders occur on Hallowe'en.

E587.2.1. *Ghost most numerous on St. Thomas Eve and St. Thomas Day.* England: Baughman.

E587.3. *Ghosts walk from curfew to cockcrow.* (Cf. E452.) England: Baughman.

E587.4. *Spirits are always in the air.* England: Baughman.

E587.5. *Ghost walk at midnight.* U.S.: Baughman.

E587.6. *Ghosts walk at full moon.* Hawaii: Beckwith Myth 198.

E588. *Ghost leaves stench behind.* Fb "stank"; Eskimo (Greenland): Rink 276, Rasmussen II 275.

E591. *Ghost travels under ground.* Fb "jord" II 45b.

E592. *Ghost carries burden.*

E592.1. *Ghost carries own dead body.* Kai (German New Guinea): Dixon 142.

E592.2. *Ghost carries coffin on back.* Wimberly 238.

E593. *Ghost takes things from people.*

E593.1. *Ghost steals collar of priest.* Evil therefore befalls priest. *Fb "gjenganger" I 443.

E593.2. *Ghost steals book from priest.* *Fb "bog" IV 53b.

E593.3. *If no lamp is lighted in a house for a period of fourteen days, ghosts take it for their dwelling.* India: Thompson-Balys.

E593.4. *Ghost takes bones from grave.* Eskimo (Greenland): Holm 81.

E593.5. *Ghost steals food and treasure.* Hawaii: Beckwith Myth 123.

E594. *Dead man wanders with torch.* (Cf. E599.7.) Tobler 84; Eskimo (Ungava): Turner RBAE XI 266.

F491. Will o'the Wisp.

E595. *Cures by transferring disease to dead.* Ghoulish charm used for this purpose. Kittredge Witchcraft 143, 461 n. 34.

D1278. Ghoulish charm. Charm made from parts of a corpse or things associated with corpse. D2161.4.1. Cure by transferring disease to animal.

E596. *Living person in service of a dead man.* BP I 214.

E596.1. *Ghost works for human being.* India: Thompson-Balys.

E597. *Corpse leaps up in emotion at saint's passing nearby.* Irish myth: Cross.

E598. *Death and return to life rids man of disease.* India: Thompson-Balys.

E599. *Other actions of revenants.*

E599.1. *Ghost searches for breath.* U.S.: Baughman.

E599.2. *Ghostly corpses seen on floor of house, disappear when coroner comes.* U.S.: Baughman.

E599.3. *Ghost watches (follows) its own corpse.* England, U.S.: *Baughman.

E599.4. *Ghost asks alms (from one who does not know that asker has died) at usual place and time.* England: Baughman.

E599.5. *Ghost travels swiftly.* (Cf. D2122.) England: Baughman.

E599.6. *Ghosts move furniture.* U.S.: *Baughman.

E599.7. *Ghost carries lantern.* (Cf. E371.10, E472, E594, E530.1, F491.1.) U.S.: Baughman.

E599.8. *Ghost vanishes when taken home.* (Cf. E332.3.3.1.) U.S.: *Baughman.

E599.9. *Ghost seen in two places simultaneously.* England: Baughman.

E599.10. *Playful revenant.* England: Baughman.

E599.11. *Locked doors open at touch of ghosts.* India: Thompson-Balys.

E599.12. *Human being transported by a ghost.* India: Thompson-Balys.

E599.13. *Dead person bathes.* Jewish: Neuman.

E600—E699. Reincarnation.

E600. Reincarnation. Return from the dead in another form. India: Penzer X 336 s.v. "Transmigration", *Cowell Jātaka Index s.v. "Bodhisatta" and "Rebirth", Keith 100, *Thompson-Balys; Irish myth: *Cross, Nutt "The Irish Vision of the Happy Otherworld and the Celtic Doctrine of Rebirth" in K. Meyer Voyage of Bran; Icelandic: *Boberg; Estonian: Loorits Grundzüge I 321ff.; Jewish: *Neuman; Siberian: Holmberg Siberian 473; Chinese: Werner 314; N. A. Indian: *Thompson Tales 337 n. 216a, Alexander N. Am. 280 n. 18; Eskimo (West Hudson Bay): Boas BAM XV 359, (Greenland): Rasmussen I 115, III 171, (Central Eskimo): Boas RBAE VI 639; S. A. Indian (Brazil): Oberg 109.

A510.2. Culture hero reborn. A511.1.3. Culture hero reincarnated from birth through virgin. A511.1.7. Culture hero born three times. A512.3. Culture hero son of god. A1232.1. Mankind from bones of dead brought from underworld. A2275.6. Son accidentally kills father, who returns to life as cuckoo and tells people how to sow grain. B81.1. Mermaids from Pharaoh's children. They were drowned in the Red Sea. D610. Repeated transformation. D1850. Immortality. D1889.7. Rejuvenation by being reborn. E0. Resuscitation. E501.4.0.1. Animals in wild hunt reincarnation of murdered person. H19.1.1. Recognition of reincarnated person by ability to identify former weapons. V311. Belief in the life to come.

E600.1. *Origin of reincarnation: miscarried message of immortality.* India: Thompson-Balys.

E600.2. *Science of reincarnation taught.* India: Thompson-Balys.

E601. *Reincarnation: former lives remembered.* Jewish: *Neuman, *Penzer X 154 s.v. "Former births"; India: Thompson-Balys.

A2275.3. Animal cries reminiscent of former life as man. D1323.16. Magic feather gives clairvoyance.

E601.1. *Man by magic sees his wives in their former incarnations as dog and sow.* India: Thompson-Balys.

A1371.3. Bad women from transformed hog and goose.

E601.2. *Reincarnated benefactor helped by man he has befriended in former life.* India: Thompson-Balys.

E601.3. *Punishments earned on one life paid in next reincarnation.* India: Thompson-Balys.

E602. *Reincarnation in form determined at death.* India: Thompson-Balys, Tawney II 145.

E603. *Limited number of souls in world necessitates reincarnation.* India: Thompson-Balys.

E700. The soul.

E604. *Definite number of reincarnations.*

E604.1. *Seven reincarnations.* *Zachariae 33ff.; India: Thompson-Balys.

E605. *Reincarnation in another human form.* *M. Bloomfield Proc. Am. Philosophical Soc. LVI 1ff.; Jewish: Neuman; India: *Thompson-Balys.

E605.1. *Reincarnation with change of sex.* *Penzer VII 230; India: Thompson-Balys.

D10. Transformation to person of different sex. M454. Curse: change of sex.

E605.1.1. *Reincarnation: woman reborn as man.* Chinese: Werner 256.

E605.1.2. *Man reborn as woman.* India: Thompson-Balys; Korean: Zong in-Sob 76.

Q551.3.6.1. Punishment: man reborn as girl.

E605.2. *Reincarnation: god reborn as man.* Icelandic: Olrik Kilderne til Sakses Oldhistorie I (1892) 30ff., 60ff., Boberg; India: *Thompson-Balys, Keith 168; Buddhist myth: Malalasekera II 907, 1258; Hawaii: Beckwith Myth 119; Marquesas: Handy 109; N. A. Indian (Mandan): Curtis N. A. Indian V 39ff.

E651. God reincarnated as dwarf. E652. God reincarnated as monster.

E605.2.1. *Reincarnation: spirit reborn as man.* Eskimo (Greenland): Rasmussen III 57.

E605.3. *Reincarnation: man becomes god.* India: *Thompson-Balys; Chinese: Werner 212.

E605.4. *Reincarnation: man becomes spirit.* India: Thompson-Balys.

E605.5. *Reincarnation: prince becomes common man.* India: Thompson-Balys.

E605.6. *Reincarnation: common man becomes prince.* India: Thompson-Balys.

E605.7. *Man reincarnated as child.* (Cf. E607.2.) India: Thompson-Balys.

E605.7.1. *Reincarnation as child which is within a fish.* India: Thompson-Balys.

E605.8. *Horse-headed men reborn as money-lenders.* India: Thompson-Balys.

E605.9. *Reincarnation as conjurer.* Eskimo (Cumberland Sound): Boas BAM XV 234, 247, (Greenland): Rasmussen III 130.

E606. *Reasons for reincarnation.* (Cf. E693.)

E606.1. *Reincarnation as punishment for sin.* India: *Thompson-Balys.

Q220. Impiety punished.

E606.2. *Reincarnation to complete unfinished work.* India: Thompson-Balys.

E607. *Methods of reincarnation.*

E607.1. *Bones of dead collected and buried.* Return in another form directly from grave. *Type 720; S. A. Indian (Warrau): Alexander Lat. Am. 272

E30. Resuscitation by arrangement of members.

E607.1.1. *Bones of dead collected and thrown into river.* India: Thompson-Balys.

E607.2. *Person transforms self, is swallowed and reborn in new form.* (Cf. D605.7, D610.) Irish myth: *Cross; Welsh: MacCulloch Celtic 110; India: Thompson-Balys; N. A. Indian: Thompson Tales 282 n. 44.

A1411.2. Theft of light by being swallowed and reborn. F392. Fairy transforms self to fly, allows self to be swallowed by woman, and is reborn as fairy. T511. Conception from eating. T539.1. Hero enters womb of sleeping woman and is reborn.

E607.2.1. *Person is swallowed and then reborn.* India: Thompson-Balys.

E607.2.2. *Rebirth by crawling into woman's womb.* Eskimo (Greenland): Rasmussen III 57.

E607.3. *Hauling canoe over dead man's body causes return from dead in new form.* Maori: Dixon 55.

E607.4. *Reincarnation by fasting.* Irish myth: Cross.

E607.5. *Cauldron of regeneration (reincarnation).* Irish myth: *Cross.

E610. Reincarnation as animal. Encyc. Rel. and Ethics I 493b; Irish myth: Cross; Breton: Sébillot Incidents s.v. "animaux"; Jewish: bin Gorion VI 110, 310; Africa: Werner African 192.

A1724. Animals from transformed parts of body of slain giant. A2001. Insects from body of slain monster. B313.1. Helpful animal reincarnation of parent. D610. Repeated transformation. D842.3. Magic object found on grave of slain helpful animal. E322.4. Dead wife returns in form of bird. E423. Revenant in animal form. E730. Soul in animal form. F167.1. Animals in otherworld. F234.1. Fairy in form of animal.

E610.1. *Reincarnation: man to animal to man.* Irish myth: Cross.

D100. Transformation: man to animal. D300. Transformation: animal to person. D610. Repeated transformation. E648. Reincarnation: man-object-man.

E610.1.1. *Reincarnation: boy to bird to boy.* Boy returns as bird, who later becomes the boy. *Type 720; *BP I 422.

E610.1.2. *Reincarnation: man to fish to man.* Eskimo (Greenland): Rasmussen I 115, II 151.

E611. *Reincarnation as domestic animal.*

E611.1. *Reincarnation as horse.* (Cf. D131.) Gaster Exempla 248 No. 349; Buddhist myth: Malalasekera I 851.

E611.1.1. *Reincarnation: man as horse-head.* Hindu: Keith 121 (Vishnu).

E611.1.2. *Reincarnation as donkey.* India: Thompson-Balys; Chinese: Eberhard FFC CXX 131.

E611.2. *Reincarnation as cow.* (Cf. D133.1.) *Type 510, 511; BP *I 187, III 61ff.; Wesselski Deutsche Märchen vor Grimm (1938) vii ff.; *MacCulloch Childhood 108; India: *Thompson-Balys.

E611.2.0.1. *Divinity reincarnated as cow.* India: Thompson-Balys.

E611.2.1. *Reincarnation as bull.* Buddhist myth: Malalasekera I 166, II 29.

E611.2.1.0.1. *Divinity reincarnated as bull.* (Cf. A132.9.) Irish: MacCulloch Celtic 152, *Cross; India: Thompson-Balys.

A132.9. Bull-god. D101. Transformation: god to animal. D133.2. Transformation: man to bull.

E611.2.1.1. *Reincarnation as bullock.* India: *Thompson-Balys.

E611.2.2. *Reincarnation as an ox.* Buddhist myth: Malalasekera II 1124.

E611.2.3. *Reincarnation as calf.* Chinese: Eberhard FFC CXX 54, 189.

E611.2.4. *Reincarnation as a buffalo.* Buddhist myth: Malalasekera II 592; Chinese: Graham (E612.11).

E611.3. *Man reincarnated as swine.* Fb "svin" III 676a, "sjæl" III 214a; India: *Thompson-Balys; Buddhist myth: Malalasekera I 423, 1031; Chinese: Eberhard FFC CXX 189, 199.

D136. Transformation: man to swine. F460.1.1.1. Mountain-man in shape of hog. F480.1. House-spirit in form of a sow.

E611.3.1. *Man reincarnated as wild boar.* Irish myth: Cross; India: Thompson-Balys; Hindu: Keith 121 (Vishnu).

A132.7. Swine-god. D114.3.2. Transformation: man to boar. F234.1.3. Fairy in form of wild boar.

E611.4. *Man reincarnated as goat.* (Cf. D134.) *Type 510, 511; *BP I 187, III 60ff.; India: Thompson-Balys; Africa (Angola): Chatelain 53 No. 2.

E611.5. *Man reincarnated as cat.* Fb "sjæl" III 214a.

D142. Transformation: man to cat. H1385.4.1. Quest for husband who has been reincarnated as a cat.

E611.5.1. *God reincarnated as cat.* India: Thompson-Balys.

E611.6. *Man reincarnated as dog.* (Cf. D141.) Fb "sjæl" III 214a; India: *Thompson-Balys; Buddhist myth: Malalasekera I 267, 827; Korean: Zong in-Sob 92; Eskimo (Greenland): Rasmussen I 115.

E612. *Reincarnation as wild animal.* Estonian: Loorits Grundzüge I 325ff.

E612.1. *Reincarnation as lion.* Hindu: Keith 121 (Vishnu).

D112.1. Transformation: man to lion.

E612.2. *Reincarnation as wolf.* Fb "pebersvend" II 795a (werwolf); Irish myth: Cross.

D113.1. Transformation: man to wolf. D113.1.1. Werwolf. E751.5.1. Wandering soul assumes shape of wolf. F234.1.13. Fairy in form of wolf.

E612.3. *Reincarnation as hare.* Fb "sjæl" III 214a; Gaster Exempla 248 No. 349; Eskimo (Central Eskimo): Boas RBAE VI 639.

D117.2. Transformation: man to hare. F234.1.12. Fairy in form of hare. G211.4. Witch in form of hare.

E612.4. *Reincarnation as fox.* (Cf. D113.3.) *Type 506; BP III 494ff.; Fb "sjæl" III 214a.

E612.5. *Reincarnation as deer.* Irish myth: *Cross; Buddhist myth: Malalasekera I 421, II 27f., 69.

D114.1.1. Transformation: man to deer. F234.1.4. Fairy in form of stag.

E612.6. *Reincarnation as seal.* (Cf. D127.1.) Irish myth: Cross; Eskimo (Greenland): Rasmussen I 115, III 56.

E612.7. *Reincarnation as mongoose.* India: Thompson-Balys.

E612.8. *Reincarnation as bear.* India: Thompson-Balys.

E612.9. *Reincarnation as hyena.* India: Thompson-Balys.

E612.10. *Reincarnation as jackal.* India: Thompson-Balys; Buddhist myth: Malalasekera 267, 1034, 1131.

E612.11. *Reincarnation as elephant.* Buddhist myth: Malalasekera I 157, II 603, 1158.

E612.12. *Reincarnation as monkey.* Buddhist myth: Malalasekera I 996, II 27, 471, 519, 847, 939.

E612.13. *Reincarnation as rat.* Buddhist myth: Malalasekera I 290, 1885.

E612.14. *Reincarnation as otter.* Buddhist myth: Malalasekera I 267.

E613. *Reincarnation as bird.* Fb "sjæl" III 214a; Gjerdman Nattskärran och nogra andra Spökfåglar (Arv I 27—68); Estonian: Loorits Grundzüge I 347—363; India: *Thompson-Balys; Buddhist myth: Malalasekera I 870, II 17; Japanese: Ikeda; Chinese: Eberhard FFC CXX 264ff, Graham; Aztec: Alexander Lat. Am. 61.

A132.6.2. Goddess in form of bird. D150. Transformation: man to bird. E423.3. Revenant as bird. E732. Soul in form of bird.

E613.0.1. *Reincarnation of murdered child as bird.* *Type 720; *BP I 422; *Fb "fugl" I 380b; English: Child I 126, 180f.; India: *Thompson-Balys; Africa: Werner African 211, (Basuto): Jacottet 56.

E231. Return from dead to reveal murder. E413. Murdered person cannot rest in grave. N271. Murder will out. N271.6. Murder revealed by child. P230. Parents and children.

E613.0.2. *Reincarnation of unbaptized child as bird.* *Fb "udøbt" III 960a; *Dh III 484.

E412.2. Unbaptized person cannot rest in grave. F251.3. Unbaptized children as fairies. F360.1. Fairies pursue unbaptized children.

E613.0.3. *Reincarnation of old maids as birds.* Dh III 485; Fb "pebersvend" II 795a.

E613.0.4. *Reincarnation of drowned persons as birds.* Dh III 482.

E613.0.5. *Severed heads of monster become birds.* Hindu: Keith 88.

A1716.1. Animals from different parts of body of slain giant.

E613.0.6. *Reincarnation of girl eaten by tiger as bird.* India: Thompson-Balys.

E613.1. *Reincarnation as duck.* Tobler 53; Lithuanian: Balys Index No. 453*; Chinese: Eberhard FFC CXX 264.

E613.1.1. *Reincarnation as sheldrake.* India: Thompson-Balys.

E613.2. *Reincarnation as owl.* Tobler 97; India: Thompson-Balys.

A1958. Creation of owl. D153.2. Transformation: man to owl.

E613.3. *Reincarnation as hawk.* (Cf. D152.1.) Tobler 97; Irish myth: Cross.

E613.3.1. *Reincarnation as eagle.* India: Thompson-Balys.

E613.4. *Reincarnation as swallow.* (Cf. D151.1.) Fb "pebersvend" II 795a. — Finnish: Aarne FFC VIII 15 No. 83; Estonian: Aarne FFC XXV 147 No. 50.

E613.5. *Reincarnation as cuckoo.* Lithuanian: Balys Index No. 3134, Legends Nos. 248ff.; Livonian: Loorits FFC LXVI 89 No. 77.

A1993. Creation of cuckoo.

E613.6. *Reincarnation as dove.* Italian: Basile Pentamerone V 9.

E613.6.1. *Reincarnation as pigeon.* Buddhist myth: Malalasekera I 520, 557.

E613.7. *Reincarnation as raven.* England: *Baughman.

E613.8. *Reincarnation as quail.* Buddhist myth: Malalasekera II 816, 986, 1065.

E613.8.1. *Reincarnation as partridge.* Buddhist myth: Malalasekera II 226.

E613.9. *Reincarnation as heron.* India: Thompson-Balys.

E613.9.1. *Reincarnation as crane.* Buddhist myth: Malalasekera II 1182.

E613.10. *Reincarnation as goose.* Buddhist myth: Malalasekera I 267, II 1264.

E613.11. *Reincarnation as peacock.* Buddhist myth: Malalasekera I 1052, II 671.

E613.12. *Reincarnation as parrot.* Buddhist myth: Malalasekera I 266, 578, II 247, 572, 730f., 1122, 1173.

E614. *Reincarnation as reptile.*

E614.1. *Reincarnation as snake.* (Cf. D191.) Fb "sjæl" III 214a; Estonian: Loorits Grundzüge I 339ff.; India: *Thompson-Balys; Buddhist myth: Malalasekera I 857; Chinese: Eberhard FFC CXX 166f.

E614.2. *Reincarnation as lizard.* India: Thompson-Balys; Buddhist myth: Malalasekera I 813; Tonga: Gifford 108.

E614.3. *Reincarnation as crocodile.* India: Thompson-Balys; Buddhist myth: Malalasekera I 365, 479, II 555.

E614.4. *Reincarnation as tortoise.* India: Thompson-Balys; Buddhist myth: Malalasekera I 267.

E614.5. *Reincarnation as iguana.* Buddhist myth: Malalasekera I 267.

E615. *Reincarnation as amphibian.*

E615.1. *Reincarnation as frog.* (Cf. D195.) Tobler 28; Fb "sjæl" III 214a; India: Thompson-Balys; Buddhist myth: Malalasekera II 1322.

E616. *Reincarnation as insect.* Estonian: Loorits Grundzüge I 331ff.; India: *Thompson-Balys.

A2001. Insects from body of slain monster. D180. Transformation: man to insect.

E616.1. *Reincarnation as bee.* (Cf. D182.) Fb "sjæl" III 214a.

E616.2. *Reincarnation as butterfly.* Chinese: Eberhard FFC CXX 266.

E616.3. *Reincarnation as flea.* India: Thompson-Balys.

E616.4. *Reincarnation as weevil.* India: Thompson-Balys.

E616.5. *Reincarnation as bedbug.* (Cf. E693.2.) India: Thompson-Balys.

E617. *Reincarnation as fish.* (Cf. D170, E713.1.) Irish myth: Cross; India: *Thompson-Balys; Buddhist myth: Malalasekera I 999, 1148, II 691.

E617.1. *Reincarnation as salmon.* (Cf. B124.1, D176.) Irish myth: *Cross; Eskimo (Greenland): Rasmussen I 115, II 15.

E617.2. *Reincarnation as goldfish.* India: Thompson-Balys.

E617.3. *Reincarnation as shark.* Solomon Islands: Beckwith Myth 13.

E617.4. *Reincarnation as whale.* Eskimo (Greenland): Rasmussen I 115.

E618. *Reincarnation as worm.* Buddhist myth: Malalasekera I 222.

E618.1. *Reincarnation as leech.* India: Thompson-Balys.

E629. *Reincarnation as animal—miscellaneous.*

E629.1. *Reincarnation as scorpion.* India: Thompson-Balys.

E629.2. *Reincarnation as crab.* Buddhist myth: Malalasekera I 267

E630. Reincarnation in object.

A978.1. Origin of minerals from body of dead culture hero. D200. Transformation: man to object. E745. Soul as object.

E631. *Reincarnation in plant (tree) growing from grave.* (Cf. E632, D1610.2.) Type 510; BP I 187; *Cox 477 n. 7; *Fb "sjæl" III 214b, "blod" IV 49a, "juletræ" II 57a; Saintyves Contes de Perrault (Paris, 1923) 36ff., 144ff. — English: *Child V 481. s.v. "grave", V 491 s.v. "plants"; Irish myth: *Cross; Breton: Sébillot Incidents s.v. "arbres", "cadavre", "tombeau"; Swiss: Jegerlehner Oberwallis 298 No. 7, 311 No 41; Spanish: Boggs FFC XC 92 No. 780B*; Greek: Fox 198 (Adonis), 201 (Pyramus and Thisbe); Italian: Basile Pentamerone I No. 6; Finnish-Swedish: Wessman 2 Nos. 12, 13; India: *Thompson-Balys; Indonesian: Dixon 238, De Vries Volksverhalen I 300; Chinese: Eberhard FFC CXX 50f.; Papua: Ker 131; N. A. Indian (Zuñi): Cushing 183, (Kato): Goddard UCal V 219 n. 1; Amazon: Alexander Lat. Am. 294; Africa (Kaffir): Theal 147, (Ekoi): Talbot 133.

A1251. Creation of man from tree. A2611. Plants from body of slain person or animal. D215. Transformation: man to tree. D842.1. Magic objects found on mother's grave. T543.1. Birth from a tree.

E631.0.1. *Twining branches grow from graves of lovers.* (Cf. E419.6.) *Gaidoz Mélusine IV No. 4; Type 966*; *Fb "rose" III 80a, "lilie" II 427b, "træ" III 867a; Chauvin V 107 No. 37; Irish myth: *Cross; India: Thompson-Balys; Chinese: Eberhard FFC CXX 264f.; Japanese: Anesaki 253, 346f.

T86. Lovers buried in same grave.

E631.0.1.1. *Tops of trees from lovers' graves show shapes of their heads.* Irish myth: *Cross.

E631.0.1.2. *Tablets made of trees from lovers' graves magically unite.* Irish myth: *Cross.

E631.0.2. *Flower from grave bears letters.* These commemorate the buried person. *Fb "grav" I 478a, "skrift"; Irish myth: Cross; Finnish-Swedish: Wessman 2 No. 11; Greek: *Frazer Apollodorus I 19 n. 3 (Hyacinth).

A2732. Indentions on plants from biting. F970. Extraordinary behavior of trees and plants.

E631.0.2.1. *Flower with "ave" on leaves.* Crows from tomb as reward for faithful sayings of "Ave Maria". *Ward Catalogue of Romances II 654 No. 21; Herbert ibid. III 342; Von der Hagen Nos. 73, 88; Spanish Exempla: Keller.

E631.0.3. *Plant from blood of slain person.* *Fb "blod" IV 49a, "juletræ", II 57a; Swiss: Jegerlehner Oberwallis 311 No. 41; Greek: Fox 198, 201; India: *Thompson-Balys; Africa: Frobenius Atlantis IV 225f.

E631.0.3.1. *Red plant from blood of slain person.* *Fb "blod" IV 49a; BP II 532 n. 2.

E631.0.4. *Speaking and bleeding trees.* Reincarnated persons. *Reinhard PMLA XXXVIII 456 n. 106; Hdwb. d. Märchens I 200 s.v. "Baum"; Swiss: Jegerlehner Oberwallis 299 No. 8; India: *Thompson-Balys; Chinese: Ferguson 177.

D1610.2. Speaking tree. E765.3.3. Life bound up with tree.

E631.0.5. *Tree from innocent man's blood.* Fb "juletræ" II 57a, "sjæl" III 214b. — English: Child I 143; India: Thompson-Balys.

E631.0.5.1. *Dry branch on innocent man's grave blossoms as proof of innocence.* Fb "uskyldig".

D1318. Magic object reveals guilt. F971.1. Dry rod blossoms.

E631.0.6. *Tree from sinner's grave.* Hdwb. d. März. I 200 s.v. "Baum".

E631.1. *Flower from grave.* BP II 126; Hungarian: Solymossy Hongaarache Sagen (1929) 243 No. 68, Moór Ungarisches Jahrbuch V 430; India: *Thompson-Balys; Korean: Zong in-Sob 207.

A2650. Origin of flowers. D212. Transformation: man (woman) to flower. H31.12. Calumniated wife alone able to pluck lotus flower, her reincarnated abandoned son.

E631.1.1. *Lily from grave.* Fb "lilie" II 427b, "sjæl" III 214b; BP III 461; English: Child I 143; India: Thompson-Balys.

E631.1.2. *Rose from grave.* *Fb "rose" III 80a.

E631.1.3. *Reincarnation as lotus.* India: Thompson-Balys; Buddhist myth: Malalasekera II 527.

E631.1.4. *Reincarnation as cockscomb.* India: Thompson-Balys.

E631.2. *Grass does not grow on murderer's grave.* (Cf. H271.) Fb "græs"; England: Baughman.

E631.2.1. *Reincarnation as a grass straw.* Eskimo (Greenland): Rasmussen I 115.

E631.3. *Herbs grow from grave of healer.* Brouwer Das Volkslied in Deutschland, Frankreich, Belgien und Holland (Groningen, 1930) 196ff.; Irish myth: *Cross.

E631.4. *Dead ogress reincarnated as bramble-bush which prevents escape of fugitive.* Chinese: Graham.

E631.5. *Reincarnation as plant.*

E631.5.1. *Reincarnation as tobacco plant.* Chinese: Graham; India: Thompson-Balys.

E631.5.2. *Reincarnation as peanut plant.* S. A. Indian (Yuracare): Métraux BBAE CXLIII (3) 503.

E631.5.3. *Reincarnation as eggplant.* Africa (Luba): LeClerq Zs. f. Kolonialsprachen IV 226f.

E631.6. *Reincarnation in tree from grave.* Japanese: Ikeda; Easter Island: Métraux Ethnology 376; Papua: Ker 92. Cf. Virgil Aeneid III 22ff.

E632. *Reincarnation as musical instrument.* The Singing Bone. A musical instrument made from the bones of a murdered person, or from a tree growing from the grave, speaks and tells of the crime. *Type 780; **Mackensen FFC XLIX; BP I 260, II 532; *Fb "streng" III 603a, "harpe" I 559b, IV 201b, "ben" IV 32b; Child I 121—135, 494, IV 449; Breton: Sébillot Incidents s.v. "os"; India: *Thompson-Balys; Japanese: Ikeda.

D1610.2. Speaking tree. E231. Return from dead to reveal murder. K1911.3.4. True bride reincarnated as reed reveals truth. N271. Murder will out. Q211. Murder punished.

E632.1. *Speaking bones of murdered person reveal murder.* India: Thompson-Balys; Japanese: Ikeda; Africa (Ibo [Nigeria]): Thomas 58, 67, (Fang): Tessman 124ff.

G64. Human flesh being cooked speaks out.

E633. *Reincarnation as dish.* Bones made into dish. These speak. (Cf. E632.) English: Child I 126; Japanese: Ikeda.

D251. Transformation: man to dish. E231. Return from dead to reveal murder.

E635. *Reincarnation as fountain.* Fb "kilde" II 119b; Child V 287a.

E636. *Reincarnation as water.* (Cf. D283.) India: Thompson-Balys.

E636.1. *Reincarnation as bag of water.* Irish myth: Cross (E636).

E637. *Reincarnation as ball (of gold and iron).* India: Thompson-Balys.

E641. *Reincarnation as whirlwind.* Ila (Rhodesia): Smith and Dale II 414 No. 12.

D281.1.1. Transformation: man to whirlwind.

E642. *Reincarnation as stone.*

E642.0.1. *Reincarnation as salt.* India: Thompson-Balys.

E642.1. *Dead lovers are now two stones lying together.* India: Thompson-Balys.

E643. *Reincarnation as smoke.*

E643.1. *Smoke from funeral fires of two lovers mingles in sky.* India: Thompson-Balys.

E644. *Reincarnation as rainbow.* India: Thompson-Balys.

E645. *Reincarnation as mineral.*

E645.1. *Reincarnation of slain boy as gold and silver.* India: Thompson-Balys.

E646. *Reincarnation as meteor.* S. A. Indian (Gran Chaco): Belaieff BBAE CXLIII (1) 380.

E648. *Reincarnation: man-object-man.* In most of the versions of E632 (Reincarnation as musical instrument) the hero (heroine) finally comes back to life in his usual form. See also BP II 126f.; India: *Thompson-Balys.

D610. Repeated transformation. E251.2.2. Prince plucks from grave of vampire a flower which later becomes a girl.

E648.1. *Reincarnation: woman - bird - nettles - stone - woman.* Chinese: Graham.

E648.2. *Reincarnation: man - woman - stone image.* Korean: Zong in-Sob 76.

E649. *Reincarnation to object—miscellaneous.*

E649.1. *Reincarnation as hill.* Head made into hill. Cheremis: Sebeok-Nyerges.

E649.2. *Reincarnation as flour vat.* Stomach made into flour vat. Cheremis: Sebeok-Nyerges.

E649.3. *Reincarnation as hoe.* Feet made into hoe. Cheremis: Sebeok-Nyerges.

E649.3.1. *Reincarnation as hoe-handle.* Back made into hoe-handle. Cheremis: Sebeok-Nyerges.

E649.4. *Reincarnation as mussel shell.* Ears made into mussel shell. Cheremis: Sebeok-Nyerges.

E649.5. *Reincarnation as currants.* Eyes made into currants. Cheremis: Sebeok-Nyerges.

E650. Reincarnation: other forms.

E651. *God reincarnated as dwarf.* Hindu: Keith 121 (Vishnu).
A134. Dwarf god. F451. Dwarf as underground spirit.

E652. *God reincarnated as monster.* India: Thompson-Balys; Buddhist myth: Malalasekera II 792, 934; Chinese: Werner 207.
A123. Monstrous gods.

E653. *Reincarnation: man as nature spirit.*

E653.1. *Reincarnation: man as water spirit.* (Cf. F420.) Buddhist myth: Malalasekera I 421.

E653.2. *Reincarnation: man as tree spirit.* (Cf. F441.2.) Buddhist myth: Malalasekera I 445, 940, II 507, 820, 952.

E656. *Reincarnation: animal to man.* India: *Thompson-Balys; Korean: Zong in-Sob 57, 96.

E656.1. *Men who behave irrationally (without plans) reincarnations of animals.* India: Thompson-Balys.

E657. *Reincarnation: animal to god.* Buddhist myth: Malalasekera I 828.

E658. *Reincarnation: animal to other animal.* Jewish: Neuman.

E670. Repeated reincarnation. Irish myth: *Cross; Gaster Exempla 248 No. 349; Italian: Basile Pentamerone V No. 9; Buddhist myth: Malalasekera I 421, II 518, 1117; India: *Thompson-Balys; Marquesas: Handy 106; S. A. Indian (Toba): Métraux MAFLS XL 142.
D610. Repeated transformations. S401. Unsuccessful attempts to kill person in successive reincarnations (transformations).

E671. *Reincarnation: man - object - object.*

E671.1. *Reincarnation: body becomes marble wall; robe, grass; eyes, pools, etc.* India: Thompson-Balys.

E690. Reincarnation: miscellaneous.

E691. *Reincarnation: animal to object.*

E691.1. *Reincarnation: snake into flowers.* India: Thompson-Balys.

E692. *Reincarnation as punishment.* India: Thompson-Balys.

E692.1. *Bad woman cursed to be reborn as bat.* India: Thompson-Balys.

E692.2. *Mean person reborn as hyena.* India: Thompson-Balys.

E692.3. *Tricky potter reborn as crab.* India: Thompson-Balys.

E692.4. *Jealous woman reborn as chilly.* India: Thompson-Balys.

E692.5. *Cruel woman reborn as firefly.* India: Thompson-Balys.

E692.6. *Youth reincarnated as root in punishment for incest.* India: Thompson-Balys.
Q242. Incest punished.

E693. *Reincarnation for revenge.* India: Thompson-Balys.

E693.1. *Drowned girl reborn as leech to take revenge on murderers.* India: Thompson-Balys.

E693.2. *Woman reborn as bedbug to take revenge on husband.* (Cf. E616.5.) India: Thompson-Balys.

E693.3. *Woman reborn as scorpion to take revenge on husband.* India: Thompson-Balys.

E694. *Reincarnation as compensation.* India: Thompson-Balys.

E694.1. *Hungry ghost reborn as jackal.* India: Thompson-Balys.

E694.2. *Frustrated woman reborn as tobacco plant.* India: Thompson-Balys.

E694.3. *Frustrated boy reborn as lizard.* India: Thompson-Balys.

E694.4. *Childless woman reborn as fish.* India: Thompson-Balys.

E695. *Gradual reincarnation — man to tiger.* Chinese: Graham.

E696. *Reincarnated person restored to original form.*

E696.1. *Bird, reincarnated murdered girl, resumes her original form when persecutor's blood is poured on her.* India: Thompson-Balys.

E697. *Vulture eats only those who will be reborn as human beings in their next birth.* India: Thompson-Balys.

E700. The Soul. **Tobler; **Feilberg Sjæletro (København, 1914); Åke Hultkrantz Conceptions of the Soul among the North American Indians (Stockholm, 1953); Hilda R. Ellis The Road to Hell, A Study in the Conception of the Dead in Old Norse Literature (London, 1943) 170ff. — Greek: Waser Über die äussere Erscheinung der Seele in den Vorstellungen der Völker, zumal der alten Griechen (Archiv für Religionswissenschaft XVI [1914] 336); Irish myth: *Cross; Skandinavian: *K. S. Kramer Die Dingbeseelung in der germanischen Überlieferung (München, 1939); Estonian: Loorits Grundzüge I 182—190, 251—266, 491—506; German: Meyer Germanen 68ff.; Jewish: Neuman; N. A. Indian (Iroquois): Hewitt The Iroquoian Concept of the Soul (JAFL VIII 107).

A45. Souls of pious as Creator's advisers. A185.12. Deity provides man with soul. A185.12.2. God removes mortal's soul. A778.2. Milky Way as path of souls (demons). D1346. Magic object gives immortality. D1850. Immortality. E480.1. Abode of animal souls. E603. Limited number of souls in the world necessitates reincarnation. E730.1. Souls of animals. F251.5. Fairies as sprites who have been given immortality. F642.7. Person of remarkable sight can see the soul. V311. Belief in the life to come.

E700.1. *Names given the soul.* Jewish: Neuman.

E701. *Soul of object.* Finnish: Holmberg Finno-Ugric 13; Siberian: Holmberg Siberian 464.

E701.1. *Soul of the earth.* Cheremis: Holmberg Finno-Ugric 240.

E701.2. *Soul of water.* Cheremis: Holmberg Finno-Ugric 214.

E701.3. *Soul of tree.* Feilberg Am Urquell V 88ff., 119ff.

E701.4. *Soul of fire.* Cheremis: Holmberg Finno-Ugric 236.

E701.5. *Soul of corn.* Cheremis: Holmberg Finno-Ugric 241.

E702. *Composition of the soul.* Jewish: *Neuman.

E703. *Creation of souls.* Jewish: *Neuman.

E705. *Soul forgets everything at birth.* Jewish: Neuman. Cf. Wordsworth "Ode on Intimations of Immortality".

E706. *Abode of unborn souls.* Jewish: *Neuman.

E707. *Person with more than one soul.* Jewish: Neuman.

E708. *Soul sustained on pleasant odors.* Jewish: Neuman.

E710. External soul. A person (often a giant or ogre) keeps his soul or life separate from the rest of his body. *Type 302; *BP III 440; *Krappe in Penzer Ocean of Story VIII 107; *MacCulloch Childhood 118ff.; *Chauvin V 176 No. 100, II 193 No. 12; Fb "hjærte" IV 318b; Mélusine XI 263; *Penzer X 143 s.v. "External Soul"; Clouston Tales I 347; Köhler-Bolte I 161, 515; Gittée RTP II 283; Krappe Revue Archéologique (May-June 1933) 195—211. — Irish myth: *Cross; Breton: Sébillot Incidents s.v. "corps", "âme"; Icelandic: Friþjofssaga (Wenz ed., Halle 1914) 16; French Canadian: Barbeau JAFL XXIX 11; Greek: Grote I 136f.; India: *Thompson-Balys; Philippine: Fansler MAFLS XII 178; N. A. Indian: *Thompson Tales 346 n. 246a, *Hultkrantz 330—341; Africa (Swahili): Steere 3ff.

E765. Life dependent on external object or event. F408.2. Spirit in heart of man (fairy). F557. Removable organs. K544. Escape by alleged possession of external soul. K956. Murder by destroying external soul. K975.2. Secret of location of external soul learned by deception.

E710.1. *Ferocious animal guardian of separable soul of ogress.* India: Thompson-Balys.

B292. Animal in service to man. G300. Other ogres.

E710.2. *External soul avenges murder.* Eskimo (Greenland): Rasmussen III 145.

E711. *Soul kept in object.* (Cf. E765.) *Penzer I 129ff, VIII 107; Indonesian: Dixon 237 n. 50; India: Thompson-Balys; Irish myth: *Cross.

D1651.10. Apple (or ball) containing man's soul can be split only by man's own sword.

E711.1. *Soul in egg.* *Type 302; *BP III 439; Krappe in Penzer Ocean of Story VIII 107; *Fb "hjærte" I 631a, "liv" II 438b, "æg" III 1141b. — Icelandic: *Boberg; Breton: Sébillot Incidents s.v. "œuf"; Missouri French: Carrière; Scotch: Campbell Tales I 1ff.; Cape Verde Islands: Parsons MAFLS XV (1) 355, 217 No. 73; India: Thompson-Balys.

D1024. Magic egg. G275.4. Seven-headed witch defeated by throwing egg at each head.

E711.1.1. *Soul in three separate eggs.* Cheremis: Sebeok-Nyerges.

E711.2. *Soul in plant.* India: *Thompson-Balys.

N699.5. Boy, while cutting trees, comes to one which happens to be bound up with the life of an ogre. Ogre bribes him with large fortune not to cut tree.

E711.2.1. *Soul in calabash (gourd).* Africa (Hottentot): Bleek 55 No. 24; N. A. Indian (Seneca): Curtin-Hewitt RBAE XXXII 572 No. 116.

E765.3.2. Life bound up with calabash.

E711.2.2. *Soul in flower.* India: *Thompson-Balys.

E711.2.3. *Soul in chilly plant.* India: Thompson-Balys.

E711.2.4. *Soul in pomegranate.* India: Thompson-Balys.

E711.2.5. *Soul in coconut.* India: Thompson-Balys; Hawaii: Beckwith Myth 148.

E711.2.6. *Soul in bamboo.* India: Thompson-Balys.

E711.3. *Soul in jewel.* BP III 439. — India: *Thompson-Balys.

E711.4. *Soul in necklace.* BP III 439. — India: *Thompson-Balys.

E711.5. *Soul in sack.* Fb "pose" II 864.

E711.6. *Life in stick.* India: Thompson-Balys.

E711.7. *Soul in stone.* (Cf. E761.5.5.) Irish myth: *Cross; Icelandic: Boberg.

F451.4.1.10. Dwarfs live in stones.

E711.8. *Soul in golden apple.* (Cf. F813.1.1.) Irish myth: *Cross.

E711.9. *Soul in golden ball.* Irish myth: Cross.

E711.10. *Soul in sword.* India: *Thompson-Balys.

E142. Resuscitation by polishing sword that contains dead man's life.

E711.11. *Soul in snow.* India: Thompson-Balys.

E711.12. *Soul in dice.* India: Thompson-Balys.

E711.13. *Soul in arrow.* India: Thompson-Balys.

E711.14. *Soul in axe.* India: Thompson-Balys.

E711.15. *Soul in bird cage.* India: Thompson-Balys.

E712. *Hidden soul (life).*

E712.1. *Soul hidden in tree.* *BP III 440; India: *Thompson-Balys, *Penzer V 127 n. 1.

E712.2. *Soul hidden in safe.* India: Thompson-Balys.

E712.3. *Soul hidden in urn.* India: Thompson-Balys.

E712.4. *Soul hidden in box.* India: Thompson-Balys.

E712.5. *Soul hidden in pillar.* India: Thompson-Balys.

E712.6. *Soul hidden in fish basket.* India: Thompson-Balys.

E712.7. *Soul hidden in water bottle.* Tuamotu: Stimson MS (z-G 13/174).

E713. *Soul hidden in a series of coverings.* This motif is combined with several others. Usually the soul will be hidden in an egg, in a duck, in a well, in a church, or a similar series. *BP III 439; MacCulloch Childhood 134; Penzer I 131; Irish myth: *Cross; India: *Thompson-Balys.

E713.1. *Soul hidden in apple (ball) in a salmon which appears every seven years in certain fountain.* (Cf. D1651.10.) Irish myth: *Cross.

E714. *Soul (or life) kept in special part of body.* *Krappe in Penzer Ocean of Story VIII 107; Greek: Frazer Apollodorus II 117 n. 3; N. A. Indian: *Hultkrantz 166-178.

E714.1. *Soul (life) in the blood.* *Fb "blod" IV 46b, "sjæl" III 213b; Paris

Zs. f. Vksk. XIII 12 n. 1; Finnish: Holmberg Finno-Ugric 4; Jewish: Neuman.

C165. Tabu: marriage with person whose blood one has drunk. D1041. Blood as magic drink. D1335.2.1. Blood as magic strengthening drink. P312.1. Drinking mixture of blood, milk, and wine as pledge of covenant. T61.1. Betrothal by lovers' drinking each other's blood.

E714.2. *Serpent's life in its gold crown.* Type 672B; *BP II 463; Chinese: Graham.

E714.3. *Soul in head.* Eskimo (Greenland): Holm 83.

E714.3.1. *Troll's life in his brother's forehead.* *Fb "hjærte" I 631a.

E714.4. *Soul (life) in the heart.* Finnish: Holmberg Finno-Ugric 4; India: Thompson-Balys.

E714.4.1. *Eaten heart gives one the owner's qualities.* Fb "hjærte" IV 218b; N. A. Indian: *Hultkrantz 397—411; Jewish: Neuman; Icelandic: *Boberg.

D1335.1.2. Heart of enemy eaten produces strength. D1357.1. Eating ferocious animal's heart makes one cruel. D1358.1. Eating courageous animal's heart makes one courageous. D1782. Sympathetic magic.

E714.5. *Soul (life) in the liver.* Finnish: Holmberg Finno-Ugric 4.

E714.6. *Soul (life) in the breath.* Finnish: Holmberg Finno-Ugric 7; Jewish: Neuman; India: Thompson-Balys; N. A. Indian: *Hultkrantz 179—208.

E714.7. *Soul (life) in left hand.* Penzer I 127, VIII 109 n. 3.

E714.7.1. *Soul (life) in thumb.* India: Thompson-Balys.

E714.8. *Monster with life in his neck.* (One vulnerable place.) India: Thompson-Balys.

Z310. Unique vulnerability.

E714.9. *Giant's soul in a mole in the hollow of his palm.* Irish myth: Cross.

E714.10. *Ogre's soul in "pale spot" below his right ear.* (Cf. Z311.2.) Irish myth: Cross.

E714.11. *Life (soul) in entrails.* India: Thompson-Balys.

E714.12. *Soul in hair.* Greek: *Grote I 203.

D1831. Magic strength resides in hair. K976. Daughter pulls out father's magic life-containing hair.

E714.13. *Soul fastened to spine.* Jewish: Neuman.

E715. *Separable soul kept in animal.* *Krappe in Penzer Ocean of Story VIII 107; Fb "liv" II 438b.

E715.1. *Separable soul in bird.* BP III 440; India: *Thompson-Balys.

E29.5. Resuscitation by cutting off heads of birds which contain the soul of dead person.

E715.1.1. *Separable soul in duck.* *Fb "and" IV 12b.

E715.1.2. *Separable soul in crop of sparrow.* Penzer I 131f.

E715.1.3. *Separable soul in parrot.* India: *Thompson-Balys, Penzer I 131.

S22. Parricide.

E715.1.3.1. *Ogre's life in parrot's feather in man's pocket.* India: Thompson-Balys.

G512.5. Ogre killed by burning feather containing his life.

E715.1.3.2. *Ogre with life in parrot, speaks from inside parrot.* India: Thompson-Balys.

F915. Victim speaks from swallower's body. T575.1. Child speaks in mother's womb.

E715.1.4. *Soul in crane.* India: Thompson-Balys.

E715.1.5. *Soul in starling.* India: Thompson-Balys.

E715.1.6. *Soul in raven.* Eskimo (Greenland): Rasmussen III 56.

E715.2. *Separable soul in fish.* (Cf. B175.) BP III 440; Irish myth: *Cross; India: Thompson-Balys.

E715.3. *Separable soul in insect.*

E715.3.1. *Separable soul in bee.* BP III 440; India: *Thompson-Balys.

E715.3.2. *Separable soul in fly.* Africa (Bambara): Equilbecq II 88ff. No. 25.

E715.3.3. *Separable soul in hornet.* India: Thompson-Balys.

E715.4. *Separable soul in wild animal.*

E715.4.1. *Separable soul in deer.* Eskimo (Greenland): Rasmussen III 55.

E715.4.2. *Separable soul in wolf.* Eskimo (Greenland): Rasmussen III 55.

E715.4.3. *Separable soul in walrus.* Eskimo (Greenland): Rasmussen III 55.

E715.4.4. *Separable soul in seal.* Eskimo (Greenland): Rasmussen III 55.

E715.5. *Separable soul in snake.* India: Thompson-Balys.

E715.5.1. *Separable soul in toad.* India: Thompson-Balys.

E715.6. *Separable soul in hydra's head.* Penzer I 132.

E718. *Multiple separable souls: ogre's separable spirits live in a tree (plant), fish, honey bee.* India: Thompson-Balys.

E720. Soul leaves or enters the body.

E720.1. *Souls of human beings seen in dream.* Icelandic: *Boberg.

E721. *Soul journeys from the body.* *Frazer Golden Bough III 36ff.; Penzer I 37 n. 1. — *Celtic: H. Hartmann Ueber Krankheit, Tod und Jenseitsvorstellungen in Irland (Erster Teil: Krankheit und Fairyentrückung) (Halle, 1942); Irish myth: *Cross; Norwegian: Solheim Register 16; Estonian: Loorits Grundzüge I 289—295, 305—311; Slavic: Máchal 227; India: Thompson-Balys; Chinese: Werner 267; Japanese: Ikeda; Eskimo (Greenland): Rasmussen III 171, 178, (West Hudson Bay): Boas BAM XV 326; N. A. Indian: Hultkrantz 241—291.

G229.1. Soul of witch leaves the body.

E721.0.1. *Mark inflicted on wandering soul seen on body after soul's return.* Irish myth: Cross.

E721.1. *Soul wanders from body in sleep.* Dreams explained as experiences of the soul on these wanderings. *Frazer Golden Bough III 36ff.;

Fb "sjæl" III 213a; Tobler 22, 37, 67; Herbert III 209; Oesterley Gesta Romanorum No. 172. — English: Guy of Warwick (EETS extra ser. XXV) lines 9358ff.; Icelandic: Boberg; Irish: Plummer clxxii, *Cross; Spanish Exempla: Keller; Lithuanian: Balys Index No. 3520; Jewish: *Neuman; India: *Thompson-Balys; Chinese: Werner 93; Siberian: Holmberg Siberian 473f.; Hawaii: Beckwith Myth 144, 173f.; Cook Islands: Clark 81; Marquesas: Handy 81; Easter Island: Métraux Ethnology 56, 363; Eskimo (Greenland): Holm 62; Africa (Fang): Trilles 133.

D1731.2. Marvels seen in dreams. G251.1. Witch recognized by seeing wasp (beetle) enter her mouth while asleep. Only when it enters can she be awakened. V510. Religious visions.

E721.1.1. *Sleeper not to be awakened, since soul is absent.* *Frazer Golden Bough III 37ff.; Tobler 38.

E721.1.2. *Soul of sleeper prevented from returning to his body.* Frazer Golden Bough III 38; India: Thompson-Balys; Eskimo (Greenland): Rasmussen II 320.

E721.1.2.1. *Soul of sleeper prevented from returning when it is captured in animal form.* Frazer Golden Bough III 38.

E721.1.2.2. *Soul of sleeper prevented from returning by moving the sleeper's body.* (Cf E431.7.2.1.) Frazer Golden Bough III 41; Irish myth: Cross.

E721.1.2.3. *Soul of sleeper prevented from returning by burning the body.* India: Thompson-Balys, *Penzer I 39 n. 2.

E721.1.2.3.1. *Body dismembered so soul cannot return.* Eskimo (Greenland): Rink 287.

E721.1.2.4. *Soul of sleeper prevented from returning to his body when soul as bee leaves body and enters hole in wall beside which he is sleeping.* (Cf. E734.2.) England: Baughman.

E721.1.2.5. *Frightened soul cannot return to body.* Eskimo (Greenland): Rink 452.

E721.2. *Body in trance while soul is absent.* *Fb "legeme" II 393a, "heks" I 581a, "sjæl" III 215a; Icelandic: MacCulloch Eddic 299—300.

E721.3. *Wandering soul cause of sickness.* Frazer Golden Bough III 53ff.; Finnish: Holmberg Finno-Ugric 6; Siberian: Holmberg Siberian 473f.; N. A. Indian: *Hultkrantz 448—463.

E721.3.1. *Madness from spirit leaving body: comes back with cough.* India: Thompson-Balys.

E721.4. *Wandering soul detained by ghosts.* Frazer Golden Bough III 52ff.

E721.5. *Wandering soul assumes various shapes.* Fb "sjæl" III 214a.

E721.5.1. *Wandering soul assumes shape of wolf.* (Cf. D113.1.1, E731.) Irish myth: Cross.

E721.6. *On return to body soul crosses on scythe-blade as bridge.* *Fb "høle" I 747a; Spanish Exempla: Keller.

A661.0.5.1. Soul-bridge. F152. Bridge to otherworld.

E721.7. *Soul leaves body to visit hell (heaven).* (Cf. V511.1, V511.2.) Irish myth: *Cross; Jewish: *Neuman.

C542.1. Tabu: contact with things on journey to hell. F81. Descent to lower world of dead (Hell, Hades).

E721.8. *Soul leaves body to converse with dead.* Irish myth: Cross.

E721.9. *Soul of embryo wanders.* Jewish: Neuman.

E721.10. *Soul takes voyage.* Cook Islands: Beckwith Myth 157.

E722. *Soul leaves body at death.* India: Thompson-Balys; Irish myth: Cross.

E722.1. *Form of soul as it leaves body at death.*

E722.1.1. *Soul as black or white spirit over coffin.* Black if condemned. Can be seen by peeping between horse's ears. Fb "sjæl" III 214b.

D1821.3.4. Magic sight by looking between dog's ears. D1825.3.2. Man sees angels over the heads of the good and black stars over the bad. E750. Perils of the soul.

E722.1.2. *Soul as black or white entity.* Black if condemned. Irish myth: *Cross.

E722.1.3. *Soul leaves body as small point of light.* England: Baughman.

E722.1.4. *Soul leaves the body in form of bird.* (Cf. E732.) England: Baughman; Korean: Zong in-Sob 30.

E722.2. *Manner of soul's leaving body.* Jewish: Neuman.

E722.2.1. *Soul borne away on cloud.* (Cf. E754.6.) Chinese: Werner 267.

E722.2.2. *Soul borne away on wind.* Chinese: Werner 314.

E722.2.3. *Roof taken off above sick man who cannot die.* This done so that the soul can escape. Zachariae Zs. f. Vksk XVIII 445; *Fb "engel" I 250.

E722.2.4. *Condemned soul forked from body by Satan.* (Cf. E752.2.) Irish myth: Cross.

E722.2.5. *Saved soul leaps from body on hearing heavenly music.* (Cf. E754.) Irish myth: Cross.

E722.2.6. *Doors fly open when one dies.* North Carolina: Brown Collection I 685.

E722.2.7. *Soul weeps when departing from body.* (Cf. E551.) Lithuanian: Balys Index No. 3504.

E722.2.8. *Soul reluctant to leave body.*

E722.2.8.1. *Soul lingers in body at death.* Lithuanian: Balys Ghosts, Balys Index No. 3503.

E722.2.8.2. *Soul hovers over body, reluctant to part.* India: Thompson-Balys.

E722.2.9. *Dead friends come for dying man's soul.* Lithuanian: Balys Index No. 3501, Balys Ghosts.

E722.2.10. *Soul taken away by God (angel).* Jewish: Neuman.

E722.2.10.1. *Chariot of gods bears astral bodies of dead to heaven.* India: Thompson-Balys.

E722.2.11. *Soul leaves body through eye.* Hawaii: Beckwith Myth 144.

E722.2.12. *Soul leaves body because of God's kiss on mouth.* Jewish: Neuman.

E722.3. *Circumstances of soul on leaving dead body.*

E722.3.1. *Soul cannot go far from grave.* Fb "sjæl" III 214b.

E722.3.1.1. *Soul remains about dead body.* Chinese: Graham.

E722.3.2. *Soul wanders till corpse decays.* Fb "lig" II 413a; Finnish: Holmberg Finno-Ugric 3f.; Jewish: *Neuman; Marshall Islands: Davenport 222; Chinese: Graham.

E422. The living corpse.

E722.3.3. *Soul visits places of birth, death, baptism, and burial after leaving body.* Irish myth: Cross.

E723. *Wraiths of persons separate from body.* England, U.S.: Baughman.

E723.1. *Person sees his own wraith.* U.S., Wales: *Baughman.

E723.1.1. *Person sees his own wraith; the wraith saves his life.* (Cf. E363.2.) England: Baughman.

E723.2. *Seeing one's wraith a sign that person is to die shortly.* (Cf. F405.4.) England, U.S., Wales: *Baughman.

E723.3. *Wraith takes place of person unable to do duty at the necessary time.* Scotland: Baughman.

E723.4. *Wraith does what person wishes to do but is unable to do in the flesh.*

E723.4.1. *Wraith returns to home and goes to bed while body is at home of friends in deep reverie.* Ireland: Baughman.

E723.4.2. *Wraith of murderer tells authorities where to find girl he has murdered.* The murderer is in church at the time. Scotland: Baughman.

E723.4.3. *Wraith of debtor tries to find his creditor at time of death.* England: Baughman.

E723.4.4. *Wraith of dying woman goes to see children for last time before death.* England: Baughman.

E723.4.5. *Wraith gives information of death in family.* England: Baughman.

E723.4.6. *Wraith investigates welfare of absent person.* England, U.S.: *Baughman.

E723.5. *Wraith of sweetheart stays in room where lover has died.* It disappears only after her death at far distant point twenty years after death of lover. U.S.: Baughman.

E723.6. *Appearance of his wraith as announcement of person's death.* (Cf. E723.2.) England, Scotland, Wales, U.S.: *Baughman.

E723.7. *Actions of wraith.*

E723.7.1. *Wraith speaks.* England, Wales: *Baughman.

E723.7.2. *Wraith rings doorbell.* Scotland: Baughman.

E723.7.3. *Wraith opens and closes door.* England: Baughman.

E723.7.4. *Wraith slams gate.* England: Baughman.

E723.7.5. *Wraith selects wood for coffin.* Scotland: Baughman.

D1322.1.1. Hammer in coffin-maker's shop makes noise to announce a death.

E723.7.6. *Wraith binds grain in field.* Scotland: Baughman.

E723.7.7. *Wraith rides horse.* (Cf. E922.1.1.3.1.) Scotland: Baughman.

E723.7.8. *Wraiths of persons drowning appear in dripping clothes.* England: *Baughman.

E723.8. *Appearance of wraith as calamity omen.*

E723.8.1. *Wraith appears before mine disaster.* England: Baughman.

E725. *Soul leaves one body and enters another.* *L. Bloomfield Proc. Am. Philosophical Soc. LVI 1; Penzer I 38; Hartland Science 227; Slavic: Máchal 228; India: *Thompson-Balys; N. A. Indian: *Hultkrantz 438—440.

F1034. Person concealed in another's body. G303.18. Devil enters body of another.

E725.1. *Soul leaves man's body and enters animal's.* *Bolte Reise der Söhne Giaffers 208; India: Thompson-Balys.

E725.2. *Ghost possesses girl and she speaks in dialect unknown to her.* India: Thompson-Balys.

E726. *Soul enters body and animates it.* *Chauvin V 287 No. 171; Irish myth: *Cross; Jewish: *Neuman; India: Thompson-Balys; Chinese: Werner 266; N. A. Indian: *Hultkrantz 149—179.

E38. Resuscitation by replacement of soul.

E726.1. *Soul received at birth.* Jewish: Neuman; Siberian: Holmberg Siberian 472.

E726.2. *Soul of unborn son comes out of mother's mouth (in form of stone), is kept by her, and later is given to son.* (Cf. E711.7.) Irish myth: Cross.

E726.3. *Soul reunited with body.* Eskimo (Greenland): Rasmussen II 89.

E727. *Relation of body to soul.*

E727.1. *Debate of body and soul.* Soul having left body enters into debate with the body concerning relative merits of body and soul. (Cf. H500.) English: *Wells 411; Irish: Gaidoz and Dottin Revue Celtique X part 4, *Cross.

E727.1.1. *Soul curses body.* (Cf. M400.) Irish myth: *Cross; India: Thompson-Balys.

E727.2. *Soul as vital principle.* N. A. Indian: *Hultkrantz 149—179.

E727.3. *Body dependent on soul.* N. A. Indian: Hultkrantz 430—440.

E728. *Evil spirit possesses person.* India: *Thompson-Balys.

E728.1. *Evil spirit cast out of person.* England, U.S.: Baughman; Spanish Exempla: Keller.

D1385. Magic object protects from evil spirits (demons). D2161. Magic healing power. D2176.3. Evil spirit exorcised. K2325. Devil frightened by threatening to bring mother-in-law. K2385. Demon enters person and refuses to leave until his wishes have been fulfilled.

E728.1.1. *Evil spirit cast out of person by killing and resuscitating.* Köhler-Bolte I 442ff.

E0. Resuscitation. D1865.2. Beautification by boiling and resuscitation.

E730. Soul in animal form. (Cf. E721.1.2.4, E722.1.4, E734.2.) Bugiel RTP XVII 602; Tobler 19; England: Baughman; Icelandic: *MacCulloch Eddic 233; Montenegrin: Máchal 228; Siberian: Holmberg Siberian 473; N. A. Indian: Hultkrantz 266f., 496.

E423. Revenant in animal form. E610. Reincarnation as animal. E722.1. Form of soul as it leaves body. F167.1. Animals in otherworld. F234.1. Fairy in form of animal.

E730.1. *Souls of animals.* Slavic: Máchal 227; Jewish: *Neuman.

E480.1. Abode of animal souls. E520. Animal ghosts.

E731. *Soul in form of mammal.*

E731.1. *Soul in form of dog.* Tobler 49, 54, 68; Icelandic: Boberg; Chinese: Eberhard FFC CXX 213.

E731.2. *Soul in form of cat.* Tobler 42, 47, 56.

E731.3. *Soul in form of mouse.* Tobler 13ff.; *Fb "heks" I 581a, "høle" I 747a, "mus" II 631b; Sébillot RTP XX 189, 489; J. Grimm Kleinere Schriften VI 192ff.; Germanic: De la Saussaye 296, E. H. Meyer Germanische 64; Finnish: Holmberg Finno-Ugric 7f.; Indonesia: Kruyt 176f.

E731.4. *Soul in form of weasel.* Tobler 19; Herbert Catalogue of Romances III 209; Oesterley Gesta Romanorum No. 172; *E. H. Meyer Germanische 64.

E731.5. *Soul in form of hare.* Tobler 20.

E731.6. *Soul in form of seal.* *Fb "sælhund"; Eskimo (Greenland): Rasmussen III 56, 172.

E731.7. *Soul in form of bat.* Hdwb. d. Abergl. II 1591; Finnish: Holmberg Finno-Ugric 7.

E731.8. *Soul in form of bear.* Icelandic: *Boberg.

E731.9. *Soul in form of wolf.* Icelandic: *Boberg.

E731.10. *Soul in form of fox.* Icelandic: Boberg.

E731.11. *Soul in form of lion.* Icelandic: *Boberg.

E731.12. *Soul in form of hog.* Icelandic: *Boberg.

E731.13. *Soul in form of bull.* Icelandic: *Boberg.

E731.14. *Soul in form of deer.* Icelandic: Boberg.

E732. *Soul in form of bird.* (Cf. G251.1.1.) **Weicker Der Seelenvogel in der alten Literatur und Kunst; *Dh III 482; *Fb "fugl" I 380b, "sjæl" III 214a; *Patch PMLA XXXIII 626 n. 88; De Gubernatis Die Thiere in der indogermanischen Mythologie (Leipzig, 1874) 469ff.; Meyer Germanische 64; *Krappe Balor 95ff., Romanic Review XV 94ff.; *Penzer VI 283; *BP II 394 (Type 707); Tobler 30f.; Wimberly 44; Kruyt 175f.; J. E. Harrison Prolegomena to the Study of Greek Religion 199ff.; Irish myth: *Cross, Beal XXI 322, O'Suilleabhain 99; Icelandic: *Boberg; Slavic: Máchal 229f.; Finnish: Holmberg Finno-Ugric 7f.; Siberian: Holmberg Siberian 398, 473; Egyptian: Müller

174; Jewish: *Neuman; Japanese: Ikeda; Marquesas: Handy 36; N. A. Indian: Hultkrantz 266f., 363; Africa (Basuto): Jacottet 60 No. 9.

A132.6.2. Goddess (god) in form of bird. E423.3. Revenant as bird. E751.2. Souls await Judgment Day in shapes of birds. F234.1.15. Fairy in form of bird. V231.1. Angel in bird shape.

E732.1. *Soul in form of dove.* (Cf. E423.3.1.) Type 756B; Andrejev FFC LXIX 154; Tobler 28f.; *Crane Miraculis 93 No. 27; Alphabet Nos. 204, 269; Meyer Germanische 63; *Loomis White Magic 66; Irish: *Cross, Beal XXI 317, 320, 332, O'Suilleabhain 45, 99, 53; Swiss: Jegerlehner Oberwallis 320 No. 35, 323 No. 133; Spanish Exempla: Keller; Jewish: *Neuman.

V345. Dove flies out of man's mouth.

E732.2. *Soul in form of crow.* (Cf. B141.4.) Tobler 31; Fb "krage" II 285b.

E752.4. Lost soul in raven feathers.

E732.3. *Soul in form of hen.* Tobler 36; Fb "sjæl" III 214a.

E732.4. *Soul in form of magpie.* Tobler 34.

E732.5. *Soul in form of seagull.* Tobler 34; Fb "måge" II 655b.

E732.6. *Soul in form of eagle.* Icelandic: *Boberg.

E732.7. *Soul in form of swan.* Icelandic: *Boberg

E732.8. *Soul in form of raven.* Danish: Kristensen Danske Sagn II (1893) 127—31, (1928) 91—95; Icelandic: Boberg.

E732.9. *Soul in form of hawk, or falcon seen in dream.* (Cf. E720.1.) Icelandic: Boberg.

E733. *Soul in form of reptile.*

E733.1. *Soul in form of serpent.* Tobler 22ff., 74; Fb "lindorm" II 433b; Meyer Germanische (1891) 63f.; Lévy-Bruhl L'âme primitive 369ff.; Kruyt 177ff.; Schreuer Zs. f. vgl. Rechtsgeschichte XXXIII (1916) 406f. — Icelandic: MacCulloch Eddic 217, Boberg; Japanese: Ikeda; Oceanic: Dixon 119; Africa: Werner African 193.

F480.2. Serpent as house-spirit.

E734. *Soul in form of insect.* *Krappe Balor 95 n. 8.

G225.1. Insect as witch's familiar.

E734.1. *Soul in form of butterfly.* Tobler 37; Meyer Germanische 63; Hdwb. d. Abergl. II 1627f.; Güntert Kalypso 215ff.; Frazer Golden Bough I 259. — Irish: Beal XXI 307, O'Suilleabhain 24; Breton: Sébillot Incidents s.v. "âme", "papillon"; Finnish: Holmberg Finno-Ugric 7f.; Jewish: Neuman; Siberian: Holmberg Siberian 473; Japanese: Anesaki 337; Chinese: Eberhard FFC CXX 266; Hawaii: Dixon 76, Beckwith Myth 148.

E734.2. *Soul in form of bee.* Type 808**; Hdwb. d. Abergl. IV 468; Tobler 37; Siberian: Holmberg Siberian 473; Japanese: Ikeda.

E734.3. *Soul in form of spider.*[1] Tobler 38.

E734.4. *Soul in form of wasp.* Siberian: Holmberg Siberian 473.

G251.1. Witch recognized by seeing wasp (beetle) enter her mouth while asleep. Only when it enters can she be awakened.

E734.5. *Soul in form of cricket.* Meyer Germanische 63.

[1] In folk thought, an insect.

E734.6. *Soul in form of beetle.* Hdwb. d. Abergl. IV 906.

E734.7. *Soul in form of fly.* Japanese: Ikeda; Chinese: Eberhard FFC CXX 201.

E734.8. *Soul in form of grasshopper.* Jewish: *Neuman.

E735. *Soul in form of fish.* Dh. III 482.

E736. *Soul in form of amphibian.*

E736.1. *Soul in form of frog.* Tobler 26, 75.

E736.2. *Soul in form of toad.* Tobler 25, 29; Meyer Germanische (1891) 64.

E738. *Soul in form of a mythical animal.*

E738.1. *Soul in form of dragon.* (Cf. B11.) Tobler 81; Icelandic: *Boberg.

E740. Other forms of the soul.

E741. *Soul in form of heavenly body.*

E741.1. *Soul in form of star.* (Cf. V515.1.2.)
F961. Extraordinary behavior of stars.

E741.1.1. *Shooting star signifies that someone is dying.* One star for each person. At his death it falls. *BP III 235; *G. Bellucci Le stelle cadenti e le lore leggende (Perugia, 1895); *Handwb. d. Abergl. IX n. 770f.; Fb "lys" II 483a, "stjerne" III 577b. — Lithuanian: Balys Index No. 3906; Slavic: Máchal 273; India: Thompson-Balys.
E765.1.3. Life-lights in lower world. Each light mystically connected with the life of a person. When light is extinguished, person dies. F962.3. Star drops from heaven: is money. V231.2. Shooting star as angel.

E741.1.1.1. *New star for each birth.* A star in the sky for each person. Fb "menneske" II 577b.
T589.5. Newborn child reincarnation of recently deceased person.

E741.1.1.2. *Star as sign of birth of hero.* Irish myth: Cross.

E741.1.2. *Shooting star signifies a birth.* Stars are the dead. When they fall they are being reborn. At death they are replaced in the sky. *Hdwb. d. Abergl. IX N. 770f.; Siberian: Holmberg Siberian 395; N. A. Indian (Mandan): Alexander N. Am. 96.
A760. Creation of the stars.

E742. *Soul as light.* *Type 332; Fb "sjæl" III 214b, "lys" II 482a; BP I 377ff., *388; Icelandic: *Boberg; Irish: Plummer cxxxviii, Cross, Beal XXI 315, O'Suilleabhain 41; Breton: Sébillot Incidents s.v. "vie"; French Canadian: Barbeau JAFL XXIX 24; Spanish: Boggs FFC XC 82 No. 708A*; Jewish: Neuman; Eskimo (Greenland): Rasmussen III 48; N. A. Indian: *Hultkrantz 260ff.; Africa (Fang): Trilles 133.
A1412.2. Origin of light: souls of dead in heaven. E530.1. Ghostlike lights. E761.7.4. Life token: light goes out. E765.1. Life bound up with light (flame).

E742.1. *Soul as taper (candle).* Swiss: Jegerlehner Oberwallis 313 No. 82.
E765.1.1. Life bound up with candle. When the candle goes out, person dies. E765.1.2. Life bound up with burning brand (torch).

E742.2. *Soul as will-o-the-wisp.* Appears as a ball or fire or a figure in a fiery garment. — Tobler 82—86 passim; Meyer Germanische 63; Fb "ild" II 11b; Swiss: Jegerlehner Oberwallis 313 No. 84;

Lithuanian: Balys Ghosts; Slavic: Máchal 229ff.; North Carolina: Brown Collection I 677.

F491. Will o' the Wisp (Jack o' Lantern.) Light seen over marshy places.

E742.3. *Souls of dead as Aurora Borealis.* Finnish: Holmberg Finno-Ugric 81; Estonian: Loorits Grundzüge I 284ff.

E743. *Soul as shadow.* Tobler 89; Meyer Germanische 66; Fb "skygge" (1) III 347b, "sjæl" III 214b; Wundt Völkerpsychologie IV 125ff.; *Hdwb. d. Abergl. IX Nachträge 137; *Frazer Golden Bough III 77ff.; Finnish: Holmberg Finno-Ugric 6, 12; Jewish: Neuman; N. A. Indian: Hultkrantz 257ff, 302ff.

K1227.7. Girl asks undesired lover to follow her but not to step on her shadow.

E743.1. *Soul as smoke.* Tobler 87; Fb "sjæl" III 214b.

F407.1. Spirit vanishes in smoke.

E743.2. *Soul as reflection or image.* N. A. Indian: Hultkrantz 309—316.

E744. *Soul as weather phenomenon.*

E744.1. *Soul as mist (fog).* Fb "sjæl" III 214b.

E744.2. *Soul as cloud.* Tobler 87f.

E744.3. *Soul as whirlwind.* Tobler 89.

E745. *Soul as object.* (Cf. E765.) N. A. Indian: Hultkrantz 268; Eskimo (Kodiak): Golder JAFL XXII 11, (Greenland): Rasmussen 1 136.

E630. Reincarnation in object. E765.3. Life bound up with object.

E745.1. *Soul as feather.* Tobler 51; Fb "sjæl" III 214b (shower of feathers).

E745.2. *Soul as needle.* Tobler 51.

E745.3. *Soul as straw.* Tobler 51.

E745.4. *Soul as flower.* BP II 394; Icelandic: Boberg.

E745.4.1. *Soul as lotus flower.* India: Thompson-Balys.

E745.5. *Soul as fruit.*

E745.5.1. *Souls as golden apples.* Later turn into birds and fly away. Hdwb. d. Märch. I 91b s.v. "Apfel".

E745.5.2. *Soul as bulb.* Icelandic: Boberg.

E745.6. *Soul as ghi (clarified butter).* India: Thompson-Balys.

E747. *Soul as mannikin (child).* Frazer Golden Bough III 26ff.; Tobler 67; Meyer Germanische 66; N. A. Indian: Hultkrantz 262—266.

E747.1. *Soul as small replica of body.* India: Thompson-Balys.

E748. *The soul as a guardian spirit.* Hilda R. Ellis The Road to Hell, A Study of the Conception of the Dead in Old Norse Literature (Cambridge [Eng.], 1943) 127ff.; Icelandic: *Boberg.

F494.1. Guardian spirit of land. N110. Luck and fate personified. N810.1. Invisible guardians.

E750. **Perils of the soul.** *Frazer Golden Bough III 26ff.; Irish myth: *Cross; India: Thompson-Balys; N. A. Indian: Hultkrantz 464—480.

A311. Conductor of the dead. B161.4. Power of seeing whether dead go to heaven or hell is gained from serpent. D1389.11. Magic armature protects soul from hurt. D1821.7. Deaf and dumb man can see soul taken to happiness or punishment. E722.1.1. Soul as black or white spirit over coffin. Black if condemned. K210. Devil cheated of his promised soul. The man saves it through deceit. V233. Angel of death. V520. Salvation.

E750.0.1. *Soul cannot enter heaven till body is buried.* (Cf. E235.2.) Irish myth: *Cross.

E750.1. *Souls wander after death.* *v. Negelein Zs. f. Vksk. XI 16ff., 149ff., 263ff.; Jewish: *Neuman; Japanese: Anesaki 237ff.

E750.1.1. *Virgins condemned to wander at death.* Korean: Zong in-Sob 39.

E750.2. *Perilous path for soul to world of dead.* (Cf. F151.1.) Siberian: Holmberg Siberian 484.

E750.2.1. *Dead person of good life goes over bridge to otherworld without fear.* India: Thompson-Balys.

E481.2.1. Bridge to land of dead.

E750.2.2. *Perilous valley in (on way to) land of dead.* Irish myth: Cross.

A671.2.4.5. Fiery glens in hell. F151.1.1. Perilous valley. F151.1.2. Perilous glen on way to otherworld.

E750.2.3. *Branching tree as roadway for souls.* Hawaii: Beckwith Myth 154.

E750.3. *Journey of soul to world of dead on reindeer.* Siberian: Holmberg Siberian 485.

E750.4. *Soul leaves possessions on road to final resting place.* India: Thompson-Balys.

E751. *Souls at Judgment Day.* Irish: *Cross; O'Suilleabhain 62, 78, Beal XXI 324, 327; Spanish Exempla: Keller; Jewish: *Neuman.

A1002. Doomsday. E178. Resurrection at Judgment Day. V313. Last Judgment. V520. Salvation.

E751.0.1. *There are to be two resurrections.* Irish myth: Cross.

E751.1. *Souls weighed at Judgment Day.* (Cf. Q155.1.) Fb "veje" III 1025b; Irish myth: Cross.

E751.2. *Souls await Judgment Day in shapes of birds.* Irish myth: *Cross.

A693. Intermediate future world. E732. Soul in form of bird.

E751.3. *Souls of Irish to be judged by St. Patrick on Judgment Day.* (Cf. Q173.) Irish myth: Cross.

E751.4. *Four (five) groups on Judgment Day.* (Cf. A661.0.5.1.) Irish myth: *Cross.

E751.5. *Souls of sinners to spend seven years under waters of the sea before Doomsday.* Irish myth: Cross.

E751.6. *Resurrection to take place on Sunday.* Irish myth: Cross.

E751.7. *Judgment day on Monday.* Irish myth: Cross.

E752. *Lost souls.* Hdwb. d. Abergl. s.v. "Arme Seelen"; Irish myth: *Cross.

A671.2.4. The fires of hell. D2061.2.4.1. Death in sin by cursing. Q560. Punishments in hell.

E752.1. *Soul in jeopardy after leaving body.* Fb "sjæl" III 214b.

E752.1.1. *Devil in disguise hunts souls.* (Cf. G303.7.1.3.) French Canadian: Barbeau JAFL XXIX 13; Spanish: Boggs FFC XC 91 No. *773A.

H1463. Three-night watch over grave to guard man from devil.

E752.1.2. *Fiends play ball with a soul.* Alphabet No. 699.

E752.1.2.1. *Demons amuse themselves by plaguing souls in hell.* Irish myth: *Cross.

E752.1.3. *Souls of dead captured on leaving corpse.* Africa (Fang): Einstein 70ff., Trilles Bulletin de la Société Neuchâteloise de Géographie XVI 190ff.

E752.2. *Soul carried off by demon (Devil).* Frazer Golden Bough III 60; *Fb "djævel" IV 99b. — Irish myth: *Cross; Spanish Exempla: Keller; Jewish: *Neuman; Eskimo (Greenland): Rink 464.

D2121.5. Magic journey: man carried off by spirit or devil. E722.2.4. Condemned soul forked from body by Satan. E727. Debate of body and soul. F402.1.5.1. Demons seek to carry off king's soul. G303.9.5. The Devil as an abductor. Q568.3. Sinners in hell fall into the mouth of Devil. R11.2. Abduction by Devil.

E752.3. *Raven carries off souls of damned.* Tobler 31; Fb "ravn" III 22a.

E752.4. *Lost soul in raven feathers.* Fb "ravn" III 22a.

E732.2. Soul in form of crow.

E752.5. *Hell-hounds accompany soul to lower world.* Wimberly 120.

A673. Hound of Hell.

E752.6. *Soul bound for hell given sight of heaven.* Irish myth: Cross.

E752.7. *Lost soul gnawed by worms.* Irish myth: Cross.

E752.7.1. *Abandoned souls feed on spiders and night moths.* Hawaii: Beckwith Myth 154.

E752.8. *Souls of dead eaten by sky-spirits.* India: Thompson-Balys.

E752.9. *Souls of wicked eaten by deity.* Easter Island: Métraux Ethnology 312.

E752.10. *Precautions taken with corpse before burial to prevent evil spirits from getting, using body.* (Cf. E431.)

E752.10.1. *Corpse must be watched carefully before burial.* England: Baughman.

E752.10.2. *Light must be kept burning by corpse to keep evil spirits away.* England: Baughman.

E754. *Saved souls.* *Frazer Golden Bough III 55ff.; Irish: *Cross, Beal XXI 327.

Q172. Reward: admission to heaven.

E754.1. *Condemned soul recovered.* Irish myth: *Cross.

K210. Devil cheated of his promised soul.

E754.1.1. *Condemned soul saved by prayer.* Alphabet No. 592; Wells 171 (The Gast of Gy); Irish: *Cross, Beal XXI 331, O'Suilleabhain 98; Spanish: Boggs FFC XC 89 No. 760C*, Keller; Swiss: Jegerlehner Oberwallis 294 No. 7.

V50. Prayer. V51.5. Beatus best prayer for saving condemned souls.

E754.1.1.1. *Demons powerless over souls commended to God before sleep.* Jewish: bin Gorion I 238.

E754.1.2. *Condemned soul saved by Virgin Mary.* (Cf. V250.) Crane Miraculis 84 No. 5, 86 No. 10, 87 No. 12, 93 No. 27; Ward II 605 No. 11, *607 No. 16, 635 No. 36, 670 No. 3, 672 No. 7; Wells 167 (Vernon Miracles).

E754.1.3. *Condemned soul saved by penance.* (Cf. Q520.) Alphabet No. 697; Irish myth: Cross.

E754.1.4. *Condemned soul saved by holy person.* Irish myth: *Cross.

D1713. Magic power of hermit (saint). D1766.1. Magic results produced by prayer. Q155. Religious and political requests of saint granted by god. Q560.0.2. Certain number of persons released from hell every Saturday through virtue of saint. V211.7.1. The harrowing of hell. V229.15. Saint disguised as poor man saves almsgiving king from punishment in hell.

E754.1.5. *Condemned soul released by God.* Irish myth: Cross.

E754.1.6. *Condemned soul released from hell by Christ.* Irish myth: Cross.

E754.1.7. *Few grains of earth from river bed translates soul destined to an evil future to Paradise.* India: Thompson-Balys.

E754.1.8. *Condemned soul released because of tears of living.* Irish: O'Suilleabhain 21, 74.

E754.2. *Saved soul goes to heaven.* Fb "sjæl" III 213b; Wells 50, 175; Alphabet No. 316; Irish: *Cross, Beal XXI 307f., 322, O'Suilleabhain 24, 27, 99; Spanish Exempla: Keller.

A661. Heaven. F11. Journey to heaven (upper-world paradise).

E754.2.0.1. *Souls of warriors go to Valhalla.* *Hdwb. d. Abergl. IX Nachträge 239.

A661.1. Valhalla.

E754.2.1. *Souls carried to heaven by doves.* Tobler 31; *Fb "himmerige" I 610b.

B457.1. Helpful dove. B552. Man carried by bird.

E754.2.2. *Souls carried to heaven by angels.* (Cf V232.2.) Hdwb. d. Märch. s.v. "Engel"; Irish myth: *Cross; Jewish: *Neuman.

E754.2.2.1. *Angels of death fail to bring soul to heaven.* India: Thompson-Balys.

E754.2.3. *Dead and living go together to gate of heaven.* Fb "død" I 228a.

E754.2.4. *Dead children invited to eat at God's table.* BP III 463.

E754.3. *Burial in certain ground assures going to heaven.* Irish myth: Cross.

D1588. Magic object assures going to heaven.

E754.4. *Soul of hermit who fasts to death for worldly fame would be damned but for past good deeds.* Nouvelles de Sens No. 20.

E754.5. *Souls carried to heaven in chariot of light.* Jewish: *Neuman.

E754.6. *Souls climb pillars of smoke and light on way to heaven.* (Cf. E722.2.1.) Jewish: *Neuman.

E754.7. *Souls of pious as angels.* Jewish: *Neuman.

E755. *Destination of the soul.*

E755.0.1. *Resurrected boys choose to return to heaven.* Irish myth: Cross.
E0. Resuscitation. Q172.6. Heaven as reward for renouncement of long life.

E755.0.2. *Angels separate souls going to heaven or hell.* Jewish: Neuman.

E755.0.3. *Souls of dead presented to Adam.* Jewish: Neuman.

E755.1. *Souls in heaven.* (Cf. A661.) K. Kohler Heaven and Hell in Comparative Religion (New York, 1923); Irish myth: Cross.
F11. Journey to heaven (upper-world paradise). Q565. Man admitted to neither heaven nor hell.

E755.1.1. *Heavenly hierarchy.* Irish myth: Cross; Jewish: Neuman; Maori: Clark 182.
A651.1.4. Seven heavens. A651.1.2.1. The nine ranks of heaven.

E755.1.2. *River in heaven burns wicked and gives joy to righteous.* Irish myth: *Cross.
A661.0.1.1.1. Doors of heaven guarded by rivers of fire. A671.2.2.6. Other rivers in hell.

E755.1.3. *Souls on way to heaven pass through Garden of Eden.* Jewish: Neuman.

E755.1.4. *Sixty thousand Jewish souls in heaven.* Jewish: Neuman.

E755.2. *Souls in hell (Hades).* A. Graf Miti, leggende et superstizioni del medio evo I 241ff.; K. Kohler Heaven and Hell in Comparative Religion (New York, 1923); Fb "helvede" I 589; Pauli (ed. Bolte) Nos. 122, 281, 406; Alphabet No. 43; Irish: *Cross, Beal XXI 320, O'Suilleabhain 53; *Icelandic: Boberg; Jewish: *Neuman.
A671. Hell. Lower world of torment. E481.1. Land of dead in lower world. Q560. Punishments in hell. Q565. Man admitted to neither heaven nor hell.

E755.2.0.1. *Souls leave hell on Sundays.* (Cf. Q560.0.1.) Irish myth: Cross.

E755.2.1. *Souls of drowned in heated kettles in hell.* *Type 475; BP II 423, III 487; Köhler-Bolte I 69; Fb "potte" II 867a.
C325. Tabu: looking into the pots in hell. C741. Tabu: relieving souls in hell. Q561.2. Kettle heating in hell for certain person.

E755.2.1.1. *Souls in hell wrenched from bodies with hot pitchforks by devils.* Spanish Exempla: Keller.

E755.2.2. *Souls in chains in hell.* (Cf. A671.2.4.7, Q566.1.) Chinese: Werner 268.

E755.2.3. *Lost soul to serve as porter in hell for seven years.* Köhler-Bolte I 320; Wimberly 416, 426.
A671.1. Doorkeeper of hell.

E755.2.4. *Ghosts gather wood for hell fires.* Jewish: bin Gorion II 154ff., 348.

E755.2.4.1. *Hell fires kindled according to sins of sinners.* Irish myth: Cross.

E755.2.5. *Icy hell.* (Cf. A677, Q567f.) Alphabet No. 662.
A671.3. Frigidity of hell.

E755.2.6. *Dead flailed by demons.* Irish myth: *Cross.
E752.1.2.1. Demons amuse themselves by plaguing souls in hell.

E755.2.7. *Devils torment sinners in hell.* India: Thompson-Balys.
G303. Devil. Q560. Punishments in hell.

E755.2.8. *Dialogue between Christ and the souls in hell.* (Cf. V211.7.2.) Irish myth: Cross.

E755.2.8. *Series of hells.* (Cf. A651.2.) Jewish: Neuman.

E755.3. *Souls in purgatory.* **Landau Hölle und Fegefeuer in Volksglaube, Dichtung und Kirchenlehre (Heidelberg, 1909); Pauli (ed. Bolte) Nos. 464, 467, 469, Crane Liber de Miraculis 86 No. 10; Hdwb. d. Abergl. s.v. "Fegefeuer"; Ward Catalogue of Romances II 440ff.; Herbert ibid. III 330; Alphabet Nos. 504, 661. — Irish: *Cross, Beal XXI 330—333, O'Suilleabhain 95, 100, 102f.
A693. Intermediate future world. Q482.3. Nobleman after death must serve as menial. V511.3. Visions of purgatory.

E755.3.1 *Soul in purgatory sends letter bidding his son reward one who has prayed him from purgatory.* Lithuanian: Balys Index No. *769.
E754.1.1. Condemned soul saved by prayer. Q564. Letter sent to the relatives from man in Hell.

E755.4. *Other destinations of souls.*

E755.4.1. *Souls of dead imprisoned in tree.* Icelandic: De la Saussaye 298; Irish: Beal XXI 332.

E755.4.2. *Soul of dead in a temple.* Chinese: Werner 314.
V112. Temples.

E756. *Contest over souls.* (Cf. E754.1.) Type 808**.

E756.1. *Devils and angels contest for man's soul.* *Wesselski Märchen 199; *Fb "djævel" IV 99b; *Crane Miraculis 87 No. 11; Irish myth: *Cross; Spanish Exempla: Keller; Italian Novella: Rotunda; Livonian: Loorits FFC LXVI No. 808*; Lithuanian: Balys Index No. *808; Estonian: Aarne in FFC XXV No. 808*; Jewish: *Neuman.

E756.2. *Soul won from devil in card game.* Fb "spille" III 487b; Irish: Beal XXI 329, O'Suilleabhain 90; Spanish: Boggs FFC XC 52 No. 345.

E756.3. *Raven and dove fight over man's soul.* Type 756B; *Andrejev FFC LXIX 157f., *249ff.; Hdwb. d. Märchen I 356a. s.v. "Busse des Räubers"; England, Wales: Baughman.

E756.4. *Saint wrests soul from demons.* (Cf. V229.5.) Irish myth: *Cross.

E756.4.1. *Soul of gambler won by saint in dice game.* Dice miraculously split to make higher score for saint. — Spanish Exempla: Keller.

E756.5. *Saved soul of woman assists her husband's soul in battle against demons.* (Cf. E754.) Irish myth: Cross.
T210. Faithfulness in marriage.

E757. *The soul prays.* Jewish: *Neuman; Chinese: Werner 268.

E758. *Rejoicing at arrival of rich man in heaven.* Event so rare as to cause rejoicing. Poor man enters unnoticed. — Type 802; BP III 274; Fb "rig" III 55a; Hdwb. d. Märch. I 351a s.v. "Burli im Himmel".

E759. *The soul—miscellaneous.* Irish myth: Cross.

E759.1. *Soul strives to be heard by the living.* Irish myth: Cross.

E759.2. *Angel gives soul information concerning mortal.* Irish myth: Cross.

E760. Life Index. Object or animal has mystic connection with person. Changes in one correspond to changes in the other. — India: Thompson-Balys.

B2. Animal totems. D1310. Magic object gives supernatural information. D1310.4.2. Magic plant bears fruit to indicate that heroine is ready to marry. D1782. Sympathetic magic. F755.4. Mountain grows concurrently with child reared upon it. H430. Chastity index.

E761. *Life token.* (Cf. E760.) Object (animal, person) has mystic connection with the life of a person, so that changes in the life-token indicate changes in the person, usually disaster or death. *Type 303; **Polivka The Life Tokens in Folk-Tales, Custom, and Belief (Národopisný Vestnik Ceskoslovanský XII [Prague, 1917]); *Chauvin V 87 No. 27 n. 1, V 295, VII 98 No. 375 n. 1; Penzer I 130, III 272 n. 1, X 210; Clouston Tales I 169ff.; Jacobs' list s.v. "Life index"; *BP I 545, II 392; *Hartland Legend of Perseus II 1—54; **Nelson The Life-Index, a Hindu Fiction Motif (Studies in Honor of Maurice Bloomfield) 211ff. — Irish myth: Cross; Breton: Sébillot Incidents s.v. "danger"; India: *Thompson-Balys; Oceanic (New Hebrides, Torres Straits, New Guinea, Indonesia): Dixon 133 n. 5; N. A. Indian: *Thompson Tales 317 n. 149, *Hultkrantz 338—340, (California): Gayton and Newman 69; S. A. Indian (Quiché): Alexander Lat. Am. 173; Africa (Kaffir): Theal 81, (Basuto): Jacottet 212, 218 Nos. 31, 32.

B311. Congenital helpful animal. D1310.4. Magic object tells how another fares. D1323.12.1. Clairvoyant spring.

E761.1. *Blood as life token.*

D1003. Magic blood — human.

E761.1.1. *Life token: water turns to blood.* (Cf. F961.3.1, V211.2.3.2.) Fb "vand" III 1000b. — England: Baughman; Irish myth: *Cross; India: Thompson-Balys.

D474. Transformation: object becomes bloody. D477.1. Transformation: water becomes wine. D1812.5.1.1.6. Washers at the ford.

E761.1.2. *Life token: horn fills with blood.* Africa (Congo): Weeks 203.

E761.1.3. *Life token: track fills with blood.* *Type 303; Icelandic: Boberg.

E761.1.3.1. *Life token: earth, water, or blood in footprint.* Earth: dead by disease; water: drowned; blood: killed in battle. Icelandic: Boberg.

E761.1.4. *Life token: blood of fish calls out.* Africa (Ekoi): Talbot 187.

D1016. Magic blood of animal. D1610. Magic speaking objects.

E761.1.5. *Life token: blood boils.* French: Cosquin Lorraine No. 5; Jewish: *Neuman.

D1318.5.6. Blood bubbles at place of murder.

E761.1.5.1. *Blood stops boiling.* Gaster Exempla 224 No. 194.

E761.1.6. *Life token: blood changes color.* Gaster Exempla 251 No. 373; Russian: Ralston Russian Folk-Tales 102.

E761.1.7. *Life token: comb drips blood.* Finnish: Kalevala runes 12, 15.

E761.1.7.1. *Life token: gloves drip blood.* Russian: Ralston Russian Folk-Tales 67.

E761.1.7.2. *Life token: scissors (razor, knife) drip blood.* Chauvin VII 198; Armenian: Macler Contes Arméniens 28.

E761.1.8. *Life token: cloth becomes bloody.* *Bolte Zs. f. Vksk. XX 70 n. 3.

E761.1.9. *Life token: hero's horse stands in stable in blood up to his knees.* Russian: Rambaud La Russie Epique (Paris, 1876) 378.

E761.1.10. *Life token: milk becomes bloody.* England: Baughman; India: *Thompson-Balys.

E761.1.11. *Life token: roof spouts of castle run with blood.* England: Baughman.

E761.1.12. *Life token: meal ground in mill is the color of blood.* England: Baughman.

E761.1.13. *Blood stops flowing from wound when captives escape.* Papua: Ker 64.

E761.2. *Life token: staff stuck in ground.* India: Thompson-Balys.

D1254. Magic staff.

E761.2.1. *Life token: staff stuck in ground shakes.* Africa (Basuto): Jacottet 212 No. 31, (Kaffir): Theal 82.

E761.2.2. *Life token: staff stuck in ground falls.* *Bolte Zs. f. Vksk. XX 70 n. 8; Africa (Basuto): Jacottet 220 No. 32.

E761.3. *Life token: tree (flower) fades.* *Bolte Zs. f. Vksk. XX 70 n. 1; Fb "lilie"; Böckel Psychologie der Volksdichtung 255; *Loomis White Magic 125f. — Breton: Sébillot Incidents s.v. "flétrissement"; French: Sébillot France III 433; India: *Thompson-Balys; Japanese: Ikeda; Philippine (Tinguian): Cole 93, 96 n. 3, 97; Papua: Ker 61; Indonesian, Polynesian: Dixon 234 n. 46; Africa (Angola): Chatelain 87 No. 5, (Kaffir): Kidd 225, (Madagascar): Dandouau Contes Populaires de Sakalava 231.

D950. Magic tree. H1556.4.6. Rose given by supernatural wife to husband when he leaves for home will shed as many petals as times he thinks of her. T589.3. Birth trees. Spring forth as hero is born, act as life tokens, etc.

E761.3.1. *Life token: bamboo stalks grow with joints upside down.* India: Thompson-Balys.

E761.3.1.1. *Life token: bananas ripen from bottom up.* Papua: Ker 61.

E761.3.2. *Lifen token: fruit decays on tree.* India: Thompson-Balys.

E761.3.3. *Life token: fruit falls from tree.* India: Thompson-Balys.

E761.3.4. *Life token: trees prostrate themselves.* Jewish: Neuman.

E761.4. *Life token: object darkens or rusts.*

E761.4.1. *Life token: knife stuck in tree rusts (becomes bloody).* *Bolte Zs. f. Vksk. XX 70 n. 2; *Fb "kniv" II 221a.

D1083. Magic knife. D1173. Magic carving knife.

E761.4.2. *Life token: picture burns black.* *Bolte Zs. f. Vksk. XX 70 n. 4.

E761.4.3. *Life token: mirror becomes black (misty).* (Cf. D1163.) *Bolte Zs. f. Vksk. XX 70 n. 5; Armenian: Macler contes Arméniens 28; Japanese: Ikeda.

E761.4.4. *Life token: ring rusts.* English: Child I 201; Italian: Basile Pentamerone III No. 4.

E761.4.5. *Life token: silver object turns dark.* Russian: Ralston Russian Folk-Tales (London, 1875) 91.

E761.4.6. *Life token: charm dries.* Africa (Lamba): Doke MAFLS XX 14 No. 11.

E761.4.7. *Life token: sword rusts.* India: *Thompson-Balys.

E761.4.8. *Life token: beads cling together.* India: Thompson-Balys.

E761.4.9. *Life token: milk turns dark.* India: Thompson-Balys.

E761.5. *Life token: object breaks (bursts).* India: Thompson-Balys.

E761.5.1. *Life token: pot breaks.* (Cf. D1171.1.) Africa (Basuto): Jacottet 188 No. 27.

E761.5.2. *Life token: zither string breaks.* *Bolte Zs. f. Vksk. XX 70 n. 9.

E761.5.3. *Life token: ring springs asunder.* *Bolte Zs. f. Vksk. XX 68f. n. 4; Fb "ring" III 60a.

D1076. Magic ring. D1818.9.1. Ring springs asunder when faithlessness of lover is learned.

E761.5.4. *Life token: cup springs asunder.* (Cf. D1171.6.) *Bolte Zs. f. Vksk. XX 70 n. 7.

E761.5.5. *Life token: stone breaks.* (Cf. E711.7.) Irish myth: *Cross.

E761.5.5.1. *Life token: stones prostrate themselves.* Jewish: Neuman.

E761.5.6. *Life token: sheaves prostrate themselves.* Jewish: Neuman.

E761.6. *Life token: troubled liquid.* (Cf. D1242.)

E761.6.1. *Life token: troubled water.* *Bolte Zs. f. Vksk. XX 70 n. 1; Italian: Basile Pentamerone No. 9; India: Thompson-Balys.

E761.6.2. *Life token: milk becomes red.* *Bolte Zs. f. Vksk. XX 70 n. 1; England: Baughman; India: Thompson-Balys.

E761.6.3. *Life token: boiling liquid.* *Jamaica: Beckwith MAFLS XVII 270 No. 82.

E761.6.4. *Life token: beer foams.* (Cf. D1045.) *Bolte Zs. f. Vksk. XX 69 n. 5.

E761.6.5. *Life token: wine turns to vinegar.* Gaster Exempla 219 No. 156 (155.)

D477.1. Transformation: water becomes wine. D1046. Magic wine.

E761.6.6. *Life token: milk becomes agitated in pan at death of relative.* (Cf. E761.6.2.) England, U.S.: Baughman.

E761.7. *Life token: miscellaneous.*

E761.7.1. *Life token: ring presses finger.* (Cf. D1076.) *Bolte Zs. f. Vksk. XX 70 n. 6.

E761.7.2. *Life token: spring goes dry.* (Cf. D927.) *Bolte Zs. f. Vksk. XX 70 n. 10.

E761.7.3. *Life token: leaves fall from tree.* (Cf. D955.) Africa (Ekoi): Talbot 185.

E761.7.4. *Life token: light goes out.* (Cf. E765.1.) *Bolte Zs. f. Vksk. XX 70 n. 11; Gaster Thespis 275ff.

D1162. Magic light. E742. Soul as light.

E761.7.5. *Life token: dogs pulling on leash.* Cape Verde Islands: Parsons MAFLS XV (1) 123.

B121.1.1. Infallible hunting-dog.

E761.7.6. *Life token: bird sent each day to tell of hero's condition; when owl comes it will be to announce death.* Carib: Alexander Lat. Am. 265.

B147.2.2. Bird of ill-omen. B291.1. Bird as messenger.

E761.7.7. *Life token: bird feathers sink in river at hero's death.* Kirghiz: Radloff Proben der Volksliteratur der türkischen Stämme Südsiberiens III 85.

E761.7.8. *Life token: great wind blows.* Irish myth: Cross.

E761.7.9. *Life token: flaming shield goes out.* (Cf. D1101.1.) Irish myth: Cross.

D1663.5. Well rises or sinks to indicate long or short life.

E761.7.10. *Life token: armor rattles at home when owner is killed away from home.* England: Baughman.

E761.7.11. *Life token: music box plays by itself as owner awaits burial.* U.S.: Baughman.

E761.7.12. *Life token: arrow falls down.* India: Thompson-Balys.

E761.7.13. *Life token: paddy productive or unproductive.* India: Thompson-Balys.

E761.7.14. *Life token: rings will exchange places on girls' fingers.* India: Thompson-Balys.

E761.7.15. *Life token: direction dagger points determines if ogress has been killed.* India: Thompson-Balys.

E765. *Life dependent on external object or event.* Person's life is mystically connected with something else and comes to an end when that thing is destroyed. India: Thompson-Balys.

D2061.2.2. Murder by sympathetic magic. An object or an animal is abused or destroyed to bring about the death of a person. E710. External soul. F531.1.6.13. Giant's strength in hair. Z310. Unique vulnerability.

E765.1. *Life bound up with light (flame).* Breton: Sébillot Incidents s.v. "vie"; Fb "lys" II 483ab; Gaster Thespis 275f.; Icelandic: *Boberg.

D2064.2. Sickness of princess dependent on witch's fire. D2065.4. Insanity of princess dependent on height of fire. E742. Soul as light.

E765.1.1. *Life bound up with candle.* When the candle goes out, person dies. — *Krappe in Penzer Ocean of Story VIII 107; Anderson Die Meleagrossage bei den Letten (Philologus N. F. XXXIII [1923]); Icelandic: De la Saussaye 315, *Boberg; Spanish: Boggs FFC XC 82 No. 708*A.

D1162.2. Magic candle. E742.1. Soul as taper (candle). K551.9. Let me live as long as this candle lasts.

E765.1.2. *Life bound up with burning brand (torch).* Hartland Science 205 (Olger the Dane); Greek: *Frazer Apollodorus I 65 n. 5 (Meleager).

E742.1. Soul as taper (candle).

E765.1.3. *Life-lights in lower world.* Each light mystically connected with the life of a person. When light is extinguished, person dies. *Type 332; BP I 377ff., *388.

E741.1.1. Shooting star signifies that someone is dying. One star for each person. At his death it falls.

E765.2. *Life bound up with that of animal.* Person to live as long as animal lives. *Krappe in Penzer Ocean of Story VIII 107; Irish myth: *Cross (Diarmaid); Italian: Basile Pentamerone IV No. 5; India: *Thompson-Balys; N. A. Indian: Hultkrantz 364—374.

B192.0.1. Magic birds die when owner is killed. B311. Congenital helpful animal. Born at same time as master and (usually) by same magic means. C841.7. Tabu: killing totem animal. T589.7.1. Simultaneous birth of domestic animal and child.

E765.3. *Life bound up with object.* *Krappe in Penzer Ocean of Story VIII 107; India: Thompson-Balys; N. A. Indian: Hultkrantz 364.

E711.10. Soul in sword. E745. Soul as object.

E765.3.0.1. *Life bound up with magic object.* When magic object is lost, person dies. Irish myth: *Cross.

E765.3.1. *Person to live as long as church stands.* Fb "kirke" II 126a, "leve" II 401b.

E765.3.2. *Life bound up with calabash.* As calabash grows, so does girl. Africa (Hottentot): Bleek 55 No. 24.

E711.2.1. Soul in calabash (gourd).

E765.3.3. *Life bound up with tree.* India: Thompson-Balys.

E631.0.4. Speaking and bleeding trees.

E765.3.4. *Girl lives until her cowslip is pulled.* England: Baughman.

E765.3.5. *Man's magic contains his life essence.* Hawaii: Beckwith Myth 541.

E765.4. *Life bound up with external event.* Death to come when certain thing happens.

M341. Death prophesied.

E765.4.1. *Father will die when daughter marries.* (Cf. E765.4.3.) Irish myth: Cross; Welsh: MacCulloch Celtic 187.

M343. Parricide prophecy. T97. Father opposed to daughter's marriage.

E765.4.2. *Mother will die when daughter is wooed.* Irish myth: Cross.

E765.4.3. *Father will die when daughter bears son.* (Cf. E765.4.1.) Irish myth: *Cross.

A525.2. Culture hero slays grandfather. M372. Confinement in tower to avoid fulfillment of prophecy. S11.4.1. Jealous father vows to kill daughter's suitors. T97. Father opposed to daughter's marriage.

E765.4.3.1. *Father (and mother) will die on same day as daughter.* Irish myth: Cross.

E765.4.4. *Person will die year he marries.* Irish myth: *Cross.

E765.4.5. *Person will die when he drinks from horn.* (Cf. D1793.) Irish myth: Cross.

E765.4.6. *Snake can die only if it gives away hoarded treasure.* India: Thompson-Balys.

E765.4.7. *Man dies when tortoise shell is dug up.* Tonga: Gifford 52.

E765.5. *One person's life dependent on another's.* Penzer I 131.

E766. *Object dies or stops when owner dies.*

E766.1. *Clock stops at moment of owner's death.* England, U.S.: *Baughman.

E766.2. *Tree dies when owner dies.* England: *Baughman.

E766.3. *Post falls when owners lose estate.* England: Baughman.

E767. *Affinity of person and object.*

E767.1. *Ash pole appears at doorway several times on day owner's daughter dies.* (It is used for coffin rests. The pole has previously mysteriously escaped being used for other purposes.) — Canada: Baughman.

E767.2. *Clothes of wicked person burn when owner dies.* U.S.: Baughman.

E770. **Vital objects.** Objects that have life in them. (Cf. D1620, D1640.)

D779. Feathered ends of arrows become alive when breathed upon.

E771. *Ring with life in it.* Breton: Sébillot Incidents s.v. "animisme".

E772. *Sickle with life in it.* Breton: Sébillot Incidents s.v. "animisme".

E780. **Vital bodily members.** They possess life independent of the rest of the body. (Cf. F1096.) India: Thompson-Balys; N. A. Indian: *Thompson Tales 346 n. 246b.

E714.1. Soul (life) in the blood. F557. Removable organs. G635. Ogre revives after limbs are severed.

E780.1. *Vital body: kills attacking enemies.* India: Thompson-Balys.

E780.2. *Animal bodily members transferred to person or other animal retains animal powers and habits.* (Cf. E781, E782.) Type 660; Haiti: Parsons MAFLS XVII (1) 59—62.

E781. *Eyes successfully replaced.* Jacobs' list s.v. "Eyes exchanged"; Fb "øje" III 1166a; Köhler-Bolte I 434ff.; Irish myth: *Cross; Gaster Thespis 333f.; India: *Thompson-Balys; Africa (Angola): Chatelain 139 No. 13.

D2161.3.1. Blindness magically cured. D2161.3.1.1 Eyes torn out magically replaced. F668.1. Skillful surgeon removes and replaces vital organs. F952. Blindness miraculously cured. F952.7. Eyes restored by bathing in spring. V52.15. Prayer said by saint into his right hand restores displaced eye of opponent.

E781.1. *Substituted eyes.* Lost eyes are replaced by those of another person or animal. (Cf. F512.1.4.) *Type 660; BP II 552; Irish myth: Cross; Japanese: Ikeda; N. A. Indian: *Thompson Tales 299 n. 94.

A2241.5. Nightingale borrows blindworm's eye. F281. Fairy replaces man's heart with heart of straw, eyes with wood, etc. J2423. The eye-juggler.

E781.1.1. *Prince regains his eyesight after theft of eyes from water maidens.* India: Thompson-Balys.

E781.2. *Eyes bought back and replaced.* *Type 533; *BP II 278 n. 1; *Köhler-Bolte I 463; Spanish: Boggs FFC XC 83 No. 711A*; Missouri French: Carrière.

M225. Eyes exchanged for food. S165. Mutilation: putting out eyes.

E781.3. *Eyes borrowed by animal.* Later returned. — Africa (Kaffir): Theal 166.

A2241.5. Nightingale borrows blindworm's eye.

E782. *Limbs successfully replaced.* Africa (Basuto): Jacottet 248 No. 36.

D1500.1.19.1. Magic healing salve restores severed feet. E780.1. Vital body: kills attacking enemies. F668.1. Skillful surgeon removes and replaces vital organs.

E782.0.1. *Substituted limbs.* Man borrows various limbs and successfully uses them. Africa (Yoruba): Ellis 267 No. 4.

E782.1. *Hands restored.* *Type 706; *BP I 295; Fb "hånd" I 765b; Irish myth: Cross; Spanish Exempla: Keller, Nouvelles de Sens No. 12; Italian: Basile Pentamerone III No. 2; India: Thompson-Balys; Japanese: Ikeda.

D2161.3.2. Magic restoration of severed hand.

E782.1.1. *Substituted hand.* Man exchanges his hand for that of another. *Type 660; BP II 552.

E782.2. *Substituted ribs (chariot ribs).* Irish myth: Cross.

E782.3. *Arms restored.* Irish myth: *Cross; Breton: Sébillot Incidents s.v. "bras".

E782.3.1. *Substituted arm.* Injured arm replaced by another. (Cf. A128.4.1.) Irish myth: Cross.

E782.4. *Horse's leg cut off and replaced.* *Type 753; *BP III 198; *Lowes Romanic Review V 368; Saintyves Saints Successeurs 248—251; Köhler-Bolte I 132, 297 n. 1; Dh II 169; Hoefler Zs. f. Vksk. I 304; Ons Volksleven III 43, V 28, 136f.

J2411.2. Imitation of miraculous horse-shoeing unsuccessful. Christ takes off a horse's foot to shoe it and then successfully replaces it.

E782.4.1. *Substituted leg.* Injured leg replaced by another. Alphabet No. 219.

E782.4.2. *Severed leg(s) regrow(s).* Africa (Somali): Kirk A Grammar of the Somali Language (Cambridge [Eng.], 1905) 162f., (Ishhak): Kirk FL XV 391ff. No. 3, (Saho): Reinisch Die Saho-Sprache I 76ff. No. 3.

E782.5. *Substituted tongue.* Haiti: Parsons MAFLS XVII (1) 59—62.

E783. *Vital head.* Retains life after being cut off. (Cf. D992, F511.) Irish myth: *Cross; Icelandic: Boberg; Spanish Exempla: Keller; Jewish: *Neuman; India: *Thompson-Balys; West Indies: Flowers 432.

B11.5.5. Self-returning dragon's head. D1400.1.20.1. Magic (human) head causes fortress to crumble. D1602.12. Self-returning head. When head is cut off it returns to proper place without harm to owner. D1610.5. Speaking head. D1615.7. Singing head. F511.0.4. Man carries his head under his arm. G223. Head of beheaded witch mends if rubbed with salt. G461.1. Boy in ogre's house sees many human heads placed in rows. Heads smile and weep. G635. Ogre revives after limbs are severed. R261.1. Pursuit by rolling head.

E783.1. *Head cut off and successfully replaced.* *Kittredge Gawain 147ff.; Irish: MacCulloch Celtic 61, *Cross; India: Thompson-Balys; S. A. Indian (Quiché): Alexander Lat. Am. 175; Africa (Angola): Chatelain 113 No. 8, (Bushman): Bleek and Lloyd 10.

E34. Resuscitation with misplaced head. F668.1. Skillful surgeon removes and replaces vital organs. M221. Beheading bargain. Q551.8.5. Head falls off when man lies to saint.

E783.2. *Severed head regrows.* Penzer III 268 n. 1. — Greek: Fox 81.

E783.2.1. *Origin of Pegasus from neck of slain Medusa.* Greek: Fox 34.

B41.1. Pegasus.

E783.3. *Severed head reddens and whitens.* Irish myth: *Cross.

E783.4. *Severed head opens eyes.* Irish myth: Cross.

E783.5. *Vital head speaks.* India: Thompson-Balys.

E783.6. *Headless body vital.* Irish myth: Cross.

D1615.8. Headless body sings.

E783.7. *Headless man lives four (seven) years.* (Cf. Q551.8.5.) Irish myth: Cross.

E783.8. *Dead head grateful for burying it.* Chinese: Eberhard FFC CXX 34.

E784. *Flesh regrows.* Icelandic: *Boberg; Breton: Sébillot Incidents s.v. "chair"; India: Thompson-Balys.

D1318.7. Flesh reveals guilt. G635.2. Ogre's limbs reassemble after they are cut off.

E785. *Vital skin.* Retains life after death of owner. Africa (Bushman): Bleek and Lloyd 3.

E785.1. *Substituted skin.* Irish myth: Cross.

E785.1.1. *Ewe's hide grafted to skinless head of wounded man.* Irish myth: Cross.

D2161.3.4.1. Feathered skin magically grafted to bald head.

E786. *Heart successfully replaced.* *Type 660.

F281. Fairy replaces man's heart with heart of straw, eyes with wood, etc.

E787. *Stomach borrowed by animal.* Later returned. Africa (Kaffir): Theal 167.

E788. *Severed pap regrows when woman bears child.* Child V 177.

E789. *Vital bodily members—miscellaneous.* India: Thompson-Balys.

E789.1. *Organs exchanged with those of animal.* India: Thompson-Balys.

E790. The soul — miscellaneous.

E791. *Man who forgets to count himself dies immediately after.* India: Thompson-Balys.

J2031. Counting wrong by not counting one's self.

www.ingramcontent.com/pod-product-compliance
Lightning Source LLC
LaVergne TN
LVHW040202080826
844660LV00001B/75